Lecture Notes in Computer Science   15053

Founding Editor

Juris Hartmanis

Series Editor

Gerhard Goos, *Karlsruhe Institute of Technology, Karlsruhe, Germany*

Editorial Board Members

Elisa Bertino, *Purdue University, West Lafayette, USA*
Wen Gao, *Peking University, Beijing, China*
Bernhard Steffen, *TU Dortmund University, Dortmund, Germany*
Moti Yung, *Columbia University, New York, USA*

The series Lecture Notes in Computer Science (LNCS), including its subseries Lecture Notes in Artificial Intelligence (LNAI) and Lecture Notes in Bioinformatics (LNBI), has established itself as a medium for the publication of new developments in computer science and information technology research, teaching, and education.

LNCS enjoys close cooperation with the computer science R & D community, the series counts many renowned academics among its volume editors and paper authors, and collaborates with prestigious societies. Its mission is to serve this international community by providing an invaluable service, mainly focused on the publication of conference and workshop proceedings and postproceedings. LNCS commenced publication in 1973.

Zhe Xia · Jiageng Chen
Editors

Information Security Practice and Experience

19th International Conference, ISPEC 2024
Wuhan, China, October 25–27, 2024
Proceedings

 Springer

Editors
Zhe Xia **ⓘ**
Wuhan University of Technology
Wuhan, China

Jiageng Chen **ⓘ**
Central China Normal University
Wuhan, China

ISSN 0302-9743   ISSN 1611-3349 (electronic)
Lecture Notes in Computer Science
ISBN 978-981-97-9052-4   ISBN 978-981-97-9053-1 (eBook)
https://doi.org/10.1007/978-981-97-9053-1

This Springer imprint is published by the registered company Springer Nature Singapore Pte Ltd.
The registered company address is: 152 Beach Road, #21-01/04 Gateway East, Singapore 189721, Singapore

If disposing of this product, please recycle the paper.

Preface

This volume contains the papers that were selected for presentation and publication at the 19th International Conference on Information Security Practice and Experience (ISPEC 2024), which was organized by Wuhan University of Technology and Central China Normal University on 25–27 October 2024.

The main goal of the ISPEC 2024 conference was to promote research on new information security technologies, including their applications and their integration with IT systems in various vertical sectors. Previous ISPEC conferences have taken place in Singapore (2005), Hangzhou, China (2006), Hong Kong, China (2007), Sydney, Australia (2008), Xi'an, China (2009), Seoul, South Korea (2010), Guangzhou, China (2011), Hangzhou, China (2012), Lanzhou, China (2013), Fuzhou, China (2014), Beijing, China (2015), Zhangjiajie, China (2016), Melbourne, Australia (2017), Tokyo, Japan (2018), Kuala Lumpur, Malaysia (2019), Nanjing, China (2021), Taipei, Taiwan (2022), and Copenhagen, Denmark (2023). For all editions, the conference proceedings were published by Springer in the Lecture Notes in Computer Science series. Note that ISPEC 2020 was postponed to 2021 due to the COVID-19 pandemic.

This year, we received 70 submissions in total. Each submission was carefully reviewed (double-blinded) by an average of three Program Committee members in terms of novelty, practical application, and technical quality to reach a common conclusion. Eventually, the Program Committee decided to accept 22 full papers with an acceptance rate of 31.4%. The accepted papers cover multiple topics of cyber security and applied cryptography. In addition to paper presentations, the program also featured three invited keynote speakers: Man Ho Allen Au from Hong Kong Polytechnic University in China, Atsuko Miyaji from Osaka University in Japan, and Willy Susilo from the University of Wollongong in Australia.

For the success of ISPEC 2024, we would like to first thank the authors of all submissions and all the PC members for their great efforts in selecting the papers. We also thank all the organizing committee members and local chairs. Finally, we thank everyone else, student helpers and session chairs, for their contribution to the program.

October, 2024

Zhe Xia
Jiageng Chen

Organization

General Chairs

Jianwen Xiang   Wuhan University of Technology, China
Xingpeng Jiang   Central China Normal University, China
Shitao Zuo   Topsec, China

Program Chairs

Zhe Xia   Wuhan University of Technology, China
Jiageng Chen   Central China Normal University, China

Publication Chairs

Pei Li   Central China Normal University, China
Weizhi Meng   Technical University of Denmark, Denmark

Local Chairs

Liming Zhai   Central China Normal University, China
Cheng Tan   Wuhan University of Technology, China

Program Committee

Joonsang Baek   University of Wollongong, Australia
Aniello Castiglione   University of Salerno, Italy
Jiageng Chen   Central China Normal University, China
Chi Cheng   China University of Geosciences (Wuhan), China
Kim Kwang Raymond Choo   University of Texas at San Antonio, USA
He Debiao   Wuhan University, China
Feng Hao   University of Warwick, UK
Jinguang Han   Southeast University, China
Shoichi Hirose   University of Fukui, Japan
Albert Levi   Sabanci University, Turkey

Zhe Liu   Nanjing University of Aeronautics and
                          Astronautics, China
Rongxing Lu   University of New Brunswick, Canada
Weizhi Meng   Technical University of Denmark, Denmark
Kazumasa Omote   University of Tsukuba, Japan
Baodong Qin   Xi'an University of Posts and
                          Telecommunications, China
Jun Shao   Zhejiang Gongshang University, China
Chunhua Su   University of Aizu, Japan
Yan Tong   Huazhong Agricultural University, China
Yuntao Wang   University of Electro-Communications, Japan
Ding Wang   Nankai University, China
Edgar Weippl   University of Vienna, Austria
Xun Yi   RMIT University, Australia
Zhe Xia   Wuhan University of Technology, China
Zheng Yan   Xidian University, China
Mingwu Zhang   Hubei University of Technology, China
Yanwei Zhou   Shaanxi Normal University, China

Contents

Secure Federated Distillation Framework for Encrypted Traffic Classification

Long Teng[1], Qi Feng[1,2], Wei Zhao[2(✉)], Min Luo[1], and Debiao He[1]

[1] School of Cyber Science and Engineering, Wuhan University, Wuhan, China
{longteng,fengqi.whu,mluo,hedebiao}@whu.edu.cn
[2] Science and Technology on Communication Security Laboratory, Chengdu, China
zhaowei9801@163.com

Abstract. Encrypted traffic classification is essential for cyberspace governance. However, due to the privacy issues associated with network traffic, most organizations, such as hospitals, government agencies, and universities, are reluctant to disclose their network traffic. Malicious users can spread illegal information or commit cybercrime on the intranet via VPN or TOR. In this paper, we adopt federated learning to provide a new solution for encrypted traffic classification in darknet. Meanwhile, we introduce federated distillation to solve the problems of excessive communication overhead and Non-IID data. In addition, secret sharing is used for privacy federated distillation. By introducing sharpening coefficients, we effectively improve the robustness of the framework against data poisoning attacks and Byzantine attacks under an honest majority. We conduct extensive experiments on public dataset ISCX CICDarknet2020 and real dataset DarkCSE2023 containing popular application traffic, including VPN and Tor. Experiments show that our proposed framework achieves precision of **96.63%** and recall of **96.76%** in centralized setting, precision of **90.02%**, and recall of **89.60%** in federated setting, which is superior to other state-of-the-art methods.

Keywords: Encrypted Traffic classification · Federated Learning · Knowledge distillation · Secure Multi-party Computation

1 Introduction

Encrypted traffic is network traffic protected by encryption protocols to ensure the confidentiality and integrity of the data being transmitted. However, some cyber-attacks utilize encryption to evade detection by network security products, and malware can use encrypted communication to download malicious payloads or exfiltrate sensitive data. Anonymous applications such as The Onion Router (Tor), Virtual Private Networks (VPN), Invisible Internet Project (I2P), Jon-Donym, etc. [2], can combat traffic monitoring systems through encryption techniques and P2P transmissions. In the first half of 2023, nearly 3,000,000 people worldwide connected directly to the Tor network every day [2]. Due to their confidentiality and anonymity, these applications are widely used in cybercrime, increasing the risk of cyber-attacks and leading to the distribution of prohibited information, such as pornography, weapons, and drugs [3]. As a result, the classification of encrypted traffic is becoming increasingly important in detecting malicious activity and combating cybercrime. Although the payloads are encrypted, network traffic with specific inherent characteristics is still generated when end-users access these applications [4].

To protect intranet privacy, most organizations, such as universities, hospitals, government agencies, etc., do not share traffic, which is the "data silos" [6]. Federated Learning (**FL**) presents a new viable solution, and different organizations can collaboratively train their personalized models without disclosing traffic privacy. Currently, the limitations of FL for applications in reality mainly include the following three aspects: 1) significant communication overhead, 2) inconsistent performance, and 3) risk of privacy breaches [8]. Non-IID data can also degrade the performance of the final model, as the data distributions of the datasets held by the clients are not the same [9]. In addition, traditional FL frameworks may even get the wrong models under data poisoning attacks and Byzantine attacks. Moreover, some research shows that adversaries can recover private data through Generative Adversarial Networks (GAN) even if they only have gradient information, which raises concerns about FL frameworks [11].

To tackle the abovementioned problems, we propose a novel and practical secure federated distillation framework for encrypted traffic classification. This paper proposes a new network traffic preprocessing method capable of extracting content and spatial-temporal feature vectors from raw network flow. In order to balance efficiency and accuracy, we adopt a variant of ResNeXt as the classification model [12]. The deep model is capable of automatically extracting hidden content features and local spatial-temporal relationships from the input to achieve accurate classification [13]. We employ a federated distillation mechanism in order to allow all clients to train classification models collaboratively without compromising privacy. We introduce secret sharing mechanism compared to the traditional federated distillation technique [14]. The client uploads the secret shares of its **Logit vector**, i.e., the output of softmax, to two non-colluding servers, respectively, which compute the distillation and return the results to clients. The clients recover logit vector locally. To resist the Byzantine attack and the data poisoning attack, we introduce a **Sharpening** coefficient to increases the robustness of the framework in an honest majority setting.

In summary, the main contributions of this paper are as follows:

- First, we propose a novel end-to-end deep learning-based classification framework that combines content and spatial-temporal features and adapts a ResNeXt-like model to efficiently capture hidden relationships for accurate classification.
- Moreover, to the best of our knowledge, this is the first study that applys federated distillation to encrypted traffic classification, which can solve the problem of client data heterogeneity. Also, this can significantly reduce the communication cost during federated training.

– Finally, we present a secure federated distillation approach for aggregation by secretly sharing the logit vectors with two non-colluding servers. Clients locally recover the value of the global average logit vectors and adjust their training as soft labels. We also optimize the computation under the framework such that the efficiency can be further improved.

2   Related Work

In this section, we review the related works that classify encrypted traffic and federated distillation in recent years.

2.1   Encrypted Traffic Classification

Existing work on traffic classification can be divided into three types: port-based techniques, Deep Packet Inspection(DPI), and statistical feature-based techniques. Port-based techniques depend on the specific TCP port of known services. However, this method is inaccurate due to dynamic ports. DPI is to mine specific content in payloads, but it is not easy to obtain content information for encrypted traffic. Statistical feature-based approaches rely on statistical features of network flow, use machine learning algorithms to train classification models and distinguish different types of traffic. Due to the good performance of deep learning in the field, it has become the most popular method for traffic classification nowadays [16].

Deep learning techniques have recently been widely used in encrypted traffic classification. Shapira et al. proposed FlowPic, which transforms the bytes of network flow into grayscale images and utilizes LeNet for classification [17]. This work provides a generic framework for encrypted traffic classification, consisting of model representation and feature transformation. Singh et al. transform the spatial features of encrypted traffic to 3-dimensional images, extract the features by deep model, and classify traffic through traditional ML model [18]. They test many combinations of ML algorithms and select VGG19 and Random Forest as the best. Habibi Lashkari et al. use CICFlowMeter to extract spatial features from raw traffic and obtain 80 statistical features [19]. They leverage RF to select and convert essential features into 2D images and a 2D CNN model for classification. Lan et al. use CNN, RNN, and multi-head attention mechanisms for classification [20]. They extract the payload, time-based, and space-based features as the input, and the different module is adapted to process different features and concatenate the output of three modules as the input of fully connected layer.

2.2   Federated Distillation

Federated distillation is a valuable approach to address Non-IID data in FL. Some papers focus on ensemble distillation; Li et al. leverage transfer learning on public datasets and ensemble distillation on clients in order to improve performance and reduce communication costs [21]. Lin et al. combine knowledge distillation with FL to fine-tune the global model on a public dataset and obtain more robusted model [22]. Cheng et al. design a system that server holds a large model and carries out self-distillation to preserve global knowledge better [23]. Lin et al. proposed FedDF, which is a server-side integration method that approximates the set of client models outputs on proxy datasets by fine-tuning the global model [24]. FedAUX is an optimization of FedDF that utilizes unsupervised training to properly initialize models on the clients. In addition, FedAUX introduces (ϵ, δ)-differential privacy mechanisms for joint prediction on proxy datasets [25].

However, all the above methods require a public dataset for knowledge distillation, similar to the private dataset on clients. This condition is not always available in reality. Some recent works aim at knowledge distillation without public dataset. Zhu et al. average the logit vectors in different labels uploaded by each client on the server [14]. The average logit vector is the soft label in the local model training phase. He et al. split the model into a feature extractor and a classification network and upload intermediates to the classifier on the server for distillation [26]. The problem of these methods is that it is difficult to defend against possible Byzantine or data poisoning attacks in the system.

3   The Proposed System

In this section, we show the overview and design details of our proposed system, a federated-based end-to-end classification framework for encrypted traffic. The details of the system are in Fig. 1. The system in this paper consists of three layers: Pre-processing layer, Encrypted traffic classification layer, and Secure federated distillation layer.

3.1   Pre-processing Layer

The format of raw network traffic is usually pcapng or pcap file with inconsistent size, which does not serve as the input to deep learning model. The task of this layer is to generate a fixed-length input vector for each network flow of varying length. In this paper, we define a **network flow** as a set of consecutive packets generated between two hosts due to the same application. These packets have the same source/destination IP address, source/destination port, and transport layer protocol. The most crucial difference is that the source and destination addresses of upstream and downstream flows are opposite. The data preprocessing layer consists of 4 steps: stream splitting, payload extraction & truncation, spatial-temporal features extraction, and normalization.

The first step is dividing all network flow packets according to L. L consecutive packets will be considered as a **packet group**. In the second step, we keep only the payload of packets and remove the protocol headers. The packets with empty payloads, wrong packets, loop packets, and retransmitted packets

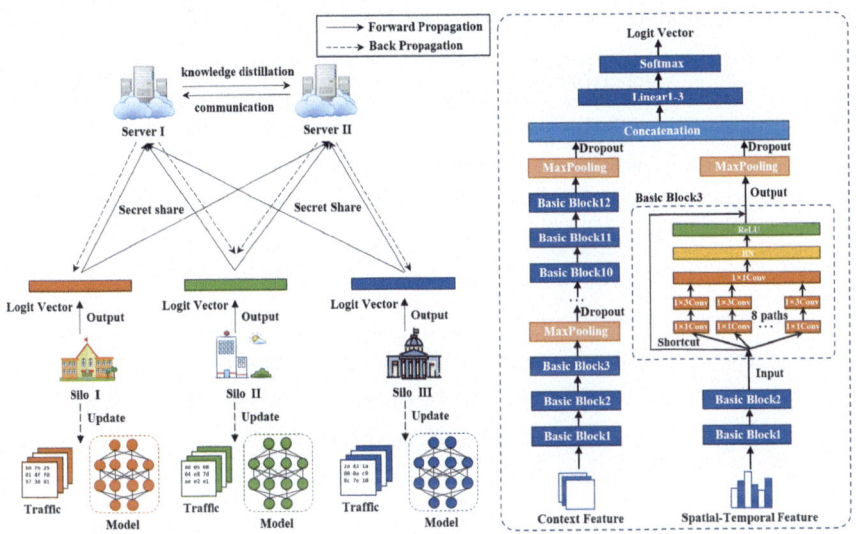

Fig. 1. The details of our proposed system and the structure of our model. The left half shows the workflow of the federated distillation framework and the right half shows the structure of the encrypted traffic classification model.

in the network traffic are also discarded in this step. In the third step, we need to normalize the length of all the loads. We analyzed the payload length of all data packets in the CICDarknet2020 dataset[20] and observed that 96.92% of the packets are less than 1500 bytes. This is because the size of packets is affected by the Maximum Transmission Unit(MTU), which in most networks is 1500[29]. Therefore, when the length of payload is less than 1500 bytes, we pad the payload with 0 bytes. Otherwise, we truncate it as the context features. The context feature of a network flow is denoted as: $x_{con} = [P_1, P_2, \cdots, P_L], P_i = [b_1^i, b_2^i, \cdots, b_B^i], b_j^i \in [0, 255], i \in [1, L], j \in [1, B]$.

The third step is extracting spatial and temporal features of the packets within a **packet group** without decryption. The temporal and spatial features of different applications are special, which can effectively improve the accuracy of classification. The details of features vector are shown in Table 1. Since the range of each feature is different, Min-Max normalization is utilized: $\bar{x} = \frac{x - x_{min}}{x_{max} - x_{min}}, \bar{x} \in [0, 1]$, where x is one of the elements in x_{st}, x_{max} and x_{min} is the maximum and minimum of x respectively.

In the last step, we normalize the feature vectors by dividing all bytes by 255, ensuring that all elements in the vectors are between $[0, 1]$. At the end of preprocessing layer, x_{con} and x_{st} will be obtained, which are used as the input of the encrypted traffic classification layer.

Table 1. The detailed temporal and spatial features list

	Description
Temporal features	Flow duration
	Time intervals among network packets
	Number of total packets/bytes per second*
	Number of upstream network packets/bytes per second*
	Number of downstream network packets/bytes per second*
Spatial features	Packet length*
	Upstream network packet/bytes length*
	Downstream network packet/bytes length*
	Number of total packets/bytes
	Number of total upstream network packets/bytes
	Number of total downstream network packets/bytes
	Ratio of upstream and downstream packets/bytes

* This contains the maximum, minimum, mean, standard deviation, and median of the measurements.

3.2 Encrypted Traffic Classification Layer

Encrypted traffic classification layer can automatically mine hidden features and potential connections from feature vectors using multiplayer convolutions and finally identify applications. We use 12 **basic blocks** to mine the hidden content features and 3 **basic blocks** to find local spatial-temporal relationships in the vector. The reason is that the length of content vector is generally long, about 48,000 bytes, requiring a deeper structure to extract higher-dimensional feature representations, while the spatial-temporal vector is shorter, only about 300 bytes, so shallow networks are sufficient.

We adopt a ResNeXt-like design with a multi-path, small convolutional kernel structure in each block. Due to the introduction of **cardinality**, it is possible to effectively improve accuracy of the model when the increase in depth does not bring gains to performance. The 1-dimensional convolutional kernels are able to obtain sparser relational mappings, significantly reducing the over-fitting risk of the model while keeping the overall complexity unchanged, which is better than 2-dimensional convolutional kernels.

$$o_{bb}(\boldsymbol{x}) = \mathcal{T}_{relu}(\mathcal{T}_{bn}(\sum_{i=1}^{C=8} \mathcal{T}_{conv}(\boldsymbol{x}) + \boldsymbol{x})) \tag{1}$$

$$\mathcal{T}_{conv}(\boldsymbol{x}) = \boldsymbol{W}_{conv} \otimes \boldsymbol{x} + \boldsymbol{b}_{conv} \tag{2}$$

$$\mathcal{T}_{bn}(\boldsymbol{x}) = (\alpha\hat{x}_1 + \beta, \alpha\hat{x}_2 + \beta, \cdots, \alpha\hat{x}_b + \beta), \ \hat{x}_i = \frac{x_i - \mu}{\delta + \xi} \tag{3}$$

where x and $o_{bb}(x)$ are the input and output of the basic block. $\mathcal{T}_{conv}$, $\mathcal{T}_{bn}$, $\mathcal{T}_{relu}$ are the 1-dimensional convolution, batch normalization, and ReLU function, respectively. W_{conv} is the convolution matrix, b_{conv} is the bias matrix, $\otimes$ is the convolution operation. We leverage 1-dimensional convolution kernels to capture the relationship in input vectors. Batch normalization is used to improve stability of the model and speed up the training. x is the input of batch normalization, μ is the mean of x, ξ is the standard deviation of x.

A maximum pooling layer and a dropout layer are added for every three basic blocks in the model to reduce the parameter size and enhance the non-linear properties. Finally, there are three consecutive fully connected layers, a ReLU layer and a Softmax layer, to determine the network type. o^i is the output of the i-th fully connected layers, W^i and b^i are the weight and bias matrix of the i-th layer, $\sigma(\cdot)$ is a non-linear function.

$$o^1 = \sigma(W^1 x + b^1), \; o^i = \sigma(W^1 o^{i-1} + b^i), i = 2, 3 \qquad (4)$$

Compared to simple CNN methods [17], we dramatically increase the depth of model through residual blocks for obtaining higher dimensional feature mappings that are more accurate. Compared to Transformer [20] and Graph Neural Network [30], our proposed model has a smaller parameter size, lower training costs, and is easier to deploy on the devices with limited computing resources.

3.3 Secure Federated Distillation Layer

We utilize a two-server setup with two central servers that do not collude. Client c_i secretly share their logit vectors to servers, which perform distillation operations on the shares. Nevertheless, additive secret sharing can only be done for elements in integral domain. Therefore, we have to encode the decimals in the vector as elements on the integral domain firstly, and then send the secret shares of the logit vector to two servers. For each $x_i \in \overline{V}_{i,j}^{(k)}$, c_i first calculate $\chi_i = encode(x_i) = x_i << 128$, and then randomly choose $r \in \mathbb{Z}_p$. Finally, c_i let $\langle x_i \rangle_0^P = \chi_i - r$, $\langle x_i \rangle_1^P = r$ and send to corresponding servers. In the secure distillation phase, the two servers perform computations on the secret share, containing three steps:

1. In j-th iteration, servers locally sum up the shares submitted by all users under k-th label respectively, i.e., compute $\sum_{i=0}^{n} \langle \overline{V}_{i,j}^{(k)} \rangle_d^P, d \in \{0, 1\}$.
2. For a-th client, servers compute $(\sum_{i=0}^{n} \langle \overline{V}_{i,j}^{(k)} \rangle_d^P - \langle \overline{V}_{a,j}^{(k)} \rangle_d^P)/(n-1), d \in \{0, 1\}$ as soft label $\langle \tilde{V}_{i,j}^{(k)} \rangle_d^P$.
3. Servers sharpen the labels obtained by $SoftmaxT(\langle \tilde{V}_{i,j}^{(k)} \rangle_d^P, T)$.

Softmax-T is a special Softmax function with **temperature** coefficient, which sharpens labels to avoid ambiguity caused by data heterogeneity among multiple parties. Our experiments show that this method can greatly accelerate convergence and enhance the robustness of the model:

$$SoftmaxT(\langle \tilde{V}_{i,j}^{(k)} \rangle_d^P | T) = \frac{e^{\langle v_{i,j}^{(k)} \rangle_d^P / T}}{\sum_{j=0}^m e^{\langle v_{i,j}^{(k)} \rangle_d^P / T}} \tag{5}$$

$$\langle v_{i,j}^{(k)} \rangle_d^P \in \langle \tilde{V}_{i,j}^{(k)} \rangle_d^P, d \in \{0,1\}, T = \frac{1}{t}, t = 1, 2, \cdots \tag{6}$$

Algorithm 1 Secure Distillation and Reconstruct

Input: $\langle \overline{V}_{i,j}^{(k)} \rangle_d^P$, $d \in \{0,1\}$, the secret shares of all logit vectors, $i \in [1,n], k \in [1,m]$.

Output: $\langle \hat{V}_{i,j}^{(k)} \rangle_d^P$, $d \in \{0,1\}$, the secret shares of all sharpen labels, $i \in [1,n], k \in [1,m]$

1: **for** each c_i, s_d **do**

2:     $\langle \tilde{V}_{i,j}^{(k)} \rangle_d^P = \Pi_{Division}^{(s)} (\sum_{i=0}^n \langle \overline{V}_{i,j}^{(k)} \rangle_d^P - \langle \overline{V}_{i,j}^{(k)} \rangle_d^P)$.

3:     $\langle \hat{V}_{i,j}^{(k)} \rangle_d^P = \Pi_{SoftmaxT}(\langle \tilde{V}_{i,j}^{(k)} \rangle_d^P)$.

4:     s_d send $\langle \hat{V}_{i,j}^{(k)} \rangle_d^P$ to c_i.

5: **end for**

6: c_i compute $\hat{V}_{i,j}^{(k)} = \langle \hat{V}_{i,j}^{(k)} \rangle_0^P + \langle \hat{V}_{i,j}^{(k)} \rangle_1^P$

7: c_i update model: $w^{(j+1)} = w^{(j)} - \eta \nabla \{\phi(F(w^{(j)}, x), \hat{y}) + \gamma \cdot \phi(F(w^{(j)}, x), \hat{V}_{i,j}^{(k)})\}$

8: $V_{i,j}^{(k)} \leftarrow V_{i,j}^k + F(w^{(j)}, x)$

9: $cnt_{i,j}^{(k)} \leftarrow cnt_{i,j}^{(k)} + 1$

10: **for** label $j = 1, 2, \cdots, m$ **do**

11:     $\overline{V}_{i,j}^{(k)} \leftarrow V_{i,j}^{(k)} / cnt_{i,j}^{(k)}, k \in [1, \cdots, m]$

12:     c_i shares $\overline{V}_{i,j}^{(k)}$ to two servers.

13: **end for**

14: **return**

Finally, clients reconstruct the secret locally and adjust the training process of the model. The detailed workflow is shown in Algorithm 1, where c_i is the i-th client, and s_i is the i-th server. In this algorithm, $\Pi_{Division}^{(s)}$ and $\Pi_{SoftmaxT}$ are invoked. $\Pi_{division}^{(s)}$ is the protocol that divide s on secret shares. For the element $v_d \in \langle \overline{V}_{i,j}^{(k)} \rangle_d^P$, $d \in \{0,1\}$, we leverage the protocol to compute a division $\frac{v_d}{n-1}$ and a truncation $v_d \gg 128$, which is equal to $\frac{v_d}{s}$, where $s = (n-1) \times 2^{128}$. If we divide v_d by s directly, the result may be incorrect when $v = v_0 + v_1 > p$, we define the modified coefficient θ_v:

$$v = v_0 + v_1 \mod p = v_0 + v_1 - \theta_v \times p \tag{7}$$

Therefore, we leverage Algotithm 3 to calculate the secret shares of warp count θ_v and modify the result of division:

$$\frac{v}{s} = \frac{v_0 + v_1}{s} - \frac{\theta_v \times p}{s}, \ \langle\frac{v}{s}\rangle_d^P = \langle\frac{v_d}{s}\rangle_d^P - \frac{\langle\theta_v\rangle_d^P \times p}{s} \tag{8}$$

$\Pi_{softmaxT}$ is used to compute the Softmax function on the shares of secret, where the key is $e^x = e^{x_0} \times e^{x_1}$, $x = x_0 + x_1$. Notice that we do not need to consider $x_0 + x_1 > p$ because we have already modified the result in the last step. The detailed workflow of $\Pi_{softmaxT}$ is shown in Algorithm 2.

Algorithm 2 $\Pi_{SoftmaxT}$

Input: $\langle\tilde{V}_{i,j}^{(k)}\rangle_d^P, d \in \{0,1\}$

Output: $\langle\hat{V}_{i,j}^{(k)}\rangle_d^P, d \in \{0,1\}$

1: **for** $\langle v\rangle_d^P \in \langle\tilde{V}_{i,j}^{(k)}\rangle_d^P$ **do**

2:   c_i randomly select $a, b \in \mathbb{Z}_p$, and corresponded shares $\langle a\rangle_d^P$, $\langle b\rangle_d^P$, compute $c = a \times b$ and it's share $\langle c\rangle_d^P$.

3:   c_i send $\langle a\rangle_0^P$, $\langle b\rangle_0^P$, $\langle c\rangle_0^P$ to s_0, send $\langle a\rangle_1^P$, $\langle b\rangle_1^P$, $\langle c\rangle_1^P$ to s_1.

4:   s_0 calculate $e^{v_0} = e^{t \cdot \langle v\rangle_0^P}$, s_1 calculate $e^{v_1} = e^{t \cdot \langle v\rangle_1^P}$

5:   s_0 calculate $\langle\alpha\rangle_0^P = e^{v_0} - \langle a\rangle_0^P$, s_1 calculate $\langle\alpha\rangle_1^P = -\langle a\rangle_1^P$, and exchange to reconstruct α.

6:   s_0 calculate $\langle\beta\rangle_0^P = -\langle b\rangle_0^P$, s_1 calculate $\langle\beta\rangle_1^P = e^{v_1} - \langle b\rangle_1^P$, and exchange to reconstruct α.

7:   s_0 calculate $\langle z\rangle_0^N = \langle c\rangle_0^N + \alpha\langle b\rangle_0^N + \beta\langle a\rangle_0^N + \alpha\beta$.

8:   s_1 calculate $\langle z\rangle_1^N = \langle c\rangle_1^N + \alpha\langle b\rangle_1^N + \beta\langle a\rangle_1^N$.

9: **end for**

10: s_0 calculate $\sum_{j=1}^m \langle z\rangle_0^P$, s_1 calculate $\sum_{j=1}^m \langle z\rangle_1^P$, exchange to reconstruct $\mathcal{V} = \sum_{j=1}^m \tilde{V}_{i,j}^{(k)}$.

11: s_0 calculate $\langle\hat{V}_{i,j}^{(k)}\rangle_0^P = \Pi_{division}^{(\mathcal{V})}(\langle z_j\rangle_0^N), j \in [1, m]$, and send back to c_i

12: s_1 calculate $\langle\hat{V}_{i,j}^{(k)}\rangle_1^P = \Pi_{division}^{(\mathcal{V})}(\langle z_j\rangle_1^N), j \in [1, m]$, and send back to c_i

13: **return**

At the end of $\Pi_{softmaxT}$, the two servers send the shares of sharpened labels to c_i. The clients recover the sharpen label locally, $\hat{V}_{i,j}^{(k)} = \langle\hat{V}_{i,j}^{(k)}\rangle_0^P + \langle\hat{V}_{i,j}^{(k)}\rangle_1^P$. c_i utilized $\hat{V}_{i,j}^{(k)}$ to adjust the local training process and update the local model $w^{(j+1)}$. Subsequently, the client c_i repeats this process until the model no longer converges, then sends a training termination signal to the server and exits the FL training process. Clients can freely join or exit FL, which increases the system's resilience.

Algorithm 3 Compute the Wrap Count

Input: $\langle v \rangle_d^P$, $d \in \{0, 1\}$

Output: $\langle \theta_v \rangle_d^P$, $d \in \{0, 1\}$

1: c_i randomly select $r \in \mathbb{Z}_p$, calculate the $r_0 + r_1 \mod N = r_0 + r_1 - \theta_r \cdot p$.
2: c_i send r_0 and $\langle \theta_r \rangle_0^P$ to s_0, r_1 and $\langle \theta_r \rangle_1^P$ to s_1.
3: s_d calculate $z_d = r_d + v_d \mod p$, $d \in \{0, 1\}$
4: s_d calculate $\langle \lambda_{xr} \rangle_d^P = (r_d + v_d - z_d)/p$, $d \in \{0, 1\}$, and exchange $\langle \lambda_{xr} \rangle_d^P$, reconstruct λ_{xr}.
5: s_d exchange z_d and reconstruct z, and calculate $\theta_z = (z_0 + z_1 - z)/p$.
6: s_d calculate $\langle \kappa_{xr} \rangle_d^P = z < r_d, d \in \{0, 1\}$.
7: s_0 calculate $\langle \theta_v \rangle_0^P = \theta_z - \langle \lambda_{xr} \rangle_0^P - \langle \theta_r \rangle_0^P - \langle \kappa_{xr} \rangle_0^P$.
8: s_1 calculate $\langle \theta_v \rangle_1^P = \theta_z - \langle \lambda_{xr} \rangle_1^P - \langle \theta_r \rangle_1^P - \langle \kappa_{xr} \rangle_1^P$.
9: **return**

---

4   Experimental Evaluation

In this section, we focus on evaluating the performance of our proposed system. We conduct experiments on the CICDarknet2020[19] and DarkCSE2023 datasets, which consists of various application traffic. The data distribution of these two datasets is shown in Table 2.

All network flow can be categorized into normal and darknet(including **VPN** and **Tor**). In order to collect the real network dataset DarkCSE2023, we utilized 12-users wireless intranet setup and captured user traffic on the gateway during 8 h, to emulate a real network environment. Due to the limited number of devices in our intranet, we have attempted to capture as many packets as possible. The dataset includes: Normal network traffic and Chat, Email, File Transfer, VOIP, Video, Browsing, Audio, and P2P on the darknet.

We outline the experimental configuration and metrics for evaluation, followed by a thorough assessment of our proposed system from four standpoints: Firstly, we evaluate the model's performance in a centralized scenario, comparing it with prior studies. Moreover, we train the classification model under our proposed federated framework and discusses the communication overhead and computational costs incurred during the train process. In addition, we also conduct experiments using FedAvg [31], FedProx [32], SCAFFOLD [33], FedBE [34], SEAR [35], PBFL [36] and the secure distillation algorithm introduced in this paper, in Non-IID data distribution to assess the steadiness of this framework. Finally, we undertook model training and testing concerning Byzantine or malicious nodes to illustrate the framework's resilience against attacks.

4.1   Experimental Settings

Before each experiment, we randomly divide the dataset into ten equally sized and disjoint subsets, among which eight subsets are the training set and the other two are the testing set. We conduct training and testing ten times for

Table 2. The number of flows under each label in CICDarknet2020 and DarkCSE2023

Traffic type	Number of flows in datasets	
	CICDarknet2020	DarkCSE2023
Normal network	4137	1856
Chat: AIM, ICQ	532	607
Email: Gmail, Outlook	401	629
File Transfer: FTPS, SFTP	887	987
VOIP: VoipBuster	2257	1005
Video: Vimeo, Netflix	2596	1119
Browsing: Youtube, Spotify	517	867
Audio: Hangouts, Facebook	482	978
P2P:BitTorrent	648	849

each experiment and calculate the average as final result. In all experiments, we deploy the clients on several laptops with Intel i7-12700H 2.3GHz CPU, 32 GB of memory, and NVIDIA GeForce RTX3060 GPU and the servers on two AWS r5.8xlarge instances with 32 vCPUs and 10Gbps bandwidth.

We adopt three metrics for our experiments, i.e., the precision(Pre), recall(Rec), and F1-score(F1), which is widely used in classification tasks and are based on True Positive(TP), True Negative(TN), False Positive(FP), and False Negative(TN).

$$Pre = \frac{TP}{TP+FP}, \ Rec = \frac{TP}{TP+FN}, \ F1 = \frac{(2 \times Pre \times Rec)}{(Pre+Rec)} \qquad (9)$$

4.2 Centralized Traffic Classification Test

In this experiment, we employed a centralized setup, trained and tested the model on global dataset, and compared our proposed model with some recent work to demonstrate the merits of our system. We adopt four deep learning-based model as baselines in centrilized traffic classification test and utilize average precision, recall, and F1 score to evaluate the performance of all tested methods. As shown in Fig. 2, our proposed method obtains better results on the above three metrics than existing state-of-the-art methods. At the same time, the convergence speed of our proposed system is significantly higher than other algorithms.

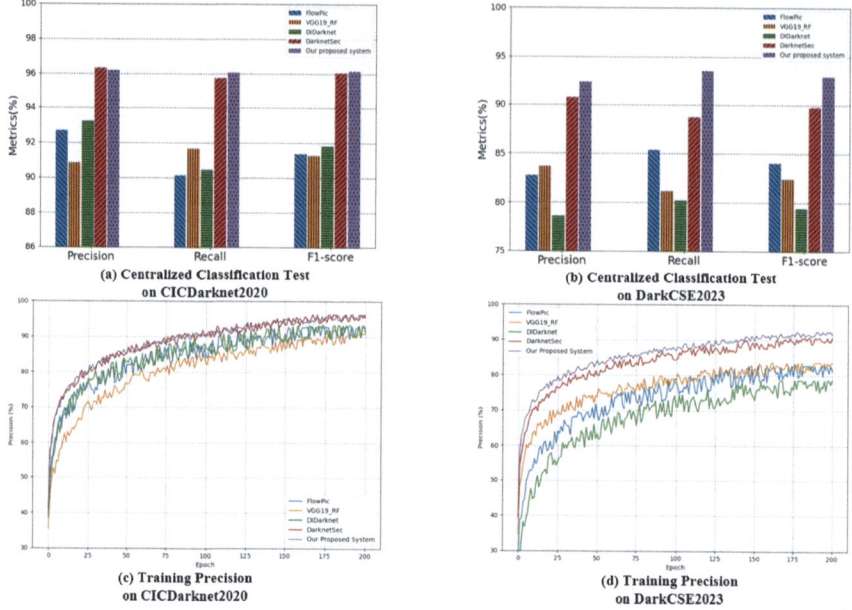

Fig. 2. Average precision, recall, F1-score and the training loss of all methods in Centralized Setting on CICDarknet2020 and DarkCSE2023. **FlowPic** [17] is a LetNet-style model that converts traffic bytes into grayscale images for classification. **VGG19-RF** [18] converts the temporal features into 3-dimensional images and combines VGG19 and Random Forest for classification. **DIDarknet**[19] extracts 80 statistical features from network flows, employs RF to select those essential features, and uses 2D-CNN for classification. **DarknetSec**[20] leverage multi-head self-attention model and LSTM for content features, convolutional module for spatial-temporal features, and several fully connected layers for prediction.

Our proposed model has marginally lower precision than DarknetSec, approximately 0.1%. However, its recall and F1-score surpass all other methods, attributed to our comprehensive feature extraction on the network flow, significantly enhancing the model's classification performance. In addition, our approach can be applied to a broader range of scenarios as the computational cost of 1D convolution is significantly lower than that of LSTM and multi-head self-attention modules.

4.3   Federated Traffic Classification Test

In this experiment, our FL framework was tested in a standard FL scenario. We established 12 benign clients, each with a disjoint subset of the global dataset and the same data distribution. These clients and servers followed the steps in Section III until the model on each client converged. We calculated the precision, recall, and F1-score of all models under nine labels and compared them with the centralized trained model on two datasets, as is shown in Fig. 3.

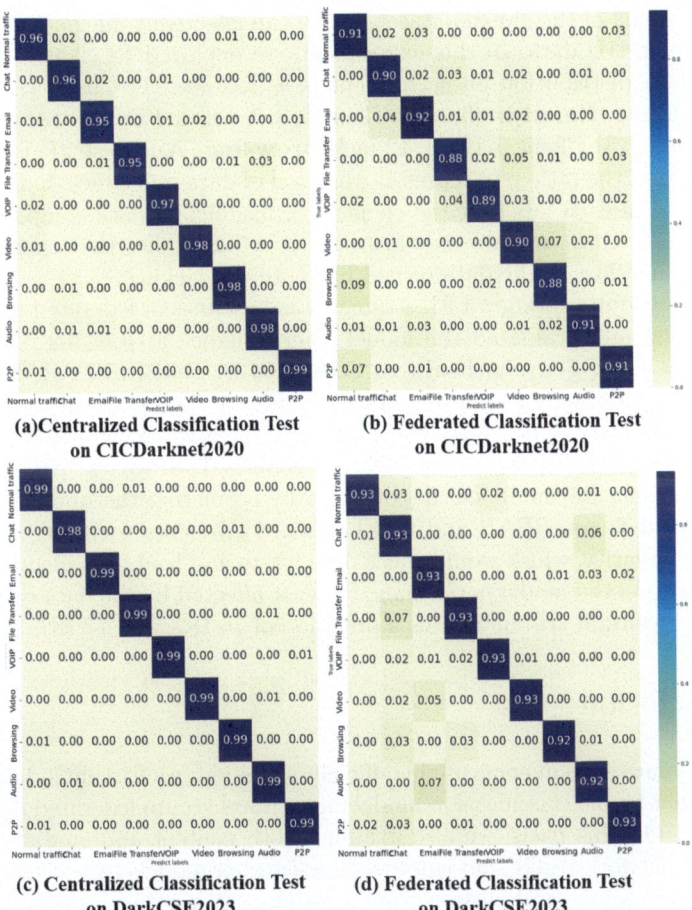

Fig. 3. Average precision, recall, and F1-score of Centralized and Federated models on CICDarknet2020 and DarkCSE2023.

We focus on the **communication and computational overhead** of the federated distillation and multi-party secure computation components. Since this scheme is based on logit vector, the communication overhead is only related to the number of classification labels m and federated clients n, and is independent of the complexity of the model on each client. Both secret sharing and reconstruction phase incurs communication cost of $2\,nm$ and the time cost is mainly in transmission delay. The communication cost of $\Pi_{Division}^{(s)}$ is $8nm$, and $\Pi_{SoftmaxT}$ has a communication cost of $26\,nm + 2$.

4.4 Non-IID Data Distribution Test

In this subsection, FL tests are performed under Non-IID data distributions. Within our framework, the knowledge distillation approach enables clients to learn a mapping of the global dataset, which can effectively alleviate the adverse effects of Non-IID data. In this experiment, we deployed 12 clients separately, and the data distribution on each client is as follows: (1) Client $1, 2, 3, 4$ lack **Normal**, **Chat**, **Email** traffic. (2) Client $5, 6, 7, 8$ lack **File Transfer**, **VOIP**, **Video** traffic. (3) Client $9, 10, 11, 12$ lack **Browsing**, **Audio**, **P2P** traffic.

We utilized the ratio ρ to represent the level of data imbalance, indicating the ratio of data in each label for the client with insufficient data compared to the other clients with more data. For instance, $\rho = 0.2$ implies that clients lacking data hold only 20% of the data owned by those not lacking.

We adopt four well-known FL strategies as baselines in federated traffic classification test and evaluated the model's performance at $\rho = 0.2, 0.3, \cdots, 0.8$, respectively, using FedAvg, FedProx, SCAFFOLD, FedBE, SEAR, PBFL and our work. The detailed results are shown in Fig. 4. The performance of model aggregated by FedAvg decreases the most as ρ increases. When $\rho = 0.2$, the performance of model is as low as 34.69% and 28.69%. FedProx, SCAFFOLD, and FedBE can mitigate the model degradation by correcting the updating process via **proximal term**. SEAR and PBFL discard gradients with large difference by cosine similarity, which would cause data waste and lead to inadequate model convergence. As the model performance is least affected by the data distribution in our framework, it still maintains a precision of 76.18% and 77.78% at $\rho = 0.2$.

5   Conclusion

To address data silos in encrypted traffic classification, we first introduce an efficient darknet traffic classification model and a novel secure federated distillation framework. On this basis, we also examine both content and spatial-temporal features of network traffic and employ deep learning models to construct a classifier that offers powerful classification capability at a reduced computing cost. Our experiments with publicly available datasets indicate that our suggested model performs better than current state-of-the-art approaches. In addition, we utilize secure multi-party computation and federated distillation methods to present fresh solutions for addressing the data silo issue in encrypted traffic classification. The thesis' federation framework meaningfully diminishes communication overheads during training while ensuring the logit vector's privacy. For cases involving Non-IID data distribution, Byzantine nodes, or data poisoning attacks, our framework can effectively guarantee the classification performance of the model. Even though, our scheme requires clients to share logit vectors frequently for better result, this will increase the communication cost, and we will explore improving this in future work.

Acknowledgment. The work was supported by the Key Research and Development Program of ShanDong Province (Grant No. 2021CXGC010107), the National Natural Science Foundation of China (Nos. 62202339, 62172307, U21A20466), and the Science and Technology on Communication Security Laboratory Foundation (Nos. 6142103022202), the New 20 Project of Higher Education of Jinan (No. 202228017) and the Fundamental Research Funds for the Central Universities (No. 2042023KF0203, 2042024kf1013). What's more, we would like to thank the anonymous reviewers.

A   Byzantine and Data Poisoning Attack Test

This subsection examines the scenario where Byzantine and malicious nodes exist among the clients. We arranged 12 clients in two honest-majority scenarios: (1) 10 benign nodes, 1 Byzantine node, and 1 malicious node, and (2) 8 benign nodes, 2 Byzantine nodes, and 2 malicious nodes. The Byzantine node uploads a random vector with average of 0.5 and standard deviation of 0.1. Malicious nodes will exchange the labels for Chat and Video in dataset and train the model, resulting in incorrect logit vector. The comparative experimental result is shown in Tables 3 and 4.

Table 3. Average precision, recall and F1-score of FedAvg, FedProx, SCAFFOLD, FedBE, SEAR, PBFL and our proposed framework on CICDarknet2020 under attack

Federated learning strategy	Experiment on CICDarknet2020					
	Scenario 1			Scenario 2		
	Precision(%)	Recall(%)	F1-Score(%)	Precision(%)	Recall(%)	F1-Score(%)
FedAvg	61.76±2.46	53.31±2.07	57.23±2.25	42.11±3.84	37.86±3.31	39.87±3.52
FedProx	68.62±1.99	63.77±2.29	66.11±2.07	50.27±2.77	47.03±2.49	48.60±2.68
SCAFFOLD	67.20±1.85	62.12±2.17	64.56±2.01	50.07±2.54	49.96±2.30	50.02±2.37
FedBE	71.08±1.48	70.78±1.83	70.93±1.66	55.04±2.19	50.29±2.07	52.60±2.14
SEAR	72.46±1.67	73.84±1.59	73.14±1.63	62.39±2.87	60.96±2.55	61.67±2.71
PBFL	76.44±1.42	77.89±1.50	77.16±1.46	67.43±1.77	69.85±1.92	68.62±1.84
Our System	**83.13±0.99**	**84.07±0.61**	**83.60±0.82**	**76.50±1.08**	**76.28±0.85**	**76.39±1.04**

Table 4. Average precision, recall and F1-score of FedAvg, FedProx, SCAFFOLD, FedBE, SEAR, PBFL and our proposed framework on DarkCSE2023 under attack

Federated learning strategy	Experiment on DarkCSE2023					
	Scenario 1			Scenario 2		
	Precision(%)	Recall(%)	F1-Score(%)	Precision(%)	Recall(%)	F1-Score(%)
FedAvg	64.53±3.37	52.76±3.18	58.05±3.29	38.41±3.96	36.72±3.57	37.56±3.77
FedProx	67.56±2.71	59.51±2.88	63.28±2.80	52.19±3.15	49.82±3.26	50.98±3.19
SCAFFOLD	69.24±2.47	66.93±2.61	68.06±2.54	55.98±2.81	53.47±2.67	54.70±2.72
FedBE	69.43±1.88	68.61±2.06	69.01±1.98	58.76±2.39	60.23±2.11	59.49±2.20
SEAR	77.83±2.05	76.94±2.20	77.38±2.13	65.73±2.31	67.21±2.42	66.46±2.36
PBFL	79.49±1.97	80.02±1.85	79.75±1.91	74.57±2.22	73.29±2.38	73.93±2.30
Our System	**85.94±0.87**	**86.77±0.72**	**86.35±0.78**	**79.54±1.01**	**78.93±0.94**	**79.23±0.98**

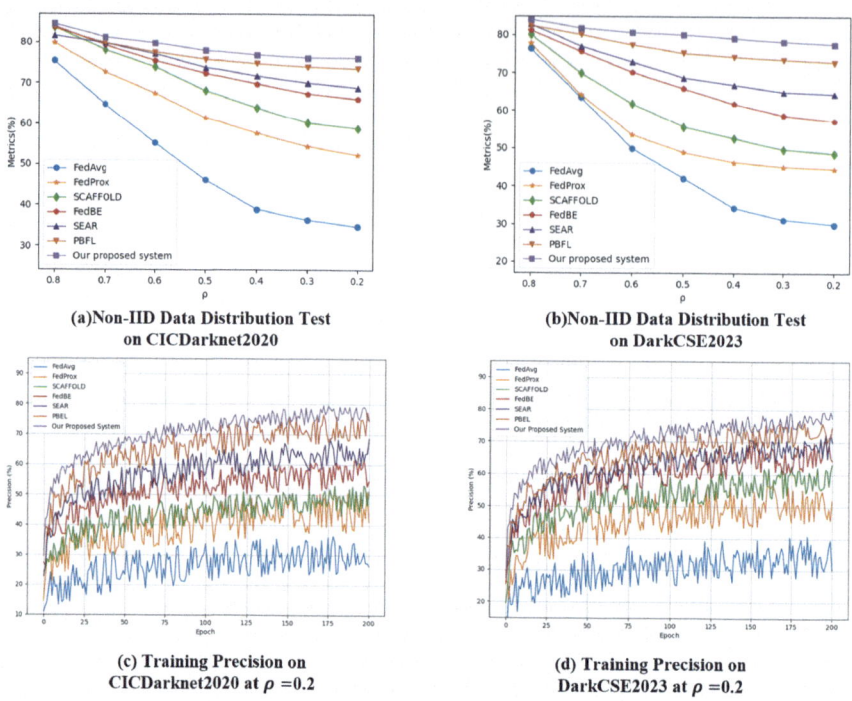

Fig. 4. Average precision and training precision of FedAvg, FedProx, SCAFFOLD, FedBE, SEAR, PBFL and our proposed framework on Non-IID data. **FedAvg** [31] is a classical FL framework, which directly computes the average of all gradients uploaded by clients. **FedProx** [32] will perform the aggregation computation with a proximal term to alleviate the problem of heterogeneous distribution of data. **SCAFFOLD** [33] introduces control vectors to control the local and global gradient updating process on the client and server respectively during the aggregation process to effectively solve the client drift problem. **FedBE** [34] proposes an FL strategy based on knowledge distillation, where after the clients upload models, the server constructs a model distribution for sampling using Dirichlet and Bayesian, combined with ensemble learning approach for prediction. **SEAR** [35] applies the trusted execution environment(TEE) for Byzantine Robust FL, which optimizes the format of the data is stored to perform efficient aggregations. **PBFL** [36] utilize fully homomorphic encryption(FHE) for secure aggregation and cosine similarity to determine whether the gradient uploaded by the client is malicious. It runs on the blockchain and guarantees a transparent process.

Traditional aggregation protocols, such as FedAvg, FedProx, SCAFFOLD, FedBE are helpless against malicious and Byzantine nodes as the precision and recall of the models decrease significantly. Methods such as SEAR, PBEL, although they can mitigate the attack, they often require the gradient to be selected based on the vector similarity, and the global gradient will still be shifted when the attacker carefully constructs the gradient. In our proposed framework, the influence of malicious nodes is significantly reduced due to eliminate the

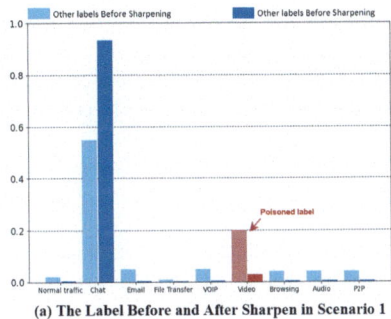
(a) The Label Before and After Sharpen in Scenario 1

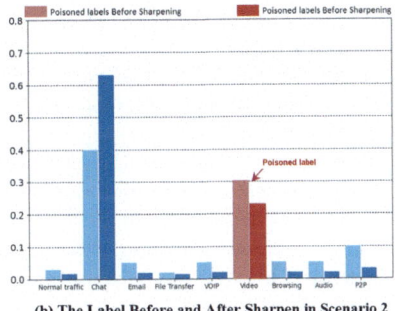
(b) The Label Before and After Sharpen in Scenario 2

Fig. 5. The comparison of soft labels before and after sharpening.

ambiguity of the average logit vector and mitigate the effect of mislabeling by introducing the label sharpening process, and the comparison of soft labels before and after sharpening is shown in Fig 5.

References

1. Zhang, X., Zhao, Z., Tsiligkaridis, T., Zitnik, M.: Self-supervised contrastive pre-training for time series via time-frequency consistency. Adv. Neural. Inf. Process. Syst. **35**, 3988–4003 (2022)
2. Aminuddin, M.A.I.M., Zaaba, Z.F., Samsudin, A., Zaki, F., Anuar, N.B.: The rise of website fingerprinting on tor: analysis on techniques and assumptions. J. Netw. Comput. Appl. **212**, 103582 (2023)
3. Mohanty, H., Roudsari, A.H., Lashkari, A.H.: Robust stacking ensemble model for darknet traffic classification under adversarial settings. Comput. Secur. **120**, 102830 (2022)
4. Khandkar, V.S., Hanawal, M.K., Kulkarni, S.G.: Challenges in adapting ech in tls for privacy enhancement over the Internet. arXiv preprint arXiv:2207.01841 (2022)
5. Dong, C., Zhang, C., Lu, Z., Liu, B., Jiang, B.: Cetanalytics: comprehensive effective traffic information analytics for encrypted traffic classification. Comput. Netw. **176**, 107258 (2020)
6. Zhang, C., Xie, Y., Bai, H., Yu, B., Li, W., Gao, Y.: A survey on federated learning. Knowl.-Based Syst. **216**, 106775 (2021)
7. Aledhari, M., Razzak, R., Parizi, R.M., Saeed, F.: Federated learning: a survey on enabling technologies, protocols, and applications. IEEE Access **8**, 140699–140725 (2020)
8. Lyu, L., Yu, H., Yang, Q.: Threats to Federated Learning: A Survey. arXiv preprint arXiv:2003.02133 (2020)
9. Li, T., Hu, S., Beirami, A., Smith, V.: Ditto: fair and robust federated learning through personalization. In: International Conference on Machine Learning, pp. 6357–6368. PMLR (2021)
10. Issa, W., Moustafa, N., Turnbull, B., Sohrabi, N., Tari, Z.: Blockchain-based federated learning for securing internet of things: a comprehensive survey. ACM Comput. Surv. **55**(9), 1–43 (2023)

11. Zhu, L., Liu, Z., Han, S.: Deep leakage from gradients. Adv. Neural Inf. Process. Syst. **32** (2019)
12. He, K., Zhang, X., Ren, S., Sun, J.: Deep residual learning for image recognition. In: Proceedings of the IEEE Conference on Computer Vision and Pattern Recognition, pp. 770–778 (2016)
13. Jin, D., Lu, Y., Qin, J., Cheng, Z., Mao, Z.: Swiftids: real-time intrusion detection system based on lightgbm and parallel intrusion detection mechanism. Comput. Secur. **97**, 101984 (2020)
14. Zhu, Z., Hong, J., Zhou, J.: Data-free knowledge distillation for heterogeneous federated learning. In: International Conference on Machine Learning, pp. 12878–12889. PMLR (2021)
15. Velan, P., Čermák, M., Čeleda, P., Drašar, M.: A survey of methods for encrypted traffic classification and analysis. Int. J. Netw. Manage. **25**(5), 355–374 (2015)
16. Xie, G., Li, Q., Jiang, Y.: Self-attentive deep learning method for online traffic classification and its interpretability. Comput. Netw. **196**, 108267 (2021)
17. Shapira, T., Shavitt, Y.: Flowpic: encrypted internet traffic classification is as easy as image recognition. In: IEEE INFOCOM 2019-IEEE Conference on Computer Communications Workshops (INFOCOM WKSHPS), pp. 680–687. IEEE (2019)
18. Singh, D., Shukla, A., Sajwan, M.: Deep transfer learning framework for the identification of malicious activities to combat cyberattack. Futur. Gener. Comput. Syst. **125**, 687–697 (2021)
19. Habibi Lashkari, A., Kaur, G., Rahali, A.: Didarknet: a contemporary approach to detect and characterize the darknet traffic using deep image learning. In: 2020 the 10th International Conference on Communication and Network Security, pp. 1–13 (2020)
20. Lan, J., Liu, X., Li, B., Li, Y., Geng, T.: Darknetsec: a novel self-attentive deep learning method for darknet traffic classification and application identification. Comput. Secur. **116**, 102663 (2022)
21. Li, D., Wang, J.: Fedmd: Heterogenous Federated Learning via Model Distillation. arXiv preprint arXiv:1010.03581 (2019)
22. Lin, T., Kong, L., Stich, S.U., Jaggi, M.: Ensemble distillation for robust model fusion in federated learning. Adv. Neural Inf. Process. Syst. **33**, 2351–2363 (2020)
23. Cheng, S., Wu, J., Xiao, Y., Liu, Y.: Fedgems: Federated Learning of Larger Server Models via Selective Knowledge Fusion. arXiv preprint arXiv:2110.11027 (2021)
24. Lin, T., Kong, L., Stich, S.U., Jaggi, M.: Ensemble distillation for robust model fusion in federated learning. Adv. Neural Inf. Process. Syst. **33**, 2351–2363 (2020)
25. Sattler, F., Korjakow, T., Rischke, R., Samek, W.: Fedaux: leveraging unlabeled auxiliary data in federated learning. IEEE Trans. Neural Netw. Learn. Syst. (2021)
26. He, C., Annavaram, M., Avestimehr, S.: Group knowledge transfer: federated learning of large CNNS at the edge. Adv. Neural Inf. Process. Syst. **33**, 14068–14080 (2020)
27. Feng, D., Yang, K.: Concretely efficient secure multi-party computation protocols: survey and more. Secur. Saf. **1**, 2021001 (2022)
28. Boneh, D., Komlo, C.: Threshold signatures with private accountability. In: Annual International Cryptology Conference. pp. 551–581. Springer (2022)
29. Xu, S.J., Geng, G.G., Jin, X.B., Liu, D.J., Weng, J.: Seeing traffic paths: encrypted traffic classification with path signature features. IEEE Trans. Inf. Forensics Secur. **17**, 2166–2181 (2022)
30. Zheng, J., Li, D.: Gcn-tc: combining trace graph with statistical features for network traffic classification. In: ICC 2019 IEEE International Conference on Communications (ICC), pp. 1–6. IEEE (2019)

31. McMahan, B., Moore, E., Ramage, D., Hampson, S., Arcas, B.A.: Communication-efficient learning of deep networks from decentralized data. In: Artificial Intelligence and Statistics, pp. 1273–1282. PMLR (2017)
32. Li, T., Sahu, A.K., Zaheer, M., Sanjabi, M., Talwalkar, A., Smith, V.: Federated optimization in heterogeneous networks. Proc. Mach. Learn. Syst. **2**, 429–450 (2020)
33. Karimireddy, S.P., Kale, S., Mohri, M., Reddi, S., Stich, S., Suresh, A.T.: Scaffold: stochastic controlled averaging for federated learning. In: International Conference on Machine Learning, pp. 5132–5143. PMLR (2020)
34. Chen, H.Y., Chao, W.L.: Fedbe: Making Bayesian Model Ensemble Applicable to Federated Learning. arXiv preprint arXiv:2009.01974 (2021)
35. Zhao, L., Jiang, J., Feng, B., Wang, Q., Shen, C., Li, Q.: Sear: secure and efficient aggregation for byzantine-robust federated learning. IEEE Trans. Dependable Secure Comput. **19**(5), 3329–3342 (2021)
36. Miao, Y., Liu, Z., Li, H., Choo, K.K.R., Deng, R.H.: Privacy-preserving byzantine-robust federated learning via blockchain systems. IEEE Trans. Inf. Forensics Secur. **17**, 2848–2861 (2022)

TriNT: A Framework for ROV Identification Based on Triplet

Yujing Liu[✉], Jiangbin Chen, and Shuhui Chen

College of Computer, National University of Defense Technology, Changsha, China
liuyujing@nudt.edu.cn

Abstract. The inter-domain routing system of the Internet is composed of Autonomous Systems (ASes), with their security mechanisms affecting the overall security of the Internet. Route Origin Validation (ROV) is a security technique for curbing malicious attacks against the routing system. The use of ROV by ASes is the basis for studying many aspects of the Internet, such as assessing Internet security and robustness. Previous research for passively measuring the status of ROV operation have been limited to specific types of ASes, such as Vantage Points (VPs) or stub ASes. We propose an ROV identification framework called TriNT that measures the path triplet difference between valid and invalid routing paths. The ROV identification results of the TriNT closely match the implementation of ROV as announced by the AS operators. Compared with previous methods, TriNT has a low network overhead, a short experimental cycle, and recognition of a wide range of ASes.

Keywords: Autonomous System · Route Origin Validation · Path Triplet

1 Introduction

The Internet is formed from the interconnection of many autonomous systems (ASes) using the Border Gateway Protocol (BGP). The security mechanisms employed by ASes affect the security of the Internet. Those mechanisms are the basis for studying Internet security, robustness [1], route hijacking, and route bottlenecks [2]. Deficiencies in BGP security have led to route leaks [3] and malicious route hijackings [4]. A large BGP route leak that occurred on April 16, 2021, affected more than 20,000 ASes [5]. The primary cause of route leakage and route hijacking events is that BGP lacks a route source authentication mechanism to verify whether the prefixes declared by neighbors truly belong to the corresponding AS.

To compensate for the lack of a route source authentication mechanism in BGP, the SIDR working group began to develop the Resource Public Key Infrastructure (RPKI) in April 2008 [6] as a hierarchical authentication system. Through the RPKI Trust Anchor operated by the five global Regional Internet Registries (RIRs), RIR members can obtain RPKI certificates and generate Route Origin Authorization (ROA) objects. Each ROA object binds an AS number (ASN) to an IP address prefix, and BGP routers implement Route Origin Validation (ROV) using the ROA object to discard invalid BGP announcements and avoid route leakage or malicious route hijacking events.

Z. Xia and J. Chen (Eds.): ISPEC 2024, LNCS 15053, pp. 20–32, 2024.
https://doi.org/10.1007/978-981-97-9053-1_2

Theoretically, RPKI improves the security of the network when most ASes perform ROV, but various problems in the actual network lead to a low rate of actual RPKI deployments [7]. The ROV process itself leads to an additional burden on routers, and internet service providers (ISPs) lack an economic incentive to deploy RPKI [8]. Enforcing ROVs and filtering invalid BGP announcements may lead to legitimate targets being unreachable [9], as with invalid BGP announcements due to ROAs that are not updated in a timely manner or announcements that are too specific to IP prefixes [8]. Although the percentage of ROA registrations of IPv4 exceeds 48% [10], the benefit of ROA registrations depends on whether an AS performs ROV and filters invalid BGP announcements [11].

Through the information released by a few ISPs [12, 13] we know that a few ASes perform ROV. Otherwise, it is difficult to determine whether ASes perform mandatory ROV; we currently find information on only 18 ASes performing ROV from the Internet. The real-time monitoring system [14] deployed by Reuter et al. [9] is no longer operational, with the last measurement being from August 31, 2020.

Existing measurement methods use active detection, inevitably causing additional network burden. The active detection approach identifies whether the stub AS [14–16] or VP [17] performs ROV, making it difficult to identify the transmitting AS on the BGP path. The measurement of the Reuter monitoring system et al. [9] showed 127 ASes, with 120 of them belonging to the VP. The same passive identification method using a full feeder only identifies whether the VP performs ROV [11]. The BeCAUSe identification method uses Reuter's experimental results et al. [9] as a given, which fails to avoid these problems.

To solve these difficulties, we deeply analyze the differences between valid and invalid paths and propose our TriNT algorithm framework for accurately identifying whether an AS performs ROV. Compared with previous research methods, TriNT has a low overhead and good accuracy. TriNT uses an ROV identification framework using the path triplet measurement. It leverages the bypassing phenomenon of invalid and non-invalid AS paths. Using information collected for multiple AS releases performing ROV, we validated the performance of our method through actual experiments. The implementation time of ROV is almost consistent with our experimental results. TriNT effectively identifies whether the ASes chosen for testing (from the top 100 listed in ASRank) performs ROV or not. Our validation set is significantly more complete, and the validation results are more credible than previous approaches, which used only three or four ASes [9, 11] performing ROV to validate the experimental results.

This paper is organized as follows. Section 2 describes the existing research on measuring ROV deployment. Section 3 describes the challenges of current ROV identification methods and our contributions. Section 4 describes our datasets. Section 4.2 details the design and implementation of TriNT. Section 5 analyses the results of TriNT experiments. Section 6 presents our conclusions.

2 Related Works

The BGP is used for communication between ASes. To avoid security breaches caused by flaws in the BGP itself, the SIDR working group began to develop RPKI based on a public key infrastructure in April 2008 and officially started to deploy it in 2011. RPKI verifies the validity of IP prefixes declared by neighboring routers to prevent malicious route hijacking. Chung et al. [8] have conducted a comprehensive longitudinal study on the basic information of RPKI from its initial deployment. Most of the information about RPKI such as the registration status of the latest ROA and the number of valid and invalid prefixes declared by the ASes is available in real-time from the NIST RPKI Monitor. However, information on the actual implementation of ROV for ASes is difficult to obtain, and the NIST RPKI Monitor explicitly states that it does not perform measurements in this area.

Gilad et al. [7] were the first to measure ROV enforcement using a passive approach, and they found that the actual deployment rate of ROV is low, with only three of the top 100 ASes in the ASRank [18] ranking enforcing ROV and filtering invalid BGP route announcements, and that the Internet remains largely insecure. Reuter et al. [9] found that the uncontrolled experiments of Gilad et al. [7] may lead to experimental errors. To avoid the errors, Reuter used controlled experiments by actively declaring valid and invalid IP prefixes using the PEERING platform [19] and found three ASes performing ROV, all verified by the ISP. They deployed a real-time monitoring system [20] for measuring ASes performing ROVs, but this monitoring system has not been updated since August 31, 2020. Testart et al. [11] studied ROV filtering behavior longitudinally using BGP routing information base data. They first extracted a set of all-feeder ASes and then searched for those with significantly fewer RPKI invalid routes and determined that 21 ASes performed ROV. Gray et al. [17] proposed an algorithmic framework for identifying whether an AS initiates Route Flap Damping and used it to identify ASes performing ROV.

Cartwright-Cox [14] proposed a new method to measure whether an AS performs ROV proactively. An ICMP scan of the entire IPv4 address space identifies hosts that can respond and indicates that the AS performs ROV if the host replies to servers in the RPKI valid address space but not to servers in the RPKI invalid address space. Huston and Damas [15] used a similar approach to determine the share of users protected by RPKI. Hlavacek et al. [21] used a controlled measurement experimental approach, measuring 12 ASes performing ROV based on the data plane and 4 ASes performing ROV based on the control plane. Rodday et al. [22] revisited previous methods for identifying ASes performing ROV and proposed a novel measurement based on RIPE Atlas [23], where they inferred that 206 ASes perform ROV, of which 10 had high confidence, 12 had low confidence, and 184 performed ROV indirectly through IXP routing servers.

In summary, the challenges include the following aspects.

Limited VPs. Previous study shows that the number of VPs is growing at a much slower rate than the number of ASes [24–26]. in January 2022, the number of global ASes was over 70,000 versus only 2,000 VPs. The current control plane research method focuses on identifying whether the VP performs ROV or not. The experimental results are influenced by the VP, making it difficult to identify whether an AS other than the VP performs ROV or not. The monitoring system deployed by Reuter et al. [9] discovered that, out of a total of 127 AS performing ROVs, 120 were VPs. The passive identification method based on the full feeder [11] can only identify whether a VP performs ROV. Identification using the BeCAUSe framework does not address how to calibrate the path to perform ROV but takes the experimental results of Reuter et al. [9] as a given, which also fails to avoid the influence of the VP. The latest research results [22] are still based on the VP measurement method.

Impact of Upstream AS. Most of the data plane measurement methods are end-to-end measurements, i.e., scanning end hosts or end hosts accessing servers to test whether the AS where the end hosts are located performs ROV. This method is only able to infer whether the end-to-end path is affected by ROV and does not indicate whether a stub AS performs ROV as any AS on that path performing ROV will show the same experimental results. Huston and Damas [15] point out that the reason for not receiving ICMP responses in the Cartwright-Cox [14] experimental results is most likely that the provider of the stub AS enables ROV, rather than the stub AS performing ROV. In replicating the experiments of Cartwright-Cox [15], Rodday [22] et al. found that the number of ASes labelled as performing ROV increased considerably the closer the AS performing ROV was to the PEERING testbed [19].

Long Experimental Cycles and High Overhead. The active detection methods in the control plane and data plane require repeated declarations of valid and invalid prefixes, and the declarations of valid and invalid prefixes have a long period. The prefix announcement period was 12 h in the experiments of Huston and Damas [15] and 24 h in Rodday's [22]. The experimental period of the control plane-based measurement method is even longer. Reuter et al. [16] had a weekly experimental period, and the results are not identical from week to week. The active detection of invalid prefixes announced in the control plane is similar to a route leak event, and invalid BGP announcements cause unnecessary network overhead. Data plane probing requires constant ICMP scans or HTTP requests, also increasing network overhead.

To address the above-mentioned challenges. We adopt a passive detection approach, deeply analyze the difference between valid declaration paths and invalid declaration paths, and propose the TriNT algorithm framework to accurately identify whether an AS performs ROV. Our contributions are as follows.

First, we propose an algorithm to passively identify whether an AS performs ROV or not. The algorithm is based on an AS path triplet measure that is independent of a VP and is able to identify whether an AS other than a VP performs ROV or not.

Second, our experimental data are derived from publicly available routing data, and our method does not require additional active probing in the control and data planes. It has the advantages of a short experimental period, low experimental cost, and no additional network overhead and enables continuous real-time measurements.

3 Datasets

The main data used in this paper are BGP update data [13, 27], PeeringDB data [28], and ROA data [29].

BGP Update Data. Route Views and RIPE RIS store both RIB and Update types of data. In this paper, we use BGP Update data to analyze the basic status of RPKI deployment. BGP Update data for the first day of each month from July 2020 to June 2022 were used to derive the AS performing ROV.

PeeringDB Data. PeeringDB is an online database operated by a non-profit organization, and PeeringDB data include copious basic information about ASes. We use these data to find the ASNs corresponding to IXPs and perform preliminary processing of BGP paths to remove ASNs corresponding to IXPs from the paths.

ROA Data. ROA is signed proof that the holder of a set of IP prefixes has authorized the AS to initiate route announcements for those prefixes. It contains an ASN and multiple IP prefixes and their prefix lengths, and the AS has the authority to announce these prefixes and their prefix lengths. The RIPE NCC provides daily ROA history data, which include the ASN, IP prefixes, maximum length, and effective start and end times of the ROA. With the ROA data provided by the RIPE NCC, we validate the BGP update data collected by the collectors.

4 Methodology

4.1 Heuristic Observations

We consider a BGP announcement to be invalid if the IP prefix in the announcement is covered by an ROA object but doesn't match the ASN, to be unknown if it is not covered by any ROA object, and to be valid if it matches an ROA object accurately. Then we classify the AS paths in BGP announcements into two categories. An invalid path is when the AS path is in invalid announcement, and a non-invalid path is when the AS path is in a valid or unknown announcement.

When an AS performs ROV and filters invalid BGP route announcements, invalid BGP announcements continue to be announced by ASes that do not perform ROV, which means that announcements of invalid IP prefixes may bypass ASes that perform ROV and continue to propagate. As shown in Fig. 1, B is an AS that performs ROV. When H declares an invalid BGP announcement, C receives the invalid BGP announcement from H and propagates the invalid BGP announcement to its neighbors B and G. Since B performs ROV and G does not, B will filter the invalid announcement, and G will further propagate the invalid BGP announcement until reaching A. The path from A to H is not the shorter path A-B-C-H, but the longer path A-F-G-C-H due to B's performance of ROV. Conversely, when such a path bypassing phenomenon exists, it may be due to the performance of ROV by an AS, and we derive the "potential AS" by finding the path bypassing phenomenon of invalid and non-invalid paths.

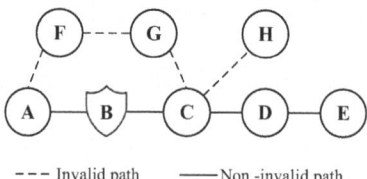

Fig. 1. Diagram of an invalid path detour. Dashed paths are invalid paths and solid paths are non-invalid paths.

4.2 TriNT Framework

The framework of our TriNT method is shown in Fig. 2. The specific steps include parsing and classifying paths, extracting non-invalid triplets, extracting invalid multiplets, finding 'Potential ASes', and identifying ROV status.

Parsing and classifying paths: We extract AS paths from BGP Update data and classify them as invalid and non-invalid paths. Route Views and RIPE RIS provide BGP Update data collected by the collectors in MRT format. First, we use the BGPStream tool to parse the MRT-format data, which include information such as the IP prefix, AS path, time, collector name, and data type. We filter out the withdraw data and IPv6 data, then compress paths from duplicate ASes (i.e., from "A-B-B-C" to "A-B-C") and delete AS paths containing AS sets, and reserved ASes. For example, if a path is A-B-C-D, where C is the reserved ASN, then that path will be deleted. Second, we delete the ASN of IXPs in the BGP path. IXP is a centralized exchange platform established by different telecom operators to connect their respective networks. An IXP may have its own ASN, but it does not actually participate in routing. We retrieve the list of IXPs from PeeringDB and remove the ASNs of IXPs from the BGP path. For example, if a path is A-B-C-D, where C is the ASN of an IXP, then this path is processed as A-B-D. Third, we use the ROA object data of five RIRs maintained by RIPE NCC to validate the BGP announcements and classify the corresponding AS paths into invalid and non-invalid paths as defined above.

Extracting non-invalid triplets: A triplet is defined as three consecutive ASes in an AS path. To obtain all triplets of non-invalid paths, we traverse the non-invalid path and find three adjacent ASes on the path as triplets. As shown in Fig. 3(a), if the non-invalid path is A-B-C-D-E, we can extract three triplets: A-B-C, B-C-D, and C-D-E.

Extracting invalid multiplets: A multiplet is defined as multiple consecutive ASes on a BGP path, where the number of ASes is greater than or equal to 4. When there is a multiplet in the invalid path, and the head and tail nodes of the multiplet are the same as the head and tail nodes of a triplet, then the invalid multiplet can match the non-invalid triplet. If there exists an invalid path A-F-G-C-H, then the triplet matched by this invalid path is A-B-C, where the matched multiplet is A-F-G-C, as in Fig. 3(b).

Finding 'Potential ASes': When an AS performs ROV, the invalid announcement is filtered by the AS, and the announcement looks for one or more other ASes that are not performing ROV to bypass the ROV filtering. There are two cases of this bypassing phenomenon. One is to find an AS that does not perform ROV to replace it, and the other is to find multiple ASes that do not perform ROV to replace the AS that performs ROV. The new path length of the first case is the same as the old path length, and we believe that this case may also be caused by the normal adjustment of the BGP path, not necessarily the result of the AS performing ROV. In the second case, the new path length is greater than the old path length, which is against the principle of minimum hop count in the BGP protocol, so we believe that this situation is most likely caused by ROV filtering. In previous steps, we find the invalid multiplet and its corresponding non-invalid triplet, with the triplet meaning the old path and the multiplet meaning the new path. When the intermediate node in a triplet does not belong to the intermediate node set of the corresponding multiplet, we consider the intermediate node of the triplet as a "Potential AS". For example, when the triplet is A-B-C and the corresponding multiplet is A-F-G-C, B is a "Potential AS" when B does not belong to F and G, as shown in Fig. 3(c).

Identifying ROV status: When an AS enforces ROV and filters invalid BGP announcements, theoretically the AS should not appear in the invalid path, but on the actual Internet, the ISP may not check the ROV status for traffic engineering [9], resulting in the AS performing ROV appearing in the invalid path. Through our previous study, we found that the proportion of these ASes appearing in invalid paths is less than the proportion of invalid paths to the total path. Therefore, we confirm the condition for an AS to perform ROV is that the proportion of it in invalid paths should be less than the ratio of invalid paths to the total paths.

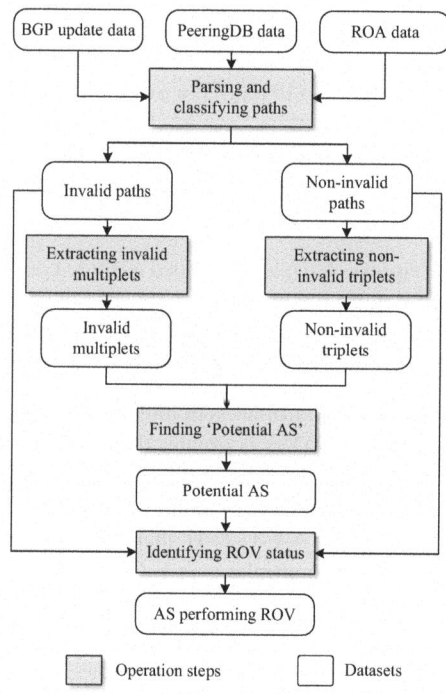

Fig. 2. TriNT framework.

5 Experimental Results

We used the TriNT framework to identify ASes that have executed ROV from July 2020 to June 2022. Then we verified the identification effect of TriNT by announcement information published by network operators.

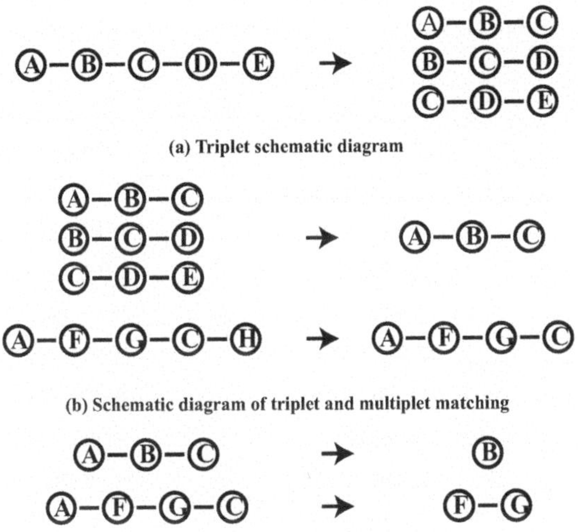

(a) Triplet schematic diagram

(b) Schematic diagram of triplet and multiplet matching

(c) Diagram of "Potential AS"

Fig. 3. Schematic diagram of determining a 'potential AS'.

5.1 Validation Dataset

The information about ASes performing ROV through ISPs can be used to verify the accuracy and reliability of the TriNT framework. At present, we know the details of 17 ASes performing ROV, as shown in Table 1.

The quantity of BGP data affects the accuracy of identification, especially when the target AS is small and the routing data are insufficient. Therefore, we select the top 100 ASes in ASRank to validate our experimental results. The eligible ASes are: AS7018, AS3257, AS6939, AS2914, AS1299, AS1221, AS4637, AS9002, AS3356, AS4826.

AS7018, AS3257, AS6939, AS2914, and AS1299 were announced to be doing ROV by July 2020, which places them all in our experimental time period. Both AS1299 and AS6939 were identified as performing ROV in the experimental results from July 2020 to June 2022 (Fig. 4). AS3257 was not identified as performing ROV during one month. AS2914 was not identified as performing ROV during two months. AS7018 was not identified as performing ROV during four months. We found that AS3257, AS2914, and AS7018 were not identified because the proportion of invalid paths was too high, which we believe is likely due to the AS turning off ROV part of the time. The proportion of invalid paths for AS7018 in both January and February 2022 was much greater than 1, and an AS performing ROV should not appear in invalid paths so frequently. During March 2021, AS2914 was not identified as performing ROV because the threshold was not set properly. The proportion of invalid paths in AS2914 suddenly increased and exceeded 3 in March 2022, and then suddenly decreased in April 2020. We believe that the reason why AS2914 was not identified as performing ROV in March may be due to anomalies in the dataset.

AS1221 was expected to formally perform ROV in June 2020, and our experimental results show that AS1221 actually performed ROV in August 2020. The experimental results do not differ much from the time when ROV was to begin and when we identified

Table 1. Schedule for AS implementation of ROV.

Organization	ASN	Time
Noris	AS12337	2018.10 [30]
AT&T	AS7018	2019.02 [31]
SEACOM	AS37100	2019.04 [32]
Workonline	AS37271	2019.04 [32]
KPN	AS286	2019.09 [12]
GTT	AS3257	2019.09 [12]
Hurricane	AS6939	2020.02 [33]
Telia	AS1299	2020.03 [34]
NTT	AS2914	2020.03 [35]
MobiCom	AS55805	2020.05 [36]
Telstra	AS1221	2020.06 [37]
SUPERLOOP	AS38195	2020.06 [38]
Telstra	AS4637	2020.10 [37]
RETN	AS9002	2020.12 [39]
RIPE	AS3333	2021.03 [40]
LLC	AS3356	2021.03 [41]
Obenetwork	AS4826	2021.03 [42]

AS1221 as performing ROV after August 2020. AS4637 actively deployed RPKI in October 2020, and experimental results show that AS4637 performed ROV in February 2021. AS9002 and AS3356 were announced to begin ROV were December 1, 2020, and March 25, 2021, respectively, and AS9002 and AS3356 were identified as performing ROV in December 2020 and April 2021. Our experimental results were consistent with the information released by each AS. AS4826 started deploying RPKI in 2020 and completed deployment in March 2021. Our experimental results show that AS4826 had already started performing ROV in October 2020, stopped doing ROV in March 2021, and resumed ROV after April 2021. AS7018, AS3257, AS6939, AS2914, AS1299, AS1221, AS4637, AS9002, AS3356, and AS4826 announced the time to perform ROV is basically consistent with our experimental results showing the time to perform ROV, which indicates that our method can effectively identify whether the AS performs ROV or not.

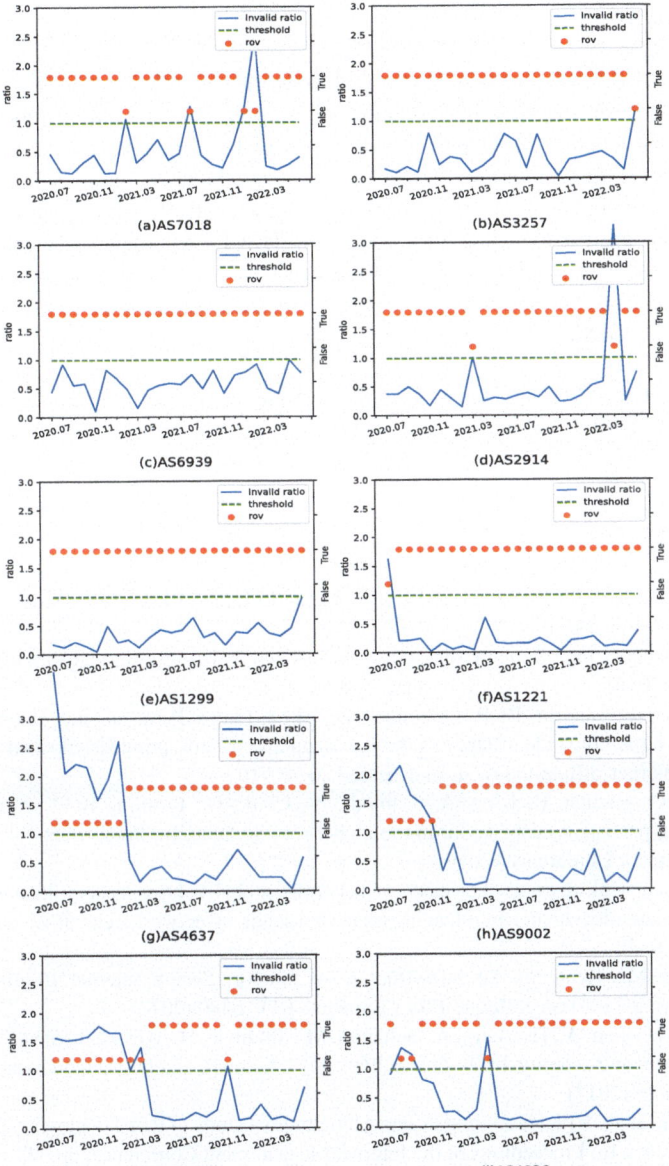

Fig. 4. Plot of heuristic experiment results for AS7018, AS3257, AS6939, AS2914, AS1299, AS1221, AS4637, AS9002, AS3356, and AS4826 for July 2020 to June 2022. The meaning of the left vertical coordinate is the ratio, and the meaning of the right vertical coordinate is the result of ROV (True means ROV performed, and False means no ROV was performed). 'Invalid ratio' indicates the ratio of invalid paths, 'rov' indicates whether the AS performed ROV, and 'threshold' indicates the set threshold value of the invalid path ratio.

6 Conclusion

To understand the security of ASes in real network networks, we deeply analyze the difference between valid and invalid paths and propose the TriNT algorithm framework for identifying whether an AS performs ROV using the path triplet measure. Compared with previous research methods, TriNT has a low overhead and good accuracy.

We collected information from ISPs indicating when ROV was implemented in their networks and used it to validate the results of TriNT experiments. The times TriNT determined ROV was being performed are nearly identical to those published dates, with AS9002 and AS3356 releases giving special confirmation of ROV operation as determined by TriNT.

Acknowledgments. This research is supported by the project of National Key R&D Program of China (No. 2022YFB3104800).

References

1. Doyle, J.C., et al.: The 'robust yet fragile' nature of the Internet. Proc. Natl. Acad. Sci. **102**(41), 14497–14502 (2005)
2. Yang, Y., et al.: Inter-domain routing bottlenecks and their aggravation. Comput. Netw. **162**, 106839 (2019)
3. How Verizon and a BGP Optimizer Knocked Large Parts of the Internet Offline Today. https://blog.cloudflare.com/how-verizon-and-a-bgp-optimizer-knocked-large-parts-of-the-internet-offline-today/. Last accessed 2024/7/10
4. Testart, C., Richter, P., King, A., Dainotti, A., Clark, D.: Profiling BGP serial hijackers: capturing persistent misbehavior in the global routing table. In: Proceedings of the Internet Measurement Conference (2019)
5. Major BGP leak disrupts thousands of networks globally. https://www.bleepingcomputer.com/news/security/major-bgp-leak-disrupts-thousands-of-networks-globally/. Last accessed 2024/7/10
6. Lepinski, M., Kent, S.: An Infrastructure to Support Secure Internet Routing. Internet Engineering Task Force, Request for Comments RFC 6480 (2012)
7. Gilad, Y., Cohen, A., Herzberg, A., Schapira, M., Shulman, H.: Are we there yet? On RPKI's deployment and security. In: In Proceedings 2017 Network and Distributed System Security Symposium (2017)
8. Chung, T., et al.: RPKI is coming of age: a longitudinal study of RPKI deployment and invalid route origins. In: Proceedings of the Internet Measurement Conference, pp. 406–419 (2019)
9. Reuter, A., Bush, R., Cunha, I., Katz-Bassett, E., Schmidt, T.C., Wählisch, M.: Towards a rigorous methodology for measuring adoption of RPKI route validation and filtering. SIGCOMM Comput. Commun. Rev. **48**(1), 19–27 (2018)
10. Li, W., et al.: RoVista: measuring and analyzing the route origin validation (ROV) in RPKI. In: Proceedings of the 2023 ACM on Internet Measurement Conference (2023)
11. Testart, C., Richter, P., King, A., Dainotti, A., Clark, D.: To filter or not to filter: measuring the benefits of registering in the RPKI today. In: Passive and Active Measurement, pp. 71–87 (2020)
12. AS286 Routing Policy. https://as286.net/AS286-routing-policy.html. Last accessed 2024/7/10

13. RIPE Forum, RIPE Network Coordination Centre. https://www.ripe.net/participate/mail/ripe-forum. Last accessed 2024/7/10
14. Are BGPs security features working yet? https://blog.benjojo.co.uk/post/are-bgps-security-features-working-yet-rpki. Last accessed 2024/7/10
15. ISP Column, June 2020. https://www.potaroo.net/ispcol/2020-06/rov.html. Last accessed 2024/7/10
16. RPKI Full Path Test. https://rpkitest.nlnetlabs.net/. Last accessed 2024/7/10
17. Gray, C., et al.: BGP beacons, network tomography, and Bayesian computation to locate route flap damping. In: Proceedings of the ACM Internet Measurement Conference, pp. 492–505 (2020)
18. AS Rank: A ranking of the largest Autonomous Systems (AS) in the Internet, https://asrank.caida.org/. Last accessed 2024/7/10
19. Schlinker, B., Zarifis, K., Cunha, I., Feamster, N., Katz-Bassett, E.: PEERING: an AS for us. In: Proceedings of the 13th ACM Workshop on Hot Topics in Networks, HotNets 2014 (2014)
20. ROV Deployment Monitoring. https://rov.rpki.net/. Last accessed 2024/7/10
21. Hlavacek, T., Herzberg, A., Shulman, H., Waidner, M.: Practical experience: methodologies for measuring route origin validation. In: 2018 48th Annual IEEE/IFIP International Conference on Dependable Systems and Networks (DSN), pp. 634–641 (2018)
22. Rodday, N.: Revisiting RPKI route origin validation on the data plane. In: 5th Network Traffic Measurement and Analysis Conference, TMA 2021 (2021)
23. RIPE NCC Staff: Ripe atlas: a global internet measurement network. Internet Protocol J. **18**, 3
24. Chen, J., Liu, Y., Chen, S., Shi, X.: Research on the derivation of AS hidden links and the discovery of critical AS. In: 2022 IEEE 47th Conference on Local Computer Networks (LCN), pp. 267–270 (2022)
25. Deng, W., Mühlbauer, W., Yang, Y., Zhu, P., Lu, X., Plattner, B.: Shedding light on the use of AS relationships for path inference. J. Commun. Netw. **14**(3), 336–345 (2012)
26. Hou, B., Cai, Z., Wu, K., Yang, T., Zhou, T.: 6Scan: a high-efficiency dynamic internet-wide IPv6 scanner with regional encoding. IEEE/ACM Trans. Netw. **31**(4), 1–16 (2023)
27. Route Views—University of Oregon Route Views Project. http://www.routeviews.org/routeviews/. Last accessed 2024/7/10
28. PeeringDB. https://www.peeringdb.com/. Last accessed 2024/7/10
29. Index of /rpki. https://ftp.ripe.net/rpki/. Last accessed 2024/7/10
30. AS12337 RPKI Validation deployed. https://www.mail-archive.com/routing-wg@ripe.net/msg00837.html. Last accessed 2024/7/10
31. AT&T/as7018 now drops invalid prefixes from peers. https://mailman.nanog.org/pipermail/nanog/2019-February/099501.html. Last accessed 2024/7/10
32. RPKI Route Origin Validation—Africa. https://mailman.nanog.org/pipermail/nanog/2019-April/100445.html. Last accessed 2024/7/10
33. RPKI_at_Hurricane_Electric-DKNOG10. https://events.dknog.dk/event/8/contributions/92/attachments/39/50/RPKI_at_Hurricane_Electric-DKNOG10.pdf. Last accessed 2024/7/10
34. Dropping RPKI invalid prefixes. https://blog.arelion.com/2020/02/05/dropping-rpki-invalid-prefixes/. Last accessed 2024/7/10
35. NTT/AS2914 enabled RPKI OV 'invalid = reject' EBGP policies, https://www.mail-archive.com/routing-wg@ripe.net/msg01261.html. Last accessed 2024/7/10
36. Dropping invalids in Mongolia. https://blog.apnic.net/2020/09/03/dropping-invalids-in-mongolia/. Last accessed 2024/7/10
37. Major ANZ operators at risk of traffic hijack as they lag on RPKI. https://www.manrs.org/2020/10/major-anz-operators-at-risk-of-traffic-hijack-as-they-lag-on-rpki/. Last accessed 2024/7/10

38. AS38195/Superloop+RPKI. https://lists.ausnog.net/pipermail/ausnog/2020-June/044256. html. Last accessed 2024/7/10
39. RETN deployed RPKI origin validation on AS9002. https://retn.net/cn/news-events/retn-dep loyed-rpki-origin-validation-on-as9002. Last accessed 2024/7/10
40. RPKI Route Origin Validation and AS3333. https://www.mail-archive.com/routing-wg@ ripe.net/msg01448.html. Last accessed 2024/7/10
41. Lumen enhances routing security with Resource Public Key Infrastructure (RPKI)— Lumen. https://blog.lumen.com/lumen-enhances-routing-security-with-resource-public-key-infrastructure-rpki/. Last accessed 2024/7/10
42. Vocus AS4826 RPKI. https://www.mail-archive.com/ausnog@lists.ausnog.net/msg05895. html. Last accessed 2024/7/10

Lattice-Based Universal Designated Multi-verifiers Signature Scheme

Yanhua Zhang[1,2]($\boxtimes$), Willy Susilo[3], Yan Chen[1], Fuchun Guo[3], and Jiaming Wen[3,4]

[1] School of Computer Science and Technology, Zhengzhou University of Light Industry, Zhengzhou 450001, China
yhzhang@email.zzuli.edu.cn
[2] Henan Key Laboratory of Network Cryptography Technology, Zhengzhou, China
[3] School of Computing and Information Technology, University of Wollongong, Wollongong NSW 2522, Australia
{wsusilo,fuchun}@uow.edu.au, wenjm@whu.edu.cn
[4] School of Cyber Science and Engineering, Wuhan University, Wuhan 430072, China

Abstract. In a universal designated multi-verifiers signature (UDMVS) scheme, any signature holder, not necessarily the signer, can non-interactively prove to a set of specific verifiers the fact that the signature holder holds a valid signature from the signer, but the designated verifiers are unable to convince any third party of this fact. However, the existing UDMVS schemes based on the large integer factorization problem and the discrete logarithm problem on finite field or elliptic curve are no longer secure in the post quantum era. To overcome this limitation, we propose a lattice-based UDMVS scheme, which is resistant to quantum computing attacks, it also avoids the risk of online eavesdropping attacks on existing universal designated verifier signature schemes. Moreover, based on the small integer solution (SIS) problem and the learning with errors (LWE) problem, the proposed lattice-based UDMVS scheme is provably secure in the random oracle model for the strong unforgeability, the non-transferability and the privacy of signer's identity.

Keywords: Lattice · Universal designated verifier signature · Multi-verifiers · Non-transferability

1 Introduction

As for a conventional digital signature, its authenticity is often considered to be public and transferable. However, these properties may not be desirable in some special applications with a requirement of privacy protection, such as electronic voting, electronic auction, cloud medical, and so on. A representative solution is designated verifier signature (DVS), first introduced by Jakobsson et al. [8] in 1996, which provides an innovative property called non-transferability (NT): any third party cannot distinguish whether a given signature was actually produced

Z. Xia and J. Chen (Eds.): ISPEC 2024, LNCS 15053, pp. 33–54, 2024.
https://doi.org/10.1007/978-981-97-9053-1_3

by the signer or simulated by a designated verifier. In 1998, Krawczyk and Rabin [10] proposed chameleon signature, which achieves the NT security by embedding a chameleon hash function (CHF) into the signing algorithm. However, these two primitives are vulnerable to online eavesdropping attacks. In 2003, Saeednia et al. [21] constructed a strong DVS (SDVS) scheme to avoid the above risk. SDVS also holds the privacy of signer's identity (PSI), which means that given two potential signing public keys and a valid signature, it is computationally infeasible for an eavesdropper to determine which of these two keys the signature is associated with. Subsequently, Laguillaumie and Vergnaud [11] suggested an extension of SDVS with a single designated verifier to the multi-verifiers setting.

Motivated by privacy issues associated with the dissemination of signed digital certificates, in 2003, Steinfeld et al. [24] proposed the notion of universal DVS (UDVS). UDVS focuses on protecting the privacy of a signature holder, by allowing any holder (not necessarily the signer) of a signature to convert a publicly verifiable signature (PV-Sig) into a designated verifiable signature (DV-Sig) that is similar to designated verifiable signature generation in SDVS just by adopting the public keys of the signer and the designated verifier. In 2005, based on the bilinear Diffie-Hellman hardness assumption, Ng et al. [17] proposed a universal designated multi-verifiers signature (UDMVS) scheme, which allows a signature holder to designate the signature for a fixed number of verifiers. In fact, UDMVS can be regarded as a generalization of the applications of non-transferable signatures, which divides the operations of signing and designating into two different roles [12,13,22,28,30].

Unfortunately, almost all existing UDVS (and UDMVS) schemes are based on the traditional number theory problems such as the large integer factorization problem and the discrete logarithm problem on finite field or elliptic curve, which are insecure as their underlying assumptions will be compromised on quantum computers [23]. Since the creative works of Ajtai [1], Regev [20] and Gentry et al. [7], lattice has a solid theoretical foundation as a cryptographic design tool. Up to now, lattice-based cryptography (LBC) is still considered as one of the most promising and firm candidates for post-quantum cryptography [9]. In addition to the lightweight algebraic operations, the hardness problems over lattices enjoy a connection from the *average-case* to the *worst-case*. Before the advent of post-quantum era, it is considered essential to transfer classical cryptosystems to the world of lattice-based cryptography.

Related Works. The first UDVS scheme, based on the bilinear Diffie-Hellman hardness assumption, was creatively proposed by Steinfeld et al. [24] in order to address privacy issues associated with dissemination of signed digital certificates. Subsequently, they showed how to construct a UDVS from a standard Schnorr or RSA signature [25]. For the issues of dependence on certificate and key management, Zhang et al. [29] proposed an identity-based UDVS scheme. Furthermore, Ng et al. [17] and Seo et al. [22] proposed the first UDMVS scheme and the first identity-based UDMVS scheme, respectively.

Recently, in the multi-verifiers setting, Rastegari et al. [19] proposed a generic new pattern for a designated multi-verifiers signature scheme in which a threshold number of the set of designated multi-verifiers can check the validity of the signature. Lin [14] proposed a time-constrained strong designated multi-verifiers signature scheme based on bilinear pairings. Wang et al. [28] proposed a UDMVS scheme with content extraction in the random oracle model, and the computation costs and signature lengths are independent of the number of designated multi-verifiers. Arora and Sharma [3] constructed several multi-signers strong designated multi-verifiers signature schemes based on bilinear pairings, the large integer factorization problem and the discrete logarithm problem.

Compared with the above works, more attention is paid to the post-quantum schemes. As far as we know, the unique lattice-based UDVS scheme designed by Li et al. [12] is vulnerable to online eavesdropping attacks, it is mainly because the designated verifier's secret key is not involved in any computation of the verifying algorithm. Zhang et al. [31] proposed a lattice-based DVS which is also vulnerable to online eavesdropping attacks due to the same issue as [12]. Noh and Jeong [18] constructed an SDVS based on the small integer solution (SIS) problem over lattices, however, a public-key encryption is adopted to realize the PSI security, resulting in an increase in the size of final signature. Cai et al. [5] proposed an identity-based SDVS based on the ring-SIS assumption, however, the generation of public keys for the signer and a designated verifier strictly depends on a selected square matrix, and once this square matrix is reversible, there is a serious security vulnerability that any adversary can calculate the secret keys. Thanalakshmi et al. [26,27] constructed a hash-based chameleon signature and a hash-based DVS, however, in the former both the signer and a designated verifier need to store a complex directed acyclic graph, and in the latter the PSI security does not hold.

Our Contributions. We construct the first (to our knowledge) lattice-based UDMVS scheme, which is conjectured resistant to quantum attacks. In particular, our construction only requires a single secret key of any designated verifier for verification, and all secret keys of designated multi-verifiers for simulation, which enjoys an optimal trade-off between efficiency and security, and makes up for the vulnerability that all existing UDVS cannot resist online eavesdropping attacks simultaneously. To sum up, our UDMVS scheme achieves the following features:

- One designation for all designated multi-verifiers: A signature holder converts PV-Sig into DV-Sig for multi-verifiers only with a single designation operation.
- Avoidance of online eavesdropping attacks: The verification operations of DV-Sig have strict limits of authorities (only for designated multi-verifiers) even in the public channel.
- Provable security: Under the harness assumptions of SIS and learning with errors (LWE) problems, our scheme satisfies the strong unforgeability of PV-Sig and DV-Sig under adaptive chosen-message attacks, the non-transferability of DV-Sig and the privacy of signer's identity.

Organization. The organization of the paper is as follows. In Sect. 2, we review the definition of UDMVS and some background knowledge on lattices. A lattice-based UDMVS scheme in the random oracle model is described and analyzed in Sect. 3. In the final Sect. 4, we conclude our whole paper.

2   Definition and Security Model

Table 1 refers to the notations used in this paper.

Table 1. Notations of this paper

Notations	Explanation
$\|\mathbf{A}\|, \|\mathbf{a}\|$	Euclidean norm of matrix $\mathbf{A}$, and vector $\mathbf{a}$
$\widetilde{\mathbf{A}}$	Gram-Schmidt orthogonalization of matrix $\mathbf{A}$
$\xleftarrow{\$}$	Sampling uniformly at random
$\log n$	Logarithmic of n with base 2
$\lceil n \rceil$	The smallest integer not less than n
$[l]$	The set $\{1, 2, \cdots, l\}$
ppt	Probabilistic polynomial-time

2.1   Universal Designated Multi-verifiers Signature

Definition 1. *(UDMVS) A* UDMVS *involves at least 3 distinct entities: a signer* S, *a signature holder* D *and a set of designated multi-verifiers* $\{V_i\}_{i \in [l]}$, *and consists of 8 polynomial time algorithms which are described as follows:*

– Setup(1^n): *This is the setup algorithm on input a security parameter n, outputs a string consisting of public parameters* pp *that is publicly available to all entities and as an implicit input of all other algorithms.*
– SKeyGen(pp): *This is the signer's key generation algorithm on input parameters* pp, *outputs the signer's public-secret key pair* (pk_S, sk_S).
– VKeyGen(pp): *This is the designated verifier's key generation algorithm on input parameters* pp, *outputs the verifier's public-secret key pair* (pk_{V_i}, sk_{V_i}).
– Sig(pk_S, sk_S, m): *This is the signing algorithm run by a signer* S. *On input* S*'s public-secret key pair* (pk_S, sk_S) *and a message* m, *outputs a PV-Sig σ.*
– Ver(pk_S, m, σ): *This is the verifying algorithm run by a signature holder* D. *On input* S*'s public key* pk_S, *a message* m *and a PV-Sig σ, outputs a verification decision as* Acc *or* Rej.
– Des($pk_S, \{pk_{V_i}\}_{i \in [l]}, m, \sigma$): *This is the designation algorithm run by a signature holder* D. *On input* S*'s public key* pk_S, *a set of designated multi-verifiers' public keys* $\{pk_{V_i}\}_{i \in [l]}$, *a message* m *and a PV-Sig σ, outputs a DV-Sig $\hat{\sigma}$.*
– DesVer($pk_S, \{pk_{V_i}\}_{i \in [l]}, sk_{V_i}, m, \hat{\sigma}$): *This is the designated verifying algorithm run by any designated verifier* V_i. *On input* S*'s public key* pk_S, *a set of designated multi-verifiers' public keys* $\{pk_{V_i}\}_{i \in [l]}$, *a verifier's secret key* sk_{V_i}, *a message* m *and a DV-Sig $\hat{\sigma}$, outputs a verification decision as* Acc *or* Rej.

– Sim(pk$_S$, {(pk$_{V_i}$, sk$_{V_i}$)}$_{i\in[l]}$, m): *This is the simulation algorithm jointly run by all designated multi-verifiers. On input* S*'s public key* pk$_S$*, a set of designated multi-verifiers' public-secret key pairs* {(pk$_{V_i}$, sk$_{V_i}$)}$_{i\in[l]}$ *and a message* m*, outputs a simulated* DV-Sig $\hat{\sigma}'$.

A *UDMVS scheme requires the correctness of* Ver*,* DesVer*, and* Sim*:*

– Ver *correctness: It requires that the* PV-Sig *generated by algorithm* Sig *should be verified as a valid signature by algorithm* Ver*, i.e.,*

$$Pr[\mathsf{Ver}(pk_S, m, \mathsf{Sig}(pk_S, sk_S, m)) = Acc] = 1$$

– DesVer *correctness: It requires that the* DV-Sig *generated by algorithm* Des *should be verified as a valid signature by algorithm* DesVer*, i.e.,*

$$Pr[\mathsf{DesVer}(pk_S, \{pk_{V_i}\}_{i\in[l]}, sk_{V_i}, m, \mathsf{Des}(pk_S, \{pk_{V_i}\}_{i\in[l]}, m, \sigma)) = Acc] = 1$$

– Sim *correctness: It requires that the* DV-Sig *simulated by algorithm* Sim *should be verified as a valid signature by algorithm* DesVer*, i.e.,*

$$Pr[\mathsf{DesVer}(pk_S, \{pk_{V_i}\}_{i\in[l]}, sk_{V_i}, m, \mathsf{Sim}(pk_S, \{(pk_{V_i}, sk_{V_i})\}_{i\in[l]}, m)) = Acc] = 1$$

Next, we define the security model for UDMVS. A practical UDMVS scheme is mainly concerned with the following 4 security properties: PV-unforgeability (PV-UF), DV-unforgeability (DV-UF), non-transferability (NT) and the privacy of signer's identity (PSI).

The unforgeability of UDMVS is categorized into PV-UF and DV-UF, and the former is defined to prevent attacks to fool the signature holder D, and the latter is defined to prevent attacks to fool the designated multi-verifiers {V$_i$}$_{i\in[l]}$. In particular, PV-UF is just the strong unforgeability of a standard digital signature and as it was proved in [24] that DV-UF security implies PV-UF security, thus we omit the detailed definition of PV-UF and only introduce the DV-UF security.

Definition 2. *(DV-UF) The* DV-UF *security under adaptive chosen-message attacks of a* UDMVS *scheme is described by the following game between a* ppt *adversary* $\mathcal{A}$ *and a challenger* $\mathcal{C}$*:*

– Setup: $\mathcal{C}$ *runs algorithms* Setup*,* SKeyGen *and* VKeyGen *to obtain* pp*,* (pk$_S$, sk$_S$) *and* {(pk$_{V_i}$, sk$_{V_i}$)}$_{i\in[l]}$*, then provides* (pp, pk$_S$, {pk$_{V_i}$}$_{i\in[l]}$) *to* $\mathcal{A}$.
– Sig queries: *Given a message* m*,* $\mathcal{C}$ *returns a* PV-Sig σ *on* m *which is generated by running* Sig(pk$_S$, sk$_S$, m).
– Des queries: *Given a message* m*,* $\mathcal{C}$ *returns a* DV-Sig $\hat{\sigma}$ *on* m *which is generated by running* Des(pk$_S$, {pk$_{V_i}$}$_{i\in[l]}$, m, σ).
– Sim queries: *Given a message* m*,* $\mathcal{C}$ *returns a* DV-Sig $\hat{\sigma}'$ *on* m *which is generated by running* Sim(pk$_S$, {(pk$_{V_i}$, sk$_{V_i}$)}$_{i\in[l]}$, m).
– DesVer queries: *Given a message* m *and a* DV-Sig $\hat{\sigma}$ *or* $\hat{\sigma}'$*,* $\mathcal{C}$ *returns a verification decision as* Acc *or* Rej *by running* DesVer (pk$_S$, {pk$_{V_i}$}$_{i\in[l]}$, sk$_{V_i}$, m, $\hat{\sigma}$ *or* $\hat{\sigma}'$).

– Output: *Finally, $\mathcal{A}$ outputs a message-DV-Sig pair $(\mathrm{m}^*, \hat{\sigma}^*)$, and the following restrictions should be satisfied:*

1. $\mathsf{DesVer}(\mathsf{pk_S}, \{\mathsf{pk_{V_i}}\}_{i\in[l]}, \mathsf{sk_{V_i}}, \mathrm{m}^*, \hat{\sigma}^*) = \mathsf{Acc}.$
2. m^* *has never been queried to the* Sig *queries.*
3. *The pair* $(\mathrm{m}^*, \hat{\sigma}^*)$ *is not a query-response to* Des *queries and* Sim *queries.*

The probability that $\mathcal{A}$ wins the above game, denoted by $\mathsf{SuccPT}_{\mathcal{A}}$, is taken over the randomness of $\mathcal{A}$, algorithms Sig, Ver, Des, Sim and DesVer. The advantage of $\mathcal{A}$ is defined as $\mathsf{Adv}^{\mathsf{DV\text{-}UF}}_{\mathsf{UDMVS},\mathcal{A}}(n) = \mathsf{SuccPT}_{\mathcal{A}}$, and we say that a UDMVS is unforgeable if $\mathsf{Adv}^{\mathsf{DV\text{-}UF}}_{\mathsf{UDMVS},\mathcal{A}}(n)$ is negligible in the security parameter n.

Informally, the purpose of NT security is to prevent designated multi-verifiers from convincing any third party that the message m was indeed signed by the signer, even if all designated multi-verifiers disclose their secret keys. Generally, it is closely related to the Sim correctness.

Definition 3. *(NT) The* NT *security of a UDMVS scheme is described by the following game between a* ppt *adversary $\mathcal{A}$ and a challenger $\mathcal{C}$:*

– Setup: *$\mathcal{C}$ runs algorithms* Setup, SKeyGen *and* VKeyGen *to obtain* pp, $(\mathsf{pk_S}, \mathsf{sk_S})$ *and* $\{(\mathsf{pk_{V_i}}, \mathsf{sk_{V_i}})\}_{i\in[l]}$, *then provides* $(\mathsf{pp}, \mathsf{pk_S}, \{(\mathsf{pk_{V_i}}, \mathsf{sk_{V_i}})\}_{i\in[l]})$ *to $\mathcal{A}$.*
– Sig queries: *Given a message* m, *$\mathcal{C}$ returns a PV-Sig σ on* m *which is generated by running* $\mathsf{Sig}(\mathsf{pk_S}, \mathsf{sk_S}, \mathrm{m})$.
– Challenge: *$\mathcal{A}$ submits a message* m^*, *$\mathcal{C}$ runs* $\mathsf{Sig}(\mathsf{pk_S}, \mathsf{sk_S}, \mathrm{m}^*)$ *to obtain a PV-Sig σ^*, then runs* $\mathsf{Des}(\mathsf{pk_S}, \{\mathsf{pk_{V_i}}\}_{i\in[l]}, \mathrm{m}^*, \sigma^*)$ *to obtain a DV-Sig $\hat{\sigma}_0^*$, and runs* $\mathsf{Sim}(\mathsf{pk_S}, \{(\mathsf{pk_{V_i}}, \mathsf{sk_{V_i}})\}_{i\in[l]}, \mathrm{m}^*)$ *to obtain a DV-Sig $\hat{\sigma}_1^*$, chooses a random bit* $b \in \{0,1\}$, *and returns $\hat{\sigma}_b^*$ to $\mathcal{A}$.*
– Output: *Finally, $\mathcal{A}$ outputs a bit $b^* \in \{0,1\}$, and wins if $b^* = b$.*

The advantage of $\mathcal{A}$ is defined as $\mathsf{Adv}^{\mathsf{NT}}_{\mathsf{UDMVS},\mathcal{A}}(n) = |\Pr[b^* = b] - 1/2|$, and we say that a UDMVS scheme is non-transferable if $\mathsf{Adv}^{\mathsf{NT}}_{\mathsf{UDMVS},\mathcal{A}}(n)$ is negligible in the security parameter n.

Informally, the purpose of PSI security is to prevent any third party, not having the secret key of anyone of the designated multi-verifiers, from distinguishing between the DV-Sig from two different signers.

Definition 4. *(PSI)The* PSI *security of a UDMVS scheme is described by the following game between a* ppt *adversary $\mathcal{A}$ and a challenger $\mathcal{C}$:*

– Setup: *$\mathcal{C}$ runs algorithms* Setup, SKeyGen *(twice) and* VKeyGen *to obtain* pp, $(\mathsf{pk_{S_0}}, \mathsf{sk_{S_0}})$, $(\mathsf{pk_{S_1}}, \mathsf{sk_{S_1}})$ *and* $\{(\mathsf{pk_{V_i}}, \mathsf{sk_{V_i}})\}_{i\in[l]}$, *then except* $\{\mathsf{sk_{V_i}}\}_{i\in[l]}$, *provides* $(\mathsf{pp}, \mathsf{pk_{S_0}}, \mathsf{sk_{S_0}}, \mathsf{pk_{S_1}}, \mathsf{sk_{S_1}}, \{\mathsf{pk_{V_i}}\}_{i\in[l]})$ *to $\mathcal{A}$.*
– Sim queries: *Given a message* m *and a bit* $b \in \{0,1\}$, *$\mathcal{C}$ returns a DV-Sig $\hat{\sigma}_b'$ on* m *which is generated by running* $\mathsf{Sim}(\mathsf{pk_{S_b}}, \{(\mathsf{pk_{V_i}}, \mathsf{sk_{V_i}})\}_{i\in[l]}, \mathrm{m})$.
– DesVer queries: *Given a message* m, *a DV-Sig $\hat{\sigma}$ and a bit $b \in \{0,1\}$, $\mathcal{C}$ returns a verification decision as* Acc *or* Rej *by running* $\mathsf{DesVer}(\mathsf{pk_{S_b}}, \{\mathsf{pk_{V_i}}\}_{i\in[l]}, \mathsf{sk_{V_i}}, \mathrm{m}, \hat{\sigma})$.

– Challenge: $\mathcal{A}$ submits a message m^*, $\mathcal{C}$ runs $\mathsf{Sig}(\mathsf{pk}_{\mathsf{S}_0}, \mathsf{sk}_{\mathsf{S}_0}, \mathsf{m}^*)$ to obtain a PV-Sig σ_0^*, then runs $\mathsf{Des}(\mathsf{pk}_{\mathsf{S}_0}, \{\mathsf{pk}_{\mathsf{V}_i}\}_{i\in[l]}, \mathsf{m}^*, \sigma_0^*)$ to obtain a DV-Sig $\hat{\sigma}_0^*$, and runs $\mathsf{Sig}(\mathsf{pk}_{\mathsf{S}_1}, \mathsf{sk}_{\mathsf{S}_1}, \mathsf{m}^*)$ to obtain a PV-Sig σ_1^*, then runs $\mathsf{Des}(\mathsf{pk}_{\mathsf{S}_1}, \{\mathsf{pk}_{\mathsf{V}_i}\}_{i\in[l]}, \mathsf{m}^*, \sigma_1^*)$ to obtain a DV-Sig $\hat{\sigma}_1^*$, chooses a random bit $b \in \{0,1\}$, and returns $\hat{\sigma}_b^*$ to $\mathcal{A}$.
– Output: Finally, $\mathcal{A}$ outputs a bit $b^* \in \{0,1\}$, and wins if the followings hold:

1. $b^* = b$,
2. $(\mathsf{m}^*, \hat{\sigma}_b^*)$ was not queried to DesVer queries for any $b \in \{0,1\}$.

The advantage of $\mathcal{A}$ is defined as $\mathsf{Adv}_{\mathsf{UDMVS},\mathcal{A}}^{\mathsf{PSI}}(n) = |\Pr[b^* = b] - 1/2|$, and we say that a UDMVS scheme has the privacy of signer's identity if $\mathsf{Adv}_{\mathsf{UDMVS},\mathcal{A}}^{\mathsf{PSI}}(n)$ is negligible in the security parameter n.

2.2 Lattices

In this subsection, we recall the knowledge on integer lattice Λ.

Definition 5. *(Lattice) Let $\boldsymbol{B} = [\boldsymbol{b}_1|\boldsymbol{b}_2|\cdots|\boldsymbol{b}_m] \in \mathbb{Z}_q^{m\times m}$ be a matrix whose columns are linearly independent vectors. An m-dimensional full-rank lattice generated by $\boldsymbol{B}$ is defined as $\Lambda(\boldsymbol{B}) = \{\sum_{i=1}^m z_i \cdot \boldsymbol{b}_i : z_i \in \mathbb{Z}\}$. Given n, m, $q \geq 2$, $\boldsymbol{A} \in \mathbb{Z}_q^{n\times m}$ and $\boldsymbol{u} \in \mathbb{Z}_q^n$, define the following q-ary lattice $\Lambda_q^\perp(\boldsymbol{A})$ and its coset:*

$$\Lambda_q^\perp(\boldsymbol{A}) = \{\boldsymbol{e} \in \mathbb{Z}^m \mid \boldsymbol{A} \cdot \boldsymbol{e} = \boldsymbol{0} \bmod q\}, \ \Lambda_q^{\boldsymbol{u}}(\boldsymbol{A}) = \{\boldsymbol{e} \in \mathbb{Z}^m \mid \boldsymbol{A} \cdot \boldsymbol{e} = \boldsymbol{u} \bmod q\}$$

Definition 6. *(SIS) The (q,n,m,β)SIS problem is: given an integer q, a uniformly random matrix $\boldsymbol{A} \in \mathbb{Z}_q^{n\times m}$ and a real $\beta > 0$, the goal is to find a non-zero integer vector $\boldsymbol{e} \in \mathbb{Z}^m$ such that $\|\boldsymbol{e}\| \leq \beta$ and $\boldsymbol{A} \cdot \boldsymbol{e} = \boldsymbol{0} \bmod q$.*

Definition 7. *(LWE) The (q,n,m,χ)LWE problem is: given a uniformly random matrix $\boldsymbol{A} \in \mathbb{Z}_q^{n\times m}$, a secret vector $\boldsymbol{s} \xleftarrow{\$} \mathbb{Z}_q^n$, a β-bounded error distribution χ over $\mathbb{Z}^m$ and a vector $\boldsymbol{b} = \boldsymbol{A}^\top \cdot \boldsymbol{s} + \boldsymbol{e} \bmod q$, the goal is to get the hidden vectors $\boldsymbol{s} \in \mathbb{Z}_q^n$ and $\boldsymbol{e} \in \chi$.*

As noted in [1,20], the average-case (q,n,m,β)-SIS problem and (q,n,m,χ)-LWE problem are as hard as approximating the shortest independent vectors problems $\mathsf{SIVP}_{\beta\cdot\tilde{\mathcal{O}}(\sqrt{n})}$ and $\mathsf{SIVP}_{\tilde{\mathcal{O}}(nq/\beta)}$ in the worst-case, respectively.

Definition 8. *(Gaussian on lattice) Given an integer m, a center $\boldsymbol{c} \in \mathbb{Z}^m$, and a Gaussian parameter $s > 0$, we define: $\rho_{s,c}(\boldsymbol{x}) = exp(-\pi\|\boldsymbol{x} - \boldsymbol{c}\|^2/s^2)$: a discrete Gaussian function over $\mathbb{Z}^m$ with $\boldsymbol{c}$ as the center and s as the Gaussian parameter; $\mathcal{D}_{\Lambda,s,c}(\boldsymbol{x}) = \rho_{s,c}(\boldsymbol{x})/\sum_{\boldsymbol{x}\in\Lambda}\rho_{s,c}(\boldsymbol{x})$: a discrete Gaussian distribution with $\boldsymbol{c}$ as the center and s as the parameter over Λ. We omit the subscript and denote it as $\mathcal{D}_{\Lambda,s}$ if $\boldsymbol{c} = \boldsymbol{0}$.*

2.3   Sampling Algorithms

Lemma 1. *([1,2,16]). Let $n \geq 1$, $q \geq 2$, $m = 2n\lceil \log q \rceil$, there is a* ppt *algorithm* TrapGen(q, n, m) *that returns $\boldsymbol{A}$ and a trapdoor $\boldsymbol{T_A}$ of $\Lambda_q^\perp(\boldsymbol{A})$, where $\boldsymbol{A}$ is statistically close to uniform distribution over $\mathbb{Z}_q^{n \times m}$, and $\|\widetilde{\boldsymbol{T_A}}\| \leq \mathcal{O}(\sqrt{n \log q})$.*

Lemma 2. *([6]). Let $n \geq 1$, $q \geq 2$, $m = 2n\lceil \log q \rceil$, given $\boldsymbol{A} \in \mathbb{Z}_q^{n \times m}$, $\boldsymbol{A}' \in \mathbb{Z}_q^{n \times m'}$ and a trapdoor $\boldsymbol{T_A}$ of $\Lambda_q^\perp(\boldsymbol{A})$, there is a deterministic polynomial time algorithm* ExtBasis$(\boldsymbol{T_A}, [\boldsymbol{A}|\boldsymbol{A}'])$ *that returns a trapdoor $\boldsymbol{T}_{[\boldsymbol{A}|\boldsymbol{A}']} \in \mathbb{Z}^{(m+m') \times (m+m')}$ of $\Lambda_q^\perp([\boldsymbol{A}|\boldsymbol{A}'])$, and $\|\widetilde{\boldsymbol{T}_{[\boldsymbol{A}|\boldsymbol{A}']}}\| = \|\widetilde{\boldsymbol{T_A}}\|$.*

Gentry et al. [7] proposed an algorithm to sample a small vector (or matrix) from a discrete Gaussian distribution, and an optimized version was shown by Micciancio and Peikert [16]. Moreover, Micciancio and Peikert also proposed the algorithm of inverting an LWE instance.

Lemma 3. *([7,16]). Let $n, k \geq 1$, $q \geq 2$, $m = 2n\lceil \log q \rceil$, given $\boldsymbol{A} \in \mathbb{Z}_q^{n \times m}$, a trapdoor $\boldsymbol{T_A}$ of $\Lambda_q^\perp(\boldsymbol{A})$, a Gaussian parameter $s = \|\widetilde{\boldsymbol{T_A}}\| \cdot \omega(\sqrt{\log n})$ and $\boldsymbol{u} \in \mathbb{Z}_q^n$ or $\boldsymbol{U} \in \mathbb{Z}_q^{n \times k}$, there is a* ppt *algorithm* SamplePre$(\boldsymbol{A}, \boldsymbol{T_A}, \boldsymbol{u} \text{ or } \boldsymbol{U}, s)$ *that returns $\boldsymbol{e} \in \mathbb{Z}^m$ or $\boldsymbol{E} \in \mathbb{Z}^{m \times k}$, where $\boldsymbol{e}$ or each column of $\boldsymbol{E}$ is sampled from a distribution statistically close to $\mathcal{D}_{\Lambda_q^u(\boldsymbol{A}),s}$ or $\mathcal{D}_{\Lambda_q^{u_i}(\boldsymbol{A}),s}$, here $\boldsymbol{u}_i$ is the i-th column of $\boldsymbol{U}$.*

Note: In the followings we default SamplePre$([\boldsymbol{A}|\boldsymbol{A}'], \boldsymbol{T_A}, \boldsymbol{u} \text{ or } \boldsymbol{U}, s)$ consists of two steps, i.e., first running ExtBasis$(\boldsymbol{T_A}, [\boldsymbol{A}|\boldsymbol{A}'])$ to get $\boldsymbol{T}_{[\boldsymbol{A}|\boldsymbol{A}']}$, then running SamplePre$([\boldsymbol{A}|\boldsymbol{A}'], \boldsymbol{T}_{[\boldsymbol{A}|\boldsymbol{A}']}, \boldsymbol{u} \text{ or } \boldsymbol{U}, s)$ to get $\boldsymbol{e} \in \mathbb{Z}^{m+m'}$ or $\boldsymbol{E} \in \mathbb{Z}^{(m+m') \times k}$.

Lemma 4. *([16]). Let $n \geq 1$, $q > 2$, $m = 2n\lceil \log q \rceil$, given a β-bounded error distribution χ over $\mathbb{Z}^m$, an LWE instance $\boldsymbol{b} = \boldsymbol{A}^\top \cdot \boldsymbol{s} + \boldsymbol{e} \bmod q$ and a trapdoor $\boldsymbol{T_A}$ of $\Lambda_q^\perp(\boldsymbol{A})$, there is a deterministic polynomial time algorithm* Invert$(\boldsymbol{A}, \boldsymbol{b}, \boldsymbol{T_A})$ *that returns the secret $\boldsymbol{s} \in \mathbb{Z}_q^n$ and error $\boldsymbol{e} \in \chi$.*

Lemma 5. *([15]). For any $\boldsymbol{A} \in \mathbb{Z}_q^{n \times m}$ where $m > 64 + n \log q / \log(2s+1)$, for a uniformly random $\boldsymbol{s} \xleftarrow{\$} \{-s, \cdots, 0, \cdots, s\}^m$, with a probability $1 - 2^{-100}$, there exists another $\boldsymbol{s}^* \in \{-s, \cdots, 0, \cdots, s\}^m$ such that $\boldsymbol{A} \cdot \boldsymbol{s} = \boldsymbol{A} \cdot \boldsymbol{s}^* \bmod q$.*

2.4   Rejection Sampling

The rejection sampling technique, first proposed by Lyubashevsky [15], is usually used in lattice-based schemes to make the distribution of signatures independent of certain secret values.

Lemma 6. *([15]) Given $\boldsymbol{c} \in \mathbb{Z}^m$ and a parameter $s = \omega(\|\boldsymbol{c}\|\sqrt{\log m})$, then*

$$Pr[\mathcal{D}_{\mathbb{Z}^m,s}(\boldsymbol{z})/\mathcal{D}_{\mathbb{Z}^m,\boldsymbol{c},s}(\boldsymbol{z}) = \mathcal{O}(1) : \boldsymbol{z} \xleftarrow{\$} \mathcal{D}_{\mathbb{Z}^m,s}] = 1 - 2^{-\omega(\log m)}$$

In particular, for any $\boldsymbol{c} \in \mathbb{Z}^m$, if $s = \alpha \cdot \|\boldsymbol{c}\|$ for any $\alpha > 0$, then $Pr[\mathcal{D}_{\mathbb{Z}^m,s}(\boldsymbol{z})/\mathcal{D}_{\mathbb{Z}^m,\boldsymbol{c},s}(\boldsymbol{z}) < exp(12/\alpha + 1/(2\alpha^2)) : \boldsymbol{z} \xleftarrow{\$} \mathcal{D}_{\mathbb{Z}^m,s}] > 1 - 2^{-100}$

Lemma 7. ([15]). *Let $\mathcal{T}$ be a subset of $\mathbb{Z}^m$ in which all elements have norms less that t, real $s = \omega(t\sqrt{\log m})$, and $\mathcal{G}$ be a probability distribution over $\mathcal{T}$, there is a constant $M = \mathcal{O}(1)$ s.t. the distribution of the following algorithm $\mathcal{A}_1$:*

1. Sample $v \xleftarrow{\$} \mathcal{G}$ and $z \xleftarrow{\$} \mathcal{D}_{\mathbb{Z}^m, v, s}$.
2. Output (z, v) with probability $min(\frac{\mathcal{D}_{\mathbb{Z}^m, s}(z)}{M \cdot \mathcal{D}_{\mathbb{Z}^m, v, s}(z)}, 1)$.

is within a statistical distance $\frac{2^{-\omega(\log m)}}{M}$ of the distribution of the following algorithm $\mathcal{A}_2$:

1. Sample $v \xleftarrow{\$} \mathcal{G}$ and $z \xleftarrow{\$} \mathcal{D}_{\mathbb{Z}^m, s}$.
2. Output (z, v) with probability $1/M$.

Moreover, the probability that $\mathcal{A}_1$ outputs something is at least $\frac{1 - 2^{-\omega(\log m)}}{M}$.

3 Our Lattice-Based UDMVS Scheme

Our UDMVS scheme consists of 8 polynomial time algorithms: Setup, SKeyGen, VKeyGen, Sig, Ver, Des, DesVer and Sim. Let the message space $\mathcal{M} = \{0,1\}^*$, $\mathcal{V} = \{V_1, V_2, \cdots, V_l\}$ be a set of designated multi-verifiers, and $|\mathcal{V}| = l$.

3.1 Description of the Scheme

- Setup(1^n): On input a security parameter n, set a prime modulus $q = \widetilde{\mathcal{O}}(n^2)$, dimension $m = 2n\lceil \log q \rceil$, two hash parameters $k = \mathcal{O}(n)$ and κ satisfying $2^\kappa \binom{k}{\kappa} \geq 2^{100}$, two Gaussian parameters $s_0 = \omega(\sqrt{n \log q \log n})$ and $s_1 = \omega(s_0 \kappa \sqrt{m \log m})$, and a distribution $\chi = \mathcal{D}_{\mathbb{Z}^m, s_1}$, the system specifies the following steps:

1. Select two collision-resistance cryptographic hash functions $\mathcal{H}_0 : \{0,1\}^* \rightarrow \{c : c \in \{-1, 0, 1\}^k, 0 < \|c\| \leq \sqrt{\kappa}\}$ and $\mathcal{H}_1 : \{0,1\}^* \rightarrow \mathbb{Z}_q^{n \times k}$.
2. Output the public parameters $\mathsf{pp} = (n, q, m, k, \kappa, s_0, s_1, \chi, \mathcal{H}_0, \mathcal{H}_1)$, which is an implicit input of the following algorithms.

- SKeyGen(pp): On input pp, the signer S specifies the following steps:

1. Run TrapGen(q, n, m) to generate the trapdoor $\mathbf{T}_{\mathbf{A}_S}$ of $\Lambda_q^\perp(\mathbf{A}_S)$
2. Output $(\mathsf{pk}_S, \mathsf{sk}_S) = (\mathbf{A}_S, \mathbf{T}_{\mathbf{A}_S})$.

- VKeyGen(pp): On input pp, a verifier $V_i \in \mathcal{V}$ specifies the following steps:

1. Run TrapGen(q, n, m) twice to generate the trapdoor $\mathbf{T}_{\mathbf{A}_{V_i,0}}$ of $\Lambda_q^\perp(\mathbf{A}_{V_i,0})$, and the trapdoor $\mathbf{T}_{\mathbf{A}_{V_i,1}}$ of $\Lambda_q^\perp(\mathbf{A}_{V_i,1})$.
2. Outputs $(\mathsf{pk}_{V_i}, \mathsf{sk}_{V_i}) = (\mathbf{A}_{V_i,0}, \mathbf{A}_{V_i,1}, \mathbf{T}_{\mathbf{A}_{V_i,0}}, \mathbf{T}_{\mathbf{A}_{V_i,1}})$.

Note: There is a CHF associated with $V_i \in \mathcal{V}$: $\mathcal{CH}_{V_i}(\mathbf{e}_0, \mathbf{e}_i) = \mathbf{A}_S \cdot \mathbf{e}_0 + \mathbf{A}_{V,0} \cdot \mathbf{e}_i \bmod q$. It achieves the chameleon property by choosing any $\mathbf{e}_0' \in \mathcal{D}_{\mathbb{Z}^m, s_1}$ and sampling a new $\mathbf{e}_i' \neq \mathbf{e}_i \in \mathcal{D}_{\mathbb{Z}^m, s_1}$ with the trapdoor $\mathbf{T}_{\mathbf{A}_{V_i,0}}$.

– Sig($\mathsf{pk}_S, \mathsf{sk}_S, \mathsf{m}$): On input S's public-secret key pair ($\mathsf{pk}_S, \mathsf{sk}_S$) and a message $\mathsf{m} \in \mathcal{M}$, the signer S specifies the following steps:

1. Check whether the local PV-Sig list has already stored the pair $(\mathsf{m}, \mathbf{E})$. If yes, do step 3 directly, otherwise, do step 2.
2. Run SamplePre($\mathbf{A}_S, \mathbf{T}_{\mathbf{A}_S}, \mathcal{H}_1(\mathsf{m}), s_0$) to generate $\mathbf{E} \in \mathbb{Z}^{m \times k}$, and store the pair $(\mathsf{m}, \mathbf{E})$ into the local PV-Sig list.
3. Output a PV-Sig $\sigma = (\mathbf{E})$ on m.

– Ver($\mathsf{pk}_S, \mathsf{m}, \sigma$): On input S's public key pk_S, a message $\mathsf{m} \in \mathcal{M}$ and a PV-Sig $\sigma = (\mathbf{E})$, the signature holder D specifies the following steps:

1. Check whether $0 < \|\mathbf{E}\| \leq s_0 \sqrt{m}$, and $\mathbf{A}_S \cdot \mathbf{E} = \mathcal{H}_1(\mathsf{m}) \bmod q$.
2. Output Acc if the above are satisfied, otherwise Rej.

– Des($\mathsf{pk}_S, \{\mathsf{pk}_{V_i}\}_{V_i \in \mathcal{V}}, \mathsf{m}, \sigma$): On input S's public key pk_S, a set of designated multi-verifiers' public keys $\{\mathsf{pk}_{V_i}\}_{V_i \in \mathcal{V}}$, a message $\mathsf{m} \in \mathcal{M}$ and a PV-Sig $\sigma = (\mathbf{E})$, the signature holder D specifies the following steps:

1. Sample uniformly random $\mathbf{s} \xleftarrow{\$} \mathbb{Z}_q^n$, and $\mathbf{y}, \mathbf{e}_1, \mathbf{e}_2, \cdots, \mathbf{e}_l \xleftarrow{\$} \chi$.
2. Compute $\mathbf{h}_i = \mathbf{A}_S \cdot \mathbf{y} + \mathbf{A}_{V,0} \cdot \mathbf{e}_i \bmod q \in \mathbb{Z}_q^n$, where $i \in [l]$.
3. Compute $\mathbf{b} = [\mathbf{A}_{V_1,1} | \mathbf{A}_{V_2,1} | \cdots | \mathbf{A}_{V_l,1}]^\top \cdot \mathbf{s} + \begin{bmatrix} \mathbf{e}_1 \\ \vdots \\ \mathbf{e}_l \end{bmatrix} \bmod q \in \mathbb{Z}_q^{lm}$.
4. Set $\mathbf{c} = \mathcal{H}_0(\mathbf{h}_1, \mathbf{h}_2, \cdots, \mathbf{h}_l, \mathbf{s}, \mathsf{m}) \in \{-1, 0, 1\}^k$.
5. Compute $\mathbf{z} = \mathbf{E} \cdot \mathbf{c} + \mathbf{y} \in \mathbb{Z}^m$.
6. Output a DV-Sig $\hat{\sigma} = (\mathbf{z}, \mathbf{c}, \mathbf{b})$ with a probability $\min(\frac{\mathcal{D}_{\mathbb{Z}^m, s_1}(\mathbf{z})}{M \cdot \mathcal{D}_{\mathbb{Z}^m, \mathbf{E} \cdot \mathbf{c}, s_1}(\mathbf{z})}, 1)$.

– DesVer($\mathsf{pk}_S, \{\mathsf{pk}_{V_i}\}_{V_i \in \mathcal{V}}, \mathsf{sk}_{V_i}, \mathsf{m}, \hat{\sigma}$): On input S's public key pk_S, a set of designated multi-verifiers' public keys $\{\mathsf{pk}_{V_i}\}_{V_i \in \mathcal{V}}$, a designated verifier's secret key sk_{V_i}, a message $\mathsf{m} \in \mathcal{M}$ and a DV-Sig $\hat{\sigma} = (\mathbf{z}, \mathbf{c}, \mathbf{b})$, the verifier V_i specifies the following steps:

1. Check whether $0 < \|\mathbf{z}\| \leq \eta \cdot s_1 \sqrt{m}$, where $1 < \eta < 2$ is a constant.
2. Run ExitBasis($\mathbf{T}_{\mathbf{A}_{V_i,1}}, [\mathbf{A}_{V_1,1} | \cdots | \mathbf{A}_{V_l,1}]$) to get a trapdoor $\mathbf{T}_{[\mathbf{A}_{V_1,1} | \cdots | \mathbf{A}_{V_l,1}]}$.
3. Run Invert($[\mathbf{A}_{V_1,1} | \cdots | \mathbf{A}_{V_l,1}], \mathbf{b}, \mathbf{T}_{[\mathbf{A}_{V_1,1} | \cdots | \mathbf{A}_{V_l,1}]}$) to get $\mathbf{e} = \begin{bmatrix} \mathbf{e}_1 \\ \vdots \\ \mathbf{e}_l \end{bmatrix}$ and $\mathbf{s}$.
4. Compute $\mathbf{h}_i' = \mathbf{A}_S \cdot \mathbf{z} - \mathcal{H}_1(\mathsf{m}) \cdot \mathbf{c} + \mathbf{A}_{V,0} \cdot \mathbf{e}_i \bmod q$, where $i \in [l]$.
5. Check whether $\mathbf{c} = \mathcal{H}_0(\mathbf{h}_1', \mathbf{h}_2', \cdots, \mathbf{h}_l', \mathbf{s}, \mathsf{m})$.
6. Output Acc if the above are satisfied, otherwise Rej.

– $\mathsf{Sim}(\mathsf{pk_S}, \{(\mathsf{pk_{V_i}}, \mathsf{sk_{V_i}})\}_{V_i \in \mathcal{V}}, \mathsf{m})$: On input S's public key $\mathsf{pk_S}$, a set of designated multi-verifiers' public-secret key pairs $\{(\mathsf{pk_{V_i}}, \mathsf{sk_{V_i}})\}_{V_i \in \mathcal{V}}$, and a message $\mathsf{m} \in \mathcal{M}$, the multi-verifiers $\{V_i\}_{i \in [l]}$ jointly specify the following steps:

1. Sample $\mathbf{z}_i \xleftarrow{\$} \mathcal{D}_{\mathbb{Z}^m, \eta s_1/l}$, $\mathbf{h}_i, \mathbf{s}_i \xleftarrow{\$} \mathbb{Z}_q^n$, and send them to $V_{j \in [l] \setminus i}$.
2. Check whether $0 < \|\mathbf{z}_i\| \le \eta \cdot s_1/l \cdot \sqrt{m}$, $i \in [l]$, if not, abort the simulation.
3. Otherwise, compute $\mathbf{z} = \sum_{i=1}^l \mathbf{z}_i$, $\mathbf{s} = \sum_{i=1}^l \mathbf{s}_i$ and $\mathbf{c} = \mathcal{H}_0(\mathbf{h}_1, \mathbf{h}_2, \cdots, \mathbf{h}_l, \mathbf{s}, \mathsf{m})$.
4. Run $\mathsf{SamplePre}(\mathbf{A}_{V_i,0}, \mathbf{T}_{\mathbf{A}_{V_i,0}}, \mathbf{h}_i - \mathbf{A_S} \cdot \mathbf{z} + \mathcal{H}_1(\mathsf{m}) \cdot \mathbf{c}, s_1)$ to generate $\mathbf{e}_i \in \mathbb{Z}^m$, and send it to $V_{j \in [l] \setminus i}$.
5. Check whether $0 < \|\mathbf{e}_i\| \le s_1 \sqrt{m}$ and $\mathbf{h}_i = \mathbf{A_S} \cdot \mathbf{z} - \mathcal{H}_1(\mathsf{m}) \cdot \mathbf{c} + \mathbf{A}_{V_i,0} \cdot \mathbf{e}_i \bmod q$, where $i \in [l]$, if not, abort the simulation.
6. Otherwise, compute $\mathbf{b} = [\mathbf{A}_{V_1,1} | \mathbf{A}_{V_2,1} | \cdots | \mathbf{A}_{V_l,1}]^\top \cdot \mathbf{s} + \begin{bmatrix} \mathbf{e}_1 \\ \vdots \\ \mathbf{e}_l \end{bmatrix} \bmod q \in \mathbb{Z}_q^{lm}$.
7. Output a simulated DV-Sig $\hat{\sigma}' = (\mathbf{z}, \mathbf{c}, \mathbf{b})$ with a probability $1/M$.

3.2 Analysis

In this subsection, we will analysis the Correctness, Efficiency and Security of our lattice-based UDMVS scheme in the random oracle model.

Correctness: We provide a correctness analysis as follows:

– Ver correctness: By algorithm $\mathsf{SamplePre}(\mathbf{A_S}, \mathbf{T}_{\mathbf{A_S}}, \mathcal{H}_1(\mathsf{m}), s_0)$ in $\mathsf{Sig}(\mathsf{pk_S}, \mathsf{sk_S}, \mathsf{m})$, we obtain a short $\mathbf{E} \in \mathbb{Z}^{m \times k}$ satisfying $\mathbf{A_S} \cdot \mathbf{E} = \mathcal{H}_1(\mathsf{m}) \bmod q$ and $0 < \|\mathbf{E}\| \le s_0 \sqrt{m}$ with an overwhelming probability. Thus, we have the conclusion that the PV-Sig σ is valid and will be accepted with overwhelming probability.
– DesVer correctness: By algorithm $\mathsf{Des}(\mathsf{pk_S}, \{\mathsf{pk_{V_i}}\}_{V_i \in \mathcal{V}}, \mathsf{m}, \sigma)$, we have that $\mathbf{h}_i = \mathbf{A_S} \cdot \mathbf{y} + \mathbf{A}_{V_i,0} \cdot \mathbf{e}_i \bmod q$, $\mathbf{A_S} \cdot \mathbf{z} = \mathbf{A_S} \cdot (\mathbf{E} \cdot \mathbf{c} + \mathbf{y}) = \mathbf{A_S} \cdot \mathbf{E} \cdot \mathbf{c} + \mathbf{A_S} \cdot \mathbf{y} \bmod q$. In addition, $\mathbf{A_S} \cdot \mathbf{E} = \mathcal{H}_1(\mathsf{m}) \bmod q$, we have that $\mathbf{A_S} \cdot \mathbf{z} = \mathbf{A_S} \cdot \mathbf{y} + \mathcal{H}_1(\mathsf{m}) \cdot \mathbf{c} \bmod q$. Furthermore, by algorithm $\mathsf{Invert}([\mathbf{A}_{V_1,1} | \cdots | \mathbf{A}_{V_l,1}], \mathbf{b}, \mathbf{T}_{[\mathbf{A}_{V_1,1} | \cdots | \mathbf{A}_{V_l,1}]})$, we have that $\{\mathbf{e}_i\}_{i \in [l]} \in \mathcal{D}_{\mathbb{Z}^m, s_1}$ and $\mathbf{s} \in \mathbb{Z}_q^n$. Finally, we have that

$$
\begin{aligned}
\mathcal{H}_0(\mathbf{h}_1', \cdots, \mathbf{h}_l', \mathbf{s}, \mathsf{m}) &= \mathcal{H}_0(\mathbf{A_S} \cdot \mathbf{z} - \mathcal{H}_1(\mathsf{m}) \cdot \mathbf{c} + \mathbf{A}_{V_1,0} \cdot \mathbf{e}_1, \cdots, \mathbf{A_S} \cdot \mathbf{z} \\
&\quad - \mathcal{H}_1(\mathsf{m}) \cdot \mathbf{c} + \mathbf{A}_{V_l,0} \cdot \mathbf{e}_l, \mathbf{s}, \mathsf{m}) \\
&= \mathcal{H}_0(\mathbf{A_S} \cdot \mathbf{y} + \mathbf{A}_{V_1,0} \cdot \mathbf{e}_1, \cdots, \mathbf{A_S} \cdot \mathbf{y} + \mathbf{A}_{V_l,0} \cdot \mathbf{e}_l, \mathbf{s}, \mathsf{m}) \\
&= \mathcal{H}_0(\mathbf{h}_1, \cdots, \mathbf{h}_l, \mathbf{s}, \mathsf{m}) = \mathbf{c} \in \{-1, 0, 1\}^k
\end{aligned}
$$

Thus, we have the conclusion that the DV-Sig $\hat{\sigma}$ is valid and will be accepted with overwhelming probability.

- Sim correctness: By algorithm $\mathsf{SamplePre}(\mathbf{A}_{V_i,0}, \mathbf{T}_{\mathbf{A}_{V_i,0}}, \mathbf{h}_i - \mathbf{A}_\mathsf{S} \cdot \mathbf{z} + \mathcal{H}_1(\mathsf{m}) \cdot \mathbf{c}, s_1)$ in $\mathsf{Sim}(\mathsf{pk}_\mathsf{S}, \{(\mathsf{pk}_{V_i}, \mathsf{sk}_{V_i})\}_{V_i \in \mathcal{V}}, \mathsf{m})$, we have that $\mathbf{A}_{V_i,0} \cdot \mathbf{e}_i = \mathbf{h}_i - \mathbf{A}_\mathsf{S} \cdot \mathbf{z} + \mathcal{H}_1(\mathsf{m}) \cdot \mathbf{c} \mod q$. In addition, by algorithm $\mathsf{Invert}([\mathbf{A}_{V_1,1}|\cdots|\mathbf{A}_{V_l,1}], \mathbf{b}, \mathbf{T}_{[\mathbf{A}_{V_1,1}|\cdots|\mathbf{A}_{V_l,1}]})$, we have that $\{\mathbf{e}_i\}_{i \in [l]} \in \mathcal{D}_{\mathbb{Z}^m, s_1}$ and $\mathbf{s} \in \mathbb{Z}_q^n$. Finally, we have that

$$
\begin{aligned}
\mathcal{H}_0(\mathbf{h}_1', \cdots, \mathbf{h}_l', \mathbf{s}, \mathsf{m}) &= \mathcal{H}_0(\mathbf{A}_\mathsf{S} \cdot \mathbf{z} - \mathcal{H}_1(\mathsf{m}) \cdot \mathbf{c} + \mathbf{A}_{V_1,0} \cdot \mathbf{e}_1, \cdots, \mathbf{A}_\mathsf{S} \cdot \mathbf{z} \\
&\quad - \mathcal{H}_1(\mathsf{m}) \cdot \mathbf{c} + \mathbf{A}_{V_l,0} \cdot \mathbf{e}_l, \mathbf{s}, \mathsf{m}) \\
&= \mathcal{H}_0(\mathbf{A}_\mathsf{S} \cdot \mathbf{z} - \mathcal{H}_1(\mathsf{m}) \cdot \mathbf{c} + \mathbf{h}_1 - \mathbf{A}_\mathsf{S} \cdot \mathbf{z} + \mathcal{H}_1(\mathsf{m}) \cdot \mathbf{c}, \cdots, \\
&\quad \times \mathbf{A}_\mathsf{S} \cdot \mathbf{z} - \mathcal{H}_1(\mathsf{m}) \cdot \mathbf{c} + \mathbf{h}_l - \mathbf{A}_\mathsf{S} \cdot \mathbf{z} + \mathcal{H}_1(\mathsf{m}) \cdot \mathbf{c}, \mathbf{s}, \mathsf{m}) \\
&= \mathcal{H}_0(\mathbf{h}_1, \cdots, \mathbf{h}_l, \mathbf{s}, \mathsf{m}) = \mathbf{c} \in \{-1, 0, 1\}^k
\end{aligned}
$$

Thus, we have the conclusion that the simulated DV-Sig $\hat{\sigma}'$ is valid and will be accepted with overwhelming probability. Efficiency: The efficiency aspect of our UDMVS scheme is as follows:

- The requirement of designated multi-verifiers' secret keys: Since our UDMVS is the first (to our knowledge) lattice-based non-transferable signature (including DVS, SDVS and UDVS) with designated multi-verifiers, it is difficult to provide an intuitive comparison of lattice-based constructions in terms of the number of designated multi-verifiers' secret keys involved in algorithms DesVer and Sim, therefore, we compare several schemes based on the traditional number theory problems, such as the large integer factorization and discrete logarithm problems with ours in Table 2.

Table 2. Comparison of requirement of designated multi-verifiers' secret keys

Schemes	DesVer	Sim
Rastegari et al. [19]	Threshold	All
Wang et al. [28]	All	All
Lin [14]	All	All
Arora-Sharma [3]	All	All
Ours	One	All

Compared with the schemes in [3,14,19,28], every verifier of designated multi-verifiers can check the validity of DV-Sig independently, thus, our UDMVS scheme eliminates the hassle that all designated multi-verifiers are needed to cooperate in order to verify the signature. For a UDMVS scheme in which only one designated verifier's secret key is involved in algorithm Sim, we consider the following scenario: a designated verifier $V_i \in \mathcal{V}$ simulates a DV-Sig $(\mathsf{m}^*, \hat{\sigma}^*)$ by using the secret key sk_{V_i}, then V_i can send $(\mathsf{m}^*, \hat{\sigma}^*)$ to the set of designated multi-verifiers $\mathcal{V} = \{V_1, V_2, \cdots, V_l\}$. For such a DV-Sig $(\mathsf{m}^*, \hat{\sigma}^*)$, every designated verifier can verify it in algorithm DesVer, however, obviously the DV-Sig

$(m^*, \hat{\sigma}^*)$ is a forge and should be reject. Therefore, there is a risk that the designated verifiers will deceive each other in this designated multi-verifiers model.

- The cost of transmission and storage: We compare the cost of transmission and storage of post-quantum non-transferable signature schemes with ours in Table 3 and define some notations as follows: $|\cdot|$ is the bit-size of an item, σ is the PV-Sig and $\hat{\sigma}$ is the DV-Sig. Furthermore, l' is the output length of a CHF in [18], in our scheme, l is the number of designated multi-verifiers and " $-$ " means that such an item does not exist in the corresponding scheme.

Table 3. Comparison of the cost of transmission and storage

Schemes	$|pp|$	$|pk_S|$	$|pk_{V_i}|$	$|sks|$	$|skv_i|$	$|\sigma|$	$|\hat{\sigma}|$
Zhang et al. [31]	$\tilde{\mathcal{O}}(n^2)$	$\tilde{\mathcal{O}}(n^2)$	$\tilde{\mathcal{O}}(n^2)$	$\tilde{\mathcal{O}}(n^2)$	$\tilde{\mathcal{O}}(n^2)$	-	$\tilde{\mathcal{O}}(n)$
Noh-Jeong [18]	$\tilde{\mathcal{O}}(l'n^2)$	$\tilde{\mathcal{O}}(n^2)$	$\tilde{\mathcal{O}}(n^2)$	$\tilde{\mathcal{O}}(n^2)$	$\tilde{\mathcal{O}}(n^2)$	-	$\tilde{\mathcal{O}}(n)$
Li et al. [12]	$\tilde{\mathcal{O}}(n)$	$\tilde{\mathcal{O}}(n^2)$	$\tilde{\mathcal{O}}(n^2)$	$\tilde{\mathcal{O}}(n^2)$	$\tilde{\mathcal{O}}(n^2)$	$\tilde{\mathcal{O}}(n)$	$\tilde{\mathcal{O}}(n)$
Cai et al. [5]	$\tilde{\mathcal{O}}(n^2)$	$\tilde{\mathcal{O}}(n^2)$	$\tilde{\mathcal{O}}(n^2)$	$\tilde{\mathcal{O}}(n^2)$	$\tilde{\mathcal{O}}(n^2)$	-	$\tilde{\mathcal{O}}(n)$
Thanalakshmi et al. [27]	$\tilde{\mathcal{O}}(n)$	$\tilde{\mathcal{O}}(n^2)$	$\tilde{\mathcal{O}}(n^2)$	$\tilde{\mathcal{O}}(n^2)$	$\tilde{\mathcal{O}}(n^2)$	-	$\tilde{\mathcal{O}}(n)$
Ours	$\tilde{\mathcal{O}}(n^2)$	$\tilde{\mathcal{O}}(n^2)$	$\tilde{\mathcal{O}}(n^2)$	$\tilde{\mathcal{O}}(n^2)$	$\tilde{\mathcal{O}}(n^2)$	$\tilde{\mathcal{O}}(n^2)$	$\tilde{\mathcal{O}}(ln)$

Compared with the post-quantum schemes in [5,12,18,27,31], the set of designated multi-verifiers has l verifiers, thus, the DV-Sig $\hat{\sigma}$ in our scheme has a l-fold extension and the PV-Sig σ is a short matrix $\mathbf{E} \in \mathcal{D}_{\mathbb{Z}^{m \times k}, s_0}$, while in [12], it is a short vector $\mathbf{e} \in \mathcal{R}$ where $\mathcal{R} = \mathbb{Z}_q[x]/(x^n + 1)$. Specifically, in our scheme, any designated verifier's key generation involves running the same algorithm adopted by the signer's key generation twice, thus, the bit-sizes of pk_{V_i} and sk_{V_i} are twice that of pk_S and sk_S, but all enjoy the same asymptotic sizes. In [18], a semantically secure public-key encryption is adopted to hide some random intermediate vectors, thus causing a relatively larger public parameters.

- The security and functionality: We compare the security and functionality of the post-quantum non-transferable signature schemes mentioned above with ours in Table 4 and define some notations as follows: Universal means that the scheme supports the operations of signing and designating into two different roles; Multi means that the scheme supports the designated multi-verifiers; STM denotes the standard model and ROM denotes the random oracle model.

Compared with the post-quantum schemes in [5,18,27,31], any signature holder, not necessarily the signer can non-interactively prove to a specific verifier the fact that the holder holds a valid signature from the signer, the scheme in [12] and ours can directly address the privacy issues associated with the dissemination of signed digital certificate. In [18], the authors claimed that a strong unforgeability has been obtained, in fact, it only satisfies a weaker security called

Table 4. Comparison of the security and functionality

Schemes	DV-UF	NT	PSI	Universal	Multi	Model
Zhang et al. [31]	✓	✓	✗	✗	✗	ROM
Noh-Jeong [18]	✗	✓	✓	✗	✗	STM
Li et al. [12]	✗	✓	✗	✓	✗	ROM
Cai et al. [5]	✗	✓	✓	✗	✗	ROM
Thanalakshmi et al. [27]	✗	✓	✓	✗	✗	ROM
Ours	✓	✓	✓	✓	✓	ROM

the existential unforgeability against adaptive chosen-message attacks. In our scheme, instead of using a burdensome public-key encryption, a random encoding strategy based on the LWE hardness assumption is adopted in the algorithm Des, which encodes a random $\mathbf{s} \in \mathbb{Z}_q^n$ and the short vectors $\mathbf{e}_1, \mathbf{e}_2, \cdots, \mathbf{e}_l \in \mathcal{D}_{\mathbb{Z}^m, s_1}$ into $\mathbf{b} \in \mathbb{Z}_q^{lm}$. In particular, our scheme only requires a single secret key of any designated verifier for verification, and all secret keys of designated multi-verifiers for simulation, which enjoys an optimal trade-off between efficiency and security requirements, and makes up for the vulnerability that the existing UDVS schemes cannot resist online eavesdropping attacks simultaneously.

Security: For DV-UF security, NT security and PSI security of our UDMVS scheme, we show the following theorems.

Theorem 1. *Our lattice-based* UDMVS *scheme is* DV-*unforgeable against strong forgery under adaptive chosen-message attacks if the* SIS *assumption holds.*

Proof. Assume that $\mathcal{A}$ is a ppt adversary who makes at most q_s queires to the signer and q_h queries to the random oracles $\mathcal{H}_0$ and $\mathcal{H}_1$, and launches an adaptive chosen-message attack on our UDMVS scheme, and is able to forge a DV-Sig $\hat{\sigma}^*$ on a message $\mathsf{m}^* \in \mathcal{M}$ with a non-negligible probability ϵ, then the simulator $\mathcal{B}$ can use $\mathcal{A}$ to solve the $(q, n, 2m, \beta)$-SIS problem instance $(\mathbf{A}_0^* | \mathbf{A}_1^*) \cdot \mathbf{v}_1 = \mathbf{0} \bmod q$ or $(\mathbf{A}_0^* | \mathbf{A}_2^*) \cdot \mathbf{v}_2 = \mathbf{0} \bmod q$ or $\cdots (\mathbf{A}_0^* | \mathbf{A}_l^*) \cdot \mathbf{v}_l = \mathbf{0} \bmod q$ where $\mathbf{A}_0^*, \mathbf{A}_1^*, \cdots, \mathbf{A}_l^* \in \mathbb{Z}_q^{n \times m}$ and the bound $\beta = \widetilde{\mathcal{O}}(n)$, with a probability $\epsilon^2/(2q_s + 2q_h)$.

Similar to Lyubashevsky [15], to make sure that the usage of a random oracle $\mathcal{H}_0$ in our DV-UF security proof provides a qualified simulation to the adversary $\mathcal{A}$, a simulation, named as Hybrid UDMVS, in which no secret keys are involved and cannot be distinguished from a real UDMVS is first defined. In algorithms Des and Sim, a designated multi-verifiers signature is generated as follows:

1. Sample uniformly random $\mathbf{s} \xleftarrow{\$} \mathbb{Z}_q^n$, and $\mathbf{e}_1, \mathbf{e}_2, \cdots, \mathbf{e}_l \xleftarrow{\$} \mathcal{D}_{\mathbb{Z}^m, s_1}$.

2. Define $\mathbf{b} = [\mathbf{A}_{V_1,1} | \mathbf{A}_{V_2,1} | \cdots | \mathbf{A}_{V_l,1}]^\top \cdot \mathbf{s} + \begin{bmatrix} \mathbf{e}_1 \\ \vdots \\ \mathbf{e}_l \end{bmatrix} \bmod q \in \mathbb{Z}_q^{lm}$.

3. Sample uniformly random $\mathbf{c} \xleftarrow{\$} \{-1,0,1\}^k$, $\mathbf{z} \xleftarrow{\$} \mathcal{D}_{\mathbb{Z}^m, \eta s_1}$, and program
$\mathcal{H}_0(\mathbf{A}_0^* \cdot \mathbf{z} - \mathcal{H}_1(\mathsf{m}) \cdot \mathbf{c} + \mathbf{A}_{V_1,0} \cdot \mathbf{e}_1, \cdots, \mathbf{A}_0^* \cdot \mathbf{z} - \mathcal{H}_1(\mathsf{m}) \cdot \mathbf{c} + \mathbf{A}_{V_l,0} \cdot \mathbf{e}_l, \mathbf{s}, \mathsf{m}) = \mathbf{c}$.

4. Output $\sigma = (\mathbf{z}, \mathbf{c}, \mathbf{b})$ with a probability $1/M$.

Throughout the proof, let $\mathcal{D}_{\mathcal{H}_0} = \{\mathbf{c} : \mathbf{c} \in \{-1,0,1\}^k, 0 < \|\mathbf{c}\| \leq \sqrt{\kappa}\}$ denote the range of the oracle $\mathcal{H}_0$ and $t = q_h + q_s$ be the bound on the number of times the oracles $\mathcal{H}_0$ and $\mathcal{H}_1$ are called or programmed during $\mathcal{A}$'s attack (*Note*: A random oracle query can be made by $\mathcal{A}$ directly, or the random oracles can be programmed by algorithms Sig, Des and Sim when $\mathcal{A}$ asks to see a signature of a message). The interactions between $\mathcal{A}$ and a simulator $\mathcal{B}$ are as follows:

– Setup: Given $\mathbf{A}_0^*, \mathbf{A}_1^*, \cdots, \mathbf{A}_l^* \in \mathbb{Z}_q^{n \times m}$, $\mathcal{B}$ specifies the following steps:

1. Run $\mathsf{TrapGen}(q, n, m)$ to generate a trapdoor $\mathbf{T}_{\mathbf{A}_{V_1,1}}$ of $\Lambda_q^{\perp}(\mathbf{A}_{V_1,1})$.

2. Sample uniformly random $\mathbf{A}_{V_2,1}, \mathbf{A}_{V_3,1}, \cdots, \mathbf{A}_{V_l,1} \xleftarrow{\$} \mathbb{Z}_q^{n \times m}$.

3. Sample random coins ϕ for $\mathcal{A}$ and φ for $\mathcal{B}$, and random $\mathbf{c}_1, \mathbf{c}_2, \cdots, \mathbf{c}_t \xleftarrow{\$} \mathcal{D}_{\mathcal{H}_0}$, which will correspond to the responses of the random oracle $\mathcal{H}_0$.

4. Define $\mathsf{pk}_\mathsf{S} = \mathbf{A}_0^*$ and $\mathsf{pk}_{V_i} = (\mathbf{A}_i^*, \mathbf{A}_{V_i,1})$, where $i \in [l]$.

5. Keep $(\mathbf{T}_{\mathbf{A}_{V_1,1}}, \mathbf{c}_1, \mathbf{c}_2, \cdots, \mathbf{c}_t, \varphi)$ in secret, and send the public parameters $\mathsf{pp} = (\mathbf{A}_0^*, \mathbf{A}_1^*, \cdots, \mathbf{A}_l^*, \mathbf{A}_{V_1,1}, \cdots, \mathbf{A}_{V_l,1}, \phi)$ to $\mathcal{A}$.

– $\mathcal{H}_1$ queries: Given a message $\mathsf{m} \in \mathcal{M}$, $\mathcal{B}$ specifies the following steps:

1. Check whether a corresponding hash vector $\mathcal{H}_1(\mathsf{m})$ is stored in the hash list $l_{\mathcal{H}_1}$, if yes, return it directly.

2. Otherwise, sample $\mathbf{E} \xleftarrow{\$} \mathcal{D}_{\mathbb{Z}^{m \times k}, s_0}$, store $(\mathsf{m}, \sigma = (\mathbf{E}))$ in the local PV-Sig list and $(\mathsf{m}, \mathcal{H}_1(\mathsf{m}) = \mathbf{A}_0^* \cdot \mathbf{E} \bmod q)$ in $l_{\mathcal{H}_1}$, and return $\mathcal{H}_1(\mathsf{m})$ to $\mathcal{A}$.

– Sig queries: Given a message $\mathsf{m} \in \mathcal{M}$, $\mathcal{B}$ specifies the following steps:

1. Check whether a corresponding PV-Sig $\sigma = (\mathbf{E})$ is stored in the PV-Sig list, if yes, return it directly.

2. Otherwise, sample $\mathbf{E} \xleftarrow{\$} \mathcal{D}_{\mathbb{Z}^{m \times k}, s_0}$, store $(\mathsf{m}, \mathcal{H}_1(\mathsf{m}) = \mathbf{A}_0^* \cdot \mathbf{E} \bmod q)$ in $l_{\mathcal{H}_1}$ and $(\mathsf{m}, \sigma = (\mathbf{E}))$ in the local PV-Sig list, and return $\mathbf{E}$ to $\mathcal{A}$.

– $\mathcal{H}_0$ queries: Given $(\mathbf{A}_0^* \cdot \mathbf{y} + \mathbf{A}_1^* \cdot \mathbf{e}_1, \mathbf{A}_0^* \cdot \mathbf{y} + \mathbf{A}_2^* \cdot \mathbf{e}_2, \cdots, \mathbf{A}_0^* \cdot \mathbf{y} + \mathbf{A}_l^* \cdot \mathbf{e}_l, \mathbf{s}, \mathsf{m})$, $\mathcal{B}$ specifies the following steps:

1. Check whether a corresponding hash vector $\mathbf{c}$ is stored in the hash list $l_{\mathcal{H}_0}$, if yes, return it directly.

2. Otherwise, sample a random $\mathbf{c}_i \xleftarrow{\$} \{\mathbf{c}_1, \mathbf{c}_1, \cdots, \mathbf{c}_t\}$ that has not been used yet, store $(\mathbf{A}_0^* \cdot \mathbf{y} + \mathbf{A}_1^* \cdot \mathbf{e}_1, \mathbf{A}_0^* \cdot \mathbf{y} + \mathbf{A}_2^* \cdot \mathbf{e}_2, \cdots, \mathbf{A}_0^* \cdot \mathbf{y} + \mathbf{A}_l^* \cdot \mathbf{e}_l, \mathbf{s}, \mathsf{m}, \mathbf{c} = \mathbf{c}_i)$ in $l_{\mathcal{H}_0}$ and return $\mathbf{c}_i$ to $\mathcal{A}$.

– Des queries: Given a message $\mathsf{m} \in \mathcal{M}$, $\mathcal{B}$ specifies the following steps:

1. Check whether a PV-Sig $\sigma = (\mathbf{E})$ is stored in the PV-Sig list or adopt the method in $\mathcal{H}_1$ queries to obtain the pair $(\mathsf{m}, \mathcal{H}_1(\mathsf{m}) = \mathbf{A}_0^* \cdot \mathbf{E} \bmod q)$.
2. Run the algorithm in Hybrid UDMVS by adopting the random coins φ to produce a signature $\hat{\sigma} = (\mathbf{c}, \mathbf{z}, \mathbf{b})$.
3. Store the hash inputs $(\mathbf{A}_0^* \cdot \mathbf{z} - \mathbf{A}_0^* \cdot \mathbf{E} \cdot \mathbf{c} + \mathbf{A}_1^* \cdot \mathbf{e}_1, \mathbf{A}_0^* \cdot \mathbf{z} - \mathbf{A}_0^* \cdot \mathbf{E} \cdot \mathbf{c} + \mathbf{A}_2^* \cdot \mathbf{e}_2, \cdots, \mathbf{A}_0^* \cdot \mathbf{z} - \mathbf{A}_0^* \cdot \mathbf{E} \cdot \mathbf{c} + \mathbf{A}_l^* \cdot \mathbf{e}_l, \mathbf{s}, \mathsf{m})$ and output $\mathbf{c}$ into $l_{\mathcal{H}_1}$.
4. Return $\hat{\sigma}$ to $\mathcal{A}$.

- Sim queries: Given a message $\mathsf{m} \in \mathcal{M}$, $\mathcal{B}$ does as in Des queries and returns a signature $\hat{\sigma} = (\mathbf{c}, \mathbf{z}, \mathbf{b})$ to $\mathcal{A}$.
- DesVer queries: Given a signature $\hat{\sigma} = (\mathbf{z}, \mathbf{c}, \mathbf{b})$ and a message $\mathsf{m} \in \mathcal{M}$, $\mathcal{B}$ specifies the following steps:

1. Check whether $0 < \|\mathbf{z}\| \leq \eta \cdot s_1 \sqrt{m}$, where $1 < \eta < 2$ is a constant.
2. Run $\mathsf{ExitBasis}(\mathbf{T}_{\mathbf{A}_{V_1,1}}, [\mathbf{A}_{V_1,1}| \cdots |\mathbf{A}_{V_l,1}])$ to get a trapdoor $\mathbf{T}_{[\mathbf{A}_{V_1,1}|\cdots|\mathbf{A}_{V_l,1}]}$.
3. Run $\mathsf{Invert}([\mathbf{A}_{V_1,1}| \cdots |\mathbf{A}_{V_l,1}], \mathbf{b}, \mathbf{T}_{[\mathbf{A}_{V_1,1}|\cdots|\mathbf{A}_{V_l,1}]})$ to get $\begin{bmatrix} \mathbf{e}_1 \\ \vdots \\ \mathbf{e}_l \end{bmatrix}$ and $\mathbf{s}$.
4. Check whether $(\mathsf{m}, \mathcal{H}_1(\mathsf{m}))$ is stored in the hash list $l_{\mathcal{H}_1}$.
5. Check whether $(\mathbf{A}_0^* \cdot \mathbf{z} - \mathcal{H}_1(\mathsf{m}) \cdot \mathbf{c} + \mathbf{A}_1^* \cdot \mathbf{e}_1, \mathbf{A}_0^* \cdot \mathbf{z} - \mathcal{H}_1(\mathsf{m}) \cdot \mathbf{c} + \mathbf{A}_2^* \cdot \mathbf{e}_2, \cdots, \mathbf{A}_0^* \cdot \mathbf{z} - \mathcal{H}_1(\mathsf{m}) \cdot \mathbf{c} + \mathbf{A}_l^* \cdot \mathbf{e}_l, \mathbf{s}, \mathsf{m}, \mathbf{c})$ is stored in the hash list $l_{\mathcal{H}_0}$.
6. Outputs Acc if the above are satisfied, otherwise Rej.

- Output: With a probability ϵ, $\mathcal{A}$ outputs a message $\mathsf{m}^* \in \mathcal{M}$ and its designated multi-verifiers signature $\hat{\sigma}^* = (\mathbf{z}^*, \mathbf{c}^*, \mathbf{b}^*)$ which satisfies $0 < \|\mathbf{z}^*\| \leq \eta s_1 \sqrt{m}$ and $\mathbf{c}^* = \mathcal{H}_0(\mathbf{A}_0^* \cdot \mathbf{z}^* - \mathcal{H}_1(\mathsf{m}^*) \cdot \mathbf{c}^* + \mathbf{A}_1^* \cdot \mathbf{e}_1^*, \mathbf{A}_0^* \cdot \mathbf{z}^* - \mathcal{H}_1(\mathsf{m}^*) \cdot \mathbf{c}^* + \mathbf{A}_2^* \cdot \mathbf{e}_2^*, \cdots, \mathbf{A}_0^* \cdot \mathbf{z}^* - \mathcal{H}_1(\mathsf{m}^*) \cdot \mathbf{c}^* + \mathbf{A}_l^* \cdot \mathbf{e}_l^*, \mathbf{s}^*, \mathsf{m}^*)$, where $\mathbf{e}_1^*, \mathbf{e}_2^*, \cdots, \mathbf{e}_l^* \in \chi$ and $\mathbf{s}^* \subset \mathbb{Z}_q^n$ are the hidden vectors in $\mathbf{b}^*$.

With a probability $1 - 1/|\mathcal{D}_{\mathcal{H}_0}|$, $\mathbf{c}^*$ must be one of the $\mathbf{c}_i$ in $\{\mathbf{c}_1, \mathbf{c}_2, \cdots, \mathbf{c}_t\}$, so the probability that $\mathcal{A}$ succeeds in the forgery and $\mathbf{c}^*$ must be one of the $\mathbf{c}_i$'s, is at least $\epsilon - 1/|\mathcal{D}_{\mathcal{H}_0}|$. Let $\mathbf{c}^* = \mathbf{c}_j \in \{\mathbf{c}_1, \mathbf{c}_1, \cdots, \mathbf{c}_t\}$, there are two cases: $\mathbf{c}_j$ was programmed during Des queries (or Sim queries) made by $\mathcal{A}$, or it was a response to $\mathcal{H}_0$ queries made by $\mathcal{A}$.

- If $\mathbf{c}^* = \mathbf{c}_j$ was programmed during Des queries (or Sim queries): Assume that the simulator $\mathcal{B}$ programmed the random oracle $\mathbf{c}^* = \mathcal{H}_0(\mathbf{A}_0^* \cdot \mathbf{z} - \mathcal{H}_1(\mathsf{m}) \cdot \mathbf{c}^* + \mathbf{A}_1^* \cdot \mathbf{e}_1, \mathbf{A}_0^* \cdot \mathbf{z} - \mathcal{H}_1(\mathsf{m}) \cdot \mathbf{c}^* + \mathbf{A}_2^* \cdot \mathbf{e}_2, \cdots, \mathbf{A}_0^* \cdot \mathbf{z} - \mathcal{H}_1(\mathsf{m}) \cdot \mathbf{c}^* + \mathbf{A}_l^* \cdot \mathbf{e}_l, \mathbf{s}, \mathsf{m})$ when signing a message $\mathsf{m} \in \mathcal{M}$. Because $\mathcal{A}$ outputs a valid forgery $\hat{\sigma}^* = (\mathbf{z}^*, \mathbf{c}^*, \mathbf{b}^*)$ for a message $\mathsf{m}^* \in \mathcal{M}$, then we have that $\mathcal{H}_0(\mathbf{A}_0^* \cdot \mathbf{z} - \mathcal{H}_1(\mathsf{m}) \cdot \mathbf{c}^* + \mathbf{A}_1^* \cdot \mathbf{e}_1, \mathbf{A}_0^* \cdot \mathbf{z} - \mathcal{H}_1(\mathsf{m}) \cdot \mathbf{c}^* + \mathbf{A}_2^* \cdot \mathbf{e}_2, \cdots, \mathbf{A}_0^* \cdot \mathbf{z} - \mathcal{H}_1(\mathsf{m}) \cdot \mathbf{c}^* + \mathbf{A}_l^* \cdot \mathbf{e}_l, \mathbf{s}, \mathsf{m}) = \mathcal{H}_0(\mathbf{A}_0^* \cdot \mathbf{z}^* - \mathcal{H}_1(\mathsf{m}^*) \cdot \mathbf{c}^* + \mathbf{A}_1^* \cdot \mathbf{e}_1^*, \mathbf{A}_0^* \cdot \mathbf{z}^* - \mathcal{H}_1(\mathsf{m}^*) \cdot \mathbf{c}^* + \mathbf{A}_2^* \cdot \mathbf{e}_2^*, \cdots, \mathbf{A}_0^* \cdot \mathbf{z}^* - \mathcal{H}_1(\mathsf{m}^*) \cdot \mathbf{c}^* + \mathbf{A}_l^* \cdot \mathbf{e}_l^*, \mathbf{s}^*, \mathsf{m}^*)$. Thus, according to the collision-resistance property of oracle $\mathcal{H}_0$, $\mathcal{B}$ computes $\begin{bmatrix} \mathbf{e}_1 \\ \vdots \\ \mathbf{e}_l \end{bmatrix} = \mathbf{b} - [\mathbf{A}_{V_1,1}| \cdots |\mathbf{A}_{V_l,1}]^\top \cdot \mathbf{s}^*$, $\begin{bmatrix} \mathbf{e}_1^* \\ \vdots \\ \mathbf{e}_l^* \end{bmatrix} = \mathbf{b}^* - [\mathbf{A}_{V_1,1}| \cdots |\mathbf{A}_{V_l,1}]^\top \cdot \mathbf{s}^*$, and we have that $\mathcal{H}_1(\mathsf{m}) = \mathcal{H}_1(\mathsf{m}^*)$ and

$$\mathbf{A}_0^* \cdot \mathbf{z} - \mathcal{H}_1(\mathsf{m}) \cdot \mathbf{c}^* + \mathbf{A}_i^* \cdot \mathbf{e}_1 = \mathbf{A}_0^* \cdot \mathbf{z}^* - \mathcal{H}_1(\mathsf{m}^*) \cdot \mathbf{c}^* + \mathbf{A}_1^* \cdot \mathbf{e}_i^*$$

$$\Rightarrow (\mathbf{A}_0^* | \mathbf{A}_i^*) \cdot \begin{bmatrix} \mathbf{z} - \mathbf{z}^* \\ \mathbf{e}_i - \mathbf{e}_i^* \end{bmatrix} = \mathbf{0} \bmod q$$

Let $\mathbf{v}_i = \begin{bmatrix} \mathbf{z} - \mathbf{z}^* \\ \mathbf{e}_i - \mathbf{e}_i^* \end{bmatrix}$, it can be easily checked that there must be at least one $\mathbf{v}_i$, $i \in [l]$, satisfying $\mathbf{v}_i \neq \mathbf{0}$, because otherwise $\hat{\sigma}^* = (\mathbf{z}^*, \mathbf{c}^*, \mathbf{b}^*)$ is exactly the same as the old signature $\hat{\sigma} = (\mathbf{z}, \mathbf{c}^*, \mathbf{b})$. In addition, since $0 < \|\mathbf{z}^*\|, \|\mathbf{z}\| \leq \eta s_1 \sqrt{m}$ and $0 < \|\mathbf{e}_i^*\|, \|\mathbf{e}_i\| \leq s_1 \sqrt{m}$, we have that $0 < \|\mathbf{v}_i\| \leq 2s_1 \sqrt{(\eta^2 + 1)m} = \tilde{\mathcal{O}}(n)$.

- If $\mathbf{c}^* = \mathbf{c}_j$ was a response to $\mathcal{H}_0$ queries: $\mathcal{B}$ records $\hat{\sigma}^* = (\mathbf{z}^*, \mathbf{c}_j, \mathbf{b}^*)$ of $\mathcal{A}$ on the message $\mathsf{m}^* \in \mathcal{M}$, and generates fresh elements $\mathbf{c}_j', \mathbf{c}_{j+1}', \cdots, \mathbf{c}_t' \xleftarrow{\$} \mathcal{D}_{\mathcal{H}_0}$. $\mathcal{B}$ runs again with $(\mathbf{A}_0^*, \mathbf{A}_1^*, \cdots, \mathbf{A}_l^*, \mathbf{A}_{V_1,1}, \cdots, \mathbf{A}_{V_l,1}, \mathbf{c}_1, \cdots, \mathbf{c}_{j-1}, \mathbf{c}_j', \cdots, \mathbf{c}_t', \phi, \varphi)$. By the General Forking Lemma of Bellare and Neven [4], $\mathcal{B}$ obtains the probability that $\mathbf{c}_j' \neq \mathbf{c}_j$ and $\mathcal{A}$ uses the random oracle response in its forgery is at least $\epsilon^* = (\epsilon - 1/|\mathcal{D}_{\mathcal{H}_0}|)^2/t - (\epsilon - 1/|\mathcal{D}_{\mathcal{H}_0}|)/|\mathcal{D}_{\mathcal{H}_0}|$, and thus with the probability ϵ^*, $\mathcal{A}$ outputs a new signature $\hat{\sigma} = (\mathbf{z}, \mathbf{c}_j', \mathbf{b})$ of the message $\mathsf{m}^* \in \mathcal{M}$ and $(\mathbf{A}_0^* \cdot \mathbf{z} - \mathcal{H}_1(\mathsf{m}^*) \cdot \mathbf{c} + \mathbf{A}_1^* \cdot \mathbf{e}_1, \mathbf{A}_0^* \cdot \mathbf{z} - \mathcal{H}_1(\mathsf{m}^*) \cdot \mathbf{c} + \mathbf{A}_2^* \cdot \mathbf{e}_2, \cdots, \mathbf{A}_0^* \cdot \mathbf{z} - \mathcal{H}_1(\mathsf{m}^*) \cdot \mathbf{c} + \mathbf{A}_l^* \cdot \mathbf{e}_l, \mathbf{s}) = (\mathbf{A}_0^* \cdot \mathbf{z}^* - \mathcal{H}_1(\mathsf{m}^*) \cdot \mathbf{c}^* + \mathbf{A}_1^* \cdot \mathbf{e}_1^*, \mathbf{A}_0^* \cdot \mathbf{z}^* - \mathcal{H}_1(\mathsf{m}^*) \cdot \mathbf{c}^* + \mathbf{A}_2^* \cdot \mathbf{e}_2^*, \cdots, \mathbf{A}_0^* \cdot \mathbf{z}^* - \mathcal{H}_1(\mathsf{m}^*) \cdot \mathbf{c}^* + \mathbf{A}_l^* \cdot \mathbf{e}_l^*, \mathbf{s}^*)$ where $\mathbf{c}^* = \mathbf{c}_j$, $\mathbf{c} = \mathbf{c}_j'$ and $\mathbf{s} = \mathbf{s}^*$. $\mathcal{B}$ also computes

$$\begin{bmatrix} \mathbf{e}_1 \\ \vdots \\ \mathbf{e}_l \end{bmatrix} = \mathbf{b} - [\mathbf{A}_{V_1,1} | \cdots | \mathbf{A}_{V_l,1}]^\top \cdot \mathbf{s} \text{ and } \begin{bmatrix} \mathbf{e}_1^* \\ \vdots \\ \mathbf{e}_l^* \end{bmatrix} = \mathbf{b}^* - [\mathbf{A}_{V_1,1} | \cdots | \mathbf{A}_{V_l,1}]^\top \cdot \mathbf{s}^*,$$

thus by plugging in $\mathcal{H}_1(\mathsf{m}^*) = \mathbf{A}_0^* \cdot \mathbf{E}^* \bmod q$ obtained in $\mathcal{H}_1$ queries, we have that

$$\mathbf{A}_0^* \cdot \mathbf{z} - \mathcal{H}_1(\mathsf{m}^*) \cdot \mathbf{c} + \mathbf{A}_i^* \cdot \mathbf{e}_i = \mathbf{A}_0^* \cdot \mathbf{z} - \mathbf{A}_0^* \cdot \mathbf{E}^* \cdot \mathbf{c} + \mathbf{A}_i^* \cdot \mathbf{e}_i$$

$$= \mathbf{A}_0^* \cdot \mathbf{z}^* - \mathbf{A}_0^* \cdot \mathbf{E}^* \cdot \mathbf{c}^* + \mathbf{A}_i^* \cdot \mathbf{e}_i^*$$

$$\Rightarrow (\mathbf{A}_0^* | \mathbf{A}_i^*) \begin{bmatrix} \mathbf{z} - \mathbf{z}^* + \mathbf{E}^* \cdot (\mathbf{c}^* - \mathbf{c}) \\ \mathbf{e}_i - \mathbf{e}_i^* \end{bmatrix} = \mathbf{0} \bmod q$$

Let $\mathbf{v}_i = \begin{bmatrix} \mathbf{z} - \mathbf{z}^* + \mathbf{E}^* \cdot (\mathbf{c}^* - \mathbf{c}) \\ \mathbf{e}_i - \mathbf{e}_i^* \end{bmatrix}$, since $\|\mathbf{e}_i^*\|, \|\mathbf{e}_i\| \leq s_1 \sqrt{m}$, $\|\mathbf{z}^*\|, \|\mathbf{z}\| \leq \eta s_1 \sqrt{m}$, $\|\mathbf{E}^* \cdot \mathbf{c}^*\|, \|\mathbf{E}^* \cdot \mathbf{c}\| \leq s_0 \kappa \sqrt{m}$, we have $\|\mathbf{v}_i\| \leq 2\sqrt{m} \sqrt{(\eta s_1 + s_0 \kappa)^2 + s_1^2} = \tilde{\mathcal{O}}(n)$. Let $i \in \{1, 2, \cdots, k\}$ be a position in which $\mathbf{c}_i^* \neq \mathbf{c}_i$, then by Lemma 5, with a probability $1 - 2^{-100}$, there is another $\mathbf{E}' \in \{-s_0, \cdots, 0, \cdots, s_0\}^{m \times k}$ such that all columns, except for i-th, of $\mathbf{E}'$ are the same as $\mathbf{E}^*$ and $\mathbf{A}_0^* \cdot \mathbf{E}^* = \mathbf{A}_0^* \cdot \mathbf{E}' \bmod q$. So, if $\mathbf{z} - \mathbf{z}^* + \mathbf{E}^* \cdot (\mathbf{c}^* - \mathbf{c}) = 0$, then $\mathbf{z} - \mathbf{z}^* + \mathbf{E}' \cdot (\mathbf{c}^* - \mathbf{c}) \neq 0$, and since $\mathcal{B}$ does not take these secret keys as input and use them for simulating the Sig and Sim oracles, $\mathcal{A}$ does not know whether $\mathcal{B}$ holds a secret key $\mathbf{E}'$ or $\mathbf{E}^*$, $\mathcal{B}$ will obtain a non-zero $\mathbf{z} - \mathbf{z}^* + \mathbf{E}^* \cdot (\mathbf{c}^* - \mathbf{c})$ with a probability at least $1/2$, thus the answer $\mathbf{v}_i \neq \mathbf{0}$ is with a probability at least $(1/2 - 2^{-100})\epsilon^* \approx \epsilon^2/(2q_s + 2q_h)$. This concludes the proof.

Theorem 2. *Our lattice-based* UDMVS *scheme is non-transferable against adaptive chosen-message attacks.*

Proof. According to the security model in Definition 3, a game between a simulator $\mathcal{B}$ and a ppt adversary $\mathcal{A}$ is as follows:

– Setup: $\mathcal{B}$ specifies the following steps:

1. Run Setup(1^n), SkeyGen(pp) and VkeyGen(pp) as in Sec. 3.1 to output pp, ($\mathsf{pk_S}, \mathsf{sk_S}$) for the signer S and ($\mathsf{pk_{V_i}}, \mathsf{sk_{V_i}}$) for a designated verifier V_i.
2. Send ($\mathsf{pp}, \mathsf{pk_S}, \{(\mathsf{pk_{V_i}}, \mathsf{sk_{V_i}})\}_{i \in [l]}$) to $\mathcal{A}$.

– Sig queries: Given a message $\mathsf{m} \in \mathcal{M}$, $\mathcal{B}$ checks whether a corresponding PV-Sig $\sigma = (\mathbf{E})$ is stored in the PV-Sig list, if yes, return it directly, otherwise, runs Sig($\mathsf{pk_S}, \mathsf{sk_S}, \mathsf{m}$), store ($\mathsf{m}, \sigma = (\mathbf{E})$) in the local PV-Sig list, and return $\mathbf{E}$ to $\mathcal{A}$.
– Challenge: Given a message $\mathsf{m}^* \in \mathcal{M}$, $\mathcal{B}$ specifies the following steps:

1. Run Sig($\mathsf{pk_S}, \mathsf{pk_S}, \mathsf{m}^*$) to output a PV-Sig $\sigma^* = (\mathbf{E}^*)$, and Des($\mathsf{pk_S}, \{\mathsf{pk_{V_i}}\}_{i \in [l]}, \mathsf{m}^*, \sigma^*$) to obtain a real designated multi-verifiers signature DV-Sig $\hat{\sigma}_0^* = (\mathbf{z}_0^*, \mathbf{c}_0^*, \mathbf{b}_0^*)$.
2. Run Sim($\mathsf{pk_S}, \{\mathsf{pk_{V_i}}, \mathsf{sk_{V_i}}\}_{i \in [l]}, \mathsf{m}^*$) to obtain a simulated designated multi-verifiers signature DV-Sig $\hat{\sigma}_1^* = (\mathbf{z}_1^*, \mathbf{c}_1^*, \mathbf{b}_1^*)$.
3. Sample a random bit $b \xleftarrow{\$} \{0,1\}$, and send ($\mathsf{m}^*, \hat{\sigma}_b^*$) to $\mathcal{A}$.

– Output: $\mathcal{A}$ outputs a bit $b^* \in \{0,1\}$.

In the above operation processes, by the property of $\mathcal{H}_0$, we can conclude that $\mathbf{c}_0^*$ and $\mathbf{c}_1^*$ are random over $\{\mathbf{c} : \mathbf{c} \in \{-1,0,1\}^k, 0 < \|\mathbf{c}\| \le \sqrt{\kappa}\}$. According to the distribution of rejection sampling in Lemma 7, $(\mathbf{z}_0^* = \mathbf{E}^* \cdot \mathbf{c}_0^* + \mathbf{y}^*, \mathbf{c}_0^*)$ is only within a statistical distance $2^{-\omega(\log m)}/M$ of $(\mathbf{z}_1^* \in \mathcal{D}_{\mathbb{Z}^m, \eta s_1}, \mathbf{c}_1^*)$ where $\mathbf{z}_1^* = \sum_{i=1}^l \mathbf{z}_i$ and $\mathbf{z}_i \xleftarrow{\$} \mathcal{D}_{\mathbb{Z}^m, \eta s_1/l}$. Furthermore, $\mathbf{b}_0^* = [\mathbf{A}_{V_1,1}|\cdots|\mathbf{A}_{V_l,1}]^\top \cdot$

$$\mathbf{s}_0 + \begin{bmatrix} \mathbf{e}_{0,1} \\ \vdots \\ \mathbf{e}_{0,l} \end{bmatrix}, \mathbf{b}_1^* = [\mathbf{A}_{V_1,1}|\cdots|\mathbf{A}_{V_l,1}]^\top \cdot \mathbf{s}_1 + \begin{bmatrix} \mathbf{e}_{1,1} \\ \vdots \\ \mathbf{e}_{1,l} \end{bmatrix}, \text{ where } \mathbf{s}_1 = \sum_{i=1}^l \mathbf{s}_{1,i} \in \mathbb{Z}_q^n,$$

$\mathbf{s}_0 \xleftarrow{\$} \mathbb{Z}_q^n, \{\mathbf{e}_{0,i}\}_{i \in [l]} \xleftarrow{\$} \mathcal{D}_{\mathbb{Z}^m, s_1}$, and $\{\mathbf{e}_{1,i}\}_{i \in [l]} \in \mathbb{Z}^m$ is an output of SamplePre, according to Lemma 3, $\mathbf{b}_0^*$ and $\mathbf{b}_1^*$ are statistically indistinguishable.

Given a signature $(\mathsf{m}^*, \hat{\sigma}_b^*) = (\mathsf{m}^*, \mathbf{z}_b^*, \mathbf{c}_b^*, \mathbf{b}_b^*)$, $\mathcal{A}$ specifies the following steps:

1. Check whether $0 < \|\mathbf{z}_b^*\| \leq \eta s_1 \sqrt{m}$, where $1 < \eta < 2$ is a constant.
2. Run $\mathsf{ExitBasis}([\mathbf{A}_{V_1,1}| \cdots |\mathbf{A}_{V_l,1}], \mathbf{T}_{\mathbf{A}_{V_i,1}})$ to get a trapdoor $\mathbf{T}_{[\mathbf{A}_{V_1,1}|\cdots|\mathbf{A}_{V_l,1}]}$.
3. Run $\mathsf{Invert}([\mathbf{A}_{V_1,1}| \cdots |\mathbf{A}_{V_l,1}], \mathbf{b}_b^*, \mathbf{T}_{[\mathbf{A}_{V_1,1}|\cdots|\mathbf{A}_{V_l,1}]})$ to get $\begin{bmatrix} \mathbf{e}_{b,1} \\ \vdots \\ \mathbf{e}_{b,l} \end{bmatrix}$ and $\mathbf{s}_b$.

Obviously, the condition 5 in algorithm DesVer is satisfied, namely, $\mathcal{A}$ checks that the equation $\mathbf{c}_b^* = \mathcal{H}_0(\mathbf{A}_\mathsf{S} \cdot \mathbf{z}_b^* - \mathcal{H}_1(\mathsf{m}^*) \cdot \mathbf{c}_b^* + \mathbf{A}_{V_1,0} \cdot \mathbf{e}_{b,1}, \mathbf{A}_\mathsf{S} \cdot \mathbf{z}_b^* - \mathcal{H}_1(\mathsf{m}^*) \cdot \mathbf{c}_b^* + \mathbf{A}_{V_2,0} \cdot \mathbf{e}_{b,2}, \cdots, \mathbf{A}_\mathsf{S} \cdot \mathbf{z}_b^* - \mathcal{H}_1(\mathsf{m}^*) \cdot \mathbf{c}_b^* + \mathbf{A}_{V_l,0} \cdot \mathbf{e}_{b,l}, \mathbf{s}_b, \mathsf{m}^*)$ holds. The real designated multi-verifiers signature $(\mathsf{m}^*, \hat{\sigma}_0^*)$ and the simulated signature $(\mathsf{m}^*, \hat{\sigma}_1^*)$ are statistically indistinguishable for $\mathcal{A}$. Although any $\mathcal{A}$ can check the validity of $(\mathsf{m}^*, \hat{\sigma}_b^*)$, $\mathcal{A}$ cannot determine which one is the real producer, and $\mathcal{A}$'s advantage in the above game is $\mathsf{Adv}_{\mathsf{UDMVS}, \mathcal{A}}^{\mathsf{NT}}(n) \approx 0$. This concludes the proof.

Theorem 3. *Our lattice-based* UDMVS *scheme satisfies the privacy of signer's identity if the* LWE *assumption holds.*

Proof. According to the security model in Definition 4, a game between a simulator $\mathcal{B}$ and a ppt adversary $\mathcal{A}$ is as follows:

– Setup: $\mathcal{B}$ specifies the following steps:

1. Run $\mathsf{Setup}(1^n)$ and $\mathsf{VkeyGen}(\mathsf{pp})$ as in Sec. 3.1 to output pp and $(\mathsf{pk}_{V_i}, \mathsf{sk}_{V_i})$ for a designated verifier V_i.
2. Run $\mathsf{SkeyGen}(\mathsf{pp})$ twice to output $(\mathsf{pk}_{\mathsf{S}_0}, \mathsf{sk}_{\mathsf{S}_0}) = (\mathbf{A}_{\mathsf{S}_0}, \mathbf{T}_{\mathbf{A}_{\mathsf{S}_0}})$ for the signer S_0 and $(\mathsf{pk}_{\mathsf{S}_1}, \mathsf{sk}_{\mathsf{S}_1}) = (\mathbf{A}_{\mathsf{S}_1}, \mathbf{T}_{\mathbf{A}_{\mathsf{S}_1}})$ for the signer S_1.
3. Send $(\mathsf{pp}, \mathsf{pk}_{\mathsf{S}_0}, \mathsf{sk}_{\mathsf{S}_0}, \mathsf{pk}_{\mathsf{S}_1}, \mathsf{sk}_{\mathsf{S}_1}, \{\mathsf{pk}_{V_i}\}_{i \in [l]})$ to $\mathcal{A}$.

– Sim queries: Given $\mathsf{m} \in \mathcal{M}$ and a bit $b \in \{0,1\}$, $\mathcal{B}$ runs $\mathsf{Sim}(\mathsf{pk}_{\mathsf{S}_b}, \{(\mathsf{pk}_{V_i}, \mathsf{sk}_{V_i})\}_{i \in [l]}, \mathsf{m})$ to obtain a simulated signature $\mathsf{DV}\text{-}\mathsf{Sig}\ \hat{\sigma}_b = (\mathbf{z}_b, \mathbf{c}_b, \mathbf{b}_b)$, and sends it to $\mathcal{A}$.
– DesVer queries: Given a message $\mathsf{m} \in \mathcal{M}$, a $\mathsf{DV}\text{-}\mathsf{Sig}$ $\hat{\sigma}$ and a bit $b \in \{0,1\}$, $\mathcal{B}$ runs $\mathsf{DesVer}(\mathsf{pk}_{\mathsf{S}_b}, \{\mathsf{pk}_{V_i}\}_{i \in [l]}, \mathsf{sk}_{V_i}, \mathsf{m}, \hat{\sigma})$ to obtain a verification decision as Acc if $\hat{\sigma}$ is valid, or Rej otherwise, and send the verification decision to $\mathcal{A}$.
– Challenge: Given a message $\mathsf{m} \in \mathcal{M}$, $\mathcal{B}$ specifies the following steps:

1. Run $\mathsf{Sig}(\mathsf{pk}_{\mathsf{S}_0}, \mathsf{sk}_{\mathsf{S}_0}, \mathsf{m}^*)$ and $\mathsf{Sig}(\mathsf{pk}_{\mathsf{S}_1}, \mathsf{sk}_{\mathsf{S}_1}, \mathsf{m}^*)$ to output a $\mathsf{PV}\text{-}\mathsf{Sig}$ $\sigma_0^* = (\mathbf{E}_0^*)$ and a $\mathsf{PV}\text{-}\mathsf{Sig}$ $\sigma_1^* = (\mathbf{E}_1^*)$, respectively.
2. Run $\mathsf{Des}(\mathsf{pk}_{\mathsf{S}_0}, \{\mathsf{pk}_{V_i}\}_{i \in [l]}, \mathsf{m}^*, \sigma_0^*)$ and $\mathsf{Des}(\mathsf{pk}_{\mathsf{S}_1}, \{\mathsf{pk}_{V_i}\}_{i \in [l]}, \mathsf{m}^*, \sigma_1^*)$ to obtain a real designated multi-verifiers signature $\mathsf{DV}\text{-}\mathsf{Sig}$ $\hat{\sigma}_0^* = (\mathbf{z}_0^*, \mathbf{c}_0^*, \mathbf{b}_0^*)$ and a $\mathsf{DV}\text{-}\mathsf{Sig}$ $\hat{\sigma}_1^* = (\mathbf{z}_1^*, \mathbf{c}_1^*, \mathbf{b}_1^*)$, respectively.
3. Sample a random bit $b \xleftarrow{\$} \{0,1\}$, and send $(\mathsf{m}^*, \hat{\sigma}_b^*)$ to $\mathcal{A}$.

– Output: $\mathcal{A}$ outputs a bit $b^* \in \{0,1\}$.

In the above operation processes, by the property of $\mathcal{H}_0$, we can also conclude that $\mathbf{c}_0^*$ and $\mathbf{c}_1^*$ are random over $\{\mathbf{c} : \mathbf{c} \in \{-1, 0, 1\}^k, 0 < \|\mathbf{c}\| \leq \sqrt{\kappa}\}$. According to the distribution of rejection sampling, $(\mathbf{z}_0^* = \mathbf{E}_0^* \cdot \mathbf{c}_0^* + \mathbf{y}_0^*, \mathbf{c}_0^*)$ is within the same distribution as $(\mathbf{z}_1^* = \mathbf{E}_1^* \cdot \mathbf{c}_1^* + \mathbf{y}_1^*, \mathbf{c}_1^*)$. Further, $\mathbf{b}_0^* = [\mathbf{A}_{V_1,1} | \cdots | \mathbf{A}_{V_l,1}]^\top \cdot \mathbf{s}_0 +$

$$\begin{bmatrix} \mathbf{e}_{0,1} \\ \vdots \\ \mathbf{e}_{0,l} \end{bmatrix} \bmod q, \mathbf{b}_1^* = [\mathbf{A}_{V_1,1} | \cdots | \mathbf{A}_{V_l,1}]^\top \cdot \mathbf{s}_1 + \begin{bmatrix} \mathbf{e}_{1,1} \\ \vdots \\ \mathbf{e}_{1,l} \end{bmatrix} \bmod q, \text{ where } \mathbf{s}_0, \mathbf{s}_1 \xleftarrow{\$} \mathbb{Z}_q^n,$$

$\mathbf{e}_{0,i}, \mathbf{e}_{1,i} \in \chi$, so $\mathbf{b}_0^*$ (and $\mathbf{b}_1^*$) is statistically close to a random vector in $\mathbb{Z}_q^{lm}$.

Given a real designated multi-verifiers signature $(\mathsf{m}^*, \hat{\sigma}_b^*)$, $\mathcal{A}$ specifies the following steps:

1. Parse the signature $(\mathsf{m}^*, \hat{\sigma}_b^*) = (\mathsf{m}^*, \mathbf{z}_b^*, \mathbf{c}_b^*, \mathbf{b}_b^*)$.
2. Check whether $0 < \|\mathbf{z}_b^*\| \leq \eta s_1 \sqrt{m}$, where $1 < \eta < 2$ is a constant.

Obviously, according to Definition 7, without the secret key $\mathsf{sk}_{V_i} = \mathbf{T}_{\mathbf{A}_{V_i}}$ of any designated verifier in $\mathcal{V}$, the hidden $\mathbf{s}_b \in \mathbb{Z}_q^n$ and $\{\mathbf{e}_{b,i}\}_{i\in[l]} \in \chi$ cannot be computed and the condition 5 in algorithm DesVer cannot be checked by $\mathcal{A}$. Thus, $\mathcal{A}$ cannot check the validity of a given signature $(\mathsf{m}^*, \hat{\sigma}_b^*)$ and determine which one is the real signer, and $\mathcal{A}$'s advantage in the above game is $\mathsf{Adv}_{\mathsf{UDMVS}, \mathcal{A}}^{\mathsf{PSI}}(n) \approx 0$. This concludes the proof.

4   Conclusion

In this paper, we propose a lattice-based UDMVS scheme that can resist quantum attacks. The scheme allows any signature holder, not necessarily the signer, to convert a publicly verifiable signature into a designated verifiable signature for designated multi-verifiers within a single designation operation, and only one designated verifier's secret key is involved in the verifying algorithm, which makes up the vulnerability that the existing lattice-based UDVS schemes cannot resist online eavesdropping attacks. Furthermore, based on the classical SIS and LWE hardness assumptions, we prove the strong DV-unforgeability, non-transferability and privacy of signer's identity in the random oracle model. However, the bite-size of DV-Sig is directly proportional to the number of designated multi-verifiers. In the future, we try to design a scheme that is not affected by this number and the security reduction does not depend on a random oracle.

Acknowledgment. The authors are grateful to Khoa Nguyen for his insightful discussions, and to anonymous reviewers of ISPEC 2024 for their very helpful comments that improve this work. Yanhua Zhang is partially supported by the Henan Key Laboratory of Network Cryptography Technology Project (No. LNCT 2022-A09), the CSC Visiting Fellow Scholarship (No. 202308410421), the Key Foundation of Science and Technology Development of Henan Province (No. 242102211078) and the Key Scientific Research Project of Higher Education of Henan Province (No. 24A520054). Willy Susilo is partially supported by the Australian Laureate Fellowship (No. FL230100033) and the ARC Discovery Project (No. DP200100144). Fuchun Guo is partially supported by the ARC Future Fellowship (No. FT220100046). Jiaming Wen is partially supported by the CSC Visiting PhD Scholarship (No. 202306270167).

References

1. Ajtai, M.: Generating hard instances of lattice problems (extended abstract). In: STOC, pp. 99–108. ACM (1996). https://doi.org/10.1145/237814.237838
2. Alwen, J., Peikert, C.: Generating shorter bases for hard random lattices. Theor. Comput. Syst. **48**(3), 535–553 (2011). https://doi.org/10.1007/s00224-010-9278-3
3. Arora, N., Sharma, R.: Multi-signer strong designated multi-verifier signature schemes based on multiple cryptographic algorithms. CoRR abs/2209.03682 (2022). https://doi.org/10.48550/arXiv.2209.03682
4. Bellare, M., Neven, G.: Multi-signatures in the plain public-key model and a general forking lemma. In: CCS, pp. 390–399. ACM (2006). https://doi.org/10.1145/1180405.1180453
5. Cai, J., Jiang, H., Zhang, P., et al.: ID-based strong designated verifier signature over R-SIS assumption. Secur. Commun. Netw. **2019**(2019), 9678095 (2019). https://doi.org/10.1155/2019/9678095
6. Cash, D., Hofheinzy, D., Kiltz, E., et al.: Bonsai trees, or how to delegate a lattice basis. In: Gilbert, H. (ed.) EUROCRYPT 2010. LNCS, vol. 6110, pp. 523–552. Springer, Heidelberg (2010). https://doi.org/10.1007/978-3-642-13190-5_27
7. Gentry, C., Peikert, C., Vaikuntanathan, V.: Trapdoor for hard lattices and new cryptographic constructions. In: STOC, pp. 197–206. ACM (2008). https://doi.org/10.1145/1374376.1374407
8. Jakobsson, M., Sako, K., Impagliazzo, R.: Designated verifier proofs and their applications. In: Maurer, U. (ed.) EUROCRYPT 1996. LNCS, vol. 1070, pp. 143–154. Springer, Heidelberg (1996). https://doi.org/10.1007/3-540-68339-9_13
9. Joseph, D., Misoczki, R., Manzano, M., et al.: Transitioning organizations to post-quantum cryptography. Nature **2022**(605), 237–243 (2022). https://doi.org/10.1038/S41586-022-046232
10. Krawczyk, H., Rabin, T.: Chameleon hashing and signatures. In: IACR Cryptology. ePrint Arch. (1998). https://eprint.iacr.org/1998/010
11. Laguillaumie, F., Vergnaud, D.: Multi-designated verifiers signatures. In: Lopez, J., Qing, S., Okamoto, E. (eds.) ICICS 2004. LNCS, vol. 3269, pp. 495–507. Springer, Heidelberg (2004). https://doi.org/10.1007/978-3-540-30191-2_38
12. Li, B., Liu, Y., Yang, S.: Lattice-based universal designated verifier signatures. In: ICEBE, pp. 329–334. IEEE (2018). https://doi.org/10.1109/ICEBE.2018.00062
13. Lin, C., Wu, W., Huang, X., et al.: A new universal designated verifier transitive signature scheme for big graph data. Comput. J. Comput. Sys. Sci. **2017**(83), 73–83 (2017). https://doi.org/10.1016/j.jcss.2016.06.003
14. Lin, H.: Time-constrained strong multi-designated verifier signature suitable for internet of things-based collaborative fog computing systems. Int. J. Distrib. Sens. Netw. **2021**(17), 155014772110017 (2021). https://doi.org/10.1177/15501477211001760
15. Lyubashevsky, V.: Lattice signatures without trapdoors. In: Pointcheval, D., Johansson, T. (eds.) EUROCRYPT 2012. LNCS, vol. 7237, pp. 738–755. Springer, Heidelberg (2012). https://doi.org/10.1007/978-3-642-29011-4_43
16. Micciancio, D., Peikert, C.: Trapdoors for lattices: simpler, tighter, faster, smaller. In: Pointcheval, D., Johansson, T. (eds.) EUROCRYPT 2012. LNCS, vol. 7237, pp. 700–718. Springer, Heidelberg (2012). https://doi.org/10.1007/978-3-642-29011-4_41
17. Ng, C., Susilo, W., Mu, Y.: Universal designated multi verifier signature schemes. In: ICPADS, pp. 305–309. IEEE (2005). https://doi.org/10.1109/ICPADS.2005.287

18. Noh, G., Jeong, I.: Strong designated verifier signature scheme from lattices in the standard model. Secur. Commun. Netw. **2016**(9), 6202–6214 (2016). https://doi.org/10.1002/sec.1766
19. Rastegari, P., Dakhilalian, M., Berenjkoub, M., et al.: Multi-designated verifiers signature schemes with threshold verifiability: generic pattern and a concrete scheme in the standard model. IET Inf. Secur. **2019**(13), 459–468 (2019). https://doi.org/10.1049/iet-ifs.2018.5063
20. Regev, O.: On lattices, learning with errors, random linear codes, and cryptography. In: STOC, pp. 84–93. ACM (2005). https://doi.org/10.1145/1060590.1060603
21. Saeednia, S., Kremer, S., Markowitch, O.: An efficient strong designated verifier signature scheme. In: Lim, J.I., Lee, D.H. (eds.) ICISC 2003. LNCS, vol. 2971, pp. 40–54. Springer, Heidelberg (2003). https://doi.org/10.1007/978-3-540-24691-6_4
22. Seo, S., Hwang, J., Choi, K., et al.: Identity-based universal designated multi-verifiers signature schemes. Comput. Stand. Interfaces **2008**(30), 288–295 (2008). https://doi.org/10.1016/j.csi.2007.08.020
23. Shor, P.: Polynomial-time algorithms for prime factorization and dislogarithms on a quantum computer. SIAM Rev. **1999**(41), 303–332 (1999). https://doi.org/10.1504/IJCSE.2020.105212
24. Steinfeld, R., Bull, L., Wang, H., et al.: Universal designated-verifier signatures. In: Laih, C.S. (ed.) ASIACRYPT 2003. LNCS, vol. 2894, pp. 523–542. Springer, Heidelberg (2003). https://doi.org/10.1007/978-3-540-40061-5_33
25. Steinfeld, R., Wang, H., Pieprzyk, J.: Efficient extension of standard Schnorr/RSA signatures into universal designated-verifier signatures. In: Bao, F., Deng, R., Zhou, J. (eds.) PKC 2004. LNCS, vol. 2947, pp. 86–100. Springer, Heidelberg (2004). https://doi.org/10.1007/978-3-540-24632-9_7
26. Thanalakshmi, P., Anitha, R., Anbazhagan, N., et al.: A hash-based quantum-resistant chameleon signature scheme. Sensors **2021**(21), 8417 (2021). https://doi.org/10.3390/s21248417
27. Thanalakshmi, P., Anitha, R., Anbazhagan, N., et al.. A hash-based quantum-resistant designated verifier signature scheme. Mathematics **2022**(10), 1642 (2022). https://doi.org/10.3390/math10101642
28. Wang, M., Zhang, Y., Ma, J., et al.: A universal designated multi verifiers content extraction signature scheme. Int. J. Comput. Sci. Eng. **2020**(21), 49–59 (2020). https://doi.org/10.1504/IJCSE.2020.105212
29. Zhang, F., Susilo, W., Mu, Y., et al.: Identity-based universal designated verifier signatures. In: Enokido, T., et al. (eds.) EUC 2005. LNCS, vol. 3823, pp. 825–834. Springer, Heidelberg (2005). https://doi.org/10.1007/11596042_85
30. Zhang, L., Zhang, J., Xin, X., et al.: Quantum designated multi-verifier signature. Int. J. Theor. Phys. **2024**(63), 11 (2024). https://doi.org/10.1007/s10773-023-05534-2
31. Zhang, Y., Liu, Q., Tang, C., et al.: A lattice-based designated verifier signature for cloud computing. Int. J. High Perform. Comput. Netw. **2015**(8), 135–143 (2015). https://doi.org/10.1504/IJHPCN.2015.070013

Differential Cryptanalysis Against SIMECK Implementation in a Leakage Profiling Scenario

Hailong Zhang[1,2,3](✉)(iD)

[1] Key Laboratory of Cyberspace Security Defense, Institute of Information
Engineering, Chinese Academy of Sciences, Beijing, China
[2] School of Cyber Security, University of Chinese Academy of Sciences, Beijing,
China
[3] Advanced Cryptography and System Security Key Laboratory of Sichuan Province,
Chengdu, Sichuan, China
zhanghailong@iie.ac.cn

Abstract. Even though SIMECK as a lightweight block cipher can be secure against differential cryptanalysis, the practical security of SIMECK implementation against differential cryptanalysis is not clear. In light of this, the security of three versions of SIMECK implementation against differential cryptanalysis is considered in a leakage profiling scenario. In a leakage profiling scenario, the leakages of three versions of SIMECK implementation can be characterized and template attack can be used to recover the eighth round output. Then, eight-round differential cryptanalysis based on some three-round differentials can be performed to recover the secret key used by SIMECK implementation. We evaluate the efficiency of this combinatorial analysis style in simulated scenario where the values of different parameters that can influence the efficiency of template attack are under full control. The evaluation results show that about 340, 720 and 1040 correct pairs of samples can be enough to recover the secret key of three versions of SIMECK implementation with at most 2^{21} exhaustive search, and the success rate of key-recovery can be higher than 90%. Therefore, inner rounds of SIMECK implementation should also be protected to counteract side-channel attacks.

Keywords: Differential cryptanalysis · SIMECK · Template attack · Leakage profiling scenario · Success rate

1 Introduction

With the advancement of technology in chip manufacturing, the size of electronic chips becomes smaller and smaller. Therefore, it is very necessary to design

This work is supported by the National Natural Science Foundation of China 62272451, the Beijing Natural Science Foundation L234079 and the Open Fund of Advanced Cryptography and System Security Key Laboratory of Sichuan Province under Grant SKLACSS-202116.

lightweight block ciphers that are suitable to be used in resource constraint chip. In June 2012, Beaulieu et al. from the U.S. National Security Agency proposed two lightweight block ciphers, i.e., SIMON and SPECK [1]. Later on, this work was published at DAC 2015 [2]. According to their different design principles, SIMON can be more suitable to be used in hardware chips (like ASIC and FPGA) while SPECK can be more suitable to be used in software chips (like microcontroller and smartcard). Since then, the security of both SIMON and SPECK against traditional cryptanalyses such as differential cryptanalysis [3–7], linear cryptanalysis [8–13] and other styles of cryptanalyses [14–16] were reported. According to the published works, all versions of SIMON and SPECK can be computationally secure against traditional cryptanalyses according to the computing power of the adversary. At CHES 2015 Yang et al. proposed SIMECK [17] with the aim of combining the merits of SIMON and SPECK so as to make SIMECK perform well on both hardware and software. After that, the security of SIMECK against traditional cryptanalyses such as differential cryptanalysis and linear cryptanalysis [18–21] and other styles of cryptanalyses [22–24] were reported. According to the published works, compared with SIMON, SIMECK may be easier to be attacked, even if it is still computationally secure against traditional cryptanalyses according to the computing power of the adversary. Then, one may concern the security of SIMECK when it is implemented into a chip (either a hardware one or a software one).

Different styles of side-channel leakage (like timing information [25], electromagnetic emanation [26] and power consumption [27]) exist when a SIMECK implementation is in operation. In this case, side-channel attacks (SCA) may pose a serious threat to the physical security of a SIMECK implementation. Among them, power analysis attacks can be the most notorious one. The reason is that the power consumption of a chip can be measured relatively easily and different styles of SCA can be methodologically the same. Accordingly, different styles of power analysis attacks such as template attack (TA) [28], correlation power analysis (CPA) [29], stochastic model (SM) [30] and mutual information analysis (MIA) [31] were proposed. Among them, TA can be the strongest one from information theory point of view, because one can use a reference device under full control to accurately characterize the leakage of a target device. Of course, compared with other attack styles, the conditions for performing TA can be more complex. In fact, in order to accurately characterize the leakage of the target device, a large number of power traces should be used in the profiling phase. Therefore, TA can be suitable to be used in an evaluation scenario where the resources needed to perform profiling are sufficient.

Different styles of power analysis attacks can use the first round side-channel leakage of a block cipher implementation to recover the secret key. In order to secure a block cipher implementation, one can use countermeasure to protect the first round encryption. For example, masking [32] or even its combination with shuffling [33] can be used to randomize the processed sensitive intermediate value. Then, the statistical relationship between the power consumption of a block cipher implementation and the sensitive intermediate value is eliminated, and different styles of power analysis attacks may lose their effects. Of course, adding countermeasure will increase the price of a block cipher implementation. In this case, it seems that it is only necessary to protect the first round of block cipher encryption. Unfortunately, advanced power analysis attacks such as soft analytical side-channel attacks (SASCA) [34–36] can fully use the leakage of a block cipher implementation at multiple rounds to recover the secret key. In light of this, full rounds of a block cipher implementation should be protected, which means a huge overhead. In practice, in order to lower down the overhead of a block cipher implementation, only some outer rounds are protected while some inner round (nonconsecutive) may be unprotected. In this case, how to use the inner round leakage of a block cipher implementation to recover the secret key becomes a practical security concern.

In light of this, differential cryptanalysis against SIMECK implementation is proposed to recover the secret key in a leakage profiling scenario. In detail, the eighth round outputs of SIMECK implementation should be recovered with TA in a leakage profiling scenario. Then, based on the searched three-round differentials, eight-round distinguishers can be constructed and which can be used to recover secret key bits of three versions of SIMECK implementation. Finally, an exhaustive search can be used to recover the remaining secret key bits. In order to verify the soundness of the proposed attack technique, the eighth round outputs of three versions of SIMECK implementation are recovered with TA in simulated scenarios where different factors that can influence the effect of TA can be under full control to simulate a perfect leakage profiling scenario. When the eighth round outputs of three versions of SIMECK implementation are recovered, some eight-round distinguishers can be used to recover secret key bits used by three versions of SIMECK implementation. In detail, for SIMECK 32/64 implementation, 2 eight-round distinguishers can be used to recover 44 secret key bits; for SIMECK 48/96 implementation, 4 eight-round distinguishers can be used to recover 75 secret key bits; for SIMECK 64/128 implementation, 8 eight-round distinguishers can be used to recover 110 secret key bits. Then, smaller than 2^{21} exhaustive search can be enough to recover the remaining secret key bits used by three versions of SIMECK implementation, which is computationally feasible in practice.

In order to evaluate the price of the attack technique, the success rate (SR) metric proposed by Standaert et al. at EUROCRYPT 2009 [37] is used. The evaluation results show that about 340, 720 and 1040 correct pairs of samples can be enough to recover the secret key used by three versions of SIMECK implementation with at most 2^{21} exhaustive search, and the success rate can be higher than 90%. The contribution of this work is that an effective attack technique is proposed to recover the secret key used by three version of SIMECK implementation. In light of this, this contribution may shed light on the physical security of three versions of SIMECK implementation in practice.

The organization of the rest part of this paper is as follows. In Sect. 2, the necessary preliminary knowledge is presented. In Sect. 3, the methodology for the proposed attack technique and its details are shown. In Sect. 4, the key-recovery efficiency of the attack technique against three versions of SIMECK implementation is evaluated in the simulated scenario and the evaluation results are shown. Finally, conclusions are given in Sect. 5.

2 Preliminary

In this section, some knowledge necessary to understand the contribution of this work is presented. First, the details of SIMECK is presented. Then, the principle of differential cryptanalysis is presented. Finally, the procedure to perform TA in practice is presented.

2.1 Details of SIMECK

SIMECK is a block cipher with a Feistel structure. The designers of SIMECK proposed three versions of SIMECK corresponding to different lengths of the block and the secret key. In detail, SIMECK 32/64 denotes one version of SIMECK with the block length equals to 32 bits and the secret key length equals to 64 bits; SIMECK 48/96 denotes one version of SIMECK with the block length equals to 48 bits and the secret key length equals to 96 bits; SIMECK 64/128 denotes one version of SIMECK with the block length equals to 64 bits and the secret key length equals to 128. The number of rounds contained in SIMECK 32/64, SIMECK 48/96 and SIMECK 64/128 can be 32, 36 and 44 respectively. In practice, one version of SIMECK may be used according to the application scenario.

In SIMECK, the input of a block can be separated into the left part and the right part. If the left part of the input block of round i is denoted as L_i and the right part of the input block of round i is denoted as R_i, the left part of the input block of round $i+1$ and the right part of the input block of round $i+1$ can be expressed as:

$$L_{i+1} = L_i \& (L_i <<< 5) \oplus (L_i <<< 1) \oplus R_i \oplus K_i. \tag{1}$$

$$R_{i+1} = L_i. \tag{2}$$

Here, $<<<$ is used to denote left cyclic shift, $\&$ is used to denote bit-wise and operation, while $\oplus$ is used to denote the bit-wise exclusive-or between two values. The key expansion of SIMECK is irrelevant to the proposed attack technique. So, we do not present the details of the key expansion part of SIMECK. However, according to the key expansion part of SIMECK, four continuous round keys need to be known in order to recover the secret key of SIMECK.

2.2 Principle of Differential Cryptanalysis

For one pair of round inputs with a certain differential, the differential of the pair of round outputs can be statistically non-uniformly distributed, which may induce the result that the round key be recovered. One can concatenate the input differentials and the output differentials of multiple rounds to obtain multi-round differential trails. In detail, if we denote the input differential of the ith round as δ_i and the output differential of the ith round as δ_{i+1}, one differential trail DT that covers r rounds can be expressed as:

$$DT_{\delta_0 \to \delta_r} = \delta_0 \to \delta_1 \to \dots \to \delta_{r-1} \to \delta_r. \tag{3}$$

Under the assumption that different rounds of a block cipher can be statistically independent, the probability that a given multi-round differential trail happens equals to the multiplication of the probability that one-round differential trail happens, which can be expressed as:

$$Pr(DT_{\delta_0 \to \delta_r}) = \prod_{i=1}^{r} Pr(\delta_{i-1} \to \delta_i). \tag{4}$$

Usually, there are multiple r-round differential trails that correspond to the same input differential δ_0 and the same output differential δ_r. In this case, all r-round differential trails corresponding to the same input differential δ_0 and the same output differential δ_r together can be seen as a differential $D_{\delta_0 \to \delta_r}$, and the probability that a differential $D_{\delta_0 \to \delta_r}$ happens can be the sum of the probability that each differential trail happens. If the number of differential trails that correspond to the same input differential δ_0 and the same output differential δ_r is n, we have:

$$Pr(D_{\delta_0 \to \delta_r}) = \sum_{j=1}^{n} Pr(DT_{\delta_0 \to \delta_r}^{j}). \tag{5}$$

Obviously, the value of $Pr(D_{\delta_0 \to \delta_r})$ can be larger than the value of $Pr(DT_{\delta_0 \to \delta_r})$. In order to optimize the key-recovery efficiency of differential cryptanalysis, it is a differential rather than a differential trail that is usually considered.

Usually, a distinguisher can be several rounds longer than the differential considered, and the constructed distinguisher depends on several bits of the secret key. Then, one can recover bits of the secret key with the constructed distinguisher. According to the diffusion property and the confusion property of block cipher design, the larger the number of rounds attacked, the larger the number of secret key bits may be recovered. However, the larger the number of rounds attacked, the higher the computational complexity of the attack. When the number of rounds attacked is too large, the attack becomes computationally infeasible. Therefore, a trade-off between the number of rounds attacked and the computational complexity of the attack should be built.

2.3 Procedure of Template Attack

There are two phases in TA, i.e., the profiling phase and the key-recovery phase. In the profiling phase, a large number n_p of power traces can be measured from the reference device. The target intermediate value v can be of length b-bit. One needs to divide n_p power traces into 2^b groups according to the value of v.

The number of power traces contained in the gth group with $g \in [1, 2^b]$ can be $n_{p,g}$. Then, we have $n_p = \sum_{g=1}^{2^b} n_{p,g}$. One can use power traces contained in 2^b groups to characterize the leakage of the target device and 2^b templates can be obtained. Totally, l interesting points are assumed to be chosen. Here, interesting points are samples in power traces related to the processing of v. In TA, the power consumption of the target device at l interesting points is assumed to be composed of two parts, i.e., the signal part $\mathbf{S}$ and the noise part $\mathbf{N}$. The mean vector $\mathbf{m}_g$ can be used to characterize the signal part $\mathbf{S}_g$ while the covariance matrix $\mathbf{C}_g$ can be used to characterize the noise part $\mathbf{N}_g$. The leakage contained in the gth group can be denoted as $\mathbf{t}_g^1, ..., \mathbf{t}_g^{n_{p,g}}$. Then, the profiling phase can be expressed as:

$$\mathbf{m}_g = \frac{1}{n_{p,g}} \sum_{j=1}^{n_{p,g}} \mathbf{t}_g^j, \mathbf{C}_g = \frac{1}{n_{p,g}} \sum_{j=1}^{n_{p,g}} (\mathbf{t}_g^j - \mathbf{m}_g)^T (\mathbf{t}_g^j - \mathbf{m}_g), \tag{6}$$

where T denotes the transposition of a vector. Here, $(\mathbf{m}_g, \mathbf{C}_g)$ can be referred to as one template. In the key-recovery phase, a small number n_a of power traces can be measured from the target device. The leakage contained in n_a power traces can be denoted as $\mathbf{t}^1, ..., \mathbf{t}^{n_a}$. Then, the key-recovery phase can be expressed as:

$$D_g = \prod_{j=1}^{n_a} \frac{exp\{-\frac{1}{2}(\mathbf{t}^j - \mathbf{m}_g)^T \mathbf{C}_g^{-1}(\mathbf{t}^j - \mathbf{m}_g)\}}{\sqrt{(2\pi)^l |\mathbf{C}_g|}}, \tag{7}$$

where $\mathbf{C}_g^{-1}$ denotes the inverse of $\mathbf{C}_g$, $|\mathbf{C}_g|$ denotes the determinant of $\mathbf{C}_g$ and $exp\{\cdot\}$ denotes the exponent function. One should compare the values of D_g computed under different key hypotheses. The template that induces the largest value of D_y may be related to the secret key with the largest probability. In this way, the secret key used by the target device may be recovered.

3   Details of the Combinatorial Analysis Style

In the combinatorial analysis style, some three-round differentials should be searched, based on which eight-round distinguishers can be constructed. The eighth round outputs of three versions of SIMECK implementation should be recovered with TA in the leakage profiling scenario. Then, correct samples of pairs of the eighth round outputs of SIMECK implementation can be used in the constructed eight-round distinguishers to recover round key bits. However, only a part of round key bits used by three versions of SIMECK can be recovered with the constructed eight-round distinguishers, while the remaining secret key bits used by three versions of SIMECK implementation should be recovered with exhaustive search.

3.1   Attack on SIMECK 32/64 Implementation

According to Liu et al. [20], the statistical probability that the optimal three-round differential trail occurs can be 2^{-4}. In order to reduce the data complexity of the attack technique, the optimal three-round differential trails that occur with probability 2^{-4} should be used. Besides, the number of optimal three-round differential trails considered can determine the data complexity of the attack technique. In fact, in order to obtain 1 correct sample, about 16 samples should be recovered with TA. In light of this, in order to control the data complexity of the attack technique, the number of optimal three-round differential trails that should be considered needs to be controlled. We will show that only 2 optimal three-round differential trails can be enough to recover the secret key used by SIMECK 32/64 implementation with smaller than 2^{21} exhaustive search. Totally, there are 144 optimal three-round differential trails available according to the search result. In our case, the following two optimal three-round differential trails shown in Table 1 are selected.

Table 1. Three-round optimal differential trails selected for SIMECK 32/64.

Number	Differential trail
1	(0x0001, 0x8023) $\rightarrow$ (0x8000, 0x0000)
2	(0x0010, 0x0238) $\rightarrow$ (0x0008, 0x0000)

According to Table 1, the Hamming weight of the output differentials of two optimal three-round differential trails can be only 1, which has the merit that the number of secret key bits involved in eight-round distinguishers is small. Therefore, the computational complexity of the attack technique can be low. Comparatively, if the Hamming weight of the output differential of the selected optimal three-round differential trail is larger than 1, then the computational complexity of this combinatorial analysis style can be high, which may induce the result that this combinatorial analysis style is practically infeasible. Besides, according to the search result, there exists only one differential trail for the given input differential and the given output differential of an optimal three-round differential trail. In this case, two selected optimal three-round differential trails can be seen as two three-round differentials. Then, we will show the truncated differentials by extending two optimal three-round differential trails four rounds, which can be shown in Table 1 as follows.

In Table 2, * can denote uncertain bits in the truncated differential, while 1 or 0 can denote bit values in the truncated differential. Then, according to Table 2, as the number of rounds considered increases, we have the number of uncertain bits in the truncated differentials also increases. Besides, round key bits involved in the constructed eight-round distinguishers can be known. In detail, there can be four phases in order to use the constructed eight-round distinguishers to recover the secret key used by SIMECK 32/64 implementation. In each phase, some secret key bits can be recovered according to the truncated differentials in two consecutive rounds.

For example, when the differential trail $(0 \times 0001, 0 \times 8023) \rightarrow (0 \times 8000, 0 \times 0000)$ is considered, Table 2 shows that the left part truncated differential at round 6

Table 2. Seven-round truncated Differentials by extending three-round differentials of SIMECK 32/64 four rounds.

Round	Δ_L	Δ_R
3	1000000000000000	0000000000000000
4	*0000000000*0001	1000000000000000
5	*00000*000**001**	*0000000000*0001
6	**000**00***01**	*00000*000**001*
7	**00***0*********	**000**00***01**

Round	Δ_L	Δ_R
3	0000000000001000	0000000000000000
4	0000000*0001*000	0000000000001000
5	00*000**001**000	0000000*0001*000
6	0**00***01****00	00*000**001**000
7	***0**********00	0**00***01****00

can be $\Delta_{L,6} = **000**00***01**$ and the left part truncated differential at round 7 can be $\Delta_{L,7} = **00***0*********$. Then, by inverting the truncated differential one round, one obtains the right part of the truncated differential at round 6, which can be denoted as $\Delta^*_{R,6} = **00***0*********$. By comparing $\Delta^*_{R,6}$ with $\Delta_{R,6}$, one observes that two truncated differentials can be different at bits 14,11,10,7,6,3,2,1. Therefore, one needs to guess bits of round key 7 related to bits 14,11,10,7,6,3,2,1 of the right part of the truncated differential of round 6. According to the round function of SIMECK, bis 0–3, 5–7 and 9–14 of round key 7 can be related to bits 14,11,10,7,5,3,2,1 of the right part of the truncated differential of round 6. Therefore, bits 0–3, 5–7 and 9-14 of round key 7 should be recovered in phase 1 of eight-round distinguisher. By inverting the truncated differential one more round, the right part pf the truncated differential at round 5 can be obtained, which can be denoted as $\Delta^*_{R,5} = **000**00***00**$. Then, by comparing $\Delta^*_{R,5}$ with $\Delta_{R,5}$, one knows that two truncated differentials can be differential at bits 14,10,9,6,5,1,0. In light of this, round key bits related to bits 14,10,9,6,5,1,0 of the right part of the truncated differential of round 6 should be recovered. According to the round function of SIMECK, one knows that bits 0,1,4-6,8-15 of round key 6 and bits 0,1,3-15 of round key 7 should be guessed in phase 2. Similarly, round key bits need to be guessed in phase 3 and phase 4 can be known, which can be shown in Table 3.

Table 3. Secret key bits of SIMECK 32/64 implementation recovered in each phase.

Phase	Bit number	Bit number
1	$k_7\{0-3,5-7,9-14\}$	$k_7\{0-2,4-7,9-11,13-15\}$
2	$k_6\{0,1,4-6,8-15\}k_7\{0,1,3-15\}$	$k_6\{0-5,8-10,12-15\}k_7\{0-5,7-15\}$
3	$k_5\{0,3-5,8-11,14,15\}k_6\{0,2-11,13-15\}k_7\{0-15\}$	$k_5\{2-4,7-9,12-15\}k_6\{1-4,6-15\}k_7\{0-15\}$
4	$k_4\{3,4,10,14,15\}k_5\{2-5,9,10,13-15\}k_6\{0-5,8-10,12-15\}k_7\{0-5,7-15\}$	$k_4\{2,3,7,8,14\}k_5\{1-3,6-9,13-14\}k_6\{0-9,12-15\}k_7\{0-9,11-15\}$

According to Table 3, the number of secret key bits need to be guessed in phase 1 can be the smallest while the number of secret key bits need to be guessed in phase 4 can be the largest. Therefore, the secret key bits can be recovered phase-by-phase. The main idea is to reduce the number of secret key bits that should be guessed in each phase. For example, one can notice that some secret key bits of round 7 that should be guessed in phase 1 should also be guessed in phase 2. Therefore, if these bits can be recovered in phase 1, they do not need to be guessed in phase 2. In this way, the number of secret key bits that should be guessed in each phase can be controlled. Under this idea, phase 1 should be performed first while phase 4 should be performed last. Reminder that a continuous four rounds secret key bits should be known in order to recover the secret key of SIMECK 32/64. However, Table 3 shows that some secret key bits cannot be recovered with the constructed eight-round distinguishers. Therefore, the remaining secret key bits should be recovered with exhaustive search. The computational complexity of exhaustive search can be smaller than 2^{21}, which is feasible in practice. Overall, the procedure of the attack technique against SIMECK 32/64 implementation can be shown in Algorithm 1 as follows.

Algorithm 1 Differential cryptanalysis against SIMECK 32/64 Implementation in a leakage profiling scenario.

Require: A number of templates which can characterize the leakage property of the eighth round output of SIMECK 32/64 implementation. A small number of power traces measured from the target device related to the eighth round encryption of SIMECK 32/64.

Ensure: Whole 64 bits of the secret key used by SIMECK 32/64 implementation.

1: (**Correct Samples Collection**) Use TA to recover the eighth round output of SIMECK 32/64 implementation with the given templates and a small number of power traces measured from the target device. Decrypt and obtain the seventh round output differential of each pair of samples, and keep only those pairs of samples that follow one of the seven-round truncated differentials shown in Table 2;

2: (**Partial Secret Key Bits Recovery**) Guess the secret key bits shown in Table 3 and partially decrypt each remaining pair of samples with the guessed secret key bits to obtain the differential after three-round encryption of SIMECK 32/64. The secret key bits should be recovered phase-by-phase to control the computational complexity. In each phase, if the output differential can match with the one shown in Table 2, one should add the success time of the corresponding key hypothesis to one; otherwise, the success time of the corresponding key hypothesis does not need to be added. Finally, among different key hypotheses, the key hypothesis that results in the highest success time can be the correct one;

3: (**Full Secret Key Bits Recovery**) In order to recover the secret key used by SIMECK 32/64 implementation, one needs to use an exhaustive search to obtain the remaining secret key bits. In detail, for each candidate, one needs to combine it with the partial secret key bits recovered in step 2 to compute and obtain one candidate of the secret key used by SIMECK 32/64 implementation. Then, one correct sample can be used to verify the correctness of the candidate;

In Algorithm 1, the effect of recovering the eighth round output of SIMECK 32/64 implementation with TA can be influenced by multiple factors such as the signal-to-noise (SNR) of the SIMECK 32/64 implementation, the number of interesting points and the number of power traces available in the attack phase of TA. In the evaluation part, we will show the influence of different parameters on the efficiency of TA in the simulated scenario where the values of different parameters can be under full control. Besides, the number of samples needed can depend on the probability of the differentials considered and the number of differentials considered. If the probability that the considered differentials occur is large, the number of correct pairs of samples needed can be small; otherwise, the number of samples needed can be large. Besides, the number of correct pairs of samples can increase with the number of differentials considered. In our case, one optimal three-round differential trail can be not enough to recover the secret key used by SIMECK 32/64 implementation, while two optimal three-round differential trails are considered to recover the secret key used by SIMECK 32/64 implementation, which can result in a low data complexity.

3.2   Attack on SIMECK 48/96 Implementation

In order to recover the secret key used by SIMECK 48/96 implementation, 96 bits of four continuous round keys need to be recovered. Compared with the case to recover the secret key used by SIMECK 32/64 implementation, we have the number of optimal three-round differential trails that should be chosen should be increased. In detail, four eight-round distinguishers based on four optimal three-round differential trails are used to recover the secret key used by SIMECK 48/96 implementation. In light of this, the number of optimal three-round differential trails that should be chosen to recover the secret key used by SIMECK 48/96 implementation can be two times the number of optimal three-round differential trails that should be chosen to recover the secret key used by SIMECK 32/64 implementation. Besides, as in the case of recovering the secret key used by SIMECK 32/64 implementation, if the Hamming weight of the output differential of an optimal three-round differential trail is equal to 1, it will be selected. In this way, the number of round key bits need to be guessed can be small and the computational complexity of the attack technique can be low. While if the Hamming weight of the output differential of an optimal three-round different trail is larger than 1, it will not be considered anymore. The optimal three-round differential trails selected can be shown in Table 4 as follows.

It can be seen from Table 4 that four optimal three-round differential trails of SIMECK 48/96 can follow the rotation invariant property, which means that if the input differential and the output differential of a differential trail rotate to the left the same number of bits, the probability that the new differential trail occurs can be the same with the probability that the original differential trail occurs. Besides, as in the case of SIMECK 32/64, the search result shows that the number of differential trails related to the same input differential and the same output differential of an optimal three-round differential trail of SIMECK 48/96 is only one. In light of this, four selected optimal three-round differential

Table 4. Three-round optimal differential trails selected for SIMECK 48/96.

Number	Differential trail
1	(0x000001, 0x800023) → (0x800000, 0x000000)
2	(0x000004, 0x00008e) → (0x000002, 0x000000)
3	(0x000010, 0x000238) → (0x000008, 0x000000)
4	(0x000040, 0x0008e0) → (0x000020, 0x000000)

trails of SIMECK 48/96 can be seen as four three-round differentials of SIMECK 48/96. Then, the seven-round truncated differentials that extend four optimal three-round differential trails of SIMECK 48/96 four rounds can be known. In Appendix A, Table 6 shows seven-round truncated differentials that extend the first two optimal three-round differential trails of SIMECK 48/96 four rounds, the rest two can be obtained based on the rotation invariant property.

Then, four eight-round distinguishers can be constructed, and round key bits involved in four eight-round distinguishers can be recovered phase by phase. In Appendix A, Table 7 shows round key bits need to be guessed in four phases of the first two eight-round distinguishers, One can know round key bits need to be guessed in four phases of the last two eight-round distinguishers based on the rotation invariant property. According to Table 7, the number of round key bits need to be recovered in phase 1 can be the smallest, while the number of round key bits need to be recovered in phase 4 can be the largest. Therefore, as in the case of recovering the secret key used by SIMECK 32/64 implementation, in order to recover the secret key used by SIMECK 48/96 implementation, the constructed eight-round distinguishers can work phase by phase. In this way, the number of round key bits need to be recovered in each phase can be small and the computational complexity of the attack technique can be low. However, one can notice that four continuous round keys of SIMECK 48/96 cannot be fully recovered with four right-round distinguishers. Therefore, the remaining bits of four continuous round keys should be recovered with an exhaustive search. Overall, one can follow the procedure shown in Algorithm 1 to recover the secret key used by SIMECK 48/96 implementation.

3.3 Attack on SIMECK 64/128 Implementation

In order to recover the secret key used by SIMECK 64/128 implementation with differential cryptanalysis in a leakage profiling scenario, some optimal three-round differential trails of SIMECK 64/128 should be selected to construct eight-round distinguishers. In order to reduce the data complexity of the attack technique, 8 optimal three-round differential trails are selected. The Hamming weight of the output differential of each selected optimal three-round differential trail can be equal to 1 so as to reduce the number of round key bits need to be guessed and to lower down the computational complexity of the constructed eight-round distinguishers. The selected optimal three-round differential trails of SIMECK 64/128 can be shown in Table 5 as follows.

Table 5. Three-round optimal differential trails selected for SIMECK 64/128.

Number	Differential trail
1	$(0x00000001, 0x80000023) \rightarrow (0x80000000, 0x00000000)$
2	$(0x00000010, 0x00000238) \rightarrow (0x00000008, 0x00000000)$
3	$(0x00000100, 0x00002380) \rightarrow (0x00000080, 0x00000000)$
4	$(0x00001000, 0x00023800) \rightarrow (0x00000800, 0x00000000)$
5	$(0x00010000, 0x00238000) \rightarrow (0x00008000, 0x00000000)$
6	$(0x00100000, 0x02380000) \rightarrow (0x00080000, 0x00000000)$
7	$(0x01000000, 0x23800000) \rightarrow (0x00800000, 0x00000000)$
8	$(0x10000000, 0x38000002) \rightarrow (0x08000000, 0x00000000)$

It can be seen from Table 5 that 8 optimal three-round differential trails can follow the rotation invariant property. For example, by rotating the 1st optimal three-round differential trail 4 bits to the left, one can obtain the 2nd optimal three-round differential trail. In fact, because the block size of SIMECK 64/128 can be 32, the number of rotation invariant differential trails of SIMECK 64/128 can be 32. In our case, only 8 of them can be enough to recover the secret key used by SIMECK 64/128 implementation. With 8 optimal three-round differential trails selected, the seven-round truncated differentials that extend 8 optimal three-round differential trails of SIMECK 64/128 four rounds should be obtained. In Appendix A, Table 8 shows the seven-round truncated differentials that extend the first two optimal three-round differential trails of SIMECK 64/128 four rounds, while the rest six can be obtained based on the rotation invariant property.

One can see from Table 8 that the number of uncertain bits contained in the truncated differentials can increase with the number of rounds considered. Based on 8 seven-round truncated differentials, eight-round distinguishers can be constructed. As in the former case, in order to control the number of round key bits need to be guessed, eight-round distinguishers should work phase by phase. Then, one needs to figure out bits of four continuous rounds need to be guessed in each phase according to 8 truncated differentials. In Appendix A, Table 9 shows round key bits need to be guessed in for phases of the first two eight-round distinguishers, while round key bits need to be guessed in four phases of the rest six eight-round distinguishers can be known based on the rotation invariant property. According to Table 9, the number of round key bits need to be guessed can be small in phase 1, while the number of round key bits need to be guessed can be large in phase 4. Therefore, eight-round distinguishers should start from phase 1 while end with phase 4. However, even if 8 eight-round distinguishers are considered, full 128 bits of four continuous round keys cannot be recovered.

In this case, the remaining round key bits should be recovered with exhaustive search. Comparatively, if less than eight distinguishers are considered, the number of remaining round key bits can be large, which can be computationally infeasible. Overall, one can follow Algorithm 1 to recover the secret key used by SIMECK 64/128 implementation.

4 Efficiency Evaluation in the Simulated Scenario

TA can recover 8 bits inner round output at a time. Therefore, one needs to perform TA 4, 6, 8 times respectively in order to recover the eighth round output of three versions of SIMECK implementation. In practice, the efficiency of TA can be influenced by different factors such as the SNR level of the target device, the number of interesting points, the number of power traces available in the attack phase of TA. In the simulated scenario, values of different factors can be under full control and the influence of different factors on the efficiency of TA can be quantitatively evaluated.

In detail, the signal part of three versions of SIMECK implementation at one interesting point is assumed to follow the bit weight leakage model [38]. Under the bit weight leakage model, different bits can leak independently and differently. The leakage weight of each bit can be randomly selected from the interval $(1,10)$ in the simulated scenario. The noise part at multiple interesting points can be assumed to follow the multivariate normal distribution. By setting the mean vector and the covariance matrix, noise part samples at multiple interesting points can be simulated. In detail, the mean vector of the noise part at multiple interesting points can be a zero vector, while the covariance matrix of the noise part at multiple interesting points can depend on the SNR of the target device and the cross correlation between the noise part at different interesting points. The SNR of three versions of SIMECK implementation can be empirically set to 10^{-1} and 10^{-2} to simulate low level noise scenario and high level noise scenario. The cross correlation between the noise part at different interesting points can be empirically set to 0.4. The number of interesting points can be varied from 4 to 16 to evaluate its influence on the efficiency of TA. Then, we vary the number of power traces available in the attack phase of TA to evaluate the efficiency of TA with the SR metric. The evaluation experiments are performed with MATLAB software. The evaluation results can be shown in Fig. 1 as follows.

According to Fig. 1, the influence of different parameters on the efficiency of TA can be known, and the following three observations can be obtained.

- First, the influence of the SNR level on the efficiency of TA can be large. Indeed, the number of power traces needed to recover 8 bits of inner round output in the high level noise scenario can be larger than the number of power traces needed to recover 8 bits of inner round output in the low level noise scenario. Therefore, the number of power traces needed in order to recover one pair of inner round outputs with TA can be significantly influenced by the SNR level of the target device.

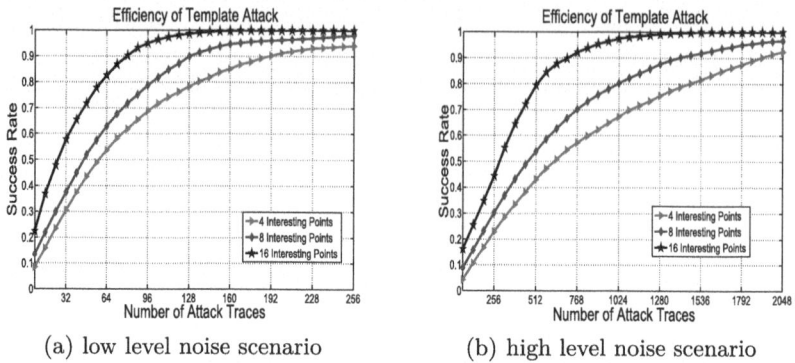

(a) low level noise scenario   (b) high level noise scenario

Fig. 1. Evaluation on the efficiency of TA influenced by different factors in the simulated scenario. (a) low level noise scenario. (b) high level noise scenario.

– Second, the number of interesting points can influence the efficiency of TA. Indeed, when only 4 interesting points are used, the efficiency of TA can be low. Comparatively, when 16 interesting points are used, the efficiency of TA can be high. The reason is that the leakage amount contained in 16 interesting points can be larger than the leakage amount contained in 4 interesting points, and the leakage amount available can judge the efficiency of TA. Therefore, in order to optimize the efficiency of TA, one should use a sufficient number of interesting points.

– Third, the efficiency of TA can increase with the number of attack traces. In the low level noise scenario, when 16 interesting points are used, less than 160 power traces available in the attack phase can already make the success rate reach 1. In the high level noise scenario, when 16 interesting points are used, about 1600 power traces available in the attack phase can make the success rate reach 1. Therefore, it is feasible to recover pairs of the eight-round output of three versions of SIMECK implementation with TA.

Then, with pairs of the eighth round output of three versions of SIMECK implementation recovered with TA in a leakage profiling scenario available, one can use differential cryptanalysis to recover the secret key. In our case, we vary the number of pairs used and evaluate its influence on the efficiency of differential cryptanalysis against three versions of SIMECK implementation. The evaluation result can be shown in Fig. 2 as follows.

Figure 2 shows that the efficiency of differential cryptanalysis against SIMECK implementation in a leakage profiling scenario can be high. First, 170 pairs can be enough for each eight-round distinguisher to recover the secret key used by SIMECK 32/64 implementation with a success rate higher than 90%. Therefore, totally 340 pairs can be enough for differential cryptanalysis to recover the secret key used by SIMECK 32/64 implementation with a success rate higher than 90%. Second, 180 pairs can be enough for each eight-round distinguisher to recover the secret key used by SIMECK 48/96 implementation with a success

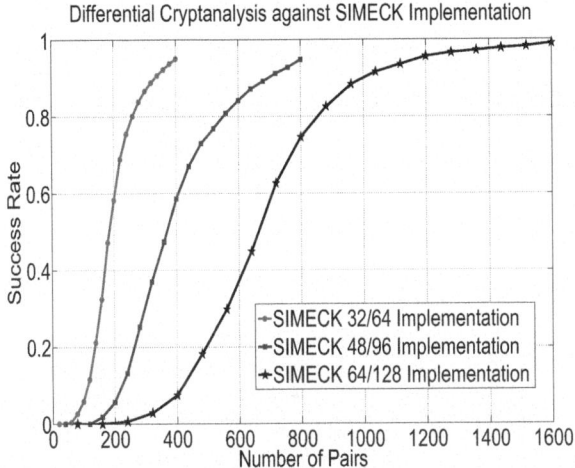

Fig. 2. Evaluation on the efficiency of differential cryptanalysis against three-versions of SIMECK implementation in a leakage profiling scenario.

rate higher than 90%. Therefore, totally 720 pairs can be enough for differential cryptanalysis to recover the secret key used by SIMECK 48/96 implementation with a success rate higher than 90%. Third, 130 pairs can be enough for each eight-round distinguisher to recover the secret key used by SIMECK 64/128 implementation with a success rate higher than 90%. Therefore, totally 1040 pairs can be enough for differential cryptanalysis to recover the secret key used by SIMECK 64/128 implementation with a success rate higher than 90%.

Then, we can evaluate the computation time of differential cryptanalysis against three versions of SIMECK implementation. We can vary the number of pairs used in each eight-round distinguisher from 10 to 200 to evaluate the time consumption of differential cryptanalysis against three versions of SIMECK implementation with a variable numbers of pairs available. Here, the evaluation is performed on a PC with a single core (Intel ® Core(TM) i7-8650U CPU 2.11GHz). The evaluation result can be shown in Fig. 3 as follows.

Figure 3 shows that the time consumption of differential cryptanalysis against three versions of SIMECK implementation can be small, which means that it is feasible to use differential cryptanalysis to recover the secret key used by three versions of SIMECK implementation in a leakage profiling scenario. This can be the most important contribution of this work compared with previous works. Besides, Fig. 3 shows that the difference between the time consumption of differential cryptanalysis against SIMECK 32/64 implementation and the time consumption of differential cryptanalysis against SIMECK 48/96 can be large, while the gap between the time consumption of differential cryptanalysis against SIMECK 48/96 implementation and the time consumption of differential cryptanalysis against SIMECK 64/128 implementation can be small. The reason can be that the number of round key bits need to be recovered with exhaustive search

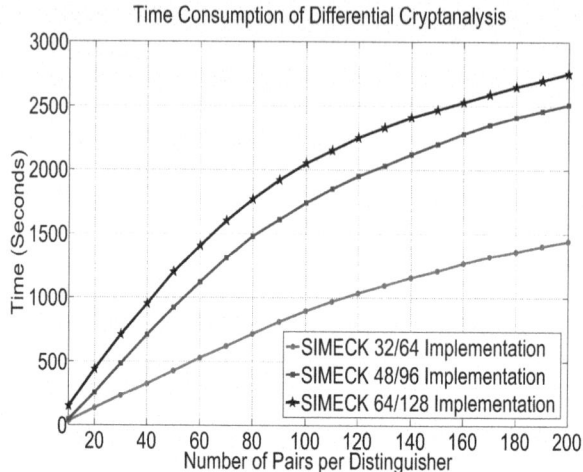

Fig. 3. Evaluation on the time consumption of differential cryptanalysis against three versions of SIMECK implementation.

in order to recover the key used by SIMECK 32/64 implementation, SIMECK 48/96 implementation and SIMECK 64/128 implementation can be 20, 21 and 18. Here, because the computational complexity of exhaustive search to recover the secret key used by SIMECK 48/96 implementation can be the highest among three cases, while the computational complexity of exhaustive search to recover the secret key used by SIMECK 64/128 implementation can be the lowest among three cases, we have the phenomenon shown in Fig. 3.

In fact, the deeper round output of SIMECK implementation can be used by differential cryptanalysis to recover the used secret key, except that the data complexity of the attack can be large. For example, the probability that the optimal four-round differential trail of three versions of SIMECK occurs can be 2^{-6}. In this case, one can select the optimal four-round differential trails to construct nine-round distinguishers to recover the secret key used by three versions of SIMECK implementation, while the data complexity of the attack can be four times the data complexity when eight-round distinguishers are used to recover the secret key used by three versions of SIMECK implementation.

5   Conclusions

In this paper, a combinatorial analysis style against three versions of SIMECK implementation is proposed. In this technique, one needs to use TA to recover the eighth round output of three versions of SIMECK implementation. Then, differential cryptanalysis based on the constructed eight-round distinguishers can be used to recover the secret key. The evaluation results show that only 340, 720 and 1040 pairs of the eight-round output can be enough to recover the secret key with a success rate higher than 90%. Apart from that, the time consumption of the proposed attack technique can be small. In fact, only several seconds can be enough to perform the attack once. Hence, compared with previous works about differential cryptanalysis against three versions of SIMECK, this work shows that in a leakage profiling scenario where the inner round output of three versions of SIMECK implementation may be recovered with TA in a leakage profiling scenario, differential cryptanalysis may pose a serious threat to the physical security three versions of SIMECK implementation.

Appendix A

Table 6 shows seven-round truncated differentials of SIMECK 48/96, while Table 7 shows round key bits of SIMECK 48/96 need to be recovered in each phase.

Table 6. Seven-round truncated differentials by extending three-round differentials of SIMECK 48/96 four rounds.

Round Δ_L		Δ_R
3	100000000000000000000000	000000000000000000000000
4	*00000000000000000*0001	100000000000000000000000
5	*0000000000000*000**001*	*000000000000000000*0001
6	*00000000*000**00***01**	*0000000000000*000**001*
7	*000*000**00***0****1***	*00000000*000**00***01**

Round Δ_L		Δ_R
3	000000000000000000000010	000000000000000000000000
4	0000000000000000*0001*0	000000000000000000000010
5	000000000000*000**001**0	0000000000000000000*0001*0
6	0000000*000**00***01***0	000000000000*000**001**0
7	00*000**00***0****1****0	0000000*000**00***01***0

Table 7. Round key bits of SIMECK 48/96 need to be recovered in each phase.

Phase	Bit Number
1	$k_7\{0-2,5-7,9-11,13-15,18-21\}$
2	$k_6\{0,1,4-6,8-10,13,14,19,20,23\}k_7\{0,1,3-10,12-15,18-20,22,23\}$
3	$k_5\{0,3-5,8,9,18,19,22,23\}k_6\{0,2-5,7-9,13,14,17-19,21-23\}k_7\{0-9,12-14,16-23\}$
4	$k_4\{3,4,18,22,23\}k_5\{2-4,13,17,18,21-23\}k_6\{1-4,8,12,13,16-18,20-23\}k_7\{0-4,7,8,11-13,15-23\}$
1	$k_7\{2-4,7-9,11-13,15-17,20-23\}$
2	$k_6\{1-3,6-8,10-12,15,16,21,22\}k_7\{0-3,5-12,14-17,20-22\}$
3	$k_5\{0-2,5-7,10,11,20,21\}k_6\{0-2,4-7,9-11,15,16,19-21,23\}k_7\{0-11,14-16,18-23\}$
4	$k_4\{0,1,5,6,20\}k_5\{0,1,4-6,15,19,20,23\}k_6\{0,1,3-6,10,14,15,18-20,22,23\}k_7\{0-6,9,10,13-15,17-23\}$

Table 8. Seven-round truncated Differentials by extending three-round differentials of SIMECK 64/128 four rounds.

Round	Δ_L	Δ_R
3	10000000000000000000000000000000	00000000000000000000000000000000
4	*000000000000000000000000000*0001	10000000000000000000000000000000
5	*0000000000000000000*000**001**	*0000000000000000000000000*0001
6	*0000000000000000*000**00***01**	*00000000000000000000*000**001*
7	*00000000000*000**00***0****1***	*0000000000000000*000**00***01**

Round	Δ_L	Δ_R
3	00000000000000000000000000001000	00000000000000000000000000000000
4	000000000000000000000*0001*000	00000000000000000000000000001000
5	00000000000000000*000**001**000	0000000000000000000000*0001*000
6	0000000000000*000**00***01***000	0000000000000000000*000**001**000
7	00000000*000**00***0****1****000	0000000000000*000**00***01***000

Table 9. Round key bits of SIMECK 64/128 need to be recovered in each phase.

Phase	Bit number
1	$k_7\{0-2, 5-7, 9-11, 13-15, 18, 19, 28, 29\}$
2	$k_6\{0, 1, 4-6, 8-10, 13, 14, 27, 28, 31\}k_7\{0, 1, 3-10, 12-14, 22, 23, 26-28, 30, 31\}$
3	$k_5\{0, 3-5, 8, 9, 26, 27, 30, 31\}k_6\{0, 2-5, 7-9, 21, 22, 25-27, 29-31\}k_7\{0-9, 16, 17, 20-22, 24-31\}$
4	$k_4\{3, 4, 26, 30, 31\}k_5\{2-4, 21, 25, 26, 29-31\}k_6\{1-4, 16, 20, 21, 24-26, 28-31\}k_7\{0-4, 11, 15, 16, 19-21, 23-31\}$
1	$k_7\{0, 1, 4-6, 9-11, 13-15, 17-19, 22, 23\}$
2	$k_6\{0, 3-5, 8-10, 12-14, 17, 18, 31\}k_7\{0, 2-5, 7-14, 16-18, 26, 27, 30, 31\}$
3	$k_5\{2-4, 7-9, 12, 13, 30, 31\}k_6\{1-4, 6-9, 11-13, 25, 26, 29-31\}k_7\{0-13, 20, 21, 24-26, 28-31\}$
4	$k_4\{2, 3, 7, 8, 30\}k_5\{1-3, 6-8, 25, 29, 30\}k_6\{0-3, 5-8, 20, 24, 25, 28-30\}k_7\{0-8, 15, 19, 20, 23-25, 27-31\}$

Then, Table 8 shows seven-round truncated differentials of SIMECK 64/128 by extending the first two optimal three-round differential trails shown in Table 5 four rounds, while Table 9 shows round key bits of SIMECK 64/128 need to be recovered in each phase of the first two eight-round distinguishers.

References

1. Beaulieu, R., Shors, D., Smith, J., Treatman-Clark, S., Weeks, B., Wingers, L.: The SIMON and SPECK families of lightweight block ciphers. Cryptography ePrint Archive, Report 2013/404 (2013)
2. Beaulieu, R., Shors, D., Smith, J., Treatman-Clark, S., Weeks, B., Wingers, L.: The SIMON and SPECK lightweight block ciphers. IN: DAC 2015, pp. 175:1–175:6 (2015)
3. Abed, F., List, E., Lucks, S., Wenzel, J.: Differential cryptanalysis of round-reduced simon and speck. In: FSE 2014, LNCS 8540, pp. 525–545 (2015)
4. Biryukov, A., Roy, A., Velichkov, V: Differential analysis of block ciphers SIMON and SPECK. FSE 2014, LNCS 8540, pp. 546–570 (2015)

5. Dinur, I.: Improved differential cryptanalysis of round-reduced speck. SAC 2014, LNCS 8781, pp. 147–164 (2014)
6. Biryukov, A., Velichkov, V.: Automatic search for differential trails in ARX ciphers. In: CT-RSA 2014, LNCS 8366, pp. 227–250 (2014)
7. Sun, S., Hu, L., Wang, P., Qiao, K., Ma, X., Song. L.: Automatic security evaluation and (related-key) differential characteristic search: application to SIMON, PRESENT, LBlock, DES(L) and other Bit-oriented block ciphers. In: ASIACRYPT 2014, part I, LNCS 8873, pp. 158–178 (2014)
8. Kölbl, S., Leander, G., Tiessen, T.: Observations on the SIMON block cipher family. In: CRYPTO 2015, Part I, LNCS 9215, pp. 161–185 (2015)
9. Abdelraheem, M.A., Alizadeh, J., Alkhzaimi, H.A., Aref, M.R., Bagheri, N., Gauravaram, P.: Improved linear cryptanalysis of reduced-round SIMON-32 and SIMON-48. In: INDOCRYPT 2015, LNCS 9462, pp. 153–179 (2015)
10. Yao, Y., Zhang, B., Wu, W.: Automatic search for linear trails of the SPECK family. In: ISC 2015, LNCS 9290, pp. 158–176 (2015)
11. Liu, Y., Wang, Q., Rijmen, V.: Automatic search of linear trails in ARX with applications to SPECK and Chaskey. In: ACNS 2016, LNCS 9696, pp. 485–499 (2016)
12. Biryukov, A., Velichkov, V., Le Corre, Y.: Automatic search for the best trails in ARX: application to block Cipher SPECK. In: FSE 2016, LNCS 9783, pp. 289–310 (2016)
13. Fu, K., Wang, M., Guo, Y., Sun, S., Hu, L.: MILP based automatic search algorithms for differential and linear trails for SPECK. In: FSE 2016, LNCS 9783, pp. 268–288 (2016)
14. Wang, Q., Liu, Z., Varici, K., Sasaki, Y., Rijmen, V., Todo, Y.: Cryptanalysis of reduced-round SIMON 32 and SIMON 48. In: INDOCRYPT 2014, LNCS 8885, pp. 143–160 (2014)
15. Alizadeh, J., ALkhzaimi, H.A., Aref, M.R., Bagheri, N., Gauravaram, P., Kumar, A., Lauridsen, M.M., Sanadhya, S.K.: Cryptanalysis of SIMON variants with connections. In: RFIDSec 2014, LNCS 8651, pp. 90–107 (2014)
16. Sun, L., Fu, K., Wang, M.: Improved zero-correlation cryptanalysis on SIMON. In: Inscrypt 2015, LNCS 9589, pp. 125–143 (2016)
17. Yang, G., Zhu, B., Suder, V., Aagaard, M.D., Gong, G.: The SIMECK family of lightweight block ciphers. In: CHES 2015, LNCS 9293, pp. 307–329 (2015)
18. Beierle, C.: Pen and paper arguments for SIMON and SIMON-like designs. In: SCN 2016, LNCS 9841, pp. 431–446 (2016)
19. Kölbl, S., Roy, A.: A brief comparison of SIMON and SIMECK. In: LIghtSec 2016, LNCS 10098, pp. 69–88 (2017)
20. Liu, Z., Li, Y., Wang, M.: Optimal differential trails in SIMON-like ciphers. IACR Trans. Symmetr. Cryptol. 2017(1), 358–379 (2017)
21. Leurent, G., Pernot, C., Schrottenloher, A.: Cluster effect in SIMON and SIMECK. In: ASIACRYPT 2021, Part I, LNCS 13090, pp. 272–302 (2021)
22. Bagheri, N.: Linear cryptanalysis of reduced-Round SIMECK variants. In: INDOCRYPT 2015, LNCS 9462, pp. 140–152 (2015)
23. Wang, X., Wu, B., Hou, L., Lin. D.: Automatic search for related-key differential trails in SIMON-like block ciphers based on MILP. In: ISC 2018, LNCS 11060, pp. 116–131 (2018)
24. Sadeghi, S., Bagheri, N.: Improved zero-correlation and impossible differential cryptanalysis of reduced-round SIMECK block cipher. IET Inf. Secur. 12(4), 314–325 (2018)

25. Kocher, P.C.: Timing attacks on implementations of diffie-Hellman, RSA, DSS, and other systems. In: CRYPTO 1996, LNCS 1109, pp. 104–113 (1996)
26. Agrawal, D., Archambeault, B., Rao, J.R., Rohatgi, P.: The EM side-channel(s). In: CHES 2002, LNCS 2523, pp. 29–45 (2002)
27. Kocher, P.C., Jaffe, J., Jun, B.: Differential power analysis. In: CRYPTO 1999, LNCS 1666, pp. 388–397 (1999)
28. Chari, S., Rao, J.R., Rohatgi, P.: Template attacks. In: CHES 2002, LNCS 2523, pp. 13–28 (2002)
29. Brier, E., Clavier, C., Olivier, F.: Correlation power analysis with a leakage model. In: CHES 2004, LNCS 3156, pp. 16–29 (2004)
30. Schindler, W., Lemke, K., Paar, C.: A stochastic model for differential side channel cryptanalysis. In: CHES 2005, LNCS 3659, pp. 30–46 (2005)
31. Girelichs, B., Batina, L., Tuyls, P., Preneel, B.: Mutual information analysis. In: CHES 2008, LNCS 5154, pp. 426–442 (2008)
32. Rivain, M., Prouff, E.: Provably secure higher-order masking of AES. In: CHES 2010, LNCS 6225, pp. 413–427 (2010)
33. Rivain, M., Prouff, E., Doget, J.: Higher-order masking and shuffling for software implementations of block ciphers. In: CHES 2009, LNCS 5747, pp. 171–188 (2009)
34. Veyrat-Charvillon, N., Gérard, B., Standaert, F.: Soft analytical side-channel attacks. In: ASIACRYPT 2014, LNCS 8873, pp. 282-296 (2014)
35. Grosso, V., Standaert, F.-X.: ASCA, SASCA and DPA with enumeration: which one beats the other and when? In: ASIACRYPT 2015. LNCS **9453**, 291–312 (2015)
36. Guo, Q., Grosso, V., Standaert, F.-X., Bronchain, O.: Modeling soft analytical side-channel attacks from a coding theory viewpoint. IACR Trans. Cryptogr. Hardw. Embed. Syst. **2020**(4), 209–238 (2020)
37. Standaert, F.-X., Malkin, T., Yung, M.: A unified framework for the analysis of side-channel key recovery attacks. EUROCRYPT 2009, LNCS 5479, pp. 443–461 (2009)
38. Doget, J., Prouff, E., Rivain, M., Standaert, F.-X.: Univariate side channel attacks and leakage modeling. J. Cryptogr. Eng. **1**(2), 123–144 (2011)

Shrinkable Ring Signatures: It Wasn't Them!

Tuong Ngoc Nguyen[1]([envelope]) [iD], Willy Susilo[1] [iD], Dung Hoang Duong[1] [iD], Fuchun Guo[1] [iD], Kazuhide Fukushima[2] [iD], and Shinsaku Kiyomoto[2] [iD]

[1] Institute of Cybersecurity and Cryptology, School of Computing and Information Technology, University of Wollongong, Wollongong, Australia
ntn807@uowmail.edu.au, {wsusilo,hduong,fuchun}@uow.edu.au
[2] Information Security Laboratory, KDDI Research, Inc., Fujimino, Japan
{ka-fukushima,kiyomoto}@kddi-research.jp

Abstract. Ring signatures facilitate a signer to arbitrarily form a set of ring members and produce a signature on their behalf without exposing his own identity. Once signed, the signature is fixed to these particular participants. However, what if, in the future, due to problems with other members, the signatory wants to exclude them from the initial ring, making the signature represent fewer members? For instance, an entrepreneur wishes to remove his arrested business partners from his previously signed ring signatures to stay out of trouble; he desires to prove that it wasn't them who signed the signatures while keeping himself anonymous among the remaining ring members. Unfortunately, no existing variants of ring signatures can provide a feasible solution for this situation. To address this issue, we introduce a new notion of *Shrinkable Ring Signature* (SRS), which allows a signatory to prove later that his already signed signature is actually on behalf of a smaller ring than the original one. We also formalize the syntax and security models for SRS. In terms of construction, we design a generic framework for an SRS from a Merkle-tree-based accumulator, a collision-resistant one-way function, a public key encryption scheme, a string commitment scheme, and a non-interactive zero-knowledge argument system. We show that our scheme is anonymous, unforgeable and shrinkable under the random oracle model. With regards to efficiency, the size of the produced signature only grows logarithmically with the number of ring members. Additionally, we present a concrete instantiation from lattices whose security relies on the SIS and LWE assumptions.

Keywords: Shrinkable ring signatures · Merkle tree-based accumulator · Lattice-based cryptography

This work is partially supported by the ARC Linkage Project LP190100984. Willy Susilo is supported by the ARC Australian Laureate Fellowship FL230100033. Fuchun Guo is supported by the ARC Future Fellowship FT220100046. Dung Hoang Duong is partially supported by AEGiS 2023 grant from University of Wollongong.

1   Introduction

1.1   Motivation

Rivest et al. [24] presented the term "ring signature" (RS) in which a ring member can sign on behalf of a set of arbitrary users without revealing his identity. Due to the anonymity property, it is beneficial to use RS in many concrete applications such as whistle-blowing [24], e-voting [27], blockchain privacy data storage [16], and cryptocurrencies [21], etc. Over the years, besides a huge number of works related to ring signatures [3,6,17], there is a range of different variants of RS have been proposed, such that Linkable ring signature [4,19], Traceable ring signature [8,10], Unique ring signature [9,20,26], Deniable ring signature [15], Threshold ring signature [5,12], Repudiable, Unrepdiable, Claimable, Unclaimable ring signatures [22], etc.; and, each variant has its own advantage in particular circumstances. Unfortunately, none of these proposals can provide a possible resolution for the below scenario.

A board of directors (BOD) of a company has 4 members: Alice, Bob, Charlie and David. The company's policy is that documents provided by any BOD member must be signed on behalf of the BOD. Following the policy, Bob signed several documents representing all BOD members. One day, Charlie and David are arrested because of their financial fraud. The police request to investigate all the documents they signed to gather evidence. To stay out of trouble, Bob wishes to prove that Charlie or David did not generate signatures on the documents he produced. Furthermore, Bob also wants to keep these documents anonymously signed on behalf of himself and Alice (the current legal BOD members).

Firstly, Bob can think of signing again on the same documents but with a new smaller ring only containing Alice and Bob. However, this solution is futile as it does not show that arrested members did not sign the documents before; moreover, some documents can be signed only once at a specific point in time, e.g., tax statements or financial reports of 2010 cannot be re-signed in 2023. Bob also cannot use claimable ring signatures (CRS) [22], a variant that lets a signer later claim his ownership of a signature, since Bob will reveal his identity after claiming that makes the documents no longer anonymously signed representing BOD. Either repudiable [22] or deniable ring signatures [15], two types of RS that allow a non-signer to show he did not produce a signature, are not suitable as well because they require Charlie and David (not Bob) to take action saying that they did not sign these documents; obviously, Charlie and David would not do that as it does not bring any benefits for them. Bob can also conceive of using linkable ring signatures (LRS), an alternative that links signatures generated by the same person, to sign the documents again and link them to the previously signed ones to prove that arrested people did not produce these signatures. However, it is not appropriate in this situation as Bob must use LRS at the signing time in the past in order to link them later; however, if Charlie and David are not arrested (that Bob did not know when signing the papers at the first time), he lets everyone know these documents are from one person in the BOD for no reason. Sadly, there is no favourable solution for Bob in such a situation! At the end of the day, what he needs is simply to prove Charlie and David did not sign his produced documents, or in other words, to prove these documents were in fact signed on behalf of {Alice and Bob} instead of {Alice, Bob, Charlie and David}.

To deal with Bob's problem, we propose a new primitive called "Shrinkable ring signature" (SRS). An SRS allows a signatory to later prove that his signature is on behalf of a smaller ring than the original ring, this is what we call *shrinking* the ring. By doing so, the signer can justify that the excluded ring members did not generate the signature, while he remains anonymous among the remaining members. To the best of our knowledge, none of the current variants of ring signatures can provide this desirable property. One interesting point is that by using SRS, the signer can ultimately shrink the original ring into a ring only consisting of himself, hence, he dy-anonymizes his identity. This special case of SRS performs similarly to the CRS; nevertheless, our SRS has an improvement compared to CRS, we clearly state this advancement in Remark 1 in Sect. 3.2.

1.2 Our Contributions

In this paper, we emphasize three main contributions described as follows.

- We introduce a new variant of ring signature, called "Shrinkable Ring Signature", that lets a signer exclude non-signers from his previously produced signatures. Our proposal provides a novel property named "shrinkability" that none of the existing ring signatures can support. We formalize the syntax and security models for SRS in Sect. 3.
- We present a generic construction for SRS in Sect. 4 by smartly combining a collision-resistant one-way function, a Merkle-tree-based accumulator, a public key encryption scheme, a string commitment scheme and a non-interactive zero-knowledge (NIZK) proof/arguments. We also prove our scheme is anonymous, unforgeable and shrinkable under the random oracle model. The signature size in our design is only logarithmically dependent on the number of ring users.
- We also construct an instantiation of SRS from lattices in Sect. 5 using a Merkle-tree-based accumulator from SIS, a Stern-like zero-knowledge argument of knowledge, a KTX commitment string [14], and multi-bit version of Regev's encryption scheme [23]. Our design is anonymous, unforgeable and shrinkable under the random oracle model assuming the hardness of SIS and LWE problems.

1.3 Technical Overview

We present an instance of a Merkle-tree-based accumulator in Fig. 1. Given a ring $P = \{y_0, \cdots, y_7\}$, a real signer's public key is $y_1 = v_{001}$, then the witness proving that his public key is in P is wit $= ((001), (v_{000}, v_{01}, v_1)) = ((i_1, i_2, i_3), (w_3, w_2, w_1))$, where $i_1 i_2 i_3$ is the binary representation of $i = 1$, the

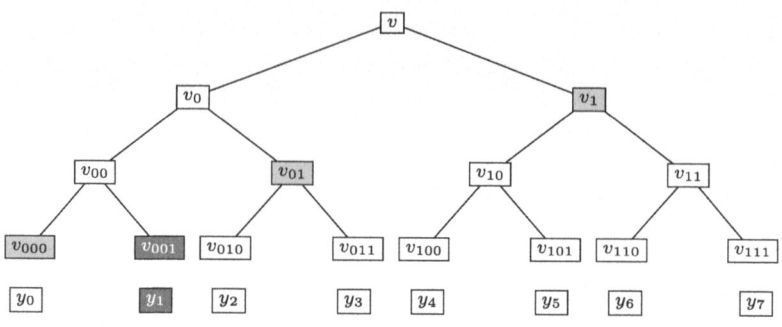

Fig. 1. An example of Merkle-tree-based accumulators

index of the signer in P, and w_t is the node at depth t of the tree. Normally, the root value v is accumulated by recursively computing digested values on its nodes using a hash function H. For instance, to check if $y_1 \in$ P, one performs the following steps using wit: (1) compute $v'_{00} = H(w_3, v_{001})$, (2) $v'_0 = H(v'_{00}, w_2)$, (3) compute $v' = H(v'_0, w_1)$. If $v' = v$, the verifier confirms that y_1 is indeed in P. In general, let $N = |$P$|, \ell = \log(N)$. To construct a ring signature based on a Merkle-tree-based accumulator, we first start with a relation below

$$\mathcal{R} = \{(v), (x, y, \text{wit} = ((i_1, \cdots, i_\ell), \{w_t\}_{t=1}^\ell)) :$$
$$\text{ACC.Verify}(v, y, \text{wit}) = 1 \ \wedge \ y = f(x)\}.$$

The first condition of $\mathcal{R}$ states that the signer is one member in the ring with a public key y, which is correctly accumulated by a value v using the accumulator ACC. The second condition requires the signer to possess a secret key x corresponding to the public key y. To provide a ring signature on a message μ, the signer applies the Fiat-Shamir Heuristic with the hash function H_{FS} to turn a zero-knowledge argument for relation $\mathcal{R}$ into a non-interactive zero-knowledge argument ZK, and obtains $\pi = (\text{CMT}, \text{CH}, \text{RSP}) \leftarrow \text{ZK.Prove}((v), (x, y, \text{wit}))$, where $\text{CH} = H_{\text{FS}}(\mu, \text{CMT}, v, P)$. Note that, by using ZK, a verifier cannot learn anything about the signer's secret information (x, y, wit). The transcript then forms the ring signature $\sigma = \pi$.

We reckon that, due to the nice property of the Merkle tree, the real signer can prove his signature is on behalf of a smaller set of public keys P$' \subset$ P by disclosing *a part* of his witness wit. For example, if he reveals v_1, everyone knows that his public key belongs to $\{y_0, \cdots, y_3\}$, or if he reveals v_{01}, his public key is indeed either y_0 or y_1, and ultimately, he can even expose himself by publishing v_{000}. This is our main idea of how the signer "shrinks" the original ring into a smaller one for a particular signature without reproducing it. However, it is not trivial to construct an SRS scheme directly from this idea.

Firstly, we cannot publish the witness at the time of signing because it reduces the anonymity of the ring signature. Therefore, we need to hide the witness at first and reveal it later in the future. To do that, we first commit to each item in wit by computing $\text{com}_t \leftarrow \text{Com}(w_t; r_t)$, for $\forall t \in [\ell]$, where Com is a statistically hiding and computationally binding string commitment scheme, and r_t is the commitment random; and then attach com_t to the signature $\sigma = (\pi, \{\mathsf{com}_t\}_{t=1}^{\ell})$. Later, the signer can open com_t by revealing $(w_t; r_t)$. Unfortunately, with this approach, there is an issue: since constructing a Merkle tree from a list of public keys is effortless, a cheating signer can pretend to be another member in the ring by computing her $\{w_t^*\}_{t=1}^{\ell}$, commit to them, and attach the "fake" commitments to the signature. In fact, the signature is still correctly verified as the verifier does not check the validity of the "fake" commitments. Then, the cheating signer can open the commitments with ease and successfully impersonate other members. To tackle this problem, we must ensure the witness that the signer commits to is indeed his. Our solution is to add one more condition to the relation $\mathcal{R}$, it then becomes

$$\mathcal{R} = \{(v, \{\mathsf{com}_{=1}^{\ell}), (x, y, \mathsf{wit} = ((i_1, \cdots, i_\ell), \{w_t\}_{t=1}^{\ell})), \{r_t\}_{t=1}^{\ell}) :$$
$$\mathsf{ACC.Verify}(v, y, \mathsf{wit}) = 1 \wedge y = f(x) \wedge \{\mathsf{Com}(w_t; r_t) = \mathsf{com}_t\}_{t=1}^{\ell}\}.$$

The extra condition asks the signer to prove the ownership of several pairs (w_t, r_t) corresponding to com_t, and the committed w_t must also be correctly verified by Acc using a public key y corresponding to his secret key x. Because the signer does not know others' secret keys, he cannot provide a valid proof for the relation if he attempts to use others' w_t^*. Next, we notice that to open com_t, the signer needs to provide a pair (w_t, r_t). Although he can easily re-compute his witness w_t (by re-constructing the Merkle tree), he has no chance to re-produce the corresponding r_t since it is uniformly sampled when signing. It is apparently unreasonable to require the signer to remember which r_t correlates to which signature; needless to say, stateless between signing and opening procedures is preferable. To deal with this, we encrypt each r_t using a public key encryption scheme PKE, and attach the ciphertexts c_t to the signature $\sigma = (\pi, \{\mathsf{com}_t\}_{t=1}^{\ell}, \{c_t\}_{t=1}^{\ell})$. Consequently, only the signer can decrypt these ciphertexts to obtain r_t later and then shrink the ring. To guarantee no cheating signer can attach a different ciphertext c_t^* of a dishonest r_t^* to the signature, we also concatenate all ciphertexts c_t to the message μ, and compute a new CH with the concatenated message.

To show the anonymity of our SRS scheme, we transform a signature produced by a user owning a secret key sk^0 into one signed by another user keeping sk^1 via a set of hybrids in an indistinguishable manner from the view of an adversary. The next hurdle encountered by the scheme is that each component in the signature must be indistinguishable between hybrids. While we can indistinguishably convert the transcript π and commitments com_t produced using sk^0 into sk^1 based on the zero-knowledge property of ZK and the hiding property of Com, respectively, it is impossible to switch the ciphertexts c_t from encrypted using pk^0 to pk^1 without noticeable changes from the view of the adversary. Our way out of this conundrum is to uniformly sample one more ciphertext $c_{t,2}$, making the signature become $\sigma = (\pi, \{\mathsf{com}_t, c_{t,1}, c_{t,2}\}_{t=1}^{\ell})$. Then, based on the pseudorandom ciphertexts property of PKE, we can indistinguishably transform ciphertexts encrypted by pk^0 into pk^1 via hybrids, and then successfully prove the anonymity of our construction. For the proof, please refer to Sect. 4.2.

2   Preliminaries

2.1   Accumulator Schemes

Definition 1. *(Accumulator)* An accumulator scheme ACC containing four algorithms (Setup, Acc, GenWit, Verify) is described as follows.

ACC.Setup(1^λ): Given security parameter λ, it outputs public parameters pp.

ACC.Acc(pp, P): Given public parameters pp, a list P, the algorithms outputs an accumulated value v for P.

ACC.GenWit(pp, P, y): Given public parameters pp, a list P and a value y, if $y \notin$ P, it outputs $\perp$; otherwise, it outputs a witness wit saying that y are correctly accumulated by ACC.Acc(pp, P).

ACC.Verify(pp, v, y, wit): Given public parameters pp, an accumulated value v, a value y, and a witness wit, if wit is the valid witness for y to accumulate the value v, then it outputs 1; otherwise, it outputs 0.

Correctness. An accumulator scheme is correct if:

$$\Pr[pp \leftarrow \text{ACC.Setup}(1^\lambda); v \leftarrow \text{ACC.Acc}(pp, \text{P}); \text{wit} \leftarrow \text{ACC.GenWit}(pp, \text{P}, y) :$$
$$y \in \text{P} \wedge \text{ACC.Verify}(pp, v, y, \text{wit}) = 1] \geq 1 - \text{negl}(n).$$

Security. An accumulator scheme is called secure if for all PPT adversaries $\mathcal{A}$:

$$\Pr[pp \leftarrow \text{ACC.Setup}(1^\lambda); (\text{P}, y^*, \text{wit}^*) \leftarrow \mathcal{A}(pp) :$$
$$y^* \notin \text{P} \wedge \text{ACC.Verify}(pp, \text{ACC.Acc}(pp, \text{P}), y^*, \text{wit}^*) = 1] \leq \text{negl}(\lambda).$$

There are instantiations of ACC based on DDH problem [2], or SIS problem [17].

2.2   String Commitment Schemes

A string commitment scheme Com consists of two phases. In the committing phase, a sender commits to a value $s \in \{0, 1\}^*$ by computing $c = \text{Com}(s; r)$, where r is a random string. In the opening phase, he opens the committed value c by revealing the pair (s, r). A string commitment scheme must satisfy the following properties:

Statistically Hiding. Given two values s_1, s_2, we have

$$\text{Com}(s_1; .) \approx_s \text{Com}(s_2; .)$$

Computationally Binding. Given security parameter λ, two pairs $(s_1; r_1), (s_2; r_2)$ and $s_1 \neq s_2$, we have

$$\Pr[\text{Com}(s_1; r_1) = \text{Com}(s_2; r_2)] = \text{negl}(\lambda)$$

There are instantiations of Com based on DDH problem [18] or SIS problem [13].

2.3 Public Key Encryption

Definition 2. *(Public Key Encryption)* A public key encryption scheme PKE containing three PPT algorithms (KeyGen, Enc, Dec) is described as follows.

PKE.KeyGen(1^λ): Given a security parameter λ, it outputs a pair of public key and secret key (pk, sk).

PKE.Enc(pk, m): Given a public key pk, a plaintext m, it outputs a ciphertext c.

PKE.Dec(sk, c): Given a secret key sk, a ciphertext c, it outputs a plaintext m.

Correctness. Given security parameter λ, for all messages m, we have

$$\Pr[(pk, sk) \leftarrow \text{PKE.KeyGen}(1^\lambda) : \text{PKE.Dec}(sk, \text{PKE.Enc}(pk, m)) = m] \geq 1 - \text{negl}(\lambda).$$

Pseudorandom Public Keys. All public keys pk are computationally indistinguishable from uniformly randomnesses.

Pseudorandom Ciphetexts. For all messages m, a uniformly random value u and public key pk, we have

$$(pk, u) \approx_c (pk, \text{PKE.Enc}(pk, m)).$$

There are instantiations of PKE based on DDH problem [7] or LWE problem [23].

3 Syntax and Security Models

3.1 Syntax

Definition 3. *(Shrinkable Ring Signatures)* A shrinkable ring signature scheme (Setup, KeyGen, Sign, Verify, Shrink, VerShrink) is described as follows.

SRS.Setup(λ): Given a security parameter λ, it outputs a public parameter pp.

SRS.KeyGen(pp): Given public parameter pp, it outputs a pair of a public key and a secret key (sk, pk).

SRS.Sign(sk, μ, R): Given a real signer's secret key sk, a message μ and a ring R, it outputs a ring signature σ.

SRS.Verify(R, μ, σ): Given a ring R, a message μ and a ring signature σ, it outputs 0/1 indicating a(an) valid/invalid ring signature.

SRS.Shrink(R, R', sk, σ): Given a ring R, a secret key sk, a ring signature σ, and a ring $R' \subseteq R$ the signer wants to shrink to, it outputs a shrink evidence ζ.

SRS.VerShrink(R, R', σ, ζ): Given a ring R, a ring R', a ring signature σ, and a shrink evidence ζ, it outputs 0/1 indicating ζ is a(an) valid/invalid shrink evidence of a signature σ for ring R'.

Definition 4. *(Correctness)* Given $pp \leftarrow \text{Setup}(\lambda)$, and a list of honest public keys $R = (pk_0, \cdots, pk_{N-1})$, a valid signature $\sigma \leftarrow \text{Signed}(sk_i, \mu, R)$, and a subset $R' \subseteq R$, a shrinkable ring signature scheme is correct if

$$\text{SRS.Verify}(\mu, R, \text{SRS.Sign}(\mu, R, sk_i)) = 1,$$

and

$$\text{SRS.VerShrink}(R, R', \sigma, \text{SRS.Shrink}(R, R', sk_i, \sigma)) = 1.$$

3.2 Security Models

Prior to presenting the security model of SRS, we define essential notations.

- Secret key oracle $\mathcal{O}_{sk}(i)$: Given an index $i \in \{0, ..., N-1\}$, the oracle returns the corresponding sk_i.
- Signing oracle $\mathcal{O}_{Sign}(i, \mu, R)$: Given an index of the i-th user, a message μ and a ring R, the oracle returns a signature σ.
- Shrinking oracle $\mathcal{O}_{shrk}(R, R', i, \sigma)$: Given a ring R, a ring R', an index of the i-th user, and a signature σ, the oracle returns a shrink evidence ζ.
- Corr is a list of users whose secret keys have been revealed to the adversary.
- $Sign_{R,\mu}$ is a list of users queried to $\mathcal{O}_{sign}(i, \mu, R)$.
- $Shrk_{R,R',\sigma}$ is a list of users queried to $\mathcal{O}_{shrk}(R, R', i, \sigma)$.
- $\mathcal{Q}$ is a list of queries the adversary makes to $\mathcal{O}_{Sign}$.

We first present the Anonymity experiment in Fig. 2.

Setup. $\mathcal{C}$ computes $pp \leftarrow$ SRS.Setup(λ). For $i \in \{0, \cdots, N-1\}$, $\mathcal{C}$ runs $\{pk_i, sk_i\} \leftarrow$ SRS.KeyGen(pp). Next, it forms $R = (pk_0, \cdots, pk_{N-1})$, and sends R to $\mathcal{A}$. $\mathcal{C}$ also sets Corr $:= \emptyset$ and $Sign_{R,\mu} := \emptyset$.

Query 1. $\mathcal{A}$ may make a polynomially bounded number of queries to $\mathcal{O}_{sk}, \mathcal{O}_{Sign}$, and $\mathcal{O}_{shrk}$, $\mathcal{C}$ responses to each query in the way mentioned above, and updates Corr, $Sign_{R,\mu}$ and $Shrk_{R,R',\sigma}$ accordingly.

Challenge. $\mathcal{A}$ chooses a tuple (i_0, i_1, μ^*, R^*) such that $i_0, i_1 \notin$ Corr and $i_0, i_1 \notin Sign_{R^*,\mu^*}$, $i_0, i_1 \notin Shrk_{R,R^*,\sigma^*}$ and sends the tuple to $\mathcal{C}$. Then $\mathcal{C}$ chooses uniformly at random a bit $b \leftarrow \{0, 1\}$ and generates $\sigma \leftarrow$ SRS.Sign(μ^*, R^*, sk_{i_b}). $\mathcal{C}$ then sends σ to $\mathcal{A}$. Then, $\mathcal{A}$ can keep sending queries to $\mathcal{O}_{shrk}(R, R', i_b, \sigma^*)$ as long as both $i_0, i_1 \in R'$.

Guess. $\mathcal{A}$ outputs a bit b'. $\mathcal{A}$ wins if $b' = b$.

Fig. 2. Anonymity experiment for SRS

Definition 5. *(Anonymity)* Given security parameter λ, a shrinkable ring signature is anonymous if for any PPT adversary $\mathcal{A}$, the advantage of $\mathcal{A}$ winning the Anonymity experiment in Fig. 2 is negligible, that is

$$\mathsf{Adv}_{\mathcal{A}}^{\mathsf{Ano}}(\lambda) \leq \frac{1}{2} + \mathsf{negl}(\lambda).$$

Next, we define the Unforgeability experiment in the Fig. 3

Definition 6. *(Unforgeability)* Given security parameter λ, a shrinkable ring signature is unforgeable if for any PPT adversary $\mathcal{A}$, the advantage of $\mathcal{A}$ winning the Unfogeability experiment in Fig. 3 is negligible, that is

$$\mathsf{Adv}_{\mathcal{A}}^{\mathsf{Unfog}}(\lambda) \leq \mathsf{negl}(\lambda).$$

> **Setup.** Same as in the anonymity experiment.
> **Query.** Same as in the anonymity experiment.
> **Forge.** $\mathcal{A}$ outputs a tuple (σ^*, μ^*, R^*) such that $(., \mu^*, R^*) \notin Q$ and $R^* \subseteq R \setminus pk_{i, i \in \mathsf{Corr}}$.
> $\mathcal{A}$ wins if $\mathsf{SRS.Verify}(\sigma^*, \mu^*, R^*) = 1$.

Fig. 3. Unforgeability experiment for SRS

We present three conditions in the definition of Shrinkability.

1. *Shrinkability correctness: A signer can always produce a valid shrink evidence for his signatures:* Given $pp \leftarrow \mathsf{Setup}(\lambda)$, and a list of honestly generated public keys $R = (pk_0, \cdots, pk_{N-1})$, a valid signature $\sigma \leftarrow \mathsf{Sign}(sk_i, \mu, R)$, and a subset $R' \subseteq R$ we have

$$Pr[\zeta \leftarrow \mathsf{SRS.Shrink}(R, R', sk_i, \sigma) :$$
$$\mathsf{SRS.VerShrink}(R, R', \sigma, \zeta) = 1] \geq 1 - \mathsf{negl}(\lambda).$$

2. *A non-signer cannot produce a valid shrink evidence for others' signatures:* We define the second experiment of Shrinkability in Fig. 4.
3. *No one (including the signer) can produce a valid shrink evidence for a signature corresponding to an invalid ring:* We define the third experiment of Shrinkability in Fig. 5.

> **Setup.** Same as in the anonymity experiment.
> **Query.** Same as in the anonymity experiment.
> **Challenge.** $\mathcal{A}$ chooses a tuple (j, μ^*, R^*) such that $pk_j \in R^*$, $R^* \subseteq R \setminus pk_{i, i \in \mathsf{Corr}}$, and sends the tuple to $\mathcal{C}$. Then $\mathcal{C}$ generates $\sigma \leftarrow \mathsf{SRS.Sign}(sk_j, \mu^*, R^*)$. $\mathcal{C}$ then sends σ to $\mathcal{A}$.
> **Forge.** $\mathcal{A}$ outputs a shrink evidence ζ^*, $\mathcal{A}$ wins if $\mathsf{VerShrink}(R^*, \tilde{R}, \sigma^*, \zeta^*) = 1$ and $j \notin \mathsf{Shrk}_{R^*, \tilde{R}, \sigma^*}$.

Fig. 4. Shrinkabilty 2 experiment for SRS

Definition 7. *(Shrinkability)* Given security parameter λ, a shrinkable ring signature is shrinkable if it is shrinkablely correct and for any PPT adversary $\mathcal{A}$, the advantage of $\mathcal{A}$ winning the Shrinkability 2 in Fig. 4 and Shrinkability 3 experiment in Fig. 5 is negligible.

Remark 1. While the shrinkability correctness for our SRS implies that any valid signature can be correctly shrunk by its signer, CRS [22] does not have this requirement. A CRS signature σ_{CRS} contains $(\sigma_{\mathsf{RS}}, c)$, where σ_{RS} is the signature of the underlying ring signature, and c is a commitment that the signer can

---

Setup. Same as in the anonymity experiment.

Query. Same as in the anonymity experiment.

Challenge. $\mathcal{A}$ chooses a tuple (j, μ^*, R^*) such that $pk_j \in \mathsf{R}^*$, $\mathsf{R}^* \subseteq \mathsf{R} \setminus pk_{i, i \in \mathsf{Corr}}$, , and sends the tuple to $\mathcal{C}$. Then $\mathcal{C}$ generates $\sigma \leftarrow \mathsf{SRS.Sign}(sk_j, \mu^*, R^*)$. $\mathcal{C}$ then sends σ to $\mathcal{A}$.

Forge. $\mathcal{A}$ outputs a shrink evidence ζ^*, $\mathcal{A}$ wins if $\mathsf{VerShrink}(\mathsf{R}^*, \tilde{\mathsf{R}}, \sigma^*, \zeta^*) = 1$ and $(pk_j \notin \tilde{\mathsf{R}} \vee \tilde{\mathsf{R}} \not\subseteq \mathsf{R}^*)$.

Fig. 5. Shrinkabilty 3 experiment for SRS

reveal later to claim his identity. To verify σ_{CRS}, a verifier only checks if σ_{RS} is valid or not and does nothing with c. This can lead to an unexpected case when the CRS signature is correctly verified, but the signer cannot claim later since c is somehow modified. With the requirement for shrinkability correctness, our SRS prevent this scenario from happening.

Remark 2. For $\mathsf{R}_1 \subset \mathsf{R}_2 \subset \mathsf{R}$, when $\mathcal{A}$ knows a shrink evidence ζ_1 for (R_1, σ), he not only reckons that the signature is on behalf of R_1 but it also represents R_2; however, the experiment in Fig. 4 requires $\mathcal{A}$ not to provide a valid shrink evidence ζ_2 for (R_2, σ). One might say that it is not essential to prevent $\mathcal{A}$ from producing ζ_2. On the contrary, we reckon that it is completely reasonable since a signer might only want to shrink his signature on behalf of a smaller ring but not a bigger one, i.e., he wants to exclude more people from his signature. Therefore, our definition ensures that no adversary can shrink the signature to represent a bigger ring (R_2) which is not the purpose of the signer (only R_1).

4 Generic Construction

First, we define the $\mathsf{GetRevealedWitnessIndex}$ algorithm that tells us which witness $w_{\mathsf{ind}} \in (w_1, \cdots, w_\ell)$ should be revealed if a signer wants to shrink from P into P' for his signature in Algorithm 1. We also present the $\mathsf{VerifyWitness}$ algorithm in Algorithm 2, which checks if w is a valid revealed witness.

Algorithm 1: GetRevealedWitnessIndex(P', P)

Input: Two lists $\mathsf{P}' = \{y_0', y_1', \cdots, y_{N'-1}'\}$ and $\mathsf{P} = \{y_0, y_1 \cdots, y_{N-1}\}$, where N and N' are powers of 2.

Output: Index ind

1 Construct a Merkle tree Tr of depth $\log(N)$ based on P using ACC

2 ind $= \log(N) - \log(N')$

3 **if** $\{y_0', y_1', \cdots, y_{N'-1}'\}$ share the same parent node at depth ind in Tr **then**

4   **return** ind

5 **return** -1

Algorithm 2: VerifyWitness(ind, w, P′, P)

Input: An index ind, a witness w, a list $\mathsf{P}' = \{y_0', y_1', \cdots, y_{N'-1}'\}$, and
$\mathsf{P} = \{y_0, y_1, \cdots, y_{N-1}\}$.
Output: 0/1
1 Construct a Merkle tree Tr of depth $\log(N)$ based on P using ACC
2 $v' = \mathsf{ACC.Acc}(\mathsf{P}')$
3 **if** $(w \neq v')$ **and** $(w, v'$ share the same parent node at depth $(\mathsf{ind} - 1)$ in Tr$)$
then
4 | **return** 1
5 **return** 0

4.1 Construction

A generic construction for logarithmic-size SRS contains the following components:

- A collision-resistant one-way function $\mathsf{F} : X \to Y$, such that, given $y = \mathsf{F}(x)$, it is hard to compute x; and it is difficult to find x_1, x_2 such that $x_1 \neq x_2$ and $\mathsf{F}(x_1) = \mathsf{F}(x_2) = y$ [17].
- A Merkle-tree based accumulator scheme ACC described in Sect. 2.1;
- A string commitment scheme Com satisfied properties defined in Sect. 2.2;
- A public key encryption scheme PKE satisfied properties in Sect. 2.3;
- A hash function H_{FS} as a random oracle;
- A NIZK argument system ZK satisfying completeness, knowledge soundness and zero-knowledge defined in [11] for the relation $\mathcal{R}$ below.

$$\mathcal{R} := \{(v, \{\mathsf{com}_t\}_{t=1}^{\ell}), (x, y, \mathsf{wit} = ((i_1, \cdots, i_\ell), \{w_t\}_{t=1}^{\ell})), \{r_t\}_{t=1}^{\ell}) :$$
$$\mathsf{ACC.Verify}(v, y, \mathsf{wit}) = 1 \land y = f(x) \land \{\mathsf{Com}(w_t; r_t) = \mathsf{com}_t\}_{t=1}^{\ell}\}.$$

Given the security parameter λ, we present our generic construction below.

SRS.Setup(λ): Given a security parameter λ, do:

1. Compute $acc.pp \leftarrow \mathsf{ACC.Setup}(1^\lambda)$.
2. Return $pp = \{acc.pp\}$.

SRS.KeyGen(pp): Given public parameters pp, a signer performs as follows:

1. Sample $x \leftarrow SK$, where SK is the space of secret keys for ring signature.
2. Compute $y = \mathsf{F}(x)$.
3. Generate $(pk_{\mathsf{PKE}}, sk_{\mathsf{PKE}}) \leftarrow \mathsf{PKE.KeyGen}(1^\lambda)$.
4. Return $(sk, pk) = ((x, sk_{\mathsf{PKE}}), (y, pk_{\mathsf{PKE}}))$.

SRS.Sign(sk, μ, R): Given a secret key sk, a ring $\mathsf{R} := \{pk_0, \cdots, pk_{N-1}\}$, and a message μ, the signer performs as follows:

1. Parse $sk = (x, sk_{\mathsf{PKE}})$. Let $pk = (y, pk_{\mathsf{PKE}})$ be the public key corresponding to sk.
2. From R, extract $\mathsf{P} = \{y_0, \cdots, y_{N-1}\}$.
3. Compute root value $v \leftarrow \mathsf{ACC.Acc}_{acc.pp}(\mathsf{P})$.
4. Compute wit $\leftarrow$ $\mathsf{ACC.GenWit}_{acc.pp}(\mathsf{P}, y)$ where wit $= \{(i_1, \cdots, i_\ell), (w_\ell, \cdots, w_1)\}$.
5. For $t \in [\ell]$:

   – Sample a randomness r_t for the string commitment.
   – Compute $\mathsf{com}_t \leftarrow \mathsf{Com}(w_t; r_t)$.
   – Encrypt r_t using pk_{PKE} as $c_{t,1} \leftarrow \mathsf{PKE.Enc}(pk_{\mathsf{PKE}}, r_t; e_t)$, where e_t is the encryption randomness.
   – Sample $c_{t,2} \leftarrow \{0,1\}^\lambda$.

6. Generate an NIZK transcript $\pi = (\mathsf{CMT}, \mathsf{CH}, \mathsf{RSP})$ as $\pi \leftarrow \mathsf{ZK.Prove}((v, \{\mathsf{com}_t\}_{t=1}^\ell), (x, y, \mathsf{wit}, \{r_t\}_{t=1}^\ell))$, where CH is computed using H_{FS}:

$$\mathsf{CH} = H_{\mathsf{FS}}(\mu || c_{1,1} || c_{1,2} || \cdots || c_{\ell,1} || c_{\ell,2}, \mathsf{CMT}, v, \mathsf{P}, \{\mathsf{com}_t\}_{t=1}^\ell).$$

7. Return $\sigma = (\pi, \{\mathsf{com}_t, c_{t,1}, c_{t,2}\}_{t=1}^\ell)$.

$\mathsf{SRS.Verify}(\mathsf{R}, \mu, \sigma)$: Given a ring R, a message μ, and a ring signature σ, a verifier performs as follows:

1. Parse $\sigma := (\pi, \{\mathsf{com}_t, c_{t,1}, c_{t,2}\}_{t=1}^\ell)$.
2. From R, extract $\mathsf{P} = \{y_0, \cdots, y_{N-1}\}$.
3. Compute root value $v \leftarrow \mathsf{ACC.Acc}_{acc.pp}(\mathsf{P})$.
4. If $\mathsf{CH} \neq H_{\mathsf{FS}}(\mu || c_{1,1} || c_{1,2} || \cdots || c_{\ell,1} || c_{\ell,2}, \mathsf{CMT}, v, \mathsf{P}, \{\mathsf{com}_t\}_{t=1}^\ell)$, return 0.
5. If $\mathsf{ZK.Verify}((v, \{\mathsf{com}_t\}_{t=1}^\ell), \pi) = 0$, return 0; otherwise, return 1.

$\mathsf{SRS.Shrink}(\mathsf{R}, \mathsf{R}', sk, \sigma)$: Given a ring signature σ on behalf of R, a real signer's secret key sk, and a ring $\mathsf{R}' \subset \mathsf{R}$ which the signer wants to shrink to, he performs as follows.

1. Parse $\sigma := (\pi, \{\mathsf{com}_t, c_{t,1}, c_{t,2}\}_{t=1}^\ell)$, and $sk = (x, sk_{\mathsf{PKE}})$.
2. Let $pk = (y, pk_{\mathsf{PKE}})$ be the public key corresponding to sk.
3. From R, R', extract $\mathsf{P} = \{y_0, \cdots, y_{N-1}\}$, $\mathsf{P}' = \{y_0', \cdots, y_{|\mathsf{R}'|-1}'\}$ respectively. If $y \notin \mathsf{P}'$, return $\perp$.
4. Compute ind $\leftarrow \mathsf{GetRevealedWitnessIndex}(\mathsf{P}', \mathsf{P})$, if ind $= -1$ return $\perp$.
5. Compute wit $\leftarrow \mathsf{ACC.GenWit}(\mathsf{P}, y)$ where wit $= \{(i_1, \cdots, i_\ell), (w_\ell, \cdots, w_1)\}$.
6. Use sk_{PKE} to decrypt either $c_{\mathsf{ind},j}$ to obtain $r_{\mathsf{ind}} \leftarrow \mathsf{PKE.Dec}(sk_{\mathsf{PKE}}, c_{\mathsf{ind},j})$, where $j \in \{1, 2\}$.
7. Compute $\mathsf{com}_{\mathsf{ind}}' \leftarrow \mathsf{Com}(w_{\mathsf{ind}}; r_{\mathsf{ind}})$, if $\mathsf{com}_{\mathsf{ind}}' \neq \mathsf{com}_{\mathsf{ind}}$ return $\perp$; otherwise, set $\zeta := (\mathsf{ind}, w_{\mathsf{ind}}, r_{\mathsf{ind}})$, return ζ.

$\mathsf{SRS.VerShrink}(\mathsf{R}, \mathsf{R}', \sigma, \zeta)$: Given a signature σ on behalf of R, a ring $\mathsf{R}' \subset \mathsf{R}$, and a shrink evidence ζ, a verifier performs as follows.

1. Parse $\zeta = (\mathsf{ind}, w_{\mathsf{ind}}, r_{\mathsf{ind}})$, if $\zeta = \perp$, return 0.
2. Parse $\sigma = (\pi, \{\mathsf{com}_t, c_{t,1}, c_{t,2}\}_{t=1}^{\ell})$.
3. From R, R', extract $\mathsf{P} = \{y_0, \cdots, y_{N-1}\}$, $\mathsf{P'} = \{y'_0, \cdots, y'_{|\mathsf{R'}|-1}\}$.
4. Compute $\mathsf{ind'} \leftarrow \mathsf{GetRevealedWitnessIndex}(\mathsf{P'}, \mathsf{P})$, if either $\mathsf{ind'} = -1$ or $\mathsf{ind'} \neq \mathsf{ind}$ return 0.
5. If $\mathsf{VerifyWitness}(\mathsf{ind}, w_{\mathsf{ind}}, \mathsf{P'}, \mathsf{P}) = 0$, return 0.
6. Compute $\mathsf{com'_{ind}} \leftarrow \mathsf{Com}(w_{\mathsf{ind}}; r_{\mathsf{ind}})$, if $\mathsf{com'_{ind}} \neq \mathsf{com_{ind}}$ return 0; otherwise return 1.

Without loss of generality, we assume the size of R and R' are powers of 2.

By using the Merkle tree as the heart of our construction, we achieve a logarithmic size signature. However, there is one limitation is that we can only shrink the original ring into several specific subsets R'. More clearly, public keys in R' must be arranged in the same order as those in R, and $\{y'_i\}_{i=1}^{N'}$ in P' (extracted from R') must also have the same parent node at the depth ind of the original Merkle tree generated by R, where ind is the revealed witness index. The Algorithm 1 ensures these conditions are satisfied. In fact, there are several existing works in the literature [25] that face the same limitation as ours because of using tree-based components in their constructions.

4.2 Security Proof

Theorem 1. *(Correctness) The* SRS *construction is correct if* ACC, Com, PKE *are correct, and* ZK *is complete.*

Theorem 2. *(Anonymity) The* SRS *construction is anonymous under the random oracle model if* Com *is computationally hiding,* PKE *has pseudorandom ciphertexts property, and* ZK *is (computationally/statistically) zero-knowledge.*

Theorem 3. *(Unforgeability) The* SRS *construction is unforgeable under the random oracle model if* ACC *is secure,* Com *is statistically binding,* ZK *is sound, and* F *is collision-resistant.*

Theorem 4. *(Shrinkability) The* SRS *construction is shrinkable under the random oracle model if* ACC, PKE *are correct,* ZK *is complete and (computationally/statistically) zero-knowledge, and* Com *is computationally binding.*

Due to the page length limit, we omit proofs of the above theorems and provide them in the full version.

5 Lattice-Based Instantiation

Notation. All vectors are in column form unless otherwise stated throughout this work. A vector is written in bold-face small letters, e.g., $\mathbf{v}$, while a matrix is in bold-face capital letters, e.g., $\mathbf{A}$. The superscript $\top$ denotes the transpose operation of a vector or a matrix; e.g., the transpose of matrix $\mathbf{A}$ is $\mathbf{A}^\top$. We let $[k]$ be the set $\{1,\ldots,k\}$ for $k \in \mathbb{N}$. Two vectors $\mathbf{u},\mathbf{v} \in \mathbb{Z}_q^n$ are concatenated by using the notation $||$, e.g., $\mathbf{u}||\mathbf{v} \in \mathbb{Z}_q^{2n}$. We define $\mathrm{bin}(\mathbf{v}) \in \{0,1\}^{n\log q}$ be the binary representation of a vector $\mathbf{v} \in \mathbb{Z}_q^n$ such that $\mathbf{v} = \mathbf{G} \cdot \mathrm{bin}(\mathbf{v})$, where $\mathbf{G}$ is the gadget matrix described as below

$$
\mathbf{G} = \begin{bmatrix} 1 \ldots 2^{\log q-1} & & & \\ & 1 \ldots 2^{\log q-1} & & \\ & & \ldots & \\ & & & 1 \ldots 2^{\log q-1} \end{bmatrix} \in \mathbb{Z}_q^{n \times n\log q}.
$$

5.1 Lattices Hardness Assumptions

Definition 8. *(SIS, [1])* Given matrix $\mathbf{A} \leftarrow \mathbb{Z}_q^{n\times m}$, Short Integer Solution problem $\mathsf{SIS}_{m,n,q,\theta}^{\infty}$ is to find $\mathbf{x} \in \mathbb{Z}^m$ s.t $\mathbf{A}\mathbf{x} = 0 \pmod q$ and $0 < \|\mathbf{x}\|_\infty \leq \theta$.

Definition 9. *(LWE, [23])* Given $n, m_e = \mathrm{poly}(n), p \geq 2$, and χ be a distribution over $\mathbb{Z}$, Learning With Errors problem $\mathsf{LWE}_{n,p,\chi}$ is to distinguish m_e samples from $\mathcal{A}_{\mathbf{s},\chi}$ and m_e uniformly random samples chosen from $\mathbb{Z}_p^n \times \mathbb{Z}_p$, where $\mathcal{A}_{\mathbf{s},\chi}$ is the distribution obtained by sampling $\mathbf{a} \leftarrow \mathbb{Z}_p^n$ and $\mathbf{e} \hookleftarrow \chi$, and ouputting $(\mathbf{a},\mathbf{s}^\top \cdot \mathbf{a} + \mathbf{e}) \in \mathbb{Z}_p^n \times \mathbb{Z}_p$, and $\mathbf{s} \leftarrow \mathbb{Z}_p^n$.

5.2 String Commitment Schemes

In this paper, we take advantage of the KTX string commitment scheme designed by Kawachi et al. [13]. We present the scheme as follows.

$\mathsf{Com}_\mathbf{C}(\mathbf{s};\mathbf{r})$: Given input $\mathbf{C} \leftarrow \mathbb{Z}_q^{n\times m}$, a message string $\mathbf{s} \in \{0,1\}^{nk}$, and a randomness $\mathbf{r} \in \{0,1\}^{nk}$, it outputs a committed value $\mathsf{com} = \mathbf{C} \cdot (\mathbf{x}||\mathbf{r}) \in \mathbb{Z}_q^n$.

Lemma 1. *([13]) The string commitment is statistically hiding and computationally binding, assuming the harness of $\mathsf{SIS}_{m,n,q,\theta}^{\infty}$ problem.*

5.3 A Stern-Like Zero-Knowledge Argument of Knowledge

We consider a ZKAoK protocol by taking advantage of a lattice-based Merkle-tree based accumulator scheme LACC in [17] for the LSRS with the below relation.

$$
\begin{aligned}
\mathcal{R}_{\mathsf{LSRS}} := \{ & (\mathbf{A},\mathbf{C},\mathbf{v},\{\mathsf{com}_t\}_{t=1}^\ell) \in \mathbb{Z}_q^{n\times m} \times \{0,1\}^{nk} \times (\mathbb{Z}_q^n)^\ell; \\
& \mathbf{x} \in \{0,1\}^m, \mathbf{p} \in \{0,1\}^{nk}, \{\mathbf{r}_t\}_{t=1}^\ell \in (\{0,1\}^{nk})^\ell \\
& \mathsf{wit} = ((i_1,\cdots,i_\ell),\{\mathbf{w}_t\}_{t=1}^\ell) \in \{0,1\}^\ell \times (\{0,1\}^{nk})^\ell : \\
& \mathsf{LACC.Verify}_\mathbf{A}(\mathbf{v},\mathbf{p},\mathsf{wit}) = 1 \ \wedge \ \mathbf{A}\mathbf{x} = \mathbf{G}\mathbf{p} \bmod q \wedge \\
& \{\mathsf{Com}_\mathbf{C}(\mathbf{w}_t,\mathbf{r}_t) = \mathsf{com}_t\}_{t=1}^\ell \}.
\end{aligned}
$$

A prover $\mathcal{P}$ wants to prove to a verifier $\mathcal{V}$ in a zero-knowledge mannner that he knows a witness $(\mathbf{x}, \mathbf{p}, \mathsf{wit}, \{\mathbf{r}_t\}_{t=1}^{\ell})$ for a given statement $(\mathbf{A}, \mathbf{C}, \mathbf{v}, \{\mathsf{com}_t\}_{t=1}^{\ell})$ such that

$$\begin{cases} \mathsf{LACC.Verify}_{\mathbf{A}}(\mathbf{v}, \mathbf{p}, \mathsf{wit}) = 1; \\ \mathbf{Ax} = \mathbf{Gp} \pmod{q}; \\ \mathsf{Com}_{\mathbf{C}}(\mathbf{w}_t, \mathbf{r}_t) = \mathsf{com}_t, \forall t \in [\ell]. \end{cases} \quad (1)$$

For the third condition, based on the definition of Com in Sect. 9, $\forall t \in [\ell]$, we transform the condition into $\mathbf{C} \cdot (\mathbf{w}_t \| \mathbf{r}_t) = \mathsf{com}_t \pmod{q}$. Let $\mathbf{u}_t = \mathbf{w}_t \| \mathbf{r}_t \in \{0, 1\}^m$, and $\mathbf{s}_t = \mathbf{G} \cdot \mathsf{bin}(\mathsf{com}_t \bmod q) \in \{0, 1\}^{nk}$, we have $\mathbf{C} \cdot \mathbf{u}_t = \mathbf{G} \cdot \mathbf{s}_t \pmod{q}$, where $\mathbf{G} \in \mathbb{Z}_q^{n \times n \log q}$ is the gadget matrix. Then, (1) is equivalent to

$$\begin{cases} \mathsf{LACC.Verify}_{\mathbf{A}}(\mathbf{v}, \mathbf{p}, \mathsf{wit}) = 1; \\ \mathbf{Ax} = \mathbf{Gp} \pmod{q}; \\ \mathbf{Cu}_t = \mathbf{Gs}_t \pmod{q}, \forall t \in [\ell]. \end{cases} \quad (2)$$

By applying the "extend-then-permute" technique [17], we build a Stern-like ZKAoK protocol for $\mathcal{P}$ to prove that he possesses a witness $(\mathbf{x}, \mathbf{p}, \mathsf{wit}, \{\mathbf{u}_t\}_{t=1}^{\ell})$ for a given statement $(\mathbf{A}, \mathbf{C}, \mathbf{v}, \{\mathbf{s}_t\}_{t=1}^{\ell})$ satisfying conditions in Eq. 2. The protocol is complete, statistical zero-knowledge and simulation-sound assuming $\mathsf{SIS}_{m,n,q,\theta}^{\infty}$ is hard, and the communication cost is $\tilde{\mathcal{O}}(\ell \cdot n)$ [17]. Due to the page length limit, we will present the ZKAoK protocol in the full version.

5.4 Shrinkable Ring Signature from Lattices

In this section, we introduce the SRS construction from lattices using the below building blocks:

- A lattice-based Merkle-tree based accumulator scheme LACC in [17],
- A KTX commitment scheme Com described in Sect. 5.2,
- A multi-bit version of Regev's encryption scheme [23], note that the scheme satisfies properties defined in Definition 2 [3],
- A hash function (as a random oracle) $H_{\mathsf{FS}} : \{0, 1\}^* \to \{1, 2, 3\}^{\kappa}$,
- A Zero-knowledge Argument of Knowledge ZKAoK described in Sect. 5.3.

Let n be the security parameter, and the number of ring users is $N = 2^{\ell} = \mathsf{poly}(n)$, a lattice-based shrinkable ring signature LSRS scheme below.

LSRS.Setup(n): Given a security parameter n, do:

1. Choose q. Let $k := \lceil \log_2 q \rceil$, $m = 2nk$.
2. Choose $p = \tilde{\mathcal{O}}(n^{1.5})$. Let $m_e = 2(n+nk)\lceil \log p \rceil$, and $\chi = D_{\mathbb{Z}, 2\sqrt{n}}$ be the LWE error distribution.
3. Sample $\mathbf{A} \leftarrow \mathbb{Z}_q^{n \times m}$, $\mathbf{C} \leftarrow \mathbb{Z}_q^{n \times m}$.
4. Choose a hash function $H_{\mathsf{FS}} : \{0, 1\}^* \to \{1, 2, 3\}^{\kappa}$,
5. Output $srs.pp := ((n, m, m_e, q, p, k, \chi, \mathbf{A}, \mathbf{C}), H_{\mathsf{FS}})$.

LSRS.KeyGen($srs.pp$): Given public parameters $scrs.pp$, a signer performs as follows:

1. Sample $\mathbf{x} \leftarrow \{0,1\}^m$. Compute $\mathbf{p} = \mathsf{bin}(\mathbf{Ax} \mod q) \in \{0,1\}^{nk}$.
2. Sample $\mathbf{S} \leftarrow \mathbb{Z}_p^{n \times nk}, \mathbf{E} \leftarrow \chi^{nk \times m_e}$. Sample $\mathbf{B} \leftarrow \mathbb{Z}_p^{n \times m_e}$. Compute $\mathbf{P} = \mathbf{S}^\top \cdot \mathbf{B} + \mathbf{E} \in \mathbb{Z}_p^{nk \times m_e}$.
3. Return $(sk, pk) = ((\mathbf{x}, \mathbf{S}), (\mathbf{p}, \mathbf{B}, \mathbf{P}))$.

LSRS.Sign(sk, μ, R): Given a secret key sk, a ring $\mathsf{R} := \{pk_0, \cdots, pk_{N-1}\}$, and a message μ, a signer performs as follows:

1. Parse $sk = (\mathbf{x}, \mathbf{S})$. Let $pk = (\mathbf{p}, \mathbf{B}, \mathbf{P})$ be the public key.
2. From R, extract $\mathsf{P} = \{\mathbf{p}_0, \cdots, \mathbf{p}_{N-1}\}$.
3. Compute $\mathbf{v} \leftarrow \mathsf{LACC}.\mathsf{Acc_A}(\mathsf{P})$ using the hash function $h_\mathbf{A}$.
4. Compute wit $\leftarrow \mathsf{LACC}.\mathsf{GenWit_A}(\mathsf{P}, \mathbf{p})$ where wit $= \{(i_1, \cdots, i_\ell) \in \{0,1\}^\ell, (\mathbf{w}_\ell, \cdots, \mathbf{w}_1) \in (\{0,1\}^{nk})^\ell\}$.
5. For $t \in [\ell]$:

   – Sample $\mathbf{r}_t \leftarrow \{0,1\}^{nk}$ and compute $\mathsf{com}_t \leftarrow \mathsf{Com_C}(\mathbf{w}_t; \mathbf{r}_t)$.
   – Encrypt $\mathbf{r}_t$ using a multi-bit version of Regev's encryption scheme:
     • Sample $\mathbf{e}_t \leftarrow \{0,1\}^{m_e}$.
     • Compute $\mathbf{c}_{t,1} = (\mathbf{c}_{t,1,1}, \mathbf{c}_{t,1,2}) = (\mathbf{B} \cdot \mathbf{e}_t \mod p, \mathbf{P} \cdot \mathbf{e}_t + \lfloor \frac{p}{2} \rfloor \cdot \mathbf{r}_t \mod p) \in \mathbb{Z}_p^n \times \mathbb{Z}_p^{nk}$.
   – Sample $\mathbf{c}_{t,2} = (\mathbf{c}_{t,2,1}, \mathbf{c}_{t,2,2}) \leftarrow \mathbb{Z}_p^n \times \mathbb{Z}_p^{nk}$.

6. Set $\mu := \mu \| \mathsf{bin}(\mathbf{c}_1) \| \mathsf{bin}(\mathbf{c}_2) \| \cdots \| \mathsf{bin}(\mathbf{c}_\ell)$, where $\forall t \in [\ell]$, $\mathsf{bin}(\mathbf{c}_t) = \mathsf{bin}(\mathbf{c}_{t,1,1}) \| \mathsf{bin}(\mathbf{c}_{t,1,2}) \| \mathsf{bin}(\mathbf{c}_{t,2,1}) \| \mathsf{bin}(\mathbf{c}_{t,2,2})$.
7. Use the Fiat-Shamir Heuristic with H_{FS} to transform the ZKAoK to a non-interactive NIZKAoK. The protocol is repeated up to $\kappa = \omega(\log n)$ Given $(\mathbf{A}, \mathbf{v}, \{\mathsf{com}_t\}_{t=1}^\ell)$ and the prover's auxiliary input $(\mathbf{x}, \mathbf{p}, \mathsf{wit}, \{\mathbf{r}_t\}_{t=1}^\ell)$ to produce a transcript $\pi = (\{\mathsf{CMT}_j\}_{j=1}^\kappa, \mathsf{CH}, \{\mathsf{RSP}_j\}_{j=1}^\kappa)$, where $\mathsf{CH} = H_{\mathsf{FS}}(\mu, \{\mathsf{CMT}_j\}_{j=1}^\kappa, \mathbf{A}, \mathbf{v}, \mathsf{P}, \{\mathsf{com}_t\}_{t=1}^\ell) \in \{1,2,3\}^\kappa$.
8. Return $\sigma = (\pi, \{\mathsf{com}_t, \mathbf{c}_{t,1}, \mathbf{c}_{t,2}\}_{t=1}^\ell)$.

LSRS.Verify(R, μ, σ): Given a ring R, a message μ, and a ring signature σ, a verifier performs as follows:

1. Parse $\sigma = (\pi, \{\mathsf{com}_t, \mathbf{c}_{t,1}, \mathbf{c}_{t,2}\}_{t=1}^\ell)$.
2. From R, extract $\mathsf{P} = \{\mathbf{p}_0, \cdots, \mathbf{p}_{N-1}\}$.
3. Compute $\mathbf{v} \leftarrow \mathsf{LACC}.\mathsf{Acc}_{acc.pp}(\mathsf{P})$ using the hash function $h_\mathbf{A}$.
4. Set $\mu := \mu \| \mathsf{bin}(\mathbf{c}_1) \| \mathsf{bin}(\mathbf{c}_2) \| \cdots \| \mathsf{bin}(\mathbf{c}_\ell)$, where $\forall t \in [\ell]$, $\mathsf{bin}(\mathbf{c}_t) = \mathsf{bin}(\mathbf{c}_{t,1,1}) \| \mathsf{bin}(\mathbf{c}_{t,1,2}) \| \mathsf{bin}(\mathbf{c}_{t,2,1}) \| \mathsf{bin}(\mathbf{c}_{t,2,2})$.
5. Parse $\pi = (\{\mathsf{CMT}_j\}_{j=1}^\kappa, \mathsf{CH}, \{\mathsf{RSP}_j\}_{j=1}^\kappa)$. Return 0 if $\mathsf{CH} \neq H_{\mathsf{FS}}(\mu, \mathsf{CMT}_j, \mathbf{A}, \mathbf{v}, \mathsf{P}, \{\mathsf{com}_t, \mathbf{c}_t\}_{t=1}^\ell)$.

6. Let CH_j be the j-th item of CH, for $j \in [\kappa]$, if $\mathsf{ZKAoK.Verify}(\mathsf{CMT}_j, s\mathsf{CH}_j, \mathsf{RSP}_j) = 0$, return 0; otherwise, return 1.

$\mathsf{LSRS.Shrink}(\mathsf{R}, \mathsf{R}', sk, \sigma)$: Given a ring signature σ on behalf of R, a real signer's secret key sk, and a ring $\mathsf{R}' \subset \mathsf{R}$ to which the signer wants to shrink to, he performs as follows.

1. Parse $\sigma = (\pi, \{\mathsf{com}_t, \mathbf{c}_{t,1}, \mathbf{c}_{t,2}\}_{t=1}^\ell)$, and $sk = (\mathbf{x}, \mathbf{S})$. Let $pk = (\mathbf{p}, \mathbf{B}, \mathbf{P})$ be the public key corresponding to sk.
2. From R, R', extract $\mathsf{P} = \{y_0, \cdots, y_{N-1}\}$, $\mathsf{P}' = \{y_0', \cdots, y_{|\mathsf{R}'|-1}'\}$ respectively. If $\mathbf{p} \notin \mathsf{P}'$, then return $\bot$.
3. Compute $\mathsf{ind} \leftarrow \mathsf{GetRevealedWitnessIndex}(\mathsf{P}', \mathsf{P})$. If $\mathsf{ind} = -1$ return $\bot$.
4. Compute $\mathsf{wit} \leftarrow \mathsf{LACC.GenWit_A}(\mathsf{P}, \mathbf{p})$ where $\mathsf{wit} = \{(i_1, \cdots, i_\ell) \in \{0,1\}^\ell, (\mathbf{w}_\ell, \cdots, \mathbf{w}_1) \in (\{0,1\}^{nk})^\ell\}$.
5. Without loss of generality, assuming $\mathbf{c}_{\mathsf{ind},1}$ is the ciphertext of $\mathbf{r}_{\mathsf{ind}}$, decrypt $\mathbf{c}_{\mathsf{ind},1}$ as follows:

   - Compute $\mathbf{r}_{\mathsf{ind}} = \mathbf{c}_{\mathsf{ind},1,2} - \mathbf{S}^\top \cdot \mathbf{c}_{\mathsf{ind},1,1} \in \mathbb{Z}_p^{nk}$.
   - For each $j \in [nk]$, if $\mathbf{r}_{\mathsf{ind},j}$ is closer to 0 than to $\lceil \frac{p}{2} \rceil \bmod p$, then set $\mathbf{r}'_{\mathsf{ind},j} := 0$; otherwise, set $\mathbf{r}_{\mathsf{ind},j} = 1$.

6. Compute $\mathsf{com}'_{\mathsf{ind}} \leftarrow \mathsf{Com_C}(\mathbf{w}_{\mathsf{ind}}; \mathbf{r}'_{\mathsf{ind}})$, if $\mathsf{com}'_{\mathsf{ind}} \neq \mathsf{com}_{\mathsf{ind}}$ return $\bot$; otherwise, return a shrink evidence $\zeta = (\mathsf{ind}, \mathbf{w}_{\mathsf{ind}}, \mathbf{r}_{\mathsf{ind}})$.

$\mathsf{LSRS.VerShrink}(\mathsf{R}, \mathsf{R}', \sigma, \zeta)$: Given a ring signature σ on behalf of R, a ring $\mathsf{R}' \subset \mathsf{R}$, and a shrink evidence ζ, a verifier performs as follows.

1. Parse $\zeta = (\mathsf{ind}, \mathbf{w}_{\mathsf{ind}}, \mathbf{r}_{\mathsf{ind}})$, if $\zeta = \bot$, return 0.
2. Parse $\sigma = (\pi, \{\mathsf{com}_t, \mathbf{c}_{t,1}, \mathbf{c}_{t,2}\}_{t=1}^\ell)$.
3. From R, R', extract $\mathsf{P} = \{y_0, \cdots, y_{N-1}\}$, $\mathsf{P}' = \{y_0', \cdots, y_{|\mathsf{R}'|-1}'\}$.
4. Compute $\mathsf{ind}' \leftarrow \mathsf{GetRevealedWitnessIndex}(\mathsf{P}', \mathsf{P})$, if either $\mathsf{ind}' = -1$ or $\mathsf{ind}' \neq \mathsf{ind}$, return 0.
5. If $\mathsf{VerifyWitness}(\mathsf{ind}, \mathbf{w}_{\mathsf{ind}}, \mathsf{P}', \mathsf{P}) = 0$, return 0.
6. Compute $\mathsf{com}'_{\mathsf{ind}} \leftarrow \mathsf{Com_C}(\mathbf{w}_{\mathsf{ind}}; \mathbf{r}_{\mathsf{ind}})$, if $\mathsf{com}'_{\mathsf{ind}} \neq \mathsf{com}_{\mathsf{ind}}$ return 0; otherwise return 1.

Next, we analyze the properties of LSRS.

Correctness. The correctness of the LSRS immediately follows the completeness of the ZKAoK, and the correctness of Com and Regev's encryption scheme.

Efficiency. The size of π dominates the size of the signature. Because the communication cost of the underlying ZKAoK is $\tilde{O}(\ell \cdot n)$, we have the size of the transcript π is $\tilde{O}(\kappa \cdot \ell \cdot n) = \tilde{O}(\log N \cdot n)$. The number of commitments com_t and ciphertexts $\mathbf{c}_t$ also grows logarithmically to the size of the ring. Hence, the size of the signature is logarithmic to the number of ring members.

Theorem 5. *(Anonymity) The shrinkable ring signature* LSRS *is anonymous under the random oracle model assuming the problem* $\mathsf{SIS}_{m,n,q,\theta}^{\infty}$ *and* $\mathsf{LWE}_{n,p,\chi}^{\infty}$ *are hard, and the underlying argument system* ZKAoK *is zero-knowledge.*

Theorem 6. *(Unforgeability) The shrinkable ring signature* LSRS *is unforgeable under the random oracle model assuming the problem* $\mathsf{SIS}_{m,n,q,\theta}^{\infty}$ *and* $\mathsf{LWE}_{n,p,\chi}^{\infty}$ *are hard, and the underlying argument system* ZKAoK *is simulation-sound.*

Theorem 7. *(Shrinkability) The shrinkable ring signature* LSRS *is shrinkable under the random oracle model assuming the problem* $\mathsf{SIS}_{m,n,q,\theta}^{\infty}$ *and* $\mathsf{LWE}_{n,p,\chi}^{\infty}$ *are hard, and the underlying argument system* ZKAoK *is zero-knowledge.*

Proof. Due to the page length limit, we will provide the proof for these theorems in the full version.

References

1. Ajtai, M.: Generating hard instances of lattice problems (extended abstract). In: Proceedings of the Twenty-eighth Annual ACM Symposium on Theory of Computing, STOC '96, pages 99–108. ACM, New York (1996)
2. Au, M.H., Tsang, P.P., Susilo, W., Mu, Y.: Dynamic universal accumulators for ddh groups and their application to attribute-based anonymous credential systems. In: Fischlin, M. (ed.) Topics in Cryptology—CT-RSA (2009)
3. Backes, M., Döttling, N., Hanzlik, L., Kluczniak, K., Schneider, J.: Ring signatures: Logarithmic-size, no setup—from standard assumptions. In: Advances in Cryptology —EUROCRYPT 2019
4. Beullens, W., Katsumata, S., Pintore, F.: Calamari and falafl: logarithmic (linkable) ring signatures from isogenies and lattices. In: Advances in Cryptology—ASIACRYPT (2020)
5. Bresson, E., Stern, J., Szydlo, M.: Threshold ring signatures and applications to ad-hoc groups. In: Advances in Cryptology—CRYPTO (2002)
6. Chatterjee, R., Garg, S., Hajiabadi, M., Khurana, D., Liang, X., Malavolta, G., Pandey, O., Shiehian, S.: Compact ring signatures from learning with errors. In: Advances in Cryptology—CRYPTO (2021)
7. ElGamal, T.: A public key cryptosystem and a signature scheme based on discrete logarithms. In: Blakley, G.R., Chaum, D. (eds.) Advances in Cryptology
8. Feng, H., Liu, J., Wu, Q., Li, Y.-N.: Traceable ring signatures with post-quantum security. In: Topics in Cryptology—CT-RSA (2020)
9. Franklin, M., Zhang, H.: Unique ring signatures: a practical construction. In: Financial Cryptography and Data Security
10. Fujisaki, E., Suzuki, K.: Traceable ring signature. In: Public Key Cryptography—PKC (2007)
11. Groth, J., Ostrovsky, R., Sahai, A.: Perfect non-interactive zero knowledge for np. In: Vaudenay, S. (ed.) Advances in Cryptology–EUROCRYPT 2006, pp. 339–358. Springer, Berlin (2006)
12. Haque, A., Scafuro, A.: Threshold ring signatures: New definitions and post-quantum security. In: Public-Key Cryptography—PKC (2020)
13. Kawachi, A., Tanaka, K., Xagawa, K.: Concurrently secure identification schemes based on the worst-case hardness of lattice problems. In: Advances in Cryptology—ASIACRYPT (2008)

14. Kawachi, A., Tanaka, K., Xagawa, K.: Multi-bit cryptosystems based on lattice problems. In: Public Key Cryptography—PKC (2007)
15. Komano, Y., Ohta, K., Shimbo, A., Kawamura, S.: Toward the fair anonymous signatures: deniable ring signatures. In: Topics in Cryptology—CT-RSA (2006)
16. Li, X., Mei, Y., Gong, J., Xiang, F., Sun, Z.: A blockchain privacy protection scheme based on ring signature. IEEE Access **8**
17. Libert, B., Ling, S., Nguyen, K., Wang, H.: Zero-knowledge arguments for lattice-based accumulators: logarithmic-size ring signatures and group signatures without trapdoors. In: Advances in Cryptology—EUROCRYPT (2016)
18. Lindell, Y.: Highly-efficient universally-composable commitments based on the ddh assumption. In: Paterson, K.G. (ed.) Advances in Cryptology—EUROCRYPT (2011)
19. Liu, J.K., Wei, V.K., Wong, D.S.: Linkable spontaneous anonymous group signature for ad hoc groups. In: Information Security and Privacy
20. Nguyen, T.N., Ta, A.T., Le, H.Q., Duong, D.H., Susilo, W., Guo, F., Fukushima, K., Kiyomoto, S.: Efficient unique ring signatures from lattices. In: Computer Security—ESORICS (2022)
21. Noether, S.: Ring signature confidential transactions for Monero. Cryptology ePrint Archive, Report 2015/1098 (2015). https://eprint.iacr.org/2015/1098
22. Park, S., Sealfon, A.: It wasn't me! In: Advances in Cryptology—CRYPTO (2019)
23. Regev, O.: On lattices, learning with errors, random linear codes, and cryptography. In: In STOC, pp. 84–93. ACM Press (2005)
24. Rivest, R.L., Shamir, A., Tauman, Y.:. How to leak a secret. In: Advances in Cryptology—ASIACRYPT (2001)
25. Safavi-Naini, R., Wang, H.: New constructions for multicast re-keying schemes using perfect hash families. In: Proceedings of the 7th ACM Conference on Computer and Communications Security, pp. 228–234 (2000)
26. Ta, A.T., Khuc, T.X., Nguyen, T.N., Le, H.Q., Duong, D.H., Susilo, W., Fukushima, K., Kiyomoto, S.: Efficient unique ring signature for blockchain privacy protection. In: Information Security and Privacy
27. Tsang, P.P., Wei, V.K.: Short linkable ring signatures for e-voting, e-cash and attestation. In: Information Security Practice and Experience

Related-Tweakey Boomerang and Rectangle Attacks on Reduced-Round Joltik-BC

Kangkang Shi[ID], Jiongjiong Ren[✉][ID], and Shaozhen Chen

Information Engineering University, Zhengzhou, China
{kkk41740,jiongjiong_fun}@163.com, chenshaozhen@vip.sina.com

Abstract. As one of the candidates for authenticated encryption in the second round of the CAESAR competition, Joltik has an internal lightweight tweakable block cipher Joltik-BC. In ASIACRYPT 2014, designers stated that the real threat to Joltik-BC comes from attacks that exploit the tweakey schedule, i.e. related-tweakey differential attacks. However, there has been no such attack against Joltik-BC currently. In the paper, we evaluate the resistance to Joltik-BC against boomerang attacks. Considering that not all distinguishers with high probability have a significant effect in key recovery attacks, we incorporate the complexity of key recovery into the search for distinguishers and turn to search for the entire truncated attack paths. Specifically, by considering truncated differential propagation, we control the number of active nibbles on the sides of plaintext and ciphertext to reduce key guessing. Then we apply it to search for appropriate distinguishers of Joltik-BC. Finally, we propose a 10-round related-tweakey boomerang attack for Joltik-BC-128 and a 14-round related-tweakey rectangle attack for Joltik-BC 192. To reduce the time complexity, we also utilize the property of components to guess partial key bits and deduce other key bits. This is the first work to evaluate the resistance of related-tweakey boomerang attack for Joltik-BC and both of them increase the round number of key recovery attacks.

Keywords: Lightweight block cipher · Tweakable cipher · Joltik-BC · MILP · Boomerang attack · Rectangle attack

1 Introduction

Since the Internet of Things and some resource-constrained devices are widely used in life, traditional ciphers suffer from the problems of high hardware implementation and high power consumption. In this direction, traditional ciphers are no longer able to meet such needs and this hinders. As a result, lightweight block ciphers arise and rapidly attract widespread attention in cryptography. In CRYPTO 2002, Liskov et al. [13] introduced an additional input tweak in traditional design and proposed tweakable block ciphers. Since altering the key is more expensive than altering the tweak, tweakable block ciphers have extensive application in fields such as resource-constrained environments.

Z. Xia and J. Chen (Eds.): ISPEC 2024, LNCS 15053, pp. 94–111, 2024.
https://doi.org/10.1007/978-981-97-9053-1_6

In ASIACRYPT 2014, TWEAKEY framework [8] is proposed to design tweakable block ciphers and the lightweight tweakable cipher Joltik-BC came into being. It is the internal block cipher of the authenticated encryption algorithm Joltik [9], which is a candidate to enter the second round of the CAESAR competition. Initially, the designers [8] pointed out that the real threat to Joltik-BC comes from attacks that exploit the tweakey schedule, i.e. related-tweakey differential attacks and meet-in-the-middle attacks. There are many meet-in-the-middle attacks on Joltik-BC currently. In 2019, Li et al. [12] utilized tweak difference to present key recovery attacks on 8-round Joltik-BC-128 and 10-round Joltik-BC-192. Then, Liu et al. [15] adopted the subtweakey difference cancellation and implemented a 9-round meet-in-the-middle attack on Joltik-BC-128. In 2021, adopting the meet-in-the-middle technique, Li et al. [11] reduced the time complexity for Joltik-BC-128 and proposed a 11-round key recovery attack for Joltik-BC-192.

However, there has been no related-tweakey differential attack against Joltik-BC. As an extension of differential attack, boomerang attack has attracted widespread attention and made significant progress, which has a better effect in cryptanalysis of AES-like ciphers [3,6], i.e. AES, SKINNY and so on. Hence, analyzing the security of Joltik-BC against related-tweakey boomerang attacks is necessary. It not only provides a comprehensive evaluation of the security, but also can help to breakthrough in design for tweakable block ciphers.

Our Contributions. Although the previous models can search for distinguishers with higher probability, not all distinguishers with high probability have a significant effect in key recovery attacks due to the possible amount of key guessing. Hence, focusing on the MILP tool, we incorporate the complexity of key recovery into the search of distinguishers and turn to search for the entire truncated attack path. Specifically, control the number of active nibbles on the sides of plaintext and ciphertext to reduce key guessing. Depending on truncated differential propagation, we divide the attack into three parts and encode them in different ways. Next, combined with the found truncated trail, we establish a bit-oriented differential model to search for two differential characteristics with the highest probability. Finally, we structure appropriate boomerang distinguishers by inspecting the dependency between two characteristics.

We apply the model to Joltik-BC and limit the attack paths to have few active nibbles on the sides of plaintext and ciphertext, which leads to a small amount of key guessing. In key recovery phase, utilizing the property of **SubNibbles** and **MixNibbles**, we also guess partial key bits to deduce other key bits that need to be guessed. These operations greatly reduce the time complexity. For Joltik-BC-128, relying on a 8-round distinguisher with probability 2^{-34}, we present a 10-round related-tweakey boomerang attack. It takes 2^{53} chosen-plaintexts-and-ciphertexts and equivalent $2^{53.58}$ 10-round encryptions to recover 64-bit key. For Joltik-BC-192, we search for a 11-round boomerang distinguisher of probability 2^{-52} and present a 14-round related-tweakey rectangle attack. The 128-bit key is guessed by $2^{59.61}$ chosen-plaintexts and equivalent $2^{123.41}$ 14-round encryptions. It summarizes all key recovery attacks on Joltik-BC in Table 1.

Table 1. Summary of analysis results against Joltik-BC. MITM = Meet-in-the-middle attack, ID = Impossible differential attack, Boom. = Boomerang attack, Rect. = rectangle attack. Our attacks are under related-tweakey scenario. Moreover, CP = Chosen-plaintexts and ACC = Chosen-plaintexts-and-ciphertexts.

Cipher	Attack	Rounds	Data	Memory	Time	References
Joltik-BC-128	MITM	8	$2^{53.5}$ CP	2^{53}	$2^{53.6}$	[12]
	MITM	9	2^{53} CP	$2^{52.91}$	$2^{56.6}$	[15]
	MITM	9	2^{53} CP	$2^{52.91}$	$2^{54.1}$	[11]
	ID	9	2^{60} CP	2^{50}	$2^{61.7}$	[24]
	Boom.	10	2^{53} ACC	2^{53}	$2^{53.58}$	Sect. 4
Joltik-BC-192	MITM	10	$2^{56.1}$ CP	$2^{123.5}$	$2^{126.5}$	[12]
	MITM	11	2^{53} CP	2^{114}	2^{123}	[11]
	Rect.	14	$2^{59.61}$ CP	2^{68}	$2^{123.41}$	Sect. 5

Outline. In the following, Sect. 2 gives a brief introduction of required preliminaries. An comprehensive summary about the MILP-based search model for boomerang distinguishers is given in Sect. 3. Then during Sect. 4 and Sect. 5, we present key recovery attacks on different variants of Joltik-BC, respectively. A conclusion is given in Sect. 6.

2 Preliminaries

2.1 Description of Joltik-BC

Based on the TWEAKEY framework, Joltik-BC [8] is a lightweight block cipher. It has an additional 64-bit input tweak T in the beginning. With 64-bit block size n, Joltik-BC has two variants: Joltik-BC-128 has a 64-bit key K, while it has a 128-bit key K for Joltik-BC-192. Moreover, the number of rounds is 24 and 32, respectively.

The Round Function. Joltik-BC adopts AES-like round function, which includes four operations. In the round function f, the state can be firstly viewed as a 4×4 matrix of nibbles, and then apply four operations in the order specified below:

- *SubNibbles*(SN): The operation applies S-box of Piccolo [19] to all nibbles.
- *ShiftRows*(SR): The operation shifts i-th row left by i nibbles, $i = 0, 1, 2, 3$.
- *MixNibbles*(MN): A 4×4 MDS matrix M is multiplied by the state.
- *AddRoundTweakey*(ART): The subtweakey can be also viewed as a 4×4 matrix of nibbles, and then XOR it to the internal state.

Moreover, an extra **AddRoundTweakey** operation is required before plaintext enters the round function. The encryption structural diagram of Joltik-BC-192 is shown in Fig. 1.

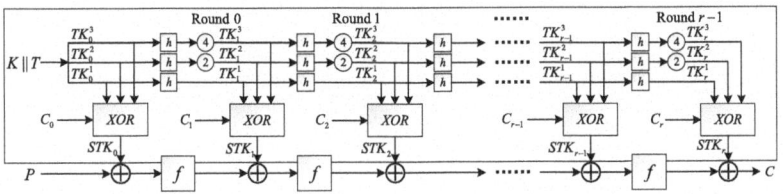

Fig. 1. The encryption structural diagram of Joltik-BC-192

Definition of the Subtweakey. We take $KT = K\|T$ to represent the concatenation of the key K and the tweak T. Firstly, split KT into several 64-bit words TK_0^j. Then, take STK_i to represent the subtweakey in the i-th round. For Joltik-BC-m, $STK_i = \bigoplus_{j=1}^{m/64} TK_i^j \oplus C_i$, where C_i is a constant and TK_i^1, TK_i^2, TK_i^3 can be deduced from TK_0^1, TK_0^2, TK_0^3 by nibble permutation and multiplication in the finite field $\mathbb{F}_{2^4}$ defined by the irreducible polynomial $x^4 + x + 1$. The process is taken as follows:

$$TK_{i+1}^1 = h(TK_i^1),\, TK_{i+1}^2 = g_2(h(TK_i^2)),\, TK_{i+1}^3 = g_4(h(TK_i^3)),$$

where h is a nibble permutation and g_α is a multiplication of every nibbles by the element α in $\mathbb{F}_{2^4}$.

Notation. For convenience, we use X_i, Y_i, Z_i to represent the state of the i-th round entering SN, MN and ART operations, respectively. And $x[i, \ldots, j]$ are used to represent the i-th, $\ldots$, j-th nibbles of state x. For boomerang attack, we use Δx and ∇x to represent the difference of state x in the upper and lower trails, respectively.

2.2 Boomerang Attack

In FSE 1999, Wagner [22] proposed the boomerang attack, with the dominant thought being to merge two short differentials to obtain a longer differential with high probability. The chart of boomerang attacks is shown in Fig. 2 (a). Boomerang attack works with chosen-plaintexts-and-ciphertexts and a right quartet can be get in the following:

1. Choose plaintext pair (P_1, P_2) satisfying $P_1 \oplus P_2 = \alpha$ randomly, and encrypt them to get the corresponding ciphertext pair (C_1, C_2);
2. Generate another ciphertext pair $(C_3 = C_1 \oplus \delta, C_4 = C_2 \oplus \delta)$, and decrypt them to get the corresponding plaintext pair (P_3, P_4);
3. Check whether the pair (P_3, P_4) satisfies $P_3 \oplus P_4 = \alpha$ or not.

We split the cipher E into sub-ciphers E_0, E_1. Assume that there exist two independent differentials $\alpha \xrightarrow{E_0} \beta$ with probability p and $\gamma \xrightarrow{E_1} \delta$ with probability q, the probability that attackers get a right quartet is $p^2 q^2$.

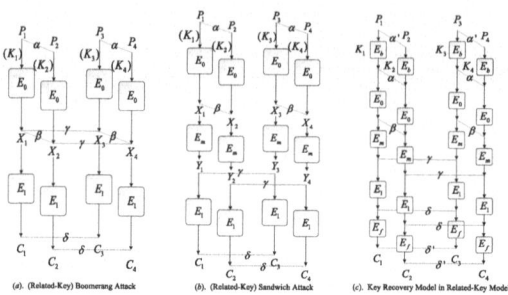

Fig. 2. Boomerang attack and key recovery model

Subsequently, boomerang attack was further extended to amplified boomerang attack [10] and rectangle attack [1]. For rectangle attack, it works in chosen-plaintext model. Therefore, the probability that attackers get a right quartet is $2^{-n}p^2q^2$. Biham et al. [1] indicated that when fixing the value of α and δ, and exhausting the possible values of β and γ except for $\beta = \gamma$ in the attack, the probability can be increased to $2^{-n}\hat{p}^2\hat{q}^2$, in which

$$\hat{p} = \sqrt{\sum_{\beta_i} Pr^2(\alpha \to \beta_i)}, \quad \hat{q} = \sqrt{\sum_{\gamma_i} Pr^2(\gamma_i \to \delta)}.$$

In EUROCRYPT 2005, Biham et al. [2] introduced related-key boomerang and rectangle attacks. Unlike single-key model, the plaintext quartet (P_1, P_2, P_3, P_4) is encrypted with different keys (K_1, K_2, K_3, K_4) in related-key model. Keys satisfy the conditions that $K_1 \oplus K_2 = \Delta K, K_1 \oplus K_3 = \nabla K, K_1 \oplus K_4 = \Delta K \oplus \nabla K$. Therefore, attackers only need to recover one of keys to deduce all in key recovery attack.

However, the above are all based on the assumption that two differentials are independent, which is not always satisfied in most cases. As studied in [3,16], the dependency between two differentials should be considered. As shown in Fig 2 (b), the sandwich attack splits cipher E into three sub-ciphers. The sub-cipher E_m includes the dependency between two differentials, whose probability can be computed by

$$r = \Pr\{E_m^{-1}(E_m(X_1) \oplus \gamma) \oplus E_m^{-1}(E_m(X_1 \oplus \beta) \oplus \gamma) = \beta\}. \tag{1}$$

2.3   The Framework of Key Recovery Attack

There have been some key recovery models [14,23] in boomerang attack currently. As shown in Fig. 2 (c), we follow the notations of previous models. For distinguishers, extend R_b rounds and R_f rounds at the beginning and end denoted as E_b and E_f. Take k to represent the master key size. Denote the number of active nibbles of input difference and guessed subtweakey involved in E_b as $r_b/4$ and $m_b/4$. Similarly denote r_f and m_f involved in E_f. The step of key recovery attack is given in the following:

1. Construct y structures of plaintext, which exhausts all the possible values of active nibbles with other nibbles fixed constants.
2. Query ciphertexts by the oracle under the corresponding keys and construct hash tables for subsequent table look-ups.
3. Guess the m_b subtweakey bits involved in E_b:
   (1) For m_f subtweakey bits involved in E_f, initialize a list of counters.
   (2) Referring to the generation of quartets in the corresponding attack, generate the quartets $((P_1, C_1), (P_2, C_2), (P_3, C_3), (P_4, C_4))$.
   (3) Filter wrong quartets. According to the known difference in plaintext and ciphertext, filter all quartets whose differences do not match up.
   (4) Guess key bits and filter quartets. All remaining quartets are used to recover the remaining subtweakeys that need to be guessed.
   (5) Select the keys with h-bit or higher advantage in the counters as the candidates.
4. Exhaust the remaining $k - m_b - m_f$ key bits and recover the right key by key schedule.

For boomerang attack, the above process can also construct structures of ciphertext. Finally, the success probability is calculated by the method in [18]:

$$P_s = \Phi(\frac{\sqrt{sS_N} - \Phi^{-1}(1 - 2^{-h})}{\sqrt{S_N + 1}}), \tag{2}$$

where s is the number of expect right quartets and $S_N = \hat{p}^2\hat{q}^2 r/2^{-n}$ is the signal-to-noise ratio.

3   MILP-Based Search Model for Boomerang Distinguishers on Joltik-BC

During the section, we introduce how to use MILP model to find an appropriate boomerang distinguisher of Joltik-BC in detail. For the model, we improve the strategy to search for distinguishers proposed by Hadipour et al. [7].

3.1   Search for Truncated Characteristic of Attack Path

The ultimate goal of a distinguisher is to use it for a key recovery attack. Therefore, as far as the effect is concerned, the probability of the distinguisher is obviously one of the important factors. However, it does not ensure that longer the number of rounds is and higher the probability is, better the effect is. Hence, we should select appropriate distinguishers to present key recovery attacks.

Before clarifying appropriate distinguishers, we firstly recall the key recovery model. With respect to the data complexity, it is mainly affected by the probability of the distinguisher. And as far as the time complexity, $r_b + r_f$ key guessing bits in the attack play an important role. Obviously, there is a positive relation between the amount of key guessing and the number of active nibbles in plaintext and ciphertext. Hence, we take the probability p^2q^2r of the distinguisher and the number of active nibbles in plaintext and ciphertext into account. Differing from the model proposed by Hadipour et al. [7], our model is to search for the entire attack path rather than the distinguishers.

As shown in Fig. 2 (c), we attempt to search for a truncated differential trail covering the entire attack path, where the middle $(R_0 + R_m + R_1)$ rounds form a distinguisher. Our model is to construct two independent truncated differential models, encoding the propagation of truncated difference passing the sub-ciphers $E_m \circ E_0 \circ E_b$ and $E_f \circ E_1 \circ E_m$, respectively. We define them as upper and lower truncated differential trails, respectively. Both of them can be divided into three parts by the different encodings. The specific classifications are illustrated in Fig. 3. In addition, we make a slight adjustment in the classifications. Specifically, for upper trail, we merge the final round of E_b into E_0. It is because that the difference remains known after $ART^{-1}, MN^{-1}, SR^{-1}$ operations. The similar procedure is performed for lower trail.

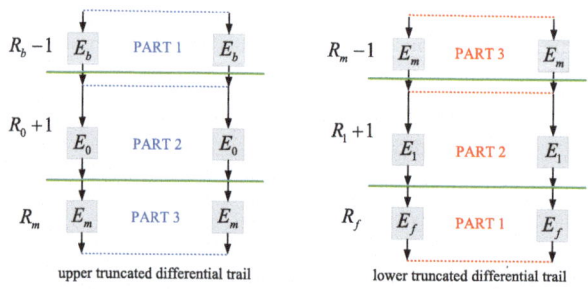

Fig. 3. The classifications in the model for truncated differential trails

During PART 2, the difference is passed in a standard way. We borrow the model to search for truncated differential characteristics proposed by Cid et al. [5]. By converting word-oriented operations to nibble-oriented operations in the model, we find truncated differential characteristics on Joltik-BC in a standard way. Specific details in the part can refer to [5].

PART 1 is concerned with the extension of the distinguisher. In upper (lower) trail, the input (output) difference changes from known to unknown after SN^{-1} (SN) operation. So there is no difference cancellation in ART in the part. Besides, in contrast to ART encoded in PART 2, we add the propagation of direction into consideration. For example, let variables x_{i+1}, stk_{i+1}, z_i to represent the activeness of a given nibble in $X_{i+1} = STK_{i+1} \oplus Z_i$ in upper trail. Based on the propagation of direction, $(z_i, stk_{i+1}, x_{i+1}) \in \{(0,0,0), (1,1,0), (1,0,1), (1,1,1)\}$ can be described as:

$$x_{i+1} + stk_{i+1} - z_i \geq 0, \quad z_i - x_{i+1} \geq 0, \quad z_i - stk_{i+1} \geq 0. \tag{3}$$

For MN in PART 1, if there exist any active nibbles in the column, all nibbles in the corresponding output column are active. We also consider the propagation of direction. Suppose that variables (y_1, y_2, y_3, y_4) and (z_1, z_2, z_3, z_4) are used to represent the activeness of input and output differences in MN respectively, the constraints are expressed by

$$\sum_{j=1}^{4} y_j - z_i \geq 0, \qquad 4z_i - \sum_{j=1}^{4} y_j \geq 0, \qquad i = 1, 2, 3, 4. \tag{4}$$

The encodings of other components are the same as that in PART 2.

PART 3 shows the dependency between two differentials. Since that upper and lower truncated differential trails are opposite in the propagation of direction, we also put the propagation of direction into consideration. In addition, to ensure that the truncated difference is propagated through the middle part with probability one, we encode ART by Eq. 3 excluding difference cancellation. MN has a property of branch number 5, which is used to exclude solutions with invalid differential propagation. Specifically, adding an additional dummy variable $d \in \{0, 1\}$ to represent whether a column is active or not, the constraints are expressed as follows:

$$5d \leq (y_1 + y_2 + y_3 + y_4) + (z_1 + z_2 + z_3 + z_4) \leq 8d. \tag{5}$$

Other components are encoded by the same way in PART 2.

Finally, we are looking for truncated trails with the minimum number of active S-boxes in the distinguisher. Taking the ladder switch effect in multiple rounds into account, we introduce $16R_m$ new binary variable $a_0^{mi}, \ldots, a_{16R_m-1}^{mi}$ to link the activeness of S-boxes at the corresponding position of upper and lower trails. Denote $a_0^{up}, \ldots, a_{16R_m-1}^{up}$ and $a_0^{lo}, \ldots, a_{16R_m-1}^{lo}$ as the activeness of S-boxes through E_m in upper and lower trails, respectively. Thus, $a_i^{mi} = 1$ if and only if $a_i^{up} = a_i^{lo} = 1$, which can be constrained by:

$$a_i^{up} - a_i^{mi} \geq 0, \quad a_i^{lo} - a_i^{mi} \geq 0, \quad -a_i^{up} - a_i^{lo} + a_i^{mi} \geq -1. \tag{6}$$

Denote $\hat{a}_0^{up}, \ldots, \hat{a}_{16R_0-1}^{up}$ and $\hat{a}_0^{lo}, \ldots, \hat{a}_{16R_1-1}^{lo}$ to represent the activeness of S-boxes through E_0 and E_1, respectively. Then the objective is set to minimize:

$$\sum_{i=0}^{16R_0-1} \hat{a}_i^{up} + \sum_{i=0}^{16R_m-1} a_i^{mi} + \sum_{i=0}^{16R_1-1} \hat{a}_i^{lo}.$$

3.2   Search for Bit-Oriented Differential Characteristics

Based on the discovered truncated attack trail, we are looking for the differentials with the highest probability on upper and lower trails. Considering that SR operation only changes the position of bits, we provide a detailed description of the differential model for the rest operations as follows.

For SN operation, the differential model of 4×4 S-boxes is well developed. In a traditional encoding, we first calculate Difference Distribution Table (DDT) of S-boxes. As described in [21], we take the concatenation of input difference, output difference and probability information to represent DDT with discrete points. There have been various studies [4, 21] to generate inequalities. In addition, to efficiently represent the S-boxes with a small number of inequalities, MILP-based approach proposed by Sasaki et al. [17] can minimize the number of inequalities. Finally, we obtained 18 inequalities to describe the S-boxes of Joltik-BC.

For MN operation, we adopt the primitive representation proposed by Sun et al. [20] to represent the MDS matrix M, which includes the elements 1, 4, 9, d in $\mathbb{F}_{2^4}$. According to that the irreducible polynomial of the field multiplication is $x^4 + x + 1$, field multiplication of elements can be represented by the primitive representation as follows:

$$\begin{pmatrix} 1 & 4 & 9 & d \\ 4 & 1 & d & 9 \\ 9 & d & 1 & 4 \\ d & 9 & 4 & 1 \end{pmatrix} \Bigg| \quad 1 = \begin{bmatrix} 1 & 0 & 0 & 0 \\ 0 & 1 & 0 & 0 \\ 0 & 0 & 1 & 0 \\ 0 & 0 & 0 & 1 \end{bmatrix}, 4 = \begin{bmatrix} 0 & 0 & 1 & 0 \\ 1 & 0 & 0 & 1 \\ 1 & 1 & 0 & 0 \\ 0 & 1 & 0 & 0 \end{bmatrix}, 9 = \begin{bmatrix} 0 & 0 & 0 & 1 \\ 1 & 0 & 0 & 0 \\ 0 & 1 & 0 & 0 \\ 0 & 0 & 1 & 1 \end{bmatrix}, d = \begin{bmatrix} 0 & 0 & 1 & 1 \\ 0 & 0 & 0 & 1 \\ 1 & 0 & 0 & 0 \\ 0 & 1 & 1 & 1 \end{bmatrix}.$$

Then denote the primitive representation of MDS matrix M as 16×16 matrix M^{PR}, which is generated by replacing the field elements with the primitive representation of elements. For the internal state Y_i, Z_i, we convert nibbles to bits and then expand them to 16×4 matrices Y_i^B, Z_i^B. Hence, MN operation can also be expressed as $Z_i^B = M^{PR} Y_i^B$. In this way, the encoding of MN can be transformed into the encoding of XOR among several variables, which can refer to the encoding of ART.

For $X_{i+1} = Z_i \oplus STK_{i+1}$ in ART operation, by representing the activeness of a given bit as previously defined, we should exclude the space of $(z_i, stk_{i+1}, x_{i+1}) \in \{(0,0,1), (0,1,0), (1,0,0), (1,1,1)\}$ out, described by:

$$\begin{cases} z_i + stk_{i+1} + (1 - x_{i+1}) > 1 \\ z_i + (1 - stk_{i+1}) + x_{i+1} \geq 1 \\ (1 - z_i) + stk_{i+1} + x_{i+1} \geq 1 \\ (1 - z_i) + (1 - stk_{i+1}) + (1 - x_{i+1}) \geq 1 \end{cases} . \tag{7}$$

For tweakey schedule, the operation consists of two functions: nibble permutation h and field multiplication g_α. Nibble permutation can be easily given as equations for the permutation between bits. For field multiplication g_α, the transformation of bits within a nibble is given in Table 2. Hence, the states TK_i^1, TK_i^2, TK_i^3 are generated by linear operations.

Table 2. The field multiplication g_α used in tweakey schedule

g_2	$x = x_3\|x_2\|x_1\|x_0 \rightarrow g_2(x) = x_2\|x_1\|(x_3 \oplus x_0)\|x_3$
g_4	$x = x_3\|x_2\|x_1\|x_0 \rightarrow g_4(x) = x_1\|(x_3 \oplus x_0)\|(x_3 \oplus x_2)\|x_2$

According to the above encodings, we try to search for two differentials. If both are found, carry out the next step to investigative the dependency in E_m. Else, search for a new truncated trail.

3.3   Search Strategy and Search Results

In the subsection, we first determine the dependency between two trails. In practice, we experimentally evaluate the probability of E_m based on the output difference of E_0 and the input difference of E_1. If it is incompatible, i.e. there are no right quartets in E_m, we should return to search for new truncated trails. Otherwise, we use Eq. 1 to compute the probability r and the probability of the distinguisher can be calculated by using the formula p^2q^2r.

In addition, as the round number increases, the size of constraints and variables also expands, causing the speed of the solution to slow down. As a result, we add extra constraints to take charge of the direction of the solution to search for appropriate attack paths. For instance, we limit the number of active nibbles on the sides of plaintext, ciphertext and subtweakeys. It is a trade-off between solution and effect. A good condition not only reduces the search space accurately and thus improves the efficiency of the model, but also avoids the loss of previous optimal results.

Finally, we apply the model to find appropriate boomerang distinguishers for Joltik-BC. We search for a 8-round distinguisher of probability 2^{-34} for Joltik-BC-128 and a 11-round distinguisher of probability 2^{-52} for Joltik-BC-192. Subsequently, as illustrated in the Appendix, both distinguishers are used for key recovery attacks.

4   Key Recovery Attack on 10-Round Joltik-BC-128

According to the boomerang distinguisher of Joltik-BC-128 with probability 2^{-34} illustrated in Table 3, we add one round both at the beginning and end to present a 10-round key recovery attack.

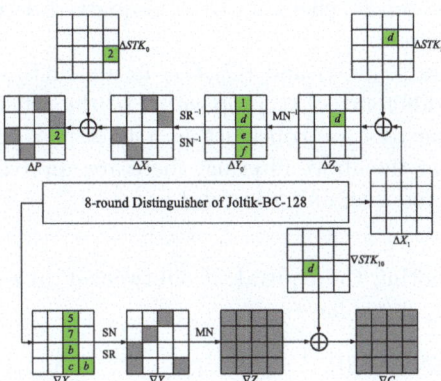

Fig. 4. 10-round related-tweakey boomerang attack on Joltik-BC-128

As shown in Fig. 4, the cells colored in green, grey and white represent that the difference is non-zero but known, unknown and zero, respectively. In practice, the ciphertext C is equivalent to the internal state Y_9 in the attack. Since MN operation is a linear operation, we can get $\nabla Y_9 = \text{MN}^{-1}(\nabla C \oplus \nabla STK_{10})$ without guessing the value of subtweakey STK_{10}. Therefore, we analyze Y_9 instead of C and the ciphertext C corresponds to the position of the internal state Y_9 in the following.

Data Collection. Following the previous definition, we have $r_b = 16, m_b = 16, r_f = 20$ and $m_f = 20$. Since the key schedule is linear, the subtweakey difference is known. We can apply subtweakey differences to compute other subtweakeys by guessing only one of them. Hence, the subtweakeys that we guess in the attack are deduced by the key schedule under key K_1.

We construct ciphertext structures in Y_9. Each structure travels all possible values of $Y_9[2, 3, 5, 8, 15]$, while other nibbles are set as some constants. For ciphertext C_1 in a structure, we query the corresponding plaintext P_1 with key K_1. As described in Fig. 4, there are 4 unknown nibbles in ΔP. So we guess the value of the 16-bit subtweakey $STK_0[2, 7, 8, 13]$ to form the set S_1 as follows:

$$
\begin{aligned}
S_1 = &\{(P_1, C_1, P_2, C_2) : P_1 = E_{K_1}^{-1}(C_1); P_2[i] = (P_1 \oplus \Delta P)[i], i = 0, 1, 3, 4, 5, 6, \\
&9, 10, 11, 12, 14, 15; P_2[j] = \mathrm{SN}^{-1}(\mathrm{SN}(P_1 \oplus STK_0)[j] \oplus \mathrm{SR}^{-1}(\Delta Y_0)[j]) \oplus \\
&(STK_0 \oplus \Delta STK_0)[j], j = 2, 7, 8, 13; C_2 = E_{K_2}(P_2)\}.
\end{aligned}
$$

We insert the set S_1 into a hash table H_1 indexed by the value of $C_2[0, 1, 4, 6, 7, 9, 10, 11, 12, 13, 14]$. For ciphertext C_3 in the similar structure that constants match the specific difference, form the set S_2 as follows:

$$
\begin{aligned}
S_2 = &\{(P_3, C_3, P_4, C_4) : P_3 = E_{K_3}^{-1}(C_3); P_4[i] = (P_3 \oplus \Delta P)[i], i = 0, 1, 3, 4, 5, 6, 9, \\
&10, 11, 12, 14, 15; P_4[j] = \mathrm{SN}^{-1}(\mathrm{SN}(P_3 \oplus STK_0 \oplus \nabla STK_0)[j] \oplus \mathrm{SR}^{-1}(\Delta Y_0) \\
&[j]) \oplus (STK_0 \oplus \nabla STK_0 \oplus \Delta STK_0)[j], j = 2, 7, 8, 13; C_4 = E_{K_4}(P_4)\}.
\end{aligned}
$$

For the elements in the set S_2, check H_1 to form quartets satisfying that $C_2 \oplus C_4$ match the specific difference.

There are 2^{20} pairs (C_1, C_2) and (C_3, C_4) in a structure, respectively. The probability that the difference ∇Y_9 propagates to the difference ∇X_9 is 2^{-20}. To get $s = 4$ right quartets, we construct $y = 4/(2^{-20} \times (2^{20})^2 \times 2^{-34}) = 2^{16}$ structures. Hence, after the above filtering, there are approximately $2^{16} \times 2^{20} \times 2^{20} \times 2^{-44} = 2^{12}$ quartets remaining in total.

Key Recovery. Denoting the equivalent subtweakey in i-th round as $IK_i = SR^{-1} \circ MN^{-1}(STK_{i+1})$, we have

$$
\begin{aligned}
X_i &= \mathrm{SN}^{-1} \circ \mathrm{SR}^{-1} \circ \mathrm{MN}^{-1}(X_{i+1} \oplus STK_{i+1}) \\
&= \mathrm{SN}^{-1} \circ \mathrm{SR}^{-1} \circ \mathrm{MN}^{-1}(X_{i+1}) \oplus \mathrm{SN}^{-1}(IK_i).
\end{aligned}
$$

Taking the example of the last round in Fig. 4, $X_9 = \mathrm{SN}^{-1} \circ \mathrm{SR}^{-1}(C) \oplus \mathrm{SN}^{-1}(IK_9)$. To get the value of $X_9[i]$, we only need to guess the value of $IK_9[i]$. Hence, the key recovery phase is as follows for 2^{12} quartets.

For remaining quartet (C_1, C_2, C_3, C_4), since the value of $\nabla X_9[8]$ is known, we can deduce the value of $IK_9[8]$ by C_1 and C_3. According to the property of S-box in Joltik-BC, we can on average get one solution for $IK_9[8]$. Then we apply subtweakey difference and partially decrypt C_2 and C_4 with corresponding subtweakeys to determine whether the difference $C_2 \oplus C_4 = \nabla X_9$ is satisfied. If satisfying, keep the value of $IK_9[8]$ and the quartet. Otherwise, filter the quartet. Recover $IK_9[9, 10, 11, 15]$ with the similar method in the following. Finally, given $h = 10$, select the key ranked within the 10-bit top to the candidates.

Complexity Analysis. In the attack, we decrypt $2 \times 2^{16+20} = 2^{37}$ ciphertexts and encrypt $2 \times 2^{16+20+16} = 2^{53}$ plaintexts. So the data complexity is $D = 2^{37} + 2^{53} \approx 2^{53}$ chosen-plaintexts-and-ciphertexts. To form the quartets, the number of table look-ups is $2^{16} \times 2^{36} = 2^{52}$. In key recovery phase, to get the equivalent subtweakeys involved in E_f, we need to decrypt one round for the remaining quartets which is equivalent to $2^{16} \times 2^{12} \times 1/10 = 2^{24.68}$ encryptions. Finally, exhaust the remaining $64 - m_b - m_f = 28$ key bits. Therefore, the time complexity is almost $2^{37} + 2^{53} + 2^{52} + 2^{24.68} + 2^{28} \approx 2^{53.58}$ in total. The memory is $2^{37} + 2^{53} + 2^{36} \approx 2^{53}$. The signal-to-noise ration is $S_N = p^2 q^2 r/2^{-n} = 2^{30}$. According to Eq. 2, the success probability is $P_s = 0.99$.

5 Key Recovery Attack on 14-Round Joltik-BC-192

Based on the boomerang distinguisher illustrated in Table 4, we take the clustering effect into account and compute the probability. For the upper differential characteristic with probability 2^{-22}, by fixing the input difference and limiting i-th nibble of the output difference to zero ($i = 1, 6, 11, 12$), there are eight trails satisfying the limitation leading to $\hat{p} = 2^{-20.61}$. To guarantee that the probability caused by the boomerang switch is always one, it means that only i-th nibble of the input difference in the lower differential characteristic may be active, and other nibbles always be inactive. There is only one characteristic of probability 2^{-4} with the output difference unchanged, i.e. $\hat{q} = 2^{-4}$. Hence, the probability of the rectangle distinguisher is $2^{-n}\hat{p}^2\hat{q}^2 = 2^{-113.22}$.

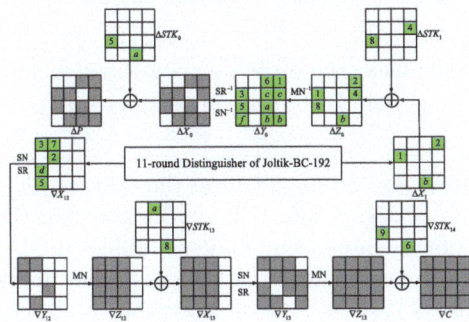

Fig. 5. 14-round related-tweakey rectangle attack on Joltik-BC-192

As illustrated in Fig. 5, we extend one round at the beginning and two rounds at the end respectively, to present a 14-round key recovery attack. Besides, we also use the internal state Y_{13} instead of the ciphertext C in the attack.

Data Collection. As shown in Fig. 5, there are 10 unknown nibbles in ΔP, which causes that the 10 nibbles of STK_0 should be considered. In E_f, the number of the unknown nibbles in ∇Y_{12} and ∇Y_{13} are 5 and 12, respectively. Hence, $r_b = 40$, $m_b = 40$, $r_f = 48$ and $m_f = 68$. Equally, the subtweakeys that we guess in the attack are deduced by the key schedule under key K_1.

We construct plaintext structures, which travel all possible values of $P[1, 2, 5, 7, 8, 10, 11, 12, 13, 15]$ and fix other nibbles as constants. Each structure consists of 2^{40} different plaintexts. In order to get $s = 4$ right quartets, we need to construct $y = \sqrt{s} \cdot 2^{n/2-r_b}/\sqrt{\hat{p}^2\hat{q}^2} = 2^{17.61}$ structures. For all plaintexts in $2^{17.61}$ structures, we query the corresponding ciphertexts with the related keys K_1, K_2, K_3, K_4 and store them in the sets L_1, L_2, L_3, L_4. Then we insert the sets L_2 and L_4 into hash tables H_1 and H_2 indexed by $P_2[i]$ and $P_4[i], i = 1, 2, 5, 7, 8, 10, 11, 12, 13, 15$, respectively. The size of hash tables both are $2^{17.61+40} = 2^{57.61}$.

We guess the 40-bit subtweakey $STK_0[1, 2, 5, 7, 8, 10, 11, 12, 13, 15]$. For $(P_1, C_1) \in L_1, (P_3, C_3) \in L_3$, we construct the sets S_1 and S_2 as follows:

$$
\begin{aligned}
S_1 =\{&(P_1, C_1, P_2, C_2) : (P_1, C_1) \in L_1, (P_2, C_2) \in L_2; P_1[i] = P_2[i], i = 0, 3, \\
&4, 6, 9, 14; \mathrm{SN}(P_1 \oplus STK_0)[j] \oplus \mathrm{SN}(P_2 \oplus STK_0 \oplus \Delta STK_0)[j] = \mathrm{SR}^{-1} \\
&(Y_0)[j], j = 1, 2, 5, 7, 8, 10, 11, 12, 13, 15\};
\end{aligned}
$$

$$
\begin{aligned}
S_2 =\{&(P_3, C_3, P_4, C_4) : (P_3, C_3) \in L_3, (P_4, C_4) \in L_4; P_3[i] = P_4[i], i = 0, 3, \\
&4, 6, 9, 14; \mathrm{SN}(P_3 \oplus STK_0 \oplus \nabla STK)[j] \oplus \mathrm{SN}(P_4 \oplus STK_0 \\
&\oplus \Delta STK_0)[j] = \mathrm{SR}^{-1}(Y_0)[j], j = 1, 2, 5, 7, 8, 10, 11, 12, 13, 15\}.
\end{aligned}
$$

The amount of elements in the sets S_1 and S_2 both are $2^{17.61+40} = 2^{57.61}$. We insert the set S_1 into a hash table H_3 indexed by $C_1[1, 6, 11, 12]$ and $C_2[1, 6, 11, 12]$. For the elements of the set S_2, check H_3 to search for the elements satisfying that $C_1[j] \oplus C_3[j] = 0 = C_2[j] \oplus C_4[j], j = 1, 6, 11, 12$ match the specific difference. Hence, after filtering, there are approximately $(2^{57.61})^2 \times (2^{-16})^2 = 2^{83.22}$ quartets remaining in total.

Key Recovery. In the phase, the subtweakeys guessed include 5 nibbles of IK_{12} and 12 nibbles of IK_{13}. For $2^{83.22}$ remaining quartets, perform the following steps:

1. To get the value of $X_{13}[8]$, we should guess the value of $IK_{13}[8]$. Hence, we can compute the values of $X_{13}[8]$ and $\nabla X_{13}[8]$ by guessing the value of $IK_{13}[8]$. Note that once there are more than 4 known nibbles in MN, other nibbles can be deduced. Hence, we can deduce the values of other nibbles in the third column of X_{13} because $\nabla Y_{12}[8, 9, 11] = 0$. Now, the input and output differences of S-boxes are known in the third column of ∇X_{13} and we can deduce one solution for $IK_{13}[9, 10, 11]$ on average. For guessed nibbles of $IK_{13}[8, 9, 10, 11]$, we apply subtweakey difference to compute other equivalent subtweakeys under K_2, K_4. Then we partially decrypt the corresponding C_2 and C_4 to compute ∇Y_{12}. If $\nabla Y_{12}[8, 9, 11] = 0$, keep the corresponding quartets and 4 nibbles of

equivalent subtweakeys. Approximately $2^{83.22} \times 2^4 \times 2^{-12} = 2^{75.22}$ quartets remain.

2. Next, for obtained quartets and 4 nibbles of equivalent subtweakeys in the previous step, we have computed the value of $\nabla Y_{12}[10]$ by C_1 and C_3. We can deduce one solution for $IK_{12}[2]$ on average since $\nabla X_{12}[2]$ is known. Then we apply subtweakey difference to compute other equivalent subtweakeys and verify them by using the corresponding C_2 and C_4. The number of remaining quartets will be $2^{75.22} \times 2^{-4} = 2^{71.22}$.

3. Guess the value of $IK_{13}[4,5]$ and partially decrypt (C_1, C_3) to calculate the value of $X_{13}[4,5]$ and $\nabla X_{13}[4,5]$. There are two inactive nibbles in the second column of ∇X_{13} so that we can deduce the value of $IK_{13}[6,7]$. Later, we partially decrypt (C_2, C_4) with corresponding equivalent subtweakeys to check whether $\nabla Y_{12}[5,6] = 0$. Keep the right quartets and equivalent subtweakeys. There are about $2^{71.22} \times 2^8 \times 2^{-8} = 2^{71.22}$ quartets remaining.

4. Because $\nabla X_{12}[3,4]$ is known, given $\nabla Y_{12}[4,7]$ for (C_1, C_3), we can get one solution for $IK_{12}[3,4]$ on average. For another pair (C_2, C_4), partially decrypt them and check whether $\nabla X_{12}[3,4]$ matches up the distinguisher. There are about $2^{71.22} \times 2^{-8} = 2^{63.22}$ quartets remaining.

5. Similarly, guess the value of $IK_{13}[0,1]$ to recover $IK_{13}[2,3], IK_{12}[0,5]$. About $2^{63.22} \times 2^8 \times 2^{-8} \times 2^{-8} = 2^{55.22}$ quartets remain.

6. Given $h = 20$, select the key ranked within the 48-bit top to the candidates.

Complexity Analysis. The data complexity is $D = 4 \times 2^{17.61+40} = 2^{59.61}$ chosen-plaintexts. We need to do $2^{40} \times (2 \times 2^{57.61} + 2^{57.61}) = 2^{99.19}$ table lookups to obtain quartets. In key recovery phase, perform one round decryption for remaining quartets which are equal to $2^{40} \times 2^{83.22} \times 2^4 \times 1/14 = 2^{123.41}$ encryptions. Hence, the time complexity is $2^{59.61} + 2^{99.19} + 2^{123.41} \approx 2^{123.41}$ in total. The memory complexity is 2^{68} based on the key counters. The signal-to-noise ration is $S_N = \hat{p}^2 \hat{q}^2 / 2^{-n} = 2^{14.78}$. According to Eq. 2, the success probability is $P_s = 0.9757$.

6 Conclusion

In the paper, we improve the search strategy for boomerang distinguishers combined with the data and time complexity in key recovery attacks and use the model for the lightweight tweakable block cipher Joltik-BC. Based on found distinguishers, we guess partial key bits rather than all to reduce the time complexity further in key recovery attacks. Finally, we propose key recovery attacks with the longest rounds on Joltik-BC. Since both have an impractical complexity in the real world and they are subjected to the chosen key scenario that attackers can only select the relationships among unknown keys, the attacks cause no real security threat to Joltik-BC. However, they extend the current understanding of the security under related-tweakey differential attacks and help to breakthrough in design for tweakable block ciphers.

Acknowledgement. The work was funded by the National Natural Science Foundation of China (Grant No. 62206312).

Appendix

Table 3. A 8-round boomerang distinguisher with probability $(2^{-13})^2 \times (2^{-2})^2 \times 2^{-4} = 2^{-34}$ of Joltik-128, with parameters as $(R_b, R_0, R_m, R_1, R_f) = (1, 4, 1, 3, 1)$.

ΔTK_0^1 : 0000000000000070 ∇TK_0^1 : 0000000090000000
ΔTK_0^2 : 0000000000000050 ∇TK_0^2 : 00000000b0000000

Round i	ΔX_i	ΔY_i	ΔZ_i	ΔSTK_{i+1}	Pr
1	0 0 0 0	0 0 0 0	0 0 0 0	0 0 0 0	1
	0 0 0 0	0 0 0 0	0 0 0 0	0 0 0 0	
	0 0 0 0	0 0 0 0	0 0 0 0	0 0 0 0	
	0 0 0 0	0 0 0 0	0 0 0 0	0 0 0 0	
2	0 0 0 0	0 0 0 0	0 0 0 0	0 0 0 0	1
	0 0 0 0	0 0 0 0	0 0 0 0	0 0 0 0	
	0 0 0 0	0 0 0 0	0 0 0 0	0 0 0 0	
	0 0 0 0	0 0 0 0	0 0 0 0	0 0 0 9	
3	0 0 0 0	0 0 0 0	1 0 0 0	0 0 0 0	2^{-2}
	0 0 0 0	0 0 0 0	2 0 0 0	0 0 0 0	
	0 0 0 0	0 0 0 0	3 0 0 0	0 8 0 0	
	0 0 0 9	4 0 0 0	4 0 0 0	0 0 0 0	
4	1 0 0 0	b 0 0 0	b 6 c 0	0 0 0 0	2^{-11}
	2 0 0 0	0 0 0 6	a c 6 a	a 0 0 0	
	3 8 0 0	0 0 b 5	c a b d	0 0 0 0	
	4 0 0 0	0 b 0 0	6 b a 4	0 0 0 0	
5	b 6 c 0	* * * 0			2^{-4}
	0 c 6 a	* * * 0			
	c a b d	* * * *			
	6 b a 4	* * * *			

Round i	∇X_i	∇Y_i	∇Z_i	∇STK_{i+1}	Pr
5	0 0 0 *	0 0 0 2	0 0 0 0	0 0 0 0	1
	* 0 0 0	0 0 0 1	0 0 0 0	0 0 0 0	
	0 * 0 0	0 0 0 4	0 0 0 4	0 0 0 4	
	0 0 * 0	0 0 0 3	0 0 0 0	0 0 0 0	
6	0 0 0 0	0 0 0 0	0 0 0 0	0 0 0 0	1
	0 0 0 0	0 0 0 0	0 0 0 0	0 0 0 0	
	0 0 0 0	0 0 0 0	0 0 0 0	0 0 0 0	
	0 0 0 0	0 0 0 0	0 0 0 0	0 0 0 0	
7	0 0 0 0	0 0 0 0	0 0 0 0	0 0 8 0	1
	0 0 0 0	0 0 0 0	0 0 0 0	0 0 0 0	
	0 0 0 0	0 0 0 0	0 0 0 0	0 0 0 0	
	0 0 0 0	0 0 0 0	0 0 0 0	0 0 0 0	
8	0 0 8 0	0 0 5 0	0 0 5 0	0 0 0 0	2^{-2}
	0 0 0 0	0 0 0 0	0 0 7 0	0 0 0 0	
	0 0 0 0	0 0 0 0	0 0 b 0	0 0 0 0	
	0 0 0 0	0 0 0 0	0 0 c 0	0 0 0 b	

Table 4. A 11-round boomerang distinguisher with probability $(2^{-22})^2 \times (2^{-4})^2 = 2^{-52}$ of Joltik-192, with parameters as $(R_b, R_o, R_m, R_1, R_f) = (1, 6, 1, 4, 1)$.

$\Delta TK_0^1 : 0010000000020000 \qquad \nabla TK_0^1 : 0000000000008a00$

$\Delta TK_0^2 : 0010000000020000 \qquad \nabla TK_0^2 : 000000000000f800$

$\Delta TK_0^3 : 00500000000a0000 \qquad \nabla TK_0^3 : 0000000000009600$

Round i	ΔX_i				ΔY_i				ΔZ_i				ΔSTK_{i+1}				Pr
1	0	0	0	2	0	0	0	5	0	0	0	a	0	0	0	a	2^{-6}
	1	0	0	0	0	0	0	9	0	0	0	7	0	0	0	7	
	0	0	0	0	0	0	0	0	0	0	0	0	0	0	0	0	
	0	0	b	0	0	0	0	1	0	0	0	0	0	0	0	0	
2	0	0	0	0	0	0	0	0	0	0	0	0	0	0	0	0	1
	0	0	0	0	0	0	0	0	0	0	0	0	0	0	0	0	
	0	0	0	0	0	0	0	0	0	0	0	0	0	0	0	0	
	0	0	0	0	0	0	0	0	0	0	0	0	0	0	0	0	
3	0	0	0	0	0	0	0	0	0	0	0	0	0	0	0	0	1
	0	0	0	0	0	0	0	0	0	0	0	0	0	0	0	0	
	0	0	0	0	0	0	0	0	0	0	0	0	0	0	0	0	
	0	0	0	0	0	0	0	0	0	0	0	0	0	0	0	0	
4	0	0	0	0	0	0	0	0	0	0	0	0	0	0	0	0	1
	0	0	0	0	0	0	0	0	0	0	0	0	0	f	0	0	
	0	0	0	0	0	0	0	0	0	0	0	0	0	0	d	0	
	0	0	0	0	0	0	0	0	0	0	0	0	0	0	0	0	
5	0	0	0	0	0	0	0	0	4	0	0	0	0	b	0	0	2^{-5}
	0	f	0	0	f	0	0	0	0	0	0	0	0	5	0	0	
	0	0	d	0	9	0	0	0	e	0	0	0	0	0	0	0	
	0	0	0	0	0	0	0	0	c	0	0	0	0	0	0	0	
6	4	b	0	0	b	3	0	0	5	a	f	0	0	2	0	0	2^{-11}
	0	5	0	0	a	0	0	0	0	d	e	0	0	0	0	0	
	e	0	0	0	0	0	d	0	7	0	d	0	0	0	0	0	
	c	0	0	0	0	2	0	0	3	6	1	0	0	0	1	0	
7	*	*	*	0	*	*	*	0									1
	0	*	*	*	*	*	*	0									
	*	0	*	*	*	*	*	0									
	*	*	0	*	*	*	*	0									

Round i	∇X_i				∇Y_i				∇Z_i				∇STK_{i+1}				Pr
7	0	0	0	*	0	0	0	*	0	0	0	b	0	0	0	b	1
	*	0	0	0	0	0	0	*	0	0	0	8	0	0	0	8	
	0	*	0	0	0	0	0	*	0	0	0	0	0	0	0	0	
	0	0	*	0	0	0	0	*	0	0	0	0	0	0	0	0	
8	0	0	0	0	0	0	0	0	0	0	0	0	0	0	0	0	1
	0	0	0	0	0	0	0	0	0	0	0	0	0	0	0	0	
	0	0	0	0	0	0	0	0	0	0	0	0	0	0	0	0	
	0	0	0	0	0	0	0	0	0	0	0	0	0	0	0	0	
9	0	0	0	0	0	0	0	0	0	0	0	0	0	0	0	0	1
	0	0	0	0	0	0	0	0	0	0	0	0	0	0	0	0	
	0	0	0	0	0	0	0	0	0	0	0	0	0	0	0	0	
	0	0	0	0	0	0	0	0	0	0	0	0	0	0	0	0	
10	0	0	0	0	0	0	0	0	0	0	0	0	0	0	0	0	1
	0	0	0	0	0	0	0	0	0	0	0	0	0	1	0	0	
	0	0	0	0	0	0	0	0	0	0	0	0	0	0	c	0	
	0	0	0	0	0	0	0	0	0	0	0	0	0	0	0	0	
11	0	0	0	0	0	0	0	0	3	0	0	0	0	7	0	0	2^{-4}
	0	1	0	0	9	0	0	0	0	0	0	0	0	2	0	0	
	0	0	c	0	2	0	0	0	d	0	0	0	0	0	0	0	
	0	0	0	0	0	0	0	0	5	0	0	0	0	0	0	0	

References

1. Biham, E., Dunkelman, O., Keller, N.: The rectangle attack—rectangling the serpent. In: Pfitzmann, B. (ed.) EUROCRYPT 2001. LNCS, vol. 2045, pp. 340–357. Springer, Heidelberg (2001). https://doi.org/10.1007/3-540-44987-6_21
2. Biham, E., Dunkelman, O., Keller, N.: Related-key boomerang and rectangle attacks. In: Cramer, R. (ed.) EUROCRYPT 2005. LNCS, vol. 3494, pp. 507–525. Springer, Heidelberg (2005). https://doi.org/10.1007/11426639_30
3. Biryukov, A., Khovratovich, D.: Related-key cryptanalysis of the full AES-192 and AES-256. In: Matsui, M. (ed.) ASIACRYPT 2009. LNCS, vol. 5912, pp. 1–18. Springer, Heidelberg (2009). https://doi.org/10.1007/978-3-642-10366-7_1
4. Boura, C., Coggia, D.: Efficient MILP modelings for sboxes and linear layers of SPN ciphers. IACR Trans. Symmetric Cryptol. **2020**(3), 327–361 (2020)
5. Cid, C., Huang, T., Peyrin, T., Sasaki, Y., Song, L.: A security analysis of deoxys and its internal tweakable block ciphers. IACR Trans. Symmetric Cryptol. **2017**(3), 73–107 (2017)
6. Delaune, S., Derbez, P., Vavrille, M.: Catching the fastest boomerangs application to SKINNY. IACR Trans. Symmetric Cryptol. **2020**(4), 104–129 (2020)
7. Hadipour, H., Nageler, M., Eichlseder, M.: Throwing boomerangs into feistel structures application to clefia, warp, lblock, lblock-s and TWINE. IACR Trans. Symmetric Cryptol. **2022**(3), 271–302 (2022)
8. Jean, J., Nikolic, I., Peyrin, T.: Tweaks and keys for block ciphers: the TWEAKEY framework. In: Sarkar, P., Iwata, T. (eds.) ASIACRYPT 2014. LNCS, vol. 8874, pp. 274–288. Springer, Heidelberg (2014). https://doi.org/10.1007/978-3-662-45608-8_15
9. Jean, J., Nikolić, I., Peyrin, T.: Joltik v1. 3. CAESAR Round **2** (2015)
10. Kelsey, J., Kohno, T., Schneier, B.: Amplified boomerang attacks against reduced-round MARS and serpent. In: Schneier, B. (ed.) FSE 2000. LNCS, vol. 1978, pp. 75–93. Springer, Heidelberg (2000). https://doi.org/10.1007/3-540-44706-7_6
11. Li, M., Chen, S.: Improved meet-in-the-middle attacks on reduced-round joltik-bc. IET Inf. Secur. **15**(3), 247–255 (2021)
12. Li, R., Jin, C., Pan, H.: Key recovery attacks on reduced-round joltik-bc in the single-key setting. Inf. Process. Lett. **151** (2019)
13. Liskov, M.D., Rivest, R.L., Wagner, D.A.: Tweakable block ciphers. In: Yung, M. (ed.) CRYPTO 2002. LNCS, vol. 2442, pp. 31–46. Springer, Heidelberg (2002). https://doi.org/10.1007/3-540-45708-9_3
14. Liu, G., Ghosh, M., Song, L.: Security analysis of SKINNY under related-tweakey settings (long paper). IACR Trans. Symmetric Cryptol. **2017**(3), 37–72 (2017)
15. Liu, Y., Shi, Y., Gu, D., Zeng, Z., Zhao, F., Li, W., Liu, Z., Bao, Y.: Improved meet-in-the-middle attacks on reduced-round kiasu-bc and joltik-bc. Comput. J. **62**(12), 1761–1776 (2019)
16. Murphy, S.: The return of the cryptographic boomerang. IEEE Trans. Inf. Theory **57**(4), 2517–2521 (2011)
17. Sasaki, Y., Todo, Y.: New algorithm for modeling s-box in MILP based differential and division trail search. In: Farshim, P., Simion, E. (eds.) SecITC 2017. LNCS, vol. 10543, pp. 150–165. Springer, Cham (2017). https://doi.org/10.1007/978-3-319-69284-5_11
18. Selçuk, A.A.: On probability of success in linear and differential cryptanalysis. J. Cryptol. **21**(1), 131–147 (2008)

19. Shibutani, K., Isobe, T., Hiwatari, H., Mitsuda, A., Akishita, T., Shirai, T.: Piccolo: An ultra-lightweight blockcipher. In: Preneel, B., Takagi, T. (eds.) CHES 2011. LNCS, vol. 6917, pp. 342–357. Springer, Heidelberg (2011). https://doi.org/10.1007/978-3-642-23951-9_23

20. Sun, L., Wang, W., Wang, M.: MILP-aided bit-based division property for primitives with non-bit-permutation linear layers. IET Inf. Secur. **14**(1), 12–20 (2020)

21. Sun, S., Hu, L., Wang, P., Qiao, K., Ma, X., Song, L.: Automatic security evaluation and (related-key) differential characteristic search: Application to simon, present, lblock, DES(L) and other bit-oriented block ciphers. In: Sarkar, P., Iwata, T. (eds.) ASIACRYPT 2014. LNCS, vol. 8873, pp. 158–178. Springer, Heidelberg (2014). https://doi.org/10.1007/978-3-662-45611-8_9

22. Wagner, D.A.: The boomerang attack. In: Knudsen, L.R. (ed.) FSE 1999. LNCS, vol. 1636, pp. 156–170. Springer, Heidelberg (1999). https://doi.org/10.1007/3-540-48519-8_12

23. Zhao, B., Dong, X., Jia, K.: New related-tweakey boomerang and rectangle attacks on deoxys-bc including BDT effect. IACR Trans. Symmetric Cryptol. **2019**(3), 121–151 (2019)

24. Zong, R., Dong, X.: MILP-aided related-tweak/key impossible differential attack and its applications to qarma, joltik-bc. IEEE Access **7**, 153683–153693 (2019)

Isogeny-Based Password-Authenticated Key Exchange Based on Shuffle Algorithm

Congrong Peng[1] , Cong Peng[1]([⊠]) , Xiaolin Yang[2], Qingcai Luo[2],
and Min Luo[1]([⊠])

[1] Key Laboratory of Aerospace Information Security and Trusted Computing,
Ministry of Education, School of Cyber Science and Engineering, Wuhan University,
Wuhan, China
{pengcongrong,cpeng,mluo}@whu.edu.cn
[2] Inspur Academy of Science and Technology, Jinan, China
{yangxl,luoqc}@inspur.com

Abstract. At CRYPTO 2022, Abdalla et al. incorporate the ability to compute the quadratic twist of elliptic curves to extend the framework of group actions introduced by Alamati et al. (ASIACRYPT 2020), and proposed two password-authenticated key exchange (PAKE) protocols. Their first protocol X-GA-PAKE$_\ell$ is a provably secure one-round isogeny-based scheme with a password length of ℓ, which improves security by increasing computation and communication overhead. In X-GA-PAKE$_\ell$, each party needs to choose 2ℓ elements and perform 5ℓ group actions. In this paper, we present an isogeny-based PAKE protocol that is more efficient than X-GA-PAKE$_\ell$. In our scheme, we reduce the number of set elements to ℓ, thus the overhead of communication between users and servers is significantly decreased. By using the shuffle algorithm, the number of group actions that each party needs to perform is reduced to 2ℓ, but our protocol can still prevent trivial attacks using twists. Due to the use of Merkle root and password in the shuffle function, the attackers cannot select a message from the received message. Also, the length of the message used for key derivation is reduced from 3ℓ to ℓ. We prove the security based on the security assumption in the isogeny-based setting.

Keywords: Password-authenticated key exchange · CSIDH · Group actions · Shuffle algorithm

1 Introduction

Password-authenticated Key Exchange (PAKE) is a cryptographic protocol that allows participants to share a key over a low-entropy secret without transferring the password over a network, allowing data to be securely transmitted over an insecure channel. In PAKE, long-term keys are derived from passwords to establish session keys securely without being leaked or stolen. The passwords are

Z. Xia and J. Chen (Eds.): ISPEC 2024, LNCS 15053, pp. 112–132, 2024.
https://doi.org/10.1007/978-981-97-9053-1_7

also used for mutual authentication between participants. Here, we focus on the two-party PAKE, primarily designed for the scenario of mutual authentication between a single server and a single user. This involves sharing the session key through negotiation and establishing a secure channel.

The ease with which passwords can be remembered has sparked considerable interest in PAKE protocols among scholars. Designing a secure PAKE protocol has thus become a task of great practical significance. To ensure that the protocol can achieve its original design goal during the protocol design phase, the current approach involves establishing an accurate communication model, providing a strict definition of security a formal security proof of the protocol.

Due to the characteristics of short passwords and low entropy, two-party PAKE is vulnerable to dictionary attacks while communicating conveniently. Therefore, the design of a two-party PAKE protocol must consider whether it can resist dictionary attacks. Dictionary attacks are classified into online dictionary attacks and offline dictionary attacks. In an online dictionary attack, the attacker impersonates a communication party with a guessed password. If the interaction fails, the attacker chooses another password to re-interact. To protect against such attacks, it is necessary to restrict the number of repeated password attempts by the attacker. In an offline dictionary attack, the attacker eavesdrops on several sessions to try to eliminate a large number of possible passwords and guess the correct one. To defend against these attacks, preventing the attacker from obtaining the message used for verifying the correctness of the password is essential.

1.1 Related Work

In 1992, Bellovin and Merritt [7] proposed the first PAKE protocol. Since then, many PAKE have been proposed, such as EKE2 [6], SPEKE [16], CPace [12], OPAQUE [17], SPAKE2 [4] and J-PAKE [14]. The main PAKE design can be classified into three types according to the use of passwords [13]: (1) password as an encryption key; (2) password as input string to derive generator; (3) passwords as integers in modular arithmetic (exponents in a multiplicative group, or scalars in an addition group on an elliptic curve). Different classifications have their own instantiation problems. Few PAKE protocols are resistant to attacks based on quantum computers, and how to design a quantum-secure PAKE protocol remains a difficult problem.

Most of the current PAKE protocols are built upon the Diffie-Hellman key exchange algorithm. Isogeny-based cryptography plays a crucial role in post-quantum cryptography, relying on the difficulty of calculating isogeny between given elliptic curves. The time complexity of this problem under quantum algorithm attack is (sub-) exponential. Compared with other post-quantum cryptography protocols, isogeny-based cryptosystems have the advantage of short key length but suffer from the disadvantage of low protocol efficiency. Currently, there are three types of isogeny-based key exchange protocols: ordinary isogeny Diffie-Hellman (OIDH), supersingular isogeny Diffie-Hellman (SIDH), and commutative supersingular isogeny Diffie-Hellman (CSIDH). The implementation efficiency of the OIDH protocol is low, and Childs et al. [10] have proposed a subexponential time quantum algorithm to address this issue, exploiting the commutative nature of the group action. While SIDH is faster than OIDH, it was discovered to be insecure due to a polynomial-time key recovery attack by Castryck and Decru in 2023 [8].

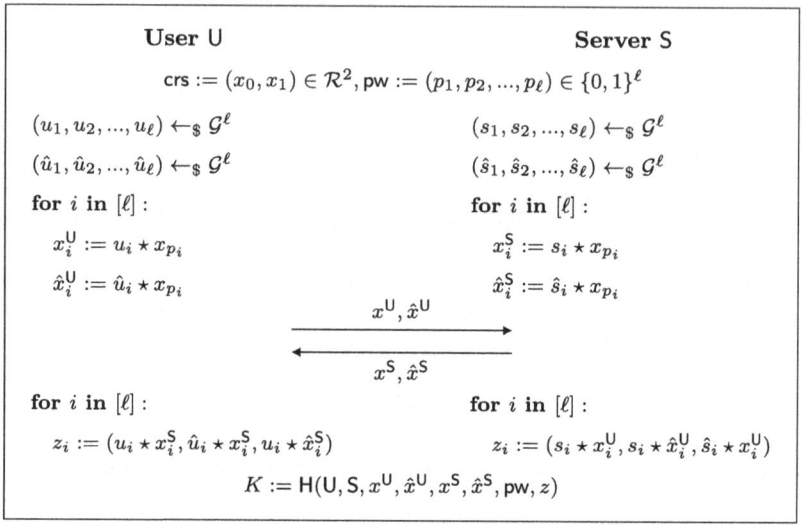

Fig. 1. PAKE protocol X-GA-PAKE$_\ell$ [1].

CSIDH is a cryptography primitive proposed by Castryck et al. [9] based on SIDH, and the Couveignes-Rostovtsev-Stolbunov scheme [11,19] was applied to supersingular elliptic curves. The size of the key, ciphertext, and signature are more compact than that of SIDH. In 2022, Abdalla et al. [1] extended the framework of group actions [5] by introducing the ability to compute the quadratic twist of an elliptic curve. They propose two PAKE protocols based on commutative group operations, the first of which, X-GA-PAKE, is an isogeny-based one-round protocol. In X-GA-PAKE$_\ell$, both parties of the protocol share the common reference string crs and ℓ-bit password. To prevent offline dictionary attacks, X-GA-PAKE$_\ell$ doubles the set elements, i.e., each party needs to choose 2ℓ elements and perform 5ℓ group actions as described in Fig 1. Additionally, the length of the shared key is tripled. Increasing the communication overhead in this protocol is a trade-off for enhanced security. Ishibashi and Yoneyama [15] carried out optimization based on X-GA-PAKE and proposed a scheme to reduce the redundant setting parameters from ℓ to $2|\text{crs}|$. However, the scheme needs further improvement in communication cost and efficiency.

1.2   Our Contribution

We design a one-round PAKE scheme based on isogeny with less communication overhead than X-GA-PAKE$_\ell$ but still proved secure tightly. Our contribution to this paper is twofold.

- We propose a isogeny-based PAKE protocol R-GA-PAKE$_\ell$. In our scheme, the overhead of communication between two parties is significantly decreased by cutting the number of set elements in half. To achieve this, we shuffle the intermediate result of group actions with a seed generated by their Merkle root and the password. Therefore, the number of group actions that each party needs to perform is reduced from 5ℓ to 2ℓ, but the protocol can still prevent offline dictionary attacks.
- With the participation of the shuffle function we defined, it is hard to choose a message depending on the message sent by the other party. We prove the security of the proposed scheme based on the security assumption in the isogeny-based setting defined in [2]. Our scheme is a one-round protocol that is secure even if both parties send messages to the other party simultaneously.

2   Preliminaries

2.1   Notation

For integer n, $[n]$ denotes the set $\{1, ..., n\}$. The process of uniformly and independently sampling an element x from a set $\mathcal{R}$ is represented as $x \leftarrow_\$ \mathcal{R}$; this notation extends naturally to probabilistic algorithms, where $y \leftarrow \mathcal{A}(x_1, ..., x_n)$ denotes that the adversary $\mathcal{A}$ inputs $(x_1, ..., x_n)$ and outputs y. The notation $\mathcal{A}^\mathcal{O}$ indicates that $\mathcal{A}$ can access to the oracle $\mathcal{O}$. For each game G_i, $\Pr[\mathsf{Succ}_i]$ denotes the probability that the game outputs 1.

2.2   Effective Group Actions (with Twists)

In this section, we recall the definition of effective group actions (with twists) (EGAT) from [5]. This concept is indispensable for the PAKE protocols to analyze security.

Definition 1 (Group Action). *Let $(\mathcal{G}, \cdot)$ be a group and $\mathcal{R}$ a set. Assuming that the identity element of $\mathcal{G}$ is e. A map $\star : \mathcal{G} \times \mathcal{R} \to \mathcal{R}$ is considered a group action if it satisfies identity and compatibility:*

1. $\forall x \in \mathcal{R}, e \star x = x$.
2. $\forall g_0, g_1 \in \mathcal{G}$ and $x \in \mathcal{R}, g_0 \star (g_1 \star x) = (g_0 \cdot g_1) \star x$.

Definition 2 (Effective Group Action (with Twists)). *Let $(\mathcal{G}, \mathcal{R}, \star)$ be a group action. We have the properties as follows:*

1. For the finite group $\mathcal{G}$, we can find efficient probabilistic polynomial-time algorithms to do membership and equality tests, as well as for (random) sample, group operation, and inversion.

2. *For the finite set $\mathcal{R}$, we can find efficient algorithms to do membership tests and compute a unique representation.*
3. *We can find a distinguished element $\tilde{x} \in \mathcal{R}$ with a known representation.*
4. *We can find an algorithm that efficiently computes $g \star x$ given g and x.*
5. *We can find an algorithm that efficiently outputs $x^t = g^{-1} \star \tilde{x}$ given $x = g \star \tilde{x} \in \mathcal{R}$.*

If the first four properties are satisfied, we call $(\mathcal{G}, \mathcal{R}, \star, \tilde{x})$ an effective group action (EGA) for the origin $\tilde{x} \in \mathcal{R}$. If all the above properties can be satisfied, we call $(\mathcal{G}, \mathcal{R}, \star, \tilde{x})$ an EGA with twists (EGAT).

2.3   Computational Assumptions

In this section, we recall the computational assumptions from [1].

We have the notion $\mathsf{GA\text{-}CDH}_x(y_0, y_1) = g_0 \star y_1$ where $g_0 \in \mathcal{G}$ such that $y_0 = g_0 \star x$, and the decision oracle $\mathsf{GA\text{-}DDH}_x(y_0, y_1, z)$. If $\mathsf{GA\text{-}CDH}_x(y_0, y_1) = z$, $\mathsf{GA\text{-}DDH}_x(y_0, y_1, z)$ outputs 1, otherwise it outputs 0. We omit the index x if $x = \tilde{x}$, which means that $\mathsf{GA\text{-}CDH}_{\tilde{x}} = \mathsf{GA\text{-}CDH}$ and $\mathsf{GA\text{-}DDH}_{\tilde{x}} = \mathsf{GA\text{-}DDH}$. The subsequent security proof of our protocol relies on $\mathsf{GA\text{-}StCDH}$, $\mathsf{SqInv\text{-}GA\text{-}StCDH}$ and $\mathsf{Sim\text{-}GA\text{-}StCDH}$ (Definitions 4 to 6). The specific definition of the above computational problems are in Appendix A.

3   PAKE Security Model

Here, we recall the security model BPR introduced by Bellare et al. [6], which is based on indistinguishability. Additionally, we recall its extension to a series of queries proposed by [3].

In the model, the two parties in PAKE create a session key using a shared password $\mathsf{pw}_{\mathsf{US}}$. Let $\mathcal{U}$ and $\mathcal{S}$ denote the name spaces of users and servers. $\mathsf{P} \in \{\mathsf{U}, \mathsf{S}\}$ has several instances denoted by π_{P}^i, each with its own distinct state. Let ℓ be the length of password and $\mathcal{PW} \subsetneq \{0,1\}^\ell$ be the password space. We denote the shared session key $K \in \mathcal{K}$.

Instance State. An instance π_{P}^i has a state tuple as follows:

- e: the (secret) ephemeral values generated by P in the instance.
- tr: the trace of the instance during the protocol execution, i.e., the name of the parties and the message each party sent and received.
- K: the session key accepted by the parties.
- acc: a flag to store whether the instance π_{P}^i accept the session key K. If yes, the flag $\pi_{\mathsf{P}}^i.\mathsf{acc} = \top$. Otherwise, $\pi_{\mathsf{P}}^i.\mathsf{acc} = \bot$.

Partnering. We define partnering through matching conversations. Specifically, $\pi_{\mathsf{U}}^{t_0}$ and $\pi_{\mathsf{S}}^{t_1}$ partner with each other iff

$$\pi_{\mathsf{U}}^{t_0}.\mathsf{acc} = \pi_{\mathsf{S}}^{t_1}.\mathsf{acc} = \top \quad \textbf{and} \quad \pi_{\mathsf{U}}^{t_0}.\mathsf{tr} = \pi_{\mathsf{S}}^{t_1}.\mathsf{tr}.$$

$PAR(\pi_U^{t_0}, \pi_S^{t_1})$ is defined as a partner predicate which outputs 1 if $\pi_U^{t_0}$ and $\pi_S^{t_1}$ are partnered and 0 otherwise.

Security Experiment. In a security experiment, the challenger randomly selects a challenge bit α and generates public parameters, which are then shared with $\mathcal{A}$. At this point, $\mathcal{A}$ can perform the queries as follows:

- EXECUTE(U, t_0, S, t_1): computes the result of protocol execution after permutation between $\pi_U^{t_0}$ and $\pi_S^{t_1}$. This kind of query is used to model passive adversaries.
- SENDINTT, SENDRESP, SENDTERM: these SEND queries are used to model active adversaries.
- CORRUPT(U, S): outputs the shared password pw_{US} of U and S.
- REVEAL(P, t): outputs the session key of π_P^t.
- TEST(P, t): if the challenge bit $\alpha = 0$, outputs the session key of π_P^t, otherwise, outputs a key that is chosen randomly and uniformly. In case π_P^t.test = **true**, π_P^t is marked as tested.

Freshness. As part of the security experiment, we keep track of whether a query is fresh or not. This is done by using a freshness predicate, denoted as $\mathsf{Fresh}(P, i)$. π_P^t is considered to be fresh or $\mathsf{Fresh}(P, i) = \mathbf{true}$, iff:

1. π_P^t accepted.
2. π_P^t has not been queried to TEST or REVEAL previously.
3. One of the conditions as follow must be true:
    - π_P^t accepted during a EXECUTE query.
    - There are multiple partner instances.
    - There is a unique and fresh partner instance.
    - There is no partner, and CORRUPT$(P, \cdot)$ was not queried.

Definition 3 (Security of PAKE). *The advantage of the adversary $\mathcal{A}$ in the experiment of PAKE protocols is defined as*

$$\mathsf{Adv}_{\mathsf{PAKE}}(\mathcal{A}) := |\Pr[\mathsf{Succ}_{\mathcal{A}}] - 1/2|.$$

If a PAKE protocol to be considered secure, online dictionary attack should be the most significant threat that an adversary $\mathcal{A}$ can pose. This implies that the advantage of $\mathcal{A}$ should be negligible close to $q_s/|\mathcal{PW}|$ when passwords $pw \leftarrow_\$ \mathcal{PW}$. Here, q_s denotes the number of SEND queries that $\mathcal{A}$ performs.

4   Our R-GA-PAKE$_\ell$ Protocol

To defend against the offline dictionary attacks, the paper [1] proposed X-GA-PAKE$_\ell$, but the deal has increased double communication overhead. Here, we present a protocol R-GA-PAKE$_\ell$, which is based on random homologous permutation. The letter R in R-GA-PAKE$_\ell$ stands for random.

4.1   Protocol

In our protocol, the original sequence is randomly replaced into a new sequence and sent to each other. After the user and the server restore the sequence sent by the other party, the two parties calculate the session key respectively and complete the key exchange. Our protocol can resist the offline dictionary attack while keeping the communication overhead as $O(\ell)$ per party as GA-PAKE$_\ell$ in [1]. The protocol is sketched in Fig 2.

During the key exchange process between the user and the server, the trusted party determines $crs = (x_0, x_1) \in \mathcal{R}^2$ and password $pw = (p_1, ..., p_\ell) \in \{0, 1\}^\ell$, which is mapped to a tuple $(x_{p_1}, ..., x_{p_\ell}) \in \mathcal{R}^\ell$. For each i, basis p_i is used for key exchange. To perform the exchange, the user generates elements $(u_1, ..., u_\ell)$ randomly and computes $x_i^{\mathsf{U}} = u_i \star x_{p_i}$, which is then sent to the server. Similarly, $(s_1, ..., s_\ell)$ is generated by the server randomly, to compute $x_i^{\mathsf{S}} = s_i \star x_{p_i}$ and sends it to the client.

Note that if $(x_1^{\mathsf{U}}, ...x_\ell^{\mathsf{U}})$ is transmitted directly, the attacker can select the message based on received messages. Therefore, certain items in the key derivation can be cancelled and the session key is no longer dependent on the input of the other party. To resist offline dictionary attacks, the shuffle algorithm is used to shuffle the order of $(x_1^{\mathsf{U}}, ...x_\ell^{\mathsf{U}})$. We denote the random permutation by σ. For σ, we set seed as $seed^{\mathsf{U}} = H(pw|root^{\mathsf{U}})$, where $root^{\mathsf{U}}$ is the Merkle roots formed by $(x_1^{\mathsf{U}}, ...x_\ell^{\mathsf{U}})$ in order of natural size. Also, we shuffle the order of $(x_1^{\mathsf{S}}, ...x_\ell^{\mathsf{S}})$ by seed $seed^{\mathsf{S}} = H(pw|root^{\mathsf{S}})$. Here, we define three functions: GetRoot is used to calculate the Merkle root of x^{P}, Shuffle is used to perform the Knuth-Durstenfeld shuffle [18] and DeShuffle is used to restore the original sequence.

Specifically, the protocol consists of the steps as follows:

1. The user generates random elements $(u_1, ..., u_\ell)$, computes $x_i^{\mathsf{U}} = u_i \star x_{p_i}$ and further computes its Merkle root $root^{\mathsf{U}}$.
2. The sever generates random elements $(s_1, ..., s_\ell)$, computes $x_i^{\mathsf{S}} = s_i \star x_{p_i}$ and further computes its Merkle root $root^{\mathsf{S}}$.
3. The user performs random permutation σ on sequence x^{U} through seed $seed^{\mathsf{U}} = H(pw\|root^{\mathsf{U}})$, obtains the sequence x_σ^{U} after random permutation, and sends it to the server.
4. The sever performs σ^{-1} to restore the sequence x_σ^{U} by seed $seed^{\mathsf{U}}$, obtains the sequence x^{U} and computes $z_i = s_i \star x_i^{\mathsf{U}}$.
5. The sever performs random permutation σ on sequence x^{S} through seed $seed^{\mathsf{S}} = H(pw|root^{\mathsf{S}})$, obtains the sequence x_σ^{S} after random permutation, and sends it to the user.
6. The user performs σ^{-1} to restore the sequence x_σ^{S} by seed $seed^{\mathsf{S}}$, obtains the sequence x^{S} and computes $z_i = u_i \star x_i^{\mathsf{S}}$.
7. Each party calculates the session key $K = H(\mathsf{U}, \mathsf{S}, x^{\mathsf{U}}, pw, z)$.

4.2   Security of R-GA-PAKE$_\ell$

In this section, we prove the security of R-GA-PAKE$_\ell$ for EGATs.

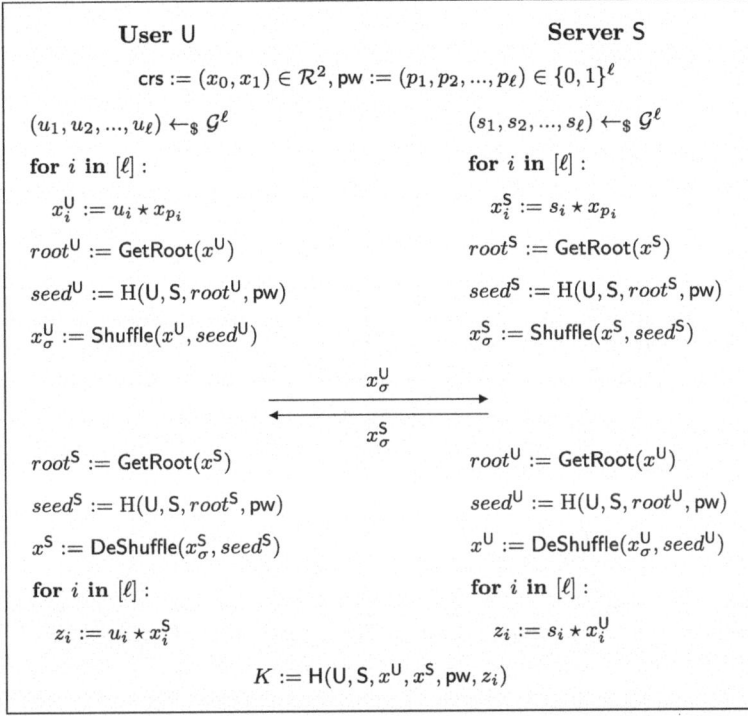

Fig. 2. PAKE protocol R-GA-PAKE$_\ell$ based on random homologous permutation.

Theorem 1. (Security of R-GA-PAKE$_\ell$) *For any adversary $\mathcal{A}$ against* R-GA-PAKE$_\ell$ *issuing up to q_e* EXECUTE *and q_s* SEND*, there exists adversaries $\mathcal{B}_1$ against* GA-StCDH *and $\mathcal{B}_2$ against* SqInv-GA-StCDH *where*

$$\mathsf{Adv}_{\text{R-GA-PAKE}_\ell}(\mathcal{A}) \leq \mathsf{Adv}_{\text{EGAT}}^{\text{GA-StCDH}}(\mathcal{B}_1) + \mathsf{Adv}_{\text{EGAT}}^{\text{SqInv-GA-StCDH}}(\mathcal{B}_2) + \frac{q_s}{|\mathcal{PW}|} + \frac{(q_s+q_e)^2}{|\mathcal{G}|^\ell}.$$

Proof (of Theorem 1). Let $\mathcal{A}$ be an adversary against R-GA-PAKE$_\ell$ and H be a random oracle.

Game G_0. As the original game, the advantage of $\mathcal{A}$ against R-GA-PAKE$_\ell$ is bounded by $|\Pr[\text{Succ}_0] - 1/2|$.

Game G_1. In this game, if an instance computes a trace that has been accepted (lines 68, 83) or the trace computed in the query collides with any accepted instance (line 29), we raise the flag $\mathbf{bad}_{\text{coll}}$ and the queries will return $\perp$. Hence, we have $|\Pr[\text{Succ}_1] - \Pr[\text{Succ}_0]| \leq \Pr[\mathbf{bad}_{\text{coll}}]$.

If $\mathbf{bad}_{\text{coll}} = \mathbf{false}$, each instance is distinct, and there can be only one corresponding partner or none. For π_P^t, the trace would consist of (U, S, x^U, x^S), where either U or S would be chosen by the game. Therefore, the occurrence of $\mathbf{bad}_{\text{coll}}$ takes place only when all ℓ set elements of one instance collide with another instance. The probability of such an occurrence for two sessions is $1/|\mathcal{G}|^\ell$, and since there are at most $q_e + q_s$ sessions, we have $|\Pr[\text{Succ}_1] - \Pr[\text{Succ}_0]| \leq \Pr[\text{bad}_{\text{coll}}] \leq \frac{(q_e + q_s)^2}{|\mathcal{G}|^\ell}$.

Game G_2. In this game, we explicitly define the freshness, and an extra variable $\pi_P^t.\text{fr}$ is updated for each oracle π_P^t.

In EXECUTE, we set all freshness variables $\pi_P^t.\text{fr} = \textbf{true}$ (line 36). In SENDRESP and SENDTERM, if the password has not been corrupted, the instance is marked as fresh (lines 72, 87). However, if the password has been corrupted, the instance is marked as non-fresh (lines 73, 90). In SENDTERM, the freshness of a partner instance is also checked (line 86). If the instance is already generated when $\mathcal{A}$ issues CORRUPT, we also update the freshness variable (line 102). Additionally, when an instance reveals its session key, we mark this instance and its partner instance as non-fresh (line 42). In TEST, the game checks the freshness of the instance only (line 45). There are only conceptual differences between G_2 and G_1, hence $\Pr[\text{Succ}_2] = \Pr[\text{Succ}_1]$.

Game G_3. In this game, we alter the method of generating K for instance queried to EXECUTE. We choose keys $K \leftarrow_\$ \mathcal{K}$ randomly instead of computing them. Here, we construct $\mathcal{B}_1$ as an adversary to against GA-StCDH and show the difference between $\Pr[\text{Succ}_3]$ and $\Pr[\text{Succ}_2]$ is bounded by $\text{Adv}_{\text{EGAT}}^{\text{GA-StCDH}}(\mathcal{B}_1)$. Adversary $\mathcal{B}_1$ takes a challenge $(x, y) = (g \star \tilde{x}, h \star \tilde{x})$ as input and has access to GA-DDH$(x, \cdot, \cdot)$. To begin the attack, $\mathcal{B}_1$ generates crs as in G_2, and takes (x_0, x_1) as input to run $\mathcal{A}$. For EXECUTE, $\mathcal{B}_1$ simulates the following process: $\mathcal{B}_1$ chooses $(u_0, ..., u_\ell)$ and $(s_0, ..., s_\ell)$ randomly for each parties. Instead of using x_{p_i}, $\mathcal{B}_1$ uses x and y to compute x^U and x^S, which means the password $\text{pw} := (p_1, ..., p_\ell)$ is not needed. This process can be rephrased as

$$x_i^U = u_i \star x = (u_i \cdot g \cdot g_{p_i}^{-1}) \star \tilde{x} = (u_i \cdot g \cdot g_{p_i}^{-1}) \star x_{p_i} = u_i' \star x_{p_i},$$

where we set $u' = u_i \cdot g \cdot g_{p_i}^{-1}$ as the group element used to acquire the session key for user. Similarly, we have $s' = s_i \cdot h \cdot g_{p_i}^{-1}$. Therefore, we can compute $z_i = (u_i' \cdot s_i') \star x_{p_i} = (u_i \cdot g) \cdot (s_i \cdot h) \cdot (g_{p_i}^{-1} \star \tilde{x})$.

We check if a value matching the session key has been queried by random oracle H before choosing a session key randomly. We iterate through the entries in Q that match the tuple $(U, S, x^U, x^S, \text{pw}_{US})$, and verify whether there is any correct entry in z. The oracle can be transformed as

$$\text{GA-CDH}_{x_{p_i}}(x_i^U, x_i^S) = z_i \quad \Leftrightarrow \quad \text{GA-CDH}(x, x_i^S) = (u_i^{-1} \cdot g_{p_i}) \star z_i.$$

In this way, we can use GA-DDH$(x, \cdot, \cdot)$ where the first input is restricted to x. If a correct entry is found, $\mathcal{B}_1$ will terminate the loop and produce the output $(g \cdot h) \star \tilde{x}$ from $(u_i^{-1} \cdot s_i^{-1} \cdot g_{p_i}) \star z_i$.

Otherwise, we add the trace, password, and values u_i, s_i to Q_e to identify relevant queries for H, then choose $K \leftarrow_\$ \mathcal{K}$. Especially if a query contains the trace $\pi_{\mathsf{P}}^{t'}$.tr and pw, we retrieve u_i and s_i to verify z_i by using the DDH oracle. If the oracle returns $\perp$ for all z_i, $\mathcal{B}_1$ will abort and produce the output $(g \cdot h) \star \tilde{x}$.

Game G_4. In this game, instead of using the basis x_{p_i}, we simply use $\tilde{x}$ to compute x^{U} and x^{S} in EXECUTE, which means we remove the password from this query. In the previous games, we used pw as the seed for shuffle. Here, we denote $\mathcal{P}$ as the namespace of permutation and simply replace the Shuffle function with PRP. The contribution of the values remains consistent with G_3. In addition, u and s are not involved in key derivation. Hence, the adversary $\mathcal{A}$ can't see the difference between the games, and $\Pr[\mathsf{Succ}_4] = \Pr[\mathsf{Succ}_3]$.

Game G_5. We show G_5 in Fig. 5. In this game, we choose K randomly for every fresh instance queried to SENTRESP and SENTTERM. Here, we introduce Q_s as a new random oracle which is independent and maps the trace to a key for an instance U or S, ensuring consistency between partner instances. In cases where the adversary $\mathcal{A}$ queries SENTTERM for an instance and a partner instance that is fresh exists, we obtain K from Q_s and give it to the instance. If an instance is not fresh, we compute the correct K by the random oracle H.

For all fresh sessions, if inconsistency exists between Q and Q_s, we set **bad = true**. The above situation happens when:

1. In SENTRESP queries, K is ready to be computed and pw has not been corrupted, yet the correct pw and z can be found in Q.
2. In SENTTERM queries, the session key is ready to be computed, there is no partner instance, pw has not been corrupted, yet the correct pw and z can be found in Q.
3. In the random oracle H, a queried trace along with the correct pw and z exists in Q_s. In case the adversary issues the correct query and the pw is corrupted, we output K obtained from Q_s.

When **bad** was not raised, G_4 is the same as G_5. Hence,

$$|\Pr[\mathsf{Succ}_5] - \Pr[\mathsf{Succ}_4]| \leq \Pr[G_5 \Rightarrow \mathbf{bad}].$$

Game G_6. In game G_6, the password is removed from SENT and generated as late as possible. To be specific, it is generated when the adversary issues CORRUPT or a result α' is returned. In SENTINIT and SENTRESP, u_i and s_i are selected uniformly at random as the previous games, but the computation of x_i^{U} and x_i^{S} is now performed using the origin element $\tilde{x}$. Now, based on the choice of the password, the messages are set as

$$x_i^{\mathsf{U}} = u_i \cdot \tilde{x} = (u_i \cdot g_{p_i}^{-1}) \star x_{p_i} = (u_i \cdot g_0^{-1}) \star x_0 = (u_i \cdot g_1^{-1}) \star x_1,$$

$$x_i^{\mathsf{S}} = s_i \cdot \tilde{x} = (s_i \cdot g_{p_i}^{-1}) \star x_{p_i} = (s_i \cdot g_0^{-1}) \star x_0 = (s_i \cdot g_1^{-1}) \star x_1.$$

Since we cannot perform shuffle using the password, we add a new table Q_σ to store the permutation order in this game. Before shuffling the order of x^{U} and x^{S}, we get the query result σ from the random oracle H_2. In case the password gets corrupted and the query accessed by the adversary is correct, we simply compute and output the correct σ. Otherwise, we return the value recorded in Q_σ or generate σ at random and record it to the table. Also, we define a new function $F_\sigma(x)$, which can permutate the input sequence x according to σ, and its corresponding inverse function $F_\sigma^{-1}(x)$. Now we replace Shuffle and DeShuffle that require password in this game. If an instance is non-fresh, we compute the correct session key by $z_i = u_i \cdot g_{p_i}^{-1} \star x_i^S$ or $z_i = s_i \cdot g_{p_i}^{-1} \star x_i^U$. We should note that the password is already generated for the above instances.

Recall that in G_5, we raise the event **bad** whenever a random oracle query does not match the key of fresh instances. But here, we specifically divide **bad** into two types as follows:

1. $\mathbf{bad_{pw}}$ is used to capture the event where there are multiple valid entries in Q that hold different pw but the trace is the same as a fresh instance.
2. $\mathbf{bad_{corr}}$ is used to capture the event where the first event does not occur, and a valid entry that contains the correct pw and the trace of a fresh instance can be found in Q. In this case, the password is not corrupted when querying H.

In SentResp and SentTerm, we check the entries in Q that contain the corresponding trace for every fresh instance. For this trace, we verify the validity of the given password and z by computing the correct z' as done for the instances that are not fresh. To identify $\mathbf{bad_{pw}}$ and $\mathbf{bad_{corr}}$, we add a new set Q_{bad}. If the values of z and z' match, the entry is added to Q_{bad}. Similarly, the attacker will specify pw when H is queried for a trace that exists in Q_s, and the validity of z is verified by using the stored u_i or s_i in Q_s for the instances. For a fresh instance, if z is valid, the query is added to Q_{bad}. If pw is corrupted at this time, the key stored in Q_s is returned. After the adversary outputs the α' as a result, we check whether $\mathbf{bad_{pw}}$ or $\mathbf{bad_{corr}}$ occurred. Note that in G_5, if **bad** is set, then either $\mathbf{bad_{pw}}$ or $\mathbf{bad_{corr}}$ flag is set in G_6 accordingly. Hence, $\Pr[G_5 \Rightarrow \mathbf{bad}] \leq \Pr[G_6 \Rightarrow \mathbf{bad_{pw}}] + \Pr[G_6 \Rightarrow \mathbf{bad_{corr}}]$.

Next, we will access the probabilities of the two events, beginning with $\mathbf{bad_{pw}}$. A new adversary $\mathcal{B}_2$, is constructed against the Sim-GA-StCDH protocol. The goal of $\mathcal{B}_2$ is to simulate the behavior of G_6 in Fig. 7. $\mathcal{B}_2$ inputs $(x_0, x_1, w) = (g_0 \star \tilde{x}, g_1 \star \tilde{x}, h \star \tilde{x})$, where $(g_0, g_1, h) \leftarrow_\$ \mathcal{G}^3$. Also, $\mathcal{B}_2$ can access to $\mathsf{GA\text{-}DDH}_{x_j}(w, \cdot, \cdot)$ where $j \in \{0, 1\}$. $\mathcal{B}_2$ runs $\mathcal{A}^\mathcal{O}(x_0, x_1)$ and simulates SentInit by choosing group elements $u \leftarrow_\$ \mathcal{G}^\ell$ and computing $x_i^U = u_i \star w = (u_i \cdot h \cdot g_0^{-1}) \star x_0 = (u_i \cdot h \cdot g_1^{-1}) \star x_1$.

Also, $\mathcal{B}_2$ sets x_i^S in SentResp in the same way. For a fresh server instance S, it's necessary to verify if there's a conflicting entry in Q. By iterating through all entries related to this instance in Q, we examine each pw and z. Specifically, we verify whether

$$z_i = \mathsf{GA\text{-}CDH}_{x_{p_i}}(x_i^U, x_i^S) \quad \Leftrightarrow \quad \mathsf{GA\text{-}CDH}_{x_{p_i}}(w, x_i^U) = s_i^{-1} \star z_i,$$

which can be simulated using $\mathsf{GA\text{-}DDH}_{x_{p_i}}(w, \cdot, \cdot)$. If z_i is correct for all i, we include the entry in Q_{bad}.

For the instances that are non-fresh, we should compute the correct key. To do so, we follow the method described above which involves verifying the existence of a valid entry z in Q. If such an entry is found, we assign its value to K. If not, we randomly choose a key from $\mathcal{K}$ and create a new entry within Q. Instead of containing z, this entry includes the secret group elements s_i, allowing us to patch the random oracle later. The simulation of SENTTERM is done similarly but with the secret group elements u_i instead.

If the trace for a random oracle query is included in Q_s, it means that the instance was fresh when querying SENT. Then, we use GA-DDH to check the validity of z as previously described. If z is a valid variable, we initially check the freshness of the instance. If so, we include the query in Q_{bad}. Otherwise, if pw has been corrupted and is specified in this query, we restore the K from Q_s. Then, we check whether the special entry added to Q for a non-fresh instance in SENTRESP or SENTTERM matches the query. In this case, we must output the same session key K as previously returned. Also, we can use GA-DDH to distinguish instances belonging to users or servers.

Once $\mathcal{A}$ completes its operation and produces the output α', $\mathcal{B}_2$ proceeds to choose the password that have not been generated in CORRUPT. In case bad_{pw} occurs, it implies that for the same trace, there are two entries in Q_{bad} but with different passwords, along with their respective values z and z'. Assuming that pw and pw' differ at the first index i, i.e., $p_i \neq p'_i$, we consider $p_i = 0$ and $p'_i = 1$. In case this isn't true, we can exchange pw and pw' to fulfill this condition. If Q_{bad} contains entries from a user instance, we can retrieve u_i from Q_s.

Here, we limit the adversary directly using twist by *root*. If the adversary uses the twist result as an input, the *root* will be recalculated. Without pw, the correct *seed* cannot be generated for shuffle. Consequently, the partner instance is incapable of restoring the actual input, and thus, it becomes impossible to share the correct session key. Recall that a group action cannot be efficiently twisted, it is believed that the Sim-GA-StCDH problem becomes hard to solve. For a user instance, $\mathcal{B}_2$ computes $y = x_i^{\mathsf{S}}$ and

$$y_0 = u_i^{-1} \star z = \mathsf{GA\text{-}CDH}_{x_0}(u_i^{-1} \star x_i^{\mathsf{U}}, x_i^{\mathsf{S}}) = \mathsf{GA\text{-}CDH}_{x_0}(w, x_i^{\mathsf{S}}),$$

$$y_1 = u_i^{-1} \star z' = \mathsf{GA\text{-}CDH}_{x_1}(u_i^{-1} \star x_i^{\mathsf{U}}, x_i^{\mathsf{S}}) = \mathsf{GA\text{-}CDH}_{x_1}(w, x_i^{\mathsf{S}}).$$

For a sever instance, $\mathcal{B}_2$ sets $y = x_i^{\mathsf{U}}$, and outputs y and

$$y_0 = s_i^{-1} \star z = \mathsf{GA\text{-}CDH}_{x_0}(s_i^{-1} \star x_i^{\mathsf{S}}, x_i^{\mathsf{U}}) = \mathsf{GA\text{-}CDH}_{x_0}(w, x_i^{\mathsf{U}}),$$
$$y_1 = s_i^{-1} \star z' = \mathsf{GA\text{-}CDH}_{x_1}(s_i'^{-1} \star x_i^{\mathsf{S}}, x_i^{\mathsf{U}}) = \mathsf{GA\text{-}CDH}_{x_1}(w, x_i^{\mathsf{U}}).$$

The analysis of bad_{pw} has concluded. If bad_{pw} raises, $\mathcal{B}_2$ can solve the Sim-GA-StCDH problem.

We then turn to the analysis of bad_{corr}. As defined above, bad_{corr} occurs only if bad_{pw} does not happen. Therefore, each instance has only one entry at most in Q_{bad}, and the size of Q_{bad} cannot exceed q_s. Since every entry is added before their corresponding pw is sampled, we have $\Pr[\mathsf{G}_6 \Rightarrow \text{bad}_{\text{corr}}] \leq \frac{q_s}{|\mathcal{PW}|}$. If

G_6 is free from any bad events, TEST generates session keys uniformly randomly. The adversary $\mathcal{A}$ can not get any information from TEST, and the value of α can only obtained by guess. Hence, $\Pr\left[\mathsf{Succ}_6\right] = \frac{1}{2}$. □

4.3 Comparison with Previous Results

In table 1, we show the comparison between the existing schemes and our scheme. Also, we provide a comparison under specific parameters.

For X-GA-PAKE$_\ell$, ℓ stands for the length of the password. In X-GA-PAKE$_\ell$, each party needs to send 2ℓ set elements as communication overhead and performs group actions for 5ℓ times. In CrsX-GA-PAKE$_\ell$, for each party, the number of set elements is reduced to $\ell + |\mathsf{crs}|$, and the number of group actions is reduced to $4\ell + |\mathsf{crs}|$. In our scheme, we also generate two random set elements crs by some trusted party. By using the shuffle function, we don't need to add any extra components to the message. Therefore, we halve the number of set elements that each party send from 2ℓ to ℓ and reduce the times of group actions to 2ℓ per party. In addition, while the message length of z, used for key derivation in X-GA-PAKE$_\ell$ and CrsX-GA-PAKE$_\ell$, is both 3ℓ, we have managed to reduce it to ℓ. We achieve optimization at the same ratio for the variant R-GA-PAKE$_{\ell,N}^t$. In X-GA-PAKE$_{\ell,N}^t$ and R-GA-PAKE$_{\ell,N}^t$, N stands for the length that divides ℓ into ℓ/N, and t stands for twists that used in the setup. Based on the sample values given in the table, we can see the optimization effect more clearly. When the value of ℓ (ℓ/N) increases, the difference in communication and computation overhead between the protocols also increases. Both X-GA-PAKE, CrsX-GA-PAKE and our scheme are one-round PAKE protocols which are provable security based on the assumption Sqinv-GA-StCDH.

5 Conclusion

In this paper, we proposed a one-round PAKE protocol based on isogeny that greatly reduces the communication overhead and the number of group actions compared to X-GA-PAKE$_\ell$. Although our solution has a considerable efficiency optimization, it still requires $O(\ell)$ communication overhead, which requires further improvement. Moreover, we have not yet proven its security in the QROM, and this remains a direction for our future work.

Acknowledgments. We thank the anonymous reviewers for their helpful discussion and feedback. The work were supported by the National Key Research and Development Program of China (No. 2022YFB4400700), the National Natural Science Foundation of China (Nos. U21A20466, U23A20302, 62272350, 62172307), the New 20 Project of Higher Education of Jinan (No. 202228017), the Fundamental Research Funds for the Central Universities (No. 2042023KF0203, 2042024KF1013) and the Henan Key Laboratory of Network Cryptography Technology(LNCT2022-A06)

game G_{0-4}

01 $(g_0, g_1) \leftarrow_\$ \mathcal{G}^2$
02 $(x_0, x_1) := (g_0 \star \tilde{x}, g_1 \star \tilde{x})$
03 $(\mathcal{C}, \mathcal{Q}) := (\emptyset, \emptyset)$
04 $\mathbf{bad_{coll}} := \mathbf{false}$ ▷ G_{0-3}
05 **for** $U \in \mathcal{U}$ **and** $S \in \mathcal{S}$
06    $pw_{US} \leftarrow_\$ \mathcal{PW}$
07 $\alpha \leftarrow_\$ \{0, 1\}$
08 $\alpha' \leftarrow_\$ \mathcal{A}^{\mathcal{O}}(x_0, x_1)$
09 **return** $[\![\alpha = \alpha']\!]$

$\underline{\text{EXECUTE}(U, t_0, S, t_1)}$

10 **if** $(\pi_U^{t_0}, \pi_S^{t_1}) \neq (\bot, \bot)$ **return** $\bot$
11 $(p_1, ..., p_\ell) := pw_{US}$ ▷ G_{0-3}
12 $u := (u_1, ..., u_\ell) \leftarrow_\$ \mathcal{G}^\ell$
13 $s := (s_1, ..., s_\ell) \leftarrow_\$ \mathcal{G}^\ell$
14 $x^U := (x_1^U, ..., x_\ell^U)$
   $:= (u_1 \star x_{p_1}, ..., u_\ell \star x_{p_\ell})$ ▷ G_{0-3}
15 $x^S := (x_1^S, ..., x_\ell^S)$
   $:= (s_1 \star x_{p_1}, ..., s_\ell \star x_{p_\ell})$ ▷ G_{0-3}
16 $root^U := \text{GetRoot}(x^U)$ ▷ G_{0-3}
17 $x_\sigma^U := \text{Shuffle}(x^U, H(U, S, root^U, pw))$ ▷ G_{0-3}
18 $root^S := \text{GetRoot}(x^S)$ ▷ G_{0-3}
19 $x_\sigma^S := \text{Shuffle}(x^S, H(U, S, root^S, pw))$ ▷ G_{0-3}
20 **for** $i \in [\ell]$ ▷ G_{0-3}
21    $z_i := u_i \star x_i^S$ ▷ G_{0-3}
22 $z := (z_1, ..., z_\ell)$ ▷ G_{0-3}
23 $x^U := (x_1^U, ..., x_\ell^U) := (u_1 \star \tilde{x}, ..., u_\ell \star \tilde{x})$ ▷ G_4
24 $x^S := (x_1^S, ..., x_\ell^S) := (s_1 \star \tilde{x}, ..., s_\ell \star \tilde{x})$ ▷ G_4
25 $\sigma \leftarrow_\$ \mathcal{P}$ ▷ G_4
26 $x_\sigma^U := \text{PRP}_\sigma(x^U)$ ▷ G_4
27 $\sigma \leftarrow_\$ \mathcal{P}$ ▷ G_4
28 $x_\sigma^S := \text{PRP}_\sigma(x^S)$ ▷ G_4
29 **if** $\exists P \in \mathcal{U} \cup \mathcal{S}, t'$ s.t.
   $\pi_P^{t'}.\text{tr} = (U, S, x^U, x^S)$ ▷ G_{1-4}
30    $\mathbf{bad_{coll}} := \mathbf{true}$ ▷ G_{1-4}
31   **return** $\bot$ ▷ G_{1-4}
32 $K := H(U, S, x^U, x^S, pw_{US}, z)$ ▷ G_{0-2}
33 $K \leftarrow_\$ \mathcal{K}$ ▷ G_{3-4}
34 $\pi_U^{t_0} := (u, (U, S, x^U, x^S), K, \mathbf{true})$
35 $\pi_S^{t_1} := (s, (U, S, x^U, x^S), K, \mathbf{true})$
36 $(\pi_U^{t_0}.\text{fr}, \pi_S^{t_1}.\text{fr}) := (\mathbf{true}, \mathbf{true})$ ▷ G_{2-4}
37 **return** $(U, x_\sigma^U, S, x_\sigma^S)$

$\underline{\text{REVEAL}(P, t)}$

38 **if** $\pi_P^t.\text{acc} \neq \mathbf{true}$ **and** $\pi_P^t.\text{test} = \mathbf{true}$ **return** $\bot$
39 **for** $\forall \pi_{P'}^{t'}$ s.t. $\text{PAR}(\pi_P^t, \pi_{P'}^{t'}) = 1$
40   **if** $\pi_{P'}^{t'}.\text{test} = \mathbf{true}$ **return** $\bot$
41 **for** $\forall \pi_{P'}^{t'}$ s.t. $\pi_P^t.\text{tr} = \pi_{P'}^{t'}.\text{tr}$ ▷ G_{2-4}
42    $\pi_{P'}^{t'}.\text{fr} := \mathbf{false}$ ▷ G_{2-4}
43 **return** $\pi_P^t.K$

$\underline{\text{TEST}(P, t)}$

44 **if** $\text{Fresh}(P, t) = \mathbf{false}$ **return** $\bot$ ▷ G_{0-1}
45 **if** $\pi_P^t.\text{fr} = \mathbf{false}$ **return** $\bot$ ▷ G_{2-4}
46 $K_0^* := \text{REVEAL}(P, t)$
47 **if** $K_0^* = \bot$ **return** $\bot$
48 $K_1^* \leftarrow_\$ \mathcal{K}$
49 $\pi_P^t.\text{test} := \mathbf{true}$
50 **return** K_α^*

$\underline{\text{SENDINIT}(U, t, S)}$

51 **if** $\pi_U^t \neq \bot$ **return** $\bot$
52 $(p_1, ..., p_\ell) := pw_{US}$
53 $u := (u_1, ..., u_\ell) \leftarrow_\$ \mathcal{G}^\ell$
54 $x^U := (x_1^U, ..., x_\ell^U) := (u_1 \star x_{p_1}, ..., u_\ell \star x_{p_\ell})$

55 $root^U := \text{GetRoot}(x^U)$
56 $x_\sigma^U := \text{Shuffle}(x^U, H(U, S, root^U, pw))$
57 $\pi_U^t := (u, (U, S, x^U, \bot), \bot, \bot)$
58 $\pi_U^t.\text{fr} := \mathbf{false}$ ▷ G_{2-4}
59 **return** (U, x_σ^U)

$\underline{\text{SENDRESP}(S, t, U, x_\sigma^U)}$

60 **if** $\pi_S^t \neq \bot$ **return** $\bot$
61 $(p_1, ..., p_\ell) := pw_{US}$
62 $s := (s_1, ..., s_\ell) \leftarrow_\$ \mathcal{G}^\ell$
63 $x^S := (x_1^S, ..., x_\ell^S) := (s_1 \star x_{p_1}, ..., s_\ell \star x_{p_\ell})$
64 $root^S := \text{GetRoot}(x^S)$
65 $x_\sigma^S := \text{Shuffle}(x^S, H(U, S, root^S, pw))$
66 $root^U := \text{GetRoot}(x^U)$
67 $x^U := \text{DeShuffle}(x_\sigma^U, H(U, S, root^U, pw))$
68 **if** $\exists P \in \mathcal{U} \cup \mathcal{S}, t'$ s.t.
   $\pi_P^{t'}.\text{tr} = (U, S, x^U, x^S)$ ▷ G_{1-4}
69    $\mathbf{bad_{coll}} := \mathbf{true}$ ▷ G_{1-4}
70   **return** $\bot$ ▷ G_{1-4}
71 **if** $U \notin \mathcal{C}$ **and** $S \notin \mathcal{C}$ ▷ G_{2-4}
72    $\pi_S^t.\text{fr} := \mathbf{true}$ ▷ G_{2-4}
73 **else** $\pi_S^t.\text{fr} := \mathbf{false}$ ▷ G_{2-4}
74 **for** $i \in [\ell]$
75    $z_i := s_i \star x_i^U$
76 $z := (z_1, ..., z_\ell)$
77 $K := H(U, S, x^U, x^S, pw_{US}, z)$
78 $\pi_S^t := (s, (U, S, x^U, x^S), K, \mathbf{true})$
79 **return** (S, x_σ^S)

$\underline{\text{SENDTERM}(U, t, S, x_\sigma^S)}$

80 **if** $\pi_U^t \neq (u, (U, S, x^U, \bot), \bot, \bot)$ **return** $\bot$
81 $root^S := \text{GetRoot}(x^S)$
82 $x^S := \text{DeShuffle}(x_\sigma^S, H(U, S, root^S, pw))$
83 **if** $\exists P \in \mathcal{U}, t'$ s.t.
   $\pi_{U'}^{t'}.\text{tr} = (U, S, x^U, x^S)$ ▷ G_{1-4}
84    $\mathbf{bad_{coll}} := \mathbf{true}$ ▷ G_{1-4}
85   **return** $\bot$ ▷ G_{1-4}
86 **if** $\exists \pi_S^{t'}$ s.t. $\pi_S^{t'}.\text{tr} = (U, S, x^U, x^S)$ ▷ G_{2-4}
      and $\pi_S^{t'}.\text{fr} = \mathbf{true}$ ▷ G_{2-4}
87    $\pi_U^t.\text{fr} := \mathbf{true}$ ▷ G_{2-4}
88 **if** $U \notin \mathcal{C}$ **and** $S \notin \mathcal{C}$ ▷ G_{2-4}
89    $\pi_U^t.\text{fr} := \mathbf{true}$ ▷ G_{2-4}
90 **else** $\pi_U^t.\text{fr} := \mathbf{false}$ ▷ G_{2-4}
91 **for** $i \in [\ell]$
92    $z_i := u_i \star x_i^S$
93 $z := (z_1, ..., z_\ell)$
94 $K := H(U, S, x^U, x^S, pw_{US}, z)$
95 $\pi_U^t := (s, (U, S, x^U, x^S), K, \mathbf{true})$
96 **return true**

$\underline{\text{CORRUPT}(U, S)}$

97 **if** $U \in \mathcal{C}$ **and** $S \in \mathcal{C}$ **return** $\bot$
98 **for** $P \in \{U, S\}$
99   **if** $\exists t$ s.t. $\pi_P^t.\text{test} = \mathbf{true}$
      and $\nexists P' \in \mathcal{U} \cup \mathcal{S}, t'$ s.t. $\text{PAR}(\pi_P^t, \pi_{P'}^{t'}) = 1$
100   **return** $\bot$
101   $\forall \pi_P^t$: **if** $\nexists P' \in \mathcal{U} \cup \mathcal{S}, t'$ s.t.
      $\text{PAR}(\pi_P^t, \pi_{P'}^{t'}) = 1$ ▷ G_{2-4}
102      $\pi_P^t.\text{fr} := \mathbf{false}$ ▷ G_{2-4}
103 $\mathcal{C} := \mathcal{C} \cup \{U, S\}$
104 **return** pw_{US}

$\underline{\text{H}(U, S, x^U, x^S, pw, z)}$

105 **if** $Q[U, S, x^U, x^S, pw, z] = K \neq \bot$ **return** K
106 $Q[U, S, x^U, x^S, pw, z] \leftarrow_\$ \mathcal{K}$
107 **return** $Q[U, S, x^U, x^S, pw, z]$

Fig. 3. Games G_{0-4} for the proof of Theorem 1. $\mathcal{A}$ can access to $\mathcal{O} := \{\text{EXECUTE},$ SENTINIT, SENTRESP, SENTTERM, REVEAL, TEST, CORRUPT, H$\}$.

Table 1. Comparison between the existing schemes and ours. X-GA-PAKE$_{\ell,N}^{t}$ is a variant of X-GA-PAKE$_\ell$, which increases the number of public parameter to 2^N and divides the length of pw into ℓ/N [1]. We obtain R-GA-PAKE$_{\ell,N}^{t}$ by the same techniques. "Comm Overhead" refers to the communication overhead. As a sample, we set $\ell = 256$ and $N = 8$, and mark the result in gray.

Protocol	Assumption	Rounds	|crs|	Comm Overhead	Group Actions
X-GA-PAKE$_\ell$ [1]	SqInv-GA-StCDH	1	2	2ℓ	5ℓ
			2	512	1280
X-GA-PAKE$_{\ell,N}^{t}$ [1]	SqInv-GA-StCDH	1	2^{N-1}	$2\ell/N$	$5\ell/N$
			128	64	160
CrsX-GA-PAKE$_\ell$ [15]	SqInv-GA-StCDH	1	2	$\ell + 2$	$4\ell + 2$
			2	258	1026
CrsX-GA-PAKE$_{\ell,N}^{t}$ [15]	SqInv-GA-StCDH	1	2^{N-1}	$\ell/N + 2^{N-1}$	$4\ell/N + 2^{N-1}$
			128	32	64
R-GA-PAKE$_\ell$	SqInv-GA-StCDH	1	2	ℓ	2ℓ
			2	256	512
R-GA-PAKE$_{\ell,N}^{t}$	SqInv-GA-StCDH	1	2^{N-1}	ℓ/N	$2\ell/N$
			128	32	64

A   Definition of Computational Problems

Definition 4. (Group Action Strong Computational Diffie-Hellman Problem (GA-StCDH)). *To solve the* GA-StCDH *problem, computing* $(g_0 \cdot g_1) \star \tilde{x}$ *based on input* $(g_0 \star \tilde{x}, g_1 \star \tilde{x}) \in \mathcal{R}^2$ *is required. Adversary* $\mathcal{A}$ *has the advantage of* EGA(T) *as*

$$\mathsf{ADV}_{\mathsf{EGA(T)}}^{\mathsf{GA\text{-}StCDH}}(\mathcal{A}) := \Pr[\mathcal{A}^{\mathsf{GA\text{-}DDH}(g_0 \star \tilde{x}, \cdot, \cdot)}(g_0 \star \tilde{x}, g_1 \star \tilde{x}) \Rightarrow (g_0 \cdot g_1) \star \tilde{x}],$$

where $(g_0, g_1) \leftarrow_\$ \mathcal{G}^2$ *and* $\mathcal{A}$ *can access decision oracle* GA-DDH$(g_0 \star \tilde{x}, \cdot, \cdot)$.

Definition 5. (Square-Inverse GA-StCDH (SqInv-GA-StCDH)). *To solve the* SqInv-GA-StCDH *problem, it's required to find* $(y, y_0, y_1) \in \mathcal{R}^3$ *based on input* $x = g \star \tilde{x}$ *that satisfies* $y_0 = g^2 \star y$ *and* $y_1 = g^{-1} \star y$. *Adversary* $\mathcal{A}$ *has the advantage of* EGA(T) *as*

$$\mathsf{ADV}_{\mathsf{EGA(T)}}^{\mathsf{SqInv\text{-}GA\text{-}StCDH}}(\mathcal{A}) := \Pr \left[\begin{array}{c} y_0 = \mathsf{GA\text{-}CDH}_{x^t}(x, y) \\ y_1 = \mathsf{GA\text{-}CDH}(x^t, y) \\ (y, y_0, y_1) \leftarrow \mathcal{A}^{\mathcal{O}}(g \star \tilde{x}) \end{array} \right],$$

where $g \leftarrow_\$ \mathcal{G}$ *and* $\mathcal{O} = \{\mathsf{GA\text{-}DDH}_{x^t}(x, \cdot, \cdot), \mathsf{GA\text{-}DDH}(x, \cdot, \cdot)\}$.

Remark 1. If we assume that the adversary is limited to using only the group and twist operations, SqInv-GA-StCDH becomes a challenging problem. Specifically, $\mathcal{A}$ can choose y based on $\tilde{x}$, x or x^t only.

For $\gamma \in \mathcal{G}$, if $\mathcal{A}$ chooses $y = \gamma \star \tilde{x}$, computing $y_1 = \mathsf{GA\text{-}CDH}(x^t, \gamma \star \tilde{x} = \gamma \star x^t$ is easy, but it's challenging to compute $y_0 = (\gamma \cdot g^2) \star \tilde{x}$. If $\mathcal{A}$ chooses $y = \gamma \star x$, it's easy to compute $y_1 = \mathsf{GA\text{-}CDH}(x^t, \gamma \star x = \gamma \star \tilde{x}$, but not $y_0 = (\gamma \cdot g^3) \star \tilde{x}$. If $\mathcal{A}$ chooses $y = \gamma \star x^t$, then it can compute $y_0 = \mathsf{GA\text{-}CDH}_{x^t}(x, \gamma \star x^t) = \gamma \star x$, but hard to compute $y_1 = (\gamma \cdot g^{-2}) \star \tilde{x}$.

Definition 6. (Simultaneous GA-StCDH (Sim-GA-StCDH)) *To solve the* Sim-GA-StCDH *problem, it's required to find* $(y, y_0, y_1) \in \mathcal{R}^3$ *based on input* $(w, x_0, x_1) = (h \star \tilde{x}, g_0 \star \tilde{x}, g_1 \star \tilde{x})$ *that satisfies* $y_0 = (g_0^{-1} \cdot h) \star y$ *and* $y_1 = (g_1^{-1} \cdot h) \star y$. *Adversary* $\mathcal{A}$ *has the advantage of* $\mathsf{EGA(T)}$ *as*

$$\mathsf{ADV}^{\mathsf{Sim\text{-}GA\text{-}StCDH}}_{\mathsf{EGA(T)}}(\mathcal{A}) := \Pr\left[\begin{matrix} y_0 = \mathsf{GA\text{-}CDH}_{x_0}(w, y) \\ y_1 = \mathsf{GA\text{-}CDH}_{x_1}(w, y) \end{matrix} \middle| \begin{matrix} (h, g_0, g_1) \leftarrow_\$ \mathcal{G}^3 \\ (w, x_0, x_1) := (h \star \tilde{x}, g_0 \star \tilde{x}, g_1 \star \tilde{x}) \\ (y, y_0, y_1) \leftarrow \mathcal{A}^\mathcal{O}(w, x_0, x_1), \end{matrix}\right]$$

where $\mathcal{O} = \{\mathsf{GA\text{-}DDH}_{x_0}(w, \cdot, \cdot), \mathsf{GA\text{-}DDH}_{x_1}(w, \cdot, \cdot)\}$.

Remark 2. Note that as mentioned in [2], the Sim-GA-StCDH problem can be solved by the adversary by simply choosing $(y, y_0, y_1) = (w^t, x_0^t, x_1^t)$. However, in cases where a group action lacks efficient twisting capabilities, it is believed that the Sim-GA-StCDH problem is hard to solve.

B   Full Version of Code-based Games

```
B₁^{GA-DDH(x,·,·)}(x, y)

01 (g₀, g₁) ←$ 𝒢²
02 (x₀, x₁) := (g₀ ⋆ x̃, g₁ ⋆ x̃)
03 (C, Q, Qₑ) := (∅, ∅, ∅)
04 bad_coll := false
05 for U ∈ 𝒰 and S ∈ 𝒮
06    pw_US ←$ 𝒫𝒲
07 α ←$ {0, 1}
08 α' ←$ 𝒜^𝒪(x₀, x₁)
09 Stop.

EXECUTE(U, t₀, S, t₁)

10 if (π_U^{t₀}, π_S^{t₁}) ≠ (⊥, ⊥) return ⊥
11 (p₁, ..., pₗ) := pw_US
12 u := (u₁, ..., uₗ) ←$ 𝒢ˡ
13 s := (s₁, ..., sₗ) ←$ 𝒢ˡ
14 x^U := (x₁^U, ..., xₗ^U) := (u₁ ⋆ x, ..., uₗ ⋆ x)
15 x^S := (x₁^S, ..., xₗ^S) := (s₁ ⋆ y, ..., sₗ ⋆ y)
16 root^U := GetRoot(x^U)
17 x_σ^U := Shuffle(x^U, H(U, S, root^U, pw_US))
18 root^S := GetRoot(x^S)
19 x_σ^S := Shuffle(x^S, H(U, S, root^S, pw_US))
20 if ∃P ∈ 𝒰 ∪ 𝒮, t' s.t. π_P^{t'}.tr = (U, S, x^U, x^S)
```

```
°21    bad_coll := true
22    return ⊥
23 for ∀z s.t. (U, S, x^U, x^S, pw_US, z) ∈ Q
24    for i ∈ [ℓ]
25       if GA-DDH(x, xᵢ^S, (uᵢ^{-1} · g_{pᵢ}) ⋆ z) = 1
26          Stop with (uᵢ^{-1} · sᵢ^{-1} · g_{pᵢ}) ⋆ z
27 Qₑ := Qₑ ∪ {U, S, x^U, x^S, pw_US, u, s}
28 K ←$ 𝒦
29 π_U^{t₀} := (u, (U, S, x^U, x^S), K, true)
30 π_S^{t₁} := (s, (U, S, x^U, x^S), K, true)
31 (π_U^{t₀}.fr, π_S^{t₁}.fr) := (true, true)
32 return (U, x_σ^U, S, x_σ^S, z)

H(U, S, x^U, x^S, pw, z)

33 if ∃(u, s) s.t. (U, S, x^U, x^S, pw, u, s) ∈ Qₑ
34    (p₁, ..., pₗ) := pw
35    for i ∈ [ℓ]
36       if GA-DDH(x, xᵢ^S, (uᵢ^{-1} · g_{pᵢ}) ⋆ z) = 1
37          Stop with (uᵢ^{-1} · sᵢ^{-1} · g_{pᵢ}) ⋆ z
38 if Q[U, S, x^U, x^S, pw, z] = K ≠ ⊥ return K
39 Q[U, S, x^U, x^S, pw, z] ←$ 𝒦
40 return Q[U, S, x^U, x^S, pw, z]
```

Fig. 4. Adversary $\mathcal{B}_1$ against GA-StCDH for the proof of Theorem 1. $\mathcal{A}$ has access to oracles $\mathcal{O}$ as in Fig. 3. Oracles except EXECUTE and H are defined in G_2.

$$\textbf{game } G_5$$

01 $(g_0, g_1) \leftarrow_\$ \mathcal{G}^2$
02 $(x_0, x_1) := (g_0 \star \tilde{x}, g_1 \star \tilde{x})$
03 $(\mathcal{C}, Q, Q_s) := (\emptyset, \emptyset, \emptyset)$
04 $\textbf{bad} := \textbf{false}$
05 $\alpha \leftarrow_\$ \{0, 1\}$
06 $\textbf{for } U \in \mathcal{U} \textbf{ and } S \in \mathcal{S}$
07 $\quad \mathsf{pw}_{US} \leftarrow_\$ \mathcal{PW}$
08 $\alpha' \leftarrow \mathcal{A}^{\mathcal{O}}(x_0, x_1)$
09 $\textbf{return } [\![\alpha = \alpha']\!]$

$\underline{\text{SENDRESP}(S, t, U, x_\sigma^U)}$

10 $\textbf{if } \pi_S^t \neq \bot \textbf{ return } \bot$
11 $(p_1, ..., p_\ell) := \mathsf{pw}_{US}$
12 $s := (s_1, ..., s_\ell) \leftarrow_\$ \mathcal{G}^\ell$
13 $x^S := (x_1^S, ..., x_\ell^S) := (s_1 \star x_{p_1}, ..., s_\ell \star x_{p_\ell})$
14 $root^S := \mathsf{GetRoot}(x^S)$
15 $x_\sigma^S := \mathsf{Shuffle}(x^S, \mathsf{H}(U, S, root^S, \mathsf{pw}))$
16 $root^U := \mathsf{GetRoot}(x_\sigma^U)$
17 $x^U := \mathsf{DeShuffle}(x_\sigma^U, \mathsf{H}(U, S, root^U, \mathsf{pw}))$
18 $\textbf{if } \exists P \in \mathcal{U} \cup \mathcal{S}, t' \text{ s.t. } \pi_P^{t'}.\mathsf{tr} = (U, S, x^U, x^S)$
19 $\quad \textbf{return } \bot$
20 $\textbf{if } U \notin \mathcal{C} \textbf{ and } S \notin \mathcal{C}$
21 $\quad \pi_S^t.\mathsf{fr} := \textbf{true}$
22 $\quad \textbf{if } \exists z \text{ s.t. } (U, S, x^U, x^S, \mathsf{pw}_{US}, z) \in Q$
       $\quad\quad \textbf{and } z_i := s_i \star x_i^U \; \forall i \in [\ell]$
23 $\quad\quad \textbf{bad} := \textbf{true}$
24 $\quad\quad K \leftarrow_\$ \mathcal{K}$
25 $\quad\quad \tilde{Q}_s[U, S, x^U, x^3] := (\tilde{S}, s, \tilde{K})$
26 $\quad \textbf{else}$
27 $\quad\quad \pi_S^t.\mathsf{fr} := \textbf{false}$
28 $\quad\quad \textbf{for } i \in [\ell]$
29 $\quad\quad\quad z_i := s_i \star x_i^U$
30 $\quad\quad z := (z_1, ..., z_\ell)$
31 $\quad\quad K := \mathsf{H}[U, S, x^U, x^S, \mathsf{pw}_{US}, z]$
32 $\quad \pi_S^t := (s, (U, S, x^U, x^S), K, \textbf{true})$
33 $\textbf{return } (S, x_\sigma^S)$

$\underline{\text{SENDTERM}(U, t, S, x_\sigma^S)}$

34 $\textbf{if } \pi_U^t \neq (u, (U, S, x^U, \bot), \bot, \bot) \textbf{ return } \bot$
35 $root^S := \mathsf{GetRoot}(x_\sigma^S)$

36 $x^S := \mathsf{DeShuffle}(x_\sigma^S, \mathsf{H}(U, S, root^S, \mathsf{pw}))$
37 $\textbf{if } \exists P \in \mathcal{U}, t' \text{ s.t. } \pi_P^{t'}.\mathsf{tr} = (U, S, x^U, x^S)$
38 $\quad \textbf{return } \bot$
39 $\textbf{if } \exists t' \text{ s.t. } \pi_S^{t'}.\mathsf{tr} = (U, S, x^U, x^S)$
     $\quad \textbf{and } \pi_S^{t'}.\mathsf{fr} = \textbf{true}$
40 $\quad \pi_U^t.\mathsf{fr} := \textbf{true}$
41 $\quad (S, s, K) := Q_s[U, S, x^U, x^S]$
42 $\textbf{else if } U \notin \mathcal{C} \textbf{ and } S \notin \mathcal{C}$
43 $\quad \pi_U^t.\mathsf{fr} := \textbf{true}$
44 $\quad \textbf{if } \exists z \text{ s.t. } (U, S, x^U, x^S, \mathsf{pw}_{US}, z) \in Q$
       $\quad\quad \textbf{and } z_i := u_i \star x_i^S \; \forall i \in [\ell]$
45 $\quad\quad \textbf{bad} := \textbf{true}$
46 $\quad\quad K \leftarrow_\$ \mathcal{K}$
47 $\quad\quad Q_s[U, S, x^U, x^S] := (U, u, K)$
48 $\quad \textbf{else}$
49 $\quad\quad \pi_U^t.\mathsf{fr} := \textbf{false}$
50 $\quad\quad \textbf{for } i \in [\ell]$
51 $\quad\quad\quad z_i := u_i \star x_i^S$
52 $\quad\quad z := (z_1, ..., z_\ell)$
53 $\quad\quad K := \mathsf{H}[U, S, x^U, x^S, \mathsf{pw}_{US}, z]$
54 $\quad \pi_U^t := (u, (U, S, x^U, x^S), K, \textbf{true})$
55 $\textbf{return true}$

$\underline{\mathsf{H}(U, S, x^U, x^S, \mathsf{pw}, z)}$

56 $\textbf{if } Q[U, S, x^U, x^S, \mathsf{pw}, z] = K \neq \bot \textbf{ return } K$
57 $\textbf{if } (U, S, x^U, x^S) \in Q_s \textbf{ and } \mathsf{pw} = \mathsf{pw}_{US}$
58 $\quad \textbf{if } Q_s[U, S, x^U, x^S] = (U, u, K)$
59 $\quad\quad \textbf{for } i \in [\ell]$
60 $\quad\quad\quad z_i' := u_i \star x_i^3$
61 $\quad\quad z' := (z_1', ..., z_\ell')$
62 $\quad \textbf{if } Q_s[U, S, x^U, x^S] = (S, s, K)$
63 $\quad\quad \textbf{for } i \in [\ell]$
64 $\quad\quad\quad z_i' := s_i \star x_i^U$
65 $\quad\quad z' := (z_1', ..., z_\ell')$
66 $\quad \textbf{if } z = z'$
67 $\quad\quad \textbf{if } U \in \mathcal{C} \textbf{ and } S \in \mathcal{C} \textbf{ return } K$
68 $\quad\quad \textbf{if } U \notin \mathcal{C} \textbf{ and } S \notin \mathcal{C}$
69 $\quad\quad\quad \textbf{bad} := \textbf{true}$
70 $Q[U, S, x^U, x^S, \mathsf{pw}, z] \leftarrow_\$ \mathcal{K}$
71 $\textbf{return } Q[U, S, x^U, x^S, \mathsf{pw}, z]$

Fig. 5. Games G_5 for the proof of Theorem 1. $\mathcal{A}$ can access to oracles $\mathcal{O}$ as in Fig. 3. EXECUTE, SENTINIT, REVEAL, CORRUPT and TEST are defined as in Fig. 3.

```
game G6
01 (g0, g1) ←$ 𝒢²
02 (x0, x1) := (g0 ⋆ x̃, g1 ⋆ x̃)
03 (𝒞, Q, Qs, Qbad, Qσ) := (∅, ∅, ∅, ∅, ∅)
04 (badcorr, badpw) := (false, false)
05 α ←$ {0, 1}
06 α' ← 𝒜^𝒪(x0, x1)
07 for U ∈ 𝒰 \ 𝒞 and S ∈ 𝒮 \ 𝒞
08   pwUS ←$ 𝒫𝒲
09 if ∃pw, pw', (U, S, x^U, x^S, z, z')
     s.t. (U, S, x^U, x^S, pw, z) ∈ Qbad
     and (U, S, x^U, x^S, pw', z') ∈ Qbad
10   badpw := true
11 else
12   if ∃U, S, x^U, x^S, z
     s.t. (U, S, x^U, x^S, pwUS, z) ∈ Qbad
13     badguess := true
14 return ⟦α = α'⟧

CORRUPT(U, S)
15 if U ∈ 𝒞 and S ∈ 𝒞 return ⊥
16 for P ∈ {U, S}
17   if ∃t s.t. π_p^t.test = true
     and ∄P' ∈ 𝒰 ∪ 𝒮, t' s.t. PAR(π_p^t, π_{p'}^{t'}) = 1
18     return ⊥
19   ∀π_p^t : if ∄P' ∈ 𝒰 ∪ 𝒮, t' s.t. PAR(π_p^t, π_{p'}^{t'}) = 1
20     π_p^t.fr = false
21 𝒞 := 𝒞 ∪ {(U, S)}
22 pwUS ←$ 𝒫𝒲
23 return pwUS

SENDINIT(U, t, S)
24 if π_U^t ≠⊥ return ⊥
25 u := (u1, ..., uℓ) ←$ 𝒢^ℓ
26 x^U := (x_1^U, ..., x_ℓ^U) := (u1 ⋆ x̃, ..., uℓ ⋆ x̃)
27 root^U := GetRoot(x^U))
28 σ = H2(U, S, root^U, pw)
29 x_σ^U = F_σ(x^U)
30 π_U^t := (u, (U, S, x^U, ⊥), ⊥, ⊥)
31 π_U^t.fr := false
32 return (U, x_σ^U)

SENDRESP(S, t, U, x_σ^U)
33 if π_S^t ≠⊥ return ⊥
34 s := (s1, ..., sℓ) ←$ 𝒢^ℓ
35 x^S := (x_1^S, ..., x_ℓ^S) := (s1 ⋆ x̃, ..., sℓ ⋆ x̃)
36 root^S := GetRoot(x^S))
37 σ = H2(U, S, root^S, pw)
38 x_σ^S = F_σ(x^S)
39 root^U := GetRoot(x_σ^U))
40 σ = H2(U, S, root^U, pw)
41 x^U = F_σ^{-1}(x_σ^U)
42 if ∃P ∈ 𝒰 ∪ 𝒮, t' s.t. π_p^{t'}.tr = (U, S, x^U, x^S)
43   return ⊥
44 if U ∉ 𝒞 and S ∉ 𝒞
45   π_S^t.fr := true
46   if ∀pw, z s.t. (U, S, x^U, x^S, pw, z) ∈ Q
47     (p_i, ..., p_ℓ) := pw
48     for i ∈ [ℓ]
49       z_i' := s_i · g_{p_i}^{-1} ⋆ x_i^U
50     z' := (z_1', ..., z_ℓ')
51     if z = z'
52       Qbad := Qbad ∪ {(U, S, x^U, x^S, pw, z)}
53   K ←$ 𝒦
54   Qs[U, S, x^U, x^S] := (S, s, K)
55 else

56 π_S^t.fr := false
57 (p_i, ..., p_ℓ) := pwUS
58 for i ∈ [ℓ]
59   z_i := s_i · g_{p_i}^{-1} ⋆ x_i^U
60 z := (z_1, ..., z_ℓ)
61 K := H[U, S, x^U, x^S, pwUS, z]
62 π_S^t := (s, (U, S, x^U, x^S, K), true)
63 return (S, x_σ^S)

SENDTERM(U, t, S, x_σ^S)
64 if π_U^t ≠ (u, (U, S, x^U, ⊥), ⊥, ⊥) return ⊥
65 root^S := GetRoot(x_σ^S))
66 σ = H2(U, S, root^S, pw)
67 x^S = F_σ^{-1}(x_σ^S)
68 if ∃P ∈ 𝒰, t' s.t. π_S^{t'}.tr = (U, S, x^U, x^S) return ⊥
69 if ∃t' s.t. π_S^{t'}.tr = (U, S, x^U, x^S) and π_S^{t'}.fr = true
70   π_U^{t'}.fr = true
71   (S, s, K) := Qs[U, S, x^U, x^S]
72 else if U ∉ 𝒞 and S ∉ 𝒞
73   π_U^t.fr := true
74   ∀pw, z s.t. (U, S, x^U, x^S, pw, z) ∈ Q
75     (p_i, ..., p_ℓ) := pw
76     for i ∈ [ℓ]
77       z_i' := u_i · g_{p_i}^{-1} ⋆ x_i^S
78     z' := (z_1', ..., z_ℓ')
79     if z = z'
80       Qbad := Qbad ∪ {(U, S, x^U, x^S, pw, z)}
81   K ←$ 𝒦
82   Qs[U, S, x^U, x^S] := (U, u, K)
83 else
84   π_U^t.fr := false
85   (p_i, ..., p_ℓ) := pwUS
86   for i ∈ [ℓ]
87     z_i := u_i · g_{p_i}^{-1} ⋆ x_i^S
88   z := (z_1, ..., z_ℓ)
89   K := H[U, S, x^U, x^S, pwUS, z]
90 π_U^t := (u, (U, S, x^U, x^S, K), true)
91 return true

H(U, S, x^U, x^S, pw, z)
92 if Q[U, S, x^U, x^S, pw, z] = K ≠⊥ return K
93 if (U, S, x^U, x^S) ∈ Qs
94   (p_1, ..., p_ℓ) := pw
95   if Qs[U, S, x^U, x^S] = (U, u, K)
96     for i ∈ [ℓ]
97       z_i' := u_i · g_{p_i}^{-1} ⋆ x_i^S
98     z' := (z_1', ..., z_ℓ')
99   if Qs[U, S, x^U, x^S] = (S, s, K)
100     for i ∈ [ℓ]
101       z_i' := s_i · g_{p_i}^{-1} ⋆ x_i^U
102     z' := (z_1', ..., z_ℓ')
103   if z = z'
104     ifU ∈ 𝒞 and S ∈ 𝒞 and pw = pwUS: return K
105   ifU ∉ 𝒞 and S ∉ 𝒞
106     Qbad := Qbad ∪ {U, S, x^U, x^S, pw, z}
107 Q[U, S, x^U, x^S, pw, z] ←$ 𝒦
108 return Q[U, S, x^U, x^S, pw, z]

H2(U, S, root, pw)
109 if Qσ[U, S, root, pw] = σ ≠⊥ return σ
110 if U ∈ 𝒞 and S ∈ 𝒞 and pw = pwUS
111   σ := Shuffle(⊥, H(U, S, root, pw))
112   Qσ[U, S, root, pw] := σ
113   return σ
114 Qσ[U, S, root, pw] ←$ 𝒫
115 return Qσ[U, S, root, pw]
```

Fig. 6. Games G_6 for the proof of Theorem 1. $\mathcal{A}$ can access to oracles $\mathcal{O}$ as in Fig. 5 and H_2. REVEAL, TEST are defined as in Fig. 3. EXECUTE is defined as in Fig. 5.

$\mathcal{B}_2^{\{\text{GA-DDH}_{x_j}(w,\cdot,\cdot)\}_{j\in\{0,1\}}}(x_0, x_1, w)$

```
01  (C, Q, Q_s, Q_bad, Q_σ) := (∅, ∅, ∅, ∅, ∅)
02  (bad_corr, bad_pw) := (false, false)
03  α ←$ {0,1}
04  α' ← A^O(x_0, x_1)
05  for U ∈ U \ C and S ∈ S \ C
06      pw_US ←$ PW
07  if ∃pw, pw', (U, S, x^U, x^S, z, z')
        s.t. (U, S, x^U, x^S, pw, z) ∈ Q_bad
        and (U, S, x^U, x^S, pw', z') ∈ Q_bad
08      (p_1, ..., p_ℓ) := pw
09      (b_1, ..., b_ℓ) := pw'
10      Find first index i such that p_i ≠ b_i
11      W.l.o.g. let p_i = 0, b_i = 1
12      if Q_s[U, S, x^U, x^S] = (U, u, K)
13          Stop with (x_i^S, u_i^{-1} ⋆ z_i)
14      if Q_s[U, S, x^U, x^S] = (S, s, K)
15          Stop with (x_i^U, s_i^{-1} ⋆ z_i)
```

SENDINIT(U, t, S)

```
16  if π_U^t ≠⊥ return ⊥
17  u := (u_1, ..., u_ℓ) ←$ G^ℓ
18  x^U := (x_1^U, ..., x_ℓ^U) := (u_1 ⋆ w, ..., u_ℓ ⋆ w)
19  root^U := GetRoot(x^U)
20  σ = H_2(U, S, root^U, pw)
21  x_σ^U = F_σ(x^U)
22  π_U^t := (u, (U, S, x^U, ⊥), ⊥, ⊥)
23  return (U, x_σ^U)
```

SENDRESP(S, t, U, x_σ^U)

```
24  if π_S^t ≠⊥ return ⊥
25  s := (s_1, ..., s_ℓ) ←$ G^ℓ
26  x^S := (x_1^S, ..., x_ℓ^S) := (s_1 ⋆ w, ..., s_ℓ ⋆ w)
27  root^S := GetRoot(x^S)
28  σ = H_2(U, S, root^S, pw)
29  x_σ^S = F_σ(x^S)
30  root^U := GetRoot(x_σ^U)
31  σ = H_2(U, S, root^U, pw)
32  x^U = F_σ^{-1}(x_σ^U)
33  if ∃P ∈ U ∪ S, t' s.t. π_P^{t'}.tr = (U, S, x^U, x^S)
34      return ⊥
35  if U ∉ C and S ∉ C
36      π_S^t.fr := true
37      if ∀pw, z s.t. (U, S, x^U, x^S, pw, z) ∈ Q
38          (p_1, ..., p_ℓ) := pw
39          if GA-DDH_{x_{p_i}}(w, x_i^U, s_i^{-1} ⋆ z_i) = 1 ∀i ∈ [ℓ]
40              Q_bad := Q_bad ∪ {(U, S, x^U, x^S, pw, z)}
41      K ←$ K
42      Q_s[U, S, x^U, x^S] := (S, s, K)
43  else
44      π_S^t.fr := false
45      (p_1, ..., p_ℓ) := pw_US
46      if ∃z s.t. (U, S, x^U, x^S, pw_US, z) ∈ Q
          and GA-DDH_{x_{p_i}}(w, x_i^U, s_i^{-1} ⋆ z_i) = 1 ∀i ∈ [ℓ]
47          K := Q[U, S, x^U, x^S, pw_US, z]
48      else
49          K ←$ K
50          Q[U, S, x^U, x^S, pw_US, (s, 0)] := K
51  π_S^t := (s, (U, S, x^U, x^S), K, true)
```

```
52  return (S, x_σ^S)
```

SENDTERM(U, t, S, x_σ^S)

```
53  if π_U^t ≠ (u, (U, S, x^U, ⊥), ⊥, ⊥) return ⊥
54  root^S := GetRoot(x_σ^S))
55  σ = H_2(U, S, root^S, pw)
56  x^S = F_σ^{-1}(x_σ^S)
57  if ∃P ∈ U, t' s.t. π_P^{t'}.tr = (U, S, x^U, x^S)
58      return ⊥
59  if ∃t' s.t. π_S^{t'}.tr = (U, S, x^U, x^S)
        and π_S^{t'}.fr = true
60      π_U^{t'}.fr = true
61      (S, s, K) := Q_s[U, S, x^U, x^S]
62  else if U ∉ C and S ∉ C
63      π_U^t.fr = true
64      ∀pw, z s.t. (U, S, x^U, x^S, pw, z) ∈ Q
65          (p_1, ..., p_ℓ) := pw
66          if GA-DDH_{x_{p_i}}(w, x_i^S, u_i^{-1} ⋆ z_i) = 1 ∀i ∈ [ℓ]
67              Q_bad := Q_bad ∪ {(U, S, x^U, x^S, pw, z)}
68      K ←$ K
69      Q_s[U, S, x^U, x^S] := (U, u, K)
70  else
71      π_U^t.fr := false
72      (p_1, ..., p_ℓ) := pw_US
73      if ∃z s.t. (U, S, x^U, x^S, pw_US, z) ∈ Q
          and GA-DDH_{x_{p_i}}(w, x_i^U, s_i^{-1} ⋆ z_i) = 1 ∀i ∈ [ℓ]
74          K := Q[U, S, x^U, x^S, pw_US, z]
75      else
76          K ←$ K
77          Q[U, S, x^U, x^S, pw_US, (u, 0)] := K
78  π_U^t := (u, (U, S, x^U, x^S), K, true)
79  return true
```

H(U, S, x^U, x^S, pw, z)

```
80  if Q[U, S, x^U, x^S, pw, z] = K ≠⊥
81      return K
82  if (U, S, x^U, x^S) ∈ Q_s
83      (p_1, ..., p_ℓ) := pw
84      if Q_s[U, S, x^U, x^S] = (U, u, K)
85          if GA-DDH_{x_{p_i}}(w, x_i^S, u_i^{-1} ⋆ z_i) = 1 ∀i ∈ [ℓ]
86              if U ∉ C and S ∉ C
87                  Q_bad := Q_bad ∪ {(U, S, x^U, x^S, pw, z)}
88              if U ∈ C and S ∈ C and pw = pw_US
89                  return K
90      if Q_s[U, S, x^U, x^S] = (S, s, K)
91          if GA-DDH_{x_{p_i}}(w, x_i^U, s_i^{-1} ⋆ z_i) = 1 ∀i ∈ [ℓ]
92              if U ∉ C and S ∉ C
93                  Q_bad := Q_bad ∪ {(U, S, x^U, x^S, pw, z)}
94              if U ∈ C and S ∈ C and pw = pw_US
95                  return K
96  if ∃u s.t. (U, S, x^U, x^S, pw, (u, 0)) ∈ Q
97      (p_1, ..., p_ℓ) := pw
98      if GA-DDH_{x_{p_i}}(w, x_i^S, u_i^{-1} ⋆ z_i) = 1 ∀i ∈ [ℓ]
99          return Q[U, S, x^U, x^S, pw, (u, 0)]
100 else if ∃s s.t. (U, S, x^U, x^S, pw, (s, 0)) ∈ Q
101     (p_1, ..., p_ℓ) := pw
102     if GA-DDH_{x_{p_i}}(w, x_i^U, s_i^{-1} ⋆ z_i) = 1 ∀i ∈ [ℓ]
103         return Q[U, S, x^U, x^S, pw, (s, 0)]
104 Q[U, S, x^U, x^S, pw, z] ←$ K
105 return Q[U, S, x^U, x^S, pw, z]
```

Fig. 7. Adversary $\mathcal{B}_2$ against Sim-GA-StCDH for the proof of Theorem 1. $\mathcal{A}$ can access to oracles $\mathcal{O}$ as in Fig. 6. REVEAL, TEST are defined as in Fig. 3. EXECUTE is defined as in Fig. 5. CORRUPT, H_2 is defined as in Fig. 6.

References

1. Abdalla, M., Eisenhofer, T., Kiltz, E., Kunzweiler, S., Riepel, D.: Password-authenticated key exchange from group actions. In: Annual International Cryptology Conference. pp. 699–728. Springer (2022)
2. Abdalla, M., Eisenhofer, T., Kiltz, E., Kunzweiler, S., Riepel, D.: Password-authenticated key exchange from group actions. Cryptology ePrint Archive, Paper 2022/770 (2022), https://eprint.iacr.org/2022/770, https://eprint.iacr.org/2022/770
3. Abdalla, M., Fouque, P.A., Pointcheval, D.: Password-based authenticated key exchange in the three-party setting. In: Public Key Cryptography-PKC 2005: 8th International Workshop on Theory and Practice in Public Key Cryptography, Les Diablerets, Switzerland, January 23-26, 2005. Proceedings 8. pp. 65–84. Springer (2005)
4. Abdalla, M., Pointcheval, D.: Simple password-based encrypted key exchange protocols. In: Topics in Cryptology–CT-RSA 2005: The Cryptographers' Track at the RSA Conference 2005, San Francisco, CA, USA, February 14-18, 2005. Proceedings. pp. 191–208. Springer (2005)
5. Alamati, N., De Feo, L., Montgomery, H., Patranabis, S.: Cryptographic group actions and applications. In: Advances in Cryptology–ASIACRYPT 2020: 26th International Conference on the Theory and Application of Cryptology and Information Security, Daejeon, South Korea, December 7–11, 2020, Proceedings, Part II 26. pp. 411–439. Springer (2020)
6. Bellare, M., Pointcheval, D., Rogaway, P.: Authenticated key exchange secure against dictionary attacks. In: International Conference on the Theory and Applications of Cryptographic Techniques, pp. 139–155. Springer (2000)
7. Bellovin, S.M., Merritt, M.: Encrypted key exchange: Password-based protocols secure against dictionary attacks (1992)
8. Castryck, W., Decru, T.: An efficient key recovery attack on sidh. In: Annual International Conference on the Theory and Applications of Cryptographic Techniques. pp. 423–447. Springer (2023)
9. Castryck, W., Lange, T., Martindale, C., Panny, L., Renes, J.: Csidh: an efficient post-quantum commutative group action. In: Advances in Cryptology–ASIACRYPT 2018: 24th International Conference on the Theory and Application of Cryptology and Information Security, Brisbane, QLD, Australia, December 2–6, 2018, Proceedings, Part III 24. pp. 395–427. Springer (2018)
10. Childs, A., Jao, D., Soukharev, V.: Constructing elliptic curve isogenies in quantum subexponential time. J. Math. Cryptol. 8(1), 1–29 (2014)
11. Couveignes, J.M.: Hard homogeneous spaces. Cryptology ePrint Archive (2006)
12. Haase, B., Labrique, B.: Aucpace: Efficient verifier-based pake protocol tailored for the iiot. Cryptology ePrint Archive (2018)
13. Hao, F., van Oorschot, P.C.: Sok: Password-authenticated key exchange–theory, practice, standardization and real-world lessons. In: Proceedings of the 2022 ACM on Asia Conference on Computer and Communications Security, pp. 697–711 (2022)
14. Hao, F., Ryan, P.Y.: Password authenticated key exchange by juggling. In: Security Protocols XVI: 16th International Workshop, Cambridge, UK, April 16-18, 2008. Revised Selected Papers 16. pp. 159–171. Springer (2011)
15. Ishibashi, R., Yoneyama, K.: Compact password authenticated key exchange from group actions. In: Australasian Conference on Information Security and Privacy, pp. 220–247. Springer (2023)

16. Jablon, D.P.: Strong password-only authenticated key exchange. ACM SIGCOMM Comput. Commun. Rev. **26**(5), 5–26 (1996)
17. Jarecki, S., Krawczyk, H., Xu, J.: Opaque: an asymmetric pake protocol secure against pre-computation attacks. In: Advances in Cryptology–EUROCRYPT 2018: 37th Annual International Conference on the Theory and Applications of Cryptographic Techniques, Tel Aviv, Israel, April 29-May 3, 2018 Proceedings, Part III 37. pp. 456–486. Springer (2018)
18. Knuth, D.E.: The art of Computer Programming, vol. 3. Pearson Education (1997)
19. Rostovtsev, A., Stolbunov, A.: Public-key cryptosystem based on isogenies. Cryptology ePrint Archive (2006)

A New Construction of Leakage-Resilient Identity-Based Encryption Scheme

Zirui Qiao[1,2], Ran Xu[1], Yonghui Lu[3(✉)], Yanwei Zhou[1(✉)], and Bo Yang[1]

[1] School of Computer Science, Shaanxi Normal University, Xi'an 710119, China
zyw@snnu.edu.cn
[2] School of Cyberspace Security, Xi'an University of Posts and Telecommunications, Xi'an 710121, China
[3] School of International Studies, Shaanxi Normal University, Xi'an 710119, China
lyhui008@snnu.edu.cn

Abstract. Although a large number of provably secure cryptographic primitives have been proposed in the literature, many of these schemes might be broken in practice because of various leakage attacks. Therefore, the leakage resilience property should be considered in designing these primitives. However, in identity-based cryptography, most of the existing leakage-resilient identity-based encryption (IBE) schemes suffer some limitations: they either resist the leakage attacks in the selective identity security model or achieve the chosen-ciphertext attack (CCA) security based on a non-static assumption. To further solve the above problems, in this paper, an IBE scheme with adaptive leakage-resilient chosen-plaintext attacks (CPA) security is proposed, and its security is rigorously proved in the random oracle model under a classic static assumption, e.g., decisional bilinear Diffie-Hellman (DBDH) assumption. In addition, the leakage-resilient CCA security can be obtained from the above CPA secure IBE scheme. That is, a generic method created leakage-resilient CCA secure public-key encryption is proposed, and the leakage-resilient CCA secure IBE scheme can also be created. Therefore, we propose a noval method to create leakage-resilient IBE scheme with CCA security from static complexity assumption.

Keywords: Identity-based encryption · Leakage resilience · Chosen-plaintext attacks · Chosen-ciphertext attacks

1 Introduction

In the traditional security definitions, e.g. security against chosen-plaintext attacks (CPA) and security against chosen-ciphertext attacks (CCA), the probabilistic polynomial time (PPT) adversary is restricted to access only the public input/output of the cryptography primitive, and she is assumed not to obtain any other information, such as the internal state. However, in the real implementation of these primitives, some information about the internal state might be

Z. Xia and J. Chen (Eds.): ISPEC 2024, LNCS 15053, pp. 133–150, 2024.
https://doi.org/10.1007/978-981-97-9053-1_8

leaked through various leakage attacks. Therefore, many of these existing cryptography primitives are unable to keep their claimed security when a certain amount of additional information regarding the internal state has been leaked. To address this issue, leakage-resilient cryptography has attracted great attention recently, and some schemes have been proposed, such as, the leakage-resilient public-key encryption (PKE) schemes [1–4], the leakage-resilient identity-based encryption (IBE) schemes [5–9], the leakage-resilient ring signature schemes [10], the leakage-resilient certificateless public-key encryption (CL-PKE) schemes [11], the leakage-resilient certificate-based encryption (CBE) schemes [12–14], the leakage-resilient attribute-based encryption (ABE) schemes [15, 16], etc.

Over the past few years, several cryptography schemes [17] with leakage resilience have been proposed. In identity-based cryptography, the previous leakage-resilient IBE schemes [5, 18, 19] either achieve CCA security in the selective-identity model, or can only satisfy CPA security. Moreover, some constructions of IBE with leakage resilience [6, 20] need to rely on a non-static assumption (e.g., q-type assumption) to achieve the adaptive CCA security. In this work, we will investigate leakage-resilient IBE schemes with adaptive CCA security under the simple static complexity assumption, e.g. decisional bilinear Diffie-Hellman (DBDH) assumption. That is, a novel method that created the leakage-resilient IBE scheme from the static assumption is proposed.

1.1 Related Works

The CPA and CCA security of IBE schemes is defined via two games performed by an adversary and a simulator, respectively. In the CPA security game, key generation queries for any identity other than the challenge identity can be submitted, and the adversary can obtain the corresponding private keys from the simulator. In the CCA security game, in addition to performing key generation queries, the adversary can submit decryption queries for arbitrary pairs of ciphertext and identity, except the challenge identity and challenge ciphertext pair. Especially, in the leakage setting, a certain amount of leaked information regarding the private key of any identity, including the challenge identity, can be obtained by the adversary through an additional leakage query. In which, if an efficiently computable hash function was submitted, the adversary can obtain a hash value on the private key of the user.

For the previous leakage-resilient IBE schemes [5, 6, 18–20], some schemes [6, 20] were created based on a non-static security assumption, and only obtained the selective identity security. Although the corresponding IBE schemes created in [18, 19] can resist leakage attacks, they only achieve CPA security. In addition, several leakage-resilient IBE systems [5, 18, 19, 21] created over the composite order bilinear groups can only achieve CPA security. However, the leakage-resilient CCA security of the IBE scheme proposed in [22] is proved in the selective-identity security model, and the adaptive CCA security is achieved in [23] based on the q-type assumption.

In addition, a leakage-resilient IBE scheme with CCA security was proposed in [24], which can resist bounded leakage attacks. However, the above method is not a direct construction of the IBE scheme, which is a leakage-resilient identity-based hybrid encryption (IB-HE) scheme. That is, the above construction is created by combining an identity-based key encapsulation mechanism (IB-KEM) with any CCA-secure symmetric-key encryption scheme. Thus, in [24], the author focuses on the design of CCA-secure leakage-resilient IB-KEM, and an instantiation of IB-KEM was proposed under the external 1-linear assumption (XDH assumption). In [25], a wicked IBE scheme resilient to continual auxiliary-inputs leakage is proposed. The scheme is proven by the subgroup decision assumption in composite-order bilinear groups and the Goldreich-Levin theorem. This leads to lower efficiency.

In this paper, we design a practical leakage-resilient IBE scheme in prime-order groups under the simple complexity assumption. As an initial goal, we focus on designing a leakage-resilient IBE scheme in the random oracle model, and the CCA security of the proposed scheme is proved based on the DBDH assumption. The adaptive CCA security in the standard model is left in future research. Furthermore, bounded leakage resilience is a basic security property of the cryptography scheme which will be studied in this work, and continuous leakage resilience can be achieved by performing an additional key update algorithm.

1.2 Our Contributions

To resist the leakage attacks and obtain adaptive CPA security from simple complexity assumption, we first present a basic leakage-resilient IBE scheme with CPA security in prime-order groups under the classic DBDH assumption. Based on this basic scheme, we develop a leakage-resilient CCA secure IBE scheme, and its security also can be proved under the DBDH assumption. Compared with the previous leakage-resilient IBE schemes [6,20,22–24], our proposed scheme enjoys the following advantages:

(1) Our construction is a leakage-resilient IBE scheme with adaptive CPA security created from the prime-order groups under the simple complexity assumption.
(2) Our construct has multi-key leakage resilience, that is, our construct not only can resist the leakage attacks on the private key of the user, but also can provide the leakage-resilient property for the master secret key.

The corresponding construction proposed in [24] is the first leakage-resilient CCA secure IBE scheme using a simple assumption (not q-type assumption). More precisely, it is an identity-based hybrid encryption scheme with leakage resilience. However, our proposed scheme is a direct construction of a leakage-resilient IBE scheme, and the corresponding CPA security is proved in the random oracle model from a classic static assumption. In other words, a novel method to construct a leakage-resilient CPA secure IBE scheme is proposed in this paper.

In [26], Boneh et al. proposed a method used to create CCA secure IBE scheme from an IBE scheme with CPA security (called BCHK transition).

According to the above BCHK transition [26], leakage-resilient CCA security can be obtained. That is, based on the strong one-time signature scheme, a generic method created leakage-resilient PKE scheme with CCA security will be proposed from an IBE scheme with leakage-resilient CPA security. Especially, the generic construction of a leakage-resilient CCA secure IBE scheme is designed from an IBE scheme with leakage-resilient CPA security.

2   Preliminaries

In this section, the basic knowledge used in our construction will be reviewed, such as bilinear groups, DBDH assumption, randomness extractor, etc.

2.1   Notations

Let $s \leftarrow_R S$ be the operation of picking an element s uniformly at random from S, and $y \leftarrow \mathcal{A}(x)$ be the operation of running $\mathcal{A}$ with input x and assigning y as the result. For the security parameter $\kappa \in \mathbb{N}$, we use $\mathsf{negl}(\kappa)$ to denote the set of all functions that are negligible in κ.

2.2   Bilinear Groups

Consider two multiplicative cyclic groups G and G_T of prime order p and let g be a generator of G. The mapping $e : G \times G \to G_T$ is an admissible bilinear pairing if and only if the following properties are satisfied:

- Bilinear. $e(P^m, Q^n) = e(P, Q)^{mn}$.
- Non-degeneracy. $e(g, g) \neq 1_{G_T}$.
- Computable. $e(P, Q)$ can be computed efficiently.

Where $P, Q \in G$, $m, n \leftarrow_R \mathbb{Z}_p^*$ and 1_{G_T} is a generator of G_T.

2.3   Complexity Assumption

Definition 1 (DBDH Assumption). *Given* $\mathbb{G} = (p, G, G_T, e(\cdot, \cdot), g) \leftarrow \mathcal{G}(1^\kappa)$ *and* $T = (g^x, g^y, g^z)$, *where* $x, y, z \leftarrow_R \mathbb{Z}_p^*$. *The challenger flips a fair binary coin* $v \leftarrow_R \{0, 1\}$, *and outputs the tuple* $(\mathbb{G}, T, T_1 = e(g, g)^{xyz})$ *if* $v = 1$. *Otherwise, the challenger outputs the tuple* $(\mathbb{G}, T, T_0)$, *where* $T_0 \leftarrow_R G_T$, *i.e.*, $T_0 = e(g, g)^{xyz^*}$, $z^* \leftarrow_R \mathbb{Z}_p^*$ *and* $z^* \neq z$. *Finally, the adversary outputs a guess* v' *of the random value* v.

The advantage of an adversary $\mathcal{S}$ *in solving DBDH problem is defined as*

$$\mathsf{Adv}_{\mathcal{S}}^{\mathrm{DBDH}}(\kappa) = |\Pr[\mathcal{S}(\mathbb{G}, T, T_1) = 0] - \Pr[\mathcal{S}(\mathbb{G}, T, T_0) = 0]|.$$

We say that the DBDH assumption holds if for all PPT adversaries $\mathcal{S}$, *we have*

$$\mathsf{Adv}_{\mathcal{S}}^{\mathrm{DBDH}}(\kappa) \leq \mathsf{negl}(\kappa).$$

2.4 Statistical Distance, Min-Entropy and Average Conditional Min-Entropy

The statistical distance of two random variables X and Y over a finite domain Ω is defined as

$$\mathsf{SD}(X, Y) = \frac{1}{2} \sum_{w \in \Omega} |\Pr[X = w] - \Pr[Y = w]|.$$

The min-entropy of a random variable X is defined as

$$H_\infty(X) = -\log(max_x \Pr[X = x]),$$

which represents the best chance of guessing X by an unbounded adversary. In addition, average conditional min-entropy captures the hardness to guess X on average, given some additional information Z (possibly related to X), and it is denoted by

$$\widetilde{H}_\infty(X|Z) = -\log(\mathbf{E}_{z \leftarrow Z}[2^{-H_\infty(X|Z=z)}]).$$

By the definition of $\widetilde{H}_\infty(X|Z)$, for any PPT adversary $\mathcal{A}$, we obtain

$$\begin{aligned}
\Pr(\mathcal{A}(Z) = A) &= \mathbf{E}_z[\Pr(\mathcal{A}(Z) = X)] \\
&\leq \mathbf{E}_z[2^{-H_\infty(X|Z=z)}] \\
&= 2^{-\widetilde{H}_\infty(X|Z)}.
\end{aligned}$$

Lemma 1. *[27] Let M, N and Q be random variables, if Q has at most 2^l possible values, then we have*

$$\widetilde{H}_\infty(M|(N, Q)) \geq \widetilde{H}_\infty(M|N) - l.$$

2.5 Extractor

Definition 2 (Randomness Extractor). *For all pairs of random variables (X, Y) such that $X \in \{0, 1\}^{l_n}$ and $\widetilde{H}_\infty(X|Y) \geq k$, if an efficient computable function $\mathsf{Ext} : \{0, 1\}^{l_n} \times \{0, 1\}^{l_t} \to \{0, 1\}^{l_m}$ is an average-case (k, ε)-strong randomness extractor, then we have*

$$\mathsf{SD}((\mathsf{Ext}(X, S), S, Y), (U_m, S, Y)) \leq \varepsilon,$$

where $S \leftarrow_R \{0, 1\}^{l_t}$ and $U_m \leftarrow_R \{0, 1\}^{l_m}$.

Lemma 2 (Leftover Hash Lemma). *[27] Let $\mathcal{H}_S = \{H_S : \mathcal{X} \to \mathcal{Y}\}_{S \in \mathcal{S}}$ be a family of universal hash functions. Let U_y is a uniform distribution over $\mathcal{Y}$. For two random variables $X \leftarrow_R \mathcal{X}$ and C, it holds that*

$$\mathsf{SD}((H_S(X), S), (U_y, S)) \leq \frac{1}{2}\sqrt{2^{-H_\infty(X)}|\mathcal{Y}|},$$

$$\mathsf{SD}((H_S(X), S, C), (U_y, S, C)) \leq \frac{1}{2}\sqrt{2^{-\widetilde{H}_\infty(X|C)}|\mathcal{Y}|}.$$

Definition 3 (Universal Hash Function). *A family of functions* $\mathcal{H}_{\mathcal{I}} = \{H_i : \mathcal{X} \to \mathcal{Y}\}$ *is universal if*

$$\Pr_{i \leftarrow \mathcal{I}}[H_i(x_1) = H_i(x_2)] \leq \frac{1}{|\mathcal{Y}|}$$

for all distinct $x_1 \neq x_2 \in \mathcal{X}$.

Example 1. [4] The family of functions $\{H_{k_1,k_2,\cdots,k_l} : \mathbb{Z}_p^{l+1} \to \mathbb{Z}_p\}_{k_i \in \mathbb{Z}_p, i=1,\cdots,l}$ is universal, where

$$H_{k_1,k_2,\cdots,k_l}(x_0, x_1, \cdots, x_l) = x_0 + k_1 x_1 + \cdots + k_l x_l.$$

All operations are in the prime field $\mathbb{F}_p$.

Example 2. [4] Let G be a multiplicative group of prime order p, and $g \in G, g \neq 1$. The family of functions $\{H_{k_1,k_2,\cdots,k_l} : G^{l+1} \to G\}_{k_i \in \mathbb{Z}_p, i=1,\cdots,l}$ is universal, where

$$H_{k_1,k_2,\cdots,k_l}(g_0, g_1, \cdots, g_l) = g_0 g_1^{k_1} \cdots g_l^{k_l}.$$

Lemma 3 (Generalized Leftover Hash Lemma). *[27] Let* X, Y *be random variables such that* $X \leftarrow_R \{0,1\}^{l_n}$ *and* $\widetilde{H}_\infty(X|Y) \geq k$. *Let* $\mathcal{H}_S = \{H_S : \{0,1\}^{l_n} \to \{0,1\}^{l_m}\}$ *be a family of universal hash functions. Then, for* $S \leftarrow_R S$ *and* $U_m \leftarrow_R \{0,1\}^{l_m}$, *we can obtain*

$$SD((Y, S, H_S(X)), (Y, S, U_m)) \leq \varepsilon$$

as long as $l_m \leq k - 2\log(1/\varepsilon)$.

Definition 4 (Two-source Extractor). *For any two random variables* $A \in \{0,1\}^{l_n}$ *and* $B \in \{0,1\}^{l_t}$ *such that* $H_\infty(A) \geq l_n$ *and* $H_\infty(B) \geq l_t$, *if*

$$SD(SD)(\mathsf{Ext}_2(A, B), U) \leq \varepsilon,$$

then, the function $\mathsf{Ext}_2 : \{0,1\}^{l_n} \times \{0,1\}^{l_t} \to \{0,1\}^{l_m}$ *is called a* (l_n, l_t, ε)-*two-source extractor, where* $U \leftarrow_R \{0,1\}^{l_m}$ *and* ε *is negligible in the security parameter* κ.

We have to stress that, for a (l_n, l_t, ε)-two-source extractor $\mathsf{Ext}_2 : \{0,1\}^{l_n} \times \{0,1\}^{l_t} \to \{0,1\}^{l_m}$, if the leakage parameter $\lambda \leq l_n + l_t - l_m - \omega(\log \kappa)$, then the output of the two-source extractor Ext_2 is indistinguishable from the uniform random value over $\{0,1\}^{l_m}$.

2.6   Difference Lemma

Lemma 4 (Difference Lemma). *[28] For the events* $\mathcal{F}_1$, $\mathcal{F}_2$ *and* $\mathcal{E}$ *defined over some probability distribution, if* $\Pr[\mathcal{F}_1|\neg\mathcal{E}] = \Pr[\mathcal{F}_2|\neg\mathcal{E}]$, *then, we have*

$$|\Pr[\mathcal{F}_1] - \Pr[\mathcal{F}_2]| \leq \Pr[\mathcal{E}].$$

3   Identity-Based Encryption

The development of identity-based cryptography which is introduced by Shamir [29] has been highly motivated, in which, the public key is an arbitrary public string such as an email address or a telephone number. The corresponding private key can only be generated by a Private Key Generator (PKG) which has knowledge of a master secret key.

3.1   Definition

Similar to previous works [6,20,29,30], an IBE scheme with the identity space $\mathcal{ID}$ and the message space $\mathcal{M}$ consists of four algorithms: Setup, KeyGen, Enc and Dec. These algorithms are described as follows:

- $(Params, S_{msk}) \leftarrow$ Setup(1^κ). The setup algorithm takes a security parameter κ as input, and outputs public parameters $Params$ and master secret key msk, where $Params$ is a common input of the following algorithms.
- $SK_{id} \leftarrow$ KeyGen(S_{msk}, id). The key generation algorithm takes S_{msk} and an identity $id \in \mathcal{ID}$ as input, and generates the private key SK_{id} for the identity id.
- $C \leftarrow$ Enc(id, M). On input a message $M \in \mathcal{M}$ and an identity id, the encryption algorithm Enc outputs the corresponding ciphertext C.
- $M/\perp \leftarrow$ Dec(SK_{id}, C). The recipient with identity id decrypts the ciphertext C by using decryption algorithm Dec, with the ciphertext C and her private key SK_{id} as input, and outputs the corresponding message M or a special symbol $\perp$, where $\perp$ denotes the inputted ciphertext is invalid.

3.2   Leakage-Resilient Security Model

Leakage Oracle. In the leakage-resilient security model, the adversary's leakage attacks can be modeled by giving the adversary access to a leakage oracle.

Definition 5 (Leakage Oracle). *A leakage oracle $\mathcal{O}_{SK_{id}}^{\lambda,\kappa}()$ is parameterized by a leakage parameter λ, a security parameter κ and a private key SK_{id} of user id. A query to the leakage oracle $\mathcal{O}_{SK_{id}}^{\lambda,\kappa}()$ consists of an efficient computable leakage function $f_i : \{0,1\}^* \to \{0,1\}^{\lambda_i}$. If $\sum_{j=1}^i \lambda_j \leq \lambda$, then the leakage oracle $\mathcal{O}_{SK_{id}}^{\lambda,\kappa}()$ computes $f_i(SK_{id})$, and outputs it to the adversary. Otherwise, $\mathcal{O}_{SK_{id}}^{\lambda,\kappa}()$ responds with the dummy value $\perp$.*

Leakage-resilient CPA Security. For an IBE scheme $\Pi = (\mathsf{Setup}, \mathsf{KeyGen}, \mathsf{Enc}, \mathsf{Dec})$, the security notion of leakage-resilient chosen-plaintext attacks (LR-CPA) security is performed by the following game between an adversary $\mathcal{A}$ and a simulator $\mathcal{S}$. The message exchange is described as follows:

- **Setup.** $\mathcal{S}$ runs $(Params, S_{msk}) \leftarrow \mathsf{Setup}(1^\kappa)$, and sends $Params$ to $\mathcal{A}$ while keeps msk as a secret.
- **Test Stage 1.** In this stage, $\mathcal{A}$ can make the following two kinds of queries. These queries may be made adaptively, i.e., each query may depend on the answers of the previous queries.
  (1) **Key Generation Queries.** On input an identity $id \in \mathcal{ID}$, $\mathcal{S}$ runs $SK_{id} \leftarrow \mathsf{KeyGen}(msk, id)$, and replies SK_{id} as the private key of identity id. We have to stress that, in the leakage and decryption queries, the corresponding private key can be created with the same method as in the key generation queries.
  (2) **Leakage Queries.** On input an identity id and an efficient computable leakage function $f_i : \{0,1\}^* \rightarrow \{0,1\}^{\lambda_i}$, if $\sum_{j=1}^{i} f_j(SK_{id}) \leq \lambda$, then $\mathcal{S}$ returns the corresponding leakage $f_i(SK_{id})$ to the adversary $\mathcal{A}$, where $SK_{id} \leftarrow \mathsf{KeyGen}(msk, id)$. Otherwise, an invalid answer $\perp$ will be outputted.
- **Challenge.** Once $\mathcal{A}$ decides that Test Stage 1 is over it outputs two equal length messages $M_0, M_1 \in \mathcal{M}$ and a challenge identity $id^* \in \mathcal{ID}$, which never appeared in a key generation query and appeared in the leakage queries with at most λ bits leakage. $\mathcal{S}$ chooses a bit $b \leftarrow_R \{0,1\}$, and produces $C_b^* \leftarrow \mathsf{Enc}(id^*, M_b)$, and then sends C_b^* as the challenge ciphertext to $\mathcal{A}$.
- **Test Stage 2.** This stage is similar to Test Stage 1, with the restriction that neither key generation queries on id^* nor leakage queries on any identity are allowed to make.
- **Output.** Finally, $\mathcal{A}$ outputs $b' \in \{0,1\}$ as the guess of random bit b picked by $\mathcal{S}$. We say that $\mathcal{A}$ wins if $b' = b$.

The advantage $\mathsf{Adv}_{IBE,\mathcal{A}}^{LR\text{-}CCA}(\kappa, \lambda)$ of adversary $\mathcal{A}$ in attacking an IBE scheme is defined as

$$\mathsf{Adv}_{IBE,\mathcal{A}}^{LR\text{-}CPA}(\kappa, \lambda) = \left| \Pr[\mathcal{A} \ wins] - \frac{1}{2} \right|.$$

Definition 6 (LR-CPA Security). *If for any PPT adversary $\mathcal{A}$ the advantage $\mathsf{Adv}_{\Pi,\mathcal{A}}^{LR\text{-}CPA}(\kappa, \lambda)$ in above game is negligible, then the corresponding IBE scheme Π is secure against leakage-resilient chosen-plaintext attacks. Also, the total amount of leakage on the same private key has to be bounded by the leakage parameter λ.*

4 Leakage-Resilient CPA Secure IBE Scheme

For easy reading, in this section, a CPA secure IBE scheme with leakage resiliece is constructed in the random oracle model.

4.1 Constructions

Our basic IBE scheme $\Pi = (\mathsf{Setup}, \mathsf{KeyGen}, \mathsf{Enc}, \mathsf{Dec})$ is described in the following.

(1) **Setup.** For the security parameter κ, the setup algorithm $(Params, S_{msk}) \leftarrow \mathsf{Setup}(1^\kappa)$ is designed as follows:

- Compute
$$\mathbb{G} = (p, G, G_T, e(\cdot, \cdot), g) \leftarrow \mathcal{G}(1^\kappa).$$

- Let $\mathsf{Ext} : G_T \times \{0,1\}^{l_t} \rightarrow \{0,1\}^{l_m}$ be an average case $(\log p - \lambda, \varepsilon)$-strong randomness extractor, where λ is the leakage parameter and ε is negligible in κ. Let $H_1 : \mathbb{Z}_p^* \rightarrow G$ be a collision resistant one-way hash function.

- Choose $\alpha \leftarrow_R \mathbb{Z}_p^*$ and $u, h, g_3 \leftarrow_R G$, and then compute
$$g_1 = g^\alpha.$$

- Let the master secret key be $msk = \alpha$, and set the public parameters
$$Params = <\mathbb{G}, g_1, g_3, u, h, \mathsf{Ext}, H_1>$$

as the common input of the following algorithms. In addition, let the identity space be $\mathcal{ID} = \mathbb{Z}_p^*$ and the message space be $\mathcal{M} = \{0,1\}^{l_m}$.

(2) **Key Generation.** For an identity $id \in \mathcal{ID}$, the key generation algorithm $SK_{id} \leftarrow \mathsf{KeyGen}(id, msk)$ is described as follows:

- Choose $r, t \leftarrow_R \mathbb{Z}_p^*$, and compute
$$sk_{id,1} = (dg_3^{-t})^\alpha (u^{id}h)^r, \quad sk_{id,2} = g^{-r} \quad \text{and} \quad sk_{id,3} = t,$$

where $d = H_1(id)$.

- Output the private key $SK_{id} = (sk_{id,1}, sk_{id,2}, sk_{id,3})$ associated with the identity id.

(3) **Encryption.** For an identity $id \in \mathcal{ID}$ and a message $M \in \mathcal{M}$, the encryption algorithm $C \leftarrow \mathsf{Enc}(id, M)$ is described as follows:

- Choose $s \leftarrow_R \mathbb{Z}_p^*$ and $S \leftarrow_R \{0,1\}^{l_t}$, and then compute
$$c_1 = g^s, \quad c_2 = (u^{id}h)^s, \quad c_3 = e(g_1, g_3)^s \quad \text{and} \quad c_4 = \mathsf{Ext}(e(d, g_1)^s, S) \oplus M,$$

where $d = H_1(id)$.

- Set $C = (c_1, c_2, c_3, c_4, S)$ as the ciphertext of M, and output the ciphertext C.

(4) **Decryption.** For a ciphertext $C = (c_1, c_2, c_3, c_4, S)$, the decryption algorithm $M \leftarrow \mathsf{Dec}(SK_{id}, C)$ is described as follows:
Compute

$$\omega = e(c_1, sk_{id,1})e(c_2, sk_{id,2})c_3^{sk_{id,3}},$$

and output $M = \mathsf{Ext}(\omega, S) \oplus c_4$ as the plaintext of C.

The correctness of our construction $\Pi = (\mathsf{Setup}, \mathsf{KeyGen}, \mathsf{Enc}, \mathsf{Dec})$ can be obtained from the following equation.

$$\begin{aligned}
\omega &= e(c_1, sk_{id,1})e(c_2, sk_{id,2})c_3^{sk_{id,3}} \\
&= e(g^s, (dg_3^{-t})^\alpha(u^{id}h)^r)e((u^{id}h)^s, g^{-r})e(g_1, g_3)^{st} \\
&= e(d, g_1)^s.
\end{aligned}$$

4.2 Proof of Security

Now, we will prove the leakage-resilient CPA security of our IBE scheme $\Pi = (\mathsf{Setup}, \mathsf{KeyGen}, \mathsf{Enc}, \mathsf{Dec})$. That is, in the random oracle model, the bounded leakage-resilient CPA security of our construction will be proved based on the DBDH assumption.

Theorem 1. *In the random oracle model, under the hardness of classic DBDH assumption, for any leakage parameter $\lambda \leq 3\log p - l_m - \omega(\log \kappa)$ (where l_m is the length of message), our construction Π is a leakage-resilient CPA secure IBE scheme.*

Proof. If there exists an adversary $\mathcal{A}$ who can break the leakage-resilient CPA security of our construction Π with non-negligible advantage $\mathsf{Adv}_{\mathcal{A},\Pi}^{\mathrm{LR\text{-}CPA}}(\lambda, \kappa)$, then, we can build an adversary $\mathcal{S}$ who can solve the DBDH assumption with obvious advantage $\mathsf{Adv}_{\mathcal{S}}^{\mathrm{DBDH}}(\kappa)$, where

$$\mathsf{Adv}_{\mathcal{S}}^{\mathrm{DBDH}}(\kappa) \geq \mathsf{Adv}_{\mathcal{A},\Pi}^{\mathrm{LR\text{-}CCA}}(\lambda, \kappa) - \frac{1}{p}.$$

In the beginning, $\mathcal{S}$ receives the challenge tuple $\mathcal{T}_v = (g, g^x, g^y, g^z, T_v)$ and public parameters $\mathbb{G} = (p, G, G_T, e(\cdot, \cdot), g)$ from the challenger of DBDH assumption, where $T_1 = e(g, g)^{xyz}$, $T_0 = e(g, g)^{xyz^*}$, $v \leftarrow_R \{0, 1\}$ and $x, y, z, z^* \leftarrow_R \mathbb{Z}_p^*$. The interactive game between $\mathcal{A}$ and $\mathcal{S}$ is described as follows:

– **Setup.** For setup, $\mathcal{S}$ chooses $e, f \leftarrow_R \mathbb{Z}_p^*$, and then computes

$$u = g^e, \quad h = g^f, \quad g_1 = g^x \quad \text{and} \quad g_3 = g^y,$$

where, $\mathcal{S}$ implicitly sets the master secret key $msk = x$.
Finally, $\mathcal{S}$ sends

$$Params = <\mathbb{G}, g_1, g_3, u, h, \mathsf{Ext}, H_1>$$

as the system public parameter to $\mathcal{A}$, where $\mathsf{Ext} : G_T \times \{0,1\}^{l_t} \to \{0,1\}^{l_m}$ is an average case strong randomness extractor, and $H_1 : \mathbb{Z}_p^* \to G$ is a random oracle.

We have to stress that, for an identity $id \in \mathcal{ID}$, the corresponding hash query H_1 submitted by $\mathcal{A}$ is responded through the following operations:

- $\mathcal{S}$ picks $\delta, t \leftarrow_R \mathbb{Z}_p^*$ and responds with $d = g^\delta g_3^t$. Also, a list $\mathcal{L}_H = <$ $id, d, \delta, t >$ is maintained by $\mathcal{S}$ to keep track answers of the corresponding H_1 queries, and this list is initially empty.

Specially, the elements x and y are picked independently and uniformly at random by the challenger of DBDH assumption from $\mathbb{Z}_p^*$, which makes the variables $Params$ properly distributed in particular. Hence, the view of $\mathcal{A}$ is completely legitimate when $\mathcal{S}$ responds with $Params$, i.e., the distribution of the public parameter is identical to the real construction.

Test Stage 1. In this stage, the following two kinds of queries are adaptively submitted by $\mathcal{A}$, and the query is depend on the previous queries, as well as the corresponding responses. We have to stress that, in the random oracle, $\mathcal{S}$ can created the complete private key for any identity, including challenge identity.

- **Key Generation Queries.** For the key generation query on the identity $id \in \mathcal{ID}$ picked by $\mathcal{A}$, the corresponding private key $SK_{id} = (sk_{id,1}, sk_{id,2}, sk_{id,3})$ can be created by performing the following operations (in this query, any identity can be submitted by $\mathcal{A}$ to obtain the corresponding private key, even the challenge identity.):

  * Compute $d = H_1(id)$. In fact, a hash query H_1 for the identity id is performed, and obtain the corresponding hash value $d = g^\delta g_3^t$ from the random oracle H_1. Also, in this query, a tuple $< id, d, \delta, t >$ will be added into $\mathcal{L}_H$, where $\delta, t \leftarrow_R \mathbb{Z}_p^*$. That is, $\mathcal{S}$ can obtain the corresponding random values δ and t from the list $\mathcal{L}_H$ with id as an index.

  * Choose $r \leftarrow_R \mathbb{Z}_p^*$, and compute

  $$sk_{id,1} = g_1^\delta(u^{id}h)^r, \quad sk_{id,2} = g^{-r} \text{ and } sk_{id,3} = t.$$

  We have to stress that, $SK_{id} = (sk_{id,1}, sk_{id,2}, sk_{id,3})$ is a valid private key of identity id, since

  $$(dg_3^{-t})^\alpha(u^{id}h)^r = (g^\delta g_3^t g_3^{-t})^\alpha(u^{id}h)^r = g_1^\delta(u^{id}h)^r.$$

- **Leakage Queries.** An efficient computable leakage function and an identity $id \in \mathcal{ID}$ will be submitted by $\mathcal{A}$, $\mathcal{S}$ returns the corresponding leakage $f_i(SK_{id})$ by performing an leakage oracle $\mathcal{O}_{SK_{id}}^{\lambda,\kappa}(\cdot)$ with the private key SK_{id} as the input, where SK_{id} can be created with the same method as the key generation queries. Specially, the total length of $f_i(SK_{id})$ which all returned from $\mathcal{O}_{SK_{id}}^{\lambda,\kappa}(\cdot)$ on the same SK_{id} must be less than the leakage parameter λ. Otherwise, an invalid answer $\perp$ will be outputted.

- **Challenge.** In the challenge stage, a challenge identity $id^* \in \mathcal{ID}$ and two equal length messages $M_0, M_1 \in \mathcal{M}$ are submitted by $\mathcal{A}$, where id^* never appeared in the key generation query and appeared in the leakage queries with at most λ bits leakage. Then, the corresponding challenge ciphertext $C^* = (c_1^*, c_2^*, c_3^*, c_4^*, S^*)$ can be created by $\mathcal{S}$ through the following operations:
  - Choose $r^* \leftarrow_R \mathbb{Z}_p^*$, and compute

$$sk_{id^*,1} = g_1^{\delta^*}(u^{id^*}h)^{r^*}, \quad sk_{id^*,2} = g^{-r^*} \quad \text{and} \quad sk_{id^*,3} = t^*,$$

  where δ^* and t^* can be obtained from the list $\mathcal{L}_H$. Set $SK_{id^*} = (sk_{id^*,1}, sk_{id^*,2}, sk_{id^*,3})$ as the private key of the challenge identity id^*.
  - Set $c_1^* = g^z$, and compute

$$c_2^* = (g^z)^{eid^*+f} \quad \text{and} \quad c_3^* = T_v,$$

  where $(g^z)^{eid^*+f} = (u^{id^*}h)^z$.
  - Choose $S^* \leftarrow_R \{0,1\}^{l_t}$ and $b \leftarrow_R \{0,1\}$, and then compute

$$\omega^* = e(c_1^*, sk_{id^*,1})e(c_2^*, sk_{id^*,2})c_3^{*sk_{id^*,3}} \quad \text{and} \quad c_4^* = \text{Ext}(\omega^*, S) \oplus M_b.$$

- **Test Stage 2.** In this stage, $\mathcal{S}$ calculates the complete private key of any identity (except the challenge identity id^*) as he did in Test Stage 1. Also, the leakage queries for any identity are unallowed.
- **Output.** Eventually, $\mathcal{A}$ outputs a guess b', then $\mathcal{S}$ returns $v' = 1$ if $b' = b$; Otherwise, $\mathcal{S}$ outputs $v' = 0$.

The challenge ciphertext $C_b^* = (c_1^*, c_2^*, c_3^*, c_4^*, S^*)$ is discussed through following two cases:

(1) If $T_v = e(g,g)^{xyz}$, i.e., $v = 1$, it is easy to see that the element c_3^* is valid, because $T_v = e(g,g)^{xyz} = e(g_1, g_3)^z$. Then, the challenge ciphertext C_b^* is a valid encryption ciphertext for id^* and M_b under random value $z \leftarrow_R \mathbb{Z}_p^*$. So, C_b^* is a valid, appropriately-distributed challenge ciphertext.

(2) If $T_v = e(g,g)^{xyz^*}$, i.e., $v = 0$, then (c_1^*, c_2^*, c_3^*) is a uniformly random and independent element of $G \times G \times G_T$. In this case, the inequalities $\log_g c_1^* \neq \log_{e(g_1,g_3)} c_3^*$ hold with probability $1 - \frac{1}{p}$. When this inequality holds, the value of

$$e(c_1^*, sk_{id^*,1})e(c_2^*, sk_{id^*,2})c_3^{*sk_{id^*,3}}$$
$$= e(c_1^*, g_1^{\delta^*}(u^{id^*}h)^{r^*}))e(c_2^*, g^{-r^*})c_3^{*t^*}$$
$$= e(g^z, (dg_3^{-t^*})^x(u^{id^*}h)^{r^*})e((u^{id^*}h)^z, g^{-r^*})e(g_1, g_3)^{z^*t^*}$$
$$= e(d, g_1)^z e(g_1, g_3)^{t^*(z^*-z)}$$

is uniformly random and independent from $\mathcal{A}$'s view, since z, z^* and t^* are uniformly random and independent from $\mathcal{A}$'s view. Thus, c_4^* is uniformly random and independent, and C_b^* can impart no information regarding the bit b.

To sum up, it is easy to see that the simulation is perfect, and C_b^* is a valid encryption ciphertext of the message M_b if $v = 1$, and we have

$$\left| \Pr[\mathcal{S}(\mathcal{T}_1) = 1] - \frac{1}{2} \right| \geq \mathsf{Adv}_{\mathcal{A},\Pi}^{\mathrm{LR\text{-}CCA}}(\lambda, \kappa)$$

On the other hand, if $v = 0$, then C_b^* is a uniformly random message in the adversary $\mathcal{A}$'s view, and gives no information about the random value b picked by $\mathcal{S}$, except the probability $\frac{1}{p}$, and we obtain

$$\left| \Pr[\mathcal{S}(\mathcal{T}_0) = 1] - \frac{1}{2} \right| \leq \frac{1}{p}.$$

Then, we can obtain that if there exists an adversary $\mathcal{A}$ who can break the leakage-resilient CPA security of our construction Π with a non-negligible advantage $\mathsf{Adv}_{\mathcal{A},\Pi}^{\mathrm{LR\text{-}CPA}}(\lambda, \kappa)$, then, we can build an adversary $\mathcal{S}$ who can solve the hardness of DBDH assumption with an obvious advantage

$$\mathsf{Adv}_{\mathcal{S}}^{\mathrm{DBDH}}(\kappa) = |\Pr[\mathcal{S}(\mathcal{T}_1) = 1] - \Pr[\mathcal{S}(\mathcal{T}_0) = 1]|$$

$$\geq \mathsf{Adv}_{\mathcal{A},\Pi}^{\mathrm{LR\text{-}CCA}}(\lambda, \kappa) - \frac{1}{p}.$$

In the leakage setting, any adversary cannot obtain information on the SK_{id^*} from the public parameter $Params$, the challenge plaintexts M_0, M_1, and the challenge identity id^*. Besides the knowledge previously, the adversary also obtains at most λ-bit leakage Leak on the private key SK_{id^*}. Also, in this construction, any leakage on the private key SK_{id^*} of challenge identity id^* cannot be captured by an adversary, thus, by Lemma 1, we have

$$H_\infty(sk_{id^*,1}, sk_{id^*,2}, sk_{id^*,3} | C_b^*, \mathsf{Leak})$$

$$= H_\infty(sk_{id^*,1}, sk_{id^*,2}, sk_{id^*,3} | \mathsf{Leak})$$

$$\geq 3 \log p - \lambda.$$

In practice, given public parameters $Params$, challenge identity id^*, challenge plaintexts M_0, M_1, challenge ciphertext C_b^*, and λ bits leakage on the private key SK_{id^*}, the average min-entropy of the inputted variable

$$e(c_1^*, sk_{id^*,1}) e(c_2^*, sk_{id^*,2}) c_3^{* sk_{id^*,3}}$$

of randomness extractor is at least $3 \log p - \lambda$. Furthermore, $\mathsf{Ext} : G_T \times \{0,1\}^{l_t} \rightarrow \{0,1\}^{l_m}$ is an average case $(\log p - \lambda, \varepsilon)$ strong randomness extractor. Therefore, the average min-entropy of $e(c_1^*, sk_{id^*,1}) e(c_2^*, sk_{id^*,2}) c_3^{* sk_{id^*,3}}$ satisfies the input requirement of randomness extractor $\mathsf{Ext} : G_T \times \{0,1\}^{l_t} \rightarrow \{0,1\}^{l_m}$. By Lemma 3, we have $l_m \leq 3 \log p - \lambda - 2 \log(\frac{1}{\varepsilon})$. Taking into account that ϵ is negligible in the security parameter κ, i.e., $2 \log(\frac{1}{\epsilon}) = \omega(\log \kappa)$, thus, we have

$$\lambda \leq 3 \log p - l_m - \omega(\log \kappa).$$

As discussed above, for any leakage parameter $\lambda \leq 3 \log p - l_m - \omega(\log \kappa)$, our construction Π is a leakage-resilient CPA secure IBE scheme.

5   Leakage-Resilient CCA Security

For an encryption scheme, CCA security is practical and important property. Thus, for the cryptography system, leakage-resilient CCA security is a strong and very useful property. In this section, we will show a generic method created leakage-resilient CCA security from leakage-resilient IBE scheme. Firstly, we improved the above leakage-resilient IBE scheme to resist the leakage attack against the master private key. After that, a novel way of constructing leakage-resilient CCA security is proposed based on the improved leakage-resilient IBE scheme.

5.1   Improved Leakage-Resilient IBE Scheme

In this subsection, the leakage-resilient IBE scheme will be improved, in which, the leakage resilience of the master secret key can be obtained by using a two source extractor $\mathsf{Ext}_2 : \{0,1\}^{l_n} \times \{0,1\}^{l_t} \to Z_q^*$. Except for the setup algorithm Setup', other algorithms KeyGen', Enc' and Dec' are consistent with the original leakage-resilient IBE scheme. Thus, the setup algorithm $(Params, S_{msk}) \leftarrow \mathsf{Setup}'(1^\kappa)$ is described in the following.

– Compute
$$\mathbb{G} = (p, G, G_T, e(\cdot, \cdot), g) \leftarrow \mathcal{G}(1^\kappa).$$

– Let $\mathsf{Ext} : G_T \times \{0,1\}^{l_t} \to \{0,1\}^{l_m}$ be an average case $(\log p - \lambda, \varepsilon_1)$-strong randomness extractor, and $\mathsf{Ext}_2 : \{0,1\}^{l_n} \times \{0,1\}^{l_t} \to Z_q^*$ be a $(l_n, l_t, \varepsilon_2)$-two source extractor, where λ is the leakage parameter, ε_1 and ε_2 are negligible in κ.

– Let $H_1 : \mathbb{Z}_p^* \to G$ be a collision resistant one-way hash function.

– Choose $a \leftarrow_R \{0,1\}^{l_n}$ and $b \leftarrow_R \{0,1\}^{l_t}$, and then compute

$$\alpha = \mathsf{Ext}_2(a, b) \quad \text{and} \quad g_1 = g^\alpha.$$

– Choose $u, h, g_2 \leftarrow_R G$. Let the master secret key be $msk = \alpha$, and set the public parameters

$$Params =< \mathbb{G}, g_1, g_2, u, h, \mathsf{Ext}, H_1 >$$

as the common input of the following algorithms.

From the security of two source extractor $\mathsf{Ext}_2 : \{0,1\}^{l_n} \times \{0,1\}^{l_t} \to Z_q^*$, the improved IBE scheme $\Pi' = (\mathsf{Setup}', \mathsf{KeyGen}', \mathsf{Enc}', \mathsf{Dec}')$ can resist the leakage of the master security key with the length

$$\lambda \leq l_n + l_t - \log q - \omega(\log \kappa).$$

5.2   Leakage-Resilient PKE Scheme with CCA Security

Let $\Pi' = (\mathsf{Setup}', \mathsf{KeyGen}', \mathsf{Enc}', \mathsf{Dec}')$ be a leakage-resilient IBE scheme with CPA security, also, the corresponding leakage parameter on the master secret key is λ_1.

Now, based on a strong one-time signature scheme $\mathsf{Sig}=(\mathcal{G}, \mathsf{Sign}, \mathsf{Vrfy})$, we can construct a leakage-resilient CCA secure PKE scheme $\Pi = (\mathsf{KeyGen}, \mathsf{Enc}, \mathsf{Dec})$ from our improved IBE scheme $\Pi' = (\mathsf{Setup}', \mathsf{KeyGen}', \mathsf{Enc}', \mathsf{Dec}')$. The construction of proceeds as follows:

- $(pk, sk) \leftarrow \mathsf{KeyGen}(1^\kappa)$.
  Outputs the public key $pk = Params$ and the secret key $sk = S_{msk}$, where
  $$(Params, S_{msk}) \leftarrow \mathsf{Setup}'(1^\kappa).$$

- $C \leftarrow \mathsf{Enc}(pk, M)$.
  Runs
  $$(vk, vsk) \leftarrow \mathcal{G}(1^\kappa).$$

  Computes
  $$c \leftarrow \mathsf{Enc}'(vk, M) \quad \text{and} \quad \delta \leftarrow \mathsf{Sign}(vsk, c).$$

  Output the final ciphertext (vk, c, δ).
- $M/\bot \leftarrow \mathsf{Dec}(sk, C)$.
  The receiver first checks whether
  $$\mathsf{Vrfy}(vk, C, \delta) \stackrel{?}{=} 1.$$

  If not, the receiver simply outputs $\bot$. Otherwise, the receiver computes
  $$sk_{id} \leftarrow \mathsf{KeyGen}'(vk, sk) \quad \text{and} \quad M \leftarrow \mathsf{Dec}'(sk_{id}, c).$$

  Outputs the corresponding plaintext M.

Theorem 2. *If $\Pi' = (\mathsf{Setup}', \mathsf{KeyGen}', \mathsf{Enc}', \mathsf{Dec}')$ is a leakage-resilient IBE scheme with master secret key leakage parameter λ, and $\mathsf{Sig} = (\mathcal{G}, \mathsf{Sign}, \mathsf{Vrfy})$ is a strong one-time signature scheme, then, for any λ, $\Pi = (\mathsf{KeyGen}, \mathsf{Enc}, \mathsf{Dec})$ is a public-key encryption scheme with leakage-resilient CCA security.*

The proof of Theorem 2 is similar to that of Theorem 1 of [26]. See [26] for details.

5.3   Leakage-Resilient IBE Scheme with CCA Security

Let $\Pi' = (\mathsf{Setup}', \mathsf{KeyGen}', \mathsf{Enc}', \mathsf{Dec}')$ be a leakage-resilient IBE scheme with CPA security, also, the corresponding leakage parameter on the private key of user is λ_2. Similarly, we can construct a leakage-resilient CCA secure IBE scheme $\Pi_{new} = (\mathsf{Setup}_{new}, \mathsf{KeyGen}_{new}, \mathsf{Enc}_{new}, \mathsf{Dec}_{new})$ from our improved IBE scheme Π'. The construction of proceeds as follows:

- $(Params, msk) \leftarrow \mathsf{Setup}_{new}(1^\kappa)$.
  Output $(Params, msk)$, where

$$(Params, msk) \leftarrow \mathsf{KeyGen}'(1^\kappa).$$

- $sk_{id} \leftarrow \mathsf{KeyGen}_{new}(id, msk)$.
  Output sk_{id}, where
$$sk_{id} \leftarrow \mathsf{KeyGen}'(1^\kappa).$$

- $C \leftarrow \mathsf{Enc}_{new}(id, M)$.
  Runs
$$(vk, vsk) \leftarrow \mathcal{G}(1^\kappa).$$

Computes

$$c \leftarrow \mathsf{Enc}'(id, vk \oplus M) \quad \text{and} \quad \delta \leftarrow \mathsf{Sign}(vsk, c).$$

Output the final ciphertext (vk, c, δ).
- $M/\bot \leftarrow \mathsf{Dec}_{new}(sk_{id}, C)$.
  The receiver first checks whether

$$\mathsf{Vrfy}(vk, C, \delta) \overset{?}{=} 1.$$

If not, the receiver simply outputs $\bot$. Otherwise, the receiver computes

$$\tilde{M} \leftarrow \mathsf{Dec}(sk_{id}, c) \quad \text{and} \quad M = \tilde{M} \oplus vk.$$

Outputs the corresponding plaintext M.

Theorem 3. *If $\Pi' = (\mathsf{Setup}', \mathsf{KeyGen}', \mathsf{Enc}', \mathsf{Dec}')$ is a leakage-resilient IBE scheme with private key leakage parameter λ_2, and $\mathsf{Sig} = (\mathcal{G}, \mathsf{Sign}, \mathsf{Vrfy})$ is a strong one-time signature scheme, then, for any λ_2, $\Pi_{new} = (\mathsf{Setup}_{new}, \mathsf{KeyGen}_{new}, \mathsf{Enc}_{new}, \mathsf{Dec}_{new})$ is an IBE scheme with leakage-resilient CCA security.*

Similarly, Theorem 3 can be proved using a method similar to that in [26].

6   Conclusions

In this work, we design a leakage-resilient CPA secure IBE scheme based on the classic DBDH assumption, in which, the leakage resilience for multi-key is achieved. That is, our construct not only can resist the leakage attacks on the private key of user, but also can provide the leakage-resilient property for the master secret key. In addition, a leakage-resilient PKE scheme with CCA security will be proposed from our leakage-resilient IBE scheme.

As an initial goal, we achieve the bounded leakage-resilient CPA security of IBE scheme in the random oracle model. After that, we will study the direct construct of IBE scheme, which has leakage-resilient CCA security.

References

1. Tseng, Y.-M., Tsai, T.-T., Huang, S.-S., Ho, T.-C.: Leakage-resilient anonymous heterogeneous multi-receiver hybrid encryption in heterogeneous public-key system settings. IEEE Access **12**, 28155–28168 (2024)
2. Chakraborty, S., Alawatugoda, J., Rangan, C.P.: New approach to practical leakage-resilient public-key cryptography. J. Math. Cryptol. **14**(1), 172–201 (2020)
3. Naor, M., Segev, G.: Public-key cryptosystems resilient to key leakage. In: CRYPTO 2009, CA, USA, August 16-20, 2009, pp. 18–35 (2009)
4. Liu, S., Weng, J., Zhao, Y.: Efficient public key cryptosystem resilient to key leakage chosen ciphertext attacks. In: CT-RSA 2013, San Francisco,CA, USA, February 25-March 1, 2013, pp. 84–100 (2013)
5. Li, J., Guo, Y., Qihong, Yu., Yang, L., Zhang, Y.: Provably secure identity-based encryption resilient to post-challenge continuous auxiliary input leakage. Sec. Commun. Netw. **9**(10), 1016–1024 (2016)
6. Li, J., Teng, M., Zhang, Y., Qihong, Yu.: A leakage-resilient cca-secure identity-based encryption scheme. Comput. J. **59**(7), 1066–1075 (2016)
7. Zhou, Y., Yang, B., Qiao, Z., Xia, Z., Zhang, M., Yi, M.: Leakage-resilient identity-based cryptography from minimal assumptions. Des. Codes Crypt. **91**(11), 3757–3801 (2023)
8. Cai, C., Qin, X., Yuen, T.H., Yiu, S.-M.: Tight leakage-resilient identity-based encryption under multi-challenge setting. In: Suga, Y., Sakurai, K., Ding, X., Sako, K., (eds.) ASIA CCS '22: ACM Asia Conference on Computer and Communications Security, Nagasaki, Japan, 30 May 2022 - 3 June 2022, pp. 42–53. ACM (2022)
9. Zhang, Y., Yang, M., Zheng, D., Zhang, T., Guo, R., Ren, F.: Leakage-resilient hierarchical identity-based encryption with recipient anonymity. Int. J. Found. Comput. Sci. **30**(4), 665–681 (2019)
10. Huang, J., Huang, Q., Susilo, W.: Leakage-resilient ring signature schemes. Theoret. Comput. Sci. **759**, 1–13 (2019)
11. Xiong, H., Yuen, T.H., Zhang, C., Yiu, S.-M., He, Y.J.: Leakage-resilient certificateless public key encryption. In: Chen, K., Xie, Q., Qiu, W., Xu, S., Zhao, Y., (eds.) Proceedings of the first ACM workshop on Asia public-key cryptography, AsiaPKC'13, Hangzhou, China, May 8, 2013, pp. 13–22. ACM (2013)
12. Guo, Y., Li, J., Yang, L., Zhang, Y., Zhang, F.: Provably secure certificate-based encryption with leakage resilience. Theoret. Comput. Sci. **711**, 1–10 (2018)

13. Jui-Di, W., Tseng, Y.-M., Huang, S.-S., Tsai, T.-T.: Leakage-resilient certificate-based key encapsulation scheme resistant to continual leakage. IEEE Open J. Comput. Soc. **1**, 131–144 (2020)
14. Tsai, T.-T., Tseng, Y.-M., Huang, S.-S.: Leakage-resilient anonymous multi-receiver certificate-based key encapsulation scheme. IEEE Access (2023)
15. Wang, Z., Cao, C., Yang, N., Chang, V.: ABE with improved auxiliary input for big data security. J. Comput. Syst. Sci. **89**, 41–50 (2017)
16. Zhang, Y., Ling, Y., Chen, J., Wang, L.: Leakage-resilient attribute-based encryption with attribute-hiding. In: International Conference on Information Security and Cryptology, pp. 113–132. Springer, 2023
17. Li, S., Zhang, F.: Leakage-resilient identity-based encryption scheme. Int. J. Grid Util. Comput. **4**(2/3), 187–196 (2013)
18. Yuen, T.H., Chow, S.S.M., Zhang, Y., Yiu, S.-M.: Identity-based encryption resilient to continual auxiliary leakage. In: Advances in Cryptology - EUROCRYPT 2012, Cambridge, UK, April 15-19, 2012. Proceedings, pp. 117–134 (2012)
19. Lewko, A.B., Rouselakis, Y., Waters, B.: Achieving leakage resilience through dual system encryption. In: TCC 2011, Providence, RI, USA, March 28–30, pp. 70–88 (2011)
20. Sun, S., Gu, D., Liu, S.: Efficient leakage-resilient identity-based encryption with CCA security. In: Pairing-Based Cryptography - Pairing 2013 - 6th International Conference, Beijing, China, November 22-24, 2013, Revised Selected Papers, pp. 149–167 (2013)
21. Sun, S., Dawu, G., Huang, Z.: Fully secure wicked identity-based encryption against key leakage attacks. Comput. J. **58**(10), 2520–2536 (2015)
22. Zhou, Y., Yang, B., Yi, M.: Continuous leakage-resilient identity-based encryption without random oracles. Comput. J. **61**(4), 586–600 (2018)
23. Zhou, Y., Yang, B., Hou, H., Zhang, L., Wang, T., Mingxiao, H.: Continuous leakage-resilient identity-based encryption with tight security. Comput. J. **62**(8), 1092–1105 (2019)
24. Tomita, T., Ogata, W., Kurosawa, K.: Cca-secure leakage-resilient identity-based key-encapsulation from simple (not q -type) assumptions. In: Advances in Information and Computer Security - 14th International Workshop on Security, IWSEC 2019, Tokyo, Japan, August 28-30, 2019, Proceedings, pp. 3–22 (2019)
25. Hou, H., Yang, B., Zhang, M., Zhou, Y., Huang, M.: Fully secure wicked identity-based encryption resilient to continual auxiliary-inputs leakage. J. Inf. Sec. Appl. **53**, 102521 (2020)
26. Boneh, D., Canetti, R., Halevi, S., Katz, J.: Chosen-ciphertext security from identity-based encryption. SIAM J. Comput. **36**(5), 1301–1328 (2007)
27. Dodis, Y., Reyzin, L., Smith, A.D.: Fuzzy extractors: how to generate strong keys from biometrics and other noisy data. In: EUROCRYPT 2004, Interlaken, Switzerland, May 2-6, 2004, pp. 523–540 (2004)
28. Shoup, V.: Sequences of games: a tool for taming complexity in security proofs. IACR Cryptology ePrint Archive **2004**, 332 (2004)
29. Shamir, A.: Identity-based cryptosystems and signature schemes. In: CRYPTO 1984, Santa Barbara, California, USA, August 19-22, 1984, pp. 47–53 (1984)
30. Chow, S.S.M., Dodis, Y., Rouselakis, Y., Waters, B.: Practical leakage-resilient identity-based encryption from simple assumptions. In: CCS 2010, Chicago, Illinois, USA, October 4-8, 2010, pp. 152–161 (2010)

Enhancing Portability in Deep Learning-Based Side-Channel Attacks Against Kyber

Peng Chen[1,2], Chi Cheng[1,2(✉)], Jinnuo Li[1,2], and Tianqing Zhu[3]

[1] School of Computer Science, China University of Geosciences, Wuhan, China
[2] Hubei Key Laboratory of Intelligent Geo-Information Processing, Wuhan, China
chengchizz@gmail.com
[3] Faculty of Data Science, City University of Macau, Macau, Macao

Abstract. Despite extensive research on side-channel attacks (SCAs) against lattice-based Key Encapsulation Mechanisms (KEMs), there has been limited attention to the portability of existing deep-learning-based SCA distinguisher, especially concerning the National Institute of Standards and Technology (NIST) KEM standard Kyber. Our work addresses the portability challenges that stem from the device and measurement variations in SCAs against Kyber. We focus on the plaintext checking oracle-based SCA against Kyber, a prominent method in the field. We propose the Ablated Multiple Leakage Point Model (Ablated-MLPM) approach to optimize deep learning models, enhancing intra-board (same device with different EM probe placement) and inter-board (different devices) portability while mitigating overfitting concerns. Our contributions include the first systematic analysis of portability issues in SCAs against Kyber, highlighting their negative impact on attack efficiency. Real-world implementations are conducted on an STM32F407G board with an ARM Cortex-M4 microcontroller, using code from the well-known open-source pqm4 library. The results demonstrate that our Ablated-MLPM approach achieves more than 99% accuracy in all datasets, significantly enhancing both intra-board and inter-board portability. Furthermore, we introduce a lightweight model, Ablated-MLPM-LW, reducing the training parameters by 79.63% at the cost of requiring more queries.

Keywords: Key Encapsulation Mechanism · Kyber · Side-Channel Attack · Portability

This work was supported by the National Natural Science Foundation of China (NO. 62172374).

1   Introduction

In July 2022, the National Institute of Standards and Technology (NIST) announced the results of the third round of the Post-Quantum Cryptography (PQC) competition [9]. CRYSTALS-Kyber [23] was selected as the candidate for the standardization of both public key encryption algorithms (PKE) and key encapsulation mechanisms (KEM). Kyber is based on the Module Learning With Errors problem, and strikes a balance between security and efficiency, making it one of the most promising lattice-based PKE/KEM candidates in the NIST PQC process [17]. Considering the large-scale practical application and deployment of algorithms in the upcoming PQC migration, NIST encourages further research into the analysis of the security of PQC schemes against side-channel attacks (SCAs) [5,12,14,19,26].

The cryptographic community has shown great interest in the development of SCAs and several new attacks against lattice-based schemes [6,11,16,18,20,22, 33]. In particular, for the plaintext-checking (PC) oracle-based electromagnetic (EM) profiled SCAs. These profiled SCAs can be broadly categorized into two main categories, Template Attacks (TA) [24,25,27,29] implemented by Test Vector Leakage Assessment (TVLA) techniques and deep learning based SCAs (DL-SCA) [8,18,30,31]. TA is a simple, straightforward, and lightweight attack, making them less suitable for more complex real-world scenarios [27,29]. Whereas, DL-SCAs can leverage a wide range of flexible optimization strategies, showing great potential in terms of robustness and scalability [8,18,30,31]. These models have the capability to address the complex challenges encountered in practical attacks. Despite the promising results of DL-SCAs [8,18,30,31], the portability problem remains a bottleneck that limits DL-SCA's practical application. The portability problem in SCA against the well-known symmetric cryptography standard AES has gained significant attention [1,4,7,10,21,28,34,35]. A closely related work is presented in [32], where Wu et al. introduce an ablation-based paradigm to overcome the inter-portability problem. By evaluating the sensitivity and resilience of each layer in a neural network, they succeed in creating a *Multiple Device Model from Single Device*, enabling the profiling model to generalize and learn leakage traces from various devices. Our approach draws inspiration from [32], although our primary focus is on lattice-based cryptography, which differs significantly from AES. Additionally, we address the intra-portability problem in our work.

1.1   Contributions

Our primary objective is to address both intra-portability and inter-portability challenges in SCAs against Kyber. We focus on PC oracle-based SCA, leveraging deep learning approaches to distinguish the EM side-channel leakage patterns. The main contributions of this work are as follows:

1. To the best of our knowledge, we are the first to consider the portability problem of PC oracle-based SCAs on Kyber KEM. We also concretely analyze the

impact of the portability problem on the attack efficiency. We systematically investigate the impact of intra-board and inter-board portability issues on the NIST-recommended platform STM32F407G board with an ARM Cortex-M4 microcontroller. Our results demonstrate that both intra-board and inter-board portability issues negatively affect the performance of existing deep learning models. This directly influences the accuracy of the PC oracle instantiation, resulting in a reduced efficiency of SCA attacks, in some cases, leading to failure.

2. We propose an enhanced method, Ablated Multiple Leakage Point Model (MLPM), to tackle model portability challenges in SCAs against Kyber. Our approach involves leveraging a more comprehensive EM leakage dataset and introducing realistic noise during training to enhance the model's robustness. Moreover, addressing the potential overfitting issue arising from the composite dataset is crucial. To overcome this challenge, we incorporate the ablation paradigm.

3. We apply our proposed Ablated-MLPM approach to optimize the CNN model proposed by Ueno et al. for SCAs against Kyber. Our real-world implementations are conducted on an STM32F407G board with an ARM Cortex-M4 microcontroller, utilizing an optimized Kyber version taken from the well-known open-source pqm4 library. The results demonstrate that our Ablated-MLPM approach achieves more than 99% accuracy in all datasets, significantly enhancing both intra-board and inter-board portability. Furthermore, we introduce a lightweight model, Ablated-MLPM-LW, which further reduces the training parameters by 79.63%, while still performing well in intra-board and inter-board scenarios at the cost of requiring more queries.

2   Background

2.1   PC Oracle Instantiation Through CNN-Based Side-Channel Distinguisher

We assume the adversary can access the clone or target device with elaborated chosen ciphertexts and get the information about the secret key through a side channel.

Algorithm 1 The PC Oracle $\mathcal{O}$

$\diamond$ $\mathcal{O}(\mathbf{ct}, \mathbf{M} := \{\mathbf{m_0}, \mathbf{m_1}\})$:

1: $\mathbf{m}' \leftarrow \mathcal{O}(\mathbf{ct})$
2: **if** $\mathbf{m}' = \mathbf{m_1}$ **then**
3:      **return** 1
4: **else**
5:      **return** 0
6: **end if**

The above process is abstracted as a PC oracle shown in Algorithm 1 and we can see that the key to the attack is to get $\mathbf{m}'$. The relationship between $\mathbf{m}'$ and the secret key could be inferred, thereby enabling a secret key recovery attack. In the following, we will describe how to instantiate the PC oracle through a CNN-based side-channel distinguisher.

We first define the candidate message set $\mathbf{M} := \{\mathbf{m_0}, \mathbf{m_1}\}$, where $\mathbf{m_0}$ is defined such that all $\mathbf{m_0}[i] = 0$ except $\mathbf{m_0}[0] = 0$, and $\mathbf{m_1}[0] = 1$, $\mathbf{m_1}[i] = 0, i \in [1, 255]$ for $\mathbf{m_1}$. Each $\mathbf{ct}$ is elaborated chosen to ensure that the message set $\mathbf{M}$ only consists of $\mathbf{m_0}$ and $\mathbf{m_1}$. Whenever an adversary queries with a chosen ciphertext $\mathbf{ct}$, it triggers a side-channel attack.

Let $\tilde{\mathbf{W}}$ denote the EM waveform collected from the target device. A distinguisher $\mathbf{Dist}_{\mathrm{CNN}}$ is utilized to recognize $\mathbf{m}'$, corresponding to the output of the oracle, as shown below:

$$\mathcal{O}(\mathbf{ct}; \mathbf{M}) = \mathbf{Dist}_{\mathrm{CNN}}(\tilde{\mathbf{W}}) \tag{1}$$

Applying Qin et al.'s encoding technique [22] to find the optimal binary recovery tree, the $\mathbf{sk}$ could be recovered efficiently.

3 Problem Definition: Portability in SCAs Against Kyber

In this section, we investigate the portability problems in SCAs against Kyber. Generally, there are two kinds of portability problems. The first is intra-portability, where the targeted device is the same as the profiling device, and portability problems arise from variations in measurement setups, such as the placement of the EM probe on the microcontroller. The second is inter-portability, which occurs when the targeted device differs from the profiling device, introducing additional portability challenges due to device variance.

3.1 Enviornment Description

The entire measurement setup is illustrated in Fig. 1a. Side-channel leakage refers to the EM waveform captured from the surface of an ARM Cortex-M4 microcontroller integrated into the STM32F407G board. The microcontroller executes an optimized implementation of Kyber-512 obtained from the open-source benchmarking library pqm4 [15]. The deep learning environment leverages CUDA 12.2, cuDNN 8.3, TensorFlow 2.10.1, and Keras 2.10.0 deployed on a PC equipped with an NVIDIA GeForce RTX 3090 GPU and an Intel i9-12900K CPU.

The board is connected to a Picoscope 3203D oscilloscope with a sampling rate of 1GS/s (Giga samples per second). The traces are captured corresponding to Kyber's decryption execution, synchronized with a board-generated trigger. The PC runs the control programs as a host computer which is used to manually adjust the measurement setups. It chooses a well-designed ciphertext as a query and, via Universal Asynchronous Receiver/Transmitter (UART), transmits it to the board and awaits decryption of the ciphertext. Upon receiving the traces

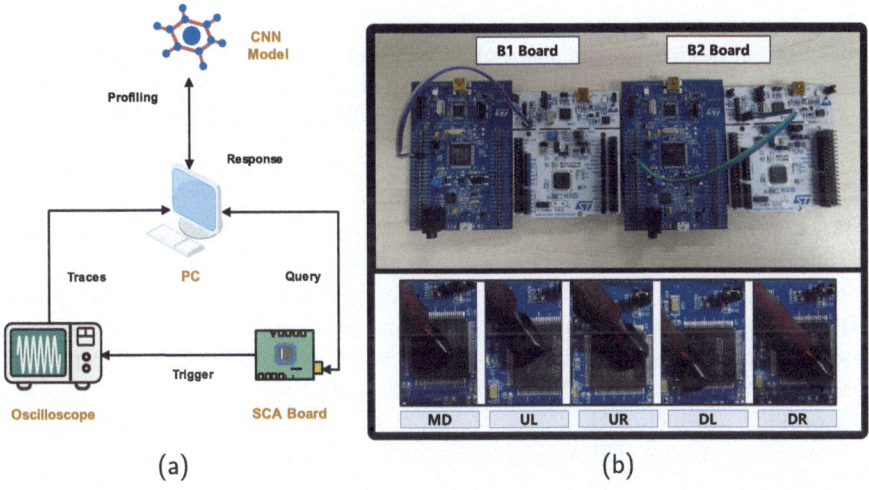

Fig. 1. Overview of deep learning-based SCA and intra-and inter-board difference.

from the oscilloscope during the decryption operation, the software then invokes a CNN-based distinguisher to recognize the EM traces as the response for the decryption query.

3.2 Scenarios Under Consideration

In the following, each dataset is denoted by the format Bx_P, where x represents the ID of the board and P indicates the position of the EM probe. For example, B1_UL represents the dataset measured at the upper left corner of board B1. As shown in Fig. 1, various datasets are collected using four corners and training/testing boards. To highlight the differences in leakages caused by different devices and EM probe placement, we calculate the Normalized Inter-Class Variance (NICV) [2]. NICV can be used to detect relevant leakage points in side-channel traces, and also to compare the quality of side-channel measurements between different datasets. To, be specific, we define

$$NICV = \frac{\sum_{k=1}^{K} n_k (\mu_k - \mu)^2}{\sum_{k=1}^{K} \sum_{x_i \in X_k} (x_i - \mu_k)^2}. \tag{2}$$

Here each x_i is a waveform. There are K classes in the dataset, and the collection of samples in the k-th class is X_k. n_k is the number of samples in the k-th class, μ_k is the mean of the samples in the k-th class, and μ is the mean of all the samples. The NICV value ranges from 0 to 1, reflecting the distinguishability of the features in the dataset. A larger NICV indicates better classification performance of the features.

In our experiments, we consider the portability issues stemming from variances between devices and measurement configurations. To further outline these two distinct sources of portability impediments, we introduce the concepts of intra-board portability and inter-board portability, respectively:

- Same device with different EM probe placement (*Intra-board portability*): In this scenario, to study the impact of measurement locations, we collect leakage datasets from different EM probe placements on the microcontroller of the same device (Device B1). This includes the middle location (B1_MD), four corners (upper left corner B1_UL, upper right corner B1_UR, down-left corner B1_DL, and down-right corner B1_DR), and four randomly selected locations near the middle region (B1-Random). B1_MD_2 is a repeated measurement of B1_MD under identical EM probe placement and code execution conditions, to provide a benchmark dataset for comparison. Although the settings are the same, there are still some differences between B1_MD and B1_MD_2 due to environmental variations during the acquisition process.
- Different devices (*Inter-board portability*): The datasets are collected from different locations on the microcontrollers of different devices. The B2_MD is the waveform dataset collected from the middle area of the microcontroller of Device B2. The B2_Corner datasets include the upper left corner (B2_UL), upper right corner (B2_UR), down-left corner (B2_DL), and down-right corner (B2_DR) of the microcontroller of Device B2, aimed to study the impact of different measurement setups and device variance.

3.3   The Analysis of Portability

Two scenarios are designed to study the impacts of different EM probe placements and devices on the SCAs. For the B1_MD, B1_Corner, B2_MD, and B2_Corner datasets in the above scenarios, we collect 1000 waveforms per dataset, and each waveform contains 10,000 sampling points (features). Among them, 800 waveforms constitute the training dataset, while 200 waveforms are assigned to the validation/test dataset. The B1-Random dataset is obtained from the B1 microcontroller, with probe positions, distances, and orientations randomly selected. This dataset comprises a total of 1,600 waveforms, all designated for testing purposes. Analyzing the model's performance on the mentioned datasets helps us intuitively grasp how the model is influenced by intra-board and inter-board portability. To establish a baseline, we consider the NICV difference between B1_MD and B1_MD_2, accounting for the inevitable discrepancies arising from environmental noise or measurement setups. Subsequent analysis is conducted based on this comparison.

NICV Analysis of Intra-Board Differences Fig. 2 illustrates the NICV values of different datasets (points taken at 1000 intervals). The NICV difference between B1_MD and B2_MD is larger than that between B1_MD and B1_MD_2, but smaller than the difference between B1_MD and B1_Corner. This suggests that the intra-board differences are more significant than inter-board differences.

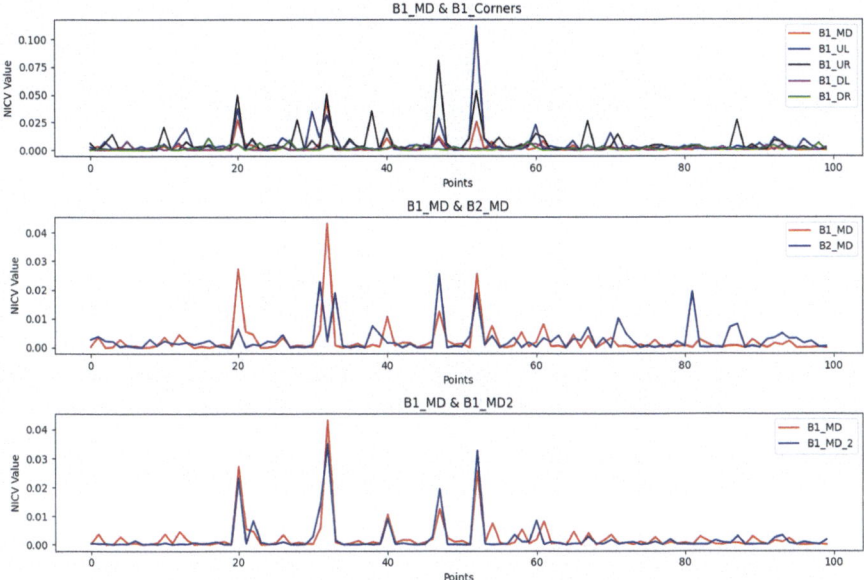

Fig. 2. NICV analysis of intra-board and inter-board difference.

Under certain circumstances, the challenge of portability stemming from different probe placements can overshadow device variance. Notably, datasets like B1_UL and B1_DR exhibit significant NICV variations, presenting a formidable obstacle to achieving high classification accuracy across both datasets. This observation finds further support in the experimental outcomes detailed in subsequent sections.

NICV Analysis of Inter-Board Differences Also depicted in Fig. 2, a notable discrepancy exists in NICV values between B1_MD and B2_MD, whereas the disparity between NICV values for B1_MD and B1_MD_2 is comparatively minor. This observation underscores that the challenges of portability across distinct boards become evident at the dataset level.

Portability Challenges of the CNN Model [31] on Boards B1 & B2 We train the original CNN model [31] on the B1_MD dataset and then test the model on other datasets corresponding to different leakage points over the Cortex-M4 microcontroller. Analyzing the results in Table 1, we observe that the model achieves the highest accuracy on the B1_MD dataset, approaching the reported accuracy of 0.998 in [31]. By comparing the performance of model B1_MD and B2_MD, we observe a decrease in accuracy on the B2_MD dataset, indicating that the inter-board portability issue degrades the model's accuracy. Additionally, when comparing the performance of model B1_MD and B1_Corners, we notice a significant deterioration in accuracy on the four B1_Corner datasets, with some even resulting in failures.

Table 1. Comparison of model [31] performance on B1 & B2 board

	MD	DL	DR	UL	UR	Avg
B1	0.9974	0.5614	0.5126	0.4889	0.7622	0.6645
B2	0.974	0.5367	0.4971	0.4894	0.8113	0.6617

The analysis highlights that, across various measurement setups, the intra-portability issue stemming from diverse leakage points presents a more significant challenge compared to the inter-portability problem arising solely from device differences. This finding aligns with our NICV analysis. Moreover, the examination of Table 1 indicates that existing models struggle with portability challenges, underscoring the necessity and practical significance of our work.

4   Ablation and Multiple Leakage Point Model

4.1   The Main Procedure

In Fig. 3, we illustrate the basic idea of the Ablated-MLPM approach. We first remove the neurons that are significantly disturbed by noise via model structure optimization, and then we extend the data diversity of the training dataset by collecting waveforms from multiple leakage points over the microcontroller surface. We summarize the main steps as follows:

Step 1: Pre-train the original model on the general dataset.

Step 2: Perform ablation and layer assessment procedures on the original model to optimize the model structure. Meanwhile, the measurement setup is updated to extend the general dataset. Specifically, collecting waveforms at the center and corners of the microcontroller surface to construct the MLPM dataset.

Step 3: Based on the ablation analysis, we adopt the extended MLPM datasets to train the ablated model.

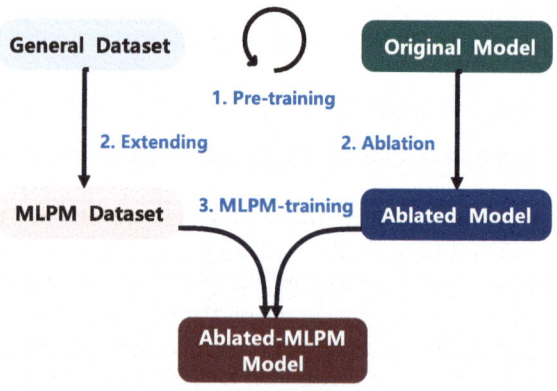

Fig. 3. Our basic idea

The major advantage of our proposed Ablated-MLPM approach is fully utilizing leakage from the entire microcontroller surfaces. By optimizing the model structure, noise-sensitive neurons are removed, enabling the model to overcome additional noise interference when training with larger and more diverse MLPM datasets. In this process, we perform an ablation procedure on each layer of the original model, analyzing the assessment results of ablated layers to obtain an appropriate model for training on the MLPM dataset. As a result, the obtained Ablated-MLPM model is capable of learning more substantial features from the microcontroller surfaces and mitigating overfitting.

In the following, we propose our Ablated-MLPM approach in detail.

4.2   Ablation

Ablation is a model analysis method in deep learning used to remove specific components of a neural network model, such as randomly deleting a fraction of neurons in a particular layer, to assess their impact on model performance.

Algorithm 2 Layer Sensitivity & Resilience Assessment.

1: **procedure** ABLATION (model M, training set $\mathbf{T}_{train}$, test set $\mathbf{T}_{test}$, repeat time σ, ablation rate ρ, noise for training $\mathsf{Noise}(\alpha)$, the model accuracy $\mathbf{Acc}_{\mathcal{O}}$, the new ablated model accuracy $\mathbf{Acc}_{\mathcal{O}_\rho}$, the Re-trained ablated model accuracy $\mathbf{Acc}'_{\mathcal{O}_\rho}$)

2:     $M \leftarrow \mathrm{train}\,(M, \mathbf{T}_{train} + \mathsf{Noise}(\alpha))$

3:     $\mathbf{Acc}_{\mathcal{O}} \leftarrow \mathrm{test}\,(M, \mathbf{T}_{test})$

4:     **for** $i = 1$ to σ **do**

5:        $M_\rho \leftarrow \mathrm{ablate}\,(M, \rho)$

6:        $\mathbf{Acc}_{\mathcal{O}_\rho} \leftarrow \mathrm{test}\,(M, \mathbf{T}_{test})$

7:        $Sens_i = \mathbf{Acc}_{\mathcal{O}} - \mathbf{Acc}_{\mathcal{O}_\rho}$ ▷ Sensitivity

8:        $M'_\rho \leftarrow \mathrm{train}\,(M_\rho, \mathbf{T}_{train} + \mathsf{Noise}(\alpha))$ ▷ Re-training

9:        $\mathbf{Acc}'_{\mathcal{O}_\rho} \leftarrow \mathrm{test}\,(M'_\rho, \mathbf{T}_{test})$

10:       $Res_i = \mathbf{Acc}_{\mathcal{O}} - \mathbf{Acc}'_{\mathcal{O}_\rho}$ ▷ Resilience

11:    **end for**

12: **end procedure**

The algorithm for assessing layer sensitivity and layer resilience is outlined in Algorithm 2.

- Sensitivity: To assess the impact of ablated network layers on overall network performance, and identify potential "critical layers" that substantially influence model outcomes. Modifying such "critical layers" induces greater changes in model predictions, hence these sensitive layers are typically prioritized during model optimization given similar constraints.
- Resilience: To evaluate whether ablated network layers induce permanent degradation in model performance. Layers that lack resilience may continue to negatively impact model accuracy even after re-training. Thus, resilience

for model optimization is a prerequisite for effective model optimization via layer removal. Our analysis identifies layers that can be safely ablated without irrecoverable damage, guiding model optimization.

The sensitivity and resilience of a layer are computed in lines 7 and 10 of the Algorithm 2, and the results are averaged by repeating the measurement σ times. We set σ to 100 to guarantee results reliability.

4.3   MLPM: Multiple Leakage Point Model

Conventional side-channel attacks restrict model training and testing to a localized region, typically the middle of the microcontroller. Based on the NICV analysis in Sect. 3, we observe that there are significant variations in EM leakage, among different leakage points. The fixed-location measurement setup not only overlooks other informative side-channel leakages elsewhere but also impairs the practicality and generalization capability of SCAs, which are critical properties of SCAs. Our proposed MLPM approach addresses this limitation by harnessing the spatial diversity of EM leakage. Specifically, we aggregate EM leakage from multiple leakage points to enhance the robustness and diversity of the training dataset. This allows us to capture more comprehensive EM leakage features on the microcontroller surface, which enhances the portability of the model across the entire microcontroller surface.

4.4   Ablated-MLPM: Ablated Multiple Leakage Point Model

In terms of layer capacity, we define it intuitively, there is redundant capacity, appropriate capacity, fully utilized capacity, and insufficient capacity. As shown in Fig. 4, we demonstrate the specific workflow of the Ablation approach. The terms train, test, and ablate represent training the model on the training dataset, testing the model on the test dataset, and performing ablation with a defined ratio ρ, respectively. The noise parameter α should be chosen to represent noise from portability. In terms of the marginal value m, ablation may lead to a decrease in $\mathbf{Acc}'_{\mathcal{O}_\rho}$. It is possible to set a certain tolerance rate, but in this paper, we set $m = 1$ to simplify the analysis.

The sensitivity and resilience of the ablated models are then evaluated by comparing $Sensi_i$ (Line 7 in Algorithm 2) and $Resi_i$ (Line 10 in Algorithm 2). Models with appropriate capacity are selected and further trained with the MLPM approach to obtain the final Ablated-MLPM optimized model. Through analyzing sensitivity and resilience, our approach identifies layers with redundant capacity (low sensitivity), insufficient capacity (low resilience), or appropriate capacity (high sensitivity and resilience). Layers with appropriate capacity enable full utilization of model capacity when trained on MLPM datasets.

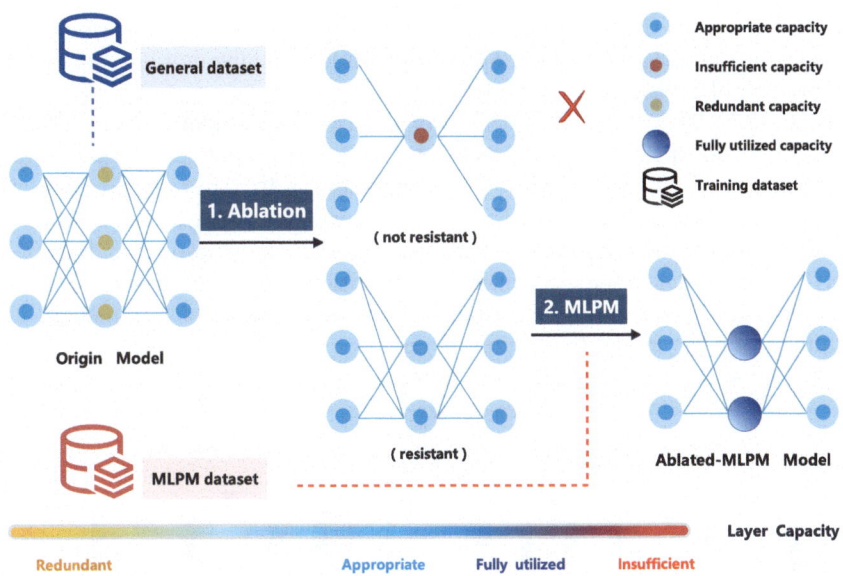

Fig. 4. Ablated-MLPM: ablation with layer assessment & training with multiple leakage point model.

5 Results

5.1 Layer Assessment

The ablation operation is performed on the convolutional layers and fully connected layers of the CNN model, with ablation ratios set to 25%, 50%, 75%, and 90%, respectively. Figure 5 shows the sensitivity and resilience of different layers in the CNN model under various ablation ratios. The ideal candidate layer for ablation should be both sensitive and resilient. When considering layer resilience, the resilience capability of the model varies after ablating different layers. In most cases, the model performance decreases after ablation, but in a few cases like (L2, ratio=0.25), (L4, ratio=0.25), (L3, ratio=0.5), (L7, ratio=0.5/0.9), (L8, ratio=0.5/0.9), the classification accuracy is improved.

– CNN-Origin: The model proposed by Ueno et al. [31] has 251,229 parameters when the input size is 100,000, with a model size of approximately 980.93 KB. The original model contains some layers that are sensitive to noise, which may lead to overfitting problems.
– Ablated-CNN: Based on the layer ablation assessment results, Ablated-CNN optimizes the model as follows: (L2, ratio = 0.25), (L3, ratio = 0.5), (L4, ratio = 0.25), (L7, ratio = 0.5), (L8, ratio = 0.5). After optimization, the model parameters are reduced to 125,724, decreasing 49.95% compared to the original model, and the optimized model size is approximately 490.79

KB. The model utilizes a lower layer ablation rate and thus possesses a certain robustness against noise disturbance while retaining more parameters for more complex classification tasks.

- Ablated-CNN-LW: Based on the layer ablation assessment results, Ablated-CNN-LW optimizes the model as follows: (L2, ratio = 0.25), (L3, ratio = 0.5), (L4, ratio = 0.25), (L7, ratio = 0.9), (L8, ratio = 0.9). After optimization, the model parameters are reduced to 25,604, decreasing 79.63% compared to the Ablated-CNN model, and the optimized model size is approximately 99.76 KB. This model adopts a higher layer ablation ratio and thus has stronger robustness against noise disturbance. However, with fewer parameters, it is difficult for the model to solve more complex classification tasks.

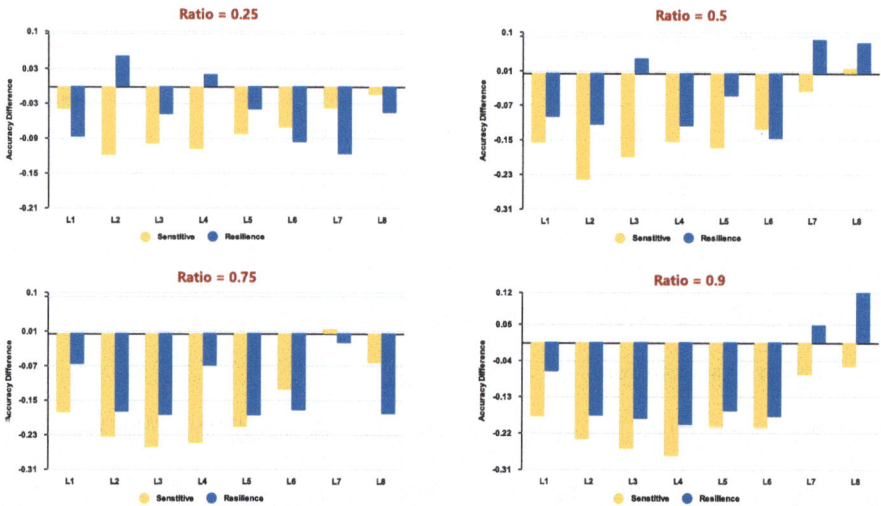

Fig. 5. Layer assessment

5.2   Performance Comparison of Ablated Models

As shown in Tables 1 and 2, CNN-Origin, Ablated-CNN, and Ablated-CNN-LW, trained on B1_MD, achieve good performance with classification accuracy above 99% on B1_MD, satisfying the requirement for a high-accuracy oracle defined in [29]. However, these models exhibit varying degrees of accuracy degradation on B2_MD. Furthermore, the model accuracy on B2_Avg decreases compared to that on B1_Avg, reflecting the impact of the portability issue across the whole microcontroller. These findings validate that inter-board portability issues can detrimentally affect model classification performance, consistent with the conclusions drawn by Bhasin et al. [1].

On the other hand, the models also show different extents of accuracy drops on the B1-Random and B1_Corner datasets. The results indicate that intra-board portability issues negatively impact model classification capabilities. Compared to performance on B2_MD, the accuracy degradation is more significant on B1_Corner. Excluding some outlier data, the three models, especially CNN-Origin, demonstrate highly similar performance at the same leakage points in different devices. All of the models perform poorly on B1_DR, and considering B1_DR has the least significant NICV among all datasets, this implies the EM side channel leakage features differ between the down-right and middle regions. Models trained solely on the MD region dataset have difficulty extracting sufficiently useful features, leading to unsatisfactory performance in the DR area. Among all the results, CNN-Origin has the lowest classification accuracy and highest loss on B1_UL and B2_UL. Given that B1_UL has the most significant NICV of all datasets, this indicates higher noise interference in the data collected from the upper left area of the microcontroller.

5.3 Performance of the Ablated-MLPM Model

When the ablated models, Ablated-CNN-LW, and Ablated-CNN, are trained with the additional B1_Corner datasets in the model training phase, the obtained Ablated-MLPM models are denoted as Ablated-MLPM-LW, and Ablated-MLPM, respectively. By introducing the additional B1_Corner datasets for training, the optimized models can capture a broader range of EM radiation features across the microcontroller during cryptographic operations, rather than being limited to the middle area.

We can see from Table 2 that the classification accuracy of Ablated-MLPM exceeds 99% on all datasets. This result demonstrates that Ablated-MLPM significantly enhances both intra-board portability and inter-board portability. Compared to Ablated-MLPM, Ablated-MLPM-LW has a smaller model parameter size, while achieving a classification accuracy higher than 99% on B1_MD and B2_MD.

In real-world scenarios, the oracle may be inaccurate due to the environment noise or measurement limitations in implementing the PC oracle, such as the inaccuracy in the deep-learning-based SCA distinguisher in [13,31]. For a more reliable full key recovery, a common technique involves majority voting. This method employs multiple rounds of recovery and selects the majority as the final result, thereby implementing a PC oracle with improved accuracy. In Table 2, we employ #**Votes** to represent the total number of votes, and #**ErrCof** denotes the average number of error coefficients in the final recovered secret key. The majority voting aims to reduce #**ErrCof** to a number less than 1.0 over 1000 iterations.

We highlight our contribution by comparing it with previous portability solutions, successfully implementing all approaches listed in Table 3, and applying them to our scenario. We chose the CNN model and applied MDMSD [32] and CDPA [3] methodologies because these schemes are designed for "Single device profiling" scenarios to solve portability issues. Additionally, the performance

Table 2. Comparison of optimized model performance in SCA against Kyber on B1 & B2

			Avg	DL	DR	UL	UR	MD	Random
Acc	Ablated-CNN-LW	B1	0.8038	0.5463	0.5125	0.9987	0.9613	1	0.9997
		B2	0.8466	0.8845	0.4975	0.9989	0.8521	1	/
	Ablated-CNN	B1	0.8026	0.8806	0.5134	0.6195	0.9993	1	0.9697
		B2	0.7193	0.9464	0.4997	0.5953	0.5549	1	/
	Ablated-MLPM-LW	B1	0.98567	0.9998	0.9997	0.9318	0.9996	0.9974	0.9348
		B2	0.97628	0.9933	0.9998	0.9052	0.9887	0.9944	/
	Ablated-MLPM	B1	0.9979	1	0.9916	0.9983	1	0.9998	0.9967
		B2	0.9971	0.9991	0.9917	0.9962	0.9991	0.9995	/
Loss	Ablated-CNN-LW	B1	1.1234	1.5552	3.9669	0.0034	0.0909	0.0005	0.0011
		B2	0.9569	0.3273	4.089	0.0027	0.3641	0.0014	/
	Ablated-CNN	B1	2.6084	0.4796	10.2855	2.2746	0.0021	0.0003	0.0815
		B2	3.0356	0.1538	10.4025	2.6763	1.9452	0.0001	/
	Ablated-MLPM-LW	B1	0.0565	0.0136	0.003	0.1674	0.0436	0.0551	0.1612
		B2	0.07752	0.0607	0.0029	0.2172	0.0439	0.0629	/
	Ablated-MLPM	B1	0.0091	0.0036	0.0255	0.01	0.0019	0.0048	0.013
		B2	0.0115	0.0057	0.0258	0.0115	0.0079	0.0064	/

Table 3. Comparison of previous work and train on B1_MD

	B2_MD	B2_DL	B2_DR	B2_UL	B2_UR	B2_Avg
MDMSD [32]	1	0.8845	0.4975	0.9989	0.8521	0.8466
CDPA [3]	1	1	0.7	0.995	0.8525	0.9095
Our	**0.9995**	**0.9991**	**0.9917**	**0.9962**	**0.9991**	**0.9971**

Table 4. Comparison of model performance in SCA against Kyber

Model	Dataset	Accuracy	#Votes (#ErrCof <1)
Ueno et al. [31]	–	0.998	3 (0.01)
Ablated-MLPM	B1-Random	0.9967	3 (0.02)
	B1_Avg	0.9979	3 (0.01)
	B1_MD	**0.9998**	**1 (0.19)**
	B2_Avg	0.9971	3 (0.01)
	B2_MD	**0.9995**	**1 (0.53)**
Ablated-MLPM-LW	B1-Random	0.9348	7 (0.76)
	B1_Avg	0.98567	3 (0.88)
	B1_MD	0.9974	3 (0.01)
	B2_Avg	0.97628	5 (0.18)
	B2_MD	0.9944	3 (0.07)

of AES portability techniques in intra-board portability scenarios is reviewed, as shown in Table 3. Our experimental results confirm that both methodologies address inter-board portability but cannot fully address our proposed intra-board portability. Table 4 illustrates the number of votes required for the model to successfully recover the secret key of Kyber-512, with an average error coefficient of less than 1. The original model achieves an accuracy of 0.998 without considering portability [31]. The CNN model optimized using the Ablated-MLPM method can achieve sufficiently high accuracy across the entire surfaces of the two microcontrollers (B1 and B2), requiring no more than three times the traces originally needed. This achieves good intra-board and inter-board portability without compromising attack efficiency. Additionally, the Ablated-MLPM optimized model can further improve the accuracy and efficiency of the attack. For instance, within the central region of the microcontroller, only one round of key recovery is necessary for the average error coefficient to fall below 1.

In summary, Ablated-CNN-LW demonstrates outstanding performance in conventional fixed-location measurement setups, due to the higher ablation rate applied to noise-sensitive layers. However, when dealing with intra-portability scenarios, the constrained model capacity of Ablated-MLPM-LW fails to meet the high-accuracy requirements of the oracle in SCAs against Kyber. Conversely, while Ablated-MLPM may be less resilient to noise disturbances compared to Ablated-MLPM-LW, its broader model capacity allows for accommodating the high-accuracy oracle across a wider range of portability scenarios.

Acknowledgment. This work was supported by the National Natural Science Foundation of China (NO.62172374)

References

1. Bhasin, S., Chattopadhyay, A., Heuser, A., Jap, D., Picek, S., Ranjan, R.: Mind the portability: a warriors guide through realistic profiled side-channel analysis. In: NDSS 2020-Network and Distributed System Security Symposium, pp. 1–14 (2020)
2. Bhasin, S., Danger, J.L., Guilley, S., Najm, Z.: Nicv: normalized inter-class variance for detection of side-channel leakage. In: 2014 International Symposium on Electromagnetic Compatibility, Tokyo, pp. 310–313. IEEE (2014)
3. Cao, P., Zhang, C., Lu, X., Gu, D.: Cross-device profiled side-channel attack with unsupervised domain adaptation. In: IACR Transactions on Cryptographic Hardware and Embedded Systems, pp. 27–56 (2021)
4. Choudary, O., Kuhn, M.G.: Template attacks on different devices. In: Constructive Side-Channel Analysis and Secure Design: 5th International Workshop, COSADE 2014, Paris, France, April 13–15, 2014. Revised Selected Papers 5, pp. 179–198. Springer (2014)
5. Heinz, D., Pöppelmann, T.: Combined fault and DPA protection for lattice-based cryptography. IEEE Trans. Comput. **72**(4), 1055–1066 (2022)
6. D'Anvers, J.P., Tiepelt, M., Vercauteren, F., Verbauwhede, I.: Timing attacks on error correcting codes in post-quantum schemes. In: Proceedings of ACM Workshop on Theory of Implementation Security Workshop, pp. 2–9 (2019)

7. Das, D., Golder, A., Danial, J., Ghosh, S., Raychowdhury, A., Sen, S.: X-deepsca: cross-device deep learning side channel attack. In: Proceedings of the 56th Annual Design Automation Conference 2019, pp. 1–6 (2019)
8. Dubrova, E., Ngo, K., Gärtner, J., Wang, R.: Breaking a fifth-order masked implementation of crystals-kyber by copy-paste. In: Proceedings of the 10th ACM Asia Public-Key Cryptography Workshop, pp. 10–20 (2023)
9. Alagic, G., Apon, D., Cooper, D., Dang, Q., Dang, T., et al.: J.: status report on the third round of the nist post-quantum cryptography standardization process (2022)
10. Gohr, A., Jacob, S., Schindler, W.: Ches 2018 side channel contest ctf—solution of the aes challenges. Cryptology ePrint Archive, Paper 2019/094 (2019). https://eprint.iacr.org/2019/094, https://eprint.iacr.org/2019/094
11. Guo, Q., Johansson, T., Nilsson, A.: A key-recovery timing attack on post-quantum primitives using the fujisaki-okamoto transformation and its application on frodokem. In: Annual International Cryptology Conference, pp. 359–386. Springer (2020)
12. Hamburg, M., Hermelink, J., Primas, R., Samardjiska, S., Schamberger, T., Streit, S., Strieder, E., van Vredendaal, C.: Chosen ciphertext k-trace attacks on masked cca2 secure kyber. In: IACR Transactions on Cryptographic Hardware and Embedded Systems, pp. 88–113 (2021)
13. Ito, A., Saito, K., Ueno, R., Homma, N.: Imbalanced data problems in deep learning-based side-channel attacks: analysis and solution. IEEE Trans. Inf. Forensics Secur. **16**, 3790–3802 (2021)
14. Kamucheka, T., Fahr, M., Teague, T., Nelson, A., Andrews, D., Huang, M.: Power-based side channel attack analysis on pqc algorithms. Cryptology ePrint Archive (2021)
15. Kannwischer, M.J., Rijneveld, J., Schwabe, P., Stoffelen, K.: pqm4: testing and benchmarking nist pqc on arm cortex-m4 (2019)
16. Lu, X., Liu, Y., Zhang, Z., Jia, D., Xue, H., He, J., Li, B., Wang, K.: Lac: practical ring-lwe based public-key encryption with byte-level modulus. Cryptology ePrint Archive (2018)
17. National Institute of Standards and Technology: Three Draft FIPS for Post-Quantum Cryptography. https://csrc.nist.gov/news/2023/threedraftfips-for-post-quantum-cryptography (2023)
18. Ngo, K., Dubrova, E., Guo, Q., Johansson, T.: A side-channel attack on a masked ind-cca secure saber kem implementation. In: IACR Transactions on Cryptographic Hardware and Embedded Systems, pp. 676–707 (2021)
19. NIST: NIST Publishes Draft Post-Quantum Cryptography Standards. https://www.nist.gov/news-events/news/2021/08/nist-publishes-draft-post-quantum-cryptography-standards (2021)
20. Kashyap, P., Aydin, F., Potluri, S., Franzon, P.D., Aysu, A.: 2deep: enhancing side-channel attacks on lattice-based key-exchange via 2-d deep learning. IEEE Trans. Comput. Aided Des. Integr. Circuits Syst. **40**(6), 1217–1229 (2020)
21. Picek, S., Perin, G., Mariot, L., Wu, L., Batina, L.: Sok: deep learning-based physical side-channel analysis. ACM Comput. Surv. **55**(11), 1–35 (2023)
22. Qin, Y., Cheng, C., Zhang, X., Pan, Y., Hu, L., Ding, J.: A systematic approach and analysis of key mismatch attacks on lattice-based nist candidate kems. In: Advances in Cryptology–ASIACRYPT 2021: 27th International Conference on the Theory and Application of Cryptology and Information Security, Singapore, December 6–10, 2021, Proceedings, Part IV 27, pp. 92–121. Springer (2021)

23. Avanzi, R., Bos, J., Ducas, L., Kiltz, , T. Lepoint, V. Lyubashevsky, et al.: Crystals-kyber: algorithm specification and supporting documentation (2019)
24. Rajendran, G., Ravi, P., D'Anvers, J.P., Bhasin, S., Chattopadhyay, A.: Pushing the limits of generic side-channel attacks on lwe-based kems-parallel pc oracle attacks on kyber kem and beyond. In: IACR Transactions on Cryptographic Hardware and Embedded Systems, pp. 418–446 (2023)
25. Ravi, P., Ezerman, M.F., Bhasin, S., Chattopadhyay, A., Roy, S.S.: Will you cross the threshold for me?-generic side-channel assisted chosen-ciphertext attacks on ntru-based kems. Cryptology ePrint Archive (2021)
26. Ravi, P., Roy, S.S.: Side-channel analysis of lattice-based pqc candidates. In: Round 3 Seminars, NIST Post Quantum Cryptography (2021)
27. Ravi, P., Roy, S.S., Chattopadhyay, A., Bhasin, S.: Generic side-channel attacks on cca-secure lattice-based pke and kems. In: IACR Transactions on Cryptographic Hardware and Embedded Systems, pp. 307–335 (2020)
28. Rioja, U., Batina, L., Armendariz, I.: When similarities among devices are taken for granted: another look at portability. In: Progress in Cryptology-AFRICACRYPT 2020: 12th International Conference on Cryptology in Africa, Cairo, Egypt, July 20–22, 2020, Proceedings 12, pp. 337–357. Springer (2020)
29. Shen, M., Cheng, C., Zhang, X., Guo, Q., Jiang, T.: Find the bad apples: an efficient method for perfect key recovery under imperfect sca oracles–a case study of kyber. In: IACR Transactions on Cryptographic Hardware and Embedded Systems, pp. 89–112 (2023)
30. Tanaka, Y., Ueno, R., Xagawa, K., Ito, A., Takahashi, J., Homma, N.: Multiple-valued plaintext-checking side-channel attacks on post-quantum kems. In: IACR Transactions on Cryptographic Hardware and Embedded Systems, pp. 473–503 (2023)
31. Ueno, R., Xagawa, K., Tanaka, Y., Ito, A., Takahashi, J., Homma, N.: Curse of re-encryption: a generic power/em analysis on post-quantum kems. In: IACR Transactions on Cryptographic Hardware and Embedded Systems, pp. 296–322 (2022)
32. Wu, L., Won, Y.S., Jap, D., Perin, G., Bhasin, S., Picek, S.: Ablation analysis for multi-device deep learning-based physical side-channel analysis. In: IEEE Transactions on Dependable and Secure Computing (2023)
33. Xu, Z., Pemberton, O., Roy, S.S., Oswald, D., Yao, W., Zheng, Z.: Magnifying side-channel leakage of lattice-based cryptosystems with chosen ciphertexts: the case study of kyber. IEEE Trans. Comput. **71**(9), 2163–2176 (2021)
34. Yu, H., Shan, H., Panoff, M., Jin, Y.: Cross-device profiled side-channel attacks using meta-transfer learning. In: 2021 58th ACM/IEEE Design Automation Conference (DAC), pp. 703–708. IEEE (2021)
35. Zhang, F., Shao, B., Xu, G., Yang, B., Yang, Z., Qin, Z., Ren, K.: From homogeneous to heterogeneous: leveraging deep learning based power analysis across devices. In: 2020 57th ACM/IEEE Design Automation Conference (DAC), pp. 1–6. IEEE (2020)

Generic CCA Secure Key Homomorphic KEM and Updatable Public Key Encryption

Kaiming Chen[1][ID], Atsuko Miyaji[1(✉)][ID], and Jiageng Chen[2][ID]

[1] Graduate School of Engineering,Osaka University, Osaka, Japan
kaiming@cy2sec.comm.eng.osaka-u.ac.jp, miyaji@comm.eng.osaka-u.ac.jp
[2] Central China Normal University, Wuhan, China
jiageng.chen@ccnu.edu.cn

Abstract. Updatable Public Key Encryption (UPKE) is a technique for updating public and private keys in secure messaging protocols, which was initially introduced by Jost et al. (EUROCRYPTO '19). Alwen et al. (CRYPTO '20) later provided an IND-CPA secure UPKE. Asano et al., in turn, applied the FO transformation to UPKE outputs to achieve IND-CCA security. However, their approach doubles the time complexity, as they treat the IND-CPA UPKE as a black box that runs the encryption process once. In this paper, we formalize an IND-CCA model for key encapsulation mechanisms that involve a one-way homomorphic function which is named key homomorphism (KhKEM). If we construct a UPKE scheme from an IND-CCA KhKEM, a one-way secure pseudorandom generator, and an IND-CCA Encrypt-then-MAC symmetric encryption scheme, we demonstrate that this generic hybrid UPKE design will be IND-CCA secure. We finally consider three KhKEM instances and discuss the parameters and efficiency. We show that our scheme has better efficiency compared with Asano et al.'s scheme.

Keywords: Updatable Public Key Encryption · Key Encapsulation Mechanism · Secure Messaging Protocols

1 Introduction

Forward Secrecy. It is an important feature that in a public key scheme if a user's private key is compromised, the previous messages will remain confidential. Forward secrecy has been considered in many standard applications like the Transportation Security Layer (TLS) and Massage Layer Security (MLS) protocols, and secure-massaging protocols like the Signal X3DH protocols [7,13]. There are many ways to achieve forward secrecy. In TLS, the $(i + 1)$-th session key is generated from the i-th one by a hash function $\mathcal{H}$ s.t. $k_{i+1} := \mathcal{H}(k_i)$, so that if k_{i+1} is leaked, the attacker cannot reveal k_i because of the one-way hash function $\mathcal{H}$. However, the TLS method is unsuitable for group messaging protocols, especially dynamic ones. While in the secure messaging protocols, the users

Z. Xia and J. Chen (Eds.): ISPEC 2024, LNCS 15053, pp. 168–185, 2024.
https://doi.org/10.1007/978-981-97-9053-1_10

will update their private and public keys and negotiate the session key with the updated keys, which ensures that the compromised private keys can only affect the last session. To analyze this key-update procedure, two different models, Key-Update Key Encapsulation Mechanism (KuKEM) [18,19] and Updatable Public Key Encryption (UPKE) [15], are proposed.

Key-Update Key Encapsulation Mechanism. A KEM scheme allows a sender to generate a secret key and a corresponding ciphertext by the public key of a receiver, and the receiver can derive the same secret key using the private key to decapsulate the ciphertext. KuKEM was first proposed by Poettering et al. [18,19]. Balli et al. [5] optimized the model that allows the adversary to manipulate the randomness for key-update, while Pijnenburg et al. [17] improved the model to catch the real-time period to expire the ciphertext. KuKEM, based on HIBE [12], takes initial associated data ad_0 and the identity as the input to generate the public key $pk_0 := (pk', ad_0)$ and the private key $sk_0 := sk'$. When updating the private key for epoch $i>0$, a new associated data ad_i will be generated and the new keys are $pk_i := (pk', ad := (ad_0, ad_1, ..., ad_i))$, $sk_i := \textbf{NEW}(sk_{i-1}, ad_i)$, where pk' and sk' are from HIBE key generation, i is the current epoch, and $\textbf{NEW}(\cdot, \cdot)$ is a key extract algorithm. Because KuKEM does not update the public key pk', some schemes with limited key size [21] are suitable for KuKEM. However, only HIBE schemes satisfy KuKEM, and the public key size has a positive relation with the epoch i, which makes KuKEM inefficient.

Updatable Public Key Encryption. The procedure of UPKE schemes to update the private keys can be described in the following steps: (1). Generate a random update data sk_{UP}, (2). Use sk_{UP} to update the public key, (3). Encrypt sk_{UP} by the public key and send the ciphertext to the receiver, (4). Decrypt the ciphertext to get sk_{UP}, (5). Use sk_{UP} to update the private key. Jost et al. [15] proposed the first UPKE scheme, then Alwen [3] proved that the UPKE scheme of Jost et al. was indistinguishable against chosen plaintext attack (IND-CPA) under the random oracle model (ROM) and computational Diffie-Hellman assumption. Dodis et al. [8] modeled the UPKE to achieve chosen-randomness plaintext attack security (IND-CR-CPA), given an extra oracle for the update randomness. They improved the model to catch the indistinguishability under the chosen update and chosen ciphertext attack (IND-CU-CCA), which permitted the attacker to ask for the update ciphertext oracle under ROM. Then, Haidar et al. [1] introduced a UPKE scheme without ROM. Eaton et al. [9] argued that the isogeny assumption cannot straightforwardly instantiate the UPKE, while Haidar et al. [2] proposed an efficient UPKE scheme based on a lattice assumption. Recently, Asano et al. [4] proved that if a UPKE scheme was IND-CPA secure, the UPKE scheme with FO-transformation [10] would be IND-CU-CCA under ROM, but it requires twice executions of the public key encryption. They also pointed out that the update operation s.t. $sk_i := sk_{i-1} + sk_i^{UP}$ (mod p) could cause $sk_0 = sk_i$ (mod p) if $sk_i^{UP} := 0$ for each update, where G_p was the private key space, p was a big prime, $sk_i^{UP} \in G_p$ was the update data, and i was the epoch number. This problem was named *non-influential random-*

ness and could break the IND-CU-CCA. They assigned the epoch number i to be one part of the public key to avoid the issue, which would increase the size of the public key.

1.1 Our Contributions

KEM with Key Homomorphism. We formalize the Key Homomorphic KEM model. In UPKE schemes, there exists a one-way homomorphic function **GetPk**: $\mathcal{SK} \rightarrow \mathcal{PK}$ over the public key space $\mathcal{PK}$ and private key space $\mathcal{SK}$. Let $(sk, up_{sk}) \in \mathcal{SK}^2$, $pk := \mathbf{GetPk}(sk)$, and $up_{pk} := \mathbf{GetPk}(up_{sk})$. $\otimes : \mathcal{SK} \times \mathcal{SK} \rightarrow \mathcal{SK}$ and $\odot : \mathcal{PK} \times \mathcal{PK} \rightarrow \mathcal{PK}$ are the operations over the key spaces respectively. Let $pk_{up} := pk \odot up_{pk}, sk_{up} := sk \otimes up_{sk}$, according to [9], $pk_{up} = \mathbf{GetPk}(sk \otimes up_{sk}) = \mathbf{GetPk}(sk) \odot \mathbf{GetPk}(up_{sk})$ holds. We name this feature key homomorphism. In this paper, we model the IND-CCA game of the KEM with key homomorphism to be the IND-CCA-KH security model.

Generic Updatable Public Key Encryption. We propose a Generic UPKE scheme. Our UPKE is constructed from an Encrypt-then-Mac hybrid symmetric encryption scheme $\prod_{EtM}$, three different pseudorandom generators($\mathbf{G}_0, \mathbf{G}_1, \mathbf{G}_2$), and a KhKEM scheme $\prod_{KEM}$. We prove that if $\prod_{EtM}$ is IND-CCA secure, pseudorandom generators are secure and one-way, $\prod_{KEM}$ is IND-CCA-KH secure, then our generic UPKE satisfies the IND-CU-CCA security and resists *non-influential randomness* with a non-negligible rate. If $\prod_{KEM}$ is secure without ROM, our UPKE scheme is also secure without ROM.

Better Performance. Table 1 illustrates the comparisons of the storage costs and communication costs between each UPKE scheme satisfying 128-bit security. Because we use the IND-CCA secure Encrypt then MAC scheme to encrypt the updated data instead of encrypting it by a public key encryption scheme, our generic UPKE scheme is more efficient than [4]. Furthermore, we use the one-way pseudorandom generators to derive the updated information so that our UPKE scheme can resist *non-influential randomness*. Above all, our generic UPKE scheme performs better than current generic UPKE schemes.

Paper Organization. In Sect. 1, we show the background of forward secrecy, two solutions for FS in group messaging protocols, and our construction. In

Table 1. The comparison of each UPKE scheme.

Scheme	Private Key	Public key	Update Ciphertext	Security Model	ROM	#PKE
Jost et al. [15]	256b	512b	512b	CR-CPA	Yes	1
Dodis et al. [8]	1.3kb	328kb	419Mb	CU-CCA	No	t
Haidar et al. [1]	4.6kb	9.2kb	105kb	CU-CCA	Yes	3
Asano et al. [4]	256b	640b	1kb	CU-CCA	Yes	2
Ours (Elgamal-UPKE with ROM [16])	256b	512b	1kb	CU-CCA	Yes	1
Ours (Elgamal-UPKE without ROM [20])	1kb	2kb	2.75kb	CU-CCA	No	1

#PKE indicates the times of the involved public key encryption operation. t is the size of the private key

Sect. 2, we list the preliminaries for our construction. In Sect. 3, we formalize the KhKEM and UPKE models. In Sect. 4, we propose our UPKE construction. In Sect. 5, we prove the correctness and security of our UPKE scheme. In Sect. 6, we illustrate three cases for KhKEM and discuss their performance. The conclusion and future work are summarized in Sect. 7.

2   Preliminaries

In this section, we introduce the preliminaries for our secure models.

Notations. $\mathcal{PK}$ is the public key space, $\mathcal{SK}$ is the private key space, $(\mathcal{K}_{KEM}, \mathcal{K}_{SE}, \mathcal{K}_{MAC})$ are KEM key space, symmetric key space, and message authentication code (MAC) key space, respectively. $(\mathcal{CT}_{SE}, \mathcal{CT}_{KEM})$ are ciphertext spaces of KEM and symmetric encryption respectively. $\mathcal{T}_{TAG}$ are the tag space, $\mathcal{R}$ are the random value space, $\mathcal{M}$ is the message space, $\mathcal{N}$ is the set of all non-negative integers. ε is a negligible probability, λ is the security parameter. The notation $function(\cdot; v)$ denotes that the random value v can be generated by $function$ itself or be one of the inputs. $A \to a$ and $a \leftarrow A$ indicate that a is generated from the space or algorithm A. $a \leftarrow \$A$ means sampling a from the space A. The adversaries in our paper are all polynomial probabilistic time (PPT) ones.

2.1   Pseudorandom Generator

A pseudorandom generator (PRG) is a deterministic algorithm:

- $\mathbf{G}(s) \to r$: It outputs a value $r \in \mathcal{R}$, given an input seed $s \in \mathcal{SD}$.

Attack Game of PRG. The challenger $\mathcal{C}$ flips a bit $b \leftarrow \${0,1}$, runs $r_0 \leftarrow \mathbf{G}(s)$, sets $r_1 \leftarrow \$\mathcal{R}$, then sends r_b to the adversary $\mathcal{A}$. $\mathcal{A}$ finally outputs a guessing bit b'. The advantage for $\mathcal{A}$ to win this game is:

$$Adv_{\mathbf{G}}(\mathcal{A}) = \left| Pr[r = r'] - \frac{1}{2} \right| \tag{1}$$

Definition 1. (Secure PRG) A PRG scheme $\mathbf{G}$ is secure if $Adv_{\mathbf{G}}(\mathcal{A}) \leq \varepsilon$ for any PPT adversary $\mathcal{A}$.

Definition 2. (Weakly One-way Function [14]) Assume $f(x)$ is weakly one-way on $\mathcal{U}$ if, for every PPT algorithm $\mathcal{L}$, the inverting probability $Pr[x = \mathcal{L}(f(x))]$ when $x \in \mathcal{U}$ is negligible.

Lemma 1. *If f is a secure PRG on $\mathcal{U}$, f is weakly one-way on $\mathcal{U}$ [14].*

2.2   Encrypt-Then-MAC

An Encrypt-then-MAC scheme is combined from a Symmetric Encryption scheme and a Message Authentication Code scheme.

Definition 3. (Symmetric Encryption) A Symmetric Encryption scheme $\prod_{SE} = (\mathbf{Enc}, \mathbf{Dec})$ has the following algorithms:

- $\mathbf{Enc}(\mathbf{k}, m) \rightarrow c$: This is a symmetric encryption algorithm that on the input of the secret key $\mathbf{k} \in \mathcal{K}_{SE}$ and a message $m \in \mathcal{M}$, it outputs a ciphertext $c \in \mathcal{CT}_{SE}$.
- $\mathbf{Dec}(\mathbf{k}, c) \rightarrow m$: This is a symmetric decryption algorithm that on the input of the secret key $\mathbf{k} \in \mathcal{K}_{SE}$ and a ciphertext $c \in \mathcal{CT}_{SE}$, it outputs a plaintext $m \in \mathcal{M}$.

Definition 4. (Message Authentication Code) A MAC scheme $\prod_{MAC} = (\mathbf{S}, \mathbf{V})$ has the following algorithms:

- $\mathbf{S}(\mathbf{k}, m) \rightarrow \tau$: This is a signing algorithm that on the input of the secret key $\mathbf{k} \in \mathcal{K}_{MAC}$ and message $m \in \mathcal{M}$, it outputs a tag $\tau \in \mathcal{T}_{TAG}$.
- $\mathbf{V}(\mathbf{k}, m, \tau) \rightarrow \{0, 1\}$: This is the verification algorithm that on the input of a secret key $\mathbf{k}$ and a tuple (m, τ), if $(\mathbf{k}, m, \tau) \in \mathcal{K}_{MAC} \times \mathcal{M} \times \mathcal{T}_{TAG}$ is a valid tuple, it outputs 1. Otherwise, it outputs 0.

Definition 5. (Encrypt-then-MAC scheme) An Encrypt-then-MAC scheme $\prod_{EtM} = (\mathbf{HEnc}, \mathbf{HDec})$ is constructed from a symmetric encryption scheme $\prod_{SE}$ and a MAC scheme $\prod_{MAC}$, it contains the following algorithms:

- $\mathbf{HEnc}((\mathbf{k}_{SE}, \mathbf{k}_{MAC}), m; ad) \rightarrow c$: It is an encryption algorithm, where ad is an associated data. It runs as follows:
  - $ct \leftarrow \prod_{SE} .\mathbf{Enc}(\mathbf{k}_{SE}, m)$, $\tau \leftarrow \prod_{MAC} .\mathbf{S}(\mathbf{k}_{MAC}, (ct, ad))$.
  - $c \leftarrow (ct, \tau)$, return c.
- $\mathbf{HDec}((\mathbf{k}_{SE}, \mathbf{k}_{MAC}), c; ad) \rightarrow m \, or \perp$: It is a decryption algorithm, where ad is an associated data. It runs as follows:
  - Parse $(ct, \tau) \leftarrow c$, $b \leftarrow \prod_{MAC} .\mathbf{V}(\mathbf{k}_{MAC}, (ct, ad), \tau)$.
  - If $b = 0$, return $\perp$. Otherwise, $m \leftarrow \prod_{SE} .\mathbf{Dec}(\mathbf{k}_{SE}, ct)$, return m.

Correctness. For all $(\mathbf{k}_{SE}, \mathbf{k}_{MAC}, m) \in \mathcal{K}_{SE} \times \mathcal{K}_{MAC} \times \mathcal{M}$, it requires:

$$Pr[\mathbf{HDec}((\mathbf{k}_{SE}, \mathbf{k}_{MAC}), \mathbf{HEnc}((\mathbf{k}_{SE}, \mathbf{k}_{MAC}), m; ad)); ad] \geq 1 - \varepsilon \quad (2)$$

Lemma 2. *(IND-CCA Security [6]) If* $\prod_{MAC}$ *and* $\prod_{SE}$ *are correct, then* $\prod_{EtM}$ *is also correct. If* $\prod_{SE}$ *is an IND-CPA secure symmetric encryption scheme,* $\prod_{MAC}$ *is an unforgeable MAC system, then the hybrid scheme* $\prod_{EtM}$ *is correct and IND-CCA secure. Let* $Adv_{\prod_{EtM}}(\mathcal{A})$ *be the advantage for any PPT adversary* $\mathcal{A}$ *to win IND-CCA game, let* $\mathcal{B}_1$ *be the adversary to attack* $\prod_{SE}$ *with the negligible advantage* $Adv_{\prod_{SE}}^{IND-CPA}(\mathcal{B}_1)$, $\mathcal{B}_2$ *be the adversary to attack* $\prod_{MAC}$ *with the negligible advantage* $Adv_{\prod_{MAC}}(\mathcal{B}_2)$, *it holds that:*

$$Adv_{\prod_{EtM}}(\mathcal{A}) \leq Adv_{\prod_{SE}}^{IND-CPA}(\mathcal{B}_1) + 2Adv_{\prod_{MAC}}(\mathcal{B}_2) \quad (3)$$

3   Secure Model

In this section, we introduce our security models .

3.1   Key Homomorphic Key Encapsulation Mechanism

In [2], the authors proposed an updatable KEM (UKEM) model with two additional key-update algorithms that were based on the one-way homomorphic functions as stated in [9]. Considering the structure of UPKE from a more basic fundamental, our KhKEM is based on the original KEM together with a one-way homomorphic function **GetPk** instead of the key-update algorithms.

Definition 6. (Key Encapsulation Mechanism) A KEM $\prod_{KEM}=$(**KGen,Encap,Decap**) contains the following three algorithms:

- **KGen**$(1^\lambda) \to (pk, sk)$: On input of the security parameter λ, this algorithm outputs a public key $pk \in \mathcal{PK}$ and a private key $sk \in \mathcal{SK}$.
- **Encap**$(pk; \alpha) \to (ct, \mathbf{k})$: On input of the public key $pk \in \mathcal{PK}$ and an optional $\alpha \in \mathcal{R}$, it outputs a secret key $k \in \mathcal{K}_{KEM}$ and a corresponding ciphertext $ct \in \mathcal{CT}_{KEM}$.
- **Decap**$(sk, ct) \to \mathbf{k}$: On input of the private key $sk \in \mathcal{SK}$ and a ciphertext $ct \in \mathcal{CT}_{KEM}$, it outputs a secret key $\mathbf{k} \in \mathcal{K}_{KEM}$.
- **GetPk**$(sk) \to pk$: On input of the private key $sk \in \mathcal{SK}$, it returns the corresponding public key $pk \in \mathcal{PK}$, where $(pk, sk) \leftarrow$ **KGen**(1^λ).

Definition 7. (Key Homomorphic Key Encapsulation Mechanism) Let $\otimes$: $\mathcal{SK} \times \mathcal{SK} \to \mathcal{SK}$ and $\odot : \mathcal{PK} \times \mathcal{PK} \to \mathcal{PK}$ be the operations over the key spaces respectively. For all $\lambda \in \mathcal{N}$, $(pk_0, sk_0) \leftarrow$ **KGen**(1^λ), and $(pk_1, sk_1) \leftarrow$ **KGen**(1^λ), if a KEM scheme $\prod_{KEM}$ satisfies the following feature, we say $\prod_{KEM}$ is a KhKEM:

$$
\begin{aligned}
Pr\left[\mathbf{k}_0 = \mathbf{k}_1 \,\middle|\, \begin{array}{l} (ct, \mathbf{k}_0) \leftarrow \mathbf{Encap}(pk_0 \odot pk_1); \\ \mathbf{k}_1 \leftarrow \mathbf{Decap}(sk_0 \otimes sk_1, ct); \end{array}\right] \geq 1 - \varepsilon \\
Pr\left[pk_2 = \mathbf{GetPk}(sk_2) \,\middle|\, \begin{array}{l} pk_2 \leftarrow pk_0 \odot pk_1; \\ sk_2 \leftarrow sk_0 \otimes sk_1; \end{array}\right] \geq 1 - \varepsilon
\end{aligned}
\tag{4}
$$

IND-CCA of Key Homomorphic KEM. The attack model of IND-CCA Key Homomorphic (IND-CCA-KH) KEM is defined by a game played between a PPT adversary $\mathcal{A}$ and its challenger $\mathcal{C}$ as follows:

- **Setup:** $\mathcal{C}$ sets a random bit $b \leftarrow \$\{0,1\}$, runs $(pk, sk) \leftarrow$**KGen**(1^λ), and returns pk to $\mathcal{A}$.
- **Query 1:** When $\mathcal{A}$ accesses the **Decap** oracle on the input of ct_i and sk_i in the i-th query, if sk_i is empty, $\mathcal{C}$ runs $\mathbf{k}_i \leftarrow$**Decap**(sk, ct_i) otherwise $\mathbf{k}_i \leftarrow$**Decap**$(sk \otimes sk_i, ct_i)$. Then $\mathcal{C}$ returns $\mathbf{k}_i$ to $\mathcal{A}$.
- **Chal:** $\mathcal{A}$ sends sk^* to $\mathcal{C}$. If sk^* is not empty, $\mathcal{C}$ runs $(ct^*, \mathbf{k}_0) \leftarrow$**Encap**$(pk \odot$ **GetPk**$(sk^*))$, otherwise, it runs $(ct^*, \mathbf{k}_0) \leftarrow$**Encap**$(pk)$. Next, it sets $\mathbf{k}_1 \leftarrow$ $\$\mathcal{K}_{KEM}$ and returns $(ct^*, \mathbf{k}_b)$ to $\mathcal{A}$. $\mathcal{A}$ finally outputs a bit b'.

– **Query 2:** It is the same as **Query 1** except that $\mathcal{A}$ cannot ask **Decap** on the input of (sk', ct^*) where $sk \otimes sk' = sk$.

The advantage $Adv_{\prod_{KEM}}^{IND-CCA-KH}(\mathcal{A}, \lambda)$ for $\mathcal{A}$ to win this game is:

$$Adv_{\prod_{KEM}}^{IND-CCA-KH}(\mathcal{A}, \lambda) := \left| Pr[b = b'] - \frac{1}{2} \right| \tag{5}$$

Definition 8. For all $\lambda \in \mathcal{N}$ and $(pk, sk) \leftarrow \mathbf{KGen}(1^\lambda)$, if the advantage $Adv_{\prod_{KEM}}^{IND}(\mathcal{A}, \lambda)$ is negligible for an PPT adversary $\mathcal{A}$ to distinguish the secret key generated by the KhKEM scheme $\prod_{KEM}$ from a random value with the same length, $\prod_{KEM}$ is said to satisfy IND-CCA-KH security.

3.2 Updatable Public Key Encryption

Definition 9. (Updatable Public Key Encryption) A UPKE scheme $\prod_{UPKE}=$ (**UGen,UEnc,UDec,UpPk,UpSk**) contains the following five algorithms:

– **UGen**$(1^\lambda) \rightarrow (upk_0, usk_0)$: With the security parameter λ, this algorithm outputs an initial public key and private key pair (upk_0, usk_0).
– **UEnc**$(upk_i, m_i) \rightarrow c_i$: On the input of the public key upk_i in epoch i and a message m_i from the message space s.t. $m_i \leftarrow \mathcal{M}$, this algorithm outputs a ciphertext c_i for current epoch.
– **UDec**$(usk_i, c_i) \rightarrow m_i \ or \perp$: Input the private key usk_i in epoch i and a ciphertext c_i, it outputs a plaintext m_i if the input usk_i and c_i are a valid tuple. Otherwise, it outputs a $\perp$ to reject the decryption.
– **UpPk**$(upk_i; seed) \rightarrow (upk_{i+1}, upd_{i+1})$: On the input of the public key upk_i in epoch i and an optional seed $seed \in \mathcal{SD}$, this algorithm outputs an update public key upk_{i+1} for next epoch $i+1$ and corresponding update information upd_i for updating the private key.
– **UpSk**$((usk_i, upk_i), (upk_{i+1}, upd_{i+1})) \rightarrow usk_{i+1} \ or \perp$: On the input of the key pair (usk_i, upk_i) in epoch i and an update tuple (upk_{i+1}, upd_{i+1}), this algorithm outputs an update private key usk_{i+1} for next epoch $i+1$, if the input (usk_i, upk_i) and (upk_{i+1}, upd_{i+1}) are a valid tuple. Otherwise, it outputs a $\perp$ to reject the update.

Correctness of UPKE. For all $\lambda, T \in \mathcal{N}$, all $(upk_0, usk_0) \leftarrow \mathbf{UGen}(1^\lambda)$, and $m_i \in \mathcal{M}$ where $i \in \{0, 1, 2, 3, ..., T-1, T\}$, it requires that:

$$Pr[\mathbf{UDec}(usk_i, \mathbf{UEnc}(upk_i, m_i)) = m_i] \geq 1 - \varepsilon \tag{6}$$

$$Pr[\mathbf{UpSk}((usk_i, upk_i), \mathbf{UpPk}(upk_i)) = usk_{i+1}] \geq 1 - \varepsilon \tag{7}$$

Security. The following secure model and security definition refer to definitions of Dodis et al. [8] and Asano et al. [4].

Attack Game of IND-Chosen-Update-CCA [8]. The IND-CU-CCA security is defined by a game where the adversary $\mathcal{A}$ can access the following phases with the challenger $\mathcal{C}$ in sequence:

- **Setup:** $\mathcal{C}$ runs $(upk_0, usk_0) \leftarrow \mathbf{UGen}(1^\lambda)$, and returns upk_0 to $\mathcal{A}$.
- **Stage 1:** The following four oracles are available for $\mathcal{A}$. $\mathcal{A}$ can call all oracles out of order.
  - **Plaintext Query:** $\mathcal{A}$ is allowed to make **UEnc** query on the plaintext m_i where i is the current epoch. $\mathcal{C}$ will run $c_i \leftarrow \mathbf{UEnc}(upk_i, m_i)$ and return c_i to $\mathcal{A}$.
  - **Ciphertext Query:** $\mathcal{A}$ is allowed to make **UDec** query on the plaintext c_i where i is the current epoch. $\mathcal{C}$ will returns the results m_i to $\mathcal{A}$ or the rejection if $\perp \leftarrow \mathbf{UDec}(usk_i, c_i)$.
  - **Seed Query:** $\mathcal{A}$ is allowed to make **UpPk** query on the value *seed*. $\mathcal{C}$ runs $(upk_{i+1}, upd_{i+1}) \leftarrow \mathbf{UpPk}(upk_i; seed)$, and return the result to $\mathcal{A}$. Then, it will run $usk_{i+1} \leftarrow \mathbf{UpSk}(usk_i, (upk_{i+1}, upd_{i+1}))$, and set current epoch to $i + 1$.
  - **Update Query:** $\mathcal{A}$ can query **UpSk** with (upk_{i+1}, upd_{i+1}). $\mathcal{C}$ returns usk_{i+1} or $\perp \leftarrow \mathbf{UpSk}((usk_i, upk_i), (upk_{i+1}, upd_{i+1}))$ to $\mathcal{A}$. If the result is not $\perp$, the current epoch moves to $i + 1$.
- **Chal:** This is the challenge phase. $\mathcal{A}$ is allowed to access this phase only once. On the input $m'_0, m'_1 \in \mathcal{M}$ of $\mathcal{A}$, where m'_0, m'_1 have the same length, $\mathcal{C}$ sets a random bit $b \leftarrow \$\{0,1\}$, runs $c'_b \leftarrow \mathbf{UEnc}(upk_t, m'_b)$, and returns c'_b to $\mathcal{A}$, where t is current epoch.
- **Stage 2:** $\mathcal{A}$ can access the same oracles as in **Stage 1**, except that $\mathcal{A}$ should call the **Update Query** or **Seed Query** successfully at least once before $\mathcal{A}$ calls the **Ciphertext Query** with c'_b. Because these two oracles will push the current epoch to the next one, it means that c'_b will be a new ciphertext and available for the **Ciphertext Query**.
- **Comp:** This is the compromise phase where $\mathcal{A}$ leaks the current private key of $\mathcal{C}$. When $\mathcal{A}$ queries "$\perp$", $\mathcal{C}$ will finish **Stage 2** and start this phase. $\mathcal{C}$ sets $seed' \leftarrow \$\mathcal{S}$, runs $(upk_l, upd_l) \leftarrow \mathbf{UpPk}(upk_{l-1}; seed')$ s.t. l is the current epoch, and $usk_l \leftarrow \mathbf{UpSk}((usk_{l-1}, upk_{l-1}), (upk_l, upd_l))$. Finally, $\mathcal{C}$ returns (upk_l, upd_l, usk_l) to $\mathcal{A}$.
- **Test:** In this phase, $\mathcal{A}$ should outputs a guess bit b' to end this game.

The advantage for $\mathcal{A}$ to win this game is:

$$Adv_{\Pi_{UPKE}}^{IND-CU-CCA}(\mathcal{A}, \lambda) := \left| \Pr[b = b'] - \frac{1}{2} \right| \tag{8}$$

Definition 10. (IND-CU-CCA Security) If $Adv_{\Pi_{UPKE}}^{IND-CU-CCA}(\mathcal{A}, \lambda) \leq \varepsilon$ under the security parameter λ for any PPT adversary $\mathcal{A}$, the UPKE scheme Π_{UPKE} is considered to satisfy the IND-CU-CCA security.

4 Our Generic UPKE Construction

Notations. Let $(\mathbf{G}_0, \mathbf{G}_1, \mathbf{G}_2)$ be three different PRGs, where $\mathbf{G}_0 : \mathcal{SD} \to \mathcal{SK}$, $\mathbf{G}_1 : \mathcal{K}_{KEM} \to \mathcal{K}_{SE}$, and $\mathbf{G}_2 : \mathcal{K}_{KEM} \to \mathcal{K}_{MAC}$. Π_{SE} is an IND-CPA symmetric encryption scheme, Π_{MAC} is a unforgeable MAC scheme, Π_{EtM} is an IND-CCA Encrypt-then-MAC scheme constructed from Π_{SE} and Π_{MAC}, Π_{KEM} is a IND-CCA-KH secure KhKEM scheme.

The details of our UPKE scheme are shown as follows.

Definition 11. (UPKE) The $\prod_{UPKE}$ has the following algorithms:

- **UGen**(1^λ) :
  1. (upk_0, usk_0)
     $\leftarrow \prod_{KEM}.\textbf{KGen}(1^\lambda)$.
  2. Return (upk_0, usk_0).
- **UEnc**(upk_i, m_i) :
  1. $(c_{KEM}, \mathbf{k}_{KEM})$
     $\leftarrow \prod_{KEM}.\textbf{Encap}(upk_i)$.
  2. $\mathbf{k}_{SE} \leftarrow \mathbf{G}_1(\mathbf{k}_{KEM})$.
  3. $\mathbf{k}_{MAC} \leftarrow \mathbf{G}_2(\mathbf{k}_{KEM})$.
  4. $c_i \leftarrow \prod_{EtM}.\textbf{HEnc}$
     $((\mathbf{k}_{SE}, \mathbf{k}_{MAC}), m_i; c_{KEM})$.
  5. $ct_i \leftarrow (c_i, c_{KEM})$.
  6. Return ct_i.
- **UDec**(usk_i, ct_i) :
  1. Parse $(c_i, c_{KEM}) \leftarrow ct_i$.
  2. $\mathbf{k}_{KEM} \leftarrow \prod_{KEM}.\textbf{Decap}$
     (usk_i, c_{KEM}).
  3. $\mathbf{k}_{SE} \leftarrow \mathbf{G}_1(\mathbf{k}_{KEM})$.
  4. $\mathbf{k}_{MAC} \leftarrow \mathbf{G}_2(\mathbf{k}_{KEM})$.
  5. $m_i \, or \perp \leftarrow \prod_{EtM}.\textbf{HDec}$
     $((\mathbf{k}_{SE}, \mathbf{k}_{MAC}), c_i; c_{KEM})$.
  6. Return $m_i \, or \perp$, terminate decryption.
- **UpPk**$(upk_i; seed)$:
  1. $seed \leftarrow \$\mathcal{SD}$

2. $sk_{i+1}^{UP} \leftarrow \mathbf{G}_0(seed)$.
3. $upk_{i+1} \leftarrow upk_i \odot$
   $\prod_{KEM}.\textbf{GetPk}(sk_{i+1}^{UP})$.
4. $(c_{KEM}, \mathbf{k}_{KEM}) \leftarrow$
   $\prod_{KEM}.\textbf{Encap}(upk_i; sk_{i+1}^{UP})$.
5. $\mathbf{k}_{SE} \leftarrow \mathbf{G}_1(\mathbf{k}_{KEM})$.
6. $\mathbf{k}_{MAC} \leftarrow \mathbf{G}_2(\mathbf{k}_{KEM})$.
7. $c_{UP} \leftarrow \prod_{EtM}.\textbf{HEnc}$
   $((\mathbf{k}_{SE}, \mathbf{k}_{MAC}), sk_{i+1}^{UP}; c_{KEM})$.
8. $up_{i+1} \leftarrow (c_{UP}, c_{KEM})$.
9. Return (upk_{i+1}, up_{i+1}).
- **UpSk**$((usk_i, upk_i), up_{i+1})$:
  1. $(c_{UP}, c_{KEM}) \leftarrow up_{i+1}$.
  2. $\mathbf{k}_{KEM} :=$
     $\prod_{KEM}.\textbf{Decap}(usk_i, c_{KEM})$.
  3. $\mathbf{k}_{SE} \leftarrow \mathbf{G}_1(\mathbf{k}_{KEM})$.
  4. $\mathbf{k}_{MAC} \leftarrow \mathbf{G}_2(\mathbf{k}_{KEM})$.
  5. $sk_{i+1}^{UP} \, or \perp \leftarrow \prod_{EtM}.\textbf{HDec}$
     $((\mathbf{k}_{SE}, \mathbf{k}_{MAC}), c_{UP}; c_{KEM})$.
  6. If $\perp$, return $\perp$ to reject.
  7. $usk_{i+1} \leftarrow usk_i \otimes sk_{i+1}^{UP}$. Return usk_{i+1} and set upk_{i+1} as $\prod_{KEM}.\textbf{GetPk}(usk_{i+1})$ Terminate update.

In our generic construction, a seed will be generated from the KEM encapsulation algorithm and derive two different keys using two PRG. The message and two keys are the inputs of the hybrid scheme. An extra PRG is assigned to generate the update data in the update procedure. This data is considered the message in the UPKE encryption and updates the current public and private keys. The KEM ciphertext and public key of the next epoch are the associated data for the hybrid scheme and will be sent to the receiver. The receiver decrypts the KEM ciphertext to get the seed and derives the duplicate symmetric keys as the sender. Then, he decrypts the symmetric ciphertext and checks its integrity to get the final results–rejection, the message, or the updated private key.

5   Security Analysis

In this section, we prove the correctness and IND-CU-CCA security of our generic UPKE scheme.

5.1   Correctness

Theorem 1. *A UPKE scheme $\prod_{UPKE}$ satisfies correctness if the hybrid scheme $\prod_{EtM}$ and the KhKEM scheme $\prod_{KEM}$ are correct, and the PRGs (G_0, G_1, G_2) are deterministic algorithms.*

Proof. First, We prove the correctness of **UEnc** and **UDec**. In epoch $i \in \{0, 1, ..., T\}$, **UEnc** takes upk_i and m_i as the inputs, and calculates:

1. $(c_{KEM}, \mathbf{k}_{KEM}) \leftarrow \prod_{KEM}.\mathbf{Encap}(upk_i)$.
2. $\mathbf{k}_{SE} \leftarrow \mathbf{G}_1(\mathbf{k}_{KEM})$, $\mathbf{k}_{MAC} \leftarrow \mathbf{G}_2(\mathbf{k}_{KEM})$.
3. $c_i \leftarrow \prod_{EtM}.\mathbf{HEnc}((\mathbf{k}_{SE}, \mathbf{k}_{MAC}), m_i; c_{KEM})$.

UDec calculates as follows:

1. $\mathbf{k}'_{KEM} \leftarrow \prod_{KEM}.\mathbf{Decap}(usk_i, c_{KEM})$.
2. $\mathbf{k}'_{SE} \leftarrow \mathbf{G}_1(\mathbf{k}'_{KEM})$, $\mathbf{k}'_{MAC} \leftarrow \mathbf{G}_2(\mathbf{k}'_{KEM})$.
3. $m'_i \; or \perp \leftarrow \prod_{EtM}.\mathbf{HDec}((\mathbf{k}'_{SE}, \mathbf{k}'_{MAC}), c_i; c_{KEM})$.

If c_{KEM} is not changed, according to the correctness and key homomorphism of $\prod_{KEM}$, we have $\mathbf{k}'_{KEM} = \mathbf{k}_{KEM}$. Because $\mathbf{G}_1$ and $\mathbf{G}_2$ are deterministic PRGs, we have $\mathbf{k}'_{SE} = \mathbf{k}_{SE}$ and $\mathbf{k}'_{MAC} = \mathbf{k}_{MAC}$. Finally, according to the correctness of $\prod_{EtM}$, we have $m'_i = m_i$.

Next, we prove the correctness of **UpPk** and **UpSk**. In epoch $i \in \{0, 1, ..., T\}$, **UpPk** takes upk_i as the input and calculates:

1. $(c_{KEM}, \mathbf{k}_{KEM}) \leftarrow \prod_{KEM}.\mathbf{Encap}(upk_i; sk_{i+1}^{UP})$.
2. $\mathbf{k}_{SE} \leftarrow \mathbf{G}_1(\mathbf{k}_{KEM})$, $\mathbf{k}_{MAC} \leftarrow \mathbf{G}_2(\mathbf{k}_{KEM})$.
3. $c_{UP} \leftarrow \prod_{EtM}.\mathbf{HEnc}((\mathbf{k}_{SE}, \mathbf{k}_{MAC}), sk_{i+1}^{UP}; c_{KEM})$.

Here, upk_{i+1} is an associated data and will be sent to the receiver, sk_{i+1}^{UP} plays the role of the message in **UEnc**. So we just consider the above four items. **UpSk** calculates the following items:

1. $\mathbf{k}'_{KEM} \leftarrow \prod_{KEM}.\mathbf{Decap}(usk_i, c_{KEM})$.
2. $\mathbf{k}'_{SE} \leftarrow \mathbf{G}_1(\mathbf{k}'_{KEM})$, $\mathbf{k}'_{MAC} \leftarrow \mathbf{G}_2(\mathbf{k}'_{KEM})$.
3. $sk'_{i+1} \; or \perp \leftarrow \prod_{EtM}.\mathbf{HDec}((\mathbf{k}_{SE}, \mathbf{k}_{MAC}), c_{UP}; c_{KEM})$.

Since $\prod_{KEM}$ and $\prod_{EtM}$ are correct, $\mathbf{G}_1$ and $\mathbf{G}_2$ are deterministic PRG, $sk'_{i+1} = sk_{i+1}^{UP}$. Above all, $\prod_{UPKE}$ is correct with non-negligible probability.

5.2   Security

Theorem 2. *Assume $\mathcal{SK}$ is a large private key. A UPKE scheme $\prod_{UPKE}$ with the secure parameter λ satisfies IND-CU-CCA security if the hybrid $\prod_{EtM}$ is IND-CCA secure scheme, $\prod_{KEM}$ is IND-CCA-KH secure scheme, and G_0, G_1, G_2 are different secure PRGs.*

*Especially, assuming there are q_{Enc_j} **Plaintext Queies**, q_{Dec_j} **Ciphertext Queries**, q_{SD_j} **Seed Queries**, and q_{UP_j} **Update Queries** in Stage j. If there* exists an adversary $\mathcal{A}$ that can break the IND-CU-CCA security of $\prod_{UPKE}$, then there exists an adversary $\mathcal{B}_{KEM}$ that can break the IND-CCA-KH of $\prod_{KEM}$, an adversary $\mathcal{B}_{EtM}$ that can break the IND-CCA of $\prod_{EtM}$, and an adversary $\mathcal{B}_{PRG}$ that can break the secure PRG. The advantage to win IND-CU-CCA game is:

$$Adv_{\prod_{UPKE}}^{IND-CU-CCA}(\mathcal{A}, \lambda) \leq \frac{q_{SD_2} + q_{UP_2}}{|\mathcal{SK}|} + Adv_{\prod_{KEM}}^{IND-CCA-KH}(\mathcal{B}_{KEM}, \lambda)$$
$$+ 3Adv_G(\mathcal{B}_{PRG}) + 2Adv_{\prod_{EtM}}(\mathcal{B}_{EtM}). \tag{9}$$

Hybrid	Description	Security
G_0	The original IND-CU-CCA game	IND-CCA security of EtM
G_1	G_0 except receiving upk_0 from the IND-CCA-KH adversary, reparse each oracle.	One-way PRG and uniform distribution of private key
G_2	G_1 except ignoring $\sum_{i=1\ to\ q} sk_i^{UP} = 0$	Secure PRG
G_3	G_2 except replacing sk_i^{UP} with a random value	IND-CCA-KH security of KEM
G_4	G_3 except replacing K_{KEM} with a random value	Secure PRG
G_5	G_4 except replacing K_{SE} with a random value	Secure PRG
G_6	G_5 except replacing K_{MAC} with a random value	IND-CCA security of EtM

Fig. 1. The game hopping of our security proof.

The overview of our proof is illustrated in Fig. 1.

Proof Skatch. Let $\mathcal{G}_0$ be the original IND-CU-CCA game, $\mathcal{G}_1$ is the same as $\mathcal{G}_0$ except that it receives the initial public key from KhKEM challenger. Because of the IND-CCA KhKEM, the challenger of $\mathcal{G}_1$ can answer the queries. To distinguish $\mathcal{G}_0$ and $\mathcal{G}_1$ means breaking the IND-CCA KhKEM. $\mathcal{G}_2$ is the same as $\mathcal{G}_1$ except that it ignores the *non-influential randomness* attack. Due to the one-way PRG, the probability of distinguishing $\mathcal{G}_2$ and $\mathcal{G}_1$ is negligible. From G_3 to G_6, we replace the updated key and secret keys step by step. Then Theorem 2 can be proven. The detail of the proof refers to the appendix.

6   The Instance of KhKEM and Performance Analysis

6.1   The Construction of Key Homomorphism KEM

In this section, we show some cases of the IND-CCA-KH KEM.

Case 1: GPV KEM. Dodis et al. [8] designed a UPKE scheme based on the GPV scheme [11]. Let $\mathcal{Z}_p$ be the Abelian group of order p, $\mathcal{Z}_p^{n \times m}$ be the set of all $n \times m$ matrices over $\mathcal{Z}_p$, $\mathcal{D}^m$ and $\mathcal{D}'$ are the Gaussian distributions over $\mathcal{Z}_p$, $< \mathbf{a}, \mathbf{b} >$ be the inner product of two vectors $\mathbf{a}$ and $\mathbf{b}$, $\lfloor d \rfloor$ be the rounding down of d. The GPV KEM is listed as follows:

- **KGen**(1^λ):
  - Sample $\mathbf{A} \leftarrow \$ \mathcal{Z}_p^{n \times m}$. Select $\mathbf{x} \leftarrow \$\{0,1\}^m$, $\mathbf{v} \leftarrow \mathbf{Ax}$.
  - Return $(pk := (\mathbf{A}, \mathbf{v}), sk := \mathbf{x})$.
- **Encap**$(pk := (\mathbf{A}, \mathbf{v}); \{\mathbf{y}_i\}_{i=1\,to\,m})$:
  - $\mathbf{k} \leftarrow \$\{0,1\}^m$.
  - For $i := 1$ to m:
  - $\mathbf{y}_i \leftarrow \$ \mathcal{Z}_p^n, \mathbf{e}_i \leftarrow \$ \mathcal{D}^m, e_i' \leftarrow \$ \mathcal{D}'$.
  - $c_{i_0} \leftarrow \mathbf{A}^T \mathbf{y}_i + \mathbf{e}_i, c_{i_1} \leftarrow <\mathbf{y}_i, \mathbf{v}> +e_i' + \mathbf{k}_i \lfloor \frac{p}{2} \rfloor$.
  - Return $(\{(c_{i_0}, c_{i_1})\}_{i=1\,to\,m}, \mathbf{k})$.
- **Decap**$(sk := \mathbf{x}, \{(c_{i_0}, c_{i_1})\}_{i=1\,to\,m})$:
  - For $i := 1$ to m:
  - $m_i' \leftarrow c_{i_1} - <c_{i_0}, \mathbf{x}> \in \mathcal{Z}_p$.
  - If m_i' is close to 0, $\mathbf{k}_i' := 0$. If m_i' is close to $\lfloor \frac{p}{2} \rfloor$, $\mathbf{k}_i' := 1$.
  - Return $\mathbf{k}'$
- **GetPk**$(sk := \mathbf{x})$: Return $\mathbf{Ax}$.
- $sk_1 \otimes sk_2$: Let $sk_1 := \mathbf{x}_1, sk_2 := \mathbf{x}_2$, return $(\mathbf{x}_1 + \mathbf{x}_2)$.
- $pk_1 \odot pk_2$: Let $pk_1 := \mathbf{Ax}_1, pk_2 := \mathbf{Ax}_2$, return $pk_1 + pk_2 = \mathbf{Ax}_1 + \mathbf{Ax}_2 = \mathbf{A}(\mathbf{x}_1 + \mathbf{x}_2) = \mathbf{A}(sk_1 \otimes sk_2)$.

GPV KEM is an IND-CPA scheme and can be IND-CCA secure with FO-transformation [10]. The security refers to the work of Dodis et al.

Case 2: EC-ElGamal KEM with Random Oralce. This is the construct of IND-CCA-KH KEM from the EC-ElGamal under the ROM model proposed by [16]. Let p, q be big prime integers, E be an elliptic curve (EC) over the finite field $\mathbf{F}_p$, $\mathbf{P}$ be a generator point of $E(\mathbf{F}_p)$, and $\mathcal{H} : E(\mathbf{F}_p)^2 \to \mathcal{K}_{KEM}$ be a random oracle (RO). The EC-ElGamal KEM has the following algorithms:

- **KGen**$(1^\lambda) : sk \leftarrow \$[1, q-1], pk \leftarrow sk \cdot \mathbf{P}$, return (pk, sk).
- **Encap**$(pk; \alpha) :$ If $\alpha = \bot, \alpha \leftarrow \$[1, q-1]$. $ct \leftarrow \alpha \cdot \mathbf{P}, u \leftarrow \alpha \cdot pk, \mathbf{k} \leftarrow \mathcal{H}(ct, u)$, return $(ct, \mathbf{k})$.
- **Decap**$(sk, ct) : u \leftarrow sk \cdot ct, \mathbf{k} \leftarrow \mathcal{H}(ct, u)$, return $\mathbf{k}$.
- **GetPk**$(sk) :$ Return $sk \cdot \mathbf{P}$.
- $\otimes$ and $\odot$: Let $sk_1, sk_2 \leftarrow \$[1, q-1], pk_1 \leftarrow sk_1 \cdot \mathbf{P}, pk_2 \leftarrow sk_2 \cdot \mathbf{P}$. $sk_1 \otimes sk_2 := sk_1 + sk_2, pk_1 \odot pk_2 := (sk_1 + sk_2) \cdot \mathbf{P} := (sk_1 \otimes sk_2) \cdot \mathbf{P}$.

Correctness and IND-CCA security follow the proof of [16]. It can be seen that (4) holds so that this KEM satisfies the key homomorphism. Therefore, the KEM is IND-CCA-KH secure under ROM.

Case 3: EC-ElGamal KEM Without Random Oralce In this section, we consider the KEM based on EC-ElGamal without ROM [20].

Let p, q be two different big prime integers, E be an elliptic curve (EC) over the finite field $\mathbf{F}_p$, v_1 be a generator point of $E(\mathbf{F}_p)$. $\mathcal{H}_0$ is a secure universal one-way hash function indexed by a random key σ. $\mathcal{H}_1$ is a pair-wise hash function with a random key ϕ, $\mathcal{H}_2 : E(\mathbf{F}_p)^2 \to \{0,1\}^n$ is a zip hash function that compresses the elements in $E(\mathbf{F}_p)^2$ to n-bit strings, where $\sqrt{2^n/p}$ is negligible. $(\sigma, \phi, n, v_1, \mathcal{H}_0, \mathcal{H}_1, \mathcal{H}_2, p, q, E)$ are public parameters. This EC-ElGamal KEM has the following algorithms:

- **KGen**(1^λ) :
  - $x_0, x_1, x_2, x_3 \leftarrow \$[1, q-1]$.
  - $v_2 \leftarrow x_0 \cdot v_1, y_1 \leftarrow x_1 \cdot v_1, y_2 \leftarrow x_2 \cdot v_1, y_3 \leftarrow x_3 \cdot v_1$.
  - $pk \leftarrow (v_2, y_1, y_2, y_3), sk \leftarrow (x_0, x_1, x_2, x_3)$.
  - return (pk, sk).
- **Encap**$(pk; \alpha)$:
  - If $\alpha = \perp, \alpha \leftarrow \$[1, q-1]$.
  - $ct_1 \leftarrow \alpha \cdot v_1, ct_2 \leftarrow \alpha \cdot v_2, \beta \leftarrow \mathcal{H}_0(\sigma, ct_1, ct_2)$.
  - $ct_3 \leftarrow \alpha \cdot (y_1 + \beta \cdot y_2), w \leftarrow \alpha \cdot y_3$.
  - $\mathbf{k} \leftarrow \mathcal{H}_1(\phi, w)$ xor $\mathcal{H}_2(ct_1, w)$, return $((ct_1, ct_2, ct_3), \mathbf{k})$.
- **Decap**(sk, ct) :
  - $\beta \leftarrow \mathcal{H}_0(\sigma, ct_1, ct_2)$.
  - If $ct_2 = x_0 \cdot ct_1$ and $ct_3 = (x_1 + \beta x_2) \cdot ct_1$ do not hold, return $\perp$.
  - Otherwise, $w \leftarrow x_3 \cdot ct_1, \mathbf{k} \leftarrow \mathcal{H}_1(\phi, w)$ xor $\mathcal{H}_2(ct_1, w)$, return $\mathbf{k}$.
- **GetPk**(sk) : $v_2 \leftarrow x_0 \cdot v_1, y_1 \leftarrow x_1 \cdot v_1, y_2 \leftarrow x_2 \cdot v_1, y_3 \leftarrow x_3 \cdot v_1$.
  Return (v_2, y_1, y_2, y_3).
- $sk_1 \otimes sk_2$: Let $sk_1 := (x_0, x_1, x_2, x_3), sk_2 := (x_0', x_1', x_2', x_3')$. $sk_1 \otimes sk_2 :=$ $(x_0 + x_0', x_1 + x_1', x_2 + x_2', x_3 + x_3')$.
- Let $pk_1 := (v_2, y_1, y_2, y_3), pk_2 := (v_2', y_1', y_2', y_3')$.

$$pk_1 \odot pk_2 = (v_2 + v_2', y_1 + y_1', y_2 + y_2', y_3 + y_3').$$
$$= ((x_0 + x_0') \cdot v_1, (x_1 + x_1') \cdot v_1, (x_2 + x_2') \cdot v_1, (x_3 + x_3') \cdot v_1)$$
$$= \mathbf{GetPk}(sk_1 \otimes sk_2).$$

The correctness and IND-CCA security follow the proof of [20].

6.2 Performance

The Communication Cost. We take **case 2** and **case 3** as examples. Let E be a 256-bit curve i.e. Curve 25519. $\mathcal{H}$ and $\mathcal{H}_i$ where $i = 0, 1, 2$ are the SHA256 hash function that has a 256-bit output string according to [20], p, q are two 256-bit primes. $\mathbf{G}_i$ are three different secure PRG with the 256-bit output. $\prod_{EtM}$ are based on the ChaCha20 and HMAC, whose key sizes and outputs are both 256 bits respectively. For **case 2**, the private key size is 256 bits, and the public key 512 bits because it is a point. The outputs of **UpPk** are the ciphertext of KEM (512 bits because it is a point), the ciphertext of the updated key (256 bits), the MAC tag of ciphertexts and associated data (256 bits), the total output of **UpPk** is 1024 bits. For **case 3**, the private key is $4 \times 256 = 1024$ bits, the public key is 2048 bits, and the output of **UpPk** is $3 \times 512 + 256 + 256 = 2048$ bits.

Efficiency. In the update phase, Asano et al. [4] applied a FO-transformation to achieve the IND-CCA security, which involves public key encryption (PKE) and symmetric encryption. Together with the original UPKE which involves PKE once, there are two PKEs and one symmetric algorithm. But in our generic UPKE, there are a KhKEM, a SE, and a MAC, thus one PKE and two symmetric algorithms in total. Because the symmetric algorithms are more efficient than the PKE operation, our generic UPKE has better performance than the one in [4].

7 Conclusion

In this paper, we first model the IND-CCA-KH security to catch the IND-CCA security and the key homomorphism of the KEM schemes. Then, we construct the generic UPKE scheme from a KhKEM, three PRGs, and an Encrypt-Then-MAC scheme. We prove that if the KhKEM is IND-CCA-KE secure, PRGs are secure and one-way, the Encrypt-then-MAC scheme is IND-CCA, the generic hybrid UPKE will be IND-CU-CCA secure and resist non-influential randomness. Finally, we illustrate three cases that satisfy IND-CCA-KH security and show that our generic UPKE has better performance. However, our IND-CCA-KH model does not satisfy those KEM schemes that do not have a uniform distribution of private key space. We leave how to construct KhKEM and UPKE schemes from those public key systems for future work.

Acknowledgment. This work is partially supported by the Quantum Leader Resources Fellowship, JSPS KAKENHI Grant Number JP21H03443, SECOM Science and Technology Foundation, the Fundamental Research Funds for the Central Universities under Grand No. CCNU24ai010, and the National Natural Science Foundation of China under Grant No. 62272189.

A Proof for Theorem 2

Proof. In the IND-CU-CCA attack game of our UPKE, let $((c_t^{SE}, \tau_t), c_t^{KEM})$ be the challenge value in **Chal** phase, t is the epoch when **Chal** is executed, i.e. $t := q_{SD_1} + q_{UP_1}$, let $seed'$ be the seed chosen in **Comp** phase, $(upk_l, upd_l := ((c_l^{SE}, \tau_l), c_l^{KEM}), usk_l)$ be the compromised value for epoch l that $l - 1$ is the epoch to execute **Comp** i.e. $l := t + q_{SD_2} + q_{UP_2} + 1$. Let $\mathcal{G}_i$ be the games played between the PPT adversary $\mathcal{A}$ and the challenger $\mathcal{C}$, $\Pr[\mathcal{W}_i]$ be the probability for $\mathcal{A}$ to win $\mathcal{G}_i$ where $i \in \{0, 1, 2, 3, 4, 5, 6\}$. The details of each game are as follows:

- $\mathcal{G}_0$: It is the original IND-CU-CCA game. There is:

$$\Pr[\mathcal{W}_0] = Adv_{\Pi_{UPKE}}^{IND-CU-CCA}(\mathcal{A}, \lambda). \tag{10}$$

- $\mathcal{G}_1$: It is the same as $\mathcal{G}_0$ except that instead of generating upk_0 and usk_0 by $\mathcal{C}$, upk_0 is received from an IND-CCA-KH challenger $\mathcal{C}_{KEM}$. $\mathcal{C}$ initiates a value sum_{i+1} with empty symbol $\perp$ to accumulate each update value sk_{i+1}^{UP} for next epoch $i + 1$. That is, $sum_0 = \perp$. In this situation, $\mathcal{C}$ does not have the usk_0. The responses to these queries and phases should be described as follows:

- **Plaintext Query**: Because this oracle does not involve anything about the private key usk_i, $\mathcal{C}$ can reply to $\mathcal{A}$ by running **UEnc**.
- **Ciphertext Query**: It is the same as the one in $\mathcal{G}_0$, except that instead running the **Decap** in **UDec**, $\mathcal{C}$ queries **Decap** from $\mathcal{C}_{KEM}$ on the input of c_{KEM}, sum_i.
- **Seed Query**: It is the same as the one in $\mathcal{G}_0$, except that in epoch $i+1$, $\mathcal{C}$ set $sum_{i+1} := sum_i \otimes sk_{i+1}^{UP}$. If $i = 0$, $sum_{i+1} := sk_{i+1}^{UP}$.
- **Update Query**: It is the same as the one in $\mathcal{G}_0$, instead running the **Decap** in **UpSk**, $\mathcal{C}$ queries **Decap** from $\mathcal{C}_{KEM}$ on the input of c_{KEM}, sum_i. When the epoch i moves to $i + 1$, $\mathcal{C}$ set $sum_{i+1} := sum_i \otimes sk_{i+1}^{UP}$. If $i = 0$, $sum_{i+1} := sk_{i+1}^{UP}$.
- **Comp**: $\mathcal{C}$ does not know usk_0, but for **Comp**, we just need to ensure that upk_l and usk_l are a valid key pair i.e. they satisfy the correctness and key-homomorphism of KEM. It can be found that $\mathcal{A}$ has no knowledge of sk_l^{UP}, so $\mathcal{C}$ runs as follows:
  * $seed' \leftarrow \$\mathcal{SD}$, $sk_l^{UP} \leftarrow \mathbf{G}_0(seed')$.
  * $(upk_l', usk_l') \leftarrow UGen(1^\lambda)$ instead of $upk_l := upk_{l-1} \odot \mathbf{GetPk}(sk_l^{UP})$ and $usk_l := usk_{l-1} \otimes sk_l^{UP}$.
  * $(c_{KEM}, \mathbf{k}_{KEM}) \leftarrow \prod_{KEM}.\mathbf{Encap}(upk_{l-1}; sk_l^{UP})$.
  * $\mathbf{k}_{SE} \leftarrow \mathbf{G}_1(\mathbf{k}_{KEM})$, $\mathbf{k}_{MAC} \leftarrow \mathbf{G}_2(\mathbf{k}_{KEM})$.
  * $c_{UP} \leftarrow \prod_{EtM}.\mathbf{HEnc}((\mathbf{k}_{SE}, \mathbf{k}_{MAC}), sk_l^{UP}; (c_{KEM}, upk_l'))$.

  Finally, $\mathcal{C}$ returns $(upk_l', upd_l := (c_{up}, c_{KEM}), usk_l')$.

Lemma 3. *If $\mathcal{A}$ can distinguish $\mathcal{G}_0$ and $\mathcal{G}_1$, there exists an adversary $\mathcal{B}_{EtM}^0$ that can make use of $\mathcal{G}_0$ and $\mathcal{G}_1$ to break the IND-CCA game of $\prod_{EtM}$ with the following probability $\Pr[EtM_0]$:*

$$\Pr[EtM_0] := |\Pr[\mathcal{W}_1] - \Pr[\mathcal{W}_0]| \leq Adv_{\prod_{EtM}}(\mathcal{B}_{EtM}^0). \tag{11}$$

Proof. · First, we prove that the queries are indistinguishable. From the view of $\mathcal{A}$, according to the key homomorphic of $\prod_{KEM}$:

$$\begin{aligned} sum_{i+1} &= sk_1^{UP} \otimes sk_2^{UP} ... \otimes sk_i^{UP}. \\ usk_{i+1} &= usk_0 \otimes sk_1^{UP} \otimes sk_2^{UP} ... \otimes sk_i^{UP} = usk_0 \otimes sum_{i+1}. \end{aligned} \tag{12}$$

Because $\mathcal{C}$ can answer the queries correctly with the help of $\mathcal{C}_{KEM}$, **Plaintext Queries**, **Ciphertext Queries Seed Queries**, **Update Queries** in $\mathcal{G}_1$ are indistinguishabe from these in $\mathcal{G}_0$.

· Second, we prove usk_l and usk_l' are indistinguishable. Assume there exist an $sk' \in \mathcal{SK}$ s.t.:

$$\begin{aligned} usk_l &= usk_0 \otimes sum_{l-1} \otimes sk_l^{UP} = usk_{l-1} \otimes sk_l^{UP} \\ usk_l' &= usk_0 \otimes sum_{l-1} \otimes sk_l' = usk_{l-1} \otimes sk_l'. \end{aligned} \tag{13}$$

Because usk_l' is generated by random, sk_l' can be seen as a random value, $\mathcal{A}$ cannot distinguish sk_l' and sk_l^{UP} so as to usk_l and usk_l'.

· Finally, we show that the main difference between $\mathcal{G}_0$ and $\mathcal{G}_1$ is that in $\mathcal{G}_0$, sk_l^{UP} is the plaintext of $\prod_{EtM}$.**HEnc** while it should be sk_l' in $\mathcal{G}_1$ but not sk_l^{UP}. If $\mathcal{A}$ can distinguish $\mathcal{G}_0$ and $\mathcal{G}_1$ and abort the game, it means that $\mathcal{A}$ can distinguish the output of $\prod_{EtM}$.**HEnc**. Then there exists an adversary $\mathcal{B}_{EtM}^0$ that can make use of $\mathcal{A}$ to break the IND-CCA game of $\prod_{EtM}$. Let $m_0 := sk_l^{UP}$, $m_1 := sk_l'$. If $\mathcal{A}$ aborts the game, $\mathcal{B}_{EtM}^0$ outputs 1 otherwise 0. Therefore:

$$\Pr[EtM_0] := |\Pr[\mathcal{W}_1] - \Pr[\mathcal{W}_0]| \le Adv_{\prod_{EtM}}(\mathcal{B}_{EtM}^0).$$

– $\mathcal{G}_2$: It is the same as $\mathcal{G}_1$ except that $\mathcal{C}$ sets sum^j to accumulate the sk_j^{UP} in **Update Queries** and **Seed Queries, Stage 2**, where $j \in [t+1, l]$, $sum^{t+1} := sk_{t+1}^{UP}$, and $sum^j := sk_{t+1}^{UP} \otimes sk_{t+2}^{UP} \dots \otimes sk_j^{UP}$ if $j > t+1$. In $\mathcal{G}_2$, if $sum^j \otimes usk_t = usk_t$ occurs, $\mathcal{C}$ aborts the game.

This is to prove that our scheme can resist the *non-influential randomness*. Assume there are q_{SD_2} **Seed Queries** and q_{UP_2} **Update Queries** in **Stage 2**. According to Lemma 1, $\mathbf{G}_0$ is weakly one-way and $\mathcal{A}$ cannot set $seed_j$ to decide sk_j^{UP} s.t. $sum^j \otimes usk_t = usk_t$. So $\mathcal{C}$ aborts the game only when $\mathcal{A}$ executes **Seed Queries** and **Update Queries**, $sum^{j-1} \otimes sk_j^{UP} \otimes usk_t = usk_t$ occurs. Therefore:

$$|\Pr[\mathcal{W}_2] - \Pr[\mathcal{W}_1]| \le \frac{q_{SD_2} + q_{UP_2}}{|\mathcal{SK}|}. \tag{14}$$

• $\mathcal{G}_3$: It is the same as $\mathcal{G}_2$, except that in **Comp**, $\mathcal{C}$ sets $sk_t^{UP} \leftarrow \$\mathcal{SK}$.

If $\mathcal{A}$ can distinguish $\mathcal{G}_3$ and $\mathcal{G}_2$, it means that $\mathcal{A}$ can distinguish the output of $\mathbf{G}_0(seed')$ from random. Then there exists an adversary $\mathcal{B}_{PRG}^0$ that can make use of $\mathcal{A}$ to break the security game of $\mathbf{G}_0$. Let $r_0 := sk_t^{UP}$, $r_1 \leftarrow \$\mathcal{SK}$. If $\mathcal{A}$ aborts the game, $\mathcal{B}_{PRG}^0$ outputs 1 otherwise 0. Therefore:

$$|\Pr[\mathcal{W}_3] - \Pr[\mathcal{W}_2]| \le Adv_{\mathbf{G}}(\mathcal{B}_{PRG}^0). \tag{15}$$

• $\mathcal{G}_4$: It is the same as $\mathcal{G}_3$, except that in **Chal**, $\mathcal{C}$ sets $\mathbf{k}_{KEM} \leftarrow \$\mathcal{K}_{KEM}$.

If $\mathcal{A}$ can distinguish $\mathcal{G}_4$ and $\mathcal{G}_3$, it means that $\mathcal{A}$ can distinguish the output of $\prod_{KEM}$.**Decap** from random. Then there exists an adversary $\mathcal{B}_{KEM}$ that can make use of $\mathcal{A}$ to break the IND-CCA-KH game of $\prod_{KEM}$. Let $k_0 := \mathbf{k}_{KEM}$, $k_1 \leftarrow \$mathcalK_{KEM}$. If $\mathcal{A}$ aborts the game, $\mathcal{B}_{KEM}$ outputs 1 otherwise 0. Therefore:

$$|\Pr[\mathcal{W}_4] - \Pr[\mathcal{W}_3]| \le Adv_{\prod_{KEM}}^{IND-CCA-KH}(\mathcal{B}_{KEM}, \lambda). \tag{16}$$

– $\mathcal{G}_5$: It is the same as $\mathcal{G}_4$, except that in **Chal**, $\mathcal{C}$ sets $\mathbf{k}_{SE} \leftarrow \$\mathcal{K}_{SE}$ instead of $\mathbf{k}_{SE} \leftarrow \mathbf{G}(\mathbf{k}_{KEM})$.

If $\mathcal{A}$ can distinguish $\mathcal{G}_5$ and $\mathcal{G}_4$, there exists an adversary $\mathcal{B}_{PRG}^1$ that can make use of $\mathcal{A}$ to break the security game of $\mathbf{G}_1$. Let $r_0 := \mathbf{k}_{SE}$, $r_1 \leftarrow \$\mathcal{K}_{SE}$. If $\mathcal{A}$ aborts the game, $\mathcal{B}_{PRG}^1$ outputs 1 otherwise 0. Therefore:

$$|\Pr[\mathcal{W}_5] - \Pr[\mathcal{W}_4]| \le Adv_{\mathbf{G}}(\mathcal{B}_{PRG}^1). \tag{17}$$

– $\mathcal{G}_6$: It is the same as $\mathcal{G}_5$, except that in **Chal**, $\mathcal{C}$ sets $\mathbf{k}_{MAC} \leftarrow \$\mathcal{K}_{MAC}$ instead of $\mathbf{k}_{MAC} \leftarrow \mathbf{G}(\mathbf{k}_{KEM})$.

If $\mathcal{A}$ can distinguish $\mathcal{G}_6$ and $\mathcal{G}_5$, there exists an adversary $\mathcal{B}_{PRG}^2$ that can make use of $\mathcal{A}$ to break the security game of $\mathbf{G}_2$. Let $r_0 := \mathbf{k}_{MAC}$, $r_1 \leftarrow \$\mathcal{K}_{MAC}$. If $\mathcal{A}$ aborts the game, $\mathcal{B}_{PRG}^2$ outputs 1 otherwise 0. Therefore:

$$|\Pr[\mathcal{W}_6] - \Pr[\mathcal{W}_5]| \leq Adv_{\mathbf{G}}(\mathcal{B}_{PRG}^2). \tag{18}$$

Because of the random $\mathbf{k}_{SE}$ and $\mathbf{k}_{MAC}$, if $\mathcal{A}$ can distinguish the outputs in $\mathcal{G}_6$, there exists an adversary $\mathcal{B}_{EtM}^1$ that can make use of $\mathcal{A}$ to break the $\prod_{EtM}$. Actually, $\mathcal{G}_6$ is the IND-CCA game of $\prod_{EtM}$. According to Lemma 2:

$$\Pr[\mathcal{W}_6] = Adv_{\prod_{EtM}}^{IND-CCA}(\mathcal{B}_{EtM}^1). \tag{19}$$

Assume $\mathcal{B}_{EtM}$ plays the roles of $\mathcal{B}_{EtM}^0$ and $\mathcal{B}_{EtM}^1$, $\mathcal{B}_{PRG}$ plays the roles of $\mathcal{B}_{PRG}^0$, $\mathcal{B}_{PRG}^1$ and $\mathcal{B}_{PRG}^2$, according to the equations (11), (14), (15), (16), (17), (18), (19), there is

$$Adv_{\prod_{UPKE}}^{IND-CU-CCA}(\mathcal{A}, \lambda) \leq \frac{q_{SD_2} + q_{UP_2}}{|\mathcal{SK}|} + Adv_{\prod_{KEM}}^{IND-CCA-KH}(\mathcal{B}_{KEM}, \lambda)$$
$$+ 3Adv_{\mathbf{G}}(\mathcal{B}_{PRG}) + 2Adv_{\prod_{EtM}}(\mathcal{B}_{EtM}). \tag{20}$$

References

1. Abou Haidar, C., Libert, B., Passelègue, A.: Updatable public key encryption from dcr: efficient constructions with stronger security. In: Proceedings of the 2022 ACM SIGSAC Conference on Computer and Communications Security, pp. 11–22 (2022)
2. Abou Haidar, C., Passelègue, A., Stehlé, D.: Efficient updatable public-key encryption from lattices. In: International Conference on the Theory and Application of Cryptology and Information Security, pp. 342–373. Springer (2023)
3. Alwen, J., Coretti, S., Dodis, Y., Tselekounis, Y.: Security analysis and improvements for the ietf mls standard for group messaging. In: Annual International Cryptology Conference, pp. 248–277. Springer (2020)
4. Asano, K., Watanabe, Y.: Updatable public key encryption with strong cca security: Security analysis and efficient generic construction. Cryptology ePrint Archive (2023)
5. Balli, F., Rösler, P., Vaudenay, S.: Determining the core primitive for optimally secure ratcheting. In: Advances in Cryptology–ASIACRYPT 2020: 26th International Conference on the Theory and Application of Cryptology and Information Security, Daejeon, South Korea, December 7–11, 2020, Proceedings, Part III 26, pp. 621–650. Springer (2020)
6. Bellare, M., Namprempre, C.: Authenticated encryption: relations among notions and analysis of the generic composition paradigm. In: International Conference on the Theory and Application of Cryptology and Information Security, pp. 531–545. Springer (2000)
7. Chen, K., Miyaji, A., Wang, Y.: Privacy-enhanced anonymous and deniable post-quantum x3dh. In: International Conference on Science of Cyber Security, pp. 157–177. Springer (2023)

8. Dodis, Y., Karthikeyan, H., Wichs, D.: Updatable public key encryption in the standard model. In: Theory of Cryptography: 19th International Conference, TCC 2021, Raleigh, NC, USA, November 8–11, 2021, Proceedings, Part III 19, pp. 254–285. Springer (2021)
9. Eaton, E., Jao, D., Komlo, C., Mokrani, Y.: Towards post-quantum key-updatable public-key encryption via supersingular isogenies. In: International Conference on Selected Areas in Cryptography, pp. 461–482. Springer (2021)
10. Fujisaki, E., Okamoto, T.: Secure integration of asymmetric and symmetric encryption schemes. In: Annual International Cryptology Conference, pp. 537–554. Springer (1999)
11. Gentry, C., Peikert, C., Vaikuntanathan, V.: Trapdoors for hard lattices and new cryptographic constructions. In: Proceedings of the Fortieth Annual ACM Symposium on Theory of Computing, pp. 197–206 (2008)
12. Gentry, C., Silverberg, A.: Hierarchical id-based cryptography. In: Advances in Cryptology-ASIACRYPT 2002: 8th International Conference on the Theory and Application of Cryptology and Information Security Queenstown, New Zealand, December 1–5, 2002 Proceedings 8, pp. 548–566. Springer (2002)
13. Hashimoto, K., Katsumata, S., Kwiatkowski, K., Prest, T.: An efficient and generic construction for signal's handshake (x3dh): post-quantum, state leakage secure, and deniable. J. Cryptol. $35(3)$, 1–78 (2022)
14. Impagliazzo, R., Levin, L.A., Luby, M.: Pseudo-random generation from one-way functions. In: Proceedings of the Twenty-First Annual ACM Symposium on Theory of Computing, pp. 12–24 (1989)
15. Jost, D., Maurer, U., Mularczyk, M.: Efficient ratcheting: almost-optimal guarantees for secure messaging. In: Advances in Cryptology–EUROCRYPT 2019: 38th Annual International Conference on the Theory and Applications of Cryptographic Techniques, Darmstadt, Germany, May 19–23, 2019, Proceedings, Part I 38, pp. 159–188. Springer (2019)
16. Kim, G.C., Sin, J.Y., Jong, Y.B.: Cca secure elgamal encryption over an integer group where icdh assumption holds. Cryptology ePrint Archive (2022)
17. Pijnenburg, J., Poettering, B.: On secure ratcheting with immediate decryption. In: International Conference on the Theory and Application of Cryptology and Information Security, pp. 89–118. Springer (2022)
18. Poettering, B., Rösler, P.: Asynchronous ratcheted key exchange. Cryptology ePrint Archive (2018)
19. Poettering, B., Rösler, P.: Towards bidirectional ratcheted key exchange. In: Advances in Cryptology–CRYPTO 2018: 38th Annual International Cryptology Conference, Santa Barbara, CA, USA, August 19–23, 2018, Proceedings, Part I 38, pp. 3–32. Springer (2018)
20. Shoup, V.: Using hash functions as a hedge against chosen ciphertext attack. In: International Conference on the Theory and Applications of Cryptographic Techniques, pp. 275–288. Springer (2000)
21. Singh, K., Rangan, C.P., Banerjee, A.: Efficient lattice hibe in the standard model with shorter public parameters. In: Information and Communication Technology: Second IFIP TC5/8 International Conference, ICT-EurAsia 2014, Bali, Indonesia, April 14–17, 2014. Proceedings 2, pp. 542–553. Springer (2014)

Breaking GEA-Like Stream Ciphers with Lower Time Cost

Zheng Wu, Lin Ding$^{(\boxtimes)}$, Zhengting Li, and Xinhai Wang

Information Engineering University, Zhengzhou 450001, China
dinglin_cipher@163.com

Abstract. GEA-1 and GEA-2 are two proprietary stream ciphers used in GPRS (General Packet Radio Service) to protect GPRS from eavesdropping. GEA-2a is an improved version of GEA-2 proposed recently. In this paper, new weaknesses of GEA-like stream ciphers (i.e., GEA-1, GEA-2 and GEA-2a) are discovered and analyzed. As the technical contribution, an automatic algorithm is proposed to search for differential paths of full GEA-like stream ciphers. By this automatic algorithm, the differential paths of full GEA-1, GEA-2 and GEA-2a are found, whose probabilities are up to $2^{-22.90}$, $2^{-19.60}$ and $2^{-18.60}$ respectively. Based on these found differential paths, practical distinguishing attacks and key recovery attacks on GEA-like stream ciphers in the chosen IV setting are presented. All these attacks have been confirmed by experimental results on a common PC. The cryptanalytic results show that the initializations of all GEA-like stream ciphers are far from being optimal and need to be strengthened.

Keywords: Differential cryptanalysis · GEA-1 · GEA-2 · Stream cipher · GPRS

1 Introduction

GPRS (General Packet Radio Service) is a mobile data standard based on GSM (Global System for Mobile) technology, widely used in the early 21st century, providing mobile internet connectivity for communication between mobile phones and base stations. To protect GPRS from eavesdropping, two proprietary stream ciphers, GEA-1 and GEA-2, were used. GEA-1 was designed by the Security Algorithms Group of Experts (SAGE) at European Telecommunications Standards Institute (ETSI) in 1998. Based on the technical report of the design process [1], the stream cipher GEA-1 takes a 64-bit key, a 32-bit initialization vector (IV), and a 1-bit flag(used to indicate the transfer direction) as input, and outputs a binary keystream sequence. GEA-2, designed approximately one year later than GEA-1, is an improvement of GEA-1 [2]. The details of the proprietary stream ciphers GEA-1 and GEA-2 had always been kept confidential and not publicly disclosed until 2021.

Z. Xia and J. Chen (Eds.): ISPEC 2024, LNCS 15053, pp. 186–204, 2024.
https://doi.org/10.1007/978-981-97-9053-1_11

The stream cipher GEA-1 was prohibited from implementing in mobile stations by ETSI since 2013, while the improved version GEA-2 and the non-encrypted mode (GEA-0) are still mandatory to be implemented [3]. In [4], the authors analyzed the support of both stream ciphers in mobile phones by testing a range of current phones. The results show that all tested phones (such as Apple iPhone XR, Samsung Galaxy S9, HMD Global Nokia 3.1, Huawei P9 lite and OnePlus 6T) support the vulnerable cipher GEA-1 and its improved version GEA-2. Once the stream cipher GEA-1 (or GEA-2) is broken and the secret key is recovered, the attacker can decrypt all traffic for the complete GPRS session until the key gets invalid, which happens in the GPRS authentication and ciphering procedure triggered by the network [4]. This fact clearly brings a serious threat to the security of today's communication.

Related Works. Up to now, there are several attacks on GEA-1 and GEA-2 published in [4–9]. In [4], Beierle et al. provided a detailed description of GEA-1 and GEA-2, and presented the first public analysis on them at EUROCRYPT 2021. At EUROCRYPT 2022, Amzaleg and Dinur [7] further improved and complemented the previous analysis in [1]. In [8], Ding et al. proposed new key recovery attacks on GEA-1 and GEA-2 by combining time-memory trade-off technique. These new attacks significantly reduce the time and memory costs compared to previous attacks on GEA-1, indicating that GEA-1 only provides 32-bit security. Additionally, they discovered and exploited the sliding property of GEA-1 and GEA-2 for the first time to explore practical related-key attacks. Finally, they proposed an improved version of GEA-2 called GEA-2a and explained the reasons behind the modifications from GEA-2. Their analysis showed that GEA-2a outperforms GEA-2 in terms of the resistance against all existing attacks and can provide 64-bit security. Recently, some new related key attacks on GEA-1 and GEA-2 were given in [9].

Our Contributions. In this paper, the security of GEA-like stream ciphers against differential cryptanalysis [10] is analyzed. As results, new distinguishing attacks and key recovery attacks on them in the single key setting are proposed. Table 1 lists all existing attacks on GEA-like stream ciphers in the single key setting, and the comparisons of our cryptanalytic results with these existing attacks are made in this table. It should be noted that the related key attacks on GEA-1 and GEA-2 proposed in [8,9] are not presented in this table, since the related key setting is often of limited practical significance. The contributions of this paper can be summarized as follows.

– In this paper, we propose an automatic algorithm, which is used to search for differential paths of full GEA-1, GEA-2 and GEA-2a. As results, the differential paths of full GEA-1, GEA-2 and GEA-2a are found, and the maximum probabilities of these differential paths can be up to $2^{-22.90}$, $2^{-19.60}$ and $2^{-18.60}$, respectively. These are quite high compared with a secure stream cipher, and indicate that the initializations of all GEA-like stream ciphers are far from optimal and need to be improved.

Table 1. Comparisons of our cryptanalytic results with the existing attacks on GEA-1 and GEA-2

Cipher	Attack	Offline\online time complexity	Memory complexity	Data complexity	Ref.
GEA-1	Key recovery	$2^{37}\backslash 2^{40}$	$2^{38.5}$ bits (44.5 GiB)	65 bits	[4]
	Key recovery	$-\backslash 2^{40}$	2^{25} bits (4 MiB)	65 bits	[7]
	Key recovery	$2^{32}\backslash 2^{26}$	2^{26} bits (8 MiB)	2^{38} bits	[8]
	Distinguishing	$-\backslash \mathbf{2^{23.90}}$	–	$\mathbf{2^{47.80}}$ **bits**	**Ours**
	Key recovery	$-\backslash \mathbf{2^{28.5}}$	–	$\mathbf{2^{52.40}}$ **bits**	**Ours**
GEA-2	Key recovery	$-\backslash 2^{45.1}$	–	12800 bits	[4]
	Key recovery	$-\backslash 2^{64}/(l-62)$	2^{39} bits (64 GiB)	l consecutive bits	[7]
	Key recovery	$-\backslash 2^{55}$	2^{28} bits (32 MiB)	11320 fragmented bits	[7]
	Key recovery	$2^{65}\backslash 2^{48.4}$	$2^{48.4}$ bits (42 TiB)	$2^{38.6}$ bits	[8]
	Distinguishing	$-\backslash \mathbf{2^{20.60}}$	–	$\mathbf{2^{51.11}}$ **bits**	**Ours**
	Key recovery	$-\backslash \mathbf{2^{25.96}}$	–	$\mathbf{2^{56.59}}$ **bits**	**Ours**

- Based on the found differential paths with maximum probabilities, practical distinguishing attacks and key recovery attacks on full GEA-1 and GEA-2 in the chosen IV setting are proposed. The cryptanalytic results show that the time complexities for recovering the key of GEA-1 and GEA-2 can be as low as $2^{28.5}$ and $2^{25.96}$ respectively, which is significantly better than the previous attacks on GEA-1 and GEA-2 in terms of the time cost, as shown in Table 1. It is important to note that both of our attacks and the existing attacks are meaningful in reality. When the message that should be encrypted by the standard stream cipher GEA-2 (or GEA-1) is so short that it only consists of a small amount of frames, the existing attacks perform better than our attaks. In contrary, our attacks are clearly more effective when a long message needs to be encrypted with the standard stream cipher.
- Based on the found differential paths with high probabilities, an efficient key recovery attack on GEA-2a is proposed for the first time. The cryptanalytic result shows that the 64-bit key of GEA-2a can be recovered with a time complexity of 2^{54}. This has been the only efficient attack on GEA-2a since GEA-2a was proposed in [8], and shows that GEA-2a can not provide 64-bit security.

The rest of this paper is structured as follows. Brief descriptions of GEA-like stream ciphers are given in Sect. 2. In Sect. 3, differential cryptanalysis of GEA-1 in the chosen IV setting is given. Differential cryptanalysis of GEA-2 and GEA-2a are given in Sect. 4. The paper is concluded in Sect. 5.

2 Brief Descriptions of GEA-Like Stream Ciphers

This section gives brief descriptions of GEA-1 and GEA-2, for full descriptions we refer to [4]. An overview of the keystream generator of GEA-1 and GEA-2 is depicted in Fig. 1. As GEA-2 is a simple extension of GEA-1 with some slight modifications, we first describe GEA-1 and explain the differences for GEA-2 latter.

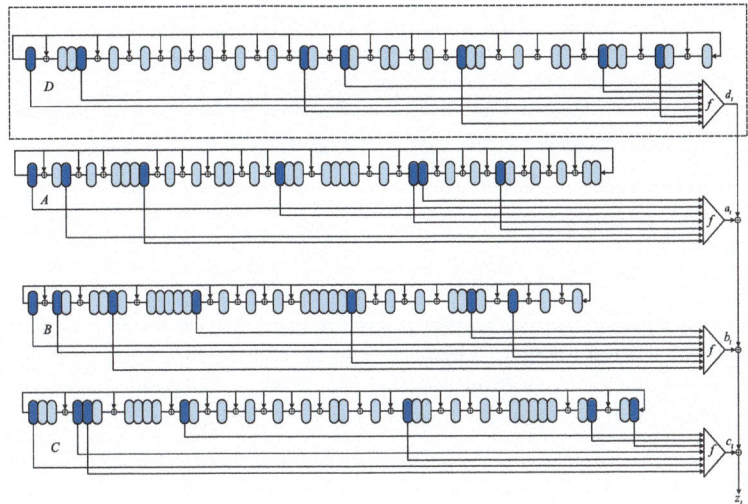

Fig. 1. An overview of the keystream generator of GEA-1 and GEA-2

2.1 A Brief Description of GEA-1

The stream cipher GEA-1 consists of three LFSRs denoted as A, B and C over $\mathbb{F}_2$, a nonlinear feedback shift register (NFSR) S and a filter function f. The lengths of three LFSRs are 31, 32, and 33 bits, respectively, and they are updated in the Galois mode. Their update functions are given as follows.

LFSR A:

$$a_i^{(t+1)} = \begin{cases} a_{i+1}^{(t)} \oplus a_0^{(t)}, \; if \; i \in TapA \\ a_{i+1}^{(t)}, \; if \; i \in \{0, ..., 29\} - TapA \\ a_0^{(t)}, \; if \; i = 30 \end{cases}$$

LFSR B:

$$b_i^{(t+1)} = \begin{cases} b_{i+1}^{(t)} \oplus b_0^{(t)}, \; if \; i \in TapB \\ b_{i+1}^{(t)}, \; if \; i \in \{0, ..., 30\} - TapB \\ b_0^{(t)}, \; if \; i = 31 \end{cases}$$

LFSR C:

$$c_i^{(t+1)} = \begin{cases} c_{i+1}^{(t)} \oplus c_0^{(t)}, \; if \; i \in TapC \\ c_{i+1}^{(t)}, \; if \; i \in \{0, ..., 31\} - TapC \\ c_0^{(t)}, \; if \; i = 32 \end{cases}$$

The three tap sets used above are listed as follows.

$$TapA = \{0, 2, 3, 7, 8, 9, 11, 12, 15, 19, 20, 22, 23, 24, 26, 27, 28\}$$
$$TapB = \{0, 2, 6, 12, 13, 14, 15, 22, 23, 24, 28, 29, 30\}$$
$$TapC = \{2, 5, 9, 11, 12, 13, 14, 15, 17, 18, 21, 22, 23, 28, 30\}$$

The filter function $f(x_0, x_1, .., x_6)$ is a nonlinear Boolean function with with an algebraic degree of 4. It can be given in algebraic normal form as

$$
\begin{aligned}
f(x_0, ..., x_6) = {} & x_0 x_1 x_5 x_6 \oplus x_0 x_2 x_3 x_6 \oplus x_0 x_2 x_5 x_6 \oplus x_0 x_3 x_5 x_6 \oplus x_1 x_2 x_5 x_6 \\
& \oplus x_1 x_3 x_4 x_6 \oplus x_1 x_3 x_5 x_6 \oplus x_0 x_1 x_3 \oplus x_0 x_1 x_4 \oplus x_0 x_1 x_6 \oplus x_0 x_2 x_3 \\
& \oplus x_0 x_2 x_4 \oplus x_0 x_2 x_6 \oplus x_0 x_3 x_5 \oplus x_1 x_2 x_5 \oplus x_1 x_2 x_6 \oplus x_1 x_4 x_6 \\
& \oplus x_2 x_5 x_6 \oplus x_0 x_2 \oplus x_0 x_3 \oplus x_0 x_5 \oplus x_1 x_3 \oplus x_1 x_5 \oplus x_1 x_6 \oplus x_2 x_3 \\
& \oplus x_2 x_5 \oplus x_2 x_6 \oplus x_4 x_5 \otimes x_5 x_6 \oplus x_1 \oplus x_2 \oplus x_3 \oplus x_5
\end{aligned}
$$

After all three LFSRs have been initialized (as described below), the actual keystream generation begins. This is done by taking bits from seven specific positions in each LFSR as input to the function f. The outputs of the three f-functions are XORed together to generate a keystream bit z_t.

$$
z_t = a_t \oplus b_t \oplus c_t, \; t \geq 0
$$

where a_t, b_t, c_t are three output bits generated by the f functions as follows.

$$
a_t = f\left(a_{22}^{(t)}, a_0^{(t)}, a_{13}^{(t)}, a_{21}^{(t)}, a_{25}^{(t)}, a_2^{(t)}, a_7^{(t)}\right)
$$

$$
b_t = f\left(b_{12}^{(t)}, b_{27}^{(t)}, b_0^{(t)}, b_1^{(t)}, b_{29}^{(t)}, b_{21}^{(t)}, b_5^{(t)}\right)
$$

$$
c_t = f\left(c_{10}^{(t)}, c_{30}^{(t)}, c_{32}^{(t)}, c_3^{(t)}, c_{19}^{(t)}, c_0^{(t)}, c_4^{(t)}\right)
$$

Initialization of GEA-1. The first step to initialize GEA-1 is to initialize the nonlinear feedback shift register S with a length of 64 bits. At the beginning of the initialization process, all bits in the NFSR S are filled with zeros. The inputs for initialization include a 32-bit public initialization vector IV, a public bit dir indicating the communication direction, and a 64-bit secret key K. In this process, the NFSR S is clocked 97 times, feeding in one input bit for each clock. These 97 input bits are sequentially loaded into the NFSR in the order of $IV_0, IV_1, ..., IV_{31}, dir, K_0, K_1, ..., K_{63}$. After this process, the NFSR S is clocked another 128 times with zeros as input bits. During this process, the output bit of feedback function is produced by XORing the input bit, the output bit of the function f, and the bit that is shifted out. The initialization process of the NFSR S is clearly described in Fig. 2.

After clocking the NFSR S 225 times, the content of S denoted as $S^{(225)} = s = (s_0, ..., s_{63})$ is named *initial state* of GEA-1. It is used as the seed for initializing the three LFSRs A, B, and C. The three LFSRs are initially filled with all zeros. After then each LFSR is clocked 64 times, and the feedback bits are produced by XORing one bit of S with the bit that is shifted out. During the initialization of LFSR A, the bits in S are loaded in the order of $s_0, s_1, ..., s_{63}$. During the initialization of LFSR B, the bits in S are loaded in the order of $s_{16}, s_{17}, ..., s_{63}, s_0, ..., s_{15}$. During the initialization of LFSR C, the bits in S are loaded in the order of $s_{32}, ..., s_{63}, s_0, ..., s_{31}$. In the event that any of the LFSRs (A, B and C) ends up with a state where all bits are zeros, the leftmost bit of that LFSR is forcibly set to 1 before generating the first keystream bit.

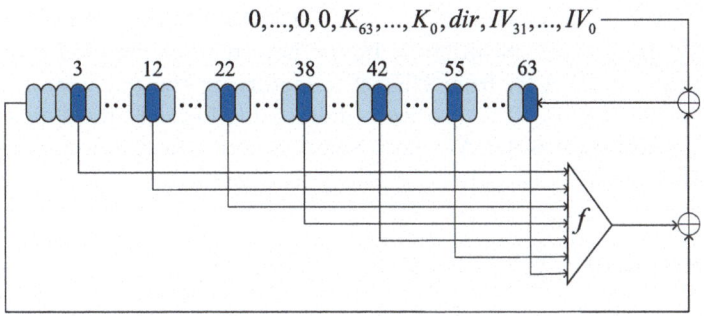

$$0,...,0,0,K_{63},...,K_0, dir, IV_{31},...,IV_0$$

Fig. 2. An overview of the initialization of the NFSR S

2.2 A Brief Description of GEA-2 and GEA-2a

GEA-2 is an improved variant of GEA-1 with some slight modifications. As shown in Fig. 1, a fourth LFSR of length 29, denoted as D, is added in the keystream generator of GEA-2. Let $D^{(t)} = \left(d_0^{(t)}, \ldots, d_{28}^{(t)}\right)$ denote the state of LFSR D at time t, and the update function of the LFSR D is given as follows.

$$d_i^{(t+1)} = \begin{cases} d_{i+1}^{(t)} \oplus d_0^{(t)}, & if \ i \in TapD \\ d_{i+1}^{(t)}, & if \ i \in \{0, \ldots, 27\} - TapD \\ d_0^{(t)}, & if \ i = 28 \end{cases}$$

where $TapD = \{0, 3, 4, 5, 6, 7, 8, 9, 11, 13, 15, 16, 19, 20, 22, 25, 27\}$.

In the keystream generation process of GEA-2, the keystream bit z_t is generated by

$$z_t = a_t \oplus b_t \oplus c_t \oplus d_t, \ t \geq 0$$

Where a_t, b_t, c_t are the same as in GEA-1, and the bit d_t is generated as follows.

$$d_t = f\left(d_{12}^{(t)}, d_{23}^{(t)}, d_3^{(t)}, d_0^{(t)}, d_{10}^{(t)}, d_{27}^{(t)}, d_{17}^{(t)}\right)$$

Initialization of GEA-2. GEA-2 also takes a 64-bit secret key, a 32-bit public IV, and a public direction bit dir as input. However, a larger NFSR of length 97, denoted as W, is used in the initialization process of GEA-2. After filling the NFSR W with all zeros, the NFSR W is clocked 97 times, feeding in one input bit with each clock. The 97 input bits are introduced in the sequence $iv_0, \ldots, iv_{31}, dir, k_0, \ldots, k_{63}$. After this, the NFSR W is clocked another 194 times with all zeros as input bits. After clocking the NFSR W 291 times, the content of NFSR W denoted as $W^{(291)} = w = (w_0, \ldots, w_{96})$ is used as a seed for initializing four LFSRs. The process of initializing four LFSRs is quite similar as in the initialization of GEA-1, so we skip it here. For a full description, we refer to [4].

GEA-2a. GEA-2a is an improved variant of GEA-2 with a similar structure, proposed by Ding et al. [8] in 2022. In the keystream generation process, the only difference of GEA-2a from GEA-2 is modifying the updates of the right most bits of four LFSRs. The process of initializing four LFSRs is quite similar as in the initialization of GEA-2, so we skip it here. For a full description, we refer to [8].

3   Differential Cryptanalysis of GEA-1

In this section, we attempt to mount practical differential attacks on the GEA-like stream ciphers, i.e., GEA-1, GEA-2 and GEA-2a. Differential attack [10] is an important cryptanalytic method for symmetric cryptographic algorithms that exploits the high probability relations between the input and output differences. It has been successfully applied to many well-known stream ciphers, e.g., 4G standard ciphers SNOW 3G [11] and ZUC [12], Loiss [13], 5G candidate ciphers SNOW-V [14] and ZUC-256 [15], Grain family of stream ciphers [16–18], DECT standard cipher [19]. Since GEA-2 (and also GEA-2a) is an improved version of GEA-1, we first introduce the differential attacks on GEA-1, and then apply them to GEA-2 and GEA-2a.

3.1   Searching for Differential Paths of Full GEA-1

Let x be a binary variable, i.e., $x \in \mathbb{F}_2$, and the difference of x and x' is denoted as $\Delta x = x \oplus x'$. Recall the nonlinear filter function $f(x_0, \ldots, x_6)$ used in the GEA-like stream ciphers, we can easily calculate all 128 probabilities $\Pr(\Delta f = 0 | \Delta x_0, \ldots, \Delta x_6)$, where $\Delta x_0, \ldots, \Delta x_6$ traverses all 128 possible values. In fact, there exists an obvious case that $\Pr(\Delta f = 0 | \Delta x_0 = \ldots = \Delta x_6 = 0) = 1$ always holds. These 128 probabilities can be easily obtained by making an exhaustive search. The results are stored in a table called T_{df}, which is listed in the supplementary document, due to the limitation of paper length.

Let $(\lambda^{(0)}, \ldots, \lambda^{(224)}) = (iv_0, \ldots, iv_{31}, dir, k_0, \cdots, k_{63}, 0, \ldots, 0)$. Since we only consider the differential paths in the single key setting, there exists no difference in the public bit dir and the 64-bit key. Thus, $\Delta\lambda^{(i)} = \Delta iv_i$ holds for $0 \leq i \leq 31$ and $\Delta\lambda^{(i)} = 0$ holds for $32 \leq i \leq 224$. When the IV difference is chosen by the attacker, it has $\Pr(\Delta\lambda^{(i)} = 0) = \Pr(\Delta iv_i = 0) = 1$ if $\Delta iv_i = 0$ and $\Pr(\Delta\lambda^{(i)} = 0) = \Pr(\Delta iv_i = 0) = 0$ if $\Delta iv_i = 1$.

Now, an automatic algorithm called **Algorithm 1** is proposed to search for differential paths of full GEA-1. In this algorithm, the input is the IV difference $\Delta IV = (\Delta iv_0, \ldots, \Delta iv_{31})$ chosen by the attacker. The output consists of two parts. The one is the differences of three LFSRs just after full initialization of GEA-1, i.e., $\left(\Delta a_0^{(64)}, \ldots, \Delta a_{30}^{(64)}\right), \left(\Delta b_0^{(64)}, \ldots, \Delta b_{31}^{(64)}\right)$ and $\left(\Delta c_0^{(64)}, \ldots, \Delta c_{32}^{(64)}\right)$. The other is the value of p_{path}, which denotes the probability of the found differential path. When the input of **Algorithm 1**, i.e., the

IV difference, is chosen by the attacker, **Algorithm 1** will give a differential path and its probability of full GEA-1 as output.

Algorithm 1 Calculating Differential Path and Its Probability of Full GEA-1

Input: The IV difference, i.e., $\Delta IV = (\Delta iv_0, \ldots, \Delta iv_{31})$.

1. Set $p_{path} \leftarrow 1$;
2. For i from 0 to 31, set $\Delta\lambda^{(i)} \leftarrow 0$ if $\Delta iv_i = 0$, otherwise $\Delta\lambda^{(i)} \leftarrow 1$ if $\Delta iv_i = 1$.
3. For i from 32 to 224, set $\Delta\lambda^{(i)} \leftarrow 0$.
4. For i from 0 to 63, set $\Delta s_i^{(0)} \leftarrow 0$.
5. For i from 0 to 224, do the following:

   – 5.1. If $\Delta s_3^{(i)} = \Delta s_{12}^{(i)} = \Delta s_{22}^{(i)} = \Delta s_{38}^{(i)} = \Delta s_{42}^{(i)} = \Delta s_{55}^{(i)} = \Delta s_{63}^{(i)} = 0$, then $\Delta s_{63}^{(i+1)} \leftarrow \Delta s_0^{(i)} \oplus \Delta\lambda^{(i)}$; otherwise, do the following:
     - $\Pr(\Delta f = 0) \leftarrow T_{df}\left(\Delta s_3^{(i)} \| \Delta s_{12}^{(i)} \| \Delta s_{22}^{(i)} \| \Delta s_{38}^{(i)} \| \Delta s_{42}^{(i)} \| \Delta s_{55}^{(i)} \| \Delta s_{63}^{(i)}\right)$;
     - If $\Delta s_0^{(i)} \oplus \Delta\lambda^{(i)} = 0$, then $\Delta s_{63}^{(i+1)} \leftarrow 0$ and $p_{path} \leftarrow p_{path} \cdot \Pr(\Delta f = 0)$;
     - Else if $\Delta s_0^{(i)} \oplus \Delta\lambda^{(i)} = 1$, then $\Delta s_{63}^{(i+1)} \leftarrow 0$ and $p_{path} \leftarrow p_{path} \cdot (1 - \Pr(\Delta f = 0))$;
   – 5.2. For j from 0 to 62, $\Delta s_j^{(i+1)} \leftarrow \Delta s_{j+1}^{(i)}$;

6. For i from 0 to 30, set $\Delta a_i^{(0)} \leftarrow 0$;
   For i from 0 to 31, set $\Delta b_i^{(0)} \leftarrow 0$;
   For i from 0 to 32, set $\Delta c_i^{(0)} \leftarrow 0$.
7. For i from 0 to 63, do the following:

   – For $j \in TapA$, $\Delta a_j^{(i+1)} \leftarrow \Delta a_{j+1}^{(i)} \oplus \Delta a_0^{(i)} \oplus \Delta s_i^{(225)}$;
   – For $j \in \{0, \ldots, 29\} - TapA$, $\Delta a_j^{(i+1)} \leftarrow \Delta a_{j+1}^{(i)}$;
   – $\Delta a_{30}^{(i+1)} \leftarrow \Delta a_0^{(i)} \oplus \Delta s_i^{(225)}$;
   – For $j \in TapB$, $\Delta b_j^{(i+1)} \leftarrow \Delta b_{j+1}^{(i)} \oplus \Delta b_0^{(i)} \oplus \Delta s_{(i+16) \bmod 64}^{(225)}$;
   – For $j \in \{0, \ldots, 30\} - TapB$, $\Delta b_j^{(i+1)} \leftarrow \Delta b_{j+1}^{(i)}$;
   – $\Delta b_{31}^{(i+1)} \leftarrow \Delta b_0^{(i)} \oplus \Delta s_{(i+16) \bmod 64}^{(225)}$;
   – For $j \in TapC$, $\Delta c_j^{(i+1)} \leftarrow \Delta c_{j+1}^{(i)} \oplus \Delta c_0^{(i)} \oplus \Delta s_{(i+32) \bmod 64}^{(225)}$;
   – For $j \in \{0, \ldots, 31\} - TapC$, $\Delta c_j^{(i+1)} \leftarrow \Delta c_{j+1}^{(i)}$;
   – $\Delta c_{32}^{(i+1)} \leftarrow \Delta c_0^{(i)} \oplus \Delta s_{(i+32) \bmod 64}^{(225)}$;

8. Output $\left(\Delta a_0^{(64)}, \ldots, \Delta a_{30}^{(64)}\right)$, $\left(\Delta b_0^{(64)}, \ldots, \Delta b_{31}^{(64)}\right)$, $\left(\Delta c_0^{(64)}, \ldots, \Delta c_{32}^{(64)}\right)$ and p_{path}.

In Step 1 of **Algorithm 1**, the initial value of the probability p_{path} is assigned to be 1. In Steps 2-3 of **Algorithm 1**, the values of $\left(\Delta\lambda^{(0)}, \ldots, \Delta\lambda^{(224)}\right)$ are assigned according to the chosen IV difference. In Step 4 of **Algorithm 1**, the initial values of $\left(\Delta s_0^{(0)}, \ldots, \Delta s_{63}^{(0)}\right)$ are assigned to be all zeros, since the NFSR is filled by all zeros at the beginning of initialization. In the following 225 clocks, the internal state of the NFSR is updated, and it has $\Delta s_{63}^{(i+1)} = \Delta s_0^{(i)} \oplus \Delta\lambda^{(i)} \oplus \Delta f$, where Δf denotes the output difference of f. If there are not differences in the seven input bits of f, i.e., $\Delta s_3^{(i)} = \Delta s_{12}^{(i)} = \Delta s_{22}^{(i)} = \Delta s_{38}^{(i)} = \Delta s_{42}^{(i)} = \Delta s_{55}^{(i)} = \Delta s_{63}^{(i)} = 0$, it has $\Delta f = 0$ and then $\Delta s_{63}^{(i+1)} = \Delta s_0^{(i)} \oplus \Delta\lambda^{(i)}$. If there are differences in the seven input bits of f, the difference $\Delta s_{63}^{(i+1)}$ is equal to $\Delta s_0^{(i)} \oplus \Delta\lambda^{(i)}$ with a probability of $\Pr(\Delta f = 0)$ or $\Delta s_0^{(i)} \oplus \Delta\lambda^{(i)} \oplus 1$ with a probability of $1 - \Pr(\Delta f = 0)$. To reduce the difference weight of the NFSR, the difference

$\Delta s_{63}^{(i+1)}$ is always assigned to be zero in Step 5.1 of **Algorithm 1**, when there are differences in the seven input bits of f. This is a natural idea in cryptanalysis, as lower weight of the input difference probably means better differential path. Thus, the probability of the differential path p_{path} should be updated to be $p_{path} \cdot \Pr(\Delta f = 0)$ if $\Delta s_0^{(i)} \oplus \Delta \lambda^{(i)} = 0$ satisfies, or $p_{path} \cdot (1 - \Pr(\Delta f = 0))$ if $\Delta s_0^{(i)} \oplus \Delta \lambda^{(i)} = 1$ satisfies. In Step 6 of **Algorithm 1**, the initial values of $\left(\Delta a_0^{(0)}, \ldots, \Delta a_{30}^{(0)}\right)$, $\left(\Delta b_0^{(0)}, \ldots, \Delta b_{31}^{(0)}\right)$ and $\left(\Delta c_0^{(0)}, \ldots, \Delta c_{32}^{(0)}\right)$ are assigned to be all zeros, since the three LFSRs are first filled by all zeros in the initialization. In Step 7 of **Algorithm 1**, the values of $\left(\Delta a_0^{(i)}, \ldots, \Delta a_{30}^{(i)}\right)$, $\left(\Delta b_0^{(i)}, \ldots, \Delta b_{31}^{(i)}\right)$ and $\left(\Delta c_0^{(i)}, \ldots, \Delta c_{32}^{(i)}\right)$ can be directly calculated, since there are only linear operations in this step and the values of $\left(\Delta s_0^{(0)}, \ldots, \Delta s_{63}^{(0)}\right)$ have been obtained in Step 5. Furthermore, the probability of the differential path p_{path} remains unchanged, since there are not nonlinear operations in Step 7.

Since the time cost of **Algorithm 1** is small enough to be negligible, the attacker can easily obtain a differential path by **Algorithm 1** for any given IV difference. To find the differential paths with high probabilities, we make an exhaustive search of all IV differences with weight no more than 6, i.e., $weight(\Delta IV) \leq 6$, in a dozen seconds on a common PC with 2.5 GHz Intel Pentium 4 processor. The amount of such IV differences is $\sum_{i=1}^{6} \binom{32}{i} \approx 2^{20.13}$. The experimental results show that the maximum probability is obtained when the weight of the IV difference is equal to one or two. More specifically, we have found 15 IV differences with weight one or two, and the probabilities of their corresponding differential paths achieve the maximum value $2^{-22.90}$. The 15 IV differences are listed as follows.

$$\Delta_{\max,i} := \{\Delta iv_{24+i} = 1, weight(\Delta IV) = 1\}, i = 0, \ldots, 7$$
$$\Delta_{\max,i+8} := \{\Delta iv_{24+i} = \Delta iv_{25+i} = 1, weight(\Delta IV) = 2\}, i = 0, \ldots, 6$$

To verify the maximum probability, we have made an experiment. In this experiment, we first choose the IV difference $\Delta_{\max,7}$, and randomly choose 10 keys and 2^{26} IVs for each key. The results show that there exist 9.2 IVs on average per key which generate the expected output difference. It leads to an experimental probability of $9.2/2^{26} = 2^{-22.80}$, which is quite close to the theoretical value $2^{-22.90}$. Furthermore, the other 14 IV differences have been also verified. The results show that all 15 experimental probabilities are quite chose to the theoretical value $2^{-22.90}$. This indicates that the differential paths with maximum probability searched by **Algorithm 1** are correct and can be used to construct distinguishers and key recovery attacks.

3.2   Differential Distinguishing Attacks on GEA-1

Let $\Delta z_0, \ldots, \Delta z_{L-1}$ denote the differences of the first L keystream bits $z_0, \ldots, z_{L-1}$ generated by GEA-1. By **Algorithm 1**, the attacker can obtain the differences of three LFSRs just after full initialization of GEA-1, and then the probabilities $\Pr(\Delta z_0 = 0), \ldots, \Pr(\Delta z_{L-1} = 0)$ can be obtained by the following algorithm.

Algorithm 2 Calculating the Probabilities $\Pr(\Delta z_0 = 0), \ldots, \Pr(\Delta z_{L-1} = 0)$

Input: $\left(\Delta a_0^{(64)}, \ldots, \Delta a_{30}^{(64)}\right)$, $\left(\Delta b_0^{(64)}, \ldots, \Delta b_{31}^{(64)}\right)$ and $\left(\Delta c_0^{(64)}, \ldots, \Delta c_{32}^{(64)}\right)$.

1. For t from 0 to $L-1$, do the followings:

1.1. $\Pr(\Delta a_t = 0) \leftarrow T_{df}\left(\Delta a_{22}^{(t+64)} || \Delta a_0^{(t+64)} || \Delta a_{13}^{(t+64)} || \Delta a_{21}^{(t+64)} || \Delta a_{25}^{(t+64)} || \Delta a_2^{(t+64)} || \Delta a_7^{(t+64)}\right)$;

1.2. $\Pr(\Delta b_t = 0) \leftarrow T_{df}\left(\Delta b_{12}^{(t+64)} || \Delta b_{27}^{(t+64)} || \Delta b_0^{(t+64)} || \Delta b_1^{(t+64)} || \Delta b_{29}^{(t+64)} || \Delta b_{21}^{(t+64)} || \Delta b_5^{(t+64)}\right)$;

1.3. $\Pr(\Delta c_t = 0) \leftarrow T_{df}\left(\Delta c_{10}^{(t+64)} || \Delta c_{30}^{(t+64)} || \Delta c_{32}^{(t+64)} || \Delta c_3^{(t+64)} || \Delta c_{19}^{(t+64)} || \Delta c_0^{(t+64)} || \Delta c_4^{(t+64)}\right)$;

1.4. $\Pr(\Delta z_t = 0) \leftarrow \mathcal{XOR}\left(\mathcal{XOR}\left(\Pr(\Delta a_t = 0), \Pr(\Delta b_t = 0)\right), \Pr(\Delta c_t = 0)\right)$;

1.5. For $j \in TapA$, $\Delta a_j^{(t+65)} \leftarrow \Delta a_{j+1}^{(t+64)} \oplus \Delta a_0^{(t+64)}$;

1.6. For $j \in \{0, \ldots, 29\} - TapA$, $\Delta a_j^{(t+65)} \leftarrow \Delta a_{j+1}^{(t+64)}$;

1.7. $\Delta a_{30}^{(t+65)} \leftarrow \Delta a_0^{(t+64)}$;

1.8. For $j \in TapB$, $\Delta b_j^{(t+65)} \leftarrow \Delta b_{j+1}^{(t+64)} \oplus \Delta b_0^{(t+64)}$;

1.9. For $j \in \{0, \ldots, 30\} - TapB$, $\Delta b_j^{(t+65)} \leftarrow \Delta b_{j+1}^{(t+64)}$;

1.10. $\Delta b_{31}^{(t+65)} \leftarrow \Delta b_0^{(t+64)}$;

1.11. For $j \in TapC$, $\Delta c_j^{(t+65)} \leftarrow \Delta c_{j+1}^{(t+64)} \oplus \Delta c_0^{(t+64)}$;

1.12. For $j \in \{0, \ldots, 31\} - TapC$, $\Delta c_j^{(t+65)} \leftarrow \Delta c_{j+1}^{(t+64)}$;

1.13. $\Delta c_{32}^{(t+65)} \leftarrow \Delta c_0^{(t+64)}$;

2. Output the probabilities $\Pr(\Delta z_0 = 0), \ldots, \Pr(\Delta z_{L-1} = 0)$.

In Steps 1.1–1.3 of **Algorithm 2**, the probabilities $\Pr(\Delta a_t = 0)$, $\Pr(\Delta b_t = 0)$ and $\Pr(\Delta c_t = 0)$ can be easily obtained by looking up the table T_{df}. When these three values are obtained, the probability $\Pr(\Delta z_t = 0)$ can be calculated by using the $\mathcal{XOR}$ operation two times, since it has $\Delta z_t = \Delta a_t \oplus \Delta b_t \oplus \Delta c_t$ in GEA-1. Here, the operation $\mathcal{XOR}$ is defined as $\mathcal{XOR}(p, q) = 2pq - p - q + 1$, where $0 \le p \le 1$ and $0 \le q \le 1$. In Steps 1.5–1.7 of **Algorithm 2**, the differences of three LFSRs can be directly updated, since there are not nonlinear operations when updating these three LFSRs.

By **Algorithm 2**, the attacker can obtain the probabilities $\Pr(\Delta z_0 = 0)$, $\ldots, \Pr(\Delta z_{L-1} = 0)$ for any given L. After analyzing these outputted probabilities, we get an observation that for a given IV difference, the difference of some keystream bit equals to zero with probability 1. Let $\Psi[\Delta_{\max,i}, L]$ be an integer set such that $\Psi[\Delta_{\max,i}, L] = \{j \mid \Pr(\Delta z_j = 0) = 1, 0 \le j \le L - 1\}$ under the given IV difference $\Delta_{\max,i}$. For each of 15 IV differences, i.e., $\Delta_{\max,0}, \ldots, \Delta_{\max,14}$, we have executed **Algorithm 2** and obtained an integer set, which are listed in Table 2.

Since the differential path under the IV difference $\Delta_{\max,i}(0 \le i \le 14)$ holds with a probability of $2^{-22.90}$, when the attacker randomly chooses $2^{22.90}$ IVs, there exists one IV on average such that the differential path is satisfied. Now, a definition is given as follows.

Table 2. The found sets $\Psi\left[\Delta_{\max,i}, L\right]$ for $0 \leq i \leq 14$

The IV difference $\Delta_{\max,i}$	The keystream length L	The set $\Psi\left[\Delta_{\max,i}, L\right]$ with $\left|\Psi\left[\Delta_{\max,i}, L\right]\right| = 30$
$\Delta_{\max,i}$ $(i = 0, \ldots, 7)$	$40529827+i$	$\{2240665+i, 2486560+i, 2700241+i, 7786720+i, 10686908+i,$ $12770795+i, 13756330+i, 14983894+i, 15931655+i, 16429393+i,$ $18429084+i, 18621403+i, 19451252+i, 19765323+i, 20070738+i,$ $20315954+i, 21719894+i, 22961509+i, 23073220+i, 24473000+i,$ $24620614+i, 25675669+i, 27290355+i, 28383282+i, 31121366+i,$ $31402806+i, 34565203+i, 37352903+i, 40499730+i, 40529826+i\}$
$\Delta_{\max,i+8}$ $(i = 0, \ldots, 6)$	$40529827+i$	$\{2240665+i, 2486560+i, 2700241+i, 7786720+i, 10686908+i,$ $12770795+i, 13756330+i, 14983894+i, 15931655+i, 16429393+i,$ $18429084+i, 18621403+i, 19451252+i, 19765323+i, 20070738+i,$ $20315954+i, 21719894+i, 22961509+i, 23073220+i, 24473000+i,$ $24620614+i, 25675669+i, 27290355+i, 28383282+i, 31121366+i,$ $31402806+i, 34565203+i, 37352903+i, 40499730+i, 40529826+i\}$

Definition 1. For a given IV and corresponding IV' satisfying the IV difference $\Delta_{\max,i}(0 \leq i \leq 14)$ of GEA-1, the IV is called **valid** if the differential path with maximum probability is satisfied. Otherwise, the IV is called **invalid**.

For a valid IV, the differential path under the IV difference $\Delta_{\max,i}$ holds directly, and then the set $\Psi\left[\Delta_{\max,i}, L\right]$ in Table 2 must exist. However, for an invalid IV, the differential path under the IV difference $\Delta_{\max,i}$ is not necessarily satisfied, and the differences will be independent and identically distributed. Thus, if enough keystream bits are available to the attacker, the valid IVs and invalid IVs can be distinguished effectively. Now, we give a distinguishing attack on GEA-1 in the chosen IV setting as follows.

In this attack, the attacker first randomly chooses m IVs, where the IV difference $\Delta_{\max,i}$ is satisfied for each IV and its corresponding IV'. After then, two keystreams are generated by the IV and IV' respectively together with the same fixed key, and then the attacker checks the two keystreams using the set $\Psi\left[\Delta_{\max,i}, L\right]$. If there is an IV which passes the test, then the attacker judges that the IV is valid and all keystreams are generated by GEA-1. Otherwise, if none of all m IVs passes the test, the attacker judges that all keystreams are random.

Note that the attacker can obtain similar distinguishing attacks for different values of i with $0 \leq i \leq 14$. Here, we take $i = 7$ as an example. It is easy to see that there are two possible errors when the attacker makes such a judgment. The one is that the keystreams are random, but at least one IV passes the test. The probability that this error happens is $\alpha = 1 - \left(1 - 2^{-\left|\Psi\left[\Delta_{\max,7}, L\right]\right|}\right)^m$. The other is that keystreams are generated by the stream cipher GEA-1, but none of all m IVs passes the test. The probability that this error happens is $\beta = \left(1 - 2^{-22.90}\right)^m$. Thus, the distinguishing attack succeeds with a probability of $1 - \alpha - \beta$. When the attacker chooses $m = 2^{22.90}$ and $L = 31402814$, it has $\left|\Psi\left[\Delta_{\max,7}, L\right]\right| = 26$ as shown in Table 2, and then $1 - \alpha - \beta \approx 0.52$. Now, we have constructed a distinguishing attack on GEA-1. The time complexity of this attack is $2m = 2^{23.90}$ GEA-1 encryptions, requiring $31402814 \approx 2^{24.90}$ keystream bits for each of $2^{22.90}$ chosen IVs. The attack has a success probability of 0.52.

To achieve a higher success probability, the attacker can choose bigger values of m and L. When the attacker chooses $m = 2^{24.5}$ and $L = 40529834$, it has $|\Psi[\Delta_{\max,7}, L]| = 30$ as shown in Table 2. The time complexity of this attack becomes $2m = 2^{25.5}$ GEA-1 encryptions, requiring $40529834 \approx 2^{25.27}$ keystream bits for each of $2^{24.5}$ chosen IVs. Now, the success probability of this attack has been improved to be 0.93.

3.3 Differential Key Recovery Attacks on GEA-1

As shown above, the valid IVs and invalid IVs can be distinguished effectively by checking the set $\Psi[\Delta_{\max,i}, L]$ for the given IV difference $\Delta_{\max,i}$. When the valid IV is obtained, the attacker can use it to recover the 64-bit key of GEA-1. In this subsection, we assume that the valid IV has been found by the distinguishing attack on GEA-1 above.

To facilitate understanding, we first propose a key recovery attack on GEA-1 using only one differential path. Here, we utilize the IV difference $\Delta_{\max,7}$. Note that a similar attack can be easily obtained when one of the other 13 IV differences is used. Once the valid IV is found for the IV difference $\Delta_{\max,7}$, the differential path in Table 3 found by **Algorithm 2** holds directly. The key bits involved in each difference of the differential path are also listed in this table. Note that there are not key bits involved in the first difference (i.e., $\Delta s_{63}^{(32)} = 0$), since only IV bits and the public bit dir are loaded into the NFSR in the first 33 clocks. Clearly, this difference can be directly satisfied in the chosen IV setting.

Table 3. The differential path under the IV difference $\Delta_{\max,7}$

The i-th difference	The probability	The key bits involved in this difference	The i-th difference	The probability	The key bits involved in this difference
1	$\Pr\left(\Delta s_{63}^{(32)} = 0\right) = 0.5$	None	12	$\Pr\left(\Delta s_{63}^{(137)} = 0\right) = 0.5$	$k_0, \ldots, k_{63}$
2	$\Pr\left(\Delta s_{63}^{(40)} = 0\right) = 0.5$	$k_0, \ldots, k_7$	13	$\Pr\left(\Delta s_{63}^{(147)} = 0\right) = 0.5$	$k_0, \ldots, k_{63}$
3	$\Pr\left(\Delta s_{63}^{(53)} = 0\right) = 0.5$	$k_0, \ldots, k_{20}$	14	$\Pr\left(\Delta s_{63}^{(156)} = 0\right) = 0.40625$	$k_0, \ldots, k_{63}$
4	$\Pr\left(\Delta s_{63}^{(57)} = 0\right) = 0.5$	$k_0, \ldots, k_{24}$	15	$\Pr\left(\Delta s_{63}^{(160)} = 0\right) = 0.5$	$k_0, \ldots, k_{63}$
5	$\Pr\left(\Delta s_{63}^{(73)} = 0\right) = 0.5$	$k_0, \ldots, k_{40}$	16	$\Pr\left(\Delta s_{63}^{(168)} = 0\right) = 0.5$	$k_0, \ldots, k_{63}$
6	$\Pr\left(\Delta s_{63}^{(83)} = 0\right) = 0.5$	$k_0, \ldots, k_{50}$	17	$\Pr\left(\Delta s_{63}^{(181)} = 0\right) = 0.5$	$k_0, \ldots, k_{63}$
7	$\Pr\left(\Delta s_{63}^{(92)} = 0\right) = 0.40625$	$k_0, \ldots, k_{59}$	18	$\Pr\left(\Delta s_{63}^{(185)} = 0\right) = 0.5$	$k_0, \ldots, k_{63}$
8	$\Pr\left(\Delta s_{63}^{(96)} = 0\right) = 0.5$	$k_0, \ldots, k_{63}$	19	$\Pr\left(\Delta s_{63}^{(201)} = 0\right) = 0.5$	$k_0, \ldots, k_{63}$
9	$\Pr\left(\Delta s_{63}^{(104)} = 0\right) = 0.5$	$k_0, \ldots, k_{63}$	20	$\Pr\left(\Delta s_{63}^{(211)} = 0\right) = 0.5$	$k_0, \ldots, k_{63}$
10	$\Pr\left(\Delta s_{63}^{(117)} = 0\right) = 0.5$	$k_0, \ldots, k_{63}$	21	$\Pr\left(\Delta s_{63}^{(220)} = 0\right) = 0.40625$	$k_0, \ldots, k_{63}$
11	$\Pr\left(\Delta s_{63}^{(121)} = 0\right) = 0.5$	$k_0, \ldots, k_{63}$	22	$\Pr\left(\Delta s_{63}^{(224)} = 0\right) = 0.5$	$k_0, \ldots, k_{63}$

The detailed process of recovering the key of GEA-1 is described as follows.

– The attacker guesses the values of 51 key bits $k_0, \ldots, k_{50}$, and then check whether the first six differences except the first difference $\Delta s_{63}^{(32)} = 0$ are simultaneously satisfied to filter the wrong guesses, which reduces the number of possible guesses from 2^{51} to about $2^{51} \cdot 2^{-5} = 2^{46}$.

– The attacker guesses the values of 9 key bits $k_{51}, \ldots, k_{59}$, which increases the number of possible guesses from 2^{46} to $2^{46} \cdot 2^9 = 2^{55}$. As shown in Table 3, the attacker can check whether the 7-*th* difference $\Delta s_{63}^{(92)} = 0$ is satisfied to filter the wrong guesses, which reduces the number of possible guesses from 2^{55} to about $2^{55} \cdot 0.40625 = 2^{53.70}$, since $\Pr\left(\Delta s_{63}^{(92)} = 0\right) = 0.40625$.

– The attacker guesses the values of the last 4 key bits $k_{60}, \ldots, k_{63}$, which increases the number of possible guesses from $2^{53.70}$ to $2^{53.70} \cdot 2^4 = 2^{57.70}$. As shown in Table 3, the attacker can check whether the remaining 15 differences, i.e., $\Delta s_{63}^{(96)} = 0, \ldots, \Delta s_{63}^{(224)} = 0$, are simultaneously satisfied to filter the wrong guesses, which reduces the number of possible guesses from $2^{57.70}$ to about $2^{57.70} \cdot 2^{-13} \cdot 0.40625^2 = 2^{42.10}$.

– Finally, the attacker makes an exhaustive search of the obtained $2^{42.10}$ possible guesses to recover the 64-bit key.

It is easy to see that the maximum number of possible guesses is no more than $2^{57.70}$ in the whole process above. Thus, the time complexity of the key recovery process is at most $2^{57.70}$. Considering the cost of the distinguishing attack to find the valid IV, the total time complexity of the attack on GEA-1 is $2^{57.70} + 2^{23.90} \approx 2^{57.70}$, requiring $2^{24.90}$ keystream bits for each of $2^{22.90}$ chosen IVs. The attack has a success probability of 0.52.

The time complexity of the key recovery attack on GEA-1 above is better than exhaustive key search, but it is still too high that makes the attack unpractical on a common PC. In fact, the time complexity can be reduced significantly using more differential paths. Now, we give a new key recovery attack on GEA-1 using eight differential paths, which are obtained by eight IV differences, i.e., $\Delta_{\max,0}, \ldots, \Delta_{\max,7}$. For each IV difference, the attacker should implement a differential distinguishing attack to find a valid IV. The detailed process of recovering the key of GEA-1 is described in Table 5 in Appendix. As shown in Table 5, in the first step, the attacker guesses the value of one key bit k_0, which leads to 2 possible guesses. Then, the attacker can check whether the condition $\Delta s_{63}^{(33)} = 0$ with $\Delta_{\max,0}$ is satisfied, reducing the number of possible guesses from 2 to about $2 \cdot 2^{-1} = 1$, since $Pr(\Delta s_{63}^{(33)} = 0) = 0.5$ holds. The following 47 steps are all similar to the first step. After all 48 steps in Table 5, about $2^{5.60}$ possible guesses are obtained. The attacker can make an exhaustive search of the obtained $2^{5.60}$ possible guesses to recover the 64-bit key of GEA-1.

It is easy to see that the maximum number of possible guesses is no more than 2^{13} in all 48 steps of Table 5. Thus, the time complexity of the key recovery process is at most 2^{13}. To achieve a higher success probability, here we choose $m = 2^{24.5}$ and $L = 40529834$, and then we have $|\Psi[\Delta_{\max,i}, L]| = 30$ $(i = 0, \ldots, 7)$ and $1 - \alpha - \beta \approx 0.93$. Considering the cost of the distinguishing attack to find the valid IVs, the total time complexity of the attack on GEA-1 is $2^{13} + 2^{25.5} \cdot 8 \approx 2^{28.5}$, requiring $2^{24.90}$ keystream bits for each of $2^{24.5} \cdot 8 = 2^{27.5}$ chosen IVs. The attack has a success probability of about $0.93^8 = 0.56$, since eight differential paths are used in this attack.

4 Differential Cryptanalysis of GEA-2 and GEA-2a

Since GEA-2 and GEA-2a have similar structures with GEA-1, the differential attacks on GEA-1 above can be easily applied to GEA-2 and GEA-2a.

4.1 Differential Distinguishing Attacks on GEA-2

By slightly modifying **Algorithm 1** and then applying it to GEA-2, the attacker can obtain a differential path of GEA-2 for any given IV difference. Like GEA-1, to find the differential paths with high probabilities, we also make an exhaustive search of all IV differences with weight no more than 6, i.e., $weight(\Delta IV) \leq 6$, in a dozen seconds on a common PC with 2.5 GHz Intel Pentium 4 processor. As results, we have found 27 IV differences with weight one or two, and the probabilities of their corresponding differential paths achieve the maximum value $2^{-19.60}$. The 27 input differences are listed as follows.

$$\Delta'_{\max,i} := \{\Delta iv_{18+i} = 1, weight(\Delta IV) = 1\},\ i = 0, \ldots, 13$$
$$\Delta'_{\max,i+14} := \{\Delta iv_{18+i} = \Delta iv_{19+i} = 1, weight(\Delta IV) = 2\},\ i = 0, \ldots, 12$$

To verify the maximum probability, we have made an experiment. In this experiment, we first choose the IV difference $\Delta'_{\max,13}$, and randomly choose 10 keys and 2^{23} IVs for each key. The results show that there exist 13.10 IVs on average per key which generate the expected output difference. It leads to an experimental probability of $13.10/2^{23} = 2^{-19.29}$, which is quite close to the theoretical value $2^{-19.60}$. Furthermore, the other 26 IV differences have been also verified. The results show that all 27 experimental probabilities are quite chose to the theoretical value $2^{-19.60}$. This indicates that the differential paths with maximum probability searched for GEA-2 are correct and can be used to construct distinguishers and key recovery attacks.

By slightly modifying **Algorithm 2** and then applying it to GEA-2, the attacker can obtained the probabilities $\Pr(\Delta z_0 = 0), \ldots, \Pr(\Delta z_{L-1} = 0)$ for any given L. Similar to GEA-1, we find that for a given IV difference, the difference of some keystream bit generated by GEA-2 also equals to zero with probability 1. Let $\Omega[\Delta'_{\max,i}, L]$ be an integer set such that $\Omega[\Delta'_{\max,i}, L] = \{j \mid \Pr(\Delta z_j = 0) = 1, 0 \leq j \leq L - 1\}$ under the given IV difference $\Delta'_{\max,i}(0 \leq i \leq 26)$. The found sets $\Omega[\Delta'_{\max,i}, L]$ for $0 \leq i \leq 26$ are listed in Table 4.

Like the distinguishing attack on GEA-1, the attacker can randomly choose m IVs, and then distinguish the valid IVs and invalid IVs of GEA-2 effectively by using the set $\Omega[\Delta'_{\max,i}, L]$. Based on this, a distinguishing attack on GEA-2 in the chosen IV setting can be easily constructed. Note that the attacker can obtain similar distinguishing attacks for different values of i with $0 \leq i \leq 26$. Here, we take $i = 13$ as an example. The distinguishing attack on GEA-2 succeeds with a probability of $1 - \alpha - \beta$, where $\alpha = 1 - \left(1 - 2^{-|\Omega[\Delta'_{\max,13}, L]|}\right)^m$ and $\beta = \left(1 - 2^{-19.60}\right)^m$. When the attacker chooses $m = 2^{19.60}$ and $L = 3048587076$, we have $|\Omega[\Delta'_{\max,13}, L]| = 23$ as shown in Table 4, and then $1 - \alpha - \beta \approx 0.54$. Now,

Table 4. The found sets $\Omega\left[\Delta'_{\max,i}, L\right]$ for $0 \leq i \leq 26$

The IV difference $\Delta'_{\max,i}$	The keystream length L	The set $\Omega\left[\Delta'_{\max,i}, L\right]$ with $\left|\Omega\left[\Delta'_{\max,i}, L\right]\right| = 27$
$\Delta'_{\max,i}$ ($i = 0, \ldots, 13$)	$3332621397+i$	$\{200040434+i,654783349+i,995597203+i,1046229278+i,$ $1343111889+i,1633866947+i,1694413527+i,1821457678+i,$ $2074066158+i,2136781936+i,2144782576+i,2318162131+i,$ $2333652506+i,2382729689+i,2406347681+i,2529724026+i,$ $2657750494+i,2749218027+i,2750992360+i,2985254692+i,$ $2996288266+i,3047146791+i,3048587062+i,3107391285+i,$ $3114411307+i,3276885606+i,3332621396+i\}$
$\Delta'_{\max,i+14}$ ($i = 0, \ldots, 12$)	$3332621397+i$	$\{200040434+i,654783349+i,995597203+i,1046229278+i,$ $1343111889+i,1633866947+i,1694413527+i,1821457678+i,$ $2074066158+i,2136781936+i,2144782576+i,2318162131+i,$ $2333652506+i,2382729689+i,2406347681+i,2529724026+i,$ $2657750494+i,2749218027+i,2750992360+i,2985254692+i,$ $2996288266+i,3047146791+i,3048587062+i,3107391285+i,$ $3114411307+i,3276885606+i,3332621396+i\}$

we have constructed a distinguishing attack on GEA-2. The time complexity of this attack is $2m = 2^{20.60}$ GEA-2 encryptions, requiring $3048587076 \approx 2^{31.51}$ keystream bits for each of $2^{19.60}$ chosen IVs. The attack has a success probability of 0.54. To achieve a higher success probability, the attacker can choose bigger values of m and L. When the attacker chooses $m = 2^{21.5}$ and $L = 3332621410$, it has $\left|\Omega\left[\Delta'_{\max,13}, L\right]\right| = 27$ as shown in Table 4. A distinguishing attack on GEA-2 with a success probability of 0.96 is obtained. The time complexity of this attack is $2m = 2^{22.5}$ GEA-2 encryptions, requiring $3332621410 \approx 2^{31.63}$ keystream bits for each of $2^{21.5}$ chosen IVs.

4.2 Differential Key Recovery Attacks on GEA-2

Like the improved key recovery attack on GEA-1, an key recovery attack on GEA-2 using more differential paths can be also proposed. Here, we utilize 11 differential paths, which are obtained by 11 IV differences, i.e., $\Delta'_{\max,0}, \ldots, \Delta'_{\max,10}$. For each IV difference, the attacker should implement a differential distinguishing attack to find a valid IV.

The detailed process of recovering the key of GEA-2 is summarized as follow. At first, the attacker guesses the value of one key bit k_0, which leads to 2 possible guesses. Then, the attacker can make a check which reduces the number of possible guesses from 2 to about $2 \cdot 2^{-1} = 1$, since $Pr(\Delta w_{96}^{(33)} = 0) = 0.5$ holds. The following steps are all similar to this step. Finally, about 2^{10} possible guesses are obtained. The attacker can make an exhaustive search of the obtained 2^{10} possible guesses to recover the 64-bit key of GEA-2. Since the maximum number of possible guesses is no more than 2^{21} in all steps. Thus, the time complexity of the key recovery process is at most 2^{21}. To achieve a higher success probability, here we choose $m = 2^{21.5}$ and $L = 3332621410$, and then we have $\left|\Omega\left[\Delta'_{\max,i}, L\right]\right| = 27(0 \leq i \leq 10)$ and $1 - \alpha - \beta \approx 0.96$. Considering the cost of the distinguishing attack to find the valid IVs, the total time complexity of the attack on GEA-2 is $2^{21} + 2^{22.5} \cdot 11 \approx 2^{25.96}$, requiring $2^{31.63}$ keystream bits for each of $2^{21.5} \cdot 11 = 2^{24.96}$ chosen IVs. The attack has a success probability of about $0.96^{11} = 0.64$, since 11 differential paths are used in this attack.

4.3 Differential Key Recovery Attacks on GEA-2a

GEA-2a is a variant of the GEA-2 stream cipher proposed by Ding et al. in [9]. It modifies the structure of GEA-2 slightly, providing a higher level of security compared to GEA-2 while retaining all the good properties of GEA-2. Now, we apply the proposed attacks on GEA-1 to GEA-2a.

By making slight modifications to **Algorithm 1** and applying it to GEA-2a, an attacker can obtain the differential path of GEA-2a for any given IV differential. Similar to GEA-1 and GEA-2, in order to find the differential paths with high probabilities, we conducted an exhaustive search on a regular PC, searching for all IV differences with a weight not exceeding 6. Our results indicate that when the IV difference has a weight of one with $\Delta iv_5 = 1$, the probability achieves the maximum $2^{-18.60}$. By using this differential path, the attacker can mount a key recovery attack on GEA-2a with a time complexity of 2^{61}.

Similarly, we can present an improved key recovery attack on GEA-2a using two differential paths with relatively high differential probabilities. Both of these two paths, i.e., $\Delta iv_8 = 1$ and $\Delta iv_{24} = 1$, have a weight of 1 and their differential probabilities are approximately $2^{-21.8}$. Similar to the key recovery attacks on GEA-1 and GEA-2, a key recovery attack on GEA-2a using two differential paths can be easily obtained. In the key recovery process, the maximum number of possible guesses does not exceed 2^{54}. Therefore, the time complexity of the key recovery process is at most 2^{54}.

5   Conclusions

In this paper, we found a new weakness in GEA-like stream ciphers that was not discovered in previous works, and new practical distinguishing attacks and key recovery attacks are proposed. The cryptanalytic results show that the initializations of all GEA-like stream ciphers are far from being optimal and need to be strengthened. We believe that the contributions of this paper can provide some new insights on how to design a secure GEA-like stream cipher.

Acknowledgement. This work was supported by the National Natural Science Foundation of China under Grant numbers 61602514, 62202493, 61802437 and 61902428.

Appendix

Table 5. The detailed process of recovering the key of GEA-1 using eight differential paths

j-th step	The key bits to be guessed	The number of possible guesses	Conditions to be checked	The number of possible guesses after checking conditions
1	k_0	2	$\Delta s_{63}^{(33)} = 0$ with $\Delta_{\max,0}$	1
2	k_1	2	$\Delta s_{63}^{(34)} = 0$ with $\Delta_{\max,1}$	1
3	k_2	2	$\Delta s_{63}^{(35)} = 0$ with $\Delta_{\max,2}$	1
4	k_3	2	$\Delta s_{63}^{(36)} = 0$ with $\Delta_{\max,3}$	1
5	k_4	2	$\Delta s_{63}^{(37)} = 0$ with $\Delta_{\max,4}$	1
6	k_5	2	$\Delta s_{63}^{(38)} = 0$ with $\Delta_{\max,5}$	1
7	k_6	2	$\Delta s_{63}^{(39)} = 0$ with $\Delta_{\max,6}$	1
8	k_7	2	$\Delta s_{63}^{(40)} = 0$ with $\Delta_{\max,7}$	1
9	$k_8,\ldots,k_{13}$	2^6	$\Delta s_{63}^{(46)} = 0$ with $\Delta_{\max,0}$	2^5
10	k_{14}	2^6	$\Delta s_{63}^{(47)} = 0$ with $\Delta_{\max,1}$	2^5
11	k_{15}	2^6	$\Delta s_{63}^{(48)} = 0$ with $\Delta_{\max,2}$	2^5
12	k_{16}	2^6	$\Delta s_{63}^{(49)} = 0$ with $\Delta_{\max,3}$	2^5
13	k_{17}	2^6	$\Delta s_{63}^{(50)} = 0$ with $\Delta_{\max,4}$, $\Delta s_{63}^{(50)} = 0$ with $\Delta_{\max,0}$	2^4
14	k_{18}	2^5	$\Delta s_{63}^{(51)} = 0$ with $\Delta_{\max,5}$, $\Delta s_{63}^{(51)} = 0$ with $\Delta_{\max,1}$	2^3
15	k_{19}	2^4	$\Delta s_{63}^{(52)} = 0$ with $\Delta_{\max,6}$, $\Delta s_{63}^{(52)} = 0$ with $\Delta_{\max,2}$	2^2
16	k_{20}	2^3	$\Delta s_{63}^{(53)} = 0$ with $\Delta_{\max,7}$, $\Delta s_{63}^{(53)} = 0$ with $\Delta_{\max,3}$	2
17	k_{21}	2^2	$\Delta s_{63}^{(54)} = 0$ with $\Delta_{\max,4}$	2
18	k_{22}	2^2	$\Delta s_{63}^{(55)} = 0$ with $\Delta_{\max,5}$	2
19	k_{23}	2^2	$\Delta s_{63}^{(56)} = 0$ with $\Delta_{\max,6}$	2
20	k_{24}	2^2	$\Delta s_{63}^{(57)} = 0$ with $\Delta_{\max,7}$	2
21	$k_{25},\ldots,k_{33}$	2^{10}	$\Delta s_{63}^{(66)} = 0$ with $\Delta_{\max,0}$	2^9
22	k_{34}	2^{10}	$\Delta s_{63}^{(67)} = 0$ with $\Delta_{\max,1}$	2^9
23	k_{35}	2^{10}	$\Delta s_{63}^{(68)} = 0$ with $\Delta_{\max,2}$	2^9
24	k_{36}	2^{10}	$\Delta s_{63}^{(69)} = 0$ with $\Delta_{\max,3}$	2^9
25	k_{37}	2^{10}	$\Delta s_{63}^{(70)} = 0$ with $\Delta_{\max,4}$	2^9
26	k_{38}	2^{10}	$\Delta s_{63}^{(71)} = 0$ with $\Delta_{\max,5}$	2^9
27	k_{39}	2^{10}	$\Delta s_{63}^{(72)} = 0$ with $\Delta_{\max,6}$	2^9
28	k_{40}	2^{10}	$\Delta s_{63}^{(73)} = 0$ with $\Delta_{\max,7}$	2^9
29	k_{41}, k_{42}, k_{43}	2^{12}	$\Delta s_{63}^{(76)} = 0$ with $\Delta_{\max,0}$	2^{11}
30	k_{44}	2^{12}	$\Delta s_{63}^{(77)} = 0$ with $\Delta_{\max,1}$	2^{11}
31	k_{45}	2^{12}	$\Delta s_{63}^{(78)} = 0$ with $\Delta_{\max,2}$	2^{11}
32	k_{46}	2^{12}	$\Delta s_{63}^{(79)} = 0$ with $\Delta_{\max,3}$	2^{11}
33	k_{47}	2^{12}	$\Delta s_{63}^{(80)} = 0$ with $\Delta_{\max,4}$	2^{11}
34	k_{48}	2^{12}	$\Delta s_{63}^{(81)} = 0$ with $\Delta_{\max,5}$	2^{11}
35	k_{49}	2^{12}	$\Delta s_{63}^{(82)} = 0$ with $\Delta_{\max,6}$	2^{11}
36	k_{50}	2^{12}	$\Delta s_{63}^{(83)} = 0$ with $\Delta_{\max,7}$	2^{11}
37	k_{51}, k_{52}	2^{13}	$\Delta s_{63}^{(85)} = 0$ with $\Delta_{\max,0}$	$2^{11.70}$
38	k_{53}	$2^{12.70}$	$\Delta s_{63}^{(86)} = 0$ with $\Delta_{\max,1}$	$2^{11.40}$
39	k_{54}	$2^{12.40}$	$\Delta s_{63}^{(87)} = 0$ with $\Delta_{\max,2}$	$2^{11.10}$
40	k_{55}	$2^{12.10}$	$\Delta s_{63}^{(88)} = 0$ with $\Delta_{\max,3}$	$2^{10.80}$
41	k_{56}	$2^{11.80}$	$\Delta s_{63}^{(89)} = 0$ with $\Delta_{\max,4}$, $\Delta s_{63}^{(89)} = 0$ with $\Delta_{\max,0}$	$2^{9.50}$
42	k_{57}	$2^{10.50}$	$\Delta s_{63}^{(90)} = 0$ with $\Delta_{\max,5}$, $\Delta s_{63}^{(90)} = 0$ with $\Delta_{\max,1}$	$2^{8.20}$
43	k_{58}	$2^{9.20}$	$\Delta s_{63}^{(91)} = 0$ with $\Delta_{\max,6}$, $\Delta s_{63}^{(91)} = 0$ with $\Delta_{\max,2}$	$2^{6.90}$
44	k_{59}	$2^{7.90}$	$\Delta s_{63}^{(92)} = 0$ with $\Delta_{\max,7}$, $\Delta s_{63}^{(92)} = 0$ with $\Delta_{\max,3}$	$2^{5.60}$
45	k_{60}	$2^{6.60}$	$\Delta s_{63}^{(93)} = 0$ with $\Delta_{\max,4}$	$2^{5.60}$
46	k_{61}	$2^{6.60}$	$\Delta s_{63}^{(94)} = 0$ with $\Delta_{\max,5}$	$2^{5.60}$
47	k_{62}	$2^{6.60}$	$\Delta s_{63}^{(95)} = 0$ with $\Delta_{\max,6}$	$2^{5.60}$
48	k_{63}	$2^{6.60}$	$\Delta s_{63}^{(96)} = 0$ with $\Delta_{\max,7}$	$2^{5.60}$

References

1. ETSI: Security algorithms group of experts (SAGE); report on the specification, evaluation and usage of the GSM GPRS encryption algorithm (GEA). Technical report (1998). https://www.etsi.org/deliver/etsi_tr/101300_101399/101375/01.01.01_60/tr_101375v010101p.pdf. Accessed 3 July (2024)
2. Brookson, C.: GPRS Security (2001). https://web.archive.org/web/20120914110208/www.brookson.com/gsm/gprs.pdf. Accessed 3 July (2024)
3. ETSI: Digital cellular telecommunications system (phase 2+) (GSM); security related network functions (3GPP TS 43.020 version 15.0.0 release 15). Technical Specification (2018). https://www.etsi.org/deliver/etsits/143000143099/143020/15.00.0060/ts143020v150000p.pdf. Accessed 3 July 2024
4. Beierle, C., Derbez, P., Leander, G., Leurent, G., Raddum, H., Rotella, Y., Rupprecht, D., Stennes L.: Cryptanalysis of the GPRS encryption algorithms GEA-1 and GEA-2. In: Canteaut, A., Standaert, F.-X. (eds.) EUROCRYPT 2021. LNCS, vol. 12697, pp. 155–183. Springer (2021)
5. Beierle, C., Felke, P., Leander, G.: To shift or not to shift: understanding GEA-1. IACR Cryptology ePrint Archive, Paper 2021/829. https://eprint.iacr.org/2021/829. Accessed 3 July (2024)
6. Beierle, C., Beyne, T., Felke, P., Leander, G.: Constructing and deconstructing intentional weaknesses in symmetric ciphers. In: Dodis, Y., Shrimpton, T. (eds.) CRYPTO 2022. LNCS, vol. 13509, pp. 748–778. Springer (2022)
7. Amzaleg, D., Dinur, I.: Refined cryptanalysis of the GPRS Ciphers GEA-1 and GEA-2. In: Dunkelman, O., Dziembowski, S. (eds.) EUROCRYPT 2022. LNCS, vol. 13277, pp. 57–85. Springer (2022)
8. Ding, L., Wu, Z., Wang, X., Guan, Z., Li, M.: New attacks on the GPRS encryption algorithms GEA-1 and GEA-2. IEEE Trans. Inf. Forensics Secur. **17**, 2878–2889 (2022)
9. Wu, Z., Ding, L., Li, Z., Wang, X., Guan, Z.: New practical attacks on GEA-1 based on a new-found weakness. IET Inf. Secur. **2024**(6674019), 1–12 (2024)
10. Biham, E., Shamir, A.: Differential Cryptanalysis of DES-like Cryptosystems. In: Menezes, A.J., Vanstone, S.A. (eds.) CRYPTO 1990. LNCS, vol. 537, pp. 2–21. Springer (1991)
11. Alex, B., Deike, P., Zhang, B.: Multiset collision attacks on reduced-round SNOW 3G and SNOW 3G$^{\oplus}$. In: Zhou, J., Yung, M. (eds.) ACNS 2010. LNCS, vol. 6123, pp. 139–153. Springer (2010)
12. Wu, H., Huang, T., Nguyen, P.H., Wang, H., Ling, S.: Differential attacks against stream cipher ZUC. In: Wang, X., Sako, K. (eds.) ASIACRYPT 2012. LNCS, vol, 7658, pp. 262–277. Springer (2012)
13. Ding, L., Guan, J.: Cryptanalysis of loiss stream cipher. Comput. J. **55**(10), 1192–1201 (2012)
14. Ma, S., Jin, C., Guan, J., Liu. S.: Improved differential attacks on the reduced-round SNOW-V and SNOW-Vi stream cipher. J. Inf. Secur. Appl. **71**(103379), 1–12 (2022)
15. Liu, F., Meier, W., Sarkar, S., Wang, G., Ito, R., Isobe, T.: New cryptanalysis of ZUC-256 initialization using modular differences. IACR Trans. Symmet. Cryptol. **2022**(3), 152–190 (2022)
16. Knellwolf, S., Meier, W., Naya-Plasencia, M.: Conditional differential cryptanalysis of NLFSR-based cryptosystems. In: Abe, M. (eds.) ASIACRYPT 2010. LNCS, vol, 6477, pp. 130–145. Springer (2010)

17. Banik, S.: Some insights into differential cryptanalysis of Grain v1. In: Susilo, W., Mu, Y. (eds.) ACISP 2014. LNCS, vol, 8544, pp. 34–49. Springer (2014)
18. Dalai, D., Pal, S., Sarkar, S.: Some conditional cube testers for grain-128a of reduced rounds. IEEE Trans. Comput. **71**(6), 1374–1385 (2022)
19. Ding, L., Li, Z., Guan, Z., Wang, X., Z. Wu: Breaking the DECT standard cipher with lower time cost. IEEE Trans. Comput. **73**(5), 1290–1299 (2024)

SNIPER: Detect Complex Attacks Accurately from Traffic

Changlong Yu[1], Bo Zhang[2], Boyu Kuang[1], and Anmin Fu[1,2(✉)]

[1] School of Cyber Science and Engineering, Nanjing University of Science and
Technology, Nanjing 210094, China
yu_cl@njust.edu.cn, kuang@njust.edu.cn
[2] School of Computer Science and Engineering, Nanjing University of Science and
Technology, Nanjing 210094, China
zhangbo07@njust.edu.cn, fuam@njust.edu.cn

Abstract. Advanced Persistent Threat (APT) is widely acknowledged
as a formidable cyberspace danger that may result in critical data leakage
and huge losses. Some processes of APT attacks inevitably expose behavioral beacons in traffic, which makes it possible to detect APT attacks
from traffic. Unlike deploying attack detectors at end devices or critical servers, anomaly detection at the network entrance provides a larger
monitoring field but has to bear a huge traffic load. In addition, traditional approaches focus on specific protocols or scenarios, making dealing
with complex and volatile APT attacks difficult. Thus, it is challenging to
catch up with the ever-growing high-speed traffic and accurately identify
complex attacks from it. In this paper, we present SNIPER, a highly efficient and accurate network-side APT detection system. SNIPER uses a
multi-task model to capture more comprehensive characterization information about the traffic. This rich characterization information provides
the basis for accurately identifying attack traffic. Then, to avoid the
additional overhead of running a large multi-tasking model and to further improve detection speed, SNIPER distills the shared feature layer
of the multi-tasking model into a lightweight model for final anomaly
detection. With this design, SNIPER can identify much of the activity
during an APT attack with extreme accuracy at a rate that matches
enterprise traffic. Finally, we evaluate SNIPER on the DAPT dataset,
and the result shows that SNIPER surpasses the baseline approach in
all metrics, obtaining an F1 score of 0.99.

Keywords: Advanced Persistent Threat · Attack Detection · Network
Security · Intrusion Detection

1 Introduction

In recent years, the size of cyber assets has been growing significantly due to
the increase in online services and telecommuting. Simultaneously, these assets
become targets for attackers, threatening trade secrets and user privacy. Some

Z. Xia and J. Chen (Eds.): ISPEC 2024, LNCS 15053, pp. 205–221, 2024.
https://doi.org/10.1007/978-981-97-9053-1_12

traditional attack methods are easily detected and filtered out by network protection systems. However, sophisticated cyber attackers have developed increasingly advanced methods to circumvent security systems, resulting in Advanced Persistent Threat (APT).

APT is known for its complexity, longevity, and invisibility [1]. APT attacks usually target large organizations or national institutions, are driven by well-funded organizations, and are carried out by powerful adversaries intending to steal sensitive or essential information [2]. A full-fledged APT attack often lasts months or even years, involves multiple advanced attack techniques (e.g., zero-day exploits), and can cause significant damage to the target.

There are already a number of methods that work in relation to identifying APT attacks from traffic. But they still faces the problem of insufficient recognition capability and detection speed. The scope of a complete APT attack is extensive. It may include multiple devices in several areas of a network system, which makes the heavy overhead of running a protection system on end devices or servers prohibitive. Deploying detectors on the network side gives a more comprehensive monitoring view and the ability to detect potential APT attacks by identifying specific behaviors [3]. However, the network-side APT attack detection systems must balance the challenge of detecting complex attacks with the required resources. Due to the high complexity of APT attacks, detection systems need have extensive learning capabilities and meet network systems' low tolerance for miss alerts. Implementing more advanced machine learning models [4,5] can aid in advancing these capabilities. Nevertheless, deploying such models often comes with high costs, and their detection speed may not keep up with the large-scale, high-speed traffic in enterprise networks. In summary, detection systems that can effectively identify the entire process of an APT attack at a rate appropriate for large-scale traffic in real-world organizations are still in short supply.

As a solution, we propose SNIPER, a network-side APT attack detection system that combines multi-task learning and knowledge distillation. SNIPER first trains a multi-task model with APT attack phases as the classification target to comprehensively learn the behavioral characteristics of these phases. This multi-task model guides a lightweight model to train as a final detector. By this way, it transfers its generalization capabilities and learning features to the detector, which could distinguish between benign and malicious traffic with high accuracy, enabling efficient detection at a low cost. To summarize, the contributions of this paper are as follows:

- We propose a multi-task learning approach to more comprehensively learn the behavioral characteristics of APT attacks from attack traffic. The richer features allow the detector to accurately distinguish between attack and benign traffic.
- We use knowledge distillation to compress the multi-task model, which avoids the extra overhead associated with multi-task models and further speeds up the detection.

– We design and implement SNIPER, a system to efficiently and accurately detect APT attacks from traffic. Then, we evaluate it on the public dataset DAPT. SNIPER is 2–4 times faster than existing methods and achieves an F1 score of 0.99.

The rest of this paper is organized as follows: Sect. 3 reviews the background. Section 2 describes related work. Section 4 details our approach. Section 5 discusses the experiments and results. Finally, Sect. 6 concludes this paper.

2 Related Work

APT attack detection methods can be categorized into network-side and host-side methods based on their deployment location [6]. SNIPER is a network-side detection method. Therefore, we analyzed both methods and focused on existing work on the network side.

2.1 Host-Side Detection Approaches

Host-side detection approaches typically rely on system audit logs as their data source and aim to identify anomalies at the system entity level by analyzing structural information from provenance graphs [7]. Rule-based methods [8–10] use known attacks to construct rules or extract attack patterns and then identify APTs on provenance graphs through matching. Statistically based methods [11,12] assume that attack activities are rare compared to benign activities. Therefore, based on rarity, they assign anomaly scores to subgraphs or paths in the provenance graph. Deep learning-based methods [13,14] use sequence-based or graph-based approaches to obtain representations of entire graphs or graph elements (e.g., edges, nodes) and then identify APTs through classification or anomaly detection.

Fine-grained details enhance the discovery of potential attacks and enable fast restoration of attack scenarios. However, they come with the challenge of high storage costs and query overheads [15], which result in minimal real-time detection methods. Additionally, unusual system entities may signal that the attacker has successfully compromised the enterprise network and may even be close to the attack target. This is not conducive to rapid response to attacks.

2.2 Network-Side Detection Approaches

APT detection systems on the network side offer better detection efficiency and enable timely proactive response to attacks, thereby reducing the potential for losses [16]. These systems are typically deployed at the network entrance to detect suspicious behaviors and malicious samples by analyzing the behavioral characteristics or payload of passing traffic. They can monitor the entire network. Simultaneously, the superiority of the deployment location enables network-side detection methods to find anomalies as attackers perform reconnaissance and put in malicious samples rather than relying on a large number of suspicious entities and interactions within the host. These anomalies in traffic typically pertain to a specific IP address, port, or URL. They can be used by security personnel to block attacks and trace further intrusions promptly. However, although network-side detection methods have considerable advantages over host-side detection methods, they still inevitably face bottlenecks in detection speed and alert fatigue due to their need to meet high-speed traffic across the network.

Niu et al. [17] combined static traffic's time series and association rule features to detect malware traffic for multiple protocols effectively. Yan et al. [18] extracted ten important features from DNS log data to identify potential APT attacks, including hosts, domains, and times. They then used unsupervised learning to identify suspicious clusters and compiled a list of malicious domains found within those clusters. He et al. [19] designed a multidimensional detection framework to detect lateral movement behavior based on the SMB protocol in an intranet environment. Liu et al. [20] analyzed DNS and TCP traffic generated by APT organizations and aid in identifying APT organizations by detecting the traffic generated when connecting with remote C&C servers and leaking data. These methods only target specific communication protocols or phases of an APT attack and are highly susceptible to attacker evasion. Marchetti et al. [21] analyzed traffic in an enterprise network by designing algorithms that represent each host as a vector. The level of suspicion is calculated based on the host's position in a multidimensional feature space and its evolution over time. The method can simultaneously monitor tens of thousands of hosts in an extensive network system. However, the detection signals are coarse-grained, making the system dependent on many human resources to participate in the threat identification of the Top-K hosts.

These methods only concentrate on particular protocols, scenarios, or attack phases based on previous attack patterns. They cannot detect the entire process of APT attacks at a higher level. Furthermore, some of the techniques still heavily rely on human involvement.

3 Background

3.1 Life Cycle of APT

A complete APT attack is a long-lasting process, and attackers tend to achieve it through a series of phases, which is called the life cycle. There have been several studies on the APT life cycle [22–24]. They all have the same APT phases: reconnaissance, establishing a foothold, lateral movement, data exfiltration, and scavenging, described as follows:

- Reconnaissance: Attackers use scanning or social engineering to gather extensive information and weaknesses in the target network. The more information they collect, the easier the attack tends to succeed.
- Establishing foothold: Attackers use phishing, vulnerability exploitation, or other methods to drop and execute malicious samples into a host to gain control and establish a foothold in the network system.

- Lateral movement: Attackers utilize the compromised host as a springboard to attack other hosts in the network with remote services, expanding their control over the network and moving towards the final target.
- Data exfiltration: Attackers steal sensitive information and transmit this data outwards using C&C(command and control) communications, web services, etc.
- Clear up: After attackers have achieved their goal, they clean up the territory to resist attack investigation. Standard cleaning techniques include modifying system logs and deleting registries and malicious files.

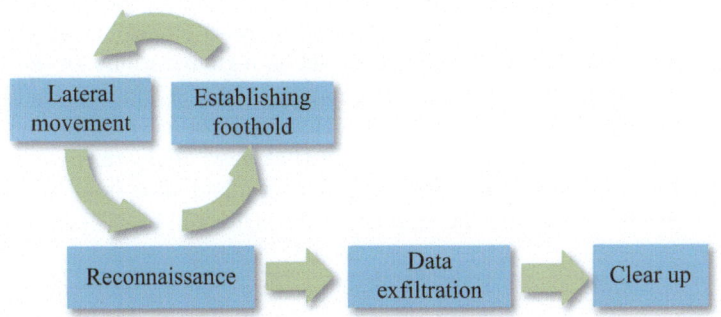

Fig. 1. APT Lifecycle.

In real-world scenarios, attackers often do not strictly follow a linear process when conducting an attack; instead, they frequently repeat certain specific steps, as illustrated in Fig. 1. Within a network system, crucial data is typically located at the network's center and it is not visible outside, making it impossible for attackers to obtain it in a single action. Consequently, attackers will start from the network's periphery, repeatedly conducting reconnaissance, establishing footholds, and lateral movement. This repetition enables them to infect more hosts and expand their control until they can access valuable information. Finally, the attackers exfiltrate the data and erase traces of their presence.

In each phase, attackers may use various techniques to progress to the next phase. Table 1 shows typical techniques.

3.2 Multi-task Learning

Multi-task learning employs one model to simultaneously learn multiple classification tasks with a shared representation layers and multiple classifiers, each corresponding to a classification task. For example, in Natural Language Processing (NLP), a multi-task model can perform sentiment analysis and topic classification. The model will use the loss functions of multiple tasks during training and optimize the joint loss of these tasks. It reduces the model parameters by sharing the representation layer and can eliminate redundant feature computations.

Table 1. APT Attack Phases and Typical Techniques.

Phases	Typical Techniques
Reconnaissance	Web scanning, Social engineering
Establishing foothold	Phishing, Exploits
Lateral movement	Legitimate Accounts, Remote Services
Data exfiltration	C&C, Web Services
Clear up	Delete samples, Modify system logs

Therefore, the multi-task model is often used to solve multimodal problems in edge devices that are resource-constrained [25]. Additionally, tasks that share related and complementary information or act as regularizations for one another have the potential to enhance task performance. It is an advantage that a multi-categorization model does not have [26]. However, the correlation among the simultaneously solved problems is weak. In that case, multi-task learning may have negative impacts because of inconsistent gradient directions across tasks, differing convergence speeds, and significant disparities in loss value magnitudes [27].

3.3   Knowledge Distillation

Knowledge distillation is a method for compressing models that transfers knowledge from a large model to a smaller model, thereby reducing the model structure while preserving knowledge in the model [28]. This helps in solving complex problems in resource-constrained scenarios. A knowledge distillation model typically includes a teacher and a student model, with the teacher model's output (soft target) used as a supervised signal to train a simpler student model. Maximizing the complexity model's entropy value enables increased information in the soft target and reduces gradient variance during each training round. Using soft targets in smaller models allows for training with less data and smaller learning rates [29]. In addition to accelerating model training, knowledge distillation produces a small model inheriting the larger model's generalization ability [30].

The knowledge employed in distillation can be categorized into response-based knowledge and feature-based knowledge [28]. Response-based knowledge typically pertains to the teacher's model's output layer. This approach enables students to mimic the teacher's final predictions directly. Feature-based knowledge refers to the teacher model's middle layer. The feature layer as a supervisory signal can facilitate the student model's learning.

4   SNIPER

In this section, we first give a general overview of SNIPER and then describe the structure of our model and its training process in detail.

4.1   Overview

SNIPER is a detection system that could accurately identify APT attacks from network traffic. Figure 2 depicts the architecture of SNIPER, including two stages, training and detection.

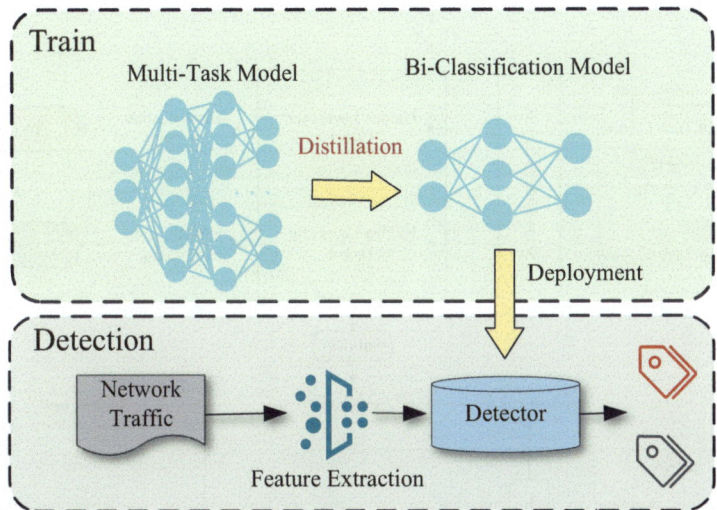

Fig. 2. Overview of SNIPER.

In training phase, SNIPER utilizes a multi-task model to learn the comprehensive characteristics of the traffic in order to identify attack traffic accurately. It also employs knowledge distillation for model compression, using the multi-tasking model as a teacher to distill the shared feature layer into a lightweight student model. Using this lightweight model for the final detection further improves the detection speed while avoiding the additional overhead of running a complex multi-task model.

During the detection stage, SNIPER first backs up the inbound traffic and extracts relevant features, then uses the student model trained in the previous step as a classifier to bi-classify the traffic in real-time and report the threats to security personnel. SNIPER has remarkable detection capabilities and generates fine-grained alerts with very low false positives, significantly reducing the amount of manual forensics and response required.

4.2   Model

Figure 3 illustrates the SNIPER model structure, comprising a multi-task teacher model and a binary classification student model. The teacher model extracts high-dimensional features, learns different attack behaviors, and directs student model training. It does not participate in the APT attack detection task, so no cost implications arise. The student model serves as the executor of the detection task, requiring a lightweight design to handle high-speed, large-scale network traffic with minimal overhead efficiently. Based on the above mentioned considerations, we establish two Deep Neural Network (DNN) models with 5 and 2 layers, T-DNN and S-DNN as the teacher and student models, respectively.

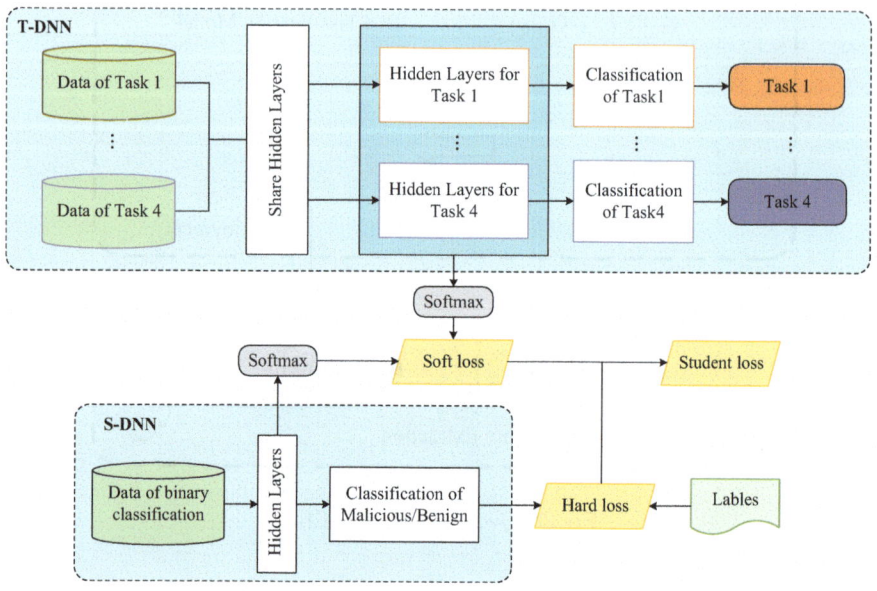

Fig. 3. Model structure of SNIPER.

T-DNN and S-DNN both utilize identical input data. Specifically, the first four layers of T-DNN function as the shared bottom feature layer across all tasks, while the ultimate layer acts as the top layer, outputting multiple task category probabilities. T-DNN's elaborate network structures enable adept learning of the input data's feature representation. Consequently, the learned feature representation vector offer a supervised signal to the student model. The bottom layer of the S-DNN serves as the feature layer, allowing for the learning of the input representation. The top layer functions as the output layer and classifies the input data categories. The S-DNN must recognize whether the input feature vector corresponds to a benign or malicious stream. It employs the T-DNN's feature representation vector as a soft target and the benign/malicious categorization label value as a hard target. A linear combination of both soft and hard targets guides the S-DNN training.

4.3   Train and Distillation

We utilize the five-phase attack model outlined in Table 1 to set the tasks for T-DNN. This model separates a complete APT attack into five distinct phases. The early four phases of the APT attack process may have abnormal network traffic performance. In light of this, we establish four binary classification tasks for T-DNN to determine if the current traffic pertains to a specific attack phase.

For input X and task-specific output $Y_i, i = 1, 2, 3, 4$, we utilize the commonly used cross-entropy function to calculate the loss of a single task:

$$\mathcal{L}(\mathbf{X}, \mathbf{Y}_i) = -\frac{1}{N} \sum_{j=1}^{N} y_j \log \widehat{y}_j, \tag{1}$$

where y denotes the actual label, $\widehat{y}$ denotes the model's prediction, and N is the BatchSize.

Among the four phases of an APT attack, suspicious behaviors in the reconnaissance phase are most clearly characterized in traffic. However, these behaviors, specific to APT attacks, can be easily confused with common low-level network attacks, resulting in many false positives. While the subsequent phases are more representative of APT attacks, they are more challenging to detect, and emphasizing them risks missing attacks. Therefore, we consider the contributions of all four phases equally. Specifically, we do not discriminate between these four tasks' variability. They equally contribute to the loss function. Hence, we formulate the overall loss function of T-DNN as the average of all tasks:

$$\mathcal{L}_T = \frac{1}{4} \sum_{i=1}^{4} \mathcal{L}_i(\mathbf{X}, \mathbf{Y}_i). \tag{2}$$

As depicted in Fig. 3, the loss function of S-DNN consists of the components of soft target $\mathcal{L}_{soft}$ and hard target $\mathcal{L}_{hard}$. The hard target is computed from the S-DNN's prediction and the true label of the input via Eq. 1.

Given the complexity of APT attacks, we use feature distillation instead of label distillation to help S-DNN better distinguish between malicious and benign traffic. It is more beneficial for students to learn the solution process rather than just the answer. This enables them to maintain good performance when facing new problems. To achieve this, we use the hidden layers of S-DNN and T-DNN to compute soft targets jointly:

$$\mathcal{L}_{soft} = -p^T \log(q^T), \tag{3}$$

where p^T and q^T are the outputs of the last hidden-layers of T-DNN and S-DNN.

SNIPER employs feature knowledge distillation to enable the teacher model to classify attack behaviors, aiding the student model in better organizing malicious traffic. This information consists of predicted values for correct and negative labels. However, using the outputs of T-DNN and S-DNN as soft targets directly yields small entropy in the probability distribution of the outputs after *softmax* function. In this situation, the predicted values for negative labels are incredibly close to zero, resulting in a negligible contribution to the loss function. To address this issue, we add the distillation temperature T to the *softmax* function to alleviate this problem.

$$softmax(x) = \frac{\exp(x/T)}{\sum \exp(x_k/T)}, \tag{4}$$

where x is any input vector.

The greater the value of T, the smoother the output probability becomes, leading to higher distribution entropy. This amplifies information carried by negative labels, prompting the model training to focus more on negative labels [29].

Similar to previous distillation methods, we define the final loss function of the S-DNN as a weighted linear combination of the soft and hard targets. Ultimately, the loss function of the S-DNN is defined as:

$$\mathcal{L}_S = \alpha\mathcal{L}_{soft} + \beta\mathcal{L}_{hard}. \tag{5}$$

Where α and β are the weight parameters of the soft target loss function $\mathcal{L}_{soft}$ and the hard target loss function $\mathcal{L}_{hard}$.

Algorithm 1 Training of S-DNN

Input: Dataset and label
Output: Trained model (S-DNN)
 1: Stochastically initialize the model parameters Θ
 2: Setting the maximum number of epoch $epoch_{max}$ and learn rating ϵ
 3: **for** $i = 1$ to T **do**
 4:     Divide the dataset into small batches D_t
 5: **end for**
 6: **for** $epoch = 1$ to $epoch_{max}$ **do**
 7:     Merging data sets $D = D_1 \cup D_2... \cup D_T$
 8:     Randomize D
 9:     **for** b_t in D **do**
10:         Calculate loss $\mathcal{L}$ by (5)
11:         Calculate gradient $\nabla(\Theta)$
12:         Update the model $\Theta = \Theta - \epsilon\nabla(\Theta)$
13:     **end for**
14: **end for**

Algorithm 1 shows the distillation process of SNIPER. The model parameters Θ are first initialized using a stochastic approach and then divide the training dataset D_t for each task t into small batches (line 1–5). In each epoch, the dataset D is first merged and randomized (line 7–8). These small batches are subsequently used to train the model. For every small batch, we compute its loss $\mathcal{L}$ and gradient $\nabla(\Theta)$ and then update the model parameters Θ by gradient descent (line 10–12). The model is then trained by iterating until the stopping condition is met.

5 Evaluation

In this section, we first describe our experimental setup and the dataset we used. Then we illustrate the actual performance of SNIPER in detecting APT attacks. Finally, we analyze the impact of different components and hyperparameters on SNIPER.

5.1 Experimental Setup

We implemented the distillation model proposed in this paper using Torch and Sklearn libraries. The number of neurons in each layer of S-DNN and T-DNN are (39, 64, 2) and (39, 256, 128, 64, 4) respectively. During the training stage, we divided the dataset into a training set and a test set in the ratio of 8:2. More parameter settings are shown in Table 2. In addition, all experiments were conducted on an Intel Core i7-12650 CPU.

Table 2. Parameters of model.

Parameters	Value
Weighting of soft targets α	0.4
Weighting of hard targets β	0.6
Learning rate	0.002
Temperature of distillation T	12

The DAPT dataset [31], developed to cover multiple phases of APT attacks, provides a test benchmark for scenarios using attack phase modeling. The dataset is constructed from network traffic collected over five days, where each day is equivalent to three months in actual systems. As shown in Table 3, the DAPT coverage includes 16 techniques across all five phases of an APT attack. Most of the attack techniques employed by renowned APT organizations in recent real-world activities are incorporated. Nonetheless, the DAPT dataset remains unbalanced like other APT attack-related datasets.

The evaluation metrics comprise accuracy, precision, recall, and F1 scores, enabling a thorough assessment of imbalanced datasets as outlined in Table 4.

5.2 Detection Performance

We first evaluate the Performance of SNIPER in detecting APT attack traffic. To demonstrate the advantages of SNIPER, we compare it with two other approaches (E-GAT-LSTM [4] and Hussain et al. [5]) that also used this dataset. Table 5 shows the evaluation results, which show that SNIPER's metrics are much better than other model. These results fully illustrate the advantages of our method in terms of classification performance.

Table 3. Attack scenarios in the DAPT Dataset.

Attack Scenarios	APT Phase
Network Scan, Application Scan, Account Bruteforce	Reconnaissance
CSRF, SQL Injection, Malware Download, Backdoor, Reverse Shell, Command Injection	Establish Foothold
Internal Scanning, Account Discovery, Password Dumping, Credential Theft, Creation of User Accounts, Privilege Escalation	Lateral Movement
Data Theft	Data Exfiltration

Table 4. Indicators for evaluation.

Metrics	Descriptions
TP	Attack flow classified as anomaly
TN	Benign flow classified as normal
FP	Benign flow classified as anomaly
FN	Attack flow classified as normal
Accuracy	$(TP+TN)/(TP+FP+TN+FN)$
Precision	$TP/(TP+FP)$
Recall	$TP/(TP+FN)$
F1-score	$2 \cdot (Precision \cdot Recall)/(Precision+Recall)$

It take us 187 s to train SNIPER and only 5.95 s to detect the entire dataset. Considering the training process is offline, the time spend on training is acceptable. In addition, thanks to the distillation design, SNIPER shows a high efficiency in the detection phase, which is far from the existing methods. Considering that the DAPT dataset includes data over five days, we believe that SNIPER can fully match the web traffic of small and medium-sized businesses. In addition, when using SNIPER for the detection task, the average CPU usage is only 1.26%. All these results meet our expectation that SNIPER is an efficient and accurate tool for detecting APT attacks.

Table 5. Performance of SNIPER and other models.

Model	Accuracy	Precision	Recall	F1-score	Detection Time (s)
E-GAT-LSTM [4]	0.92	0.81	**0.99**	0.89	12.1
Hussain et al. [5]	0.96	0.95	0.96	0.96	20.56
SNIPER	**0.99**	**0.98**	**0.99**	**0.99**	**5.95**

5.3 Ablation Studies

Distillation Effectiveness. To demonstrate the effectiveness of knowledge distillation, we set up S-DNN with knowledge distillation and DNN without knowledge distillation, respectively. Figure 4 show the change in loss and accuracy values of the two models in training. The DNN converges quickly in the first few training rounds, and the accuracy stabilizes at around 0.95. At the same time, the S-DNN undergoes a lengthy process of knowledge distillation and has a smoother training process. This is in line with our expectation that the convergence process of the student model is smoother under the influence of the teacher's model. In addition, S-DNN performs better in detection with 99% accuracy due to the richer feature information learned from the teacher's model.

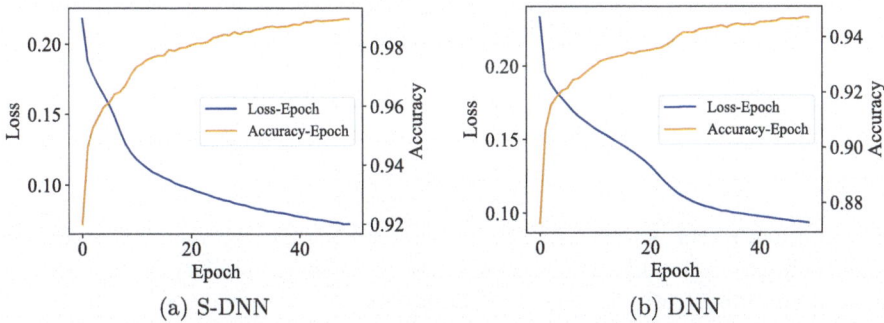

(a) S-DNN   (b) DNN

Fig. 4. Loss and Accuracy curve for S-DNN and DNN.

To further verify that the better generalizability of the distilled detection model brings advantages for detecting attack traffic, we further evaluate the performance of DNN and S-DNN. In addition, we also choose BNN and SVM, two classical machine learning models, to demonstrate the advantages of deep learning models for detection. Table 6 shows the evaluation results. S-DNN achieves better results compared to DNN without knowledge distillation. In particular, the *precision* is significantly improved by 10%, implying that knowledge distillation effectively improves the ability of S-DNN to distinguish between malicious and benign traffic.

Table 6. Performance of SNIPER and baseline.

Model	Accuracy	Precision	Recall	F1-score
BNN	0.85	0.64	0.78	0.70
SVM	0.93	0.89	0.87	0.88
DNN	0.95	0.89	0.94	0.91
S-DNN	**0.99**	**0.98**	**0.99**	**0.99**

In addition, we plot the ROC curves of the two models under study, as shown in Fig. 5. The larger area under the curve (AUC) demonstrates again that multitasking and knowledge distillation work well on S-DNN.

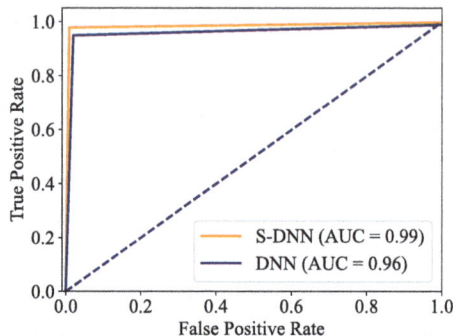

Fig. 5. ROC curve for S-DNN and DNN.

Hyper-parameter Analysis. The function of SNIPER is controlled by several hyperparameters, including two loss weights (α, β) and a distillation temperature (T). Figure 6 illustrates the effect of these hyperparameters on SNIPER.

The weighting of soft and hard target is an essential parameter in the distillation process, which balances the two processes of inherited knowledge and independent learning of the student model. If the weight of soft target is too low and the weight of hard target is too high, it will lead to the student model's tendency to learn from labels and less about the teacher's ground knowledge. Conversely, it will make the student model learn the teacher model's feature layer and weaken the supervision of data labeling. After experiments, we found the optimal parameter combination of (α, β) as $(0.4, 0.6)$.

As we mention in Sect. 4.2, the distillation temperature is correlated with the model's focus on negative labeling. Higher temperatures can help student models learn interclass similarities better but can also potentially lead to information loss. After experiments, we obtain the optimal distillation temperature $T = 12$.

6   Conclusion

In this paper, we proposed SNIPER, an efficient network-side APT attack detection system based on knowledge distillation and multi-task learning. Specifically, we trained a multi-task model to learn more comprehensive features of APT attack by identifying attack traffic at different stages of APT as sub-tasks. These rich features can help us more accurately identify APT attacks from the traffic. Considering the vast deployment cost of the model, we utilized the knowledge distillation technique to transfer the knowledge learned in the multi-task model

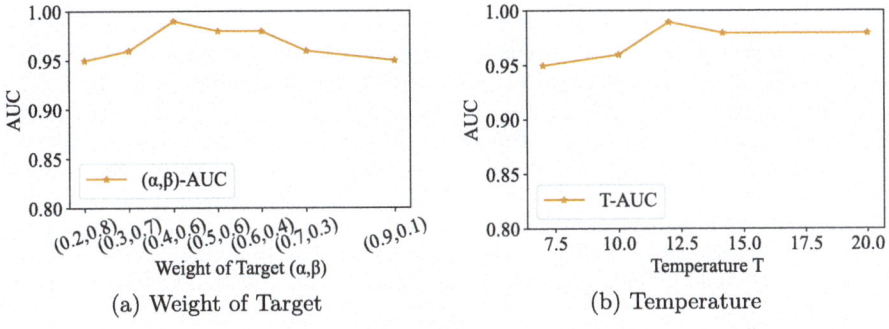

Fig. 6. Hyper-parameter and AUC curve for SNIPER.

to a lightweight model, thus achieving effective model compression while retaining the knowledge. Experimental evaluations showed that SNIPER can utilize this lightweight model to efficiently and accurately detect APT attacks from traffic.

Acknowledgement. This work is supported by National Natural Science Foundation of China (62072239, 62372236), Natural Science Foundation of Jiangsu Province, China (BK20211192), Jiangsu Funding Program for Excellent Postdoctoral Talent, Qing Lan Project of Jiangsu Province, Postdoctoral Fellowship Program of CPSF (GZB20240982).

References

1. Ye, M., Men, S., Xie, L., Chen, B.: Detect advanced persistent threat in graph-level using competitive autoencoder. In: Proceedings of the 2023 2nd International Conference on Networks, Communications and Information Technology, pp. 28–34 (2023)
2. Cole, E.: Advanced persistent threat: understanding the danger and how to protect your organization. Newnes (2012)
3. Park, N.E., Lee, Y.R., Joo, S., Kim, S.Y., Kim, S.H., Park, J.Y., Kim, S.Y., Lee, I.G.: Performance evaluation of a fast and efficient intrusion detection framework for advanced persistent threat-based cyberattacks. Comput. Electr. Eng. **105**, 108548 (2023)
4. Liao, N., Wang, J., Guan, J., Fan, H.: A multi-step attack identification and correlation method based on multi-information fusion. Comput. Electr. Eng. **117**, 109249 (2024)
5. Hussain, S., Ahmad, M.B., Asif, M., Akram, W., Mahmood, K., Das, A.K., Shetty, S.: APT adversarial defence mechanism for industrial IoT enabled cyber-physical system. IEEE Access (2023)
6. Alshamrani, A., Myneni, S., Chowdhary, A., Huang, D.: A survey on advanced persistent threats: techniques, solutions, challenges, and research opportunities. IEEE Commun. Surv. Tutorials **21**(2), 1851–1877 (2019)
7. Akoglu, L., Tong, H., Koutra, D.: Graph based anomaly detection and description: a survey. Data Min. Knowl. Disc. **29**, 626–688 (2015)

8. Altinisik, E., Deniz, F., Sencar, H.T.: ProvG-searcher: a graph representation learning approach for efficient provenance graph search. In: Proceedings of the 2023 ACM SIGSAC Conference on Computer and Communications Security, pp. 2247–2261 (2023)

9. Xiong, C., Zhu, T., Dong, W., Ruan, L., Yang, R., Cheng, Y., Chen, Y., Cheng, S., Chen, X.: Conan: a practical real-time apt detection system with high accuracy and efficiency. IEEE Trans. Dependable Secure Comput. **19**(1), 551–565 (2020)

10. Milajerdi, S.M., Eshete, B., Gjomemo, R., Venkatakrishnan, V.: POIROT: aligning attack behavior with kernel audit records for cyber threat hunting. In: Proceedings of the 2019 ACM SIGSAC Conference on Computer and Communications Security, pp. 1795–1812 (2019)

11. Hassan, W.U., Guo, S., Li, D., Chen, Z., Jee, K., Li, Z., Bates, A.: NoDoze: combatting threat alert fatigue with automated provenance triage. In: Network and Distributed Systems Security Symposium (2019)

12. Wang, Q., Hassan, W.U., Li, D., Jee, K., Yu, X., Zou, K., Rhee, J., Chen, Z., Cheng, W., Gunter, C.A., et al.: You are what you do: hunting stealthy malware via data provenance analysis. In: NDSS (2020)

13. Zengy, J., Wang, X., Liu, J., Chen, Y., Liang, Z., Chua, T.S., Chua, Z.L.: ShadeWatcher: recommendation-guided cyber threat analysis using system audit records. In: 2022 IEEE Symposium on Security and Privacy (SP), pp. 489–506. IEEE (2022)

14. Alsaheel, A., Nan, Y., Ma, S., Yu, L., Walkup, G., Celik, Z.B., Zhang, X., Xu, D.: ATLAS: a sequence-based learning approach for attack investigation. In: 30th USENIX Security Symposium (USENIX Security 21), pp. 3005–3022 (2021)

15. Zipperle, M., Gottwalt, F., Chang, E., Dillon, T.: Provenance-based intrusion detection systems: a survey. ACM Comput. Surv. **55**(7), 1–36 (2022)

16. Talib, M.A., Nasir, Q., Nassif, A.B., Mokhamed, T., Ahmed, N., Mahfood, B.: APT beaconing detection: a systematic review. Comput. Secur. 102875 (2022)

17. Niu, W., Zhou, J., Zhao, Y., Zhang, X., Peng, Y., Huang, C.: Uncovering APT malware traffic using deep learning combined with time sequence and association analysis. Comput. Secur. **120**, 102809 (2022)

18. Yan, G., Li, Q., Guo, D., Li, B.: AULD: large scale suspicious DNS activities detection via unsupervised learning in advanced persistent threats. Sensors **19**(14), 3180 (2019)

19. He, D., Gu, H., Zhu, S., Chan, S., Guizani, M.: A comprehensive detection method for the lateral movement stage of apt attacks. IEEE Internet Things J. (2023)

20. Liu, J., Liu, Y., Li, J., Sun, W., Cheng, J., Zhang, R., Huang, X., Pang, J.: Two statistical traffic features for certain APT group identification. J. Inf. Secur. Appl. **67**, 103207 (2022)

21. Marchetti, M., Pierazzi, F., Colajanni, M., Guido, A.: Analysis of high volumes of network traffic for advanced persistent threat detection. Comput. Netw. **109**, 127–141 (2016)

22. Vukalović, J., Delija, D.: Advanced persistent threats-detection and defense. In: 2015 38th International Convention on Information and Communication Technology, Electronics and Microelectronics (MIPRO), pp. 1324–1330. IEEE (2015)

23. Ussath, M., Jaeger, D., Cheng, F., Meinel, C.: Advanced persistent threats: behind the scenes. In: 2016 Annual Conference on Information Science and Systems (CISS), pp. 181–186. IEEE (2016)

24. Messaoud, B.I., Guennoun, K., Wahbi, M., Sadik, M.: Advanced persistent threat: new analysis driven by life cycle phases and their challenges. In: 2016 International Conference on Advanced Communication Systems and Information Security (ACOSIS), pp. 1–6. IEEE (2016)

25. Vandenhende, S., Georgoulis, S., Van Gansbeke, W., Proesmans, M., Dai, D., Van Gool, L.: Multi-task learning for dense prediction tasks: a survey. IEEE Trans. Pattern Anal. Mach. Intell. **44**(7), 3614–3633 (2021)

26. Thung, K.H., Wee, C.Y.: A brief review on multi-task learning. Multimedia Tools Appl. **77**, 29705–29725 (2018)

27. Zhang, Y., Yang, Q.: An overview of multi-task learning. Natl. Sci. Rev. **5**(1), 30–43 (2018)

28. Gou, J., Yu, B., Maybank, S.J., Tao, D.: Knowledge distillation: a survey. Int. J. Comput. Vision **129**, 1789–1819 (2021)

29. Hinton, G., Vinyals, O., Dean, J.: Distilling the knowledge in a neural network (2015). arXiv preprint arXiv:1503.02531

30. Wang, L., Yoon, K.J.: Knowledge distillation and student-teacher learning for visual intelligence: a review and new outlooks. IEEE Trans. Pattern Anal. Mach. Intell. **44**(6), 3048–3068 (2021)

31. Myneni, S., Chowdhary, A., Sabur, A., Sengupta, S., Agrawal, G., Huang, D., Kang, M.: DAPT 2020—constructing a benchmark dataset for advanced persistent threats. In: Deployable Machine Learning for Security Defense: First International Workshop, MLHat 2020, San Diego, CA, USA, 24 Aug 2020, Proceedings 1, pp. 138–163. Springer, Berlin (2020)

From the Perspective of Prototypes: A Privacy-Preserving Personalized Federated Learning Framework

Liwei Liu, Zijian Liu, and Na Ruan[✉]

Shanghai Jiao Tong University, Shanghai, China
naruan@cs.sjtu.edu.cn

Abstract. Federated learning, as a collaborative learning approach that protects user privacy, has garnered significant attention from researchers in recent years. However, traditional federated learning paradigm generally suffers from two major limitations: ubiquitous reliance on the IID assumption and the homogeneous architecture design of local model and global model. In contrast, prototype federated learning, a personalize federated learning (PFL) paradigm, addresses these heterogeneity problem quite well. However, its original paradigm ignores privacy risks posed by prototype leakage. To prove the risk of prototype leakage, we propose a generative attack method based on conditional generative models, using prototype information to achieve sample reconstruction and theft of training results. To the best of our knowledge, we demonstrate for the first time that prototype information leakage can lead to a series of privacy security issues. Furthermore, We propose a privacy-preserving personalized federated learning framework based on prototypes, ingeniously integrating homomorphic encryption technology into the training of prototype federated learning through equivalent transformations, thus addressing the privacy issue in prototype federated learning.

Keywords: personalized federated learning · prototype · homomorphic encryption · data privacy

1 Introduction

Federated learning has attracted widespread attention from researchers due to its ability to achieve collaborative training while preserving user privacy. Traditional federated learning realizes joint model training by transmitting gradients, enabling local data to remain on-site and thereby partially addressing the data silo problem. However, subsequent research has demonstrated that federated learning also faces significant privacy challenges, such as the DLG algorithm [2], which successfully reconstructs training samples from gradients.

Though traditional federated learning study provides unique academic insights, it also has evident limitations. Firstly, traditional federated learning are generally based on the statistical assumption of IID data, which is quite

© The Author(s), under exclusive license to Springer Nature Singapore Pte Ltd. 2025
Z. Xia and J. Chen (Eds.): ISPEC 2024, LNCS 15053, pp. 222–239, 2024.
https://doi.org/10.1007/978-981-97-9053-1_13

different from real-world scenarios where data is non-IID. Deploying traditional federated learning methods in real-world scenarios lead to client shift, significantly reducing the model performance. Secondly, traditional federated learning research typically employs homogeneous architectural design, where both clients and central server share the same model architecture. This approach not only overlooks clients' personalized needs but also exacerbates issues of fairness.

To address the issue of heterogeneity, prototype federated learning, which replaces gradient aggregation with prototype aggregation, has received considerable critical attention. However, its original framework has neglected the discussion of privacy issues. In fact, there exist potential risks of prototype information leakage. In this paper, we propose a generative attack method based on conditional generative models to reveal the potential risk empirically. Furthermore, we propose a privacy-preserving personalized federated learning framework based on prototypes, integrating homomorphic encryption technology to protect original prototype information from attackers.

Our main contributions can be summarized as follows:

- **Revealing the potential risk of prototype leakage.** We propose a feasible generative attack method based on conditional generative models. In the experimental section, with the help of prototype and auxiliary datasets, we use CGAN to achieve sample reconstruction successfully.
- **A privacy-preserving PFL framework.** We propose a novel personalized federated learning framework based on prototypes. By incorporating homomorphic encryption technology, the framework prevents direct exposure of label and prototype information,mitigating associated privacy risks.
- **Summarizing the general rules of prototype generation.** Previous research has not delved further into the discussion of prototype generation, resulting in difficulty in model selection for researchers. In our paper, we test prototypes generated by mainstream models on three datasets, summarizing the general rules of prototype generation empirically.

2   Related Work

2.1   Personalized Federated Learning (PFL)

In recent years, there has been a surge of relevant work in the field of personalized federated learning. A. Tan et al. summarized existing research on personalized federated learning and provided a reasonable explanation for the phenomenon of client drift [4]. L. Collins et al. proposed the FedRep algorithm, which innovatively integrated the alternating minimization method into the model training process of federated learning, achieving hierarchical training of models and partially addressing statistical heterogeneity issues [5]. Y. Tan et al. introduced the prototype federated algorithm, which utilizes prototype aggregation instead of traditional gradient aggregation methods, significantly improving the performance of models on heterogeneous data and achieving better results in addressing model heterogeneity issues [6]. C. Wu et al. employed knowledge distillation, guiding student model training using teacher models to facilitate knowledge transfer between different models, partially resolving model heterogeneity issues [7]. M.G. Arivazhagan et al. first introduced the concept of personalized layers to achieve personalized model architectures, which has inspired other PFL work based on model partitioning [8]. P.P. Liang et al. proposed the LG-FedAvg algorithm, which addresses data heterogeneity issues by jointly training downstream classifiers [9]. However, these studies generally focus on solving heterogeneity issues and to some extent overlook the analysis of privacy issues.

2.2   Prototype Federated Learning

The concept of prototype federated learning was first proposed by Y. Tan et al. [6]. It is inspired by the idea of prototype learning to mimic the general pattern of human knowledge acquisition. In prototype learning, data distributions and features can be represented by learning a set of prototypes. By learning a refined set of prototypes, prototype learning can significantly enhance the model's performance across various tasks. In prototype federated learning, it uses neural networks to generate class-level prototypes and control the distance between global and local prototypes with the aid of contrasive learning. Moreover, it innovatively introduces prototype aggregation instead of gradient aggregation. In conclusion, the core idea of prototype federated learning is to utilize prototypes to transfer knowledge among various clients, guiding the optimization training of downstream models while ensuring that the distance between global and local prototypes is minimized.

3   Problem Formulation

3.1   Traditional Federated Learning Scenario

Based on the framework of traditional federated learning, assuming each client has a dataset D_i collected from the probability distribution P_i, where x and y represent the input features and labels of samples respectively. The global model is denoted as $F(w; x)$, where $F(\cdot)$ represents the model architecture with hyperparameters set, w represents the model parameters. Then, the optimization objective of traditional federated learning can be formalized as follows:

$$\arg\min_{w} \sum_{i=1}^{n} \frac{\|D_i\|}{N} L_s(F(w; x), y) \tag{1}$$

where n is the number of clients in the training. In IID scenario, we assume the existence of the optimal model parameter that achieves the best performance under this distribution. Thus, the training process in high-dimensional space indicates that w gradually approaching w^*. However, in Non-IID scenario, the optimal model parameters for each distribution are w_i^*, which are usually different from each other. Traditional federated learning algorithm suffers from significant performance degradation in this scenario, leading to client shift phenomenon. It has been proved that simply averaging the gradients is insufficient to achieve the theoretical optimal solution.

3.2 Personalized Federated Learning Scenario

Personalized federated learning, is a federated learning paradigm aimed at providing customized services to users. The main challenges faced by it are how to solve the issue of statistical heterogeneity and model heterogeneity. The effectiveness of personalized federated learning algorithms is primarily evaluated based on their performance in two heterogeneous scenarios.

In personalized federated learning scenarios, each user is assumed to hold a different model. Suppose the dataset held by the user i is D_i, which follows distribution $P_i(x, y)$, and the model held is $F_i(w_i; x)$, where w_i represents the model parameters. Then, the optimization objective of personalized federated learning can be formalized as follows:

$$\arg\min_{w} \sum_{i=1}^{n} \frac{\|D_i\|}{N} L_s(F_i(w_i; x), y) \tag{2}$$

Assuming the optimal solution of the client i is w_i^*, it is difficult for traditional federated learning to meet the needs of all users by training a single global model, since the optimal solutions for different users' model parameters vary. However, in personalized scenario, because the local model parameters w_i are separated from the global parameters w, each w_i have the potential to reach their respective optimal solution w_i^*, rather than the compromise of an averaged optimal solution $\overline{w}^*$.

3.3 Generative Attack based on Conditional Generative Model

Conditional generative models are a critical field of machine learning. They can generate corresponding data samples based on given conditions or representations. In general, we can describe the role of conditional generative models with the following formula:

$$x = Gen(z|y) \tag{3}$$

In this formula, x represents sample features, z represents noise sampled from a Gaussian distribution or other synthesized feature vectors, and y represents conditional information, typically corresponding to the labels of samples.

Attack Principle Prototypes, as a form of category-level distilled knowledge, serve a similar role to the label conditional information or prompts commonly used in conditional generative models. However, unlike label information typically represented by fixed vectors generated through an Embedding layer, prototypes generated through neural networks not only have a closer relationship with sample representations but are also not static. They are closely related to the structure and training methods of prototype generation models, allowing for continuous optimization and updates. Based on the principles of conditional generative models, we propose using prototype information instead of label information as auxiliary information to guide the model in attempting to reconstruct sample data, with subsequent analysis and validation conducted in the experimental phase.

Attacker Model In personalized federated learning scenario, assume n clients participate in prototype federated training, with a third-party central server responsible for prototype aggregation during training. The goal of the clients, acting as defenders, is to obtain models that meet their individual needs without privacy leakage. All clients adopt original prototype federated learning paradigm and directly transmit prototype information. Based on these assumptions, there may be two types of attackers:

- **Semi-Honest Central Server**: In a semi-honest scenario, the central server follows the prescribed process for prototype aggregation. However, out of curiosity or for other reasons, it retains the local prototype lists and global prototype lists collected in each training round. Assuming the central server can access some public datasets, it attempts to reconstruct a client's training samples using the prototype information and conditional generative models, such as obtaining a user's private photos.
- **Malicious Third-party Attacker**: More generally, in real-world scenario, malicious attackers may use active attack methods such as eavesdropping to obtain prototype information transmitted during training. Similar to the semi-honest scenario, third-party attackers can use the collected prototype information, and even partial personal information to reconstruct training samples. Moreover, they can easily create new samples at a low cost by using the prototypes as template. For example, by stealing a prototype representing the Impressionist style, they could quickly train a model capable of generating different Impressionist paintings, indirectly stealing the client model (Fig. 1).

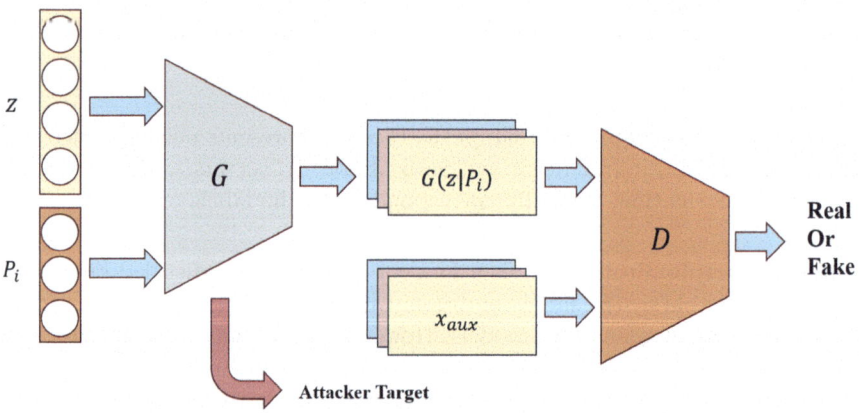

Fig. 1. Generative Attack Framework based on CGAN (The ultimate goal of attacker is to obtain a generator with ideal performance at a low cost.)

4   Methodology

4.1   Generative Attack Based on CGAN

Model Selection Conditional Generative Adversarial Network (CGAN) is one of the representative methods of conditional generative models. By introducing a conditional variable, usually label information, CGAN continuously improves the deception ability of the generator to the discriminator while satisfying the given conditional constraints. The advantage of CGAN lies in its ability to control the attributes of generated samples, making it widely applicable to tasks such as image-to-image translation, conditional image generation, and text-to-image generation. Currently, there are studies extending conditions to other forms such as video sequences and structured data, enhancing the control capability of generative models. Based on these advantages, we select CGAN as the model for generative attacks.

Optimization Objective CGAN builds upon the foundation of GAN by introducing conditional information to guide the training of the generative model. However, in the past, there has been a general focus on using structured data such as label information. Similarly, if we use prototype information as a conditional variable, theoretically, we can generate different samples under the constraints of the prototype. This idea actually aligns with the pattern of human learning and creation. Humans, during the creative process, use existing knowledge as a template and create new images based on inspiration. The process of training a generative model is aimed at improving its ability to generate images constrained by prototypes. Using prototypes as conditional information, the optimization objective of CGAN can be formalized as follows:

$$\min_{G} \max_{D} E_x[\log(D(x|P_i)] + E_z[\log(1 - D(G((z|P_i)))] \tag{4}$$

Privacy Risk of Prototype In past research on prototype federated learning, there has been a general neglect of discussions on the privacy issue of prototypes. The proposer of prototype federated learning has briefly analyzed whether prototype information leakage would lead to privacy risks. They believed that due to the irreversibility of prototype calculation and the small dimensions of prototypes, prototype federation inherently possesses strong privacy capabilities. However, through our research, we have found that using generative models for attacks, specifically conditional generative models, can leverage prototype information to achieve goals such as sample reconstruction and model theft, posing a serious threat to user privacy. Therefore, to address the privacy shortcomings of prototype federated learning, we further combine homomorphic encryption technology to propose a brand-new framework for privacy-preserving personalized federated learning.

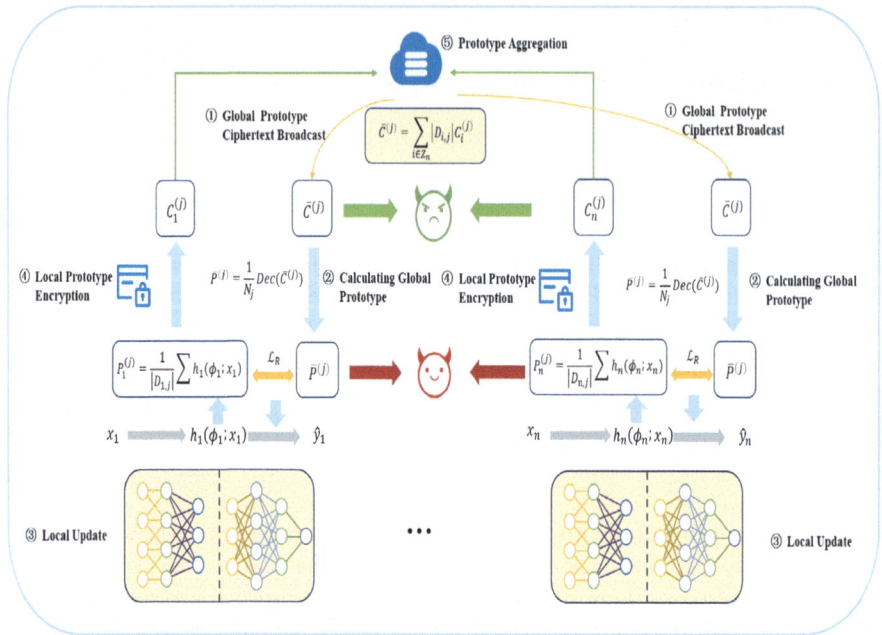

Fig. 2. Privacy-Preserving PFL Framework based on Prototype

4.2   Privacy-Preserving Personalized Federated Learning Framework

To address the heterogeneity issues that traditional federated learning struggles with and avoid prototype information leakage, we propose a prototype-based privacy-preserving personalized federated learning framework. An overview of the framework is shown in Fig. 2. A central server is responsible for sending and receiving messages from n clients, denoted as $M_1, M_2, \ldots, M_n$, where $M_i = \{(|D_{i,j}|, Y'_{i,j}, C_{i,j})|i \in Z_n, j \leq |Y_i|\}$. Here, $C_{i,j}$ represents the encrypted local prototype of client i for class j, and $Y'_{i,j}$ corresponds to the encrypted label of the prototype. Specially, in personalized scenario, each client may have a different set of prototype categories. During the prototype aggregation process, the central server needs to perform intersection operations based on label information.

Training Step The steps for each communication round in this framework are as follows:

- **Global Prototype Ciphertext Broadcast**: The central server broadcasts the global prototype ciphertext list $\overline{C}_i$.
- **Calculating Global Prototype**: The clients collect their respective global prototype ciphertext lists and decrypt them using the pre-negotiated private key, obtaining the unencrypted global prototype list $\overline{P}_i$ used in training.

- **Local Update**: Users generate their local prototype lists P_i and then train with their local datasets for the next round. After the update, the local prototype list P_i is recalculated.
- **Local Prototype Encryption**:After training, the clients encrypt their local prototype lists using the pre-negotiated public key to obtain the encrypted local prototype list C_i.
- **Prototype Aggregation**: The aggregation of prototypes is performed directly on the encrypted local prototype list C_i to obtain the global prototype ciphertext list $\overline{C}_i$ for the next communication round.

Local Model Structure Based on the different functionalities of the network, the local model can be divided into prototype generation layer and downstream task layer.

- **Prototype Generation Layer**: The function of the prototype generation layer is to generate local prototypes that guide the training of the downstream task layer. The prototype generation layer of the i-th client can be described as a function $h_i(\varphi_i)$.
- **Downstream Task Layer**: The function of the downstream task layer is to perform corresponding tasks, such as sentiment classification or text generation, based on the upstream representation vectors and prototype knowledge. Similarly, the downstream classification layer of the i-th client can be formalized as a function $c_i(\psi_i)$. The overall function of the model can be described as follows:

$$F_i(w_i) = F_i(\varphi_i, \psi_i) = c_i(\psi_i) \circ h_i(\varphi_i) \tag{5}$$

Prototype Definition We introduce partial homomorphic encryption based on the prototype federated learning framework. It involves four types of prototypes: local prototype, local prototype ciphertext, global prototype, and global prototype ciphertext.

- **Local Prototype**: $P_i^{(j)}$ represents the j-th class prototype of the i-th client. It is defined as the average of the representation vectors generated by the prototype generation network for the j-th class data. It can be formally described as follows:

$$P_i^{(j)} = \frac{1}{\|D_{i,j}\|} \sum_{(x,y) \in D_{i,j}} h_i(\varphi_i; x) \tag{6}$$

- **Local Prototype Ciphertext**: Since directly exposing prototype information may lead to privacy risks, the local prototypes are encrypted using an additive homomorphic encryption algorithm. Assuming that the clients collaboratively generate a public-private key pair $(sk, pk) = KeyGen(\lambda)$, the ciphertext of the j-th class prototype of the i-th client can be formally described as follows:

$$C_i^{(j)} = Enc(pk, P_i^{(j)}) \tag{7}$$

- **Global Prototype**: The role of the global prototype can be understood as the average perception of a certain concept by all participating clients. By calculating the difference between the global prototypes and the local prototypes, each client is guided to optimize and adjust their model. Typically, the global prototype is defined as the weighted average of the local prototypes. The j-th class global prototype can be described as follows:

$$\overline{P}^{(j)} = \sum \frac{\|D_{i,j}\|}{N_j} P_i^{(j)} \tag{8}$$

- **Glocal Prototype Ciphertext**: Since the prototype aggregation process essentially involves polynomial operations with non-integer coefficients, the additive homomorphic properties cannot be extended to perform weighted averaging directly on the ciphertexts. Therefore, through an equivalent transformation, the global prototype ciphertext is redefined to establish the relationship between the global prototype ciphertext and the global prototype. The global prototype ciphertext is defined as follows:

$$\overline{C}^{(j)} = \sum_{i \in Z_n} \|D_{i,j}\| C_i^{(j)}, \|D_{i,j}\| \in Z \tag{9}$$

At the same time, client can calculate global prototype using the following formula. The proof of equivalence for this transformation is detailed in Appendix 1.

$$\overline{P}^{(j)} = \frac{1}{N_j} \sum_{i \in Z_n} \|D_{i,j}\| Dec(C_i^{(j)}) = \frac{1}{N_j} Dec(\overline{C}^{(j)}) \tag{10}$$

Prototype Instruction The core idea of prototype federated learning is to transfer abstract knowledge among different data distributions through prototypes. In this framework, we follow the design of the original prototype federated framework, introducing regularization terms into the loss function. The formal definition of this regularization term is described as follows:

$$L_R(P_i, \overline{P}_i) = \sum_j Dist(P_i^{(j)}, \overline{P}_i^{(j)}) \tag{11}$$

Where P_i and $\overline{P}_i$ respectively represent the local prototype and global prototype list held by the i-th client, and $Dist(\cdot)$ represents the distance metric function. Therefore, the loss function for the i-th client can be expressed as:

$$L_i = L_s(F_i(w_i; x), y) + \lambda L_R(P_i, \overline{P}_i) \tag{12}$$

Estimation of Additional Costs The primary factor limiting homomorphic encryption is the significant additional overhead it incurs. Compared to models with parameters in the range of millions, the prototypes transmitted in prototype-based federated learning paradigm often are in the hundreds for dimension. This directly leads to a much lower times of encryption operations than traditional federated learning. To assess the feasibility of introducing partial homomorphic encryption in this framework, we provide a time overhead estimation formula as follows:

$$t_i = sl(\Delta t_e + \Delta t_d) + sl(n-1)\Delta t_a \tag{13}$$

In this formula, s represents the dimension of the prototype, l is the length of the prototype list, Δt_e and Δt_d denote the average time required for a single homomorphic addition and decryption operation, respectively, and Δt_a represents the average time needed for a single homomorphic addition operation between ciphertexts.Taking the CIFAR10 dataset used in the experiments of this paper as an example and substituting the corresponding values, the estimated additional overhead for a single communication round is less than 1 minute, while the duration for a single training round is over half an hour.

Discussion Firstly, in terms of privacy protection, compared to the original prototype federated framework, this framework encrypts the prototype information uploaded during the training process using partially homomorphic encryption algorithms, allowing the central server to only access the encrypted global prototypes without obtaining the actual global prototypes. This effectively eliminates the possibility of using prototype information for generative attacks. Secondly, in terms of model performance, this framework retains the advantages of prototype federated learning by using prototypes to bridge knowledge gaps between different data distributions, effectively addressing the heterogeneity issues in personalized federated learning. Finally, in terms of communication efficiency, although the introduction of partially homomorphic encryption incurs additional time overhead, based on the theoretical estimation of the additional costs mentioned above, the overhead remains within an acceptable range.

5 Experiment

5.1 Generative Attack Based on CGAN

Training Setups We selected the MNIST dataset and used the global prototype information when $n = 3$ as the constraint condition. A third of the MNIST dataset was uniformly sampled to serve as the auxiliary training set for training the CGAN. This auxiliary dataset can generally be collected by any third party through publicly available information channels. The CGAN consists of a discriminator D and a generator G. Both the discriminator and generator network structures are multilayer perceptrons. Through adversarial training, a generator is eventually obtained for testing the reconstruction attack effect. In this part of the experiment, a learning rate of 0.002 was used. The prototype dimension in the experiment was 50, and the noise was sampled from a Gaussian distribution with a dimension of 100. This noise was concatenated with the prototype and then input into the generator for subsequent training.

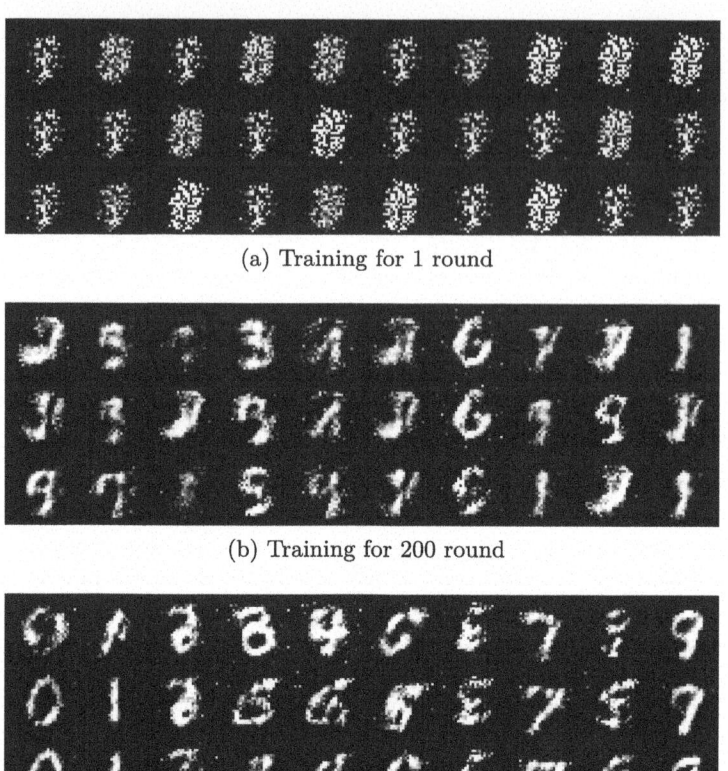

(a) Training for 1 round

(b) Training for 200 round

(c) Training for 400 round

Fig. 3. Attack Model Performance (We use the global prototype information received by the central server in the $5th$ round of prototype federated training to guide the training of the CGAN.)

Attack Effectiveness As shown in Fig. 3, with the increase in training iterations of the attack model, the images generated by the generator gradually transform from initial meaningless noise into corresponding digit images. This preliminary result indicates that by using prototypes as constraint conditions, conditional generative models can achieve attack objectives such as reconstructing samples. In other words, this experiment demonstrates that the direct leakage of prototype information can also lead to significant privacy issues.

Prototype Influence As shown in Fig. 4, the results are correspond to the CGAN training using global prototypes collected by the central server at different stages: after 5, 50, and 100 rounds of aggregation during prototype federated training, respectively. It can be noted that in the early stages of training, global prototypes collected after 5 rounds of aggregation lead to a faster achievement of a well-performing generative model. However, using global prototypes collected in the middle stages of training required more iterations but ultimately results in a better-performing generative model. This is likely because, during the prototype aggregation process, With the progress of prototype aggregation, the global prototypes tend to encapsulate more deeply hidden information, making it difficult for a simple conditional generative network to extract latent information. Due to the inherent limitations of the model's generative capabilities, the final generative performance of the model stabilizes. By replacing the conditional generative model or optimizing parameter selection, the final generative performance of the model can be improved.

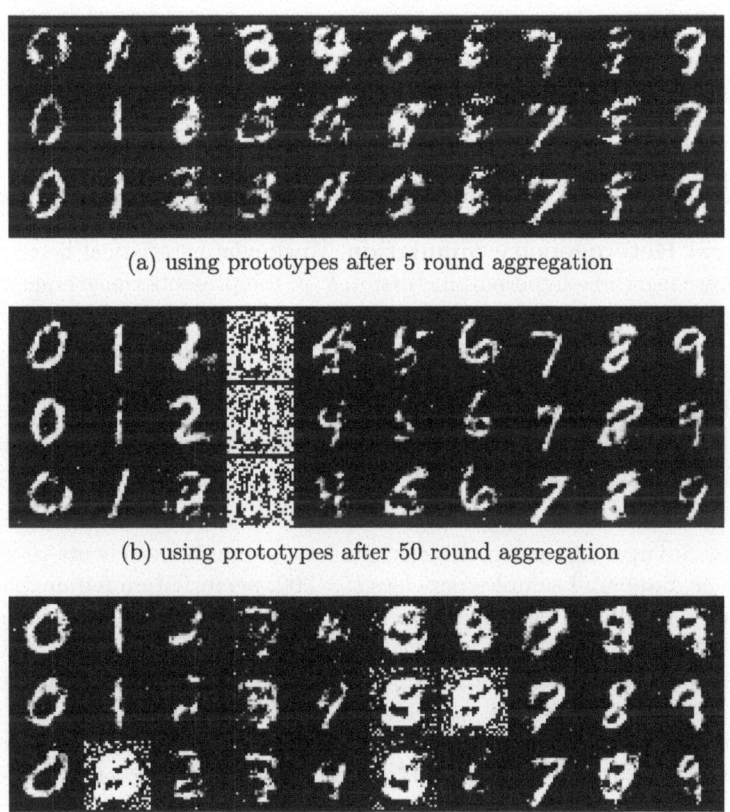

(a) using prototypes after 5 round aggregation

(b) using prototypes after 50 round aggregation

(c) using prototypes after 100 round aggregation

Fig. 4. Attack Model Performance correspond to different stage of prototype aggregation (All attack models are trained for 400 rounds.)

Table 1. Model Performance in statistical heterogeneity scenario (we select different model structures for prototype generation on three dataset)

Dataset	Model	Test Average Accuracy (%)		
		$n = 3$	$n = 4$	$n = 5$
MNIST	Baseline	96.00 ± 2.13	97.11 ± 0.41	97.85 ± 0.33
	CNNMNIST	$\mathbf{98.97 \pm 0.30}$	$\mathbf{98.55 \pm 0.19}$	$\mathbf{97.86 \pm 0.31}$
	LeNet	98.72 ± 0.54	97.82 ± 0.48	97.76 ± 0.25
FEMNIST	Baseline	65.22 ± 3.92	67.49 ± 2.77	68.46 ± 2.26
	CNNFEMNIST	$\mathbf{97.44 \pm 1.75}$	96.31 ± 1.03	95.39 ± 2.54
	LeNet	96.71 ± 1.32	$\mathbf{96.97 \pm 1.04}$	$\mathbf{96.67 \pm 1.93}$
CIFAR10	Baseline	51.76 ± 3.46	43.96 ± 3.23	42.87 ± 1.78
	ResNet18	$\mathbf{76.04 \pm 2.48}$	$\mathbf{66.54 \pm 1.78}$	$\mathbf{63.85 \pm 2.36}$
	MobileNet v2	64.76 ± 4.59	50.4 ± 4.10	40.53 ± 2.90

5.2 Performance Evaluation in Statistical Heterogeneity Scenario

Statistical Heterogeneity Simulation To simulate statistical heterogeneity scenario, we use three hyperparameters: n, k, δ. n represents the average number of sample categories held by each client, k represents the average number of samples for each category, and δ serves as a perturbation parameter. During training, the number of sample categories held by each client and the number of samples for each category are randomly selected within the ranges $[n - \delta, n + \delta]$ and $[k - \delta, k + \delta]$ respectively. Clients then generate their local datasets by randomly sampling from the corresponding datasets.

Training Setups In the experiment, we set the number of clients to 20, with the average number of samples per class $k = 200$, perturbation parameter $\delta = 1$, and average number of classes per client $n = 3, 4, 5$, to simulate varying degrees of heterogeneity. For MNIST and FEMNIST, training rounds were limited to no more than 100 rounds, with $\lambda = 1$, optimizing using SGD with a learning rate 0.01, local batch size set to 8. For CIFAR10, training rounds were limited to no more than 150 rounds, using the Adam optimizer with a regularization coefficient of $\lambda = 0.1$, a learning rate of 0.01, local batch size set to 8.

Model Performance The experimental results are shown in Table 1. It can be observed that, for MNIST and FEMNIST, using prototype-based aggregation method yields higher test accuracy compared to the traditional federated learning algorithm FedAvg, regardless of the local model structure. However, for CIFAR10, our prototype-based method shows a significant accuracy advantage over the classical algorithm when $n = 3, 4$. When $n = 5$, the accuracy is lower than baseline if pre-trained MobileNet v2 model is used. The reason for this might be that, MobileNet v2, with its inverted residuals and linear bottlenecks, focuses more on model efficiency and lightweight design compared to ResNet18.

General Rules of Prototype Generation Furthermore, for FEMNIST and CIFAR10, the proposed method demonstrates a significant advantage in test accuracy over the traditional federated algorithms across all three heterogeneity scenarios. However, this advantage is not as evident for MNIST. The reason lies in the relative simplicity of the MNIST dataset, whereas FEMNIST and CIFAR10 have higher classification and image complexity. For complex tasks, the limited number of samples amplifies the advantages of the prototype aggregation-based federated learning algorithm. Additionally, for FEMNIST, when $n = 3$, employing CNNFEMNIST as the prototype generation layer outperforms using LeNet. However, as n changes, the test accuracy of the model using CNNFEM-NIST drops from 97.4 to 95.4%, whereas the accuracy of the model using LeNet only decreases marginally from 96.7% to 96.6%.

6   Conclusion

We first propose a generative attack based on conditional generative models, revealing the potential risk of direct prototype information leakage. Secondly, we introduce a prototype-based privacy-preserving personalized federated learning framework, which ingeniously incorporates homomorphic encryption technology through equivalent transformation. Finally, we conduct extensive experiments on prototype generation, summarizing the general rules of prototype generation and providing valuable guidance for future research. For the sake of representativeness, we only used classic models and datasets in this study. Future researchers can conduct related experiments on more complex tasks. Additionally, other privacy protection methods also need to be investigated.

Acknowledgment. This research has received support from National Key R&D Program of China (2023YFB2704700), Shanghai Committee of Science and Technology, China (23511101000), Science and Technology Project of the State Grid Corporation of China (5700-202321603A-3-2-ZN). **Disclosure of Interests.** The authors declare that they have no conflict of interest relevant to this article.

Appendix 1   Proof of the Transformation Equivalence

Proof. Given that a public and private key pair $(sk, pk) = KeyGen(\lambda)$ is agreed upon among clients before training, the local prototypes are encrypted using an additive homomorphic algorithm, satisfying the following equation:

$$C_i^{(j)} = Enc(pk, P_i^{(j)}) \tag{14}$$

Given the property of additive homomorphism:

$$Enc(m_1) \oplus Enc(m_2) = Enc(m_1 + m_2) \tag{15}$$

$$Dec(c_1 + c_2) = Dec(c_1) + Dec(c_2) \tag{16}$$

Performing integer-order homomorphic addition operations, we obtain that:

$$Dec(\sum_{i \in Z_n} k_i c_i) = \sum_{i \in Z_n} k_i Dec(c_i), k \in Z \tag{17}$$

The definition of global prototype is:

$$\overline{P}^{(j)} = \sum_i \frac{\|D_{i,j}\|}{N_j} P_i^{(j)} = \sum_i \alpha_i P_i^{(j)} \tag{18}$$

To prove the equivalence of prototype aggregation operations, we need to prove the following formula:

$$Dec(\sum_{i \in Z_n} \alpha_i C_i^{(j)}) = \sum_{i \in Z_n} \alpha_i Dec(C_i^{(j)}), \alpha_i \in R \tag{19}$$

However, in fact, the above equation is usually not valid, requiring an equivalent transformation of prototype aggregation operations. Therefore, we redefine the global prototype ciphertext as follows:

$$\overline{C}^{(j)} = \sum_{i \in Z_n} \|D_{i,j}\| C_i^{(j)}, \|D_{i,j}\| \in Z \tag{20}$$

Global prototype can be transformed as follows:

$$\overline{P}^{(j)} = \sum_i \alpha_i P_i^{(j)} = \sum_i \alpha_i Dec(C_i^{(j)}) = \frac{1}{N_j} \sum_{i \in Z_n} \|D_{i,j}\| Dec(C_i^{(j)}), \ \|D_{i,j}\| \in Z \tag{21}$$

Considering Eq. 17, we can obtain that:

$$\overline{P}^{(j)} = \frac{1}{N_j} Dec(\sum_{i \in Z_n} \|D_{i,j}\| C_i^{(j)}) = \frac{1}{N_j} Dec(\overline{C}^{(j)}) \tag{22}$$

Appendix 2   Estimation of Additional Costs

In the scenario of federated learning, suppose that n clients adopt the additive homomorphic encryption algorithm to individually encrypt their local prototype lists. Assuming that the local prototype $P_i^{(j)} \in R^{1 \times s}$ is held by the i-th client, the length of the local prototype list is $l = \|Y_i\|$. Assuming that the additional time overhead brought by one round of communication is denoted as t_i, then it satisfies the following equation:

$$t_i = \Delta t_{Enc} + \Delta t_{Dec} + \Delta t_{agg} \tag{1}$$

Where t_{Enc} represents the additional time overhead brought by encrypting local prototypes, t_{Dec} represents the additional time overhead brought by decrypting, and t_{agg} represents the time overhead brought by homomorphic operations during the prototype aggregation process.

According to the definitions, they satisfy following equation:

$$t_{Enc} = sl\Delta t_e \tag{2}$$

$$t_{Dec} = sl\Delta t_d \tag{3}$$

$$t_{agg} = sl(n-1)\Delta t_a \tag{4}$$

In above equation, Δt_e and Δt_d denote the average time required for a single homomorphic addition and decryption operation, respectively, and Δt_a represents the average time needed for a single homomorphic addition operation between ciphertexts. Therefore,

$$t_i = \Delta t_{Enc} + \Delta t_{Dec} + \Delta t_{agg} = sl(\Delta t_e + \Delta t_d) + sl(n-1)\Delta t_a \tag{5}$$

References

1. McMahan, H.B., Moore, E., Ramage, D., Hampson, S., Agüera y Arcas, B.: Communication-efficient learning of deep networks from decentralized data (2016). arXiv preprint arXiv:1602.05629
2. Zhu, L., Liu, Z., Han, S.: Deep leakage from gradients (2019). arXiv preprints arXiv:1906.08935
3. Ye, M., Fang, X., Du, B., Yuen, P.C., Tao, D.: Heterogeneous federated learning: state-of-the-art and research challenges (2023). arXiv preprints arXiv:2307.10616
4. Tan, A.Z., Yu, H., Cui, L., et al.: Towards personalized federated learning. IEEE Trans. Neural Networks Learn. Syst. (2023)
5. Collins, L., Hassani, H., Mokhtari, A., et al.: Exploiting shared representations for personalized federated learning. In: International Conference on Machine Learning (ICML) (2021)
6. Tan, Y., Long, G., Liu, L., et al.: FedProto: federated prototype learning across heterogeneous clients. In: AAAI (2022)
7. Wu, C., Wu, F., Lyu, L., et al.: Communication-efficient federated learning via knowledge distillation. Nat. Commun. (2022)
8. Arivazhagan, M.G., Aggarwal, V., Singh, A.K., Choudhary, S.: Federated learning with personalization layers (2019). arXiv preprint arXiv:1912.00818
9. Liang, P.P., Liu, T., Ziyin, L., et al.: Think locally, act globally: federated learning with local and global representations. In: NeurIPS (2019)
10. Hu, R., Guo, Y., Li, H., et al.: Personalized federated learning with differential privacy. IEEE Internet Things J. (2020)
11. Jeong, E., Oh, S., Kim, H., et al.: Communication-efficient on-device machine learning: federated distillation and augmentation under non-IID private data (2018). arXiv priprints arXiv:1811.11479
12. Khosla, A., Jayadevaprakash, N., Yao, B., et al.: Novel dataset for fine-grained image categorization. In: CVPR (2011)
13. Li, D., Wang, J.: FedMD: heterogenous federated learning via model distillation. In: Advances in Neural Information Processing Systems (2020)
14. Lin, T., Kong, L., Stich, S.U., Jaggi, M.: Ensemble distillation for robust model fusion in federated learning. In: Advances in Neural Information Processing Systems (2020)

15. Jiang, J., Ji, S., Long, G.: Decentralized knowledge acquisition for mobile internet applications. World Wide Web 1–17 (2020)
16. Li, D., Wang, J.: FedMD: heterogenous federated learning via model distillation. In: Advances in Neural Information Processing Systems (2020)
17. Fallah, A., Mokhtari, A., Ozdaglar, A.: Personalized federated learning with theoretical guarantees: a model-agnostic meta-learning approach. In: Advances in Neural Information Processing Systems (2020)
18. Hoang, N., Lam, T., Low, B.K.H., Jaillet, P.: Learning task-agnostic embedding of multiple black-box experts for multi-task model fusion. In: International Conference on Machine Learning, pp. 4282–4292. PMLR (2020)
19. Du, S.S., Hu, W., Kakade, S.M., Lee, J.D., Lei, Q.: Few-shot learning via learning the representation, provably (2020)
20. Fallah, A., Mokhtari, A., Ozdaglar, A.: Personalized federated learning: a meta learning approach (2020)
21. Hanzely, F., Richtarik, P.: Federated learning of a mixture of global and local models (2020). arXiv preprint arXiv:2002.05516
22. Jiang, Y., Konečný, J., Rush, K., Kannan, S.: Improving federated learning personalization via model agnostic meta learning (2019). arXiv preprint arXiv:1909.12488
23. Singh, I., Zhou, H., Yang, K., Ding, M., Lin, B., Xie, P.: Differentially-private federated neural architecture search. In: FL-International Conference on Machine Learning Workshop (2020)
24. Wang, J., Liu, Q., Liang, H., Joshi, G., Poor, H.V.: Tackling the objective inconsistency problem in heterogeneous federated optimization. In: Advances in Neural Information Processing Systems (2020)
25. Yang, Y., Guan, Z., Li, J., Zhao, W., Cui, J., Wang, Q.: Interpretable and efficient heterogeneous graph convolutional network. IEEE Trans. Knowl. Data Eng. (2021)
26. Kong, W., Somani, R., Song, Z., Kakade, S., Oh, S.: Meta-learning for mixed linear regression. In: International Conference on Machine Learning, pp. 5394–5404. PMLR (2020)
27. Li, T., Hu, S., Beirami, A., Smith, V.: Ditto: fair and robust federated learning through personalization (2020). arXiv preprint arXiv:2012.04221
28. Zheng, Y., Jin, M., Liu, Y., Chi, L., Phan, K.T., Chen, Y.-P.P.: Generative and contrastive self-supervised learning for graph anomaly detection. IEEE Trans. Knowl. Data Eng. (2021)
29. He, C., Annavaram, M., Avestimehr, S.: FedNAS: federated deep learning via neural architecture search. In: Proceedings of the IEEE Conference on Computer Vision and Pattern Recognition (2020)
30. Pathak, R., Wainwright, M.J.: FedSplit: an algorithmic framework for fast federated optimization (2020). arXiv preprint arXiv:2005.05238
31. Xu, J., Chen, Z., Quek, T.Q.S., Chong, K.F.E.: FedCorr: multi-stage federated learning for label noise correction. In: CVPR (2022)
32. Wang, Y., Lin, L., Chen, J.: Communication-efficient adaptive federated learning. In: ICML (2022)
33. Wang, H., Sreenivasan, K., Rajput, S., Vishwakarma, H., et al.: Attack of the tails: yes, you really can backdoor federated learning. In: NeurIPS (2020)
34. Shang, X., Lu, Y., Huang, G., Wang, H.: Federated learning on heterogeneous and long-tailed data via classifier re-training with federated features. In: IJCAI (2022)
35. Sattler, F., Müller, K.-R., Samek, W.: Clustered federated learning, model-agnostic distributed multitask optimization under privacy constraints. In: IEEE TNNLS (2020)

36. Lim, W.Y.B., Ng, J.S., Xiong, Z., Jin, J., Zhang, Y., Niyato, D., Leung, C., Miao, C.: Decentralized edge intelligence: a dynamic resource allocation framework for hierarchical federated learning. In: IEEE TPDS (2021)

Efficient Large-Scale Multi-party Computation Based on Garbled Circuit

Zhusen Liu[ID], Jiafei Wu[ID], and Zhe Liu[✉][ID]

Zhejiang Lab, Hangzhou, Zhejiang, China
{liuzs,wujiafei,zhe.liu}@zhejianglab.org

Abstract. Multi-party garbled circuits employ distributed garbling strategy to achieve constant-round secure computation and authentication techniques to resist malicious adversaries. Implementations of these multi-party authenticated garbled circuits are used in constructing payment channels in blockchain and decentralized oracles for TLS. However, the high communication and computation costs limit their application in large-scale scenarios. In this paper, we propose an efficient, large-scale and constant-round multi-party computation protocol based on information-theoretic message authentication code and garbled circuit in the malicious model. Additionally, we propose a novel path-related optimization technique for multi-party authenticated garbled circuit, where parties generate a garbled circuit based on the related path in the circuit rather than the entire circuit. Through experimental evaluation and comparison with related work, the proposed scheme demonstrates dramatic improvement in computation and communication efficiency for each party when the number of parties increases.

Keywords: Garbled Circuit · Malicious Security · Path-Related Optimization · Large-Scale Parties

1 Introduction

Multi-party computation (MPC) is a technique that enables parties to collaboratively compute an agreed-upon function in a privacy-preserving manner. It was first proposed by Yao based on the garbled circuit (GC) [22]. Recently, MPC has been widely applied in scenarios such as e-voting [25] and privacy-preserving machine learning [26]. The garbled circuit is a crucial MPC technique due to its constant communication rounds. With many optimizations, such as FreeXOR [13], half gates [23], and a slice-and-dice technique [18], it is feasible to implement garbled circuit schemes directly on smart devices. Additionally, various adversarial models have been considered to deal with different adversarial behaviors in the real world. Especially, numerous schemes is designed to address the malicious model, including cut-and-choose methods [14], zero-knowledge proofs (ZK) [4], and information-theoretic message authentication codes (IT-MAC) [6,10,15,17,20]. Among these techniques, IT-MAC is the most

Z. Xia and J. Chen (Eds.): ISPEC 2024, LNCS 15053, pp. 240–257, 2024.
https://doi.org/10.1007/978-981-97-9053-1_14

efficient since it does not require expensive operations based on public-key cryptography and is homomorphic for computation authentication. Therefore, SPDZ [6] and its variants [11,12] based on IT-MAC are practical in applications such as machine learning [26,27]. In this paper, we also focus on MPC based on the garbled circuit in the malicious model.

Authenticated multi-party garbled circuit schemes based on IT-MAC, such as WRK [20] and YWZ [21], utilize a distributed garbling strategy [1,5] where participants jointly generate a garbled circuit. The development of the strategy have contributed to efficient protocols [8,19] for constant-round MPC resisting an arbitrary number of collusion. Wang et al. [20] proposed a global-scale MPC scheme based on authenticated GC, demonstrating a practical implementation of AES among 128 parties worldwide in approximately 2.5 min. Some studies [7,24] have utilized this implementation to provide additional privacy guarantees in real-world applications. Building on [20], Yang et al. proposed a more efficient MPC scheme with optimized triple generation and IT-MAC. These authenticated MPC schemes all follow a preprocessing-online paradigm. In the preprocessing phase, all parties perform both function-independent and function-dependent steps to generate a garbled circuit. In the online phase, the parties evaluate the garbled circuit generated during preprocessing.

WRK and YWZ can securely compute AES-128 among 32 parties in about one second, which can be utilized in constructing payment channels and decentralized hashes for TLS. However, increasing the number of parties results in significant communication and computation burdens for each participant. These high costs limit the application of MPC schemes in large-scale scenarios such as e-voting systems, necessitating the optimization of authenticated garbled circuit schemes. We observe that in the garbled circuit, each party's related task follows a specific path from the input wire to the output wire. In traditional approaches, all parties generate garbled tables for all gates, rather than for the specific required path. This results in unnecessary additional expenses for each party. In this paper, we optimize the authenticated garbled circuit generation to reduce computation and communication costs, making the protocol more feasible for large-scale scenarios.

Contributions. In this work, we propose an efficient, large-scale, constant-round MPC protocol based on IT-MAC and GC in malicious model. We also propose a novel path-related optimization technique for multi-party authenticated GC. In the technique, parties generate a garbled circuit based on the related path in the circuit rather than the whole circuit. It can dramatically reduce the computation and communication cost for large-scale parties. Like WRK and YWZ, our protocol guarantees correctness and security in malicious model.

We have implemented our protocol using a sum circuit common used for tallying in e-voting. In the implementation, when the number of parties is around 10,000, computation time of our protocol is around 0.1 s, while WRK and YWZ require approximately 300 and 100 s, respectively. when the number of parties exceeds 1,000, this work's communication cost is less than 10 MB, whereas both of WRK and YWZ require nearly 1 GB. Through experimental evaluation and comparison with related work, the proposed scheme demonstrates dramatic improvement in computation and communication efficiency for each party when the number of parties increases. In contrast, our protocol can support large-scale parties, allowing for high efficiency in computation and communication, and is promising in large-scale applications.

The rest of this paper is structured as follows. We introduce the preliminaries in Sect. 2 including our proposed path-related optimization technique. We present our proposed efficient large-scale MPC protocol based on GC in Sect. 3. In Sect. 4, we prove the correctness and security of our protocol. In Sect. 6, implementation results are given. Finally, in Sect. 7, we present the conclusion.

2   Preliminaries

In this section, we provide an introduction to four fundamental components: garbled circuit [20], information-theoretic message authentication code [17], almost universal linear hash functions [3], proposed path-related authenticated shares preprocessing technique.

2.1   Garbled Circuit

In a classic garbled circuit scheme in the semi-honest model, one party P_A generates garbled circuits, and then the other P_B evaluates the circuits. For the boolean circuits, the GC method can be executed as follows.

(1) **Garbled circuit generation.** Let H be a hash function and κ be a security parameter. For every gate $\mathcal{G} = (\alpha, \beta, \gamma, g)$ with input wires α, β, output wire γ, and the gate function $g : \{0,1\} \times \{0,1\} \rightarrow \{0,1\}$, P_A generates the garbled circuits as below.

    (a) For the wire $w_i \in \{\alpha, \beta, \gamma\}$, P_A generates the garbled bits and corresponding labels, $(r_{w_i,0} \in_R \{0,1\}, L_{w_i,0} \in_R \{0,1\}^\kappa)$, and $(r_{w_i,1} = 1 - r_{w_i,0}, L_{w_i,1} \in_R \{0,1\}^\kappa)$.

    (b) P_A constructs garbled table for $s \in \{0,1\}$ and $t \in \{0,1\}$ and computes,

$$G_{\gamma,s,t} = H(L_{\alpha,s}, L_{\beta,t}, \gamma) \oplus (r_{\gamma,g(s,t)}, L_{\gamma,g(s,t)}).$$

    Then, P_A sends the garbled table to P_B.

    (c) P_A sends circuit output decoding table to P_B.

(2) **Garbled circuit evaluation.** P_A sends the garbled bits and labels corresponding to its input wires to P_B. Then, P_B obtains its input wire bits and labels via the oblivious transfer technique. Next, P_B evaluates the garbled circuit gate-by-gate. For every gate $\mathcal{G} = (\alpha, \beta, \gamma, g)$ with input bits and labels $(r_\alpha, L_\alpha), (r_\beta, L_\beta)$, P_B computes

$$(r_\gamma, L_\gamma) = G_{\gamma, r_\alpha, r_\beta} \oplus H(L_\alpha, L_\beta, \gamma).$$

(3) **Ouput recovery.** P_B decodes the bits and labels of circuit ouput wires based on the output decoding tables and obtain the function result. Then, P_B sends the output to P_A.

2.2   Information-Theoretic Message Authentication Code

This work scheme is constructed based on the information-theoretic message authentication codes [17]. In IT-MAC scheme, the MAC $M_A[b]$ of P_B's bit b can be authenticated to P_A with P_A's global key Δ_A and random string $K_A[b]$, by checking $M_A[b] := K_A[b] \oplus b\Delta_A$. Similarly, the MAC $M_B[a]$ of P_A's bit a can be authenticated to P_B with P_B's global key Δ_B and random string $K_B[a]$, by checking $M_B[a] := K_B[a] \oplus a\Delta_B$. Obviously, P_A or P_B's IT-MAC is XOR-homomorphic, according to the equation $M_B[a \oplus c] := M_B[a] \oplus M_B[c] = K_B[a] \oplus K_B[c] \oplus (a \oplus c)\Delta_B$ and $M_A[b \oplus d] := M_A[b] \oplus M_A[d] = K_A[b] \oplus K_A[d] \oplus (b \oplus d)\Delta_A$.

An extended method to authenticate an unknown bit to all parties is secret sharing combined with authenticating each share, exemplified by the work [20,21]. To produce an authenticated secret bit x, XOR shares of x are generated (i.e., $\{x^i\}_{i=1}^n$ such that $\oplus_{i=1}^n x^i = x$), followed by each party authenticating their shares to the other. We denote an authenticated share of bit x as $\langle x \rangle = ([x^1]_1, \cdots, [x^n]_n)$, where each party holds $[x^i]_i = (x^i, \{M_j[x^i]\}_{j \neq i}, \{K_i[x^j]\}_{j \neq i})$. Obviously, authenticated shares are also XOR-homomorphic. Besides, for a constant bit b, $\langle x \rangle \oplus b = ([x^1]_1 \oplus b, [x^2]_2, \cdots, [x^n]_n)$, and $b\langle x \rangle = \langle 0 \rangle$ if $b = 0$ and $\langle x \rangle$ otherwise.

2.3   Almost Universal Linear Hash Functions

The almost universal linear hash functions [3,21] over Galois Field $\mathbb{F}_{2^k}$ for some parameter $k \in \mathbb{N}$ is defined as follows:

Definition 1. A family $\mathcal{H}$ of linear hash functions $\mathbb{F}_{2^k}^m \rightarrow \mathbb{F}_{2^k}$ is ϵ-almost universal, if it holds for every non-zero vector $x \in \mathbb{F}_{2^k}^m$ such that

$$\Pr_{H \leftarrow \mathcal{H}}[H(x) = 0] \leq \epsilon,$$

where H is selected uniformly randomly from $\mathcal{H}$.

We adopt almost universal linear hash functions based on a polynomial hash used in [9,21]. Sample $\chi \in \mathcal{F}_{2^k}$ to define the hash function $H : \mathbb{F}_{2^k}^m \rightarrow \mathbb{F}_{2^k}$, $H(x_1, x_2, \cdots, x_m) = x_1\chi + x_2\chi^2 + \cdots + x_m\chi^m$. In practice, given $k = 128$, the hash function can be implemented efficiently on modern CPUs using the Intel SSE instruction set.

2.4   Path-Related Authenticated Share Preprocessing

In the garbled circuit, each party's input follows a path from the input wire to the computation output wire. This is exemplified by the red path depicting the input of party P_1 in Fig. 1. All parties process garbled circuits for all wires, resulting in unnecessary additional expenses for each party. We recognize that it suffices to have participants relevant to this specific path engaged in the generation of path-related authenticated shares. There is no necessity for all parties to generate authenticated shares for unrelated wires, and shares for other unrelated wires

---

Algorithm 1 $\mathcal{P}ath\mathcal{P}arties\mathcal{I}D(\mathcal{T})$: Path-Related Parties Identification

---

Input: $\mathcal{T}$.
Output: path-related parties set $\mathcal{S}$.
1: /* Initialization of the current node n and $\mathcal{S}$ */
2: **for** n **in** $\mathcal{T}$.leafnodes_set() :
3:     $V_i \leftarrow \mathcal{T}$.leafnode_ID$(n)$
4:     $\mathcal{S}$.add$((n, V_i))$
5:     /* Traverse upward through the tree and fill $\mathcal{S}$*/
6:     **While** n **not** $\mathcal{T}$.rootnode :
7:         $n \leftarrow \mathcal{T}$.parentnode(n)
8:         **if** n **is** AND **and** n **not in** $\mathcal{S}$:
9:             $t \leftarrow \mathcal{T}$.subtree(n)
10:             $s \leftarrow t$.leafnodes_set()
11:             $\mathcal{S}$.add$((n, s))$

---

can be set to 0. Our approach shares similarities with that presented in the schemes by Ben-Efraim et al. [2] and Yang et al. [21], albeit with a focus beyond optimizations solely for input wires.

To realize the idea, we propose an algorithm, denoted as $\mathcal{P}ath\mathcal{P}arties\mathcal{I}D(\mathcal{T})$ (**Algorithm 1**). This algorithm is designed to identify parties involved in communication to generate authenticated shares along specific paths. The circuit can be envisioned as a tree $\mathcal{T}$, where leaf nodes represent the binary input (0 or 1) of each party, the root node signifies the circuit output, and branch nodes are considered as gates of the tallying circuit, including AND or XOR gates. Specifically, we employ FreeXOR for XOR gates to mitigate communication cost, so we capture only input wires and AND gates in the algorithm. For the leaf node associated with P_i, $i \subset [n]$, we add the leaf node (i.e., the input wire of P_i) and P_i to the set $\mathcal{S}$. Then, we traverse upward through the tree for each leaf node, identifying the set of parties represented by the leaf nodes of the subtree whose root node is an AND gate and not included in the current set $\mathcal{S}$. Upon completing the tree traversal, We derive the set $\mathcal{S}$ which records the nodes and the corresponding parties engaged in communication at each node of input wires and AND gates. It is easy to deduce the unique path of each party P_i in the circuit by linking the node represented as the element of $\mathcal{S}$ including P_i.

Based on the set $\mathcal{S}$, we define a useful operation called **SetShare**, which generates authenticated shares of input wire, AND output wires and AND triple to P_i. For $(\hat{n}, \hat{s})$ in $\mathcal{S}$, where $\hat{n}$ is a node and $\hat{s}$ is the set of corresponding parties engaged in communication at $\hat{n}$, **SetShare** executes as follows.

If $\hat{n} = $ INPUT, **SetShare** takes as input an authenticated bit $(r^i, \{M_k[r]\}_{k \neq i}, \{K_k[r]_{k \neq i}\})$, where $k \in [n]$, with bit r^i known for P_i in $\hat{s}$, and extends it to an authenticated share $\langle r \rangle$ as follows:

– P_i, $i \in \hat{s}$ sets

$$[r^i]_i := (r^i, \{M_k[r^i]\}_{k \neq i}, \{K_i[r^k]\}_{k \neq i})$$
$$= (r^i, \{M_k[r^i]\}_{k \neq i}, \{K_i[r^k]\}_{k \neq i, k \in \hat{s}} \cup \{0\}_{k \notin \hat{s}});$$

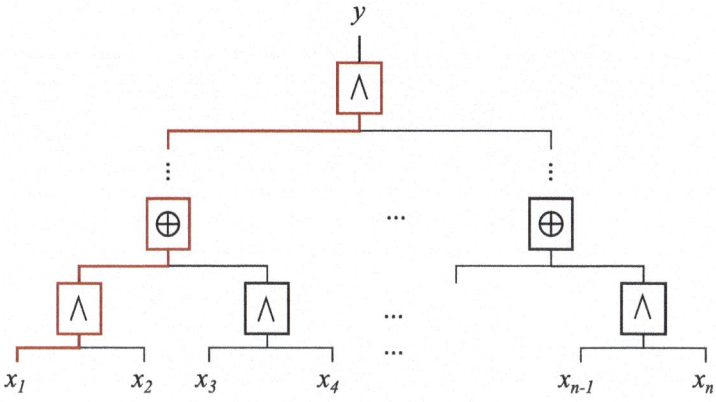

Fig. 1. A function circuit.

- P_j, $j \notin \hat{s}$ sets

$$[r^i]_j := [0]_j = (r^j, \{M_k[r^j]\}_{k \neq j}, \{K_j[r^k]\}_{k \neq j})$$
$$= (0, \{0\}_{k \neq j}, \{K_j[r^k]\}_{k \in \hat{s}} \cup \{0\}_{k \notin \hat{s}, k \neq j}).$$

In this way, just P_i holds its own bit keys for its input wires (ie. vote vector entries), because $\hat{s} = \{i\}$. For AND output wires, **SetShare** also generates authenticated shares in this way.

If $\hat{n} =$ AND, P_i, $i \in \hat{s}$ communicates with each other to generate the authenticated triple $((a_i, \{M_k[a_i]\}_{k \neq i}, \{K_k[a_i]\}_{k \neq i}), (b_i, \{M_k[b_i]\}_{k \neq i}, \{K_k[b_i]\}_{k \neq i}), (c_i, \{M_k[c_i]\}_{k \neq i}, \{K_k[c_i]\}_{k \neq i}))$, like the work in [21], such that $\oplus_{i \in \hat{s}} a^i \oplus_{i \in \hat{s}} b^i = \oplus_{i \in \hat{s}} c^i$. **SetShare** can also take the authenticated triple as input with AND triple (a_i, b_i, c_i) known for P_i, $i \in \hat{s}$, and extend it to an authenticated triple share $(\langle a \rangle, \langle b \rangle, \langle c \rangle)$ as follows:

- P_i, $i \in \hat{s}$ sets

$$[a^i]_i := (a^i, \{M_k[a^i]\}_{k \neq i}, \{K_i[a^k]\}_{k \neq i})$$
$$= (a^i, \{M_k[a^i]\}_{k \neq i}, \{K_i[a^k]\}_{k \neq i, k \in \hat{s}} \cup \{0\}_{k \notin \hat{s}})$$
$$[b^i]_i := (b^i, \{M_k[b^i]\}_{k \neq i}, \{K_i[b^k]\}_{k \neq i})$$
$$= (b^i, \{M_k[b^i]\}_{k \neq i}, \{K_i[b^k]\}_{k \neq i, k \in \hat{s}} \cup \{0\}_{k \notin \hat{s}})$$
$$[c^i]_i := (c^i, \{M_k[c^i]\}_{k \neq i}, \{K_i[c^k]\}_{k \neq i})$$
$$= (c^i, \{M_k[c^i]\}_{k \neq i}, \{K_i[c^k]\}_{k \neq i, k \in \hat{s}} \cup \{0\}_{k \notin \hat{s}});$$

– $P_j, j \notin \hat{s}$ sets

$$[a^j]_j := [0]_j = (a^j, \{M_k[a^j]\}_{k \neq j}, \{K_j[a^k]\}_{k \neq j})$$
$$= (0, \{0\}_{k \neq j}, \{K_j[a^k]\}_{k \in \hat{s}} \cup \{0\}_{k \notin \hat{s}, k \neq j})$$
$$[b^j]_j := [0]_j = (b^j, \{M_k[b^j]\}_{k \neq j}, \{K_j[b^k]\}_{k \neq j})$$
$$= (0, \{0\}_{k \neq j}, \{K_j[b^k]\}_{k \in \hat{s}} \cup \{0\}_{k \notin \hat{s}, k \neq j})$$
$$[c^j]_j := [0]_j = (c^j, \{M_k[c^j]\}_{k \neq j}, \{K_j[c^k]\}_{k \neq j})$$
$$= (0, \{0\}_{k \neq j}, \{K_j[c^k]\}_{k \in \hat{s}} \cup \{0\}_{k \notin \hat{s}, k \neq j}).$$

It is easy to prove that the triple share $(\langle a \rangle, \langle b \rangle, \langle c \rangle)$ is a correct AND triple share since the equation below holds

$$\bigoplus_{i \in [n]} a^i \bigoplus_{i \in [n]} b^i$$
$$= (\bigoplus_{i \in \hat{s}} a^i \oplus \bigoplus_{i \notin \hat{s}} a^i) \cdot (\bigoplus_{i \in \hat{s}} b^i \oplus \bigoplus_{i \notin \hat{s}} b^i) \tag{1}$$
$$= (\bigoplus_{i \in \hat{s}} a^i)(\bigoplus_{i \in \hat{s}} b^i) = \bigoplus_{i \in \hat{s}} c^i = \bigoplus_{i \in [n]} c^i.$$

3 Proposed Protocol

In the protocol, all parties $P_i, 1 \leq i \leq n$ collaboratively compute the function $f : \{0,1\}^{\mathcal{I}_i} \times \cdots \{0,1\}^{\mathcal{I}_n} \to \{0,1\}^{\mathcal{O}}$ with P_i's input $x_i \in \{0,1\}^{\mathcal{I}_i}$. In this protocol, f is transformed into the function circuits $\mathcal{C}$ with the input wire $\mathcal{I}_i$ of P_i, output wires $\mathcal{O}$, and the set of all AND gate output wires $\mathcal{W}$. x_w^i denotes the bit of x_i on the wire $w \in \mathcal{I}_i$. The protocol consists of two phases: the preprocessing phase and the online phase.

The preprocessing phase comprises **Key Initialization**, **Circuit-Independent Preprocessing** and **Circuit-Dependent Preprocessing**. In the step of **Key Initialization**, the system initializes the parties' global keys. Then, the parties generate the authenticated bits and labels of the input wires, output wires and the wires of AND gates in **Circuit-Independent Preprocessing**. Next, the parties execute the circuit-dependent preprocessing step to generate the authenticated bits, labels and the garbled tables of the AND gates according to the topological order of the function circuit in **Circuit-Dependent Preprocessing**.

The online phase comprises four steps, **Input Processing**, **Circuit Evaluation**, **Verification of Intermediate Results** and **Output Recovery**. In **Input Processing**, each parties P_i use the authenticated bits to mask their own inputs and the parties send the corresponding labels to P_1. Next, P_1 evaluates the circuit according to the topological order of the circuit in **Circuit Evaluation**. P_i sends authenticated mask bits to each other to check the validity of intermediate results in **Verification of Intermediate Results** and utilize the masked output bits from S to recover of the function result in **Output Recovery** after the checks pass.

3.1   Preprocessing Phase

Key Initialization: $P_i, i \in [n]$ can run the functionality in [21] to get global key Δ_i for P_i.

Circuit-independent preprocessing: for the wires $w \in \mathcal{I}_1 \cup \cdots \cup \mathcal{I}_n \cup \mathcal{W}$, $P_i, i \in [n]$ runs **Algorithm 1** to obtain the set $\mathcal{S}$, and executes the functionality **SetShare**, then gets the authenticated masks $[r_w^i]_i = (r_w^i, \{M_j[r_w^i], K_i[r_w^j]\}_{j \neq i})$, where $j \in [n]$. Each $P_i, i \neq 0$ selects a random κ-bit string $L_{w,0}^i \in \{0,1\}^\kappa$ for the bit 0. For each $w \in \mathcal{W}$, according to $\mathcal{S}$, P_i operate as described via **SetShare**, then P_i gets the authenticated AND triple $([a_w^i]_i, [b_w^i]_i, [c_w^i]_i) = ((a_w^i, \{M_j[a_w^i], K_i[a_w^j]\}_{j \neq i}), (b_w^i, \{M_j[b_w^i], K_i[b_w^j]\}_{j \neq i}), (c_w^i, \{M_j[c_w^i], K_i[c_w^j]\}_{j \neq i}))$.

Circuit-dependent preprocessing: Based on the topological pattern of the function circuit, for every gate $\mathcal{G} = (\alpha, \beta, \gamma, T)$, where α, β are the input wires, γ is the output wire and T is the gate type, P_i operate as shown below.

(1) If $T = \oplus$, P_i computes locally $\langle r_\gamma^i \rangle := \langle r_\alpha^i \rangle \oplus \langle r_\beta^i \rangle$. $P_i, i \neq 1$ also computes $L_{\gamma,0}^i := L_{\alpha,0}^i \oplus L_{\beta,0}^i$.

(2) If $T = \wedge$ and $(\hat{n}, \hat{s}) \in \mathcal{S}$, where $\hat{n} = \text{AND}$

    (a) The parties take the authenticated AND triple $(\langle a_\gamma \rangle, \langle b_\gamma \rangle, \langle c_\gamma \rangle)$ and computes $\langle d_\gamma \rangle := \langle r_\alpha \rangle \oplus \langle a_\gamma \rangle$ and $\langle e_\gamma \rangle := \langle r_\beta \rangle \oplus \langle b_\gamma \rangle$. Then, the parties open d_γ, e_γ and compute $\langle r_{\alpha\beta} \rangle := \langle r_\alpha \cdot r_\beta \rangle = \langle c_\gamma \rangle \oplus d_\gamma \cdot \langle b_\gamma \rangle \oplus e_\gamma \cdot \langle a_\gamma \rangle \oplus d_\gamma \cdot e_\gamma$.

    (b) $P_i \in \hat{s}, i \neq 1$ locally computes with $p, q \in \{0,1\}$

$$(r_{\gamma,p,q}^i, \{M_j[r_{\gamma,p,q}^i]\}_{j \neq i}, \{K_i[r_{\gamma,p,q}^j]\}_{j \neq i})$$
$$= (r_{\alpha\beta}^i \oplus r_\gamma^i \oplus p r_\alpha^i \oplus q r_\beta^i,$$
$$\{M_j[r_{\alpha\beta}^i] \oplus M_j[r_\gamma^i] \oplus p M_j[r_\alpha^i] \oplus q M_j[r_\beta^i]\}_{j \neq i},$$
$$\{0\}_{j \in [n] - \hat{s} - \{1\}} \cup \{K_i[r_{\alpha\beta}^1] \oplus K_i[r_\gamma^1] \oplus p K_i[r_\alpha^1] \oplus q K_i[r_\beta^1] \oplus pq\Delta_i\}_{j=1}$$
$$\cup \{K_i[r_{\alpha\beta}^j] \oplus K_i[r_\gamma^j] \oplus p K_i[r_\alpha^j] \oplus q K_i[r_\beta^j]\}_{j \in \hat{s}, j \neq i}).$$

$$(2)$$

Then, P_i locally computes $L_{\alpha,1}^i = L_{\alpha,0}^i \oplus \Delta_i$ and $L_{\beta,1}^i = L_{\beta,0}^i \oplus \Delta_i$, and for the bit $p \in \{0,1\}$ and $q \in \{0,1\}$, P_i computes

$$G_{\gamma,p,q}^i := H(L_{\alpha,p}^i, L_{\beta,q}^i, \gamma, p, q) \oplus (r_{\gamma,p,q}^i, \{M_j[r_{\gamma,p,q}^i]\}_{j \neq i}, L_{\gamma,0}^i$$
$$\oplus (\bigoplus_{j \neq i} K_i[r_{\gamma,p,q}^j]) \oplus r_{\gamma,p,q}^i \Delta_i).$$

$$(3)$$

P_i sends $\{G_{\gamma,p,q}^i\}_{p,q \in \{0,1\}}$ to P_1.

    (c) $P_i \notin \hat{s}, i \neq 1$ locally computes $L_{\alpha,1}^i = L_{\alpha,0}^i \oplus \Delta_i$ and $L_{\beta,1}^i = L_{\beta,0}^i \oplus \Delta_i$, and for the bit $p, q \in \{0,1\}$,

$$G_{\gamma,p,q}^i := H(L_{\alpha,p}^i, L_{\beta,q}^i, \gamma, p, q) \oplus L_{\gamma,0}^i \oplus \bigoplus_{j \in \hat{s}} (K_i[r_{\alpha\beta}^j] \oplus K_i[r_\gamma^j] \oplus p K_i[r_\alpha^j]$$
$$\oplus q K_i[r_\beta^j]\}_{j \in \hat{s}, j \neq i}) \oplus pq\Delta_i.$$

$$(4)$$

and sends $\{G_{\gamma,p,q}^i\}_{p,q \in \{0,1\}}$ to P_1.

(d) $P_1 \in \hat{s}$ computes locally with $p, q \in \{0, 1\}$

$$
\begin{aligned}
&(r^1_{\gamma,p,q}, \{M_j[r^1_{\gamma,p,q}]\}_{j\neq 1}, \{K_1[r^j_{\gamma,p,q}]\}_{j\neq 1})\\
&= (r^1_{\alpha\beta} \oplus r^1_{\gamma} \oplus pr^1_{\alpha} \oplus qr^1_{\beta} \oplus pq,\\
&\quad \{M_j[r^1_{\alpha\beta}] \oplus M_j[r^1_{\gamma}] \oplus pM_j[r^1_{\alpha}] \oplus qM_j[r^1_{\beta}]\}_{j\neq 1},\\
&\quad \{0\}_{j\in[n]-\hat{s}} \cup \{K_1[r^j_{\alpha\beta}] \oplus K_1[r^j_{\gamma}] \oplus pK_1[r^j_{\alpha}] \oplus qK_1[r^j_{\beta}]\}_{j\in\hat{s}}).
\end{aligned}
\tag{5}
$$

(e) $P_1 \notin \hat{s}$ computes locally with $p, q \in \{0, 1\}$

$$
\begin{aligned}
&(r^1_{\gamma,p,q}, \{M_j[r^1_{\gamma,p,q}]\}_{j\neq 1}, \{K_1[r^j_{\gamma,p,q}]\}_{j\neq 1})\\
&= (r^1_{\alpha\beta} \oplus r^1_{\gamma} \oplus pr^1_{\alpha} \oplus qr^1_{\beta} \oplus pq, \{0\}_{j\neq 1},\\
&\quad \{0\}_{j\in[n]-\hat{s}} \cup \{K_1[r^j_{\alpha\beta}] \oplus K_1[r^j_{\gamma}] \oplus pK_1[r^j_{\alpha}] \oplus qK_1[r^j_{\beta}]\}_{j\in\hat{s}}).
\end{aligned}
\tag{6}
$$

3.2   Online Phase

Input processing. For $w \in \mathcal{I}_i$, P_i broadcasts the value $x^i_w \oplus r^i_w$. For each $P_j, j \neq 1$ sends $L^j_{w, x^i \oplus r^i_w} := L^j_{w,0} \oplus (x^i \oplus r^i_w)\Delta_j$ to P_1.

Circuit Evaluation. Based on the topological order of the tallying circuit, for every gate $\mathcal{G} = (\alpha, \beta, \gamma, T)$, P_1 evaluates the circuit as described below with $(\hat{y}_\alpha, \{L^i_{\alpha,\hat{y}_\alpha}\}_{i\neq 1})$ and $(\hat{y}_\beta, \{L^i_{\beta,\hat{y}_\beta}\}_{i\neq 1})$, where $\hat{y}_\alpha = y_\alpha \oplus r_\alpha$, $\hat{y}_\beta = y_\beta \oplus r_\beta$, and y_α, y_β are the underlying values of the wire.

(1) If $T = \oplus$, P_1 computes the masked output of γ, $\hat{y}_\gamma = \hat{y}_\alpha \oplus \hat{y}_\beta$, and the labels $\{L^i_{\gamma,\hat{y}_\gamma} := L^i_{\alpha,\hat{y}_\alpha} \oplus L^i_{\beta,\hat{y}_\beta}\}_{i\neq 1}$.

(2) If $T = \wedge$ and $(\hat{n}, \hat{s}) \in \mathcal{S}$, where $\hat{n} = \text{AND}$, let $p = \hat{y}_\beta$ and $q = \hat{y}_\alpha$.

    (a) For $i \in \hat{s}, i \neq 1$, P_1 computes

$$
(r^i_{\gamma,p,q}, \{M_j[r^i_{\gamma,p,q}]\}_{j\neq i}, L^i_{\gamma}) = G^i_{\gamma,p,q} \oplus H(L^i_{\alpha,p}, L^i_{\beta,q}, \gamma, p, q).
\tag{7}
$$

    P_1 checks that $\{(r^i_{\gamma,p,q}, M_1[r^i_{\gamma,p,q}], K_1[r^i_{\gamma,p,q}])\}_{i\neq 1}$. P_1 computes $\hat{y}_\gamma := \bigoplus_{i\in\hat{s}} r^i_{\gamma,p,q}$ and $\{L^i_{\gamma,\hat{y}_\gamma} := L^i_\gamma \oplus (\bigoplus_{j\neq i, j\in\hat{s}} M_i[r^j_{\gamma,p,q}])\}_{i\in\hat{s}, i\neq 1}$.

    (b) For $i \notin \hat{s}, i \neq 1$, P_1 computes

$$
L^i_\gamma = G^i_{\gamma,p,q} \oplus H(L^i_{\alpha,p}, L^i_{\beta,q}, \gamma, p, q).
\tag{8}
$$

    Then, P_1 computes $L^i_{\gamma,\hat{y}_\gamma} := L^i_\gamma \oplus (\bigoplus_{j\in\hat{s}} M_i[r^j_{\gamma,p,q}])$.

Verification of intermediate results. After evaluating the last AND gate, P_1 computes $\{h_i := H(\{L^i_{w,\hat{y}_w}\}_{w\in\mathcal{W}})\}_{i\neq 1}$, where H is a cryptographically secure hash function and also samples a seed $\chi \leftarrow \mathbb{F}_{2^\kappa}$. Then, P_1 sends $(\{\hat{y}_w\}_{w\in\mathcal{W}}, h_i, \chi)$ to $P_i, i \neq 1$. Therefore, every P_i checks that $h_i = H(\{L^i_{w,0} \oplus \hat{y}_w\Delta_i\}_{w\in\mathcal{W}})$. If the check fails, P_i aborts.

Otherwise, P_i verifies the correctness of intermediate results of the circuit efficiently with the masked outputs of AND gates as below.

(a) For the gate $(\alpha, \beta, \gamma, \oplus)$ and $i \neq 1$, P_i computes locally $\hat{y}_\gamma := \hat{y}_\alpha \oplus \hat{y}_\beta$.
(b) For the gate $(\alpha, \beta, \gamma, \wedge)$, the parties check $z_\gamma = (\hat{y}_\alpha \oplus r_\alpha) \wedge (\hat{y}_\beta \oplus r_\beta) \oplus (\hat{y}_\gamma \oplus r_\gamma) = 0$ in a batch way. P_i computes locally

$$M_1[z_\gamma^i] := \hat{y}_\alpha \cdot M_1[r_\beta^i] \oplus \hat{y}_\beta \cdot M_1[r_\alpha^i] \oplus M_1[r_{\alpha\beta}^i] \oplus M_1[r_\gamma^i]. \tag{9}$$

P_1 computes $z_\gamma^1 = \hat{y}_\alpha \cdot \hat{y}_\beta \oplus \hat{y}_\gamma \oplus \hat{y}_\alpha r_\beta^1 \oplus \hat{y}_\beta r_\alpha^1 \oplus r_{\alpha\beta}^1 \oplus r_\gamma^1$ and the following values:

$$\{K_1[z_\gamma^i] := \hat{y}_\alpha \cdot K_1[r_\beta^i] \oplus \hat{y}_\beta \cdot K_1[r_\alpha^i] \oplus K_1[r_{\alpha\beta}^i] \oplus K_1[r_\gamma^i]\}_{i\neq 1},$$
$$M_1[z_\gamma^1] := z_\gamma^1 \Delta_1 \oplus \bigoplus_{i\neq 1} K_1[z_\gamma^i]. \tag{10}$$

(c) Let $\mathbf{H}$ be the almost universal linear hash function defined by χ. P_i computes and sends $\tau_i := \mathbf{H}(\{M_1[z_w^i]\}_{w \in \mathcal{W}}) \in \mathbb{F}_{2^\kappa}$ to P_1.
(d) P_1 computes $\tau_1 := \mathbf{H}(\{M_1[z_w^i]\}_{w \in \mathcal{W}}) \in \mathbb{F}_{2^\kappa}$ and checks $\tau_1 \oplus \bigoplus_{i \in [n]} \tau_i = 0$. If the check fails, P_1 aborts.

Result recovery. After the above verification succeed, P_1 broadcasts the output $\{\hat{y}_w\}_{w \in \mathcal{O}}$. Then, P_i broadcasts $\{\langle r_w^i \rangle\}_{w \in \mathcal{O}}$, so every P_i verifies the mask bits and recoveries $\{y_w = \hat{y}_w \oplus \bigoplus_{i \in [n]} r_w^i\}_{w \in \mathcal{O}}$.

4   Security Analysis

Theorem 1. *If each $P_i, i \in [n]$ observes the proposed protocol, each party can obtain the correct $(y_w \oplus r_w, \{L_{w, y_w \oplus r_w}^i\}_{i \in [n]})$ for $w \in \mathcal{O}$.*

Proof. During online phase, P_1 gets the labels and masked inputs of $P_i, i \neq [n]$. Then, based on the structure of the circuit, P_1 evaluates the circuit $\mathcal{C}$ for every gate $\mathcal{G} = (\alpha, \beta, \gamma, T)$.

If $T = \oplus$, P_1 can correctly compute $\hat{y}_\gamma, \{L_{\gamma, \hat{y}_\gamma}^i\}_{i \neq 1}$ on the output wires based on FreeXOR technique.

If $T = \wedge$ and $(\hat{n}, \hat{s}) \in \mathcal{S}$, P_1 gets $\{(r_{\gamma, p, q}^i, \{M_j[r_{\gamma, p, q}^i]\}_{j \neq i}, L_\gamma^i)\}_{i \in \hat{s}}$ based on Eqs. (3), (7) and $\{L_\gamma^i\}_{i \notin \hat{s}}$ based on Eqs. (4), (8), where $p = \hat{y}_\beta$ and $q = \hat{y}_\alpha$. Then, P_1 computes the masked output

$$\hat{y}_\gamma = \bigoplus_{i \in \hat{s}} r_{\gamma, p, q}^i$$
$$= pq \oplus \bigoplus_{i \in \hat{s}} (r_{\alpha\beta}^i \oplus r_\gamma^i \oplus p r_\alpha^i \oplus q r_\beta^i) \tag{11}$$
$$= r_{\alpha\beta} \oplus r_\gamma \oplus p r_\alpha \oplus q r_\beta \oplus pq.$$

Since $r_{\alpha\beta} = r_\alpha r_\beta$, $p = \hat{y}_\beta = y_\beta \oplus r_\beta$ and $q = \hat{y}_\alpha = y_\alpha \oplus r_\alpha$,

$$
\begin{aligned}
\hat{y}_\gamma &= r_\alpha r_\beta \oplus r_\gamma \oplus (y_\beta \oplus r_\beta) r_\alpha \oplus (y_\alpha \oplus r_\alpha) r_\beta \oplus (y_\alpha \oplus r_\alpha)(y_\beta \oplus r_\beta) \\
&= r_\alpha r_\beta \oplus r_\gamma \oplus y_\beta r_\alpha \oplus r_\alpha r_\beta \oplus y_\alpha r_\beta \oplus r_\alpha r_\beta \oplus y_\alpha y_\beta \oplus y_\beta r_\alpha \\
&\quad \oplus y_\alpha r_\beta \oplus r_\alpha r_\beta \\
&= y_\alpha y_\beta \oplus r_\gamma.
\end{aligned}
\tag{12}
$$

Because the true value y_γ of the wire γ is $y_\alpha y_\beta$ at the AND gate, P_1 correctly computes the masked input $\hat{y}_\gamma = y_\gamma \oplus r_\gamma$.

P_1 computes the label of the wire γ for $i \in \hat{s}$

$$
\begin{aligned}
L_{\gamma, \hat{y}_\gamma}^i &= L_\gamma^i \oplus \Big(\bigoplus_{j \neq i, j \in \hat{s}} M_i[r_{\gamma,p,q}^j] \Big) \\
&= L_{\gamma,0}^i \oplus \Big(\bigoplus_{j \neq i} K_i[r_{\gamma,p,q}^j] \Big) \oplus r_{\gamma,p,q}^i \Delta_i \oplus \Big(\bigoplus_{j \neq i, j \in \hat{s}} M_i[r_{\gamma,p,q}^j] \Big) \\
&= L_{\gamma,0}^i \oplus \Big(\bigoplus_{j \in \hat{s}} r_{\gamma,p,q}^j \Delta_i \Big) \\
&= L_{\gamma,0}^i \oplus \hat{y}_\gamma \Delta_i,
\end{aligned}
\tag{13}
$$

where $\bigoplus_{j \notin \hat{s}} K_i[r_{\gamma,p,q}^j] = pq\Delta_i$, $M_i[r_{\gamma,p,q}^j]) = K_i[r_{\gamma,p,q}^j]) \oplus r_{\gamma,p,q}^j \Delta_i$ and $r_{\gamma,p,q}^1 = pq$.

P_1 computes the labels of the wire γ for $i \notin \hat{s}$

$$
\begin{aligned}
L_{\gamma, \hat{y}_\gamma}^i &= L_\gamma^i \oplus \Big(\bigoplus_{j \in \hat{s}} M_i[r_{\gamma,p,q}^j] \Big) \\
&= L_{\gamma,0}^i \oplus pq\Delta_i \oplus \Big(\bigoplus_{j \in \hat{s}} M_i[r_{\gamma,p,q}^j] \Big) \oplus \bigoplus_{j \in \hat{s}} (K_i[r_{\alpha\beta}^j] \oplus K_i[r_\gamma^j] \\
&\quad \oplus p K_i[r_\alpha^j] \oplus q K_i[r_\beta^j] \}_{j \in \hat{s}, j \neq i}) \\
&= L_{\gamma,0}^i \oplus \Big(\bigoplus_{j \in \hat{s}} r_{\gamma,p,q}^j \Delta_i \Big) \\
&= L_{\gamma,0}^i \oplus \hat{y}_\gamma \Delta_i,
\end{aligned}
\tag{14}
$$

where $M_i[r_{\gamma,p,q}^j] = M_i[r_{\alpha\beta}^j] \oplus M_i[r_\gamma^j] \oplus p M_i[r_\alpha^j] \oplus q M_i[r_\beta^j] = K_i[r_{\alpha\beta}^j] \oplus K_i[r_\gamma^j] \oplus p K_i[r_\alpha^j] \oplus q K_i[r_\beta^j] \oplus r_{\gamma,p,q}^j \Delta_i$ for $j \in \hat{s}$. P_1 correctly computes the masked output bits and labels of AND gates. Therefore, P_1 can correctly evaluate the circuit.

Then, P_1 sends $(\{\hat{y}_w\}_{w \in \mathcal{W}}, h_i, \chi)$ to $P_i, i \neq 1$. P_i can easily verify the validity of the bit and labels for each AND gate when the parties obey the protocol. For an AND gate $\mathcal{G} = (\alpha, \beta, \gamma, \wedge)$,

$$\bigoplus_{i \neq 1}(M_1[z_\gamma^i]) \oplus M_1[z_\gamma^1]$$

$$=\bigoplus_{i \neq 1}(M_1[z_\gamma^i] \oplus K_1[z_\gamma^i]) \oplus z_\gamma^1 \Delta_1$$

$$=\bigoplus_{i \neq 1}(\hat{y_\alpha} r_\beta^i \oplus \hat{y_\beta} r_\alpha^i \oplus r_{\alpha\beta}^i \oplus r_\gamma^i)\Delta_1 \oplus z_\gamma^1 \Delta_1 \tag{15}$$

$$=(\hat{y_\alpha} r_\beta \oplus \hat{y_\beta} r_\alpha \oplus r_{\alpha\beta} \oplus r_\gamma \oplus \hat{y_\alpha}\hat{y_\beta} \oplus \hat{y_\gamma})\Delta_1$$

$$=((\hat{y}_\alpha \oplus r_\alpha)(\hat{y}_\beta \oplus r_\beta) \oplus (\hat{y}_\gamma \oplus r_\gamma))\Delta_1$$

$$=(y_\alpha y_\beta \oplus y_\gamma)\Delta_1 = 0.$$

Because the almost universal linear hash function $\mathbf{H}$ is XOR-homomorphic, $\tau_1 \oplus \bigoplus_{i \neq 1} \tau_i = \mathbf{H}(\{\bigoplus_{i \in [n]}(M_1[z_\gamma^i])\}_{w \in \mathcal{W}}) = 0$, proving the correctness of AND intermediate results in a batch way. Finally, P_i can get the same $\{\hat{y}_w\}_{w \in \mathcal{O}}$. Then, they computes $\{y_w = \hat{y_w} \oplus \bigoplus_{i \in [n]} r_w^i\}_{w \in \mathcal{O}}$ using $\{r_w^i\}_{w \in \mathcal{O}}$. In the end, **Theorem 1** has been proven.

Theorem 2. *If H and $\mathbf{H}$ are modeled as random oracles, the protocol securely computes $\mathcal{C}$ against an adversary corrupting up to $n-1$ parties based on authenticated garbled circuits.*

Because we just optimize the garbled circuit based on the same security assumption like [20,21], we provide the proof sketch of Theorem 2 here. The reader can read the article [20] for more details.

Proof. We consider the case where P_1 is honest and where P_1 is malicious. Let $\mathcal{H}$ and $\mathcal{M}$ be denoted as the index set of honest parties and malicious parties, respectively.

    Honest P_1. Considering an adversary $\mathcal{A}_1$ corrupting malicious P_i. We construct a simulator Sim capable of executing $\mathcal{A}_1$ as a subroutine in the ideal world with an ideal functionality $\mathcal{F}$ to evaluate the function f. The operation of Sim is outlined as follows:

(1) In the preprocessing phase, Sim generates mac keys $\{\Delta_i\}_{i \in [n]}$ randomly from $\{0,1\}^\kappa$, emulates semi-honest parties and records all authenticated values. If any honest party would abort, Sim also aborts.

(2) In the online phase, Sim acts as honest parties and interacts with $\mathcal{A}_1$, using input $\{x^i := 0\}_{i \in \mathcal{H}}$. Sim computes $\{x_w^i = \hat{x}_w^i \oplus r_w^i\}_{i \in \mathcal{M}, w \in \mathcal{I}_i}$ based on the masked inputs $\{\hat{x}_w^i\}_{i \in \mathcal{M}, w \in \mathcal{I}_i}$ and recorded values.

(3) Sim interacts with $\mathcal{A}_1$ acting as honest parties. If P_1 would abort, Sim outputs whatever $\mathcal{A}_1$ outputs and aborts; otherwise, Sim sends $\{x^i\}_{i \in \mathcal{M}}$ to $\mathcal{F}$.

We conduct a series of experiments to prove that the real-world output distribution of $\mathcal{A}_1$ and semi-honest parties is indistinguishable from that of Sim and semi-honest parties.

Hyb$_1$: this experiment is performed in a hybrid world where Sim simulates honest parties with the actual input $\{y_w\}_{w \in \mathcal{I}_i, i \in \mathcal{H}}$. **Hyb$_1$** is obviously computationally indistinguishable from the real world.

Hyb$_2$: the experiment is similar to **Hyb$_1$** but Sim computes $\{x_w^i = \hat{x}_w^i \oplus r_w^i\}_{i \in \mathcal{M}, w \in \mathcal{I}_i}$. If P_1 or other honest parties would abort, Sim outputs whatever $\mathcal{A}_1$ outputs and aborts; otherwise, Sim sends $\{x^i\}_{i \in \mathcal{M}}$ to $\mathcal{F}$.

The views of **Hyb$_2$** and **Hyb$_1$** are exactly the same. For the IT-MAC, P_1 can just learn the same output.

Hyb$_3$: Same as **Hyb$_2$**, except with Sim using input $\{x_w := 0\}_{i \in \mathcal{H}, w \in \mathcal{I}_i}$.

Even with different inputs in **Hyb$_3$** and **Hyb$_2$**, the views are indistinguishable for the uniform random distribution of $\{r_w^i\}_{i \in \mathcal{H}}$. P_1 aborts in both Hybrids with the same probability for independently random decrypted rows in garbled circuits. **Hyb$_3$** is the ideal-world experiment, so the proof ends when P_1 is honest.

Malicious P_1. Considering an adversary $\mathcal{A}_2$ corrupting malicious $P_i, i \in \mathcal{M}$. We construct a simulator Sim capable of executing $\mathcal{A}_2$ as a subroutine in the ideal world with an ideal functionality $\mathcal{F}$ to evaluate the function f. The operation of Sim is outlined as follows:

(1) In the preprocessing phase, Sim generates mac keys $\{\Delta_i\}_{i \in [n]}$ randomly from $\{0, 1\}^\kappa$, emulates semi-honest parties and records all authenticated values. If any honest party would abort, Sim also aborts.

(2) In the online phase, Sim acts as honest parties and interacts with $\mathcal{A}_2$, using input $\{x^i := 0\}_{i \in \mathcal{H}}$. Sim computes $\{x_w^i = \hat{x}_w^i \oplus r_w^i\}_{i \in \mathcal{M}, w \in \mathcal{I}_i}$ based on the masked inputs $\{\hat{x}_w^i\}_{i \in \mathcal{M}, w \in \mathcal{I}_i}$ and recorded values.

(3) Sim sends $\{x^i\}_{i \in \mathcal{M}}$ on behalf of $P_i, i_\mathcal{M}$ to $\mathcal{F}$. If $\mathcal{F}$ aborts, Sim aborts. Otherwise, if Sim receives z as output, Sim computes $z' = f(x'^1, \cdots, x'^n)$ where $\{x'^i := 0\}_{i_\mathcal{H}}$ and $\{x'^i := x^i\}_{i_\mathcal{M}}$. For each $i \in \mathcal{H}$, $w \in \mathcal{O}$, if $z_w' = z_w$, Sim sends $(r_w^i, M_1[r_w^i])$ on behalf of P_i to $\mathcal{A}_2$; otherwise, Sim sends $(r_w^i \oplus 1, M_1[r_w^i] \oplus \Delta_1)$.

We conduct a series of experiments to prove that the real-world output distribution of $\mathcal{A}_1$ and semi-honest parties is indistinguishable from that of Sim and semi-honest parties.

Hyb$_1$: this experiment is performed in a hybrid world where Sim simulates honest parties with the actual input $\{y_w\}_{w \in \mathcal{I}_i, i \in \mathcal{H}}$. **Hyb$_1$** is obviously computationally indistinguishable from the real world.

Hyb$_2$: the experiment is similar to **Hyb$_1$** but Sim computes $\{x_w^i = \hat{x}_w^i \oplus r_w^i\}_{i \in \mathcal{M}, w \in \mathcal{I}_i}$. If any honest party would abort, Sim outputs whatever $\mathcal{A}_2$ outputs and aborts; otherwise, Sim sends $\{x^i\}_{i \in \mathcal{M}}$ to $\mathcal{F}$.

The views of **Hyb$_2$** and **Hyb$_1$** are exactly the same for no interaction.

Hyb$_3$: Same as **Hyb$_2$**, except with Sim using input $\{x_w := 0\}_{i \in \mathcal{H}, w \in \mathcal{I}_i}$. Sim sends $\{x^i\}_{i \in \mathcal{M}}$ on behalf of $P_i, i_\mathcal{M}$ to $\mathcal{F}$. If $\mathcal{F}$ aborts, Sim aborts. Otherwise, if Sim receives z as output, Sim computes $z' = f(x'^1, \cdots, x'^n)$ where $\{x'^i := 0\}_{i_\mathcal{H}}$ and $\{x'^i := x^i\}_{i_\mathcal{M}}$. For each $i \in \mathcal{H}$, $w \in \mathcal{O}$, if $z_w' = z_w$, Sim sends $(r_w^i, M_1[r_w^i])$ on behalf of P_i to $\mathcal{A}_2$; otherwise, Sim sends $(r_w^i \oplus 1, M_1[r_w^i] \oplus \Delta_1)$.

Even with different inputs in **Hyb₃** and **Hyb₂**, the views are indistinguishable for the uniform random distribution of $\{r_w^i\}_{i\in\mathcal{H}}$. According to the security of GC, P_1 can just open one rows among every AND gate ciphertexts. Hence, even with the masked bits at each gate, marked bits and garbled keys are with the same probability between **Hyb₃** and **Hyb₂**. **Hyb₃** is the ideal-world experiment, so the proof is complete when P_1 is malicious.

5   Implementation

The experiments are implemented on the Manjaro Linux 22.0.0 operating system, running on Intel i9-12900KS 3.40 GHz CPU with 32.0 GB RAM. Similar to prior works such as WRK [20] and YWZ [21], we leverages the C++ library of emptoolkit [16] for its implementation. The security parameter κ is fixed at 128. For simulation, the function circuit is $f(x_1, \cdots, x_n) = x_1 + x_2 + \cdots + x_n$ with a bit input x_i from P_i. The function can be applied in e-voting system [25] for tallying votes.

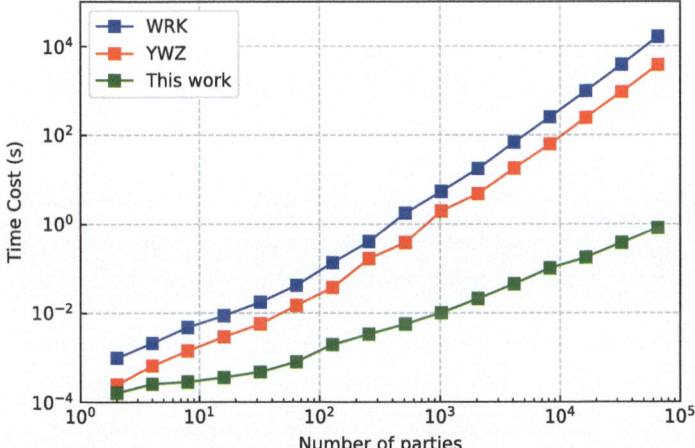

Fig. 2. Each party's computational cost comparison of between WRK, YWZ and this work in preprocessing phase.

Time cost comparison. The most time-consuming phase of authenticated GC is the preprocessing phase and this work focuses on the optimization of the phase. What is more, our protocol shares similarities with WRK and YWZ in the low-cost online phase. However, it diverges significantly in the time-consuming preprocessing phase. Thus, we exclusively compare our protocol with those of WRK and YWZ in term of each party's computational cost in the preprocessing phase, as shown in Fig. 2. The figure illustrates that this work significantly outperforms WRK and YWZ in terms of computational cost during the preprocessing phase. We employ the same efficient AND triple generation technique as YWZ, resulting in similar costs between this work and YWZ, both of which are more efficient than WRK in the two-party setting. However, as the number of parties increases, the time required for this work is substantially lower than that of WRK and YWZ, primarily due to our path-related optimizations. For instance, when the number of parties is around 10,000, this work's computation time is around 0.1 s, while WRK and YWZ require approximately 300 s and 100 s, respectively. *Communication overhead comparison.* Table 1 presents a comparison of the communication complexity among WRK, YWZ and this work. The communication complexity is the maximum amount of data sent by each party. In the table, $\mathcal{O}$ is the length of all circuit-output wires, ρ is the statistical security parameter, B is the size of each bucket, $|\mathcal{C}_A|$ is the number of AND gates in circuit and $|\mathcal{C}_P|$ is the number of communications with the parties along each party's related path of AND gates. $|\mathcal{C}_P|$ is much less than $|\mathcal{C}_A|$ with the increase of participants. By employing the efficient AND triple generation technique used in YWZ and incorporating path-related optimizations, this work demonstrates the most efficient communication complexity during the function-independent step compared to WRK and YWZ and the similar communication complexity compared to YWZ during the function-dependent step. The communication complexity of the three schemes in online phase is similar and much lower than that in the preprocessing phase.

Table 1. Communication Complexity Comparison

Scheme	Func. Ind.	Func. Dep.	Online
WRK	$(3B + \frac{\kappa}{\kappa+\rho}B + 1)(n - 1)|\mathcal{C}_A|(\kappa + \rho)+$ $(n - 1)|\mathcal{I}|(\kappa + \rho)$	$4(n - 1)|\mathcal{C}_A|\kappa + 4|\mathcal{C}_A|\rho+$ $2(n - 1)|\mathcal{C}_A| + (n - 1)|\mathcal{I}|$	$|\mathcal{I}|\kappa + |I|/n + |\mathcal{O}|$
YWZ	$(4D + 1)(n - 1)|\mathcal{C}_A|\kappa + (1 - 1/n)|\mathcal{I}|\kappa$	$(4n - 6)|\mathcal{C}_A|\kappa + (2n - 1)|\mathcal{C}_A|\max\{|\mathcal{I}|\kappa, |\mathcal{C}_A|\}+$ $|\mathcal{I}|/n + |\mathcal{O}|$	
This work	$(4B + 1)|\mathcal{C}_P|\kappa + (2n - 2+$ $(n - 1)(\lceil log(n)\rceil + 1)\lceil log(n)\rceil)\kappa$	$(4n - 4)|\mathcal{C}_A|\kappa + (2n - 1)|\mathcal{C}_A|\max\{|\mathcal{I}|\kappa, |\mathcal{C}_A|\}+$ $|\mathcal{I}|/n + |\mathcal{O}|$	

Figure 3 also demonstrates the comparison of each party's total communication cost between WRK, YWZ and this work. In the figure, we can find that when the number of parties exceeds 1,000, this work's communication cost is less than 10 MB, whereas both of WRK and YWZ require nearly 1 GB. We can find that compared with WRK and YWZ, this work presents almost 100× improvements in terms of computation and total communication efficiency of each party when the number of parties exceeds 1000 due to path-related optimizations.

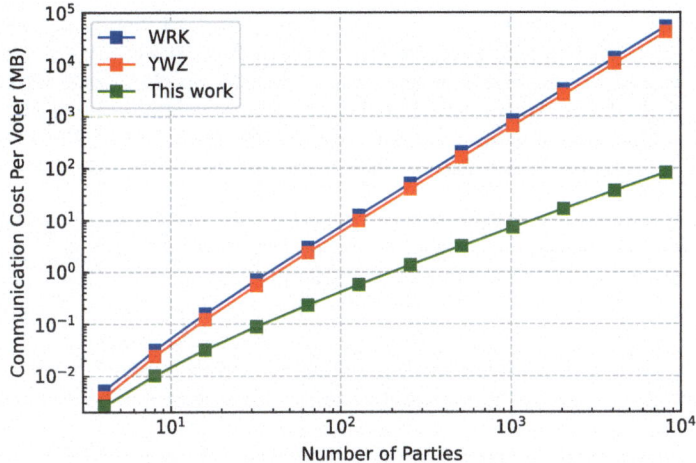

Fig. 3. Each party's total communication cost comparison between WRK, YWZ and this work.

6 Conclusion

The paper presents an efficient, large-scale and constant-round MPC protocol based on IT-MAC and GC in malicious model. Additionally, the paper proposes a path-related authenticated shares preprocessing optimization technique for efficiently generating garbled circuits in a distributed manner. The optimization dramatically reduces the computation and communication cost for large-scale parties as demonstrated in implementation analysis. The experimental evaluation illustrates the proposed scheme has shown nearly 100× improvement in terms of computation and communication efficiency of each party when the number of parties exceeds 1000. The potential advantages of our protocol are promising for large-scale applications, such as e-voting and blockchain. Future research should focus on implementing our efficient general GC protocol in practical settings using existing systems, as our current implementation has only been simulated locally on a personal computer within a specific e-voting context.

References

1. Beaver, D., Micali, S., Rogaway, P.: The round complexity of secure protocols (extended abstract). In: Proceedings of the 22nd Annual ACM Symposium on Theory of Computing, pp. 503–513. ACM (1990)
2. Ben-Efraim, A., Lindell, Y., Omri, E.: Optimizing semi-honest secure multiparty computation for the internet. In: Procceedings of the 2017 ACM SIGSAC Conference on Computer and Communications Security, CCS 2017, pp. 578–590. ACM (2016)
3. Cascudo, I., Damgård, I., David, B., Döttling, N., Nielsen, J.B.: Rate-1, linear time and additively homomorphic UC commitments. In: CRYPTO 2016, vol. 9816, pp. 179–207 (2016)

4. Chowdhury, A.R., Guo, C., Jha, S., van der Maaten, L.: Eiffel: Ensuring integrity for federated learning. In: Proceedings of the 2022 ACM SIGSAC Conference on Computer and Communications Security, CCS 2022, pp. 2535–2549 (2022)

5. Damgård, I., Ishai, Y.: Constant-round multiparty computation using a black-box pseudorandom generator. In: Advances in Cryptology—CRYPTO 2005: 25th Annual International Cryptology Conference, vol. 3621, pp. 378–394. Springer, Berlin (2005)

6. Damgård, I., Pastro, V., Smart, N.P., Zakarias, S.: Multiparty computation from somewhat homomorphic encryption. In: CRYPTO 2012, pp. 643–662 (2012)

7. Green, M., Miers, I.: Bolt: anonymous payment channels for decentralized currencies. In: Proceedings of the 2017 ACM SIGSAC Conference on Computer and Communications Security, CCS 2017, pp. 473–489. ACM (2017)

8. Hazay, C., Ishai, Y., Venkitasubramaniam, M.: Actively secure garbled circuits with constant communication overhead in the plain model. J. Cryptol. **36**(3), 26 (2023)

9. Hazay, C., Scholl, P., Soria-Vazquez, E.: Low cost constant round MPC combining BMR and oblivious transfer. J. Cryptol. **33**(4), 1732–1786 (2020)

10. Katz, J., Ranellucci, S., Rosulek, M., Wang, X.: Optimizing authenticated garbling for faster secure two-party computation. In: CRYPTO 2018, Santa Barbara, CA, USA, pp. 365–391 (2018)

11. Keller, M.: MP-SPDZ: a versatile framework for multi-party computation. In: 2020 ACM SIGSAC Conference on Computer and Communications Security, CCS, pp. 1575–1590 (2020)

12. Keller, M., Pastro, V., Rotaru, D.: Overdrive: making SPDZ great again. In: Advances in Cryptology, EUROCRYPT 2018—37th Annual International Conference on the Theory and Applications of Cryptographic Techniques. Lecture Notes in Computer Science, vol. 10822, pp. 158–189. Springer, Berlin (2018)

13. Kolesnikov, V., Schneider, T.: Improved garbled circuit: free XOR gates and applications. In: ICALP 2008, pp. 486–498 (2008)

14 Lindell, Y.: Fast cut and-choose-based protocols for malicious and covert adversaries. J. Cryptol. **29**(2), 456–490 (2015)

15. Liu, Z., Wang, L., Bao, H., Cao, Z., Zhou, L., Liu, Z.: Efficient and privacy-preserving cloud-assisted two-party computation scheme in heterogeneous networks. IEEE Trans. Industr. Inf. **20**(5), 8007–8018 (2024)

16. Malozemoff, A.J., Wang, X., Katz, J.: emp-toolkit. https://github.com/emp-toolkit

17. Nielsen, J.B., Nordholt, P.S., Orlandi, C., Burra, S.S.: A new approach to practical active-secure two-party computation. In: CRYPTO 2012, pp. 681–700 (2012)

18. Rosulek, M., Roy, L.: Three halves make a whole? Beating the half-gates lower bound for garbled circuits. In: Annual International Cryptology Conference, pp. 94–124. Springer, Berlin (2021)

19. Rotaru, D., Wood, T.: Marbled circuits: mixing arithmetic and Boolean circuits with active security. In: Progress in Cryptology, INDOCRYPT 2019—20th International Conference on Cryptology in India. Lecture Notes in Computer Science, vol. 11898, pp. 227–249. Springer, Berlin (2019)

20. Wang, X., Ranellucci, S., Katz, J.: Global-scale secure multiparty computation. In: Proceedings of the 2017 ACM SIGSAC Conference on Computer and Communications Security, CCS 2017, pp. 39–56 (2017)

21. Yang, K., Wang, X., Zhang, J.: More efficient MPC from improved triple generation and authenticated garbling. In: Proceedings of the 2020 ACM SIGSAC Conference on Computer and Communications Security, CCS 2020, pp. 1627–1646 (2020)

22. Yao, A.C.: Protocols for secure computations (extended abstract). In: 23rd Annual Symposium on Foundations of Computer Science, pp. 160–164. IEEE Computer Society (1982)
23. Zahur, S., Rosulek, M., Evans, D.: Two halves make a whole—reducing data transfer in garbled circuits using half gates. In: EUROCRYPT 2015, pp. 220–250 (2015)
24. Zhang, F., Maram, D., Malvai, H., Goldfeder, S., Juels, A.: DECO: liberating web data using decentralized oracles for TLS. In: Proceedings of the 2020 ACM SIGSAC Conference on Computer and Communications Security, CCS2020, pp. 1919–1938. ACM (2020)
25. Zhang, X., Zhang, B., Kiayias, A., Zacharias, T., Ren, K.: An efficient E2E crowd verifiable e-voting system. IEEE Trans. Dependable Secur. Comput. **19**(6), 3607–3620 (2021)
26. Zheng, W., Deng, R., Chen, W., Popa, R.A., Panda, A., Stoica, I.: Cerebro: a platform for multi-party cryptographic collaborative learning. In: Proceedings of USENIX Security Symposium 2021, pp. 2723–2740. USENIX Association (2021)
27. Zheng, W., Popa, R.A., Gonzalez, J.E., Stoica, I.: Helen: maliciously secure coopetitive learning for linear models. In: 2019 IEEE Symposium on Security and Privacy (IEEE S&P), pp. 724–738 (2019)

Parallel Implementation of Sieving Algorithm on Heterogeneous CPU-GPU Computing Architectures

Mengsi Wu⬤, Pei Li(✉)⬤, Jiageng Chen⬤, and Shixiong Yao⬤

Central China Normal University,Wuhan 430079, China
peili@ccnu.edu.cn

Abstract. Sieving algorithms currently represent the fastest approach of solving the Shortest Vector Problem (SVP). However, current sieving algorithms exclusively utilize either CPUs or GPUs. This paper introduces a novel sieving approach tailored to CPU+GPU heterogeneous computing platforms. We constructed a runtime system capable of concurrently executing both CPU and GPU versions of the sieving algorithm. The GPU version of the sieving algorithm reduces the demand for graphics memory by efficiently transferring data in batches. We used two computing platforms to evaluate our method: Hannibal is equipped with an AMD Ryzen 7 5800H CPU and an NVIDIA RTX 3060 GPU; Zeus is equipped with an Intel Xeon Platinum 8176M CPU and two Integrated Matrox G200eW3 Graphics Controllers. The experimental results show that, compared to the classical sieving algorithm implementation in G6K, the proposed method achieves a minimum speedup of 7.2x (for 30-dimensional SVP) and a maximum of 588x (for 120-dimensional SVP) on Hannibal and a minimum speedup of 4.3x (for 30-dimensional SVP) and a maximum of 1230x (for 120-dimensional SVP) on Zeus.

Keywords: SVP · Sieving · Heterogeneous Computing · CUDA

1 Introduction

Lattice-based cryptography is a robust method for creating useful cryptographic protocols. Its security relies on the difficulty of solving the shortest vector problem (SVP), which aims to find the shortest non-zero vector within lattices. There are many algorithms to solve the SVP, including LLL, BKZ, enumeration, and sieving. Among these, sieving algorithm currently stands as the fastest algorithm for solving the SVP.

Sieving algorithm was first introduced by Ajtai et al. [1] in 2001. Since then, several parallel-friendly sieving algorithms have emerged. These include Gauss Sieve [15], Hash Sieve [5], BGJ sieving [10], triple_sieve [8] and LD sieving [4]. The current parallel sieving algorithm is observed to use only one type of device, such as GPUs or CPUs. [2,9,12–14,16] only use CPUs to parallelize the above

Z. Xia and J. Chen (Eds.): ISPEC 2024, LNCS 15053, pp. 258–272, 2024.
https://doi.org/10.1007/978-981-97-9053-1_15

algorithms. And [7,19] only use GPUs to parallelize the above algorithms. In addition, [3] used multiple platforms, including CPUs and FPGAs.

The General Sieve Kernel (G6K) [2] is a lattice reduction framework based on sieving algorithms, characterized by its "stateful" design, as opposed to treating sieving as a black-box Shortest Vector Problem (SVP) oracle. It incorporates recent optimized algorithms such as progressive sieving [11] and dimensions for free [6]. In addition to an abstract state machine that facilitates the straight-forward description of different reduction strategies, it also provides an open source implementation that has successfully tackled several new TU Darmstadt SVP Challenges [18] (up to dimension 155). In G6K, parallel implementations of triple_sieve [8], BGJ sieving [10], and LD sieving [4] are based on thread pools. Although [7] improved the sieving algorithm in G6K using tensor cores, it only uses GPU devices. Table 1 shows the parallelization of the above sieving algorithms.

Therefore, the main objective of this paper is to propose a sieving algorithm suitable for CPU+GPU heterogeneous computing architecture based on the BGJ sieving algorithm. Moreover, despite the current availability of GPUs with up to 128 GB of graphics memory, the SVP challenges are evolving and the memory requirements may increase. Thus, our approach also can solve the problem of larger memory requirements.

Table 1. The parallelization of sieving algorithms.

	Using CPUs	Using GPUs	Using multiple platforms
Gauss Sieve [15]	[9,14,16]	[19]	[3] using FPGAs and CPUs
Hash Sieve [5]	[12]	-	-
BGJ sieving [10]	[2]	[7]	-
Triple_sieve [8]	[2]	[7]	-
LD sieving [4]	[2,13]	[7]	-

2   Preliminaries

2.1   Notations and Definitions

The Euclidean norm of a vector $\mathbf{v} = v_i$, $i = 1, ..., n$, in $\mathbb{R}^n$ is denoted by $\|v\|_2$ or simply $\|v\|$. Lattices are discrete subgroups of the m-dimensional Euclidean space R^n, with a strong periodicity property. A lattice $\mathcal{L}$ generated by a basis $\mathbf{B}$, a set of linearly independent vectors $\mathbf{b}_1, ..., \mathbf{b}_n$ in R^m, is denoted by:

$$\mathcal{L}(\mathbf{B}) = \{\mathbf{v} \in R^n : \mathbf{v} = \sum_{i=1}^{n} \mathbf{x}_i \mathbf{b}_i, \mathbf{x} \in \mathbb{Z}^n\} \tag{1}$$

where n is the rank of the lattice. When $n = m$, the lattice is said to be of full rank. The shortest non-zero vector in a lattice can be defined as the radius of the smallest ball containing a non-zero lattice point. This definition can be extended to define a sequence of parameters $\lambda = \lambda_1 \leq \lambda_2 \leq ... \leq \lambda_n$, called to as the successive minima of the lattice.

Definition 1 Shortest Vector Problem (SVP) Given a lattice basis $\mathbf{B}$, the task is to find the shortest non-zero lattice vector, denoted as $\mathbf{v} \in \mathcal{L}(\mathbf{B})$, such that its norm satisfies $\|v\| = \lambda_1(\mathcal{L}(\mathbf{B}))$.

2.2   The Sieving Algorithm

The basic sieving algorithm is shown in Algorithm 1. The steps of the basic sieving algorithm are as follows: (1) Sample some vectors from the lattice $\mathcal{L}$ in L. (2) Perform reductions and replace the longest vector in L. The reduction step involves adding or subtracting two vectors, and if the result is shorter than the longest vector in L, then replace the longest vector in L. Repeat step 2 until the specified proportion of short vectors is achieved in L, indicating that the list L contains short vectors that saturate the ball of radius R.

Algorithm 1 The basic sieving algorithm, described in [7]

Require: A basis $\mathbf{B}$ of a lattice $\mathcal{L}$, a saturation radius R, and a list L.
Ensure: A list L comprising short vectors that saturate the ball of radius R.
 1: Sample some vectors from the lattice $\mathcal{L}$ in L.
 2: **while** L does not cover the entire ball with a radius of R **do**
 3:    Perform reductions and replace the longest vector in L.
 4: **end while**
 5: **return** L

2.3   CUDA (Compute Unified Device Architecture)

CUDA is a parallel computing platform and programming model developed by NVIDIA specifically for general purpose computing on graphics processing units (GPUs). An NVIDIA GPU typically has thousands of CUDA cores organized into multiple execution units called Streaming Multiprocessors (SMs). These SMs use their many CUDA cores to handle a large number of resident threads, strategically deployed to hide latencies associated with computation and memory operations. Threads are grouped in sets of 32, forming a warp, and adhere to the single-instruction multiple-data (SIMD) paradigm. The execution of a GPU program, called a kernel, involves multiple blocks. Each block that consists of multiple warps is executed on a single available Streaming Multiprocessor (SM).

3   Optimization and Implementation

3.1   Basic Implementation of BGJ Sieving Algorithm

The G6K includes multiple sieving algorithms that implement the Sieve instruction. The NV sieve [17] and Gauss sieve [15] both have single-threaded implementations primarily for testing purposes. Additionally, G6K includes a fully multi-threaded and low-level optimized version of the BGJ sieve [5] with a single bucket layer (bgj1). The filtering techniques of bgj1 have also been extended and used in the triple sieve implementation [8]. The asymptotically optimal sieving algorithm, which we refer to as BDGL [4], also has a multi-threaded implementation in G6K. However, due to the parallel implementation of BDGL involving multiple tasks with dependencies on execution order, BDGL is not suitable for CPU+GPU heterogeneous computing platforms. So, we propose a CPU+GPU heterogeneous computing platform based on the BGJ sieving algorithm.

The general procedure of the BGJ sieving algorithm [5] is as follows: (1) Firstly, sample a large number of lattice vectors in the list L. (2) Then, randomly select a bucket center in the list L, denoted as $\mathbf{c}$. (3) Subsequently, compare each vector in the list with $\mathbf{c}$. If the angle between them is less than $\pi\gamma$, place the vector into the corresponding bucket. Here, γ represents a fixed angle parameter where $0 < \gamma < \frac{1}{2}$. This step is called the bucketing phase. (4) Finally, reduce all vector pairs in the bucket. If the reduced vector is shorter than the longest vector in L, then replace the longest vector in L with this vector. This step is called the reduction phase. Steps (2), (3), and (4) iterate continuously until the list L contains short vectors saturating the ball of radius R, which means the list L contains a certain proportion of short vectors. The BGJ sieving algorithm is shown in Algorithm 2.

3.2   Heterogeneous Parallel Sieving Algorithm

The Runtime System Compared to the implementation of the BGJ sieving algorithm in G6K, our implementation extends its functionality by introducing a novel sieving approach tailored to CPU+GPU heterogeneous computing platforms. This is achieved using an optimized runtime system that automatically distributes tasks and manages execution across different computing devices.

Thread scheduling is illustrated in Fig. 1. (1) Upon initialization, the runtime system creates and starts a specified number of threads, referred to as *threads*, as determined by the user. Each thread remains idle, waiting for tasks to be assigned for execution. (2) Users submit tasks to the system, specifying whether they should be executed by the CPU or GPU. These tasks are then added to the task queue. If multiple GPUs are available, GPU tasks are evenly distributed among them. (3) When idle threads are available, the system retrieves tasks from the task queue and assigns them to idle threads for execution. The task queue operates on a first-in-first-out principle. In Fig. 1, CPU task 1 is initially assigned to an idle thread for execution, followed by subsequent tasks sequentially assigned to idle threads. (4) After a thread completes its task, new tasks

---

Algorithm 2 The BGJ sieving algorithm

Require: A basis $\mathbf{B} = (\mathbf{b}_1, ..., \mathbf{b}_n)$ of a lattice $\mathcal{L}$, a saturation radius R, a list L, and
a fixed angle parameter $0 < \gamma < \frac{1}{2}$.

Ensure: A list L comprising short vectors that saturate the ball of radius R.

Sample a large number of vectors from the lattice $\mathcal{L}$ in L.

2: **while** L does not cover the entire ball with a radius of R **do**

  Randomly select a bucket center $\mathbf{c}$ from L.

4: **for** $\mathbf{v} \in L$ **do**

    if $\frac{\langle \mathbf{v}, \mathbf{m} \rangle}{\|\mathbf{v}\|\|\mathbf{m}\|} \geq \cos(\pi\gamma)$ **then**

6:      Place $\mathbf{v}$ into the *bucket*.

    end if

8: **end for**

  for every $\mathbf{l}_1, \mathbf{l}_2 \in bucket$ **do**

10:    **if** $\|\mathbf{l}_1 \pm \mathbf{l}_2\| < \max(|L|)$ **then**

      Replace the longest vector in L with $\mathbf{l}_1 \pm \mathbf{l}_2$.

12:    **end if**

  end for

14: **end while**

  return L

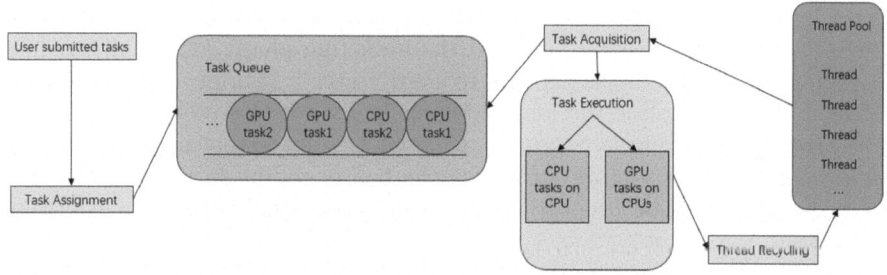

Fig. 1. The runtime system scheduling.

can be added to the task queue, and the runtime system continues to schedule available threads to execute these tasks.

Our runtime system architecture is suitable not only for sieving algorithms but also for other single-task algorithms, requiring only task modifications. Therefore, our system exhibits excellent scalability.

Before executing tasks, we calculate the number of short vectors, denoted as sn, needed for the BGJ sieving to terminate. Then, we determine the number of short vectors that each thread needs to find, which is sn divided by the number of threads. Once a thread finds a sufficient number of short vectors, it becomes idle and proceeds to execute other tasks in the task queue.

The GPU Task The CPU task involves the BGJ sieving task implemented in G6K. Regarding GPU tasks, a single iteration is illustrated in Fig. 2, and Algorithm 3 outlines the GPU task. First, we need to initialize the data we

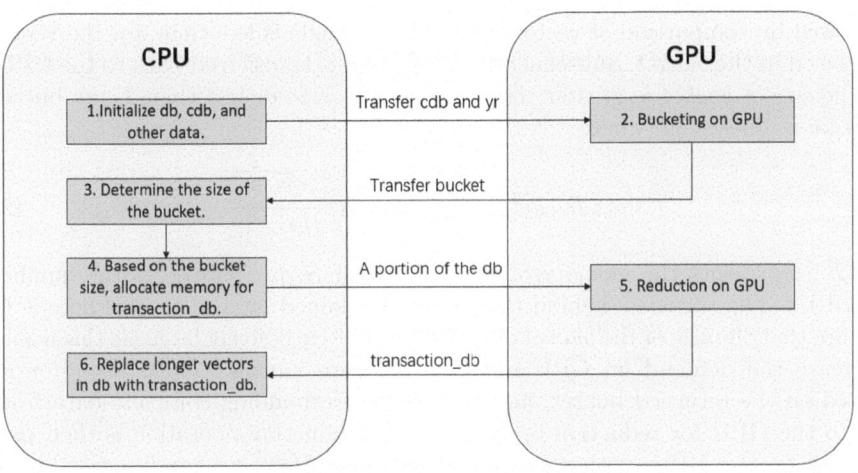

Fig. 2. An iteration of the GPU task.

will use, including the databases **db** and **cdb**, *bucket*, *transaction_db* and so on. **db** refers to the list L in the sieving algorithm, while **cdb** stores the simhash corresponding to all vectors in the list, which is a compressed representation of a vector and consumes less memory. The *transaction_db* is used to store the found short vectors, and eventually, the short vectors in *transaction_db* will replace the long vectors in **db**. The entry stored in **db** is of type *Entry* and is as follows:

- **x**: Coordinates of vectors

- **yr**: GSO(Gram-Schmidt Orthogonalization) basis

- **c**: Compressed vectors

- **uid**: Unique identifier for collision detection, i.e., a hash

- **len**: The length of the vector

The entry stored in **cdb** is of type *CompressedEntry* and is as follows:

- **c**: Compressed vectors, i.e., a simhash

- i: Index of non-compressed entry in database **db**

- **len**: Sorting value

Then the bucketing operation is performed on the GPU, where each thread compares a vector in the **cdb** with **c**. First, pre-filtering is conducted using SimHash, followed by comparison of vector angles. If the angle is less than $\pi\gamma$, the vector is placed in the *bucket*. Subsequently, the *bucket* is transferred back to the CPU. If the size of *bucket* is greater than *max_bucket_size* or less than 2, the bucket will be re-bucketing, where

$$max\_bucket\_size = N_{GPU}\sqrt{\frac{2^{m-1}}{threads}} \qquad (2)$$

2^m represents the memory of the GPU, and N_{GPU} represents the number of GPUs. The rationale behind this will be explained later. The goal here is to ensure that the size of the *bucket* does not become excessively large, as this would increase the demand on GPU memory. Allocate memory for *transaction_db* based on the returned bucket, and send the corresponding complete data from db to the GPU for reduction operations. The reduction operation is then performed on the GPU, with each thread using SimHash for pre-filtering before the reduction. If reduction is possible, only the reduced coordinates and uid are computed first, then placed in *transaction_db*.

After reduction, *transaction_db* is transmitted to the CPU. We then use the uid from both *transaction_db* and the hash table to check for collisions. The hash table contains the uid of all vectors in the db. If collisions are found, we remove the corresponding reduced vectors from *transaction_db*. Otherwise yr, len and other parameters are calculated. If the size of *transaction_db* exceeds the required number of short vectors $\frac{sn}{threads}$, the size of the *transaction_db* will be resized to $\frac{sn}{threads}$. Finally, the longer vectors in db are replaced with the remaining vectors in *transaction_db*. This entire process is repeated until the desired number of short vectors is obtained.

Our algorithm imposes limits on the size of *bucket* and transfers data in batches rather than all at once to the GPU. Despite these constraints, it does not compromise the efficiency of our algorithm. Therefore, our approach remains highly efficient even in memory-constrained situations.

Maximum Value of the Size of the Bucket If the size of the bucket is n, then the maximum number of short vectors found in the reduction phase will be $O(n^2)$. In our experiments, the memory required for tasks is allocated in advance. The bucket size is reserved as the size of cdb $* sizeof(CompressedEntry)$, and the storage for short vectors in *transaction_db* is reserved as the square of the bucket size $* sizeof(Entry)$. Therefore, if the bucket size is too large, it will necessitate reserving a substantial amount of memory for the short vectors that will be identified in the reduction phase.

During our testing of the GPU-based sieving algorithm, we observed that as the dimensionality and the number of GPU tasks increase, occurrences of GPU memory shortage become more frequent. This significantly impacts the computational efficiency of the sieving algorithm. Therefore, it is crucial to check the bucket size after transferring it to the CPU. If the bucket size is less than 2 or greater than *max_bucket_size*, we need to repeat the bucketing operation.

Algorithm 3 The GPU task

Require: Databases db and cdb, a hash table, the *bucket*, a set of *transaction_db*, a
  saturation radius R and a fixed angle parameter $0 < \gamma < \frac{1}{2}$.

Ensure: A database db comprising short vectors that saturate the ball of radius R.

1: Initialization of data.

2: **while** db does not cover the entire ball with a radius of R **do**

3:     Randomly select a bucket center **c** in cdb.

4:     Transfer cdb, yr to the GPU.

5:     Bucketing on the GPU.

6:     Pass the *bucket* back to the CPU.

7:     **if** $bucket\_size > max\_bucket\_size \| bucket\_size < 2$ **then**

8:         continue

9:     **end if**

10:     Transfer the data from the corresponding db in the *bucket* to the GPU.

11:     Reduction on the GPU.

12:     Return the set of found short vectors *transaction_db* to the CPU.

13:     Check vectors in *transaction_db* for collisions in the hash table.

14:     **if** the size of $transaction\_db > \frac{sn}{threads}$ **then**

15:         Set the size of $transaction\_db = \frac{sn}{threads}$

16:     **end if**

17:     Replace longer vectors in *db* with *transaction_db*.

18: **end while**

19: **return** db

During the bucketing phase, the data to be transferred consists of cdb and
yr. For the reduction phase, the vectors to be transmitted include all vectors
in db corresponding to the entries in *bucket*. A *CompressedEntry* occupies 40
bytes, while yr occupies 512 bytes, and an **Entry** occupies 816 bytes. Therefore,
this part of the transmitted data does not consume significant memory.

The main memory consumption comes from the short vectors found during
the reduction phase. Moreover, some of the actual GPU memory is used by
the operating system, GPU drivers, and other system components, and that
the graphics card memory system typically does not occupy half of the total
memory. Therefore, we assume that only half of the GPU memory (i.e., $2^{(m-1)}$)
is available for data storage. In the most extreme case, in which only GPU tasks
are considered, i.e., each thread needs to store data, the amount of GPU memory
available to each thread is $\frac{2^{m-1}}{threads}$. Given the utilization of multiple GPUs for
execution, the bucket size is maximized to $N_{GPU}\sqrt{\frac{2^{m-1}}{threads}}$.

This approach not only avoids extreme cases, but also ensures that performance is not compromised. As a result, our approach not only combines CPU
and GPU resources well, but also has a small demand on GPU memory.

4   Experiments

4.1   Experiments Setup

Two platforms were used in our experiment to test our algorithm, namely Hannibal and Zeus. Hannibal had a 16-core AMD Ryzen 7 5800H processor and an NVIDIA RTX 3060 graphics card with 8 GB of graphics memory. Zeus had an Intel Xeon Platinum 8176M 56-core processor and two Integrated Matrox G200eW3 Graphics Controllers. It is evident that we conducted single-GPU experiments on Hannibal and multi-GPU experiments on Zeus.

For each run of the sieving method, we randomly selected lattice bases and used a pseudo-random number generator to sample elements from a normal distribution. This ensures that each basis vector is composed of independently and identically distributed random variables. Subsequently, we generated lattice vectors using these bases, with each basis producing a set of 10^5 lattice vectors. The random selection of lattice bases has minimal impact on the overall results. For both experiments, we set the default number of threads to 16, which is also equal to the total number of tasks. We compared the BGJ sieving algorithm implemented in G6K using different task ratios. The task ratio represents the ratio of GPU-based sieving tasks to CPU-based sieving tasks. Each experiment was repeated five times and averaged. To simplify the representation, let GPUX denote X GPU tasks and CPUY denote Y CPU tasks, with X + Y = threads. In Tables 2 and 3, the first row represents the dimensions of the lattice basis, the first column indicates the number of GPU and CPU tasks, and the remaining data represent the time required for the sieving method, measured in seconds.

4.2   Evaluation on Hannibal

Table 2 presents the comprehensive results observed on the Hannibal. The data clearly shows a significant performance enhancement when GPU tasks are introduced alongside single CPU tasks. Specifically, in dimensions ranging from 30 to 80, and extending up to 90–120 dimensions, the addition of GPU tasks notably reduces the computation time. In dimensions 30–80, there is a marked improvement when the number of GPU tasks is equal to or fewer than the number of CPU tasks. However, when the number of GPU tasks exceeds that of CPU tasks, certain data points show larger time requirements. This discrepancy can be attributed to the random selection of bucket centers, which sometimes results in most short vectors found by the final GPU tasks already existing in the database (db). Moreover, the fixed number of vectors in db increases the likelihood of encountering duplicate vectors, particularly in lower dimensions. Consequently, multiple iterations of bucketing and reduction steps are necessary to discover a sufficient number of collision-free short vectors.

However, in dimensions ranging from 90 to 120, the scenario changes. When the number of GPU tasks equals or exceeds the number of CPU tasks, overall performance improves noticeably. As dimensions increase, GPU multi-threading proves capable of processing large datasets more efficiently compared to CPUs.

Table 2. The overall results on Hannibal. The data in the table are measured in (s) seconds.

Dimension	30	40	50	60	70	80	90	100	110	120
GPU0+CPU16	65	87	134	232	404	879	3523	21416	72821	218892
GPU1+CPU15	40	19	40	17	7	296	738	678	687	63853
GPU2+CPU14	10	19	12	7	5	4	498	645	539	537
GPU3+CPU13	8	16	8	6	5	4	440	429	7358	432
GPU4+CPU12	8	9	11	6	4	6	363	394	356	380
GPU5+CPU11	12	9	6	6	9	5	353	454	318	980
GPU6+CPU10	5	9	4	15	8	4	260	574	279	271
GPU7+CPU9	8	8	17	4	5	4	243	224	252	249
GPU8+CPU8	9	11	8	8	6	8	223	210	231	372
GPU9+CPU7	69	24	4	5	7	6	234	202	934	232
GPU10+CPU6	83	28	8	8	10	4	219	234	249	400
GPU11+CPU5	19	9	5	16	10	13	1055	224	279	296
GPU12+CPU4	9	26	8	10	3	8	275	212	258	340
GPU13+CPU3	16	9	7	9	92	9	277	595	211	258
GPU14+CPU2	8	9	10	5	15	5	277	213	221	234
GPU15+CPU1	15	7	5	11	7	6	350	302	358	218
GPU16+CPU0	13	10	9	9	10	12	476	228	235	246

Therefore, the algorithm performs optimally when the number of GPU tasks matches the number of CPU tasks, achieving a balanced utilization of both resources. In Table 2, we observed optimal performance when the task ratio was 1:1 (equal number of GPU and CPU tasks). This configuration allowed our algorithm to leverage both GPU and CPU resources fully. Consequently, our algorithm achieved a significant speedup, demonstrating a 7.2x improvement in 30 dimensions and a remarkable 588x improvement in 120 dimensions. According to experimental tests, if the bucket size is limited to $\frac{3N_{GPU}}{32}\sqrt{\frac{2^{m-1}}{threads}}$, there is no GPU memory shortage problem and the impact on the algorithm performance is small.

4.3 Evaluation on Zeus

Table 3 illustrates the results obtained on Zeus. On Zeus, we utilized one CPU and two GPUs, evenly distributing the GPU tasks across both GPUs for execution. Similar to Hannibal, with the addition of GPU tasks, the overall time required significantly decreased, especially in dimensions 90–120. It can be observed that in dimensions 30–60, a considerable amount of data exceeds 10. This is likely due to the use of multiple GPUs for executing GPU tasks, where the data is not shared between the two devices during the sieving process. This can lead to more duplicate short vectors being found, necessitating

Table 3. The overall results on Zeus. The data in the table are measured in (s) seconds.

Dimension	30	40	50	60	70	80	90	100	110	120
GPU0+CPU16	34	37	61	112	188	445	2039	15813	42964	111968
GPU1+CPU15	13	20	19	60	3	5	2024	3212	1707	2595
GPU2+CPU14	22	12	17	4	6	7	2035	2130	1432	1136
GPU3+CPU13	17	13	17	8	6	3	1494	635	411	647
GPU4+CPU12	15	15	11	15	3	4	897	1077	362	491
GPU5+CPU11	10	19	9	6	4	3	995	340	599	276
GPU6+CPU10	11	10	15	6	4	3	258	205	197	368
GPU7+CPU9	15	15	16	15	4	3	191	526	285	301
GPU8+CPU8	17	13	13	6	5	3	165	463	344	173
GPU9+CPU7	14	9	16	5	3	5	151	251	145	146
GPU10+CPU6	8	10	8	10	5	5	140	358	133	213
GPU11+CPU5	14	9	10	6	7	4	186	126	157	119
GPU12+CPU4	13	9	13	11	7	4	127	114	128	113
GPU13+CPU3	5	12	12	9	7	3	193	134	113	107
GPU14+CPU2	11	11	5	10	7	7	132	104	103	102
GPU15+CPU1	17	9	12	9	5	6	119	96	101	123
GPU16+CPU0	11	9	11	8	8	7	96	96	94	91

additional bucketing and reduction operations, and consequently requiring more time. However, there is still an overall improvement. In dimensions 70–80, our algorithm performs exceptionally well. It is not only very stable but also achieves significant improvements. When the number of GPU tasks is 10, the algorithm performs optimally. This corresponds to a task ratio of 5:3, achieving optimal performance from 30 dimensions to 80 dimensions.

From dimensions 90 to 120, the performance of the algorithm improves gradually as the number of GPU tasks increases. Notably, when the number of GPU tasks reaches 16, meaning only GPUs are utilized, the algorithm achieves its highest performance. This demonstrates that when utilizing multiple GPUs, relying solely on GPU tasks yields the best results. At this point, the full potential of the GPUs is realized, surpassing the performance of a single CPU. Thus, according to the Table 3, we obtained the optimal performance which achieves a 4.3x speedup in 30 dimensions and a 1230x speedup in 120 dimensions.

Table 4. The overall performance of our algorithm.

	30	40	50	60	70	80	90	100	110	120
Hannibal	7.2x	7.9x	16.7x	29x	67x	109.8x	15.8x	101x	122x	588x
Zeus	4.3x	3.7x	7.6x	11.2x	37.6x	89x	21x	165x	457x	1230x

The comprehensive performance of the algorithm, as detailed in Table 4, highlights its performance under different configurations. Specifically, experiments employing a single CPU and a single GPU demonstrate optimal performance when maintaining a 1:1 ratio of GPU tasks to CPU tasks. Conversely, scenarios utilizing a single CPU with multiple GPUs show peak performance when exclusively leveraging GPU tasks. Our runtime system exhibits good scalability, and future users of this system can refer to these task ratios for optimal performance.

However, these experiments also reveal a significant issue with our algorithm: instability during execution, particularly noticeable in lower dimensions. This instability stems from two main factors. Firstly, the random selection of a lattice vector as the bucket center results in uncertain vectors within each bucket after each bucketing. Consequently, the efficiency of each bucketing varies, leading to unstable experimental results. Secondly, each thread independently executes the sieving algorithm locally, which means a short vector found by one thread may also be discovered by others, impacting the efficiency and stability of the algorithm. Despite the instability, the experimental results show significant efficiency improvements.

4.4   Comparison of Our Experiment with [3]

In [3], various devices, including CPUs and FPGAs, were employed with Gauss Sieve, yielding impressive results. A comparison of the acceleration between our algorithm and [3] is illustrated in Fig. 3. [3] shows a steady increase. In contrast, our algorithm initially rises (from 30 to 80 dimensions), then begins to decline (from 80 to 90 dimensions), and continues to increase thereafter. For Hannibal [3] shows greater acceleration in the ranges of 30–47 dimensions and 88–92 dimensions, while Hannibal exhibits greater acceleration from 47 to 88 dimensions and 90–120 dimensions. Therefore, overall, our runtime system demonstrates better acceleration performance compared to [3]. While our system performs well across most dimensions, it does not perform as effectively at 90 dimensions. This is primarily because 90 dimensions represent a higher dimensionality, necessitating more time for both CPU and GPU operations compared to lower dimensions. As a result, the acceleration rate is relatively lower.

For Hannibal and Zeus, Hannibal shows a greater acceleration ratio when the dimensions are less than 88, while Zeus exhibits a greater acceleration ratio when the dimensions are greater than 88. As the number of devices increases, the computational capabilities of the system improve. Therefore, in dimensions above 88, performance is better with more GPU devices.

5   Conclusion

This paper introduces a novel sieving approach tailored for CPU+GPU heterogeneous computing platforms, aiming to address the Shortest Vector Problem (SVP). Our method constructs a runtime system that can simultaneously execute both CPU and GPU versions of the sieving algorithm, maximizing computational efficiency. It performs well even under memory constraints. Additionally,

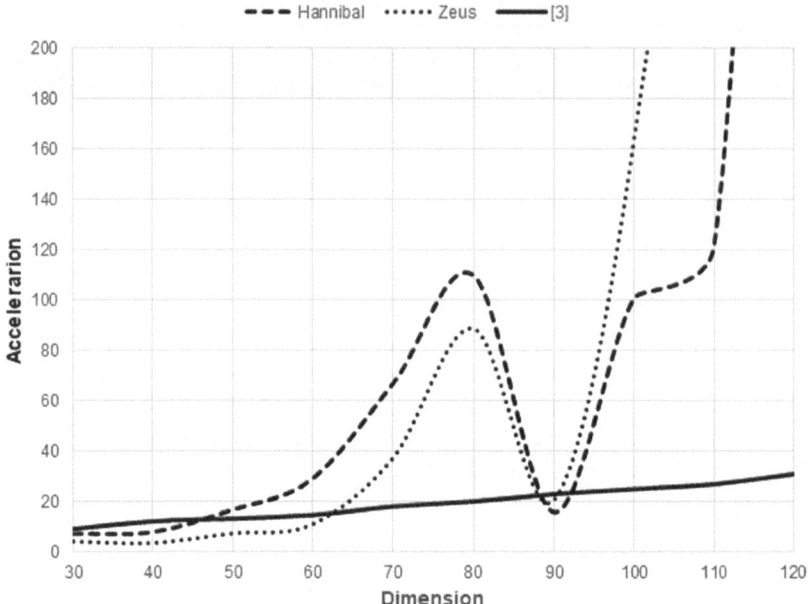

Fig. 3. Comparison of the acceleration observed in our experiments with [3].

our system exhibits excellent scalability and is also suitable for other single-task algorithms.

Our algorithm implementation outperforms the original sieving algorithm on G6K. When using a single CPU and a single GPU, we achieved a speedup of 7.2x in 30 dimensions and up to 588x in 120 dimensions. In lower dimensions, the algorithm performs better when the proportion of GPU tasks to CPU tasks is lower. Conversely, in higher dimensions, the algorithm performs better when the proportion of GPU tasks to CPU tasks is higher. Overall, the algorithm achieves optimal performance when the proportion of GPU tasks to CPU tasks is equal. When using a single GPU and multiple GPUs, we achieved a speedup of 4.3x in 30 dimensions and up to 1230x in 120 dimensions. In lower dimensions, the algorithm performs better when the ratio of GPU tasks to CPU tasks is 5:3. In higher dimensions, the algorithm performs better when only GPU tasks are utilized. Additionally, in higher dimensions, the system performs better with more GPU devices.

Acknowledgement. This work has been partly supported by the Fundamental Research Funds for the Central Universities under Grand No. CCNU24ai010 and the National Natural Science Foundation of China under Grant No. 62272189.

References

1. Ajtai, M., Kumar, R., Sivakumar, D.: A sieve algorithm for the shortest lattice vector problem. In: Proceedings of the Thirty-Third Annual ACM Symposium on Theory of Computing, pp. 601–610 (2001)
2. Albrecht, M.R., Ducas, L., Herold, G., Kirshanova, E., Postlethwaite, E.W., Stevens, M.: The general sieve kernel and new records in lattice reduction. In: Annual International Conference on the Theory and Applications of Cryptographic Techniques, pp. 717–746. Springer (2019)
3. Andrzejczak, M., Gaj, K.: A multiplatform parallel approach for lattice sieving algorithms. In: Algorithms and Architectures for Parallel Processing: 20th International Conference, ICA3PP 2020, New York City, NY, USA, October 2–4, 2020, Proceedings, Part I 20, pp. 661–680. Springer (2020)
4. Becker, A., Ducas, L., Gama, N., Laarhoven, T.: New directions in nearest neighbor searching with applications to lattice sieving. In: Proceedings of the Twenty-seventh Annual ACM-SIAM Symposium on Discrete Algorithms, pp. 10–24. SIAM (2016)
5. Becker, A., Gama, N., Joux, A.: Speeding-up lattice sieving without increasing the memory, using sub-quadratic nearest neighbor search. Cryptology ePrint Archive (2015)
6. Ducas, L.: Shortest vector from lattice sieving: a few dimensions for free. In: Annual International Conference on the Theory and Applications of Cryptographic Techniques, pp. 125–145. Springer (2018)
7. Ducas, L., Stevens, M., van Woerden, W.: Advanced lattice sieving on GPUS, with tensor cores. In: Annual International Conference on the Theory and Applications of Cryptographic Techniques, pp. 249–279. Springer (2021)
8. Herold, G., Kirshanova, E.: Improved algorithms for the approximate k-list problem in Euclidean norm. In: IACR International Workshop on Public Key Cryptography, pp. 16–40. Springer (2017)
9. Ishiguro, T., Kiyomoto, S., Miyake, Y., Takagi, T.: Parallel gauss sieve algorithm: solving the SVP challenge over a 128-dimensional ideal lattice. In: Public-Key Cryptography—PKC 2014: 17th International Conference on Practice and Theory in Public-Key Cryptography, Buenos Aires, Argentina, March 26–28, 2014. Proceedings 17, pp. 411–428. Springer (2014)
10. Laarhoven, T.: Sieving for shortest vectors in lattices using angular locality-sensitive hashing. In: Advances in Cryptology–CRYPTO 2015: 35th Annual Cryptology Conference, Santa Barbara, CA, USA, August 16–20, 2015, Proceedings, Part I 35, pp. 3–22. Springer (2015)
11. Laarhoven, T., Mariano, A.: Progressive lattice sieving. In: International Conference on Post-Quantum Cryptography, pp. 292–311. Springer (2018)
12. Mariano, A., Bischof, C., Laarhoven, T.: Parallel (probable) lock-free hash sieve: a practical sieving algorithm for the SVP. In: 2015 44th International Conference on Parallel Processing, pp. 590–599. IEEE (2015)
13. Mariano, A., Laarhoven, T., Bischof, C.: A parallel variant of LDSIEVE for the SVP on lattices. In: 2017 25th Euromicro International Conference on Parallel, Distributed and Network-Based Processing (PDP), pp. 23–30. IEEE (2017)
14. Mariano, A., Timnat, S., Bischof, C.: Lock-free Gausssieve for linear speedups in parallel high performance SVP calculation. In: 2014 IEEE 26th International Symposium on Computer Architecture and High Performance Computing, pp. 278–285. IEEE (2014)

15. Micciancio, D., Voulgaris, P.: Faster exponential time algorithms for the shortest vector problem. In: Proceedings of the Twenty-first Annual ACM-SIAM Symposium on Discrete Algorithms, pp. 1468–1480. SIAM (2010)
16. Milde, B., Schneider, M.: A parallel implementation of Gausssieve for the shortest vector problem in lattices. In: Parallel Computing Technologies: 11th International Conference, PaCT 2011, Kazan, Russia, September 19–23, 2011. Proceedings 11, pp. 452–458. Springer (2011)
17. Nguyen, P.Q., Vidick, T.: Sieve algorithms for the shortest vector problem are practical. J. Math. Cryptol. **2**(2), 181–207 (2008)
18. Schneider, M., Gama, N.: Darmstadt SVP challenges, 2010 (2018)
19. Yang, S.Y., Kuo, P.C., Yang, B.Y., Cheng, C.M.: Gauss sieve algorithm on GPUS. In: Cryptographers Track at the RSA Conference, pp. 39–57. Springer (2017)

Unveiling the Efficacy of BERT's Attention in Memory Obfuscated Malware Detection

Md Mashrur Arifin⊙, Troy Suyehara Tolman⊙, and Jyh-haw Yeh(✉)⊙

Boise State Universitya,Boise, ID83725, USA
{mdmashrurarifin,troytolman483,jhyeh}@boisestate.edu

Abstract. The study addresses the challenge of detecting obfuscated malware, particularly memory-obfuscated variants, which evade conventional detection methods by targeting a system's volatile memory. By leveraging transformer-based models, notably BERT, the research demonstrates promising advancements in malware detection. Through data augmentation and rigorous feature selection processes, the study enhances the CIC-MlMem-2022 dataset, improving its quality for training classification models. Comparative analysis with conventional machine learning techniques highlights the superior performance of BERT and DistilBERT, achieving approximately 74% accuracy in classifying malware families. Notably, BERT exhibits exceptional capability in generalizing to unseen malware, achieving a remarkable 100% success rate in categorizing new families. These findings underscore the potential of transformer-based models for effectively detecting obfuscated malware, emphasizing the need for intelligent detection mechanisms in cybersecurity.

Keywords: BERT-based Models · Malware Detection · Memory Obfuscated Malware

1 Introduction

Malicious software that uses obfuscation to hide its presence to elude detection and removal attempts is known as obfuscated malware. To avoid being discovered by anti-malware software, malware developers use a variety of obfuscation strategies, including packing, identifier renaming, polymorphic code, etc. Detecting obfuscated malware poses a formidable challenge for cybersecurity experts [1]. Some of these obfuscation techniques can greatly decrease the accuracy of malware detection; for some malware families, the detection rate can even drop by as much as 50% [10]. One variation among the obfuscated malware is Memory-obfuscated malware, which deliberately targets a system's volatile memory, making it even harder to find using conventional static and dynamic analysis techniques [23]. In addition to capturing malware footprints, memory

Z. Xia and J. Chen (Eds.): ISPEC 2024, LNCS 15053, pp. 273–291, 2024.
https://doi.org/10.1007/978-981-97-9053-1_16

analysis also collects essential characteristics that can aid in revealing the concealed original code within disguised malware. In light of these circumstances, the development of an intelligent detection mechanism becomes imperative.

In recent years, BERT (Bidirectional Encoder Representations from Transformers) [9] has shown a lot of promise as a way to find malware compared to traditional machine learning and deep learning-based systems. This is for several important reasons. It's transformer-based architecture surpasses the capability of traditional approaches in learning intricate patterns from vast datasets [11]. Because of its attention mechanism, BERT can comprehend complex correlations between characteristics, which helps it recognize sophisticated virus patterns [20]. Furthermore, BERT's huge natural language corpus pre-training provides it with contextual and semantic knowledge that aids in malware detection. BERT also shows effectiveness at creating detailed feature representations for malware samples, which improves classification accuracy. Its versatility on many systems and efficiency in identifying malware that has been obfuscated serve to emphasize its supremacy even more [3].

Our study offers a comprehensive framework based on BERT-based models for identifying memory-obfuscated malware. The primary finding of our study is

- The proposed framework assesses the performance of transformer-based models for the first time in detecting memory-obfuscated malware. The assessment compared traditional machine learning techniques with transformer-based models, revealing that BERT and DistilBERT emerge as the top-performing models. In contrast, Roberta exhibits lower performance, indicating its potential limitations in this specific categorization task.
- Our research evaluates the models' ability to generalize to unseen malware, a critical aspect of malware detection. Impressively, BERT achieves a remarkable success rate in categorizing all collected malware samples from previously unseen families. Despite its lower performance in the initial model evaluation, RoBERTa exhibits improved classification performance on unseen data, which demands further future work.
- The research also emphasizes the importance of rigorous feature selection techniques in optimizing model performance and reducing the risk of overfitting. Through a two-step feature selection process involving the chi-square test and Recursive Feature Elimination (RFE) using logistic regression, the research identified the most essential features that were deemed ideal for model training. This meticulous approach to feature selection contributes to the overall effectiveness of the classification models.

2   Related Works

The detection of obfuscated malware is a persistent difficulty in the field of cybersecurity. Recent advancements in the battle against malware detection methods, such as efficient memory analysis-based detection systems, have been observed. Through our analysis of some recent research, We identified that attention-based models possess the potential to contribute to identifying memory-obfuscated malware knowledge gaps and motivate us to make appropriate contributions to this developing field.

Obfucated Malware Detection The problem of obfuscated memory malware identification in resource-constrained IoT devices for smart city applications was tackled by Shafin et al. [23], who suggested a lightweight multiclass malware detection technique appropriate for embedded device deployment. MeMalDet is a memory analysis-based malware detection system that was introduced by Maniriho et al. [17] It uses stacked ensemble learning and deep autoencoders to detect complex obfuscated malware that has never been seen before, with high accuracy and F1-score. To examine the influence of obfuscation changes on detection methodologies, Banescu et al. [4] created FEEBO, an empirical paradigm for testing malware detection resilience against behavior obfuscation. Their study proved the usefulness of this methodology. Targeting obfuscated Windows binary files, Treadwell and Zhou [27] suggested a heuristic detection strategy that relies on risk rating systems and static checks to stop harmful process execution. The ubiquity of obfuscation in contemporary malware and the demand for novel antimalware strategies that concentrate on malware behavior as opposed to its techniques were covered by O'Kane et al. [18]. Javaheri and Hosseinzadeh [12] presented a framework based on memory dumping and filter drivers for identifying and combating obfuscated malware with the goal of analyzing malware activities and identifying new threats.

Memory Analysis in Malware Detection Leveraging memory analysis, many researchers have suggested multiple methodologies to enhance the categorization and identification of malicious software. In their study, Dai et al. [8] proposed the conversion of malware memory dump files into grayscale photographs, which led to a notable increase in accuracy when compared to conventional approaches. Yucel et al. [30] investigated a system for mapping heat in three dimensions to speed up the classification of malware, whereas Kang et al. [13] proposed the use of vectoring assembly source code with LSTM (Long Short-Term Memory) to enhance accuracy. Aghaeikheirabady et al. [2] suggested transforming malware dump data into binary pictures to improve their comparability and detection. Siwail et al. [24] created a methodology that utilizes memory forensics to forecast future malware attributes. Case et al. [6] tackled Objective-C malware risks on MacOS X computers by developing a Volatility[1] plugin for automated analysis.

BERT as Malware Detector Research in the domain of malware classification has investigated the application of transformer-based models, specifically BERT, in identifying and categorizing malware samples. Alvares and Troia [3] examined the utilization of word embeddings produced by BERT for multi-class malware classification, showcasing its efficacy in comparison to Word2Vec. In order to detect evasive malware, Wang and Xu [28] suggested a novel method that combines binary opcode analysis with BERT. Malbert, a pre-trained deep learn-

---

[1] https://volatilityfoundation.org/.

ing model for dynamic analysis-based malware detection of Windows software, was presented by Xu et al. [29], underscoring the significance of pre-training for obtaining optimal performance. MalBERTv2, a BERT-based model for malware detection that uses natural language processing approaches to proactively detect malware threats, was introduced by Rahali and Akhloufi [20]. Furthermore, Rahali and Akhloufi [19] demonstrated the good performance of MalBERT, a model based on BERT, in the static analysis of Android applications. MalBERT is intended for the automatic identification of malicious software. Empirical research on the detection and classification of Android malware by Souani et al. [25] showed that BERT is effective in obtaining high accuracy in both tasks.

These studies showcase the potential of BERT-based models for malware detection. However, as far as we know, there is no evidence of the use of attention-based models in the field of memory-obfuscated malware detection. In our response, we propose an efficient framework that aims to classify memory-obfuscated malware by leveraging BERT's attention-based mechanism.

3   Model Description

Our study uses four main transformer-based language models, i.e. BERT, RoBERTa, DistilBERT, and Electra to classify malware. BERT is a fundamental transformer model that was first presented in 2018 [9]. It is well-known for its bidirectional encoding and contextual understanding abilities, which enable it to detect malicious behavior that may be concealed in written descriptions or code. In 2019, RoBERTa [16] is designed to improve the resilience of BERT by optimizing its training process. This makes RoBERTa especially suitable for tasks that require a high degree of performance consistency. Comparably, DistilBERT, which debuted in 2019 [22], provides a quicker and lighter substitute for BERT that is designed to be used on devices with limited resources. DistilBERT is a desirable option for applications that prioritize computational efficiency as, despite its smaller size, it frequently maintains performance parity with BERT. Electra, on the other hand, debuted in 2020 [7] and uses a unique generator-discriminator framework for training, which improves the model's capacity to differentiate between masked and real language-a critical feature for malware classification tasks.

These models collectively represent potent tools for comprehending complex textual data (Comparison shown in Table 1), leveraging their capacity to extract contextual cues and identify intricate patterns to classify malware, even those previously unseen. The study underscores the unique strengths of each model, while spotlighting BERT's exceptional performance in extrapolating to novel malware families, showcasing its versatility and efficacy in real-world cybersecurity applications.

Table 1. A comparative main architectural features of the BERT, RoBERTa, ELEC-TRA, and DistilBERT models

Feature/Models	BERT	RoBERTa	ELECTRA	DistilBERT
Transformer Layers	12	12	12	6
Attention Heads	12	12	12	12
Hidden Units	768	768	768	768
Model Size	Large	Large	Large	Smaller
Number of Parameters	110 million	355 million	110 million	66 million

4 Data Description

CIC-MalMem-2022 Dataset We have utilized the obfuscated malware dataset [5] in our work, which is used as a reference to assess memory-based obfuscated malware detection techniques in many previous research works. It incorporates common malware types like ransomware, trojan horses, and spyware to mimic real-world situations. This carefully chosen dataset provides a fair representation for evaluating how well obfuscated malware detection systems work. In order to preserve authenticity, the dataset uses debug mode when performing memory dumps, which stops dumping activity from being captured in memory dumps. By simulating the usual malware attack environment, this method more closely resembles the circumstances faced by regular users.

The dataset [5] consists of an equal distribution of 50% benign memory dumps and 50% malicious memory dumps as shown in Fig. 1, resulting in a balanced dataset. The dataset contains a range of malware families, which are specified in the figure, among other malicious samples. The dataset comprises a total of 58,596 records, evenly divided into 29,298 benign samples and 29,298 malicious samples.

5 Research Framework

The methodology of this research proposes a framework where BERT-based models provide a systematic way to detect memory-obfuscated malware. Our study primarily revolves around the six steps presented in Fig. 2. The six-step framework is given below.

Step-1: Data collection We obtained the CIC-MalMem-2022 dataset directly from the official website[2] and generated a new dataset by following the procedures illustrated in Fig. 4. The new dataset expands the scope of CIC-MalMem-2022 by incorporating more types of malware variations and families.

---

[2] https://www.unb.ca/cic/datasets/malmem-2022.html.

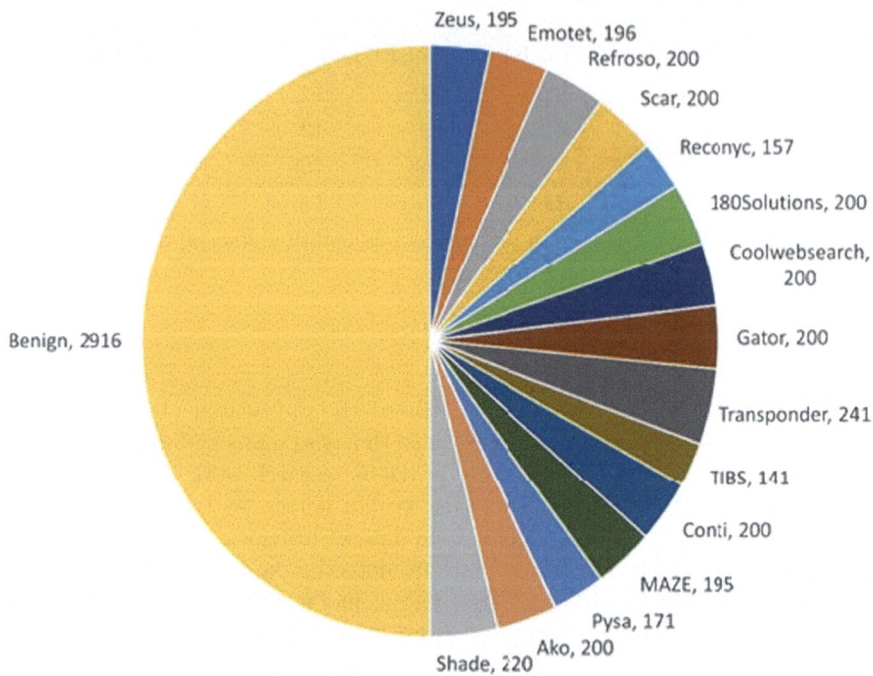

Fig. 1. Malware families in CIC-MalMem-2022 Dataset [5]

Step-2: Feature Selections Two methods were employed to identify the features: initially, the chi-square test [26] was used to determine the 40 most important features related to the target variable; Furthermore, once again, logistic regression and RFE were employed to select the top 40 most important features. By conducting a comparison of the feature sets obtained from both methods, we were able to achieve homogeneity. As a result, we identified the 25 most significant features that were utilized in the experiment. These features played a crucial role in reducing overfitting and providing reliable predictors for classification.

Step-3: Data Preprocessing We clean NaN values in the data as part of preprocessing. Originally labeled for binary classification, the dataset's 15 unique malware family types (shown in Fig. 1) were prepared for multiclass classification. We split the dataset into 70% for training and 30% for testing. Additionally, new data is labeled into 7 unique classes of malware (shown in Fig. 3).

Step-4: Model Training and Testing Four pre-trained transformer models (BERT, RoBERTa, DistilBERT, and Electra) are utilized for classification. The AdamW optimizer [14] is used to train the models over a predetermined number of epochs, and the models' performance is assessed on a testing set.

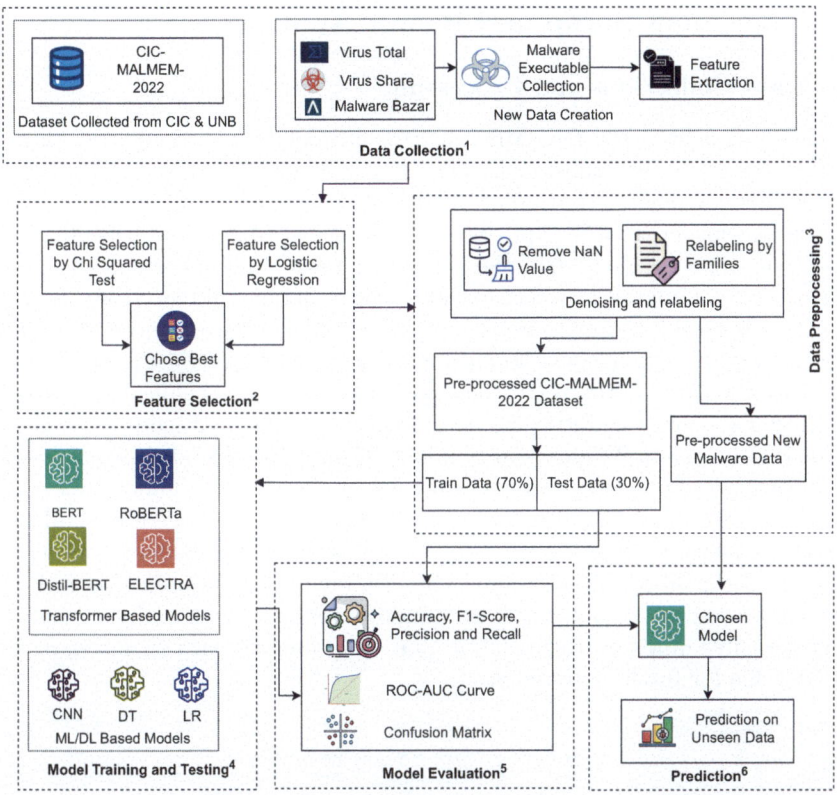

Fig. 2. Research Framework

Step-5: Model Evaluation The model's classification performance is assessed using evaluation metrics such as accuracy, precision, recall, and F1-score, along with the confusion matrix. The area under the curve (AUC) is another tool used to indicate the model, and ROC curves show how each model balances the true positive rate and false positive rate.

Step-6: Unseen Malware Prediction In step-4 and step-5, transformer-based models are trained and evaluated systematically for a multi-class classification task as part of the research procedure. In this step, we depend on the recommended pre-trained BERT-based model, chosen from Step-5, to conduct binary classification for predicting unknown malware on a new data set.

6   Experiment Setup and Result Analysis

6.1   Data Collections and Processing

We have augmented the CIC-MlMem-2022 dataset by collecting and extracting features from the malware families that are not included in the original dataset. The augmented portion of the dataset contains 7 new types of malware (bootkit, keylogger, rootkit, apt, botnet, worm, and bootsectorvirus) shown in Fig. 3 that were not present in the original dataset. Figure 4 shows the procedure of the data augmentation starts from collecting executables from the virus share,[3] virus total,[4] and malware bazaar.[5] We used the feature extractor module VolMemLyzer [15], a memory forensic tool designed based on the open-source tool named volatility, to create the expansion. Due to a challenge caused by Volatility 2's incompatibility with more recent versions of Windows, we had to use an ISO image of Windows 10 build 14393, which is found compatible with Volatility 2. We built image clones using VirtualBox to run malware tests in a separate sandbox environment. Every clone's memory was imaged by WinPmem memory imager and then exported to the host system. We extracted all 53 features out of the 56 from the original CIC-MalMem-2022 dataset; this variation happens because of the differences in Windows versions, VolMemLyzer was able to extract three different features. Later on, we preserved our new malware data in a CSV file for further operation.

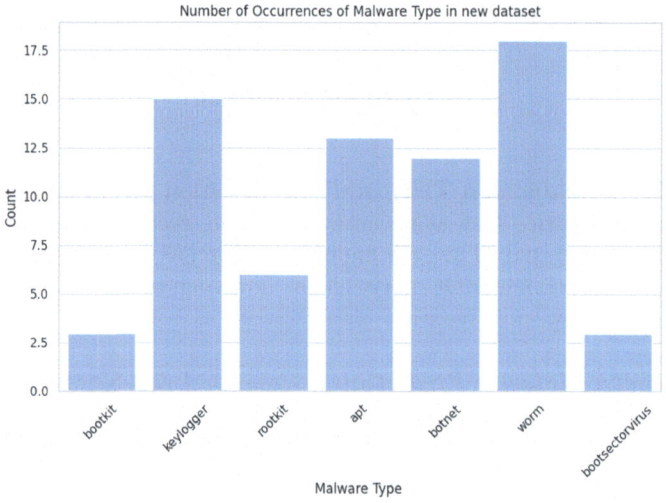

Fig. 3. New Malware Families

---

[3] https://www.virustotal.com/gui/home.
[4] https://virusshare.com/.
[5] https://bazaar.abuse.ch/.

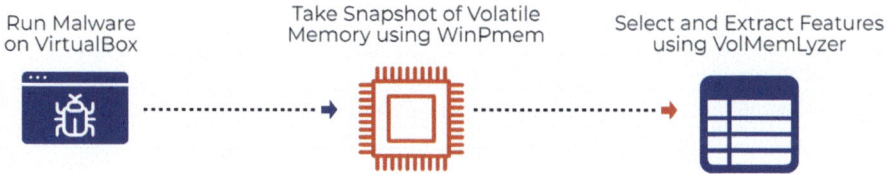

Run Malware on VirtualBox

Take Snapshot of Volatile Memory using WinPmem

Select and Extract Features using VolMemLyzer

Fig. 4. New Malware Data Creation Procedure

We denoised the dataset by removing the NaN values and relabeling them with the corresponding malware multi-classes. Next, training and testing sets are divided, with 70% of the data going to training and the rest of them for testing. We kept the newly created data separated from the training dataset as we plan to utilize them in the trained model as unseen malware and observe their classification performance.

6.2   Feature Description and Selection

We employed two techniques for feature selection: the chi-square test and recursive feature elimination (RFE) using logistic regression. Initially, the chi-square test was used to determine the 40 most significant features related to the target variable

This statistical test assesses the degree of independence between each feature and the target variable, identifying the ones that exhibit the most robust relationships. Secondly, the feature set was further refined using logistic regression and RFE. In this instance, the most informative subset is retained through the use of logistic regression as a classifier by rating the significance of features iteratively. Finally, To guarantee uniformity between the selection processes, the final features derived from comparing the two approaches, and selecting the common features were found. We found a total of 25 features common to both procedures, which is shown in Table 2. We selected the features carefully to avoid model overfitting and to improve the accuracy of the malware classification process.

6.3   Model Training and Testing

Model training was performed by initializing four distinct pre-trained transformer-based models—BERT, RoBERTa, DistilBERT, and Electra. Model-specific tokenization techniques were used to encode textual features into input IDs and attention masks for each. These models each used unique preprocessing functions that were designed to fit their unique architectures. Subsequently, DataLoader objects are generated for training and testing sets, enabling effective batch-wise data processing for model training and testing. The training of each model is conducted using the AdamW optimizer, with a learning rate of 2×10^{-5} and an epsilon value of 1×10^{-8}. In addition, to modify the learning rate during training, a linear scheduler with warmup stages is employed. Each

Table 2. Selected Feature Description

Feature names	Description
handles.nfile	Number of file handles
handles.nsemaphore	Number of semaphore handles
handles.nkey	Number of registry key handles
handles.nhandles	Total number of handles
handles.ntimer	Number of timer handles
handles.nsection	Number of section handles
svcscan.kernel_drivers	Number of kernel drivers
ldrmodules.not_in_load	Number of modules not in load
modules.nmodules	Number of loaded modules
handles.nevent	Number of event handles
handles.ndesktop	Number of desktop handles
malfind.protection	Protection of suspicious memory regions
pslist.avg_handlers	Average number of handles per process
handles.ndirectory	Number of directory handles
pslist.nproc	Number of processes
handles.avg_handles_per_proc	Average number of handles per process
ldrmodules.not_in_mem	Number of modules not in memory
svcscan.nservices	Number of services
handles.nmutant	Number of mutant handles
dlllist.ndlls	Number of DLLs
svcscan.nactive	Number of active services
callbacks.ncallbacks	Number of registered callbacks
malfind.commitCharge	Commit charge of suspicious memory regions
handles.nthread	Number of thread handles
svcscan.shared_process_services	Shared process services

epoch is iterated over by the training loop, during which the model is configured to training mode and trained on batches of input data. The model's parameters are changed in accordance with the calculated loss and backpropagation. The models are assessed on a different test dataset after training.

6.4   Model Evaluation and Prediction

The evaluation procedure begins by gathering both true and expected labels, applying inference to batches of test data, and computing predictions using the trained models. Evaluation metrics that give information about how well the model classifies the data are computed, including accuracy, precision, recall, and F1-score. The area under the curve (AUC) is used as a model indicator, and receiver operating characteristic (ROC) curves are also plotted to show the trade-off between true positive rate and false positive rate for each model. While precision (Eq. 2) measures the ratio of true positive predictions to all predicted positives, accuracy (Eq. 1) measures how accurate the model is overall. We also measured recall (Eq. 3) alternatively referred to as sensitivity formulated by the ratio of true positive predictions to actual positives in the dataset. The F1 score (Eq. 4) offers a fair evaluation of the model's performance and is calculated as the harmonic mean of precision and recall. The transformer-based models' performance is compared to one another in order to create a baseline for comparison. Furthermore, we performed a comparison with the performance of some conventional machine learning algorithms such as Convolutional Neural Networks (CNN), Decision Tree (DT), and Logistic Regression (LR) to evaluate how well transformer models perform for the memory-obfuscated malware classification task.

$$\text{Accuracy} = \frac{\text{Number of Correct Predictions}}{\text{Total Number of Predictions}} \tag{1}$$

$$\text{Precision} = \frac{\text{True Positive (TP)}}{\text{True Positive (TP) + False Positive (FP)}} \tag{2}$$

$$\text{Recall} = \frac{\text{True Positive (TP)}}{\text{True Positive (TP) + False Negative (FN)}} \tag{3}$$

$$F1\text{-score} = \frac{2 \times (\text{Precision} \times \text{Recall})}{\text{Precision} + \text{Recall}} \tag{4}$$

6.5   Result Analysis

Result from model evaluation The model evaluation results shown in Table 3 demonstrate clear performance distinctions among the four models: BERT, RoBERTa, Electra, and DistilBERT. With an overall accuracy of 74%, BERT and DistilBERT are the most accurate, closely followed by Electra at 73%, and RoBERTa at 61%. BERT and DistilBERT perform similarly in terms of the macro F1-score, circling around 0.74 to indicate strong overall classification performance. With an F1-score of 0.59, RoBERTa performs noticeably worse than Electra, which comes in second with a slightly lower F1-score of 0.73. In every metric, RoBERTa consistently performs worse than the other three BERT-based models.

Interesting insights are revealed by comparing the training behavior and evaluation metrics. BERT demonstrates a stable reduction in training loss over epochs shown in Fig. 5, suggesting efficient learning, in addition to excellent evaluation metrics, such as 74.06% accuracy and 73.90% F1 score. As shown in Table 3, DistilBERT's performance is almost identical to BERT's, indicating similar effectiveness. DistilBERT is an effective distilled version of BERT because, in spite of its smaller size and simpler architecture, it achieves similar evaluation metrics to BERT. While showing a less declining trend in training loss, RoBERTa performs worse than the other models in terms of evaluation metrics, including accuracy, precision, recall, and F1 score.

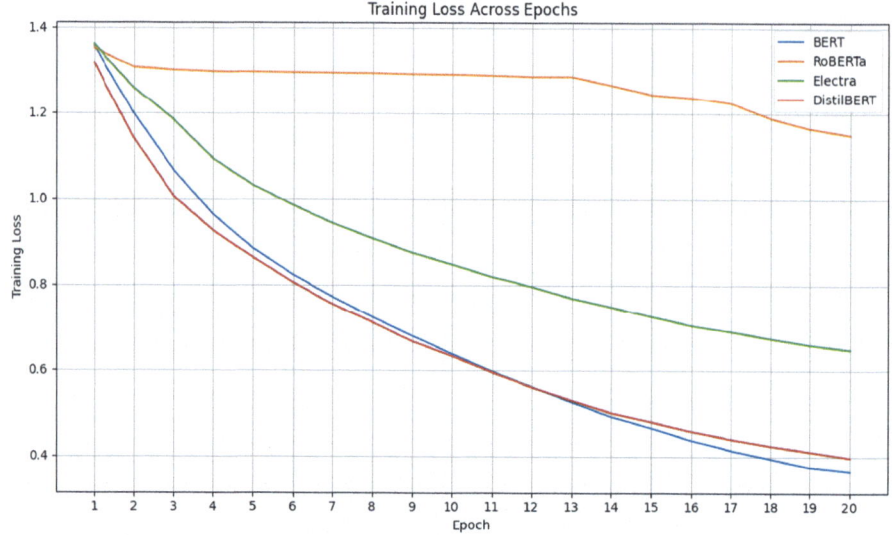

Fig. 5. Training Loss Across epoch

Confusion matrices shown in Figs. 6 and 7 reveal how well the models are able to categorize instances into various classes. Compared to RoBERTa and Electra, BERT and DistilBERT exhibit more evenly distributed predictions across classes, suggesting superior generalization. All models perform well when it comes to classifying "benignware," the majority class, but they have trouble with minority classes.

ROC AUC values shed light on how well the models rank classes. With ROC AUC values ranging from 0.65 to 0.72 shown in Fig. 8, BERT and DistilBERT perform moderately well; in contrast, RoBERTa shows comparatively better class separation with a value of roughly 0.72. Electra's ROC AUC of roughly 0.68 places it in the middle.

To sum up, BERT and DistilBERT demonstrate strong overall performance and evenly distributed predictions among the classes, making them the best algorithms for this classification task. However, RoBERTa continuously performs worse than expected on all metrics, indicating that it might not be the best option for our malware classification task. We also found that BERT, Electra and RoBERTa perform better than two baseline models MalHyStack [21] and RobustCBL [23] shown in Table 3.

Table 3. Model Evaluation Result

Types	Models				Metrics
		Accuracy	Precision	Recall	F1 Score
BERT Based Models	BERT	0.7406	0.7397	0.7406	0.7390
	RoBERTa	0.6136	0.6593	0.6136	0.5930
	Electra	0.7283	0.7282	0.7283	0.7240
	DistilBERT	0.7422	0.7421	0.7422	0.740
Other Models	CNN	0.7244	0.7277	0.7244	0.7190
	Decision Tree	0.7381	0.5141	0.5182	0.5159
	Logistic Regression	0.6115	0.3664	0.2664	0.2563
Baseline Models	MalHyStack [21]	0.6694	0.6694	0.6856	0.6671
	RobustCBL [23]	0.7260	0.7300	0.7300	0.7200

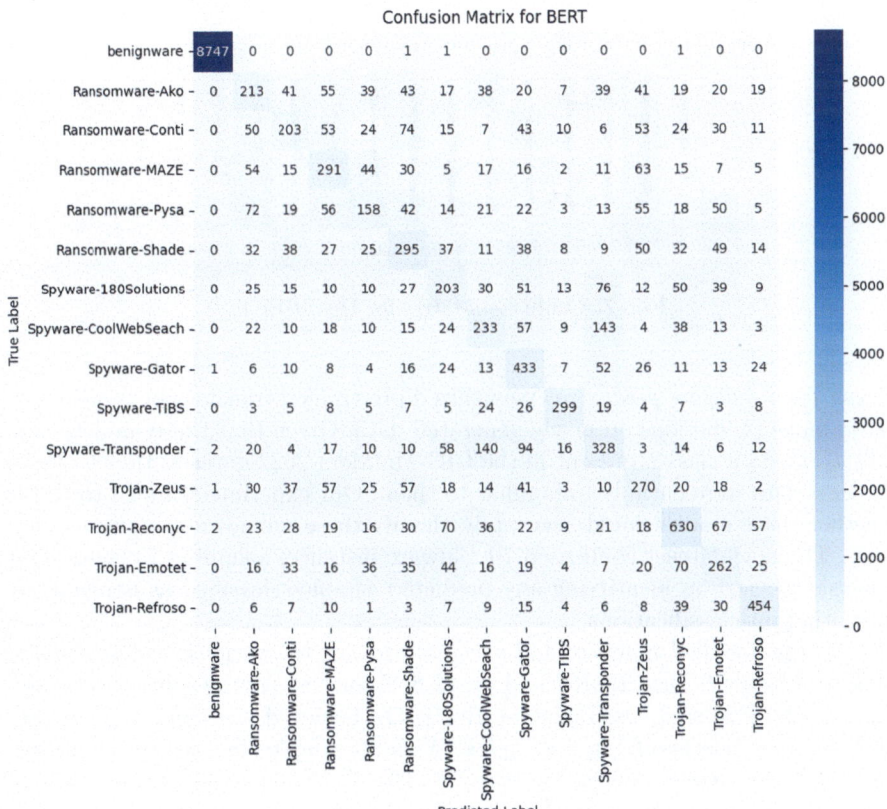

Fig. 6. Confusion Matrix for BERT

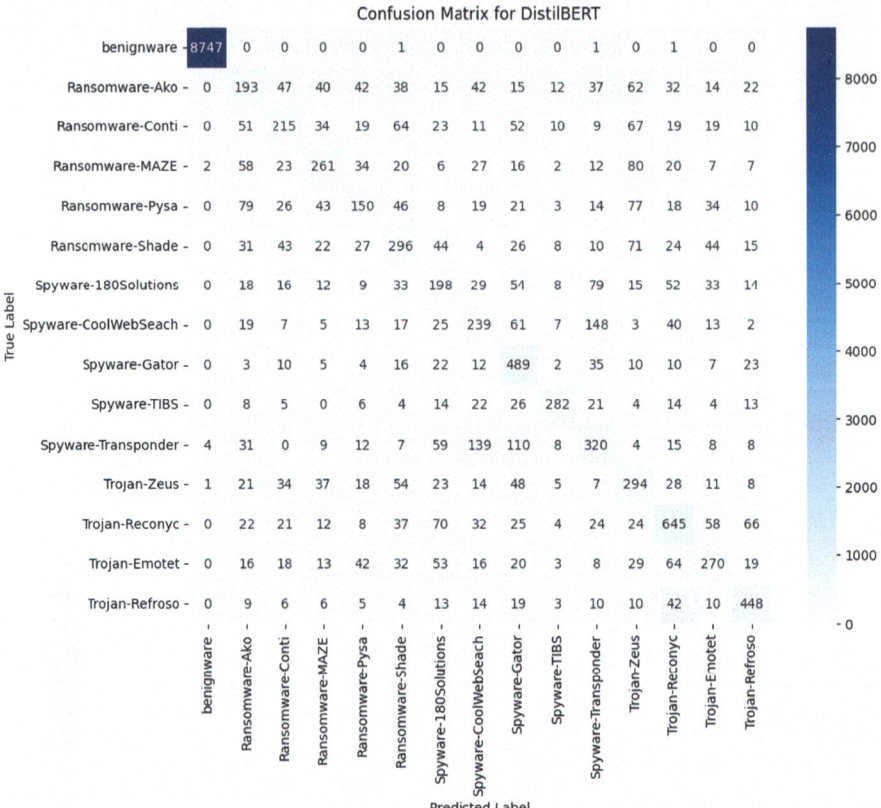

Fig. 7. Confusion Matrix for DistilBERT

Result from malware prediction We utilized pre-trained transformer-based models to make predictions on newly generated data. Given that these models were only trained on classes present in the CIC-MalMem-2022 dataset, the classes in the new data were entirely unfamiliar to them. Our experiment aimed to assess whether these models could accurately classify these unknown samples as malware. The new dataset comprised 70 malware instances spanning 7 classes. Our analysis focused on identifying any predicted samples classified as benignware, indicating misclassifications.

The misclassified malware and success rates for the various models are displayed in Table 4. DistilBERT had an 82.86% success rate despite misclassifying 12 out of 70 samples. Likewise, RoBERTa achieved a greater success rate of 92.86% by misclassifying 5 samples. With 16 samples incorrectly identified, ELECTRA's success percentage was 77.14%. With a perfect success rate of 100%, BERT scored the highest success rate by properly identifying all 70 samples.

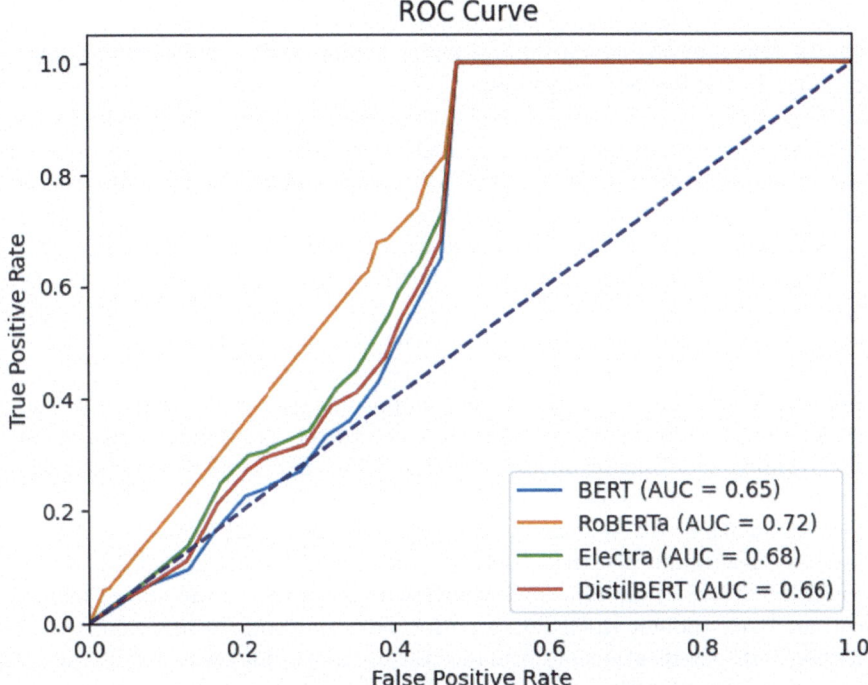

Fig. 8. ROC-AUC curve

Table 4. Prediction on Unseen Malware

Models	Misclassified Samples	Success Rate
DistilBERT	12/70	82.86%
RoBERTa	5/70	92.86%
ELECTRA	16/70	77.14%
BERT	0/70	100%

7   Outcome and Discussion

Data Augmentation and Feature Selection The primary outcome of our research is the framework that effectively investigates transformer-based models' performance for identifying the memory-obfuscated malware, especially malware from families that are unseen to the model. Another outcome of our study is we have added additional malware families in the CIC-MlMem-2022 dataset, which improves the dataset's quality and usefulness for training classification models. Additionally, we used a rigorous two-step feature selection process to guarantee the models' effectiveness and reduce the possibility of overfitting. The most relevant features were first determined using the chi-square test and

Recursive feature elimination using logistic regression was then used to further refine the selection process and produce a collection of 25 essential features that were judged ideal for model training.

Model Performance Regarding the model performance, we compared conventional machine learning techniques (CNN, Decision Tree, Logistic Regression) with four pre-trained transformer models (BERT, RoBERTa, DistilBERT, Electra), as shown in Table 3. The top two models were BERT and DistilBERT, which classified malware families in the CIC-MalMem-2022 dataset with an accuracy of approximately 74%. RoBERTa's total accuracy was lower at 61%, indicating that it may not be as suitable for this particular categorization task.

Generalization to Unseen Malware One important assessment was to see how well the models could classify malware from completely new families that weren't in the training set. This evaluation measured the models' ability to generalize their knowledge to unknown malware. It's interesting to note that BERT accomplished an amazing achievement by correctly categorizing all 70 malware samples from these new families with a 100% success rate. Both Electra (77.14%) and DistilBERT (82.86%) did remarkably well, with a reasonable amount of misclassification. Even though RoBERTa's performance in model evaluation was not satisfying but classification performance on unknown data was better than its total performance (92.86% success rate).

8   Limitation and Future Work

Transformer-based models have complex structures and require large amounts of computing power to train and optimize. However, once trained, these models are applicable and scalable to a wide range of lightweight systems. Even with these benefits, our research notes that there is still room for improvement in terms of model performance through hyperparameter tuning. For example, tuning the *batch size, maximum length of the input string* and *number of epochs* can produce different results for the four BERT-based models. Furthermore, the sample size of unknown malware utilized in our study is limited. However, we are confident that future efforts can be made with a larger number of samples that will reveal more concrete findings.

Furthermore, our research acknowledges the constraints resulting from the limited sample size used in prediction studies. Future efforts will attempt to rectify this by adding to the dataset a larger set of new malware samples, which will enable a more thorough examination. Furthermore, in addition to BERT-based models, a variety of other transformer-based architectures, such GPT-2, have the ability to detect malware that has been obfuscated with memory, therefore they should be further researched and tested in future studies.

9 Conclusion

In conclusion, this study demonstrates the effectiveness of transformer-based models in memory-obfuscated malware classification, especially when it comes to recognizing malware families that are not familiar to the model. The outcomes demonstrate how much better transformer models—particularly BERT-are than more conventional machine learning techniques. By correctly categorizing new malware samples, BERT showed off its remarkable generalization abilities. On unseen data, DistilBERT and Electra also performed well, suggesting that they have promise for use in real-world cybersecurity applications. Subsequent investigations may concentrate on refining transformer models, for example enhancing RoBERTa's performance against different metrics and observing how it behaves with unknown data. In summary, this study highlights the importance of transformer models in creating effective malware classification systems that can adjust to changing online threats. Researchers can learn a great deal about the efficacy of various models and tokenization strategies by methodically examining performance metrics and model outputs. This knowledge can subsequently be utilized in future research endeavors and optimization tactics.

References

1. Aboaoja, F.A., Zainal, A., Ghaleb, F.A., Al-Rimy, B.A.S., Eisa, T.A.E., Elnour, A.A.H.: Malware detection issues, challenges, and future directions: a survey. Appl. Sci. **12**(17), 8482 (2022). https://doi.org/10.3390/app12178482
2. Aghaeikheirabady, M., Farshchi, S.M.R., Shirazi, H.: A new approach to malware detection by comparative analysis of data structures in a memory image. In: 2014 International Congress on Technology, Communication and Knowledge (ICTCK), pp. 1–4. IEEE (2014). https://doi.org/10.1109/ICTCK.2014.7033519
3. Alvares, J., Troia, F.D.: Bert for malware classification. In: Artificial Intelligence for Cybersecurity, pp. 161–181. Springer (2022). https://doi.org/10.1007/978-3-030-97087-1_7
4. Banescu, S., Wuchner, T., Salem, A., Guggenmos, M., Ochoa, M., Pretschner, A.: A framework for empirical evaluation of malware detection resilience against behavior obfuscation. In: 2015 10th International Conference on Malicious and Unwanted Software (MALWARE), pp. 40–47. IEEE (2015). https://doi.org/10.1109/MALWARE.2015.7413683
5. Carrier, T., Victor, P., Tekeoglu, A., Lashkari, A.H.: Detecting obfuscated malware using memory feature engineering. In: ICISSP, pp. 177–188 (2022). https://doi.org/10.5220/0010908200003120
6. Case, A., Richard, G.G., III.: Detecting objective-c malware through memory forensics. Digit. Investig. **18**, S3–S10 (2016). https://doi.org/10.1016/j.diin.2016.04.017
7. Clark, K., Luong, M.T., Le, Q.V., Manning, C.D.: Electra: pre-training text encoders as discriminators rather than generators (2020). arXiv:2003.10555
8. Dai, Y., Li, H., Qian, Y., Lu, X.: A malware classification method based on memory dump grayscale image. Digit. Investig. **27**, 30–37 (2018). https://doi.org/10.1016/j.diin.2018.09.006

9. Devlin, J., Chang, M.W., Lee, K., Toutanova, K.: Bert: pre-training of deep bidirectional transformers for language understanding (2018). arXiv:1810.04805

10. Elsersy, W.F., Feizollah, A., Anuar, N.B.: The rise of obfuscated android malware and impacts on detection methods. PeerJ Comput. Sci. **8**, e907 (2022). https://doi.org/10.7717/peerj-cs.907

11. Ferrag, M.A., Ndhlovu, M., Tihanyi, N., Cordeiro, L.C., Debbah, M., Lestable, T., Thandi, N.S.: Revolutionizing cyber threat detection with large language models: a privacy-preserving Bert-based lightweight model for IoT/IIoT devices. IEEE Access (2024). https://doi.org/10.1109/ACCESS.2024.3363469

12. Javaheri, D., Hosseinzadeh, M.: A framework for recognition and confronting of obfuscated malwares based on memory dumping and filter drivers. Wireless Pers. Commun. **98**, 119–137 (2018). https://doi.org/10.1007/s11277-017-4859-y

13. Kang, J., Jang, S., Li, S., Jeong, Y.S., Sung, Y.: Long short-term memory-based malware classification method for information security. Comput. Electr. Eng. **77**, 366–375 (2019). https://doi.org/10.1016/j.compeleceng.2019.06.014

14. Kingma, D.P., Ba, J.: Adam: a method for stochastic optimization (2014). arXiv:1412.6980

15. Lashkari, A.H., Li, B., Carrier, T.L., Kaur, G.: Volmemlyzer: volatile memory analyzer for malware classification using feature engineering. In: 2021 Reconciling Data Analytics, Automation, Privacy, and Security: A Big Data Challenge (RDAAPS), pp. 1–8. IEEE (2021). https://doi.org/10.1109/RDAAPS48126.2021.9452028

16. Liu, Y., et al.: Roberta: a robustly optimized Bert pretraining approach (2019). arXiv:1907.11692

17. Maniriho, P., Mahmood, A.N., Chowdhury, M.J.M.: Memaldet: a memory analysis-based malware detection framework using deep autoencoders and stacked ensemble under temporal evaluations. Comput. Secur. **142**, 103864 (2024). https://doi.org/10.1016/j.cose.2024.103864

18. O'Kane, P., Sezer, S., McLaughlin, K.: Obfuscation: the hidden malware. IEEE Secur. Privacy **9**(5), 41–47 (2011). https://doi.org/10.1109/MSP.2011.98

19. Rahali, A., Akhloufi, M.A.: Malbert: malware detection using bidirectional encoder representations from transformers. In: 2021 IEEE International Conference on Systems, Man, and Cybernetics (SMC), pp. 3226–3231. IEEE (2021). https://doi.org/10.1109/SMC52423.2021.9659287

20. Rahali, A., Akhloufi, M.A.: Malbertv2: code aware Bert-based model for malware identification. Big Data Cogn. Comput. **7**(2), 60 (2023). https://doi.org/10.3390/bdcc7020060

21. Roy, K.S., Ahmed, T., Udas, P.B., Karim, M.E., Majumdar, S.: Malhystack: a hybrid stacked ensemble learning framework with feature engineering schemes for obfuscated malware analysis. Intell. Syst. Appl. **20**, 200283 (2023). https://doi.org/10.1016/j.iswa.2023.200283

22. Sanh, V., Debut, L., Chaumond, J., Wolf, T.: Distilbert, a distilled version of Bert: smaller, faster, cheaper and lighter (2019). arXiv:1910.01108

23. Shafin, S.S., Karmakar, G., Mareels, I.: Obfuscated memory malware detection in resource-constrained IoT devices for smart city applications. Sensors **23**(11), 5348 (2023). https://doi.org/10.3390/s23115348

24. Sihwail, R., Omar, K., Zainol Ariffin, K.A., Al Afghani, S.: Malware detection approach based on artifacts in memory image and dynamic analysis. Appl. Sci. **9**(18), 3680 (2019). https://doi.org/10.3390/app9183680

25. Souani, B., Khanfir, A., Bartel, A., Allix, K., Le Traon, Y.: Android malware detection using Bert. In: International Conference on Applied Cryptography and

Network Security, pp. 575–591. Springer (2022). https://doi.org/10.1007/978-3-031-16815-4_31

26. Tallarida, R.J., Murray, R.B., Tallarida, R.J., Murray, R.B.: Chi-square test. Manual of pharmacologic calculations: with computer programs, pp. 140–142 (1987)

27. Treadwell, S., Zhou, M.: A heuristic approach for detection of obfuscated malware. In: 2009 IEEE International Conference on Intelligence and Security Informatics, pp. 291–299. IEEE (2009). https://doi.org/10.1109/ISI.2009.5137328

28. Wang, S., Xu, B.: A novel approach of evasive malware analysis through binary opcode and Bert. Research Square (2024). https://doi.org/10.21203/rs.3.rs-3840848/v1

29. Xu, Z., Fang, X., Yang, G.: Malbert: a novel pre-training method for malware detection. Comput. Secur. **111**, 102458 (2021). https://doi.org/10.1016/j.cose.2021.102458

30. Yücel, Ç., Koltuksuz, A.: Imaging and evaluating the memory access for malware. For. Sci. Int. Dig. Investigation **32**, 200903 (2020). https://doi.org/10.1016/j.fsidi.2019.200903

An eID-Based Privacy-Enhanced Public Transportation Ticket System

Kanagaratnam Anojjan[1], Weizhi Meng[1,2(✉)], Brooke Kidmose[1], and Yu Wang[3]

[1] SPTAGE Lab, Technical University of Denmark, Kgs. Lyngby 2800, Denmark
`weizhi.meng@ieee.org`
[2] School of Computing and Communications, Lancaster University, Lancaster, UK
[3] Institute of Artificial Intelligence and Blockchain, Guangzhou University, Guangzhou, China

Abstract. The electronic ticketing (e-ticketing) network system has been widely adopted in many countries, offering numerous benefits to public transport authorities and their customers. These benefits include fast and compatible verification processes and mechanisms for replacing lost tickets. Additionally, the system provides security against forgery through cryptographic mechanisms. Most e-ticketing systems use RFID technology to facilitate authentication. RFID-based authentication publishes customer-related sensitive information—e.g., customer location—as temporary data. RFID alone does not adequately address privacy concerns. In this work, we discuss the relevant privacy and security requirements of existing e-ticketing systems and introduce an eID protocol designed to create a privacy-enhanced framework.

Keywords: E-ticketing System · Train Ticket · Privacy Preserving · Public Transport Authority · Trusted Third Party

1 Introduction

In the modern world, ticketing in the public transit sector has increasingly moved towards electronic ticketing (e-ticketing). E-tickets offer numerous benefits to both customers and public transport authorities, though they also come with certain risks [4,5]. From the public transport authority's perspective, e-tickets help reduce maintenance costs and are harder to counterfeit due to cryptographic techniques. From the customer's perspective, e-ticketing is generally automated, allowing one e-ticket to be used multiple times. The digital nature of the system provides various settings, enabling customers to save time and select fares according to their preferences [38]. Additionally, if an e-ticket is lost or damaged, it can be reclaimed with the balance intact.

However, there are also risks, particularly concerning customer privacy. When purchasing an e-ticket, customers may need to provide personal information such as their name, address, and date of birth [14]. Due to the manner in which e-ticketing systems normally operate, this sensitive information could be accessible to various parties—including unauthorized parties—if not properly secured.

These unauthorized parties could misuse the customer's information, potentially harming both the ticketing system and legitimate customers, for example, by cloning a legitimate customer's e-ticket. Additionally, some customers want to ensure that their personal information, such as travel patterns, remains private [36]. There are also protocol-related issues, as certain protocols may facilitate attacks on the e-ticketing system, like replay attacks or man-in-the-middle (MITM) attacks. In this work, we aim to explore the relationship between security and customer privacy and discuss how these aspects can be integrated into a single digital system.

Motivation. Today, most e-ticketing systems for public transport are considered part of smart transportation systems, a consequence of ubiquitous computing [20]. The front-end of these e-ticketing systems primarily relies on RFID/NFC technologies. Such systems are already in use worldwide, especially in major cities, including the Oyster system in London [2], the EZ-link system in Singapore [1], and the Rejsekort system in Denmark [3]. Additionally, advancements in mobile technology now allow for valid e-ticket verification through smartphones equipped with NFC technology [15]. This progress has created a new platform for e-ticketing in public transport, making these systems an even more integral part of ubiquitous computing.

The increasing adoption of smart e-ticketing systems for public transport brings various benefits but also raises concerns about customer privacy. Using NFC technology-based e-tickets, whether through smart cards or smartphones, significantly increases the digital traces left by customers, potentially exposing sensitive information [38]. Without privacy protection techniques or mechanisms, this could become a major issue [19]. Currently, this vulnerability has not been fully addressed; many proposed solutions are either supplementary suggestions or too complex to integrate into real systems [27,28]. Additionally, privacy protection involves significant trade-offs between security and efficiency, posing challenges for system implementation. Moreover, many modern solutions exclude—and even preclude—key features of e-ticket systems for public transportation [6,36]. Despite these challenges, e-ticket systems offer advantages such as sophisticated billing options, ease of use, and flexible pricing schemes. Therefore, effective privacy solutions are crucial to adequately protect public transport e-ticketing systems.

Related work. With the rapid development of e-ticketing systems, customer privacy has garnered significant attention from both academia and industry. In the literature, Sadeghi et al. [36] highlighted early concerns about privacy, noting that most privacy-preserving RFID schemes are unsuitable for e-tickets. They subsequently introduced a privacy-preserving e-ticket system based on established cryptographic techniques and RFID. Kerschbaum et al. [19] analyzed the privacy issues of Singapore's EZ-Link system, demonstrating how easily a customer's travel records could be obtained. They then proposed a comprehensive privacy-preserving scheme based on partially homomorphic encryption.

Gudymenko [13,14] proposed a privacy-preserving framework for public transportation systems that supports sophisticated billing. Chu et al. [12] developed a scheme which enhanced ticket transparency and provided accountable single sign-on services with privacy-preserving public logs. This scheme leveraged blind signatures, identity-based encryption, and Bloom filters to counteract fraudulent tickets. Han et al. [16] introduced a privacy-preserving electronic ticket scheme with attribute-based credentials to prevent double-spending of tickets. Recently, blockchain technology has also been explored as a privacy-preserving solution for e-ticketing [9,10] and data sharing [11]. However, most existing studies do not define a concrete attack model and lack a practical background, motivating our work.

Contributions. The main goal of this work is to enhance the existing infrastructure proposed by Gudymenko et al. [13,14] for an e-ticketing system based on loosely coupled, privacy-preserving architecture, which supports local validation of e-tickets and sophisticated billing operations. A loosely coupled design allows terminals to perform check-in and check-out processes at the front-end without needing to contact the back-end. This is crucial for the practical applicability of an e-ticketing system across a wide area. **The main contribution** of this work is the development of an eID protocol with a trusted third party (TTP) to create a privacy-enhanced framework for e-ticketing systems. This framework addresses privacy-related issues, and the framework implementation is explained in detail.

Organization. The remainder of this paper is organized as follows: Sect. 2 introduces the background on e-ticketing systems with two real-world examples. Section 3 describes the threat model and core privacy requirements for e-ticketing systems. Section 4 outlines the existing privacy-preserving framework in the literature. In Sect. 5, we explain the proposed eID protocol, step by step. We discuss the advantages and disadvantages of the protocol—as well as strategies to ameliorate the disadvantages— in Sect. 6. Finally, we conclude this work in Sect. 7.

2   Background on E-Ticketing Systems

Figure 1 depicts a global framework of e-ticketing system for public transportation. There are four main elements—the public transport authority (PTA), a customer, a reader for check-in and a reader for check-out. It is worth noting that PTA can participate several sub-components (e.g., processing computers, database, etc.). When customers—or components—communicate with the PTA, they have to communicate with some of its sub-components. Sub-components can usually communicate with each other.

The specific details depend on the design, but generally, using an e-ticketing system involves the following steps: (1) a customer requests an e-ticket and provides some personal information to the PTA, then (2) the e-ticket is then issued to the customer and registered in the system. Once the ticket is loaded with a balance, it can be used, and its holder is recognized as a legitimate, authorized customer.

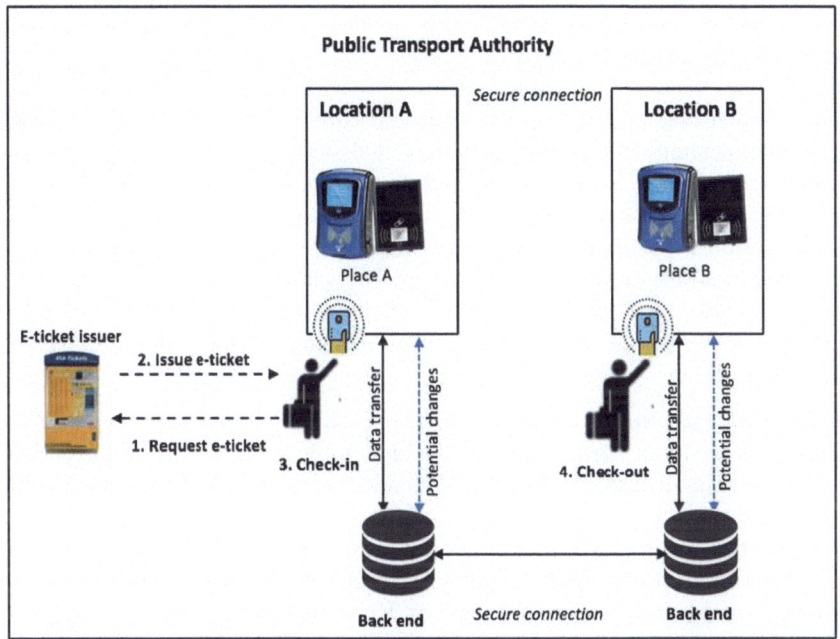

Fig. 1. General e-ticketing system.

If a customer wants to travel from place A to place B, she must first complete the check-in procedure. This involves touching her e-ticket to the check-in reader (terminal) at place A. Typically, this communication is facilitated by RFID (Radio Frequency Identification) and NFC (Near Field Communication) technologies, with the e-ticket (which could be a smartphone or a plastic card) acting as a transponder and the reader device functioning as a transceiver.

E-ticket validation occurs during check-in, where specific conditions must be met for a successful validation. At the end of the journey, the customer checks out by establishing communication between her e-ticket and a check-out reader at place B. Successful check-out is contingent upon meeting certain conditions. The fare for the journey is calculated based on predefined rules, typically involving factors such as distance, fares, and the type of e-ticket used. Throughout usage, check-in/out readers communicate with the back-end system to transfer data from travelers' e-tickets and potentially update the readers' memory.

Below we introduce two real examples of existing e-ticketing systems: the Rejsekort system and the EZ-link system.

The Rejsekort system. The Rejsekort system [3] serves as Denmark's primary e-ticketing system, comprising three interconnected components: a customer's card (the e-ticket), a reader (used for check-in or check-out at terminals), and a back-end node. A customer initiates communication with the system by presenting his card to a reader, which, if equipped with valid read and write keys, can both write data to and read data from the customer's card. The card functions as a memory card, storing unencrypted data about the customer's journeys along with a digital signature and additional parameters (such as details of inspection checks) for communication with the system. Calculations are performed by the reader for two reasons: to reduce card costs (as a more advanced chip would be more expensive) and to meet operational time constraints set by Rejsekort (e.g., check-in should take approximately 200–300 milliseconds). At intervals, the reader sends the data read from different cards to the back-end system. Essentially, the back-end node is responsible for organizing journeys from various transactions, storing data, and verifying it for accuracy and potential fraud. The Rejsekort solution prioritizes efficiency and security, albeit at the expense of privacy protection. It is evident that the security aspect heavily relies on the non-anonymous structure of the system (i.e., processing detailed, non-anonymized, unencrypted data).

The EZ-link system. The EZ-link card [1], introduced in Singapore in 2001, is a contactless payment card primarily used for public transportation fares. Additionally, it can be utilized for Electronic Road Pricing (ERP), Electronic Parking System (EPS), printing and photocopying services, payment at selected food and beverage outlets, shopping and retail outlets, vending machines, among other services. There are over eight million cards in circulation, and each card can store up to 500 SGD and has a lifespan of five years. Until September 2017, the EZ-Online service allowed passengers to view their card details, including the most recent 30 transactions (travel records), and download discount coupons onto their cards.

Kerschbaum et al. [19] then conducted a study to investigate if a CEPAS-compliant EZ-Link card leaked any sensitive or personal information related to the card owner during real top-up transactions. They used USBlyzer to intercept messages transmitted between the reader and the PC, and Wireshark to intercept messages between the PC and the EZ-Link server. They discovered that travelers' information is transmitted as plain text from the reader to the PC (and vice versa0, making it possible to trace someone's records. For instance, by carrying an EZ-Link reader and walking close enough to an EZ-Link card, one can retrieve the target's recent travel records without their knowledge in less than a second. The retention of past transaction records serves the purpose of fraud detection; for instance, the records can be used to authenticate the card by ensuring that the data matches that stored in the database.

3   Threat Model and Core Privacy Requirements

In an e-ticketing system, privacy protection encompass all system components and account for both the system itself and any external entities (e.g., third parties). In this work, similar to prior work [13,14], we consider the following attack models:

- **External observers (outsider).** Able to listen to communication between tickets and terminals.
- **Terminals (insider).** Able to access collected data and analyze it to discover travel patterns.

- **Back-end (insider).** Possesses a global overview of the system and can analyze all the data that has been gathered.

To protect the system against those threats, we define the following the core privacy requirements:

- **Privacy against external observers.** Most privacy violation attacks are carried out by external entities. Protecting travelers' privacy when faced with such attackers is particularly critical in the front-end system—due to the e-tickets, the terminals, and the contactless communication them. Therefore, external entities should not be able to obtain any identifying information—or tracking information—by monitoring the communication between terminals and e-tickets. Essentially, by fulfilling this requirement, we ensure that the front-end is secure against privacy attacks during any interaction between customers (i.e., travelers and their e-tickets) and the front-end (i.e., the terminals).
- **Privacy against front-end terminals.** In the public transportation systems, terminals are widely distributed and, realistically, cannot be constantly supervised by the PTA. Additionally, the wireless interface used for e-ticket validation can be exploited by unauthorized third parties. To minimize unauthorized access, terminals should store minimal customer information when starting and ending a journey. Regarding customer privacy, no one should be able to track or identify customers based on their tickets. The PTA must ensure that terminals store as little sensitive data as possible. This approach significantly reduces the amount of private information disclosed from the e-ticket to the terminal during check-in/out sessions. Furthermore, terminals must not be able to track valid e-tickets, differentiate them, or associate them with particular customers.
- **Privacy against the back-end terminals.** Similar to the previous requirement, the back-end must be restricted from tracking and differentiating individual interactions between e-tickets and terminals. However, the back-end is responsible for the e-ticketing system's sophisticated billing capabilities. Therefore, a compromise is necessary: the back-end should not use e-tickets to identify and differentiate customers, but it can link different travel records to a single e-ticket pseudonym for billing purposes.

4 The Privacy-Preserving Framework for Public Transportation Systems

In this work, the focused framework proposed by Gudymenko et al. [13,14] is composed of three core blocks as follows:

- At the front-end, mutual authentication is conducted between a terminal and an e-ticket. In this setup, the front-end is the focal point of the e-ticketing system, and communication can be secured using robust techniques.

- Also at the front-end, local revocation of invalid e-tickets at the terminal can be conducted without immediate communication with the back-end, facilitating loose coupling.
- At the back-end, path reconstruction correlates a number of journeys with a single customer pseudonym for billing purposes.

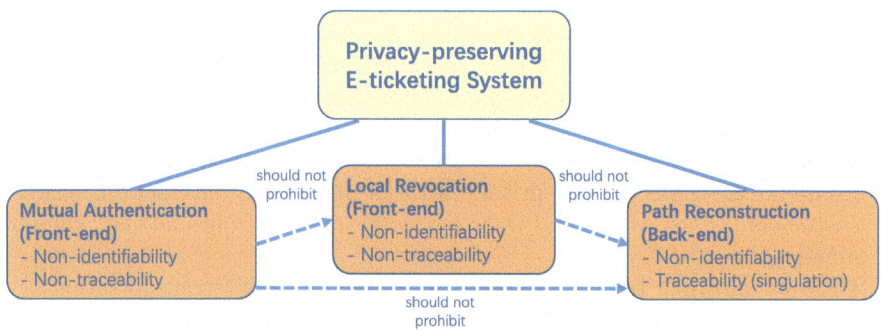

Fig. 2. The existing privacy-preserving framework with main blocks

The implementation of the three main blocks (Fig. 2) must prioritize privacy enhancement, taking into account the attacker model and the core privacy requirements outlined in Sect. 3. As illustrated in Fig. 2, there are inherent dependencies among these blocks. Privacy-enhanced authentication should not prevent local revocation at the front terminal or path reconstruction in the back-end. Similarly, local revocation should not impede path reconstruction. These dependencies present a significant challenge for system design because ensuring non-identifiability and untraceability conflicts with the need for customer revocation and path reconstruction.

Mutual Authentication. The following criteria must be satisfied during the mutual authentication between a terminal and an e-ticket:

- Only a legitimate, authorized terminal can communicate with an e-ticket
- The terminal process should only be triggered by a valid e-ticket
- Man-in-the-middle attacks should be mitigated (this type of attack is irrelevant when it comes to RFID/NFC technology [15]).

During the mutual authentication process, it is crucial to ensure that check-in/out events do not divulge additional information about the customer's e-ticket that could be exploited by terminals. Additional information might include identification, tracking, or linking and aggregating various communication sessions.

Local Revocation. The public transport system must allow access for valid e-tickets while blocking those that are invalid and have been blacklisted. Terminals must initially verify the validity of e-tickets. A crucial requirement is that a valid ticket must remain anonymous and untraceable. One possible solution is to use cryptographic techniques [8]. Instead of checking if an e-ticket is blacklisted, a zero-knowledge proof can be used to confirm that a specific value-stored on the e-ticket-matches an entry in the terminal's whitelist. Revocation involves removing this value from the whitelist and recalculating it. The updated whitelist must then be distributed to all terminals. This whitelist must be updated with each revocation. However, this approach is unsuitable for e-tickets that are mostly offline. If the updated whitelist were dynamically delivered to a customer device during check-in/out, recalculating credentials would incur additional costs and cause delays in the time-sensitive check-in/out process.

Path Reconstruction. Finally, to generate a bill, different rides need to be linked in a way that keeps the fundamental identity of each customer unknown to the transport authority. This involves several challenges: firstly, the billing fare schemes need to be extensible and flexible. The fare collection method should not be overly complex compared to the privacy-enhancement mechanism in use (e.g., [17]). Instead, it should be straightforward and capable of offering ride discounts. Secondly, the billing process must enhance privacy, avoiding direct identification of customer information and behaviors.

Information Flow. The above existing privacy-enhancement framework aims to prevent the disclosure of sensitive information and block unauthorized parties from accessing it. It essentially considers two distinct entities, as follows:

- **Public Transport Authority (PTA).** This is a public transportation company which organizes transport services.
- **Trusted Third Party (TTP).** This is a trusted intermediary between the PTA and its customers, as shown in Fig. 3.

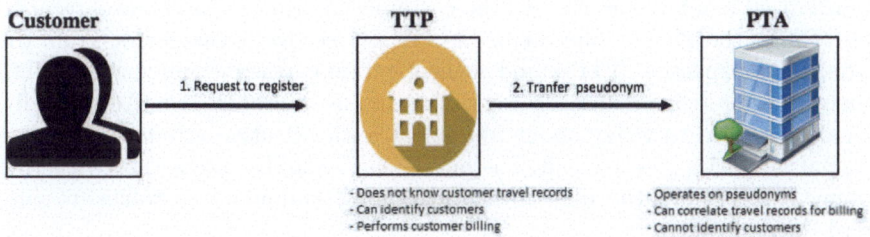

Fig. 3. Initialization phase

The process begins with the customer requesting a ticket registration, disclosing their personal information. The TTP receives and stores this information (in its own database), then creates a ticket ID combined with a pseudonym, which it sends to the PTA. The PTA converts this pseudonym to another pseudonym for internal use.

The main idea behind this system is that when issuing bills, the PTA's back-end does not need to possess any identity information about the e-ticket customer. It only needs to correlate different rides taken by a customer to a specific pseudonym agreed upon with the TTP, apply various pricing schemes, and handle billing. Periodically, based on the subscription type, the bill and pseudonym are sent to the TTP, which knows only the bill and the customer it is assigned to, without access to their travel history. Customers make payments to the PTA via the TTP.

In summary about the information flow, the PTA trusts the TTP to accurately bill customers, while customers trust the TTP to protect their privacy and forward payments to the PTA.

5   Our Approach for Enhancement

In current literature, most e-ticketing systems tend to align on framework and functionality, though their privacy protection techniques may vary. Importantly, many privacy-related issues stem from the billing process, where employees of the PTA can access customer information and travel records. Consequently, it is reasonable to assume that the billing procedure in most e-ticketing systems may inadvertently compromise privacy. To address this concern, we propose adding a trusted third party (TTP) to existing privacy-preserving frameworks. The primary objective is to mitigate privacy-related issues and enhance the robustness of billing processes. Specifically, by introducing a TTP, the PTA no longer needs to access customer information (e.g., identification information), and the TTP does not need to retrieve customer travel records. This approach offers a better chance of adequately protecting customer privacy within the e-ticketing system.

Benefits. From the PTA's perspective, authentication based on the TTP can mitigate customer privacy concerns and prevent unauthorized access—including unauthorized employee access—to the customer information and travel records. This enables the PTA to offer highly secure services to its customers. From the customers' perspective, TTP-based authentication means they no longer need to remember their login credentials every time they access the system. Additionally, they do not need to worry about fraudulent authentication attempts or online criminal activities. As a result, customers can securely access the e-ticketing system. Furthermore, this dual-authentication method allows customers to safeguard their privacy.

Another advantage of TTP-based authentication is that customers can securely access a variety of online services with the same credentials. Of course, during the initial registration phase, customers are required to register their credentials with the TTP. Upon successful registration with the TTP, customers receive an authentication code.

The billing process. With this e-ticketing scheme, a customer must prove her identity in two situations: (1) when paying for travel (e.g., top up e-ticket, buy a monthly/annual pass, pay a bill, etc.), and (2) when complaining to customer service (e.g., e-ticket lost or stolen, forgot check-in/out, etc.).

We propose an eID protocol that consists of three main entities:

- **PTA.** Provides e-ticketing service.
- **Trusted Third Party (TTP).** Provides identity confirmation.
- **Customer.** Accesses the PTA service.

If the e-ticket customer needs to access the PTA service, she first has to confirm her identity through the TTP. If the identity confirmation is successful, then she can access the PTA services; otherwise, she will be denied.

eID Protocol. The proposed protocol allows a customer to receive data confidential from a service provider after being authenticated through a TTP. Figure 4 shows the protocol written in AnB language.

```
1  Protocol: eID
2  Types:
3      Agent A,B,ca;
4      Function inv,sign,prf;
5      Number ps,cipher,compr,t20,t22,t23;
6
7  Formats:
8      client_hello(Number,Number,Number,Number,Number);
9      server_hello(Number,Number,Number,Number,Number);
10     server_cert(Msg);
11     x509(Agent,PublicKey);
12         client_key_ex(Msg);
13         pms_form(Number);
14     finished(Msg);
15     client_finished(Number,Number,Number,Msg);
16      server_finished(Number,Number,Number,Msg);
17     master_form(Number,Number,Number);
18     fh(Msg,Agent,Number,Number,Number,Number,Number,Number);
19
20     # auxiliary formats
21     fb1(Msg,Msg,Number);
22     fa1(Msg,Number,Msg);
23     fb2(Msg,Msg);
24
25 Knowledge:
26     A: A,B,pk(A),pk(ca),inv(pk(A)), sign(inv(pk(ca)),x509(A,pk(A))),eps,cipher,
27         compr, t20,t22,t23;
28     B: B, pk(B),pk(ca),inv(pk(B)), sign(inv(pk(ca)),x509(B,pk(B))),eps,cipher,
29         compr,t20,t22,t23, certType, suppAlg, certAuth
```

Fig. 4. eID protocol.

- **Types.** In the protocol, we have three agents: (1) Agent A represents a customer/user, (2) Agent B represents a service provider (in our case, the PTA), and (3) the CA represents a trusted third party that issues an authority for the service provider B. We also declare the cipher suite *cipher*, the compression algorithm *compr*, the empty string *eps*, and the tags t_{20}, t_{22} and t_{23}.

- **Formats.** eID supports several different message structures, each with specified fields. For example, the `clientHello` message structure contains the following fields: (1) timestamp, (2) session identifier, (3) cipher suites, (4) time identifier, and (4) compression function.
- **Knowledge.** The initial knowledge for each participating agent in the eID process is as follows: Initially, Agent A has knowledge of its name, the name of B and the public key of CA. Agent A also has knowledge of the compression function $compr$, the cipher suite $cipher$ and the empty string eps, as well as t_{20}, t_{22} and t_{23}. Agent B possesses the same knowledge.
- **Goals.** The protocol aims at building a secure channel between Agents A and B, so that they can securely exchange payloads. In this protocol, the agent A has a certificate issued by the CA, which can be sent to Agent B.
- **Actions.** We outline the protocol exchange between participant agents using the newly generated data, which is transmitted via Transport Layer Security (TLS). Figure 5 illustrates the primary actions of the protocol.

```
31  Actions:
32
33      #   A generates Ra and T1
34      let UM1= record(t22, clientHello(T1,Ra,eps,cipher,compr))
35  A->B : UM1
36
37      #B generates RB T2 and Id
38      B: Number Rb, Id, T2
39      let SM1= record(t22, serverHello(T2,Rb,Id,cipher,compr)),
40          record(t22, serverCert(sign(inv(pk(ca)),x509(B,pk(B))))),
41          record(t22, certRequest(certType,suppAlg,certAuth)),
42          record(serverHelloDone(eps))
43
44  A -> B: SM1
45      #A checks the certificate for a TTP ca
46      #A extracts the public key of B
47      #A generates the Pre-Mster Secret PMS
48      #A computes MS=PRF(mster -form(PMS;RA + RB))
49      # Here in certVerify(eps), eps replaces signed_hanshake
50      let MS = prf(masterForm(PMS,add(Ra,Rb)))
51      A: Number PMS
52      let UM2= record(t22, clientCert(sign(inv(pk(ca)),x509(A,pk(A))))),
53          record(t22, clientKeyExchage(crypt(pk(B), pmsForm(PMS)))), record(t22, certVerify(eps)),
54          record(t20, changeCipher(eps)),
55          record(t22, finished(prf(clientFinished(MS,add(Ra,Rb),hash(AM1, BM1)) )))
56
57  A -> B: UM2
58
59      B->A: record(t20, changeCipher(eps)), record(t22, finished(prf( serverFinished(MS,add(Ra,Rb),hash(UM1,
            SM1, UM2)))))
60
61      #A computes the key clntK=extractCK(key block(MS;RA + RB))
62      #A and B exchange payload messages as follows:
63      A: Number PAYLOADA
64
65      # A checks the certificate (assuming here ca is a trusted certificate authority that A knows the
            public key of)
66      # A extracts the public key of B and generates the pre-master secret PMS.
67      # Compute master secret MS = prf(master form(PMS,RA,RA))
68
69  A->B: record(t23, scrypt(extCK(keyBlock(MS, add(Ra,Rb))), PAYLOADA))
70      #B computes srvrK=extractSK(key block(MS;RA + RB)),
71      B: Number PAYLOADB
72      B->A: record(t23, scrypt(extSK(keyBlock(MS, add(Ra,Rb))), PAYLOADB))
```

Fig. 5. eID protocol: Actions.

– **Step 1.** Initially, the client sends the request to the PTA (agent B). In our case, the agent A sends a request with R_a (random number) and T_1 (timestamp), *eps* (empty string) to Agent B with *cipher* (encryption function priority) and *compr* (compression algorithm priority). Agent A sends the data in the clientHello format. The tag t_{22} indicates that this message is part of the Transport Layer Security (TLS) handshake sub-protocol. We denote the entire message as UM_1.

– **Step 2.** In response to the request from Agent A, Agent B generates R_b (random number), Id (session identifier) and T_2 (timestamp). With the obtained *cipher* and *compr*, agent B can format that via the serverHello. Agent B sends the certificate issued by the trusted third party CA in the serverCert format. Again, the tag t_{22} signifies that this message is part of the TLS handshake sub-protocol. We denote the entire message as UM_2.

– **Step 3.** In this step, Agent A checks the certificate provided by CA and extracts the public key of Agent B. After that, Agent A creates the PMS (pre-master secret) using the following pseudonym function:

$$(\text{prf}) \ \text{MS} = \text{psy}(\text{masterForm}(\text{PMS}, \ \text{add} \ (\text{R}_\text{a}, \text{R}_\text{b})))$$

Here, Agent A encrypts MS with the public key of Agent B using the clientKeyExchange format. The final form of the message is as follows:

$$(\text{prf}(\text{clientFinished}(\text{MS}, \ \text{add}(\text{R}_\text{a}, \text{R}_\text{b}), \text{hash}(\text{UM}_1, \text{SM}_1)))))$$

As shown above, the final form of the message requires Agent A to calculate the hashes of both UM_1 and SM_1. The t_{20} tag signifies that this message is part of the TLS handshake sub-protocol. Ultimately, this form is transmitted to Agent B.

– **Step 4.** Agent B computes the pseudonym function as follows:

$$\text{serverFinished}(\text{MS}, \text{add}(\text{R}_\text{a}, \text{R}_\text{b}))$$

To create the final message, Agent B wraps the calculated value and the hashes of all the previous messages (e.g., UM_1, SM_2, and UM_2) into the finished format, which is sent to Agent A as the final message.

– **Step 5.** Agent A calculates keyextCK(keyBlock(MS,add($\text{R}_\text{a}, \text{R}_\text{b}$))) using the client's extract-key function $extCK$ and uses it to encrypt the payload message PAYLOAD. Then, Agent A transmits the encrypted message to Agent B. The message is tagged with t_{23} to indicate that it is associated with a TLS sub-protocol.

Meanwhile, Agent B is able to calculate the key extSK(keyBlock(MS, add($\text{R}_\text{a}, \text{R}_\text{b}$))) using the server's extract-key function $extSK$ and uses it to encrypt the payload message PAYLOAD. Then, Agent B transmits the encrypted message to Agent A. Note that both $extCK$ and $extSK$ are publicly known functions, so both the customer (Agent A) and the PTA (Agent B) can compute the keys of both encrypted messages. This process allows the PTA to identify the customer.

Registration process. To register, a customer must submit his/her personal information to the TTP. Upon receiving this information, the TTP transforms the customer's personal details into a digital format and establishes a customer account associated with the relevant digital file. Subsequently, the TTP returns the customer's login credentials along with a set of authentication code keys (random numbers) to the customer.

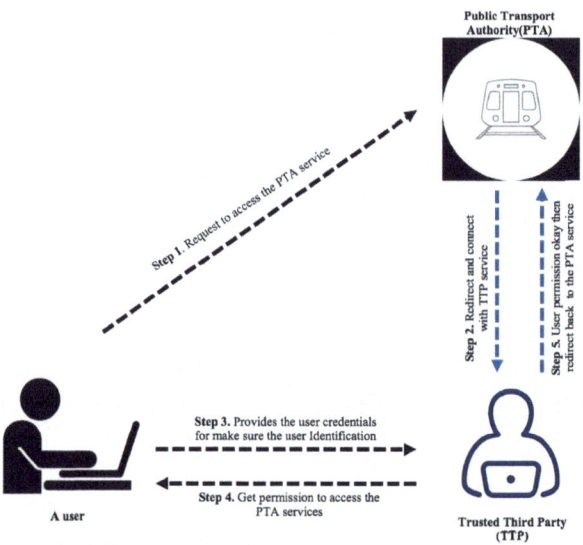

Fig. 6. Mutual authentication via TTP.

Mutual authentication via TTP. Fig. 6 describes the basic authentication procedure with important steps.

- A customer establishes a "secure" TLS connection to a website that offers eID login with an EasyID login frame where the customer username and password can be entered.
- The input information is forwarded to the TTP server, and, if the password is correct, the TTP server replies with a code from the customer's code card.
- The customer looks up the code on her code card and replies with the corresponding entry. If the customer entry is correct, eID informs the TTP server that the customer is legitimate. From there, the TTP server informs the PTA that the customer was successfully identified. When the PTA receives a positive message from the TTP server, it allows that customer to access public transportation services.

Protocol testing. The protocol has been tested for security weakness using OFMC tools [35]. OFMC was created with the aim of conducting symbolic analysis of security protocols to uncover any vulnerabilities in their design. The evaluation has three goals:

- The service provider (i.e., the PTA) must be able to authenticate the customer,
- The customer must be able to authenticate the service provider based on its response to the request,
- The result of a query must remain confidential between the customer and the service provider.

```
Anojjans-MacBook-Pro:ofmc-2016 anojjan$ ./ofmc-mac --numSess 2 3.AnB --attacktrace
Open-Source Fixedpoint Model-Checker version 2014
INPUT:
    3.AnB
SUMMARY:
  NO_ATTACK_FOUND
GOAL:
  as specified
DETAILS:
  BOUNDED_NUMBER_OF_SESSIONS
BACKEND:
  Open-Source Fixedpoint Model-Checker version 2014
STATISTICS:
  TIME 11162 ms
  parseTime 4 ms
  visitedNodes: 10957 nodes
  depth: 14 plies
```

Fig. 7. The outcome of protocol testing.

Figure 7 depicts our protocol testing process and results. With the help of OFMC, we conducted an extensive analysis of the protocol to detect vulnerabilities. Our evaluation did not uncover any vulnerabilities. Subsequently, we individually tested each component of the system—primarily using black-box testing methods—to verify that the expected behavior can match the actual behavior. Finally, we performed end-to-end tests, which included tracing a request through the entire system and checking the results. In our evaluation, the results aligned with our expectations.

6   Discussion

Compared to previous works—as well as existing e-ticketing systems—the billing process for our eID-based privacy-enhanced public transportation ticket system is markedly different. In essence, traditional check-in/out validation is eliminated. Billing-wise, it is always possible to check-in or check-out, since there is no predefined balance associated with the ticket. The bill is calculated retrospectively at the end of a defined period [13,14].

This billing scheme benefits the public transport agency: calculations can be performed offline (e.g., with heavy computation handled by the back-end node), and real-time communication is not required, reducing computational demands on the front-end. However, the unrestricted check-in/out policy may inconvenience—and even financially threaten—customers.

From the customer's perspective, lack of control over public transportation expenditures can be frustrating and stressful. Even if a customer diligently tracks his journeys and corresponding expenditures, bugs in the system could cause it to incorrectly calculate the cost of a journey [17]. If a customer receives an inflated bill at the end of a period and complains, the PTA will have to resolve it. However, without a direct communication channel between the PTA and the affected customer (due to the presence of the TTP as an intermediary) the situation becomes even more complicated. As such, the TTP would need to be involved in customer billing disputes.

We also need to consider customer risk. With a billing system similar to Denmark's Rejsekort [3], if an e-ticket is lost or stolen, they will *at most* lose the current balance of the e-ticket. However, with the proposed solution, if fraudsters steal or forge a legitimate customer's e-ticket, they use it without limitation, and the customer will be liable for the charges. Since the e-ticket does not contain customer identity information (which is instead stored by the TTP), distinguishing between fraudsters and the legitimate e-ticket holder becomes challenging.

These concerns underscore the importance of customer service, which includes the capability to provide a customer with her current bill upon her request. The billing calculation is carried out on the back-end by the PTA, which maintains a database of bills linked to pseudonyms—and regularly updates them. To request a copy of her bill, the customer submits a request to the TTP along with her personal information. Then, the TTP will contact the PTA to obtain the bill for the customer associated with the provided pseudonym. The PTA will retrieve the bill from the database, and the query result will be transmitted to the customer via the TTP.

With this functionality, the proposed solution resembles a distributed system, which leads us to several more questions, e.g., who is responsible for the customer service website? Are the additional demands on the TTP and PTA reasonable? Will the TTP, as a mediator for customer billing disputes, become a bottleneck for the system? To prevent the TTP from becoming a bottleneck, we can increase its capacity.

One more supplemental feature would allow customers to block their e-tickets via the Internet. This feature can be seamlessly integrated with the existing design. However, we still need to address the danger of stolen e-tickets, as customers must notice their absence before taking action to block them. By the time customers realize their e-tickets are missing, fraudsters may have already racked up significant bills. While it would be beneficial for customers to have online access to their journeys, such a feature would require merging identities and travel records, which contradicts the system's design principles. Conversely, providing customers with a warning notification should suffice to address the use of stolen or forged e-tickets.

As previously noted, the PTA has the capability to link multiple travel records to one customer using pseudonyms. In addition, the PTA can analyze these records using its high computation power on the back-end. Aside from fraud detection, the PTA can also uncover travel patterns (e.g., frequency, destination). If an e-ticket is used for a journey that deviates from the established patterns associated with a specific pseudonym, the PTA will alert the TTP to this pattern change. Subsequently, the TTP will notify the corresponding customer. While this technique is inherently limited—primarily due to the subjective nature of defining patterns—and may generate false positives if a legitimate customer goes on an unusual, albeit legitimate, journey, it remains a reasonable measure. This approach respects the design goals: the knowledge that something changed in a customer's travel patterns is more important than the specifics of that change.

In general, an effective solution might involve the implementation of an advanced terminal capable of direct communication with the PTA, offering customers access to their PTA profiles. Such an advanced terminal would allow customers to manually input details regarding a missing check-out, prompted by a warning from the PTA through the TTP, akin to the notification about a deviation in travel patterns.

It is worth noting that protecting the security of e-ticket systems is not an easy task, there is a need for multiple security solutions, such as traditional intrusion detection [7,29,30], trust management [21,23,31,33], and proper authentication (including user authentication [18,22,25,26], access control [37,39] and event filtration [24,32,34]).

7 Conclusion

Privacy has emerged as a major concern in existing public transportation systems, especially when it comes to electronic ticketing (e-ticketing). In this work, we addressed three main threats: external observers, front-end terminals, and back-end terminals, and we discussed pertinent privacy and security prerequisites for modern e-ticketing systems. Next, we introduced a privacy-preserving framework for e-ticketing systems, which can achieve multilateral security. Finally, we presented an eID protocol with detailed implementation specifications—including specifications for the trusted third party (TTP)—aimed at enhancing the framework's efficacy.

Our work focuses primarily on card-based e-tickets, which, in general, contain only the customer's credentials. However, with smartphone-based e-tickets, the scenario is markedly different. Due to the presence of additional data on a smartphone, such as contacts and social network cookies, smartphone-targeting malware could acquire the smartphone holder's identity and correlate it with e-ticketing credentials in the event of a breach. Moreover, determining the smartphone's location implies obtaining knowledge about the e-ticket's whereabouts. Therefore, it is evident that a dedicated protection technique must be devised to safeguard privacy against threats originating from customer devices. Isolating the e-ticketing application from all other applications on a smartphone presents a significant challenge, which necessitates collaboration with smartphone developers at a more profound level.

Acknowledgments. This work was partially supported by National Natural Science Foundation of China (U21A20463).

References

1. EZ-Link Card System and Technology. https://www.ezlink.com.sg/
2. Transport for London Oyster Online. https://oyster.tfl.gov.uk/oyster/entry.do
3. Rejsekort. https://www.rejsekort.dk/
4. Der E-Ticket-Deutschland-Standard, die VDV-Kernapplikation. Accessed on 1 May 2023. https://trid.trb.org/view/940920
5. Aguiar, A., Nunes, F.M.C., Silva, M.J.F., Silva, P.A., Elias, D.: Leveraging electronic ticketing to provide personalized navigation in a public transport network. IEEE Trans. Intell. Transp. Syst. **13**(1), 213–220 (2012)
6. Heydt-Benjamin, T.S., Chae, H.J., Defend, B., Fu, K.: Privacy for public transportation. In: Privacy Enhancing Technologies, pp. 1–19 (2006)
7. Lampe, B., Meng, W.: can-train-and-test: a curated CAN dataset for automotive intrusion detection. Comput. Secur. **140**, 103777 (2024)
8. Camenisch, J., Lysyanskaya, A.: Dynamic accumulators and application to efficient revocation of anonymous credentials. In: CRYPTO, pp. 61–76 (2002)
9. Cha, S.C., Peng, C.W., Hsu, T.Y., Chang, C.L., Li, S.W.: A blockchain-based privacy preserving ticketing service. In: GCCE, pp. 585–587 (2018)
10. Chiu, W.Y., Meng, W.: EdgeTC—a PBFT blockchain-based ETC scheme for smart cities. Peer-to-Peer Netw. Appl. **14**, 2874–2886 (2021)
11. Chiu, W.Y., Meng, W., Jensen, C.D.: My data, my control: a secure data sharing and access scheme over blockchain. J. Inf. Secur. Appl. **63**(103020), 1–11 (2021)
12. Chu, D., Lin, J., Li, F., Zhang, X., Wang, Q., Liu, G.: Ticket transparency: accountable single sign-on with privacy-preserving public logs. In: SecureComm, pp. 511–531 (2019)
13. Gudymenko, I.: Privacy-Preserving E-Ticketing Systems for Public Transport Based on RFID/NFC Technologies. Dresden University of Technology (2015)
14. Gudymenko, I.: A privacy-preserving e-ticketing system for public transportation supporting sophisticated billing and local validation. In: SIN, pp. 1–8 (2014)
15. Haselsteiner, E., Breitfub, K.: In security in near field communication (NFC). Strengths and weaknesses. In: Workshop on RFID Security (RFIDSec), pp. 1–11 (2006)
16. Han, J., Chen, L., Schneider, S., Treharne, H., Wesemeyer, S.: Privacy-preserving electronic ticket scheme with attribute-based credentials. IEEE Trans. Dependable Secur. Comput. **18**(4), 1836–1849 (2021)
17. Hoepman, J.H., Huitema, G.B.: Privacy enhanced fraud resistant road pricing. In: HCC, pp. 202–213 (2010)
18. Johnson, P.C., Kapadia, A., Tsang, P.P., Smith, S.W.: Nymble: Anonymous IP-address blocking. In: Privacy Enhancing Technologies, pp. 113–133 (2007)
19. Kerschbaum, F., Lim, H.W., Gudymenko, I.: Privacy-preserving billing for e-ticketing systems in public transportation. In: WPES, pp. 143–154 (2013)
20. Kakousis, K., Paspallis, N., Papadopoulos, G.A.: A survey of software adaptation in mobile and ubiquitous computing. Enterp. Inf. Syst. **4**(4), 355–389 (2010)
21. Li, W., Meng, W., Zhu, H.: Towards collaborative intrusion detection enhancement against insider attacks with multi-level trust. In: The 19th IEEE International Conference on Trust, Security and Privacy in Computing and Communications (TrustCom), pp. 1179–1186. IEEE (2020)
22. Li, W., Meng, W., Furnell, S.: Exploring touch-based behavioral authentication on smartphone email applications in IoT-enabled smart cities. Pattern Recogn. Lett. **144**, 35–41 (2021)

23. Li, W., Meng, W., Kwok, L.F.: Surveying trust-based collaborative intrusion detection: state-of-the-art, challenges and future directions. IEEE Commun. Surv. Tutorials **24**(1), 280–305 (2022)
24. Jin, Z., Liang, Z., Wang, Y., Meng, W.: Mobile network traffic pattern classification with incomplete a priori information. Comput. Commun. **166**, 262–270 (2021)
25. Li, W., Tan, J., Zhu, N.: Design of double-cross-based smartphone unlock mechanism. Comput. Secur. **129**, 103204 (2023)
26. Li, W., Gleerup, T., Tan, J., Wang, Y.: A security enhanced android unlock scheme based on pinch-to-zoom for smart devices. IEEE Trans. Consumer Electron. **70**(1), 3985–3993 (2024)
27. Liu, Z., Wu, L., Meng, W., Wang, H., Wang, W.: Accurate range query with privacy preservation for outsourced location-based service in IoT. IEEE Internet Things J. **8**(18), 14322–14337 (2021)
28. Milutinovic, M., Decroix, K., Naessens, V., Decker, B.D.: Privacy-preserving public transport ticketing system. In: DBSec, pp. 135–150 (2015)
29. Meng, W., Li, W., Kwok, L.F.: EFM: enhancing the performance of signature-based network intrusion detection systems using enhanced filter mechanism. Comput. Secur. **43**, 189–204 (2014)
30. Meng, W., Li, W., Xiang, Y., Choo, K.K.R.: A Bayesian inference-based detection mechanism to defend medical smartphone networks against insider attacks. J. Netw. Comput. Appl. **78**, 162–169 (2017)
31. Meng, W., Raymond Choo, K.K., Furnell, S., Vasilakos, A.V., Probst, C.W.: Towards Bayesian-based trust management for insider attacks in healthcare software-defined networks. IEEE Trans. Netw. Serv. Manag. **15**(2), 761–773 (2018)
32. Meng, W.: Intrusion detection in the era of IoT: building trust via traffic filtering and sampling. IEEE Comput. **51**(7), 36–43 (2018)
33. Meng, W., Li, W., Zhu, L.: Enhancing medical smartphone networks via blockchain-based trust management against insider attacks. IEEE Trans. Eng. Manage. **67**(4), 1377–1386 (2020)
34. Meng, W., Li, W., Zhou, J.: Enhancing the security of blockchain-based software defined networking through trust-based traffic fusion and filtration. Inf. Fusion **70**, 60–71 (2021)
35. Modersheim, S.: Open Source Fixedpoint Model Checker. https://paolo.science/anbxtutorial/tools/ofmc-manual.pdf
36. Sadeghi, A.R., Visconti, I., Wachsmann, C.: User privacy in transport systems based on RFID E-tickets. In: PiLBA (2008)
37. Shen, G., Xia, C., Li, Y., Shen, H., Meng, W., Zhang, M.: Traceable and privacy-preserving authentication scheme for energy trading in V2G networks. IEEE Internet Things J. **11**(4), 6664–6676 (2024)
38. Stopka, U., Schafer, G., Kreisel, A.: NFC-enabled eTicketing in public transport—aims, approaches and first results of the OPTIMOS project. In: HCI, pp. 582–597 (2017)
39. Zhang, Y., Meng, L., Zhang, M., Meng, W.: A secure and lightweight batch authentication scheme for internet of drones environment. Vehic. Commun. **44**(100680), 1–11 (2023)

Outsourced and Robust Multi-party Computation with Identifying Malicious Behavior and Application to Machine Learning

Hong Qin[1], Debiao He[1(✉)], Qi Feng[1], Xiaolin Yang[2], and Qingcai Luo[3]

[1] Key Laboratory of Aerospace Information Security and Trusted Computing, Ministry of Education, School of Cyber Science and Engineering, Wuhan University, Wuhan, China
{qinhong,fengqi.whu}@whu.edu.cn, hedebiao@163.com
[2] Inspur Cloud Information Technology Co., Ltd., Jinan, China
yangxl@inspur.com
[3] Inspur Academy of Science and Technology, Jinan, China
luoqc@inspur.com

Abstract. This work proposes an efficient n-party computation framework with malicious security in the outsourced case. We consider a non-symmetrical trust setting that $n-1$ parties, including P_0, is semi-honest and one party is malicious. Once the party in $\{P_1, P_2, ..., P_{n-1}\}$ misbehaves, we will caught and exclude it, achieving robustness by executing the further computations among semi-honest parties. Unlike previous works that focused on traditional robustness, we do not need to delegate the computation to an identified honest party, which contradicts the usual expectation of privacy and hinder the adoption in practice. Our framework bridges the gap between semi-honest and malicious honest-majority multi-party protocols, and is well suited for privacy-preserving machine learning. In general, machine learning depends on large amounts of data and powerful computing power, leading resource-constrained clients to resort to secure outsourced computing (SOC) approach. In this work, we utilize the n-party framework to design efficient building blocks for machine learning. We significantly improve the efficiency of blocks and implement machine learning inference in LAN and WAN setting, respectively. Theoretical analysis and experimental results show that our framework outperforms the existing honest-majority protocols, such as SWIFT (USENIX Security'21) in terms of "robustness" and Fantastic Four (USENIX Security'21) in terms of efficiency.

Keywords: multiparty computation · machine learning · robustness · secure outsourced

Z. Xia and J. Chen (Eds.): ISPEC 2024, LNCS 15053, pp. 310–328, 2024.
https://doi.org/10.1007/978-981-97-9053-1_18

1 Introduction

Secure multiparty computation (MPC) was firstly introduced by Yao [1,2]. After decades of development, most MPC protocols can be divided into two phases: preprocessing and online. The pre-processing phase is independent of the inputs, and online phase begins when the parties provide their inputs. In addition to running the protocols directly between parties, MPC can also be used for outsourcing scenarios. As described in [3], the data owners secretly share their data with n non-colluding computational parties, who evaluate the MPC protocols without knowing original data. These parties then return the output shares to receiver for reconstructing plaintext results. In practice, the n can be appropriately selected based on performance, cost and security requirements.

Once the computation is outsourced, however, the data owners will lose physical control, bringing about serious privacy breaches. Hence it is critical to provide security assurances against malicious computational parties. One may want to ensure that the computing tasks and sensitive inputs are hidden from all parties, while identifying and excluding the malicious party once they acts maliciously. Moreover, the computation should be able to continue after the exclusion of malicious party, thus achieving guaranteed output delivery (GOD) and preventing Denial-of-Service (DoS) attacks. Notice that not all parties are malicious; rather, most of them are rational. Therefore, we can assume that one of the n parties is malicious and the rest are semi-honest. This asymmetric corruption model is suitable for many real-world applications, such as machine learning inference [4–6], because of the heterogeneity of parties and difference in confidence level. Compared with static symmetric security models, these schemes do not need to verify the correct behavior of all parties and can use the nature of semi-honest party to speed up computation.

Machine learning, as one of the typical applications of MPC, has become a hot topic and representative of advanced technology. With the rapid development of cloud computing and big data, privacy-preserving machine learning (PPML) has shifted towards secure outsourced computing (SOC) paradigm. In SOC paradigm, a number of powerful and well-equipped service providers offer access to their resources for clients on a pay-per-use basis. Typically, this secure outsourced computation is also known as server-aided setting. Robustness is a highly attractive feature in outsourced PPML, which has been pointed out and explored in [7–9]. It is vital for the deployment of PPML in real world, ensuring that the output is available regardless of adversary misbehavior. Consider an outsourcing scenario where the ML model owner intends to render inference services for remuneration. In this case, the model owner will share model parameters with service providers while the client share their query requests. However, a malicious attacker can abort the above protocols, preventing the client from obtaining expected output and causing serious financial loss. To seamlessly adopt PPML solutions in outsourcing scenario, the robustness is crucial.

More recently, a series of honest-majority works [7,8] focused on the traditional robustness of identifying an honest party, making it aware of all secrets and completing the computation in plaintext. In practice, this contradicts the usual expectation of privacy and is not viable enough. Dalskov et al. [9] considered the private robustness in four-party framework Fantastic Four, which achieves robustness through complex transformations between four and three parties. Although Fantastic Four avoids the security risk of relying on honest party to know inputs, it has the obvious limitation of not being able to extend to n-party setting. In this work, we present a $n, n \geq 3$-party framework that overcomes these limitations and aims to obtain robust and secure computation system with high usability. The case of $n = 3$ is due to the fact that our scheme can still be regarded as a two-party computation after excluding the malicious party. By assuming that there is one malicious party and others are semi-honest, we bridge the gap between fully semi-honest and malicious honest-majority protocols. Either the parties execute the protocols honestly and get paid, or deviate from protocols and get caught. In the latter case, the malicious party will be blacklisted or punished. Below we introduce the specific contributions.

Robust Multi-Party Computation Framework. We construct a n-party computation framework with malicious security over a ring $\mathbb{Z}_{2^l}$. Our framework does not require any heavy-cost operations, such as zero-knowledge proofs. We consider a non-symmetrical trust setting that $n - 1$ parties, including P_0, is semi-honest and one party in $\{P_1, P_2, ..., P_{n-1}\}$ is malicious. Once a party misbehaves, we will caught and exclude it, achieving guaranteed output delivery by completing the computations between semi-honest parties.

Building Blocks for Machine Learning. Based on the n-party framework, we present the practically efficient blocks for privacy-preserving machine learning. Due to the aid provided by semi-honest party P_0 in our setting, we improves the efficiency of building blocks significantly. We take the state-of-the-art four-party protocol Fantastic Four [9] as reference. Their online communication for multiplication is $6(l+\kappa)$, while our work is $6l$ (κ is security parameter, l is the size of ring in bits). Their online communication for MSB extraction is close to $30l$, while our work is only $18l$. Other specific complexity analysis and improvements are stated in Sect. 4.

Secure Prediction. We benchmark the n-party framework through ML inference in LAN and WAN setting, respectively. We consider the inference over the MINIST dataset for linear/logistic regression, neural network and k-means clustering. The theoretical analysis and experimental results show that our framework outperforms the existing honest-majority robust protocols, such as SWIFT [8] in terms of security and Fantastic Four [9] in terms of efficiency.

Related Works. Demmler et al. [10] proposed a mixed-protocol framework ABY, which achieves the conversions between arithmetic, boolean and yao sharing. The drawback is that the online computation requires lots of oblivious transfers, resulting in lower efficiency. Other researchers [11] have improved the performance of ABY by running OTs in pre-processing phase. Their framework, named ABY2.0, allowed multi-input multiplication without inflating the online communication. Mohassel et al. [12] proposed a outsourced neural network training and inference scheme over two non-colluding servers. They considered the semi-honest adversary and permitted the collusion among clients.

For 3-party computation, Mohassel and Rindal [13] presented ABY^3 that is secure against the malicious adversary. They focused on the training and inference for regression and neural network. However, they required computationally expensive parallel prefix adder and garbled circuits. ASTRA [14] avoided this and introduced efficient computation protocols in three non-colluding servers setting. It included the computing protocols for regression but not for neural network inference. Patra et al. [15] considered the same 3-party setting and proposed the fair framework BLAZE. It required that at most one party is maliciously corrupt. SWIFT [8] firstly proposed a robust 3-party framework on the basis of joint message passing primitive. It can be extended to 4 parties that is 2x faster than [16]. The problem lies in that SWIFT needs to identify an honest party to complete computation in plaintext.

Trident [17] extended ABY^3 to the 4-party setting by introducing another honest party in offline phase. In fact, the online computation still involved 3 parties. Trident removed expensive multiplicative triples and supported secure training/inference with fairness guarantee. Based on replicated secret-sharing, Byali et al. [16] constructed the first robust 4PC protocol FLASH. They achieved secure training and inference in four non-colluding servers setting. But the robustness, like SWIFT, required sending plaintext to the identified honest party, which contradicts the usual expectation of privacy. Dalskov et al. [9] solved this problem and proposed a new 4-party robust framework Fantastic Four. They achieved the private robustness by conversion of 3-party and 4-party protocols.

2   Preliminaries

Secret Sharing. We use $[\![\cdot]\!]$ to mean the shares of additive secret sharing. A value $x \in \mathbb{Z}_{2^l}$ is $[\![\cdot]\!]$-shared among parties $P_i, i \in [n]$ if P_i holds $[\![x]\!]_i \in \mathbb{Z}_{2^l}$ and $x = \sum_{i=1}^{n} [\![x]\!]_i \bmod 2^l$. We use $[\![\cdot]\!]^2$ to mean the shares of boolean sharing on $\mathbb{Z}_2$. A value $x \in \mathbb{Z}_2$ is $[\![\cdot]\!]^2$-shared among parties $P_i, i \in [n]$ if P_i holds $[\![x]\!]_i^2 \in \mathbb{Z}_2$ and $x = \bigoplus_{i=1}^{n} [\![x]\!]_i^2 \bmod 2$. We use $\langle \cdot \rangle$ to mean the shares of vector space secret sharing [18] on $\mathbb{Z}_{2^l}$. Given the set of subsets of parties $\mathcal{Q} = \{Q_0, Q_1, ..., Q_{m-1}\}(m < 2^n)$, we define $\mathcal{Q}$ is access structure of $\langle \cdot \rangle$-sharing. The parties in an authorized set can jointly reveal secrets while others cannot. Given vector space $(Z_p)^\zeta$ where p is large prime and $\zeta \geq 2$ is an integer, there is a function $\psi : \mathcal{P} \to (Z_p)^\zeta$ satisfying $\sum_{P_i \in Q_j} a_i \cdot \psi(P_i) = (1, 0, ..., 0)$. We note that $Q_j, j \in [m]$ is authorized set and a_i is public reconstruction coefficient corresponding to $P_i, i \in [n]$. Suppose that the public matrix constructed by all vectors $\psi(P_i)$ is Ψ. To secretly share a value x, the party who holds x firstly samples $\zeta - 1$ random values $u_1, u_2, ..., u_{\zeta-1} \in Z_p$ and constructs the vector $\boldsymbol{u} = (x, u_1, u_2, ..., u_{\zeta-1})^T$. Then the party computes and sends share $\langle x \rangle_i = \psi(P_i) \cdot \boldsymbol{u}$ to P_i. Since $x = (1, 0, ..., 0) \cdot \boldsymbol{u}$, we can obtain that $x = \sum_{P_i \in Q_j} a_i \cdot \psi(P_i) \cdot \boldsymbol{u} = \sum_{P_i \in Q_j} a_i \cdot \langle x \rangle_i$. The $\langle \cdot \rangle$-sharing satisfies linearity property. That is, each party can locally compute $\langle c_1 \cdot x + c_2 \cdot y \rangle = c_1 \cdot \langle x \rangle + c_2 \cdot \langle y \rangle$ with shares $\langle x \rangle, \langle y \rangle$ and public constants c_1, c_2.

Triple sacrificing. To check whether a multiplication triple (a, b, c) is correct, the triple sacrifice approach sacrifices another correlated and potentially incorrect triple $(\tilde{a}, b, \tilde{c})$ while keeping (a, b, c) secret. It is suitable for linear secret sharing schemes, including vector space secret sharing. In Algorithm 1, we give the detailed process of triple sacrificing in semi-honest model. Obviously, the triple (a, b, c) is correct if $r(c - ab) = \tilde{c} - \tilde{a}b \mod 2^l$ with high probability.

Algorithm 1 Semi-honest triple sacrificing protocol $\Pi_{\text{tsa}}^{\text{semi}}$

Input: $(\langle a \rangle, \langle b \rangle, \langle c \rangle)$ and $(\langle \tilde{a} \rangle, \langle b \rangle, \langle \tilde{c} \rangle)$.
Output: True or False.
  1: The parties randomly select $r \in \mathbb{Z}_{2^l}$ and compute $\langle v \rangle = r \cdot \langle a \rangle - \langle \tilde{a} \rangle$.
  2: The parties reconstruct v and compute $\langle w \rangle = v \cdot \langle b \rangle - r \cdot \langle c \rangle + \langle \tilde{c} \rangle$.
  3: The parties reconstruct w.
  4: P_0 outputs True if $w = 0$ and False otherwise.

---

3   Outsourced and Robust Multi-party Computation

3.1   Three-Party Computation Protocol

Input Sharing. We define a 5×3 public matrix $\mathbf{\Psi}$ which the j-th row $\mathbf{\Psi}_j, j \in \{0, 1, 2\}$ corresponds to P_0, P_1, P_2 respectively. P_0 also holds two alternate vectors $\mathbf{\Psi}_3, \mathbf{\Psi}_4$, which $\mathbf{\Psi}_3 = \alpha \cdot \mathbf{\Psi}_1 + \beta \cdot \mathbf{\Psi}_2, \mathbf{\Psi}_4 = \alpha' \cdot \mathbf{\Psi}_1 + \beta' \cdot \mathbf{\Psi}_2$ for $\alpha, \alpha', \beta, \beta' \neq 0$. Therefore, there are fifteen public reconstruction coefficients such that

$$
\begin{aligned}
(1, 0, 0) &= a_{00} \cdot \mathbf{\Psi}_0 + a_{01} \cdot \mathbf{\Psi}_1 + a_{02} \cdot \mathbf{\Psi}_2 = \tilde{a}_{10} \cdot \mathbf{\Psi}_0 + \tilde{a}_{11} \cdot \mathbf{\Psi}_1 + \tilde{a}_{13} \cdot \mathbf{\Psi}_3 \\
&= \tilde{a}_{20} \cdot \mathbf{\Psi}_0 + \tilde{a}_{23} \cdot \mathbf{\Psi}_3 + \tilde{a}_{22} \cdot \mathbf{\Psi}_2 = \hat{a}_{10} \cdot \mathbf{\Psi}_0 + \hat{a}_{11} \cdot \mathbf{\Psi}_1 + \hat{a}_{14} \cdot \mathbf{\Psi}_4 \quad (1) \\
&= \hat{a}_{20} \cdot \mathbf{\Psi}_0 + \hat{a}_{24} \cdot \mathbf{\Psi}_4 + \hat{a}_{22} \cdot \mathbf{\Psi}_2.
\end{aligned}
$$

When a user shares x, it sets a 3-dimensional vector $\boldsymbol{u}$ to compute $\langle \cdot \rangle$-shares of x. As shown in Algorithm 2, the user firstly selects two random values $u_1, u_2 \in_R \mathbb{Z}_p$ and obtains $\boldsymbol{u} = (x, u_1, u_2)^T$. Then it computes $\langle x \rangle_j = \mathbf{\Psi}_j \cdot \boldsymbol{u}, j \in \{0, 1, 2\}$ for P_0, P_1, P_2 respectively (Additionally $\langle x \rangle_3 = \mathbf{\Psi}_3 \cdot \boldsymbol{u}, \langle x \rangle_4 = \mathbf{\Psi}_4 \cdot \boldsymbol{u}$ for P_0). After the execution, P_0 holds $\langle x \rangle_0, \langle x \rangle_3, \langle x \rangle_4$, P_1 holds $\langle x \rangle_1$ and P_2 holds $\langle x \rangle_2$.

Algorithm 2 The 3-party sharing protocol Π_{shr}^3

Input: The value x held by user.
Output: $\langle x \rangle$.
  1: The user sets a 3-dimensional vector $\boldsymbol{u} = (x, u_1, u_2)^T$ in which u_1, u_2 are randomly selected from $\mathbb{Z}_p$.
  2: The user generates and sends $\langle x \rangle_j = \mathbf{\Psi}_j \cdot \boldsymbol{u}, j \in \{0, 1, 2\}$ to P_j respectively. Additionally, it computes two alternate shares $\langle x \rangle_3 = \mathbf{\Psi}_3 \cdot \boldsymbol{u}, \langle x \rangle_4 = \mathbf{\Psi}_4 \cdot \boldsymbol{u}$ for P_0.

Computation with Semi-honest Security. For addition and multiplication with public constants, each party can locally compute $\langle c_1 \cdot x + c_2 \cdot y \rangle = c_1 \cdot \langle x \rangle + c_2 \cdot \langle y \rangle$ with inputs $\langle x \rangle, \langle y \rangle$ and constants c_1, c_2. For multiplication, we propose a semi-honest secure protocol $\Pi_{\text{mul}}^{\text{semi}}$ in Algorithm 3. The protocol requires multiple parties to collaborate to securely generate multiplication triples and involves a reconstruction process. For output reconstruction, all parties can aggregate the shares and reconstruct x by $a_{00} \cdot \langle x \rangle_0 + a_{01} \cdot \langle x \rangle_1 + a_{02} \cdot \langle x \rangle_2$, as shown in Algorithm 4. While P_1 and P_2 can collude with each other, the secret x cannot be revealed without the share of P_0.

Algorithm 3 Semi-honest secure multiplication protocol $\Pi_{\text{mul}}^{\text{semi}}$

Input: The shares $\langle x \rangle, \langle y \rangle$. The pre-shared multiplication triplet $(\langle d \rangle, \langle e \rangle, \langle f \rangle)$.

Output: $\langle z \rangle = \langle x \cdot y \rangle$.

1: P_j locally computes $\langle h \rangle_j = \langle x \rangle_j + \langle d \rangle_j, \langle v \rangle_j = \langle y \rangle_j + \langle e \rangle_j$. P_0 additionally computes $\langle h \rangle_3 = \langle x \rangle_3 + \langle d \rangle_3, \langle h \rangle_4 = \langle x \rangle_4 + \langle d \rangle_4, \langle v \rangle_3 = \langle y \rangle_3 + \langle e \rangle_3, \langle v \rangle_4 = \langle y \rangle_4 + \langle e \rangle_4$.

2: The parties interactively invoke $\Pi_{\text{rec}}^{\text{semi}}(\langle h \rangle)$ and $\Pi_{\text{rec}}^{\text{semi}}(\langle v \rangle)$.

3: P_j locally computes $\langle z \rangle_j = \langle x \rangle_j \cdot v - \langle e \rangle_j \cdot h + \langle f \rangle_j$ and P_0 additionally computes two alternate shares $\langle z \rangle_3 = \langle x \rangle_3 \cdot v - \langle e \rangle_3 \cdot h + \langle f \rangle_3$ and $\langle z \rangle_4 = \langle x \rangle_4 \cdot v - \langle e \rangle_3 \cdot h + \langle f \rangle_4$.

Algorithm 4 Semi-honest secure reconstruction protocol $\Pi_{\text{rec}}^{\text{semi}}$

Input: The shares $\langle x \rangle$.

Output: x.

1: P_j receives the shares from other two parties.

2: P_j computes x by $x = a_{00} \cdot \langle x \rangle_0 + a_{01} \cdot \langle x \rangle_1 + a_{02} \cdot \langle x \rangle_2$.

Computation with Malicious Security. Since the parties can locally perform additions and multiplications with public constants, the maliciously secure version of that is the same as semi-honest version. For multiplication, it is necessary to introduce multiplication triplets that generated by multi-party collaboration. But the existing protocol Π_{vmtgen} is semi-honest and cannot ensure correctness in the presence of malicious adversary. Hence, we propose a maliciously secure triple sacrifice protocol $\Pi_{\text{tsa}}^{\text{mal}}$ to verify correctness, and additionally introduce batch technique [6,20] for efficiency. In Algorithm 5, the parties randomly sample $r \in \mathbb{Z}_{2^l}$ non-interactively from pseudo-random function key-setup. To improve efficiency, they use the same r for all sacrifice instances in one batch.

The maliciously secure reconstruction protocol $\Pi_{\text{rec}}^{\text{mal}}$ (Algorithm 5) can identify and exclude malicious party. After that, the reconstruction of w is accomplished by semi-honest parties. Specific reconstruction process of $\Pi_{\text{rec}}^{\text{mal}}$ is described in Algorithm 6. Since P_0 is semi-honest and one of P_1, P_2 is malicious, we allow P_0 to perform reconstruction firstly and assist in identifying malicious

---

Algorithm 5 Maliciously secure triple sacrificing protocol $\Pi_{\text{tsa}}^{\text{mal}}$

Input: $(\langle a \rangle, \langle b \rangle, \langle c \rangle)$ and $(\langle \tilde{a} \rangle, \langle b \rangle, \langle \tilde{c} \rangle)$.

Output: True or False.

1: The parties randomly sample $r \in \mathbb{Z}_{2^l}$ non-interactively.
2: The parties locally compute $\langle v \rangle = r \cdot \langle a \rangle - \langle \tilde{a} \rangle$.
3: The parties invoke $\Pi_{\text{rec}}^{\text{mal}}(\langle v \rangle)$ and compute $\langle w \rangle = v \cdot \langle b \rangle - r \cdot \langle c \rangle + \langle \tilde{c} \rangle$.
4: **if** P_1 is malicious **then**
5:     P_2 sends $\langle w \rangle_2$ to P_0. P_0 computes $w = \tilde{a}_{20} \cdot \langle w \rangle_0 + \tilde{a}_{23} \cdot \langle w \rangle_3 + \tilde{a}_{22} \cdot \langle w \rangle_2$.
6: **else if** P_2 is malicious **then**
7:     P_1 sends $\langle w \rangle_1$ to P_0. P_0 computes $w = \tilde{a}_{10} \cdot \langle w \rangle_0 + \tilde{a}_{11} \cdot \langle w \rangle_1 + \tilde{a}_{13} \cdot \langle w \rangle_3$.
8: **end if**
9: P_0 outputs True if $w = 0$ and False otherwise.

---

party. Taking the reconstruction of x as an example, P_0 aggregate the shares and reconstruct x by Equations (2)–(6). If P_1 is malicious, only the reconstruction result of Equation (4) equals to Equation (6). If P_2 is malicious, only the reconstruction result of Equation (3) equals to Equation (5). We denote all the reconstruction result as x_0, x_1, x_2, x_3, x_4 respectively.

$$x_0 = a_{00} \cdot \langle x \rangle_0 + a_{01} \cdot \langle x \rangle_1 + a_{02} \cdot \langle x \rangle_2, \tag{2}$$

$$x_1 = \tilde{a}_{10} \cdot \langle x \rangle_0 + \tilde{a}_{11} \cdot \langle x \rangle_1 + \tilde{a}_{13} \cdot \langle x \rangle_3, \tag{3}$$

$$x_2 = \tilde{a}_{20} \cdot \langle x \rangle_0 + \tilde{a}_{23} \cdot \langle x \rangle_3 + \tilde{a}_{22} \cdot \langle x \rangle_2, \tag{4}$$

$$x_3 = \hat{a}_{10} \cdot \langle x \rangle_0 + \hat{a}_{11} \cdot \langle x \rangle_1 + \hat{a}_{14} \cdot \langle x \rangle_4, \tag{5}$$

$$x_4 = \hat{a}_{20} \cdot \langle x \rangle_0 + \hat{a}_{24} \cdot \langle x \rangle_4 + \hat{a}_{22} \cdot \langle x \rangle_2. \tag{6}$$

Algorithm 6 Maliciously secure reconstruction protocol $\Pi_{\text{rec}}^{\text{mal}}$

Input: The shares $\langle x \rangle$.

Output: x.

1: P_0 receives all shares from the other two parties.
2: P_0 computes x_0, x_1, x_2, x_3, x_4 by Equation (2)–Equation (6) respectively.
3: **if** $x_2 = x_4, x_0 \neq x_1 \neq x_3$ **then**
4:     P_0 outputs $x = x_2$. P_1 is malicious.
5:     P_2 receives $\langle x \rangle_0, \langle x \rangle_3$ from P_0 and computes $x = \tilde{a}_{10} \cdot \langle x \rangle_0 + \tilde{a}_{13} \cdot \langle x \rangle_3 + \tilde{a}_{12} \cdot \langle x \rangle_2$.
6: **else if** $x_1 = x_3, x_0 \neq x_2 \neq x_4$ **then**
7:     P_0 outputs $x = x_1$. P_2 is malicious.
8:     P_1 receives $\langle x \rangle_0, \langle x \rangle_3$ from P_0 and computes $x = \tilde{a}_{00} \cdot \langle x \rangle_0 + \tilde{a}_{01} \cdot \langle x \rangle_1 + \tilde{a}_{03} \cdot \langle x \rangle_3$.
9: **end if**

Up to this point, we have verified the correctness of multiplication triple in the presence of malicious party. Next we need to construct a maliciously secure multiplication protocol (Algorithm 7). Fortunately, most of the computations of semi-honest secure multiplication protocol are performed locally, except for the reconstruction process. Thus, the maliciously secure multiplication protocol can be completed by simply calling maliciously secure reconstruction protocol $\Pi_{\mathrm{rec}}^{\mathrm{mal}}$.

Algorithm 7 Maliciously secure multiplication protocol $\Pi_{\mathrm{mul}}^{\mathrm{mal}}$

Input: The shares $\langle x \rangle, \langle y \rangle$. The verified multiplication triplet $(\langle d \rangle, \langle e \rangle, \langle f \rangle)$.
Output: $\langle z \rangle = \langle x \cdot y \rangle$.
1: P_j locally computes $\langle h \rangle_j = \langle x \rangle_j + \langle d \rangle_j$ and $\langle v \rangle_j = \langle y \rangle_j + \langle e \rangle_j$. P_0 additionally computes $\langle h \rangle_3 = \langle x \rangle_3 + \langle d \rangle_3, \langle h \rangle_4 = \langle x \rangle_4 + \langle d \rangle_4$ and $\langle v \rangle_3 = \langle y \rangle_3 + \langle e \rangle_3, \langle v \rangle_4 = \langle y \rangle_4 + \langle e \rangle_4$.
2: The parties interactively invoke $\Pi_{\mathrm{rec}}^{\mathrm{mal}}(\langle h \rangle)$ and $\Pi_{\mathrm{rec}}^{\mathrm{mal}}(\langle v \rangle)$.
3: **if** P_1 is malicious **then**
4:    $P_j, j \in \{0, 2\}$ locally computes $\langle z \rangle_j = \langle x \rangle_j \cdot v - \langle e \rangle_j \cdot h + \langle f \rangle_j$.
5:    P_0 additionally computes two alternate shares $\langle z \rangle_3 = \langle x \rangle_3 \cdot v - \langle e \rangle_3 \cdot h + \langle f \rangle_3$ and $\langle z \rangle_4 = \langle x \rangle_4 \cdot v - \langle e \rangle_3 \cdot h + \langle f \rangle_4$.
6: **else if** P_2 is malicious **then**
7:    $P_j, j \in \{0, 1\}$ locally computes $\langle z \rangle_j = \langle x \rangle_j \cdot v - \langle e \rangle_j \cdot h + \langle f \rangle_j$.
8:    P_0 additionally computes two alternate shares $\langle z \rangle_3 = \langle x \rangle_3 \cdot v - \langle e \rangle_3 \cdot h + \langle f \rangle_3$ and $\langle z \rangle_4 = \langle x \rangle_4 \cdot v - \langle e \rangle_3 \cdot h + \langle f \rangle_4$.
9: **end if**

3.2   n-Party Computation Protocol

Input Sharing. We define a $(n + 2) \times n$ public matrix $\boldsymbol{\Psi}$ which the j-th row $\boldsymbol{\Psi}_j, j \in \{0, 1, ..., n - 1\}$ corresponds to $P_0, ..., P_{n-1}$ respectively. The party P_0 also holds two alternate vectors $\boldsymbol{\Psi}_n, \boldsymbol{\Psi}_{n+1}$ that equals to the linear combination of $\boldsymbol{\Psi}_0, \boldsymbol{\Psi}_1, ..., \boldsymbol{\Psi}_{n-1}$. There are public reconstruction coefficients such that

$$
\begin{aligned}
(1, 0, ..., 0) &= a_{00} \cdot \boldsymbol{\Psi}_0 + a_{01} \cdot \boldsymbol{\Psi}_1 + ... + a_{0,n-2} \cdot \boldsymbol{\Psi}_{n-2} + a_{0,n-1} \cdot \boldsymbol{\Psi}_{n-1} \\
&= \tilde{a}_{10} \cdot \boldsymbol{\Psi}_0 + \tilde{a}_{11} \cdot \boldsymbol{\Psi}_1 + ... + \tilde{a}_{1,n-2} \cdot \boldsymbol{\Psi}_{n-2} + \tilde{a}_{1,n} \cdot \boldsymbol{\Psi}_n \\
&= \tilde{a}_{20} \cdot \boldsymbol{\Psi}_0 + \tilde{a}_{21} \cdot \boldsymbol{\Psi}_1 + ... + \tilde{a}_{2,n} \cdot \boldsymbol{\Psi}_n + a_{2,n-1} \cdot \boldsymbol{\Psi}_{n-1} \\
&= ... = \tilde{a}_{n-1,0} \cdot \boldsymbol{\Psi}_0 + \tilde{a}_{n-1,n} \cdot \boldsymbol{\Psi}_n + ... + \tilde{a}_{n-1,n-1} \cdot \boldsymbol{\Psi}_{n-1} \quad (7) \\
&= \hat{a}_{10} \cdot \boldsymbol{\Psi}_0 + \hat{a}_{11} \cdot \boldsymbol{\Psi}_1 + ... + \hat{a}_{1,n+1} \cdot \boldsymbol{\Psi}_{n+1} \\
&= \hat{a}_{20} \cdot \boldsymbol{\Psi}_0 + \hat{a}_{21} \cdot \boldsymbol{\Psi}_1 + ... + \hat{a}_{2,n} \cdot \boldsymbol{\Psi}_n + \hat{a}_{2,n-1} \cdot \boldsymbol{\Psi}_{n-1} \\
&= ... = \hat{a}_{n-1,0} \cdot \boldsymbol{\Psi}_0 + \hat{a}_{n-1,n+1} \cdot \boldsymbol{\Psi}_{n+1} + ... + \hat{a}_{n-1,n-1} \cdot \boldsymbol{\Psi}_{n-1}.
\end{aligned}
$$

When a user shares the value x, it sets a n-dimensional vector $\boldsymbol{u}$ to compute $\langle \cdot \rangle$-shares of x. As shown in Algorithm 8, the user firstly selects $n - 1$ random values $u_1, ..., u_{n-1} \in_R Z_p$ and obtains $\boldsymbol{u} = (x, u_1, ..., u_{n-1})^T$. Then it computes $\langle x \rangle_j = \boldsymbol{\Psi}_j \cdot \boldsymbol{u}$ for $P_j, j \in \{0, ..., n-1\}$ respectively (Additionally $\langle x \rangle_n = \boldsymbol{\Psi}_n \cdot \boldsymbol{u}$ and $\langle x \rangle_{n+1} = \boldsymbol{\Psi}_{n+1} \cdot \boldsymbol{u}$ for P_0).
Computation with Semi-honest Security. As mentioned earlier, each party can locally compute $\langle c_1 \cdot x + c_2 \cdot y \rangle = c_1 \cdot \langle x \rangle + c_2 \cdot \langle y \rangle$ with $\langle x \rangle, \langle y \rangle$ and constants

---

Algorithm 8 The n-party sharing protocol Π_{shr}^n

Input: The value x held by a user
Output: $\langle x \rangle$.
  1: The user sets a n-dimensional vector $\boldsymbol{u} = (x, u_1, ..., u_{n-1})^T$ in which $u_1, ..., u_{n-1}$ are randomly selected from Z_p.
  2: The user generates and sends $\langle x \rangle_j = \boldsymbol{\Psi}_j \cdot \boldsymbol{u}$ to $P_j, j \in \{0, ..., n-1\}$ respectively. Additionally, it computes the alternate shares $\langle x \rangle_n = \boldsymbol{\Psi}_n \cdot \boldsymbol{u}$ and $\langle x \rangle_{n+1} = \boldsymbol{\Psi}_{n+1} \cdot \boldsymbol{u}$ for P_0.

---

c_1, c_2. For n-party multiplication, it is similar to 3-party setting except for the way of generating multiplication triples. However, the extension of triples generation from 3-party to n-party is intuitive, so we will not go into that. Remark that even if $P_1, P_2..., P_{n-1}$ collude with each other, the secret x cannot be revealed without P_0.

Computation with Malicious Security. For local additions and multiplications with public constants, the computation is the same as semi-honest version. For multiplication, we use n-party maliciously secure triple sacrificing method to verify triples correctness, which is analogous to $\Pi_{\text{tsa}}^{\text{mal}}$. The core component of multiplication is reconstruction process that can identify and exclude the malicious party. This is because reconstruction is the only process that requires interaction. Specific identification process is also based on the equivalence of reconstruction results. Concretely, the reconstruction results based on malicious party's share are unequal, while the results based on semi-honest party's share are equal. Since P_0 is semi-honest, we allow P_0 to reconstruct intermediate results firstly and exclude the malicious party in $\{P_1, P_2, ..., P_{n-1}\}$. The subsequent computations are performed locally between semi-honest participants.

4 Privacy-Preserving Machine Learning

4.1 ML Building Blocks

Secure Comparison. Given shares $\langle x \rangle, \langle y \rangle$, the comparison operation is to check if $x < y$ by extracting the most significant bit (MSB) of $x - y$. It outputs $\langle b \rangle = \langle \text{MSB}(x - y) \rangle = \langle 1 \rangle$ if $x < y$ and $\langle 0 \rangle$ otherwise. In this paper, we use the boolean variant of Parallel Prefix Adder (PPA) circuit to tackle MSB extraction, which is proposed by ABY3 [13]. This circuit has $2l$ AND gates and the multiplicative depth is $logl$. It receives two boolean format inputs and outputs the MSB of the sum of inputs. Therefore, we need to convert $\langle \cdot \rangle$-shares to $[\![\cdot]\!]$-shares firstly and then convert $[\![\cdot]\!]$-shares to $[\![\cdot]\!]^2$-shares. The first conversion of x can be achieved by Equations (2)–(6). For instance, the parties can compute locally $[\![x]\!]_0 = a_{00} \cdot \langle x \rangle_0, [\![x]\!]_1 = a_{01} \cdot \langle x \rangle_1, [\![x]\!]_2 = a_{02} \cdot \langle x \rangle_2$ according to Equation (2). About y, the conversion is the same. After that, the parties convert $[\![x]\!]$ and $-[\![y]\!]$ to $[\![x]\!]^2, -[\![y]\!]^2$ with the existing methods [13,21,22]. However, since the first conversion is done locally, a malicious party may perform an incorrect conversion without being detected. Performing subsequent computations with the wrong conversion will lead to invalid results. Fortunately, there are always two conversions (from two Equations) are correct, regardless of whether P_1 or P_2 is malicious. The parties can perform conversions and computations several times, taking the two identical results as final result. This helps to identify and exclude malicious party. Finally, the parties obtain boolean sharing of $[\![b]\!]^2 = [\![\text{MSB}(x - y)]\!]^2$. As for the conversion from $[\![b]\!]^2$ to $\langle b \rangle$, we recommend readers to refer to [19] for further details.

Secure Truncation. For two fixed-point numbers with a fractional part of l_f-bit, the result of multiplication will have $2l_f$-bit precision. In order to keep the result in the same format as inputs, we need to execute truncation operation. We assume that the random truncation pair $(\langle r \rangle, \langle r' \rangle)$ [19] which $\langle r' \rangle = \langle r/2^{l_f} \rangle, r, r' \in \mathbb{Z}_{2^l}$ has been honestly generated and pre-shared. Given shares $\langle z \rangle$, the truncation protocol needs to output $\langle z' \rangle$ where $z' = z/2^{l_f}$. As shown in Algorithm 9, the identification and exclusion of malicious party relies on the invocation of maliciously secure multiplication.

Algorithm 9 Maliciously secure truncation protocol $\Pi_{\text{tru}}^{\text{mal}}$

Input: The shares $\langle z \rangle$. The truncation pair $(\langle r \rangle, \langle r' \rangle)$ which $\langle r' \rangle = \langle r/2^{l_f} \rangle$.
Output: $\langle z' \rangle$ which $z' = z/2^{l_f}$.
1: P_j locally computes $\langle z - r \rangle_j = \langle z \rangle_j - \langle r \rangle_j$. P_0 additionally computes $\langle z - r \rangle_3 = \langle z \rangle_3 - \langle r \rangle_3$ and $\langle z - r \rangle_4 = \langle z \rangle_4 - \langle r \rangle_4$.
2: P_0 invokes $\Pi_{\text{rec}}^{\text{mal}}(\langle z - r \rangle)$ to obtain $z - r$ and identify malicious party.
3: **if** P_1 is malicious **then**
4:     P_0 computes $\langle z \rangle_0 = (z - r)/(2^{l_f} \cdot \tilde{a}_{20}) + \langle r' \rangle_0, \langle z \rangle_3 = \langle r' \rangle_3, \langle z \rangle_4 = \langle r' \rangle_4$.
5:     P_2 computes $\langle z \rangle_2 = \langle r' \rangle_2$.
6: **else if** P_2 is malicious **then**
7:     P_0 computes $\langle z \rangle_0 = (z - r)/(2^{l_f} \cdot \tilde{a}_{10}) + \langle r' \rangle_0, \langle z \rangle_3 = \langle r' \rangle_3, \langle z \rangle_4 = \langle r' \rangle_4$.
8:     P_2 computes $\langle z \rangle_2 = \langle r' \rangle_2$.
9: **end if**

Secure Activation Function. For input x, the ReLU function can be defined as $\text{ReLU}(x) = max(0, x)$. This is also viewed as $\text{ReLU}(x) = (1 \oplus b) \cdot x$, which b is the most significant bit of x. If $x < 0$, $b = 1$ and vice-versa. Given shares $\langle x \rangle$, the maliciously secure ReLU protocol (Algorithm 10) outputs $\langle \text{ReLU}(x) \rangle$, where $\text{ReLU}(x) = 0$ if $x < 0$ and x otherwise. The sigmoid function can be defined as $\text{Sigmoid}(x) = 1/(1 + e^{-x})$. We use the approximation technique as [12], that is $\text{Sigmoid}(x) = b_2 \cdot (1 \oplus b_1) \cdot (x + 1/2) + (1 \oplus b_2)$. Note that $b_1 = 1$ if $x + 1/2 < 0$ and $b_2 = 1$ if $x - 1/2 < 0$. Given shares $\langle x \rangle$, the maliciously secure sigmoid protocol that outputs $\langle \text{Sigmoid}(x) \rangle$ is similar to that of ReLU. Since only multiplication operation requires interaction, we execute multiplication protocol $\Pi_{\text{mul}}^{\text{mal}}$ for identifying and excluding malicious party.

Algorithm 10 Maliciously secure ReLU protocol $\Pi_{\text{ReLU}}^{\text{mal}}$
___
Input: The shares $\langle x \rangle$.
Output: $\langle \text{ReLU}(x) \rangle$, which $\text{ReLU}(x) = 0$ if $x < 0$ and x otherwise.
 1: The parties execute MSB extraction of $\langle x \rangle$ to obtain $\langle b \rangle$ and exclude malicious party.
 2: The remaining parties locally compute $\langle 1 \oplus b \rangle$.
 3: The remaining parties invokes $\Pi_{\text{mul}}^{\text{semi}}(\langle 1 \oplus b \rangle, \langle x \rangle)$ to obtain $\langle \text{ReLU}(x) \rangle$.
___

Secure Division. Given shares $\langle x \rangle, \langle y \rangle$, the division protocol needs to output $\langle z \rangle$ which $z = x/y$. As shown in Algorithm 11, our maliciously secure version requires the user to share a random $r \in \mathbb{Z}_{2^l}$ between the parties. The identification and exclusion of malicious party relies on the invocation of maliciously secure multiplication protocol.

Algorithm 11 Maliciously secure division protocol $\Pi_{\text{div}}^{\text{mal}}$
___
Input: The shares $\langle x \rangle, \langle y \rangle$.
Output: $\langle z \rangle$ which $z = x/y$.
 1: The user randomly selects $r \in \mathbb{Z}_{2^l}$ and invokes $\Pi_{\text{shr}}^3(r)$.
 2: $P_j, j \in \{0, 1, 2\}$ invokes $\Pi_{\text{mul}}^{\text{mal}}(\langle r \rangle, \langle x \rangle), \Pi_{\text{mul}}^{\text{mal}}(\langle r \rangle, \langle y \rangle)$ to compute $\langle r \cdot x \rangle, \langle r \cdot y \rangle$ and identify the malicious party.
 3: **if** P_1 is malicious **then**
 4:     $P_j, j \in \{0, 2\}$ sends $\langle r \cdot y \rangle_j$ to each other and compute $r \cdot y = \tilde{a}_{20} \cdot \langle r \cdot y \rangle_0 + \tilde{a}_{22} \cdot \langle r \cdot y \rangle_2 + \tilde{a}_{23} \cdot \langle r \cdot y \rangle_3$.
 5:     P_0 computes $\langle z \rangle_0 = \langle r \cdot x \rangle_0 / (r \cdot y), \langle z \rangle_3 = \langle r \cdot x \rangle_3 / (r \cdot y), \langle z \rangle_4 = \langle r \cdot x \rangle_4 / (r \cdot y)$. P_2 computes $\langle z \rangle_2 = \langle r \cdot x \rangle_1 / (r \cdot y)$.
 6: **else if** P_2 is malicious **then**
 7:     $P_j, j \in \{0, 1\}$ sends $\langle r \cdot y \rangle_j$ to each other and compute $r \cdot y = \tilde{a}_{00} \cdot \langle r \cdot y \rangle_0 + \tilde{a}_{01} \cdot \langle r \cdot y \rangle_1 + \tilde{a}_{03} \cdot \langle r \cdot y \rangle_3$.
 8:     P_0 computes $\langle z \rangle_0 = \langle r \cdot x \rangle_0 / (r \cdot y), \langle z \rangle_3 = \langle r \cdot x \rangle_3 / (r \cdot y), \langle z \rangle_4 = \langle r \cdot x \rangle_4 / (r \cdot y)$. P_1 computes $\langle z \rangle_1 = \langle r \cdot x \rangle_1 / (r \cdot y)$.
 9: **end if**
___

4.2 Secure Prediction

We consider an outsourced server-aided scenario where model owner and client outsource the $\langle \cdot \rangle$-shares of model parameters and query to cloud service providers, respectively. The service providers then securely compute ML algorithms via our multi-party protocol and return the result share to client. Finally, the client reconstructs prediction output based on the received information. Once the data is outsourced, the model owner and client will lose control. Note that not all service providers are malicious, most of them are rational. In this section, we allow for one malicious service provider and the rest are semi-honest. Our scheme ensures that the malicious service provider will be identified once it performs malicious behavior. After the service provider is identified and excluded, the computation can still continue, which is called "robustness". Such malicious service provider will be blacklisted and not be used when there are other computing demands.

In order to achieve secure prediction, the client needs to perform some special operations honestly, such as truncated pair generation in Algorithm 9 and randomness generation in Algorithm 11 (step 1). Since client is the sole receiver of outputs, the incentive for client to compute dishonestly is low. Moreover, these operations can be performed in advance without increasing the overhead of online prediction. In the following, we present a high-level overview of prediction functions. More optimization techniques, such as matrix operation, can be found in [12,13,23]. We consider linear regression, logistic regression, neural network and k-means clustering. For linear regression, the prediction output for a query vector $\langle \boldsymbol{x} \rangle$ is given by $\langle \boldsymbol{w} \odot \boldsymbol{x} \rangle = \sum_{i=1}^{d} \langle \boldsymbol{w}_i \rangle \langle \boldsymbol{x}_i \rangle$, which $\boldsymbol{w}$ is model parameters and d is the number of features. The computation of logistic remains the same as linear regression, except for an additional sigmoid function that previously described. For neural network, we consider the LeNet network [24] as in [8], which has about 431K parameters. We use ReLU function in non-linear activation layer. For k-means clustering, the basic operators include Euclidean distance, comparison and division. Specific computation about Euclidean distance can refer to [23], which the multiplication protocol is substituted by our malicious version.

5   Security Proofs

In this section, we prove that our framework can guarantee privacy in the presence of malicious adversary. The proofs for semi-honest secure protocols, such as Π_{shr} and $\Pi_{\text{mul}}^{\text{semi}}$, is intuitive and follows the considerations in [19,23]. Since the core of most maliciously protocols is the maliciously secure reconstruction protocol $\Pi_{\text{rec}}^{\text{mal}}$, we present the security proof of $\Pi_{\text{rec}}^{\text{mal}}$ firstly.

Theorem 1. *The protocol $\Pi_{\text{rec}}^{\text{mal}}$ is secure against a static, malicious adversary $\mathcal{A}$ that corrupts P_1 or P_2.*

Proof. Without prejudice to the generality, we focus on the case for corrupt P_1 while the case for corrupt P_2 is performed symmetrically. Suppose that $\mathcal{A}$ is a real-world adversary that corrupts P_1. We construct an ideal-world simulator $\mathcal{S}_{\text{rec}}$ that plays the roles of P_0, P_2 and simulates the information received by P_1. The simulator $\mathcal{S}_{\text{rec}}$ receives all shares from $\mathcal{A}$ on behalf of P_0. Then $\mathcal{S}_{\text{rec}}$ sends random $\langle x' \rangle_0, \langle x' \rangle_3 \in \mathbb{Z}_{2^l}$ to $\mathcal{A}$ on behalf of P_0. Finally, the simulator $\mathcal{S}_{\text{rec}}$ outputs $\mathcal{A}$'s output. It can be easily seen that the real-world view and simulated view of adversary are computationally indistinguishable.

Theorem 2. *The protocol $\Pi_{\text{tsa}}^{\text{mal}}$ is secure against the malicious adversary $\mathcal{A}$ that corrupts P_1 or P_2.*

Proof. Suppose that $\mathcal{A}$ is a real-world adversary that corrupts P_1. We construct an ideal-world simulator $\mathcal{S}_{\text{tsa}}$ that acts as P_0, P_2 and simulates the information received from P_1. Firstly, $\mathcal{S}_{\text{tsa}}$ simulates the protocol execution of $\Pi_{\text{rec}}^{\text{mal}}$ as $\mathcal{S}_{\text{rec}}$. On behalf of P_0, the simulator $\mathcal{S}_{\text{tsa}}$ receives a random $\langle w' \rangle \in \mathbb{Z}_{2^l}$ from $\mathcal{A}$. The case for corrupt P_2 is similar. Our proof simply obtains from that the real-world view and simulated view of adversary are computationally indistinguishable.

Theorem 3. *The protocol $\Pi_{\text{mul}}^{\text{mal}}$ is secure against the malicious adversary $\mathcal{A}$ that corrupts P_1 or P_2.*

Proof. We present the case for corrupt P_1 while the case for corrupt P_2 is similar. Suppose that $\mathcal{A}$ is a real-world malicious adversary that corrupts P_1 during the protocol. We construct an ideal-world simulator $\mathcal{S}_{\text{mul}}$ that acts as P_0, P_2 and simulates the information received by P_1. The only communication of P_1 is during the maliciously reconstruction protocols $\Pi_{\text{rec}}^{\text{mal}}(\langle h \rangle)$ and $\Pi_{\text{rec}}^{\text{mal}}(\langle v \rangle)$. Hence $\mathcal{S}_{\text{mul}}$ can easily simulate the interactive information as $\mathcal{S}_{\text{rec}}$. Not surprisingly, the real-world view and simulated view of adversary are computationally indistinguishable.

Theorem 4. *The protocol $\Pi_{\text{tru}}^{\text{mal}}$ is secure against the malicious adversary $\mathcal{A}$ that corrupts P_1 or P_2.*

Proof. We present the case for corrupt P_1 while the case for corrupt P_2 is similar. Suppose that $\mathcal{A}$ is a real-world malicious adversary that corrupts P_1 during the protocol. We construct an ideal-world simulator $\mathcal{S}_{\text{tru}}$ that acts as P_0, P_2 and simulates the information received by P_1. The only communication of P_1 is during the maliciously reconstruction protocols $\Pi_{\text{rec}}^{\text{mal}}(\langle z - r \rangle)$. Hence $\mathcal{S}_{\text{tru}}$ can easily simulate the messages as $\mathcal{S}_{\text{rec}}$. It is straight that the real-world view and simulated view of adversary are computationally indistinguishable.

Theorem 5. *The secure comparison protocol is secure against the malicious adversary $\mathcal{A}$ that corrupts P_1 or P_2.*

Proof. This protocol involves the basic reconstruction and multiplication protocol whose security is proved in Theorem 1 and Theorem 3, respectively. The security of comparison can be proved through the computational indistinguishability of corrupted party's view and simulated view. This is straight and similar with the above proofs.

Theorem 6. *The protocol $\Pi_{\text{ReLU}}^{\text{mal}}$ is secure against the malicious adversary $\mathcal{A}$ that corrupts P_1 or P_2.*

Proof. This protocol involves the secure comparison protocol whose security is proved in Theorem 4. After that, the second interaction is from the semi-honest multiplication protocol. It is obvious that the corrupted party's view and simulated view are computational indistinguishable.

Theorem 7. *The protocol $\Pi_{\text{div}}^{\text{mal}}$ is secure against the malicious adversary $\mathcal{A}$ that corrupts P_1 or P_2.*

Proof. Suppose that $\mathcal{A}$ is a real-world malicious adversary that corrupts P_1 during the protocol. We construct an ideal-world simulator $\mathcal{S}_{\text{div}}$ that acts as P_0, P_2 and simulates the information received by P_1. The only communication of P_1 is during the maliciously multiplication protocols $\Pi_{\text{mul}}^{\text{mal}}(\langle r \rangle, \langle x \rangle)$ and $\Pi_{\text{mul}}^{\text{mal}}(\langle r \rangle, \langle y \rangle)$. Hence $\mathcal{S}_{\text{div}}$ can easily simulate the messages as $\mathcal{S}_{\text{mul}}$. The case for corrupt P_2 is analogous and we omit details here. It can be easily seen that the real-world view and simulated view of adversary are computationally indistinguishable.

6 Performance and Implementation

6.1 Complexity Analysis

Table 1 details the communication comparison between our work, SWIFT [8] and Fantastic Four [9]. We use l_f to denote the number of bits for the fractional part of a ring element. Note that κ is security parameter and d is the input size. The $<$ indicates that the complexity is slightly less than a multiple of l. For multiplication, the pre-processing operations denote multiplication triplet generation and triplet sacrificing. For truncation, the pre-processing operation denotes truncation pair generation. For division, the pre-processing operation denotes the sharing of random value. For MSB extraction, the share conversion from $[\![\cdot]\!]$ to $[\![\cdot]\!]^2$ requires l parallel Full Adder circuit, each comprising of a AND gate. Additionally, the boolean variant of PPA circuit requires $2l$ AND gates. Since each AND gate requires $\Pi_{\text{mul}}^{\text{mal}}$ to be executed, the 3PC requires an amortized communication of $12l$ bits. The analysis of 4PC is similar. Although SWIFT appears to be more efficient than our solution in online phase, its security is debatable. Specifically, SWIFT relies on the honest party who learns all secrets to complete the computation in plaintext. The security definition of MPC is only concerned with protecting secret inputs from malicious party, so this approach is permissible. However, in practice, the users expect the computing framework to protect sensitive inputs from disclosure, including by any party in the framework. For 4PC, our online communication outperforms Fantastic Four [9].

6.2 Experiment Evaluation

The experiments are performed on multiple Linux servers equipped with an Intel(R) Xeon(TM) CPU, operating at 2.0GHz with 8GB RAM in Ubuntu 20.04 operating system. We consider two different network environments, i.e., the LAN setting with average latency of 0.8ms and WAN setting with average latency of 67ms. In both LAN and WAN setups, each of the two parties (i.e., server) is connected via a two-way communication channel, facilitating the simultaneous exchange of data. We implement our scheme in C++ using open source library [25] and set the ring as $Z_{2^{64}}$ (the length of fractional part $l_f = 13$). Furthermore, we set $\boldsymbol{\Psi}_0 = (1, 0, 1), \boldsymbol{\Psi}_1 = (1, 1, 2^l - 1), \boldsymbol{\Psi}_2 = (2, 2, 2^l - 3), \boldsymbol{\Psi}_3 = (3, 3, 2^l - 4), \boldsymbol{\Psi}_4 = (0, 1, 2^l - 2)$. We use the MINIST dataset containing handwritten digits from zero to nine. It has 60K training samples and 10K test samples, each with

Table 1. The comparison of amortized communication for ML building blocks

		3PC			4PC	
		Pre-processing†	Online		Pre-processing†	Online
Multiplication	SWIFT	$3l$	$3l$	Fantastic Four	–	$6(l+\kappa)$
	This work	$(2l)^{gen} + (5l)^{sac}$	$4l$	This work	$(3l)^{gen} + (8l)^{sac}$	$6l$
Dot Product	SWIFT	$3l$	$3l$	Fantastic Four	–	$6l$
	This work	–	$4ld$	This work	–	$6ld$
MSB extraction	SWIFT	$9l$	$9l$	Fantastic Four	–	$< 30l$
	This work	–	$12l$	This work	–	$18l$
Truncation	SWIFT	$12l$	$3l$	Fantastic Four	$3l$	$12l$
	This work	$4l$	$4l$	This work	$6l$	$6l$
ReLU	SWIFT	$21l$	$16l$	Fantastic Four	–	–
	This work	–	$17l$	This work	–	$26l$
Division	SWIFT	–	–	Fantastic Four	–	–
	This work	$5l$	$6l$	This work	$6l$	$9l$

† : gen, sac denote the triplet generation and sacrificing, respectively.

784 features representing 28×28 pixels. For regression, we explore a binary classification with the number "0" in one class and the number "1~9" in the other. For clustering and neural network, we explore a ten-level classification task.

ML Building Blocks. As illustrated in Fig. 1, we evaluate the computation cost of building blocks in LAN and WAN setting, respectively. Since the computation of sigmoid function is similar to that of ReLU, we only present the running time of secure ReLU protocol. We observe that the runtime of all protocols increases slightly as the number of parties increases. This is due to the fact that some operations between parties can be parallelized. In addition, the computation cost of both secure comparison and secure ReLU is higher than the others. The similarity happens because they both require multiple executions of share conversion and PPA circuit to caught the malicious party. Note that we omit the time in pre-processing phase, such as truncated pair generation. We also present the communication overhead of building blocks. As shown in Fig. 2, the online communication of truncation and division is similar, with small deviations attributed to differences in multiplication and reconstruction protocols. For comparison and ReLU function, the main bottleneck is the AND gate in PPA circuit, which requires interactive computation. Obviously, the communication cost of these protocols grows linearly as the increase of the number of parties.

Secure Prediction. In Table 2, we present the time of regression, neural network and k-means clustering for query. Runtime is measured in milliseconds in LAN setting and in seconds in WAN setting. We compare this work with SWIFT[8] and Fantastic Four[9], respectively. We use online prediction time as a metric to compare these works. For 3PC, SWIFT is around $1.25\times \sim 2.1\times$ faster than our work. We believe there are two reasons for this performance

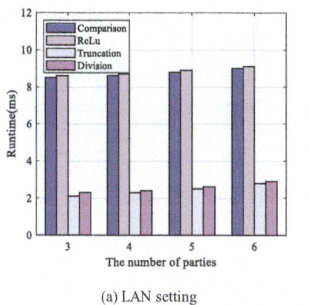
(a) LAN setting

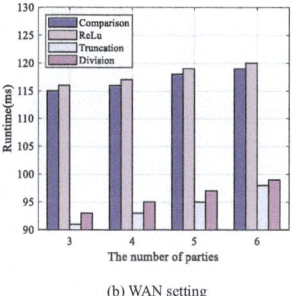
(b) WAN setting

Fig. 1. Runtime of building blocks

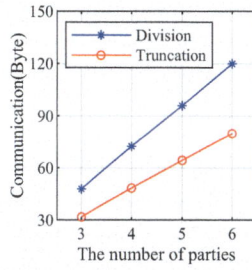

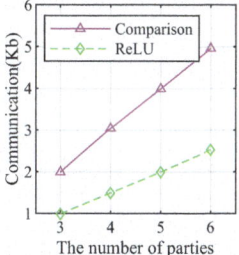

Fig. 2. The communication overhead of building blocks

Table 2. The comparison of online prediction time

		3PC			4PC	
		LAN(ms)	WAN(s)		LAN(ms)	WAN(s)
Linear Regression	SWIFT	–	0.008	Fantastic Four	1.5	0.1
	This work	0.8	0.01	This work	1.12	0.02
Logistic Regression	SWIFT	–	0.022	Fantastic Four	6.4	0.17
	This work	1.75	0.03	This work	2.4	0.05
Neural Network	SWIFT	–	0.053	Fantastic Four	56.8	0.56
	This work	12.7	0.08	This work	13.6	0.1
Clustering	SWIFT	–	–	Fantastic Four	18.3	0.2
	This work	5.3	0.05	This work	6.1	0.07

difference. Firstly, the experiment environment is different. The experimental results of SWIFT are obtained from [8,26], which equipped with 2.3 GHz Intel Xeon processors and 30GB of RAM. Secondly, the underlying dot product in SWIFT is efficient and independent of inputs dimension. However, since our solution achieves privacy robustness [9,27] and is resistant to collusion attacks, the performance difference is acceptable. For security considerations, each step of our scheme needs to identify malicious party. In practice, if a malicious party can be excluded at the beginning, the later identification can be omitted which

Table 3. The comparison of online communication overhead

		Communication(Kb)			
		Linear Regression	Logistic Regression	Neural Network	Clustering
3PC	SWIFT	0.25	0.69	358.4	–
	This work	0.31	5.7	419.84	10.5
4PC	Fantastic Four	0.86	26.35	1507.35	65.75
	This work	0.3	7.1	386.5	17.2
	Improved factor	2.87	3.71	3.9	3.76

will significantly improve efficiency. Thus, our scheme remains very promising. For 4PC, our work outperforms Fantastic Four [9] because the SPDZ-wise protocols in [9] requires lots of data authentication and verification. We can derive the communication overhead of prediction from Table 3. For regression and neural network of 3PC, the communication cost of SWIFT is smaller than our work. We attribute this to the fact that the overhead of our activation function needs complex comparison operations. For clustering, we set $k = 5$. Our 4PC framework outperforms Fantastic Four by a factor of $2.87\times \sim 3.9\times$. Notably, our scheme recognizes the malicious server and continues the computation after excluding it, without any complex operations.

Acknowledgements. The work was supported by the Shandong Provincial Key Research and Development Program (No. 2021CXGC010107), the National Natural Science Foundation of China (Nos. 62325209), the Major Program (JD) of Hubei Province (No. 2023BAA027), and the Fundamental Research Funds for the Central Universities (Nos. 2042023KF0203, 2042024kf1013).

References

1. Yao, A.C.: Protocols for secure computations. In: Proceedings of the 23rd Annual Symposium on Foundations of Computer Science, pp. 160–164. IEEE (1982)
2. Yao, A.C.-C.: How to generate and exchange secrets. In: Proceedings of the 27th Annual Symposium on Foundations of Computer Science, pp. 162–167. IEEE (1986)
3. Kamara, S., Mohassel, P., Raykova, M.: Outsourcing multi-party computation. Cryptology ePrint Archive (2011)
4. Lehmkuhl, R., Mishra, P., Srinivasan, A., Popa, R.A.: Muse: secure inference resilient to malicious clients. In: Proceedings of the 30th USENIX Security Symposium, pp. 2201–2218 (2021)
5. Chandran, N., Gupta, D., Obbattu, S.L.B., Shah, A.: SIMC: ML inference secure against malicious clients at semi-honest cost. In: Proceedings of the 31st USENIX Security Symposium, pp. 1361–1378 (2022)
6. Brüggemann, A., Schick, O., Schneider, T., Suresh, A., Yalame, H.: Don't eject the impostor: fast three-party computation with a known cheater. In: Proceedings of the 45th IEEE Symposium on Security and Privacy, pp. 164–164. IEEE Computer Society (2024)

7. Byali, M., Chaudhari, H., Patra, A., Suresh, A.: Flash: fast and robust framework for privacy-preserving machine learning. Cryptology ePrint Archive (2019)
8. Koti, N., Pancholi, M., Patra, A., Suresh, A.: Swift: super-fast and robust privacy-preserving machine learning. In: Proceedings of the 30th USENIX Security Symposium (2021)
9. Dalskov, A., Escudero, D., Keller, M.: Fantastic four: honest-majority four-party secure computation with malicious security. In: Proceedings of the 30th USENIX Security Symposium, pp. 2183–2200 (2021)
10. Demmler, D., Schneider, T., Zohner, M.: Aby-a framework for efficient mixed-protocol secure two-party computation. In: Proceedings of the 22nd Network and Distributed System Security Symposium (2015)
11. Patra, A., Schneider, T., Suresh, A., Yalame, H.: Aby2.0: improved mixed-protocol secure two-party computation. In: Proceedings of the 30th USENIX Security Symposium (2021)
12. Mohassel, P., Zhang, Y.: SECUREML: a system for scalable privacy-preserving machine learning. In: Proceedings of the 38th IEEE Symposium on Security and Privacy, pp. 19–38. IEEE (2017)
13. Mohassel, P., Rindal, P.: Aby3: a mixed protocol framework for machine learning. In: Proceedings of the 2018 ACM SIGSAC Conference on Computer and Communications Security, pp. 35–52 (2018)
14. Chaudhari, H., Choudhury, A., Patra, A., Suresh, A.: Astra: high throughput 3pc over rings with application to secure prediction. In: Proceedings of the 2019 ACM SIGSAC Conference on Cloud Computing Security Workshop, pp. 81–92 (2019)
15. Patra, A., Suresh, A.: Blaze: blazing fast privacy-preserving machine learning (2020). arXiv:2005.09042
16. Byali, M., Chaudhari, H., Patra, A., Suresh, A.: Flash: fast and robust framework for privacy-preserving machine learning. Proc. Privacy Enhancing Technol. **2020**(2), 459–480 (2020)
17. Chaudhari, H., Rachuri, R., Suresh, A.: Trident: efficient 4pc framework for privacy preserving machine learning (2019). arXiv:1912.02631
18. Brickell, E.F.: Some ideal secret sharing schemes. In: Workshop on the Theory and Application of of Cryptographic Techniques, pp. 468–475. Springer (1989)
19. Song, L., et al.: PMPL: a robust multi-party learning framework with a privileged party. In: Proceedings of the 2022 ACM SIGSAC Conference on Computer and Communications Security, pp. 2689–2703. ACM (2022)
20. Eerikson, H., Keller, M., Orlandi, C., Pullonen, P., Puura, J., Simkin, M.: Use your brain! Arithmetic 3pc for any modulus with active security. Cryptology ePrint Archive (2019)
21. Damgård, I., Escudero, D., Frederiksen, T., Keller, M., Scholl, P., Volgushev, N.: New primitives for actively-secure MPC over rings with applications to private machine learning. In: Proceedings of the 40th IEEE Symposium on Security and Privacy, pp. 1102–1120. IEEE (2019)
22. Braun, L., Demmler, D., Schneider, T., Tkachenko, O.: Motion-a framework for mixed-protocol multi-party computation. ACM Trans. Privacy Secur. **25**(2), 1–35 (2022)
23. Qin, H., He, D., Obaidat, M.S., Vijayakumar, P., Sivaraman, A.: Secure and robust three-party k-means clustering based on cloud-edge-client collaboration. ACM Trans. Multimedia Comput. Commun. Appl. (2024)
24. LeCun, Y., Bottou, L., Bengio, Y., Haffner, P.: Gradient-based learning applied to document recognition. Proc. IEEE **86**(11), 2278–2324 (1998)

25. Song, L., Wang, Z.: PMPL [online] (2022). https://github.com/FudanMPL/pMPL
26. Ajith, S.: MPCLeague: Robust MPC Platform for Privacy-Preserving Machine Learning. Ph.D. thesis. Indian Institute of Science Bangalore (2021)
27. Alon, B., Omri, E., Paskin-Cherniavsky, A.: MPC with friends and foes. In: Proceedings of the 40th Annual International Cryptology Conference, pp. 677–706. Springer (2020)

Controlled Multi-client Functional Encryption for Flexible Access Control

Mingwu Zhang[1,2](✉), Yulu Zhong[1], Yifei Wang[3], and Yuntao Wang[4]

[1] School of Computer Science and Information Security, Guilin University of Electronic Technology, Guilin, China
[2] School of Computers, Hubei University of Technology, Wuhan, China
csmwzhang@gmail.com
[3] School of Mathematics, The University of Edinburgh, Edinburgh, UK
[4] School of Informatics and Engineering, The University of Electro-Communications, Chofu, Japan

Abstract. In Controlled Functional Encryption (C-FE), a policy parameter is introduced during encryption to restrict how the decryptor can decrypt and compute the ciphertext, but C-FE shows certain limitations in complex scenarios involving multiple encryptors participating with their data remaining confidential from each other. To overcome these limitations and leverage the advantages of Multi-Client Functional Encryption (MCFE) and Attribute-Based Encryption (ABE), we extend C-FE, introducing a new primitive termed Controlled Multi-Client Functional Encryption for Flexible Access Control (CMCFE-FAC). This primitive introduces several key innovations: firstly, our CMCFE-FAC scheme combines MCFE to support multiple encryptors, enabling independent encryption and ensuring data privacy and security. Secondly, CMCFE-FAC combines attribute-based mechanisms to support dynamic access control, expanding traditional access control policies and enhancing their flexibility. Thirdly, we formalize the definition and security model for CMCFE-FAC, propose a CMCFE-FAC scheme tailored for the inner product function, and demonstrate the scheme's security based on the DBDH assumption. Finally, theoretical analysis and experimental results are provided to illustrate its effectiveness and security.

Keywords: Functional Encryption · Inner Product · Multi-Client · Access Control

1 Introduction

1.1 Backgrounds

With the advent of the big data era, the sharing of medical data has become a pivotal trend to advance medical research and enhance the quality of disease diagnosis and treatment [17]. However, this presents a significant challenge: how to ensure the privacy and security of patient data while facilitating medical research, particularly in preventing research institutions from misusing the data after decryption.

Functional Encryption (FE) can mitigate this issue, first proposed by Boneh et al. [9]. FE introduces a more flexible access control mechanism, allowing the decryption result to be the value of a function of the encrypted message. This ensures that after data sharing, only the computed results related to the private data can be obtained. However, FE cannot restrict how the decrypting party (user) computes with the private data, which requires additional access control measures to address.

Controlled Functional Encryption (C-FE) [20] introduces a policy parameter during the encryption process provided by the encryptor. When a decryptor (user) wishes to perform decryption, it must send a key request to an authority. The authority evaluates whether the decryptor meets the policy requirements and decides whether to issue the key. This ensures that data can only be computed under the specified policy.

1.2   Motivation and Application Scenarios

Motivation The current C-FE schemes are not well-suited to real-world medical scenarios.

- In real-world medical scenarios, medical data is typically fragmented and managed by different data owners who do not trust each other. In such cases, it is necessary to encrypt the data from various parties without mutual trust, which has not been adequately addressed in previous solutions.
- Additionally, previous C-FE schemes only incorporate simple policy parameters during encryption, lacking the capability to finely control access permissions and dynamically evaluate access requests.

To address these issues, we propose a multi-client FE scheme with access control capabilities in the standard model, similar to C-FE. We extend the concept of C-FE to the multi-client setting, leveraging the idea of MCFE to protect the privacy of these independent data owners. Meanwhile, the "controlled" aspect is based on Attribute-Based Encryption (ABE) [14], which supports fine-grained control over user access to data.

Scenarios In modern healthcare systems, Electronic Health Records (EHR) [16] have become essential tools for recording and managing patients' health information. These health data originate from various entities such as hospitals, clinics, and laboratories. Researchers aim to use this private data for their studies, but data owners do not want these private data to be used for other purposes and wish to restrict access to designated personnel only. Data Owners can encrypt the EHR data based on researchers' attributes (e.g., cardiology, Project A, early-stage research) and generate corresponding access policies, which are then sent to a trusted third-party authority. These encrypted data can be stored on a cloud server. If researchers wish to decrypt and analyze this private data, they must submit a request to a trusted third-party authority. The authority will evaluate whether the request meets the predefined access policies (e.g., the researcher's policy being cardiology AND Project A). If the criteria are met, the authority will issue a decryption key; otherwise, the request will be denied. Once the researchers obtain the key, they can decrypt the data and perform computations to obtain the desired research results.

1.3   Our Contributions

The following is a summary of this paper's contributions:

- We provide a definition and specific construction of Controlled Multi-Client Functional Encryption for Flexible Access Control (CMCFE-FAC) and prove that the construction is secure under the Decisional Bilinear Diffie-Hellman (DBDH) assumption. Unlike existing C-FE, we extend this to accommodate multi-client scenarios, which support multiple encryptors, i.e., multiple clients. The decentralized data input parties encrypt their data, jointly design the access policy, and send the policy to the authority, ensuring that each input party's data is not leaked.
- We expand the access policies in the existing C-FE. Drawing on the concept of ABE, we use attributes as access policies rather than simple policy parameters. We embed attributes into the ciphertext and incorporate access control into the keys. This allows our scheme to support multiple access control policies and to adjust different access control strategies to meet various security requirements. Encryptors can flexibly update access policies as needed, without the need to re-encrypt data, and the authority will enforce control over decryptors based on the new access policies.
- We conducted both theoretical and experimental analyses of the computational overhead of CMCFE-FAC to verify the practicality of the scheme.

Table 1 provides comparison of different solutions in multi-client scenarios. The remaining question is how to construct our scheme with higher security.

Table 1. Comparison of Different Encryption Solutions in Multiparty Scenarios.

Scheme	Multiple Input	Controlled	Fine-Grained Access Control
MCFE [10]	✓	X	X
MCFE [22]	✓	X	✓
C-FE [20]	X	✓	X
Section 4: CMCFE-FAC	✓	✓	✓

Our Idea We first considered a straightforward approach to implement the CMCFE-FAC scheme for the inner product. Leveraging the idea from C-FE [20], "Superfast Construction for computing actual inner product," we utilize two encryption methods, where the access policy is simply the policy parameters. The ciphertext CT is divided into two parts: the first part encrypts the message $(x + r)$ using MCFE-IP, and the second part encrypts the policy parameters and r using CCA2-secure symmetric encryption. When the decryptor receives these ciphertexts, it first submits a request to the central authority. The central authority uses the symmetric decryption algorithm to decrypt and extract the policy parameters and the vector r, then determines whether the access policy is satisfied. If the policy is satisfied, the central authority issues the MCFE-IP decryption key. Finally, the decryptor can obtain $\langle x, y \rangle = \langle (x + r), y \rangle - \langle r, y \rangle$ through MCFE-IP decryption.

The concept of our proposed approach is described as follows. We embed attributes into the ciphertext and embed the access structure into the keys. When the decryptor submits a request to the central authority, it provides partial ciphertext containing the attributes. The central authority then checks whether these attributes satisfy the access structure. If the access policy is satisfied, the central authority generates a response key along with a key containing vector y, which together form the decryption key. If the attributes do not satisfy the access structure, the central authority rejects the request and does not send anything.

Our proposed approach is superior to the initial simple scheme mainly because using two encryption methods increases the complexity of the system. Another reason is that, unlike simple policy parameters, attribute-based access policies can achieve access control more flexibly and securely.

2   Related Work

Inner-product Functional Encryption In 2015, Abdalla et al. [1] considered FE for inner products. They gave a construction under the DDH assumption [8] or LWE assumption [24] and a framework to construct schemes from public key encryption schemes. In 2016, to achieve a higher level of security, they proposed IPFE with security against adaptive adversaries in [2]. Later, Benhamouda et al. [7] relied on the projective hash functions to achieve security against the chosen ciphertext attack. In 2023, Jiaxin Guan et al. [13] proposed a registerable functional encryption scheme that supports attribute-hiding inner product predicates based on prime-order asymmetric bilinear groups. Recently, in order to further expand the practicability of the inner product function, Valerio et al. [11] proposed a novel inner product functional encryption scheme. This scheme can convert the ciphertext by updating the token even after the ciphertext is generated. At present, inner product functional encryption has many application scenarios, such as word vector training in machine learning [28], using a privacy-preserving learning algorithm to achieve privacy protection for word vector training, and privacy protection in blockchain smart contracts [15,25].

Multi-client Functional Encryption In 2018, Chotard et al. [10] explored the development of MCFE for inner-product. They demonstrate that MCFE can be effectively implemented using either the DDH or the SXDH assumptions. Although these schemes are effectively constructed, their security proofs rely on random oracles, which may not provide the expected level of security in practice. Subsequently, in 2019, Benoît Libert and Radu iiu [19] constructed a fully secure MCFE scheme under adaptive corruption, whose security proof is based on the Learning With Errors (LWE) assumption and does not require the random oracle model. Given that previous research on MCFE mainly focused on inner product functions, to further expand the application scope of MCFE, Agrawal et al. [3] in 2022 proposed an MCFE scheme that supports quadratic functions, but the scheme did not prove its security under a general corruption model. In recent years, how to combine access control with functional encryption has become a research focus. Nguyen et al. [22] proposed an MCFE framework with fine-grained access control. They combine single-input and multi-client with access control, with these schemes featuring both fine-grained control over computation and fine-grained control over access, and they satisfy both selective. To enhance system security and effectively identify malicious clients, in 2023, Ky Nguyen et al. [21] introduced the concept of Verifiable MCFE. This concept addresses the issue of decryption outputs being rendered meaningless due to erroneous data input by clients. Furthermore, in their work, they achieved decentralization, eliminating the need for any trusted third-party authority within the system model. In the same year, Li et al. [18] addressed the issue of malicious clients by proposing a robust decentralized MCFE scheme. This scheme ensures that even in the presence of malicious clients, the decryptor can still decrypt and compute the data from all honest clients. MCFE can be applied in federated learning to address many practical issues related to data sharing and privacy protection [23].

Controlled Functional Encryption To take additional protection measures for sensitive data, in 2014, C-FE was proposed by Naveed and Agrawal et al. [20]. They show that C-FE can leverage existing encryption tools to achieve finer-grained control over user access to encrypted data. Subsequently, according to C-FE, Ambrona et al. [5] proposed a quadratic multi-authority C-FE. The role of the authority is distributed across multiple parties, with an efficient instantiation achieved through the application of CCA2 encryption and linear homomorphic encryption. Nuttapong et al. [6] provide functional encryption with controlled decryption, which is different from C-FE. By using tokens in the process of encryption and decryption, this scheme provides a mechanism for the encrypting party to control the decryption of the already encrypted message. In 2023, Datta et al. [12] proposed the first decentralized multi-authority attribute-based inner product functional encryption scheme that supports unbounded vector lengths. Unbounded means that the encryptor can encrypt vectors of any length according to their chosen access policies. Similar to C-FE, it combines access control with functional encryption. Multiple authorities can independently issue decryption keys. However, unlike C-FE, there is no key request algorithm.

3   Preliminaries

In this section, the notation employed throughout the paper is introduced, which is listed in Table 2. Moreover, we will revisit familiar definitions adjusted for our notation and review well-known results or theorems that will be applied in our proof construction.

Table 2. Main abbreviations.

Notations	Descriptions	Notations	Descriptions
msk	Master secret key	$[n]$	Set of integers from 1 to n
mpk	Public parameters	γ	A set of attributes
ek_i	Encryption key	$(C_i)_{i\in[n]}$	Sequence numbered by index i
D	Respond key	$\{C_j\}_{j\in\gamma}$	Set numbered by index j
dk_f	Functional decryption key for f	$\mathcal{M}^n$	Message space
1^λ	Security parameter	V	Set of secret values of leaf nodes of the tree
n	The number of senders as well as the vector dimension	$PGGen(1^\lambda)$ $\mathbb{A}$	A pairing group generator Access structure
$\mathcal{U}$	Universe of attributes	$\mathcal{T}$	Access tree
x, x_i	An n-tuple vector and one of its components	Q_z	Polynomial of node z
ℓ	label	S_z	Set of all children of node z
$\mathcal{H}$	Hash function	ϵ	Advantage of attack scheme

3.1   Pairing Group

A pairing group generator PGGen, which is a probabilistic polynomial time (PPT) algorithm, takes the security parameter 1^λ as input and returns a group description $PG = (\mathbb{G}_1, \mathbb{G}_T, p, g, e(\cdot, \cdot))$ of pairing groups. In this context, $\mathbb{G}_1$ and $\mathbb{G}_T$ represent additive cyclic groups of prime order p, with g serving as a generator for $\mathbb{G}_1$, correspondingly, and $e : \mathbb{G}_1 \times \mathbb{G}_1 \to \mathbb{G}_T$ is a bilinear map, which satisfies bilinear, non-degenerate and computational properties. Define $g_t := e(g, g)$, which is a generator of G_T.

3.2   Intraceable Security Assumption

Our scheme uses the Decisional Bilinear Diffie-Hellman Assumption(DBDH) to prove its security. The precise definition is outlined below.

Definition 1. (DBDH Assumption). Let $\mathcal{PG} = (\mathbb{G}_1, \mathbb{G}_T, p, g, e(\cdot, \cdot)) \leftarrow$ PG Gen (1^λ), where $g \in \mathbb{G}_1$. For randomly chosen $\alpha, \beta, \eta, \delta \in \mathbb{Z}_p$, and generate two tuples $T_0 = (g^\alpha, g^\beta, g^\eta, e(g, g)^{\alpha\beta\eta}), T_1 = (g^\alpha, g^\beta, g^\eta, e(g, g)^\delta)$. Define the advantage of PPT adversary $\mathcal{A}$ to distinguish these two tuples as

$$Adv_{\mathsf{DBDH}} = \Pr\left[\mathcal{A}(T_0) \rightarrow 1\right] - \Pr\left[\mathcal{A}(T_1) \rightarrow 1\right]$$

3.3   Access Structures

Definition 2. (Access Structures). Consider $\{\rho_i\}_{i \in [n]}$ to be a set of parties. An access structure is a collection $\mathbb{A} \subseteq 2^{\rho_1, \dots, \rho_n}$ of non-empty subsets of these parties. The sets included in $\mathbb{A}$ are known as the authorized sets, and those not contained in $\mathbb{A}$ are referred to as the unauthorized sets. A collection $\mathbb{A}$ that is monotone, this means that for $\forall$ sets M, N where if M $\in \mathbb{A}$ and M $\subseteq N$, then N $\in \mathbb{A}$.

Definition 3. (Access Trees). In our concrete construction, we have used an access tree as the concrete access structure, and the principle is similar to [14]. Suppose that $\mathcal{T}$ is a tree that embodies an access structure. In this tree, each non-leaf node is associated with a threshold gate, which is characterized by the number of its children and a specific threshold value. For each node z, let num_z be the number of children of node z and k_z be the threshold value, then $0 < k_z \leq num_z$. There are two kinds of threshold gates, AND gates and OR gates. If $k_z = 1$, the threshold gate is an OR gate. On the other hand, if $k_z = num_z$, it serves as an AND gate.

Evaluating access trees. Let $\mathcal{T}(\gamma) = 1$ denote a set of attributes γ satisfying the access tree $\mathcal{T}$. Consider $\mathcal{T}_z$ to be a subtree within tree $\mathcal{T}$. We compute $\mathcal{T}_z(\gamma)$ recursively as follows.

- For a non-leaf node z, assess $\mathcal{T}_z(\gamma)$ for every child z' for node z. $\mathcal{T}(\gamma)$ yields 1 if and only if a minimum of k_z children also return 1. The root node is treated as a non-leaf node here.
- For a leaf node z, $\mathcal{T}_z(\gamma)$ yields 1 exclusively when the attribute of z is included in the authorization attribute set.

To improve our interaction with the access trees, several functions have been established. The notation $parent(z)$ refers to the node z's parent within the tree. The function $att(z)$, applicable solely to leaf nodes, signifies the attribute linked with the leaf node z. Moreover, the child nodes are sequentially numbered from 1 to num. The function $index(z)$ yields this specific ordinal number associated with the node z.

3.4 Pseudo-random Functions

A pseudo-random function is a function that applies randomness to input data. It takes a key and an input and generates a pseudo-random output. In this paper, we employ a Pseudo-random Function (PRF) to ensure that the pseudo-random numbers generated by the client are identical.

Definition 4. (Pseudo-random Function). Let PRF: $\mathcal{K} \times \mathcal{V} \to \mathcal{W}$ be a deterministic polynomial-time algorithm, with key space $\mathcal{K} = \{0,1\}^\lambda$, domain $\mathcal{V}$ and range $\mathcal{W}$.

4   Definition of Controlled Multi-Client Functional Encryption for Flexible Access Control

In this section, we give the formal definition of Controlled Multi-Client Functional Encryption for Flexible Access Control (CMCFE-FAC). Figure 1 illustrates the structure of the proposed scheme. Central Authority generates n encryption keys ek_i and public parameters and distributes encryption keys to n Data Owners. Each Data Producer uses the encryption keys ek_i to encrypt its data x_i under a set of attributes γ and then sends the generated ciphertext $Ct_{i,\ell,\gamma} = (C_i, C_j)$ where $i \in [n], j \in \gamma$ to the Decryption Party. Upon receiving the ciphertext, the Decryption Party must request the corresponding decryption key from the Central Authority to decrypt it. After receiving the application, the Central Authority will check whether the Decryption Party meets the access policies set by the Data Producer. If the conditions are met, the decryption key dk_f will be granted; otherwise, the request will be rejected.

Note that, differing from the definition of C-FE [20], only one data owner is allowed to encrypt data, in our controlled setting, we expand the data owner to multiple parties, so that our scheme provide flexible and more application scenarios. At the same time, our access control is no longer a simple policy parameter, we introduce access control in ABE, which can be compatible with a variety of policies.

A CMCFE-FAC scheme facilitates the encryption of data vectors from multiple senders (data owners), enabling controlled function computation on these diverse datasets. We proceed to formally define a CMCFE-FAC scheme as follows.

Definition 5. (Controlled Multi-Client Functional Encryption for Flexible Access Control). A CMCFE-FAC scheme on message space $\mathcal{M}$ and universe of attributes $\mathcal{U}$ and **Labels**=$\{0,1\}^*$ be a set of labels involving a set of n senders consists of five algorithms:

- Setup($1^\lambda, 1^n, \mathcal{U}$): This algorithm accepts 1^λ as the security parameter, the number of senders n and the attribute universe $\mathcal{U}$ as inputs, and produces the public parameters mpk, the master secret key msk, the n encryption keys ek_i as outputs;

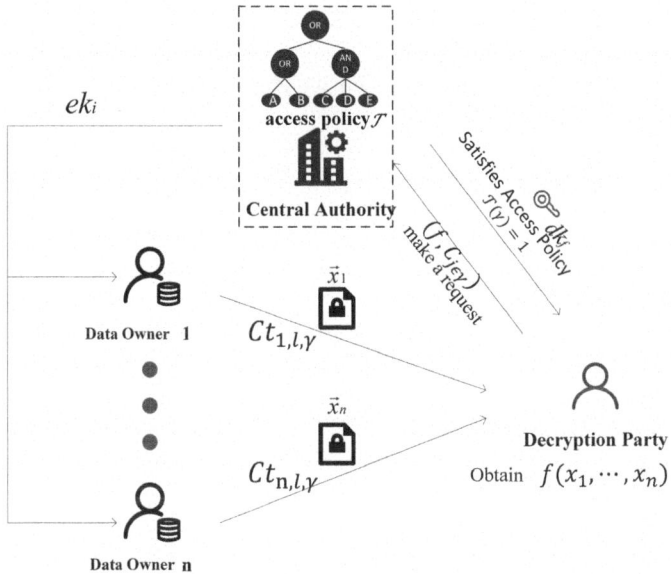

Fig. 1. Outline of our CMCFE-FAC scheme.

- **Encrypt**$(x_i, ek_i, mpk, \ell, \gamma)$: This algorithm accepts a value x_i, encryption key ek_i, the public parameters mpk, a label $\ell \in$ **Labels** and a set of attributes γ as inputs for encryption, producing the ciphertexts C_i and C_j as outputs, where $j \in \gamma$ and i is the client sequence number;
- **KeyReq**$(\{C_j\}_{j \in \gamma}, \mathbb{A}, msk)$: This algorithm accepts ciphertext $\{C_j\}_{j \in \gamma}$, an access structure $\mathbb{A}$ defined over the universe of attribute and master secret key msk as inputs. It outputs a respond key D if attribute satisfies the access policy, or $\perp$ otherwise;
- **KeyGen**(msk, f, D): This algorithm accepts a master secret key msk, a respond key D, and a function f as inputs. It outputs a functional decryption key dk_f;
- **Decrypt**$((C_i)_{i \in [n]}, dk_f, \ell)$: This algorithm accepts a functional decryption key dk_f, a sequence ciphertexts $(C_i)_{i \in [n]}$ and a label ℓ as inputs. It outputs $f(x)$, if $(C_i)_{i \in [n]}$ are valid encryption of $\boldsymbol{x} = (x_i)_{i \in [n]} \in \mathcal{M}^n$ for the label ℓ, or $\{\perp\}$ otherwise;

Correctness. The CMCFE-FAC scheme is correct if, for all $\lambda, n \in \mathbb{N}$, $\boldsymbol{x} = (x_i)_{i \in [n]} \in \mathcal{M}^n$, and any function $f : \mathcal{M}^n \to \mathcal{R}, \gamma \subseteq \mathcal{U}$, if $\gamma \in \mathbb{A}$, the following holds:

$$\Pr\left[\text{Encrypt}\left((C_i)_{i \in [n]}, dk_f, \ell\right) = f(x) : \begin{array}{l} \text{Setup}\left(1^\lambda, 1^n, \mathcal{U}\right) \to (mpk, msk, (ek_i)_{i \in [n]}); \\ \text{Encrypt}\,(x_i, ek_i, mpk, \ell, \gamma) \to (C_i, C_j)\,, \text{where}\,\forall i \in [n], \forall j \in \gamma; \\ \text{KeyReq}\,(\{C_j\}_{j \in \gamma}, \mathbb{A}, msk) \to D; \\ \text{KeyGen}\,(msk, f, D) \to dk_f; \end{array} \right] = 1.$$

Definition 6. (Security game of CMCFE-FAC scheme). Considering a CMCFE-FAC scheme with n senders. No adversary $\mathcal{A}$ should have the capability to succeed in the subsequent security game when faced with a challenger represented by $\mathcal{C}$:

- **Init.** The challenger $\mathcal{C}$ runs $\mathcal{A}$. $\mathcal{A}$ chooses the set of attributes γ and two challenge messages $\boldsymbol{x}^0 = \left(x_1^0, x_2^0, \cdots, x_n^0\right), \boldsymbol{x}^1 = \left(x_1^1, x_2^1, \cdots, x_n^1\right)$ of the desired challenge.
- **Setup.** $\mathcal{C}$ produces the public parameters mpk and provides them to the adversary the adversary $\mathcal{A}$.
- **Queries 1.** $\mathcal{A}$ can adaptively request the decryption key dk_f for access structure $\mathbb{A}$ and a function f within the function space $\mathcal{F}$, where $\gamma \notin \mathbb{A}$. But with the following limitation: $f(\boldsymbol{x}^0) = f(\boldsymbol{x}^1)$.
- **Challenge.** $\mathcal{C}$ tosses an coin $\varphi \in \{0,1\}$, and proceeds to encrypt $\boldsymbol{x}^\varphi$ with γ. The ciphertext is then transmitted to the adversary $\mathcal{A}$.
- **Queries 2.** Phase 1 continues.
- **Guess.** $\mathcal{A}$ produces a guess φ' in an attempt to determine φ. If $\varphi' = \varphi$ adversary $\mathcal{A}$ wins.

We shall elucidate the rationale behind the aforementioned constraint. If $f(\boldsymbol{x}^0) \neq f(\boldsymbol{x}^1)$ is satisfied in the queried decryption key, then the adversary can simply execute $f(\boldsymbol{x}^0)$ and then call the decryption algorithm to output $f(\boldsymbol{x}^\varphi)$. Clearly, if these two computations are equal, then the adversary can easily judge $\boldsymbol{x}^\varphi = \boldsymbol{x}^0$, otherwise, $\boldsymbol{x}^\varphi \neq \boldsymbol{x}^0$.

The advantage of adversary $\mathcal{A}$ in succeeding in the IND-CPA game is defined as

$$Adv_{\text{IND-CPA}}^{\text{CMCFE-FAC}} = |Pr[\varphi' = \varphi] - \frac{1}{2}|.$$

Definition 7. (Semantic Security against IND-CPA of CMCFE-FAC). A CMCFE-FAC is secure against IND-CPA if the advantage $Adv_{\text{IND-CPA}}^{\text{CMCFE-FAC}}$ is negligible for any PPT algorithm.

5   Construction of CMCFE-FAC for Inner Product

In this section, we detail a secure CMCFE-FAC for Inner Product scheme under the above definition. In the CMCFE-FAC for Inner Product scenario, three kinds of entities exist: data owners, clients, and authorities. Different from C-FE, we increase the number of data owners to n. The input encrypted data is decomposed from a single input $\boldsymbol{x}$ into input vectors $(\boldsymbol{x}_1, \ldots, \boldsymbol{x}_n)$, where each component is independent. The establishment of our access tree is consistent with [14]. CMCFE-FAC for Inner Product relies on a PRF instantiated with the keyspace $\mathcal{K} = \{0,1\}^\lambda$, the domain $\mathcal{V} = \textbf{Labels}$ and the range $\mathcal{W} = Z_p$.

5.1 Concrete Construction

We give the concrete construction of our CMCFE-FAC for inner product as follows.

- **Setup**$(1^\lambda, 1^n, \mathcal{U}) \rightarrow (mpk, msk, (ek_i)_{i \in [n]})$. The setup algorithm takes as input 1^λ and selects a bilinear group in the following manner

$$PGGen(1^\lambda) \rightarrow (\mathbb{G}_1, \mathbb{G}_T, p, g, e(\cdot, \cdot))$$

Sample generators $g \in \mathbb{G}_1$, $g_t = e(g, g) \in \mathbb{G}_T$ and the encryption keys $s_i \xleftarrow{\$} \mathbb{Z}_p$ and PRF key $cons \leftarrow \{0, 1\}^\lambda$. Define $\mathcal{H}$ as a full-domain hash function onto $\mathbb{G}_T$ and set $\boldsymbol{s} = (s_1, ..., s_n)$. Define the universe of attributes $\mathcal{U} = \{1, ..., m\}$. For each attribute $j \in \mathcal{U}$, generate a number $t_j \leftarrow \mathbb{Z}_p$. Finally, choose $t \leftarrow \mathbb{Z}_p$ and set public parameters $mpk = (T_1 = g^{t_1}, ..., T_{|\mathcal{U}|} = g^{t_{|\mathcal{U}|}},$ $\mathbb{G}_1, \mathbb{G}_T, g, g_t, p, Y = e(g, g)^t)$, the encryption keys $ek_i = (s_i, cons)$ and master secret key $msk = (t_1, ..., t_{|u|}, t, \boldsymbol{s})$.

- **Encrypt**$(x_i, ek_i, mpk, \ell, \gamma) \rightarrow (C_i, C_j)$. The encryption algorithm first computes $\mathcal{H}(\ell) \in \mathbb{G}_T$ and then encrypts the message vector x_i under a set of attributes γ and computes $k = PRF_{cons}(\ell)$, and outputs the ciphertext as:

$$C_i = g_t^{x_i} \mathcal{H}(\ell)^{s_i} Y^k \quad C_j = (\gamma, E_j = \{T_j^k\}_{j \in \gamma})$$

- **KeyReq**$(\{C_j\}_{j \in \gamma}, \mathcal{T}, msk) \rightarrow D$. The KeyReq algorithm generates a response key, allowing the user to decrypt a message encrypted with a set of attributes γ exclusively when $\mathcal{T}(\gamma) = 1$. Firstly, select a polynomial q_z for each node z within the tree $\mathcal{T}$, as guided by [14]. This selection process, which begins at the root node r, is conducted in a top-down approach. The degree of the polynomial is taken as $d_z = k_z - 1$, where k_z represents the threshold value for node z, and num_z denotes the number of children of z. For the root node r, set $q_r(0) = t$. For other nodes, z of the visited tree, set $q_z(0) = q_{parent(z)}(index(z))$, and the d_z nonconstant coefficients of the polynomial are chosen randomly. After the polynomial definition of all nodes is completed, for each leaf node z, the secret value on it is calculated

$$D_z = g^{\frac{q_z(0)}{t_j}} \quad \text{where } j = att(z)$$

The set of appeal secret values is set to V.

Afterwards, the DecryptNode(C_j, V, z) recursive algorithm defined in [14] is invoked, which inputs ciphertext C_j, a set of secret values V, and a node z, producing outputs in the group $\mathbb{G}_T$ or $\perp$. The algorithm DecryptNode is defined as follows, where z is a node of the tree.

  - If z represents a leaf node and let $j = att(z)$. If $j \in \gamma$, then

$$\text{DecryptNode}(C_j, V, z) = e(V, E_j) = e\left(g^{\frac{q_z(0)}{t_j}}, g^{k \cdot t_j}\right) = e(g, g)^{k \cdot q_z(0)}.$$

  Otherwise, The DecryptNode function outputs $\perp$.

– If node z not being a leaf node, DecryptNode(C_j, V, w) is called on all the children w of z and the output is stored as F_w. Let S_z be an arbitrary k_z-sized set of child nodes w such that $F_w \neq \perp$. If no such set exists, then the node is not satisfied, and the function returns $\perp$. Otherwise, let $j = index(w)$ and $S'_z = \{index(w) : w \in S_z\}$(the total number of all child nodes) and compute using the Lagrangian difference theorem

$$F_z = \prod_{w \in S_z} F_w^{\Delta_{j,S'_z}(0)} = \prod_{w \in S_z} \left(e(g,g)^{k \cdot q_w(0)} \right)^{\Delta_{j,S'_z}(0)}$$

$$= \prod_{w \in S_z} \left(e(g,g)^{k \cdot q_{\text{parent}(w)}(\text{index}(w))} \right)^{\Delta_{j,S'_z}(0)}$$

$$= \prod_{w \in S_z} e(g,g)^{k \cdot q_z(i) \cdot \Delta_{j,S'_z}(0)} = e(g,g)^{k \cdot q_z(0)}$$

With the function defined, the requesting algorithm only needs to call it at the root node of the tree. We get D through the DecryptNode algorithm. DecryptNode(C_j, V, r) $= e(g,g)^{t^k} = Y^k$ is true only when the ciphertext meets the requirements of the tree.

– **KeyGen**($msk, \boldsymbol{y}, D$) $\to dk_y$. The KeyGen algorithm inputs master secret key msk, a respond key D and vectory $\boldsymbol{y} = (y_1, ..., y_n)$ computes $sk_y = \sum_i s_i \cdot y_i$ and sets $dk_y = (sk_y, D)$.

– **Decrypt**($(C_i)_{i \in [n]}, dk_y, \ell$) $\to \langle \boldsymbol{x}, \boldsymbol{y} \rangle$. The Decrypt algorithm returns the discrete logarithm in basis g_t of

$$C_{M,i} = \frac{C_i}{D} \text{ that is, } g_t^{<\boldsymbol{x},\boldsymbol{y}>} = \frac{\prod_i (C_{M,i})^{y_i}}{H(\ell)^{sk_y}}$$

5.2   Correctness

Using Access Trees as proof of correctness and underlying algebraic structure, we highlight the main points below.

To begin with, for the access control tree $\mathcal{T}$, if the attribute γ satisfies it, then the KeyReq algorithm can recover the secret value t in the polynomial.

$$D = \text{DecryptNode}(C_j, D_z, z) = e(g,g)^{tk} = Y^k$$

After obtaining the decryption key $dk_y = (sk_y, D)$, the decryptor computes

$$C_{M,i} = \frac{C_i}{D} = \frac{g_t^{x_i} H(\ell)^{s_i} Y^k}{Y^k} = g_t^{x_i} H(\ell)^{s_i}$$

$$\frac{\prod_i C_{M,i}^{y_i}}{H(\ell)^{sk_y}} = \frac{g_t^{\langle \boldsymbol{x},\boldsymbol{y} \rangle} H(\ell)^{\langle \boldsymbol{s},\boldsymbol{y} \rangle}}{H(\ell)^{\langle \boldsymbol{s},\boldsymbol{y} \rangle}} = g_t^{\langle \boldsymbol{x},\boldsymbol{y} \rangle}$$

The final inner-product value must be computed using discrete logarithms. It should be noted that, within this discrete logarithm setting, one must evaluate $\langle \boldsymbol{x}, \boldsymbol{y} \rangle$ as small as possible for the final decryption to succeed.

5.3   Security

Using the following theorems, we prove that the CMCFE-FAC for Inner Product scheme is IND-CPA secure.

Theorem 1. (Security of CMCFE-FAC for Inner Product). *If the DBDH assumption is intractable, then CMCFE-FAC for Inner Product is secure against IND-CPA.*

Proof. Should there exist a PPT adversary $\mathcal{A}$ capable of undermining the IND-CPA security of CMCFE-FAC for Inner Product with a non-negligible advantage ϵ, it implies the existence of a challenger $\mathcal{C}$ who can challenge the DBDH assumption with a significant advantage of $\frac{1}{2}\epsilon$. Following is a description of the game between $\mathcal{A}$ and $\mathcal{C}$.

The challenger $\mathcal{C}$ does the following setup. Select the groups $\mathbb{G}_1$(including its generator g) and $\mathbb{G}_T$ with an efficient bilinear map and flip a fair binary coin μ. If $\mu = 0$, $\mathcal{C}$ sets

$$(O, P, Q, T) = \left(g^\alpha, g^\beta, g^\eta, e(g,g)^{\alpha\beta\eta}\right)$$

otherwise it sets

$$(O, P, Q, T) = \left(g^\alpha, g^\beta, g^\eta, e(g,g)^\delta\right)$$

for random $\alpha, \beta, \eta, \delta$. The universe, $\mathcal{U}$ is assumed to be defined.

Init. $\mathcal{A}$ selects the set of attributes γ to change. The two challenge vectors are as follows

$$x^0 = \left(x_1^0, x_2^0, \cdots, x_n^0\right), x^1 = \left(x_1^1, x_2^1, \cdots, x_n^1\right)$$

where $x^0 \neq x^1$.

Setup. $\mathcal{C}$ produces the public parameters. $\mathcal{C}$ lets $s_i^* \xleftarrow{\$} \mathbb{Z}_p$, $cons \leftarrow \{0,1\}^\lambda$ and sets $t = \alpha\beta$, $ek_i = (s_i^*, cons)$. Therefore, $Y = e(g,g)^{\alpha\beta}$ and $s = (s_1^*, s_2^*, \cdots, s_n^*)$. For all $j \in \mathcal{U}$, T_j is determined in this manner: if $j \in \gamma$, a random $r_j \in \mathbb{Z}_p$ is selected, leading to the assignments $T_j = g^{r_j}$ (consequently, $t_j = r_j$). If not, it chooses a random $v_j \in \mathbb{Z}_p$ and sets $T_i = g^{\beta v_j} = B^{v_j}$ (consequently, $t_j = \beta v_j$). It subsequently provides $\mathcal{A}$ with the public parameters mpk.

Queries 1. $\mathcal{A}$ is allowed to adaptively generates queries for the decryption key dk_f corresponding to the access structure $\mathbb{A}$ and a vector y from the message space $\mathcal{M}^n$, where $\gamma \notin \mathbb{A}$. For each query dk_y, $\mathcal{C}$ must first check that the query is valid. If $\langle x^0 - x^1, y \rangle \neq 0$, Then the $\mathcal{A}$'s inquiry is invalid and $\mathcal{C}$ will reject this inquiry. Otherwise, $\mathcal{C}$ carries out the operations below to address the query for the decryption key dk_f made by $\mathcal{A}$.

For each node within the access tree $\mathcal{T}$, $\mathcal{C}$ must allocate a polynomial Q_z with a degree of d_z. To do this, we define two functions as in [14]: PolySat and PolyUnsat. The purpose is to ensure the security of the system even under the most unfavourable conditions (i.e., an adversary tries to use an attribute set that does not conform to the access policy). Please refer to [14] for the specific definition and construction.

For distributing keys corresponding to the access structure $\mathcal{T}$, $\mathcal{C}$ initially executes PolyUnsat $(\mathcal{T}, \gamma, g^{\alpha})$ to establish a polynomial q_z for every node z of $\mathcal{T}$. Furthermore, $q_r(0) = \alpha$. $\mathcal{C}$ according to the following way for each node z of $\mathcal{T}$ define polynomial $Q_z(\cdot) = \beta q_z(\cdot)$, where $t = Q_r(0) = \alpha\beta$. For the leaf nodes, Let $i = att(z)$ and define the key component corresponding to node z. We consider the following two cases.

- If $j \in \gamma$, then $D_z = g^{\frac{Q_z(0)}{t_j}} = g^{\frac{\beta q_z(0)}{r_j}} = P^{\frac{q_z(0)}{r_j}}$
- If $j \notin \gamma$, the $D_z = g^{\frac{Q_z(0)}{t_j}} = g^{\frac{\beta q_z(0)}{\beta v_j}} = g^{\frac{q_z(0)}{v_j}}$.

So $\mathcal{C}$ implicitly defines a polynomial $Q_z(0) = \beta q_z(0)$ for each node of $\mathcal{T}$, such that $Q_r(0) = \alpha\beta = t$. In addition, the distribution of the private key for $\mathcal{T}$ is identical to that in the original scheme. $\mathcal{C}$ computes D by DecryptNode algorithm. Then $\mathcal{C}$ derives the decryption key as $dk_y = (sk_y, D)$

Challenge. The challenger $\mathcal{C}$ implicitly sets $k = \eta$, flips a random coin $\varphi \in \{0, 1\}$, and encrypts $\boldsymbol{x}^{\varphi}$ with γ. For every $i \in [n]$ and $j \in \gamma$, $\mathcal{C}$ sets

$$C_i = g_t^{x_i^{\varphi}} \mathcal{H}(\ell)^{s_i^*} T \qquad C_j = (\gamma, E_j = \{T_j^k\}_{j \in \gamma})$$

It is easily to see that the following conditions is satisfied.

- If $\mu = 0$, then $T = e(g,g)^{\alpha\beta\eta}$, $k = \eta$, $Y^k = (e(g,g)^{\alpha\beta})^{\eta}$, $E_j = (T_j^k) = (g^{r_j})^{\eta} = Q^{r_j}$. Therefore, it is valid ciphertext.
- If $\mu = 1$, then $T = e(g,g)^{\delta}$, $C_i = g_t^{x_i^{\varphi}} \mathcal{H}(\ell)^{s_i^*} e(g,g)^{\delta}$.

Queries 2. The same as the Queries 1 phase.

Guess. Finally, $\mathcal{A}$ outputs a guess φ' of φ. If $\varphi' = \varphi$, then $\mathcal{C}$ output $\mu' = 0$ to indicate that $T = e(g,g)^{\alpha\beta\eta}$; Otherwise, $\mathcal{C}$ output $\varphi' = 1$ to indicate that $T = e(g,g)^{\delta}$.

When $\mu = 1$, $\mathcal{A}$ does not acquire any information about φ, so $Pr[\varphi' \neq \varphi | \mu = 1] = \frac{1}{2}$, while $\mathcal{C}$ guesses $\mu = 1$ when $\varphi' \neq \varphi$, so $Pr[\mu' = \mu | \mu = 1] = \frac{1}{2}$. When $\mu = 0$, $\mathcal{A}$ is able to obtain a valid ciphertext. Since the advantage of $\mathcal{A}$ is ϵ, $Pr[\varphi' = \varphi | \mu = 0] = \frac{1}{2} + \epsilon$, while $\mathcal{C}$ guesses $\mu = 1$ when $\varphi' \neq \varphi$, so $Pr[\mu' = \mu | \mu = 0] = \frac{1}{2} + \epsilon$. In summary, we analyze the advantage of $\mathcal{C}$ successfully solving the DBDH assumption.

$$Adv_{\mathcal{C}} = \tfrac{1}{2} Pr[\mu' = \mu | \mu = 0] - \tfrac{1}{2} Pr[\mu' = \mu | \mu = 1] = \tfrac{1}{2} \cdot (\tfrac{1}{2} + \epsilon) - \tfrac{1}{2} \cdot \tfrac{1}{2} = \tfrac{\epsilon}{2}.$$

6 Performance and Experiment

We conduct simulation experiments on CMCFE-FAC for Inner Product and analyze the effectiveness and practicability of our scheme theoretically and empirically.

Table 3. Comparison of Computation Cost.

Algorithm	Our Scheme	Scheme [1]
Setup	$mE_g + e + (n + m + 1)R_p$	$nR_p + nE_g$
Encrypt	$3nE_t + 2nM_t + nH + \gamma E_g + nT_p$	$R_p + (2n + 1)E_g + nM_g$
KeyReq	$Q + zE_g + F + ze + zi + zM_p$	-
KeyGen	$(n - 1)M_p$	$(n - 1)M_p$
Decrypt	$(n + 1)I_t + H + (n + 1)E_t + 2nM_t + DL$	$(n + 1)E_g + nM_g + I_g$

6.1 Theoretical Analysis

We denote M_p, M_g, and M_t to be the multiplications in groups $\mathbb{Z}_p$, $\mathbb{G}_1$, and $\mathbb{G}_T$, respectively. E_g and E_t represent the exponentiation operations within the groups $\mathbb{G}_1$ and $\mathbb{G}_T$, respectively. i, I_g and I_t are the inversions of the groups $\mathbb{Z}_p$, $\mathbb{G}_1$ and $\mathbb{G}_T$, respectively. Define R_p as the process of randomly choosing an element from the groups $\mathbb{Z}_p$. e represents the operation of the bilinear mapping, H represents the operation of hashing, n represents the length of the vector, m represents the size of the attribute domain, Q represents specify a polynomial for each node of the policy tree, z represents the number of leaf nodes of the policy tree, F represents the time to perform polynomial interpolation on non-leaf nodes, γ represents the number of attributes in encryption, DL represents the time at which the discrete logarithm is calculated and T_p represents the time at PRF. The theoretical analysis of performance is shown in Table 3.

6.2 Empirical Analysis and Discussion

We implement our scheme on a computer equipped with AMD Ryzen 5 5600 6-Core Processor six-core CPU, 32GB RAM, ITG SSD, and virtual machine Ubuntu 64-bit. In addition, we use python charm crypto library [4] to implement our scheme, which is a cryptographic tool that provides efficient, easy to use, and extensible. All simulations use SS512 elliptic curves, where SS stands for super singular curve and 512 means the security level of this elliptic curve is 512 bits.

We set the number of clients n, the dimension of the vector, to 10,20 and 30, respectively. The number of clients is less than 30, which is also sufficient for most distributed systems. In Fig. 2, we compare the computational cost of encryption, decryption, and key generation of our CMCFE-FAC for Inner Product scheme and other schemes [1]. Meanwhile, at $n = 10$, we conduct another set of experiments according to different depths of the policy tree. The depth of the policy tree is increased from 1 to 5 to analyze the computational cost of the key request algorithm. We believe that a policy tree depth of 5 can generally cover many access control requirements and provide sufficient flexibility. The results show that the scheme [1] is more efficient than our scheme in encryption and decryption, but our scheme provides new features, including increased access control and multi-client Settings.

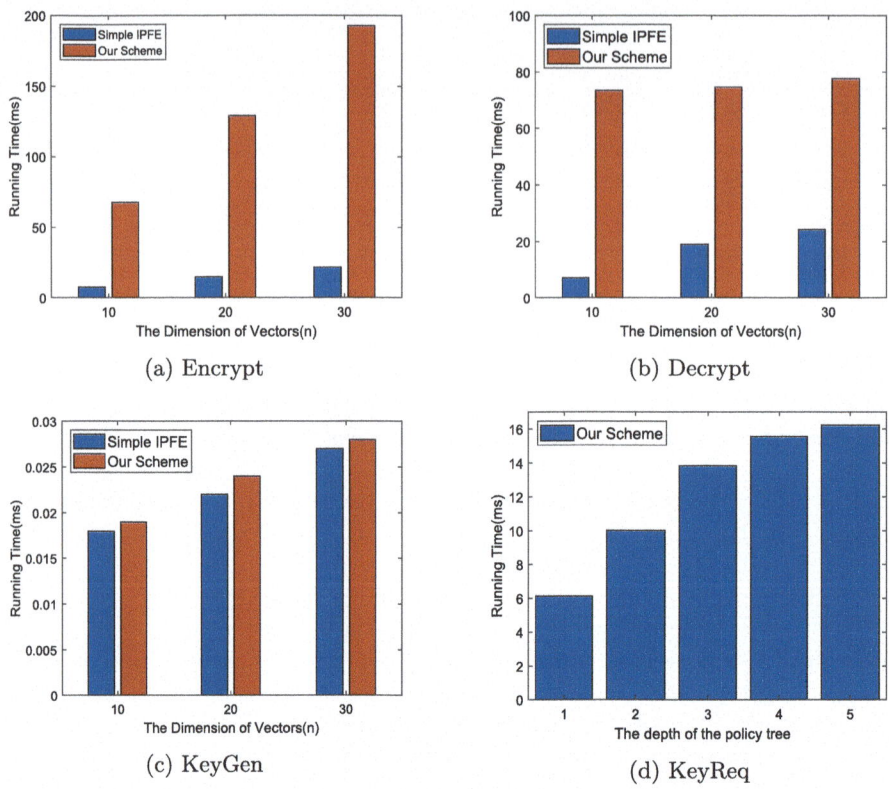

Fig. 2. Comparison of Computation Cost.

7   Conclusions

As a growing field, privacy protection is receiving more and more attention and investment [26, 27]. We gave the concrete construction of a Controlled Multi-Client Functional Encryption for Flexible Access Control scheme, which has significant value and potential in emerging application scenarios that require stronger privacy protection, such as blockchain and medical big data. For instance, in blockchain systems, users can keep sensitive data confidential, where participants can jointly calculate the function evaluation without disclosing the data to achieve more secure and private smart contract functions.

Acknowledgement. This work is supported in part by the National Natural Science Foundation of China under grants 62072134 and U2001205, and the Major Research Plan of Hubei Province under Gran No. 2023BAA027, and the Key Research and Development Program of Hubei Province under Grant 2021BEA163 and the Innovation Project of GUET Graduate Education 2024YCXS060.

References

1. Abdalla, M., Bourse, F., De Caro, A., Pointcheval, D.: Simple functional encryption schemes for inner products. In: IACR International Workshop on Public Key Cryptography, pp. 733–751. Springer (2015)
2. Abdalla, M., Bourse, F., De Caro, A., Pointcheval, D.: Better security for functional encryption for inner product evaluations. Cryptology ePrint Archive (2016)
3. Agrawal, S., Goyal, R., Tomida, J.: Multi-input quadratic functional encryption: stronger security, broader functionality. In: Theory of Cryptography Conference, pp. 711–740. Springer (2022)
4. Akinyele, J.A., Garman, C., Miers, I., Pagano, M.W., Rushanan, M., Green, M., Rubin, A.D.: Charm: a Framework for Rapidly Prototyping Cryptosystems, vol. 3, pp. 111–128. Springer (2013)
5. Ambrona, M., Fiore, D., Soriente, C.: Controlled functional encryption revisited: multi-authority extensions and efficient schemes for quadratic functions. Proc. Priv. Enhancing Technol. **2021**(1), 21–42 (2021)
6. Attrapadung, N., Hanaoka, G., Hirano, T., Kawai, Y., Koseki, Y., Schuldt, J.C.: Multi-input functional encryption with controlled decryption. IEICE Trans. Fundam. Electron. Commun. Comput. Sci. **104**(7), 968–978 (2021)
7. Benhamouda, F., Bourse, F., Lipmaa, H.: CCA-secure inner-product functional encryption from projective hash functions. In: Public-Key Cryptography—PKC 2017: 20th IACR International Conference on Practice and Theory in Public-Key Cryptography, Amsterdam, The Netherlands, March 28–31, 2017, Proceedings, Part II 20, pp. 36–66. Springer (2017)
8. Boneh, D.: The decision Diffie-Hellman problem. In: International Algorithmic Number Theory Symposium, pp. 48–63. Springer (1998)
9. Boneh, D., Sahai, A., Waters, B.: Functional encryption: definitions and challenges. In: Theory of Cryptography: 8th Theory of Cryptography Conference, TCC 2011, Providence, RI, USA, March 28–30, 2011. Proceedings 8, pp. 253–273. Springer (2011)
10. Chotard, J., Dufour Sans, E., Gay, R., Phan, D.H., Pointcheval, D.: Decentralized multi-client functional encryption for inner product. In: Advances in Cryptology—ASIACRYPT 2018: 24th International Conference on the Theory and Application of Cryptology and Information Security, Brisbane, QLD, Australia, December 2–6, 2018, Proceedings, Part II 24, pp. 703–732. Springer (2018)
11. Cini, V., Ramacher, S., Slamanig, D., Striecks, C., Tairi, E.: (inner-product) functional encryption with updatable ciphertexts. J. Cryptol. **37**(1), 8 (2024)
12. Datta, P., Pal, T.: Decentralized multi-authority attribute-based inner-product FE: large universe and unbounded. In: IACR International Conference on Public-Key Cryptography, pp. 587–621. Springer (2023)
13. Francati, D., Friolo, D., Maitra, M., Malavolta, G., Rahimi, A., Venturi, D.: Registered (inner-product) functional encryption. In: International Conference on the Theory and Application of Cryptology and Information Security, pp. 98–133. Springer (2023)
14. Goyal, V., Pandey, O., Sahai, A., Waters, B.: Attribute-Based Encryption for Fine-Grained Access Control of Encrypted Data, pp. 89–98 (2006)
15. Han, P., Zhang, Z., Ji, S., Wang, X., Liu, L., Ren, Y.: Access control mechanism for the internet of things based on blockchain and inner product encryption. J. Inf. Secur. Appl. **74**, 103446 (2023)

16. Hoerbst, A., Ammenwerth, E.: Electronic health records. Methods Inf. Med. **49**(04), 320–336 (2010)
17. Li, X., Zhao, H., Deng, W.: BFOD: blockchain-based privacy protection and security sharing scheme of flight operation data. IEEE Internet Things J. (2023)
18. Li, Y., Wei, J., Guo, F., Susilo, W., Chen, X.: Robust decentralized multi-client functional encryption: motivation, definition, and inner-product constructions. In: International Conference on the Theory and Application of Cryptology and Information Security, pp. 134–165. Springer (2023)
19. Libert, B., Ţiţiu, R.: Multi-client functional encryption for linear functions in the standard model from LWE. In: International Conference on the Theory and Application of Cryptology and Information Security, pp. 520–551. Springer (2019)
20. Naveed, M., Agrawal, S., Prabhakaran, M., Wang, X., Ayday, E., Hubaux, J.P., Gunter, C.: Controlled functional encryption. In: Proceedings of the 2014 ACM SIGSAC Conference on Computer and Communications Security, pp. 1280–1291 (2014)
21. Nguyen, D.D., Phan, D.H., Pointcheval, D.: Verifiable decentralized multi-client functional encryption for inner product. In: International Conference on the Theory and Application of Cryptology and Information Security, pp. 33–65. Springer (2023)
22. Nguyen, K., Phan, D.H., Pointcheval, D.: Multi-client functional encryption with fine-grained access control. In: International Conference on the Theory and Application of Cryptology and Information Security, pp. 95–125. Springer (2022)
23. Qian, X., Li, H., Hao, M., Xu, G., Wang, H., Fang, Y.: Decentralized multi-client functional encryption for inner product with applications to federated learning. IEEE Trans. Dependable Secure Comput. (2024)
24. Regev, O.: On lattices, learning with errors, random linear codes, and cryptography. J. ACM (JACM) **56**(6), 1–40 (2009)
25. Shakya, S., Mukherjee, A., Halder, R., Maiti, A., Chaturvedi, A.: Smartmixmodel: Machine Learning-Based Vulnerability Detection of Solidity Smart Contracts, pp. 37–44 (2022)
26. Zhang, M., Chen, Y., Susilo, W.: Decision tree evaluation on sensitive datasets for secure e-healthcare systems. IEEE Trans. Dependable Secure Comput. (2022)
27. Zhang, M., Huang, S., Shen, G., Wang, Y.: PPNNP: a privacy-preserving neural network prediction with separated data providers using multi-client inner-product encryption. Comput. Stand. Interfaces **84**, 103678 (2023)
28. Zhang, M., Li, Z.A., Zhang, P.: A secure and privacy-preserving word vector training scheme based on functional encryption with inner-product predicates. Comput. Stand. Interfaces **86**, 103734 (2023)

A Secure Incentive Mechanism in Blockchain-Based Mobile Crowdsensing

Mingwu Zhang[1,2(✉)], Qi Zou[2,3], and Bo Yang[4]

[1] School of Computer Science, Hubei University of Technology, Wuhan 430068, China

[2] School of Computer Science and Information Security, Guilin University of Electronic Technology, Guilin 541004, China
csmwzhang@gmail.com

[3] School of Cyber Science and Engineering, Wuhan University, Wuhan 430072, China

[4] School of Computer Science, Shannxi Normal University, Xi'an 710119, China

Abstract. With the widespread popularity of smart devices in recent years, mobile crowdsensing (MCS) as a new appealing data collection paradigm has gained attention in urban monitoring, traffic prediction and social networks, which deploys on decentral terminals for contribution from mobile devices of a large number of participants or crowdsensing nodes. However, traditional MCS systems are mainly based on integrated server development, which cannot fully guarantee their reliability in reality. In addition, the incentive phase of MCS is usually performed under clear-text conditions, it is easy to link the real identity of the nodes with the completed tasks. Therefore, nodes might be unwilling to participate in sensing tasks due to concerns about possible privacy leakage and lack of fair incentives. In addressing the issue of security in corwdsensing, in this work, we propose a privacy-preserving incentive mechanism in blockchain-based mobile crowdsensing systems. It applies blind signatures and zero-knowledge proofs to empower users to update their reputation and receive remuneration for contributing data without divulging the specifics of their individual contributions. In addressing the issue of equitable incentivization, we design an incentive mechanism that distributes rewards fairly based on their contributions, and provide a reputation quantification model to update participants' reputations reasonably. Finally, we design a reputation-based consensus node selection mechanism to constrain the behavior of consensus node. The experimental results indicate that the reputation quantitative model were in line with our expectations.

Keywords: Crowdsensing system · Blockchain · Privacy-protection · Incentive mechanism

This work is supported in part by the Major Research Plan of Hubei Province under Grant 2023BAA027, the National Natural Science Foundation of China under grants 62072134 and U2001205, and the Key Research and Development Program of Hubei Province under Grant 2021BEA163.

Z. Xia and J. Chen (Eds.): ISPEC 2024, LNCS 15053, pp. 347–364, 2024.
https://doi.org/10.1007/978-981-97-9053-1_20

1   Introduction

The popularity of embedded mobile smart devices enables MCS to collect data inexpensively but extensively [2]. A typical MCS scenario is mainly composed of a task publisher, a central platform, and a set of mobile nodes. By utilizing common embedded sensors, MCS already has many practical applications in environmental noise detection, traffic monitoring, and healthcare [25,26].

However, there are still some obstacles to the large-scale deployment of MCS. First, existing MCS schemes mostly rely on a central authority. But in reality, there is no guarantee that the central authority is completely creditable [4,9, 14]. The centralized architecture could lead to the collapse of the entire MCS system if a single point of failure occurs. Meanwhile, the data submitted by users to central authority will also risk the threat of privacy leakage. Such privacy concerns prevent users from participating. Second, the user's motivation could be undermined if task publishers can assess task data unfairly or even deny the receipt of data to extract extra benefits without supervision [8,20].

Currently, many privacy-preserving schemes focus on providing anonymity to users [16,23]. However, some greedy users may exploit higher anonymity to repeatedly submit data reports for the same sensing task, thereby leading to escalated data collection costs. In addition, the existing mobile sensing schemes are mostly built on the premise of a semi-honest adversary model. In this model, users are assumed to be honest, and even with attackers, they will not violate the protocol and are merely curious about privacy. However, attackers in reality will actively manipulate the protocol to gain greater benefits [3]. Traditional MCS schemes do not provide enough constraints on the potential malicious behavior of the central server and the user to avoid the problems of data rejection and identity impersonation [24]. Therefore, protecting user's sensitive privacy while ensuring the system's fairness is the key to improving users' enthusiasm for task participation.

To cope with the above problems, this paper proposes a privacy-preserving incentives mechanism in blockchain-based mobile crowdsensing to address the challenge of achieving a balance between incentive mechanism and privacy protection in an integrated way. The results of simulation experiments show that our scheme is efficient with a smaller communication overhead. it will also not increase the burden on the user's terminal, and the reputation quantification model is both reasonable and feasible. The main contributions are as follows:

- It proposes a privacy-preserving incentive mechanism in blockchain-based mobile crowdsensing. This scheme eliminates the need for third parties which ensures the completeness of data such as employment relationships and node identities in the system and enhances the trustworthiness of system participants. The scheme uses ELGamal blind signature and zero-knowledge proof technology to disassociate the participants' identities from their contributed data, thereby protecting user privacy.
- It also designs an incentive calculation and a credit update model based on the quality of data contribution. Under the premise of ensuring fair incentives,

the model broadens task participation and motivates inactive users in the system to participate in tasks. In addition, it also designed a reputation-based consensus node selection mechanism to constrain the malicious behavior of consensus nodes.

- It gives the concrete construction of our scheme and conduct the experiments on smart devices of crowdsensing. we give a comprehensive evaluation of our scheme for storage, communication and conducted comparative experiments for running time. Experimental results show that our scheme improves about 47.8% and 22% respectively, in terms of efficiency compared to existing privacy-preserving incentive schemes, respectively.

2 Related Work

In traditional MCS systems, quality control of sensing data and privacy protection of users' sensitive information have always been challenging issues [21]. To protect the privacy of participants, [22] proposed a privacy-preserving data aggregation and quality assessment protocol based on smart contracts, which achieves optimal and dependable aggregation and estimation of sensor data on the blockchain without revealing data and participant privacy. Aiming at the same problem, [1] designed a blockchain-based privacy protection quality control mechanism, including a data truth discovery method based on the secure multi-party computation and verification calculation scheme. The mechanism conducts matching degree calculations by participants during the participant selection phase to protect the user's attribute privacy. Aiming at the resource allocation problem of clients in blockchain-based joint learning, [18] designed an incentive mechanism to help model owners allocate appropriate training and mining rewards to each client, and the scheme utilizes a two-stage Stackelberg game to decide how much arithmetic power to allocate to each subtask. And the game model is transformed into two optimization problems to be solved sequentially to derive the optimal strategies for the task executors and clients. In addition, [12] proposed a distributed user privacy protection structure combining blockchain and trusted execution environment (TEE), which breaks the link between user identity and sensitive information in data by encrypting data, and utilizes smart contract signatures for user deposit management and data verification to achieve privacy protection and accurate reward distribution. To solve the problem of how to maximize the coverage under a given budget, [15] proposed an incentive mechanism and written as a smart contract to the blockchain, which protects user privacy with linkable ring signatures in addition to achieving computational efficiency and budget feasibility.

Considering the quality assurance problem of MCS, [13] proposed a lightweight quality assurance framework based on blockchain, which maintains the crowdsensing platform through two smart contracts, and also designs a reputation-based aggregator selection algorithms to reduce on-chain iteration expenses. [6] proposed an incentive-based joint learning scheme for digital twin (DT)-driven industrial mobile crowdsensing by designing a digital twin (DT)-driven industrial mobile crowdsensing architecture to realize dynamic sensing of IoT environments. An incentive-based joint learning framework is developed based on this architecture to optimize the accuracy of the model. In addition, to address the heterogeneity of non-independent and identically-distributed (Non-IID) data, the program designs a knowledge refinement algorithm. The rationality of the incentive mechanism will directly affect the enthusiasm of the participants. [17] proposed a fair awareness and privacy protection participant quality evaluation scheme based on blockchain technology, machine learning, and TEE, which uses blockchain and smart contracts to complete the crowdsensing task, then uses the machine learning method to evaluate the quality of the task data. Its advantage is that it can reduce the burden of the system when faced with a large number of tasks, and can also improve the accuracy of the evaluation. In addition, [19] proposed a blockchain-based decentralized crowdsensing architecture to resist single-point failures. At the same time, it proposed a reward-punishment mixed incentive mechanism to consider factors that affect rewards and user enthusiasm in a more diversified way, which makes the system more fair and prevents users from being cheated. MCS currently lacks an effective incentive mechanism for service requesters and staff, [5] integrated smart contracts and mobile devices, and established a secure and fair blockchain-based MCS system, which employs the Stackelberg game to assess worker participation levels and the fair reward mechanism of requesters to achieve a dynamic balance. At the same time, the system relocates the data evaluation phase off-chain, which saves the computing cost of nodes on the chain. To solve the problem that the existing privacy protection mechanism cannot guarantee the data quality of task participants, [27] proposed a privacy protection and data quality incentive scheme, which uses zero-knowledge proof technology to evaluate data quality while protecting user privacy, and based on the deviation between reliable data and true values is used to quantify data quality. Finally, monetary rewards are given to task participants based on data quality.

In this work, in accordance with the principles of equitable reward distribution and the enhancement of user motivation for task engagement, we have designed an incentive mechanism and a reputation quantification model. These models are predicated upon the assessment of data contribution quality, with the aim of justly apportioning rewards and judiciously updating user reputations. In addition, we also design a dynamic consensus node selection mechanism based on reputation to mitigate static attacks and enforce constraints on the behavior of consensus nodes.

3   Backgrounds and Preliminary

3.1   Blind Signature

Blind signatures can be used to protect the privacy of users in our scheme, and can also achieve anonymity so that the signer can still effectively sign the message m without knowing the content [11]. Let $(x_1; y_1, g, q)$ and $(x_2; y_2, g, q)$ denote the public and private keys of the user and signer, respectively, and q is the public key modulus, and $g \in Z_p^*$. If a user wants to obtain a blind signature on message m:

- **Initialization**: user calculates $m' = m \cdot t^{x_1} \bmod (q-1)$, where $t \in Z_p^*$ is a blinding factor selected by the user that is relatively prime to $(q-1)$ then send it to the signer.
- **Signing**: The signer uses the ELGamal algorithm to sign on m'. Firstly, it randomly chooses (k, ξ) in Z_p^*, then calculates $r = g^k \bmod q$, $h = y_1^{x_2 \xi} \bmod q$ and $\varphi = k^{-1} x_2 \bmod (q-1)$, $SIG' = h^{-1} k^{-1} (m' - x_2 r) \bmod (q-1)$. Then, it returns the signature (r, SIG', φ, ξ) to the user.
- **Verification**: The user verifies that the equality holds:

$$g^{m'} = y_2^r * r^{SIG' h} \bmod q \tag{1}$$

- **De-blinding**: If the equality holds, the user recovers the signature

$$SIG = SIG' t^{-x_1} + h^{-1} \varphi r (t^{-x_1} - 1) \bmod (q-1) \tag{2}$$

for the message m, otherwise rejects the signer's signature.

3.2 Partially Blind Signature

Partial blind signature allows users to obtain the signature of message m from the signer without letting the signer know it [11]. The signer can add some public information (such as a timestamp) to the signature. As many signatures contain public information, the signer cannot associate the signature with the message or the communication session in which the signature was obtained. The process involves three algorithms in this paper:

- **Generate key**: $\mathsf{PBS}(1^\lambda) \to (s', S)$. Where s' is secret key, S is public key, generate by s' through homomorphic hash function.
- **Signing**: $\mathsf{PBS}(s', S, m, info) \to \delta$. Where m is the message to be signed, $info$ is the common information, generating a signature δ for m and $info$.
- **Signature verification**: $\mathsf{PBS}(S, m, info, \delta) \to b$. Return the verification result b for any m and its signature δ, where $b \in (0, 1)$ is output as 1 when the verification is successful, otherwise it is 0.

3.3 Non-interactive Zero-Knowledge Arguments System

The zero-knowledge proof protocol is a cryptographic protocol that runs between the prover and the verifier. If they interact only once in the system, that means the verifier produces a proof and sends it directly to the verifier, who decides when to verify it. It is said that the system realizes non-interactive zero-knowledge proof (NIZK). NIZKis represented by three tuples of probabilistic polynomial time ($\mathsf{NIZK}_{Gen}, \mathsf{NIZK}_{Pro}, \mathsf{NIZK}_{Vri}$), An NIZKis correct if for a given relation R and $(x, w) \in R$:

- NIZK$_{Gen}.(1^\lambda) \rightarrow crs$, where $\lambda \in \mathbf{N}$ denotes the security parameter, generate common reference string crs.
- NIZK$_{Pro}.(crs, x, w) \rightarrow \pi$, for any statement x and a witness w generate a proof π.
- NIZK$_{Vri}.(crs, x, \pi) \rightarrow b$, for any statement x and proof π, the verifier output $b = 1$, meaning that the proof π is accepted, or 0 in case it is rejected.

4   System Model

Blockchain is typically governed by a peer-to-peer network following a predefined consensus protocol. The blockchain-based MCS system consists of three types of entities, a task publishing node S, a set of mobile nodes P, and a consensus node C. In the absence of a centralized server, MCS circumvents many associated issues. Each node can transition between the three types of entities. Our system model is illustrated in Fig. 2, and the general sensing process of the model is performed as follows (Fig. 1):

For data collection, S posts the sensing tasks onto the blockchain via C, which includes sensing quality evaluation indicators and related parameters. and then C adds them into a task queue.

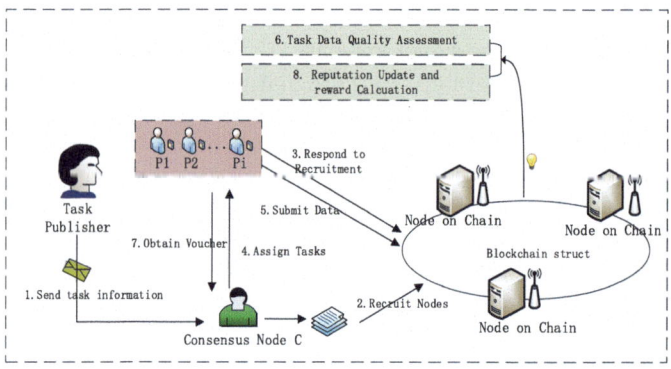

Fig. 1. Mobile Crowdsensing System Framework with Blockchain

After random time intervals, a mobile node uses a pseudonym to communicate with C for searching sensing tasks. The retrieval time is randomized to hinder C from associating the same node through a sequence of retrieval requests.

The mobile node decides for itself which tasks it wants to accept. If it wants to accept a task, it needs to send a request to the C using a new pseudonym. Then, C returns approval and marks the request as approved, which means that this task is assigned. For an assigned task, C only collects data uploaded by mobile nodes that have the approval issued by C. The mobile node collects sensing data as specified by the task, then it uses a new pseudonym submits the sensing data to C, and immediately C issues a receipt to it. Then C hands the data to the chain nodes to evaluate the data quality and returns the data quality score α_i to the data provider.

Once a task has been assigned to a sufficient number of mobile nodes, C removes it from the active task queue. Subsequently, the employment relationship between the mobile nodes and S, the reward rules (including the budget from S), and the updated reputation data of both the mobile nodes and C are encapsulated within a block, which means that the first consensus is finished. Then, mobile nodes submit sensing data to C.

Following the submission of data for respective tasks, the mobile node submits the corresponding task receipts and the data quality score α_i to C for obtaining rewards vouchers. Since C does not know the node identity, it issues encrypted vouchers to the node, which decrypts it into usable vouchers. The transform relies on a secret only known to the mobile node, so C cannot link a usable voucher to an encrypted one or tell which task the vouchers were obtained from. After a random waiting period, the mobile node submits the usable vouchers to C using its real identity. C updates reputation and calculates remuneration based on its α_i.

5   Our Scheme

5.1   Problem Overview

Privacy Threats in the Incentive All entities in the system except smart contracts deployed in advance on the blockchain are assumed to be semi-honest entities, which means that after participating in system tasks, participants will follow the established interaction procedures, but will remain curious about the privacy of other participants as much as possible during the execution of the protocol. Based on the definition of privacy by the above entities, the following definition of privacy can be derived.

1. In the crowdsensing phase: the node's real identity address eid, the correspondence between eid and the task report submitted by it is regarded as privacy data and is kept secret from other semi-honest entities to prevent other semi-honest entities from identifying themselves based on eid Correlation analysis.
2. In the incentive phase: the correspondence between eid and the incentive identifier in the incentive phase is regarded as privacy data and is kept secret from other semi-honest entities.

Design Goals This section formally describes achieving goals in designing a privacy-preserving incentive mechanism in blockchain-based mobile crowdsensing.

– Concerning privacy: our goal is to ensure that C cannot establish links between individual reports and their respective submission nodes, nor can it know whether a given node accepted a given task, link multiple tasks accepted by the same node, or associate vouchers with sensing data provisioning nodes.

– Concerning incentives: our goal is to establish a mechanism for nodes to accrue reputation in a manner that is both reasonable and compliant with the preset reputation limits defined by the task issuer. More precisely, if a node submits reports for a task, it can earn reputation based on its contribution; if it is not assigned the task or if the quality of the submitted task data is substandard, it will earn nothing and may even incur a deduction in it's reputation value.

5.2   Reputation-Based Consensus Node Selection

The proof of work algorithm is the most widely recognized method for selecting miner nodes in blockchain-based applications, such as Bitcoin. However, this approach entails significant computational resource wastage on the part of nodes. In our scheme, we proposed a reputation-based consensus node selection mechanism to achieve the election process.

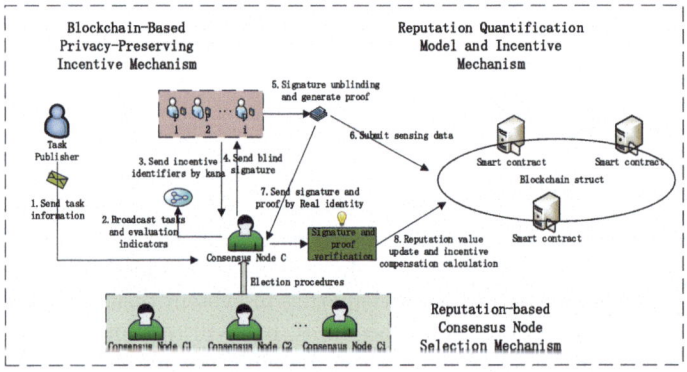

Fig. 2. System Model

Within this scheme, the nodes on chain collectively determine the consensus node set through a voting process, and the voting weight is determined by the node's reputation. After a predefined time interval, the system will re-execute the consensus algorithm to select a new consensus node set. Subsequently, we will further filter the selected consensus nodes based on their historical behavior records and their performance on similar tasks. If a node has been offline for a long time or has other malicious behavior in previous tasks, its reputation will be reduced when executing the reputation update algorithm. The possibility that it be excluded from the consensus node set will increase during the subsequent selection process. We formally the model like equation (3) about the relationship between the node's reputation and the possibility of being removed from the consensus node set upon implementing this mechanism.

$$P_{Del}(rep_{t,i}) = e^{-(\lambda rep_{t,i}+\gamma)} \qquad (3)$$

where $rep_{t,i}$ is the tth round task reputation of the mobile node P_i, λ is an integer greater than 3 to ensure that the value of $P_{Del}(rep_{t,i})$ is as close to 1 as possible at lower reputation values. The value of γ is as small as possible to ensure that the range of $P_{Del}(rep_{t,i})$ is (0,1). From Eq. 2, we can derive that the lower the reputation of the node is, the greater the probability that it will be deleted from the consensus node set. It can effectively prevent the inaction or malicious behavior of consensus nodes.

Due to the different nature of work, the reputation of the consensus node requires additional updates. The change in its value is positively correlated with its current reputation value and the data quality provided by the selected mobile node set. The specific representation of the $Rep_{t,i}$ is as follows:

$$Rep_{t,i} = Rep_{t-1,i} + \frac{\sum_1^{|Q|} Rep_{t,i}}{|Q|\beta} \tag{4}$$

where $|Q|$ represents a set of data providers that adhere to predefined quality standards, while β is an integer serving as a constraint on the occurrence of malicious behaviors by the consensus node. The change in the reputation value of the consensus node is part of the average value of the mobile nodes's reputation of the $|Q|$, regulated by the security parameter β. When $\beta = -\beta$, it indicates that the consensus node behavior is malicious. If we set its reputation value to the average reputation value of all nodes within $|Q|$, its reputation will reset to zero after consecutive β malicious actions. By formula 2, we can obtain that the possibility of it regaining consensus node status approaches nearly zero.

5.3   Blockchain-Based Privacy-Preserving Incentive Mechanism

When retrieving the task window, the mobile node generates a random incentive identifier for each task $i_{i=1,2,...,n_1}$.

$$mark_i = H(i|H(i|r_i)) \tag{5}$$

where r_i is the random number selected by the mobile node. The node will use the identifier to get the voucher for task j. Specifically, each voucher consists of an identifier and a consensus node's partially blind signature over the identifier, formally like $[mark_i, \mathsf{PBS}(mark_i)]$. It is important to note that a node cannot obtain this signature until it has submitted data reports for the given task, and this function is implemented by the following design.

Suppose that a mobile node has retrieved task i. If it intends to accept this task, it needs to utilize a pseudonym that satisfies the task reputation requirements to transmit a request to the consensus node. This request includes its report $\tau_i = H(0|H(r_i))$ for task i.

$$P_i \to C : \ PID_1, \tau_i \tag{6}$$

The consensus node employs a private key x_2 to generate blind ELGamal signatures for the mobile node's report and other information. It has four different private keys including k_1, k_2, k_3, k_4 to generate different partially blind

---

1. Consensus Node(C) generates $(k_1, k_2, k_3, k_4, x_2)$, sets $L, K = \phi$.

For all $task_i (i \in n_1)$

    2. $P_i(i = [1, D])$ generates r_i, x_1.

    3. P_i calculates all $mark_i, \tau_i$ and sends PID_1, τ_i to C.

    4. C generates all $s', S, PBS_{k_1}(s', S, \tau_i, i)$ and sends $PBS_{k_1}(s', S, \tau_i, i)$ to P_i.

After any time

    5. P_i sends $PID_1, i, \tau_i, PBS_{k_1}(s', S, \tau_i, i)$ to C.

    6. C checks $PBS_{k_1}(i, \tau_i)$ is True ?

    7. After checking, C set $L = L \cup \tau_i$.

    8. C generates $\beta_i, PBS_{k_2}(s', S, \beta_i, i)$.

    9. C sends $\beta_i, i, PBS_{k_2}(s', S, i, \beta_i)$ to P_i.

    10. P_i generates μ_j and sends $PID_2, j, \mu_j, PBS_{k_2}(s', S, \beta_i, i)$ to C.

    11. C generates $PBS_{k_3}(s', S, i, \mu_i)$ and sends $PBS_{k_3}(s', S, i, \mu_i)$ to P_i.

After n_2 tasks' data-quality assessment

    12. P_i calculates $t_j, mark'_{j,j=1...n_2}$.

    13. P_i calls $\mathsf{NIZK}_{Pro}(i, \tau_j, mark'_j, \alpha_j) \to \pi_1$

        and sends $i, \tau_j, [\mu_j, PBS_{k_3}(s', \mu_j, i)], \pi_1, [mark'_j]$ to C.

    14. C Receives parameters, then:

        (a) checks τ_j in L ? and $PBS_{k_3}(i, \mu_j)$ is True ?

        (b) calls $\mathsf{NIZK}_{Vri}(i, \tau_j, mark'_j, \pi_1)$.

        (c) checks $\mathsf{NIZK}_{Vri} = 1$?

        (d) checks $mark'_j$ is not in K?

        (e) sets $K = K \cup mark'_j$.

        (f) generates k, ξ, r, h, φ and then signs $SIG' = PBS_{x_2, r, h, \varphi}(mark'_j)$.

        (g) sends r, SIG', φ, ξ to P_i.

    15. P_i recovers $SIG = PBS_{x_1, r, h, \varphi}(mark'_j)$.

    16. P_i calls $\mathsf{NIZK}_{Pro}(i, \tau_j, mark_j, \alpha_j) \to \pi_2$.

After random time

    17. P_i sends $(eid, report, mark_j, SIG, \alpha_j, \pi_2)$ to C.

    18. C receives parameters, then:

        (a) checks $[mark_j, PBS_{k_3}(mark_j)]$ is True ?

        (b) calls $\mathsf{NIZK}_{Vri}(i, \tau_i, mark_j, \pi_2)$.

        (c) checks $\mathsf{NIZK}_{Vri} = 1$?

    19. **Update Reputation and Remuneration.**

Fig. 3. Secure MCS Process

signatures PBS. Initially, the consensus node generates the $PBS(1^\lambda) \to (s', S)$. Where s' represents the secret key, S is the public key generated from s' through a homomorphic hash function. For each report, the consensus node generates $PBS_{k_1}(s', S, \tau_i, i)$ and send it to the mobile node P_i.

$$C \to P_i : PBS_{k_1}(s', S, \tau_i, i) \tag{7}$$

Subsequently, P_i employs the same pseudonym to send a request $(i, \tau_i, PBS_{k_1}(s', S, \tau_i, i))$ for task application to the consensus node.

$$P_i \to C : PID_1, (i, \tau_i, PBS_{k_1}(s', S, \tau_i, i)) \tag{8}$$

The consensus node validates the signature to ascertain the correctness of the request for task i. In the affirmative case, it marks τ_i as approved and adds it to the set L, otherwise it marks τ_i as unapproved. In either case, the mobile node is not allowed to reuse the request, that is the precautionary measure to prevent any node from attempting to reuse the request. In the case of approval, the mobile node obtains a report denoted as R_i' for task i. Subsequently, it generates a random value β_i, and acquires a partially blind signature $PBS_{k_2}(s', S, \beta_i, i)$ from the consensus node. As a result, the mobile node acquires a reports voucher R_i'' of task i, those are $[\beta_i, i, PBS_{k_2}(s', S, \beta_i, i)]$.

$$C \to P_i : PID_1, [\beta_i, i, PBS_{k_2}(s', S, i, \beta_i)] \tag{9}$$

The mobile node can employ a new pseudonym to submit data and reports to the consensus node. The consensus node verifies the signature and accepts the report. Subsequently, it can issue a report receipt $PBS_{k_3}(s', S, \mu_i, i)$ to the mobile node, where $\mu_i = H(\tau_i|i|n_1)$ is generated by the mobile node and send to the consensus node.

Following the phase of mission data quality assessment, the mobile node computes the random blindness factor for its completed n_2 tasks associated with the identifier $mark_j$:

$$t_j = H(i|\tau_j|z)_{j=1\ldots n_2} \tag{10}$$

where z is the smallest positive integer that makes t_i relatively prime to $(q-1)$. It then blinded calculation gives:

$$mark_j' = mark_j \cdot t_j^{x_1} \bmod (q-1) \tag{11}$$

Then, the mobile node invokes the algorithm $NIZK_{Pro}(i, \tau_j, mark_j', \alpha_j)$ to generate a proof π_1 of the correspondence between the data quality score α_i of task j and the blinded identifier $mark_j'$. Then it sends:

$$P_i \to C : (i, \tau_i, [\mu_i, PBS_{k_3}(s', S, \mu_i, i)], \pi_1, [mark_j']_{j=1\ldots n_2}) \tag{12}$$

The consensus node performs the following tasks:

1. It verifies whether τ_i represents an approved report for task i, indicating that the node has been assigned task i.
2. It validates the n partially blind signatures, which indicates that the mobile node has submitted n reports for n tasks.
3. It invokes the algorithm $NIZK_{Vri}(i, \tau_j, mark'_j, \pi_1)$ to verify the proof, which signifies that the identifier corresponds to the data quality score α_i of task i.
4. Finally, it verifies that all of these $mark'_j$ values are distinct and adds the unique $mark'_j$ values to its maintained dynamic identifiers list.

If all above conditions hold, the consensus node proceeds to sign each of the $mark'_j$ values using the key x_2. To do this, it randomly selects (k, ξ) from Z_p^* and calculates $r = g^k \bmod q, h = y_1^{x_2\xi} \bmod q, \varphi = k^{-1}x_2 \bmod (q-1)$, then computes:

$$SIG' = h^{-1}k^{-1}(mark'_j - x_2r) \ bmod \ (q-1) \tag{13}$$

and return the signatures $[PBS_{x_2}(mark'_j), h, \varphi, r]$ to the mobile node. The mobile node firstly verify that the equation holds:

$$g^{mark'_j} = y_2^r r^{SIG'^{-1}h} \bmod q \tag{14}$$

Then the mobile node removes the blinding factor $t_j^{x_1} \bmod q$ from signature $PBS_{x_2}(mark'_j)$ which is the blind signature for $mark_j$ and gets $PBS_{k_3}(mark_j)$. Specifically, it gets rewards voucher $[mark_j, PBS_{k_3}(mark_j)]$ by calculating the following equation:

$$SIG = SIG't_j^{-x_1} + h^{-1}\varphi r(t_j^{-x_1} - 1) \bmod (q-1) \tag{15}$$

Then, P_i calls the NIZK algorithm $NIZK_{Pro}(i, \tau_j, mark_j, \alpha_j)$ to generate a proof π_2 of the restored $mark_j$. When a node acquires a rewards voucher, it undergoes a random waiting period ranging from 0 to T units of time. Subsequently, it employs its actual identity like 'Bob,' to perform reputation updates or reward calculations. Specifically, after C receives the parameters $[eid, report, mark_j, SIG, \alpha_j, \pi_2]$ sent by P_i:

1. It checks whether the rewards voucher $[mark_j, PBS_{k_3}(mark_j)]$ correspond correctly.
2. It calls NIZK algorithm $NIZK_{Vri}(i, \tau_i, mark_j, \pi_2)$ to verify whether the proof π_2 corresponds to the identifier $mark_j$.

5.4   Security Analysis

In this section, we firstly give the security analysis of our privacy-preserving incentive scheme, and then we analysis how the goals of incentives are achieved.

Blindness. The consensus node C signs the message without knowing its content. Specifically, the C only sees the blinded message $mark'_j$ and cannot infer the original message $mark_j$. We assume that the C is not involved in collusion with a separate MN P_1. P_1 generates the blinding factors $t_j^{x_1}$, and calculates $mark_j' = mark_j \cdot t_j^{x_1} \bmod (q-1)$. Since $t_j^{x_1}$ is randomly chosen by the user and it is independent of $mark_j'$, $mark_j'$ is a random number to C, and C cannot infer $mark_j$ from $mark_j'$.

Unforgeability. An attacker cannot generate a valid signature without the consensus node C's private key x_2. The C uses the private key x_2 to sign the blinded message $mark_j'$, generates SIG', and the P_1 gets SIG through the deblinding computation $SIG = SIG' t_j^{-x_1} + h^{-1}\varphi r(t_j^{-x_1}-1) \bmod (q-1)$. Due to the intractability of the discrete logarithm problem, an attacker cannot compute the private key x_2 and therefore cannot forge the signature.

Non-repudiation. The consensus node C cannot deny his signature on message $mark_j$. That is obtained by the P_1 through deblinding. The SIG is obtained by the P_1 through deblinding. Since the SIG' is based on the C private key x_2 and can be verified publicly like $g^{mark_j'} = y_2^r r^{SIG'^{-1}h} \bmod q$, the C cannot deny that the SIG is generated by his private key x_2.

As the P_1 employs pseudonyms both when applying for tasks and submitting task data, and given that the C can solely validate the legality of the submitted reports, it is unable to establish a direct link between the report and P_1. Although the task index can be associated with its corresponding report and request vouchers, it remains dissociated from both the assessment score and the identity of the node. Consequently, the C is incapable of determining whether P_1 has either accepted or submitted reports for a specific task. Since reports can exclusively be correlated with report vouchers, and report vouchers used by the P_1 are independently generated through the partially blind signature method, there exists no mechanism for the C to connect multiple reports submitted by P_1.

As for the incentive identifier, it is obtained by the interaction between the mobile node and the consensus node through the ELGamal blind signature algorithm, and then the participants are de-blinded.

If an attacker intercepts the blind message $mark_j'$ and wants to solve for the private key x_1 from $mark_j'$, he will face the problem of solving the discrete logarithm. And if he wants to find the original message $mark_j$, because t_j is a large random number, he will also face the factorization of a large integer Difficulties.

For attackers, reports have already been transmitted to the consensus node and cannot be resubmitted, therefore they cannot benefit from using these reports. If attackers are not assigned the task, they will be unable to submit data for that specific task. In both scenarios, attackers cannot gain any form of advantage from the system.

Attacks on Incentive. In the event of an attacker launching an assault, the attacker must initially furnish an address that aligns with the task's prerequisites to procure the reports associated with the task. Furthermore, a node is precluded from leveraging the report associated with task i to garner vouchers for another task j, since those have been committed to the task i through partially blind signatures. Consequently, all mobile nodes are constrained to employ solely the specific report and voucher pair to which they have committed within the context of task i. If an attacker is either unassigned to the task or is assigned it but refrains from submitting reports, they will not be eligible for any reward. In summary, an attacker cannot subvert the achievement of our scheme's incentive objectives.

6   Performance Analysis

In this section, To verify the performance of our scheme and the feasibility of the model, we experimentally evaluate the privacy-preserving incentive scheme and reputation quantification model in reality. Compared with previous blind signature-based PPAIM [7] and zero-knowledge proof-based PACE [27], our scheme balances security, decentralization, identity privacy, and efficiency of MCS. The feature comparison is listed in Table 1.

Table 1. Features Comparison

	PPAIM	PACE	Our Scheme
Identity-privacy	✓	✓	✓
Decentralization	×	×	✓
Quality-aware	✓	✓	✓
Reputation-quantify	×	✓	✓

We implemented our schemes in Python, and the ELGamal scheme [10] is used as our blind signature scheme, the partially blind ELGamal signature [11] is used as our PBS scheme. A private chain was built in the Ubuntu 18.04.6 environment, using the PoS consensus mechanism and performing performance tests on the blockchain test network on a single host. To ensure the same experimental environment conditions, each experiment was repeated 20 times, and the experimental data was taken 20 times Experimental average. The simulation experiment is implemented in Python, running on Intel(R) Core(TM) i5-9300H CPU @ 2.40GHz 2.40 GHz processor, 8GB RAM, and the reputation quantification model is run on Matlab of the same model computer. The mobile device used by the mobile node uses Android 12 OS, 256GB storage, 15GB RAM for running, and a 3.0GHz CPU. The platform is described in Table 2.

Table 3 summarizes our schemes' computation, communication, and storage costs. From the tabular data presented, it is evident that the costs are significantly lower for nodes with unassigned tasks. For the other nodes, the costs are mainly incurred by the submission of reports and the implementation of the NIZK protocol, as well as the necessary interactions.

We use the parameter N in Table 3 to represent the cost of a single task process. Besides, we use the parameter ε to denote the average proportion of

Table 2. Hardware Platform of the Experiments

	C	MN	P-Chain
Terminal Model	HP Pavilion	RedMi K-40	HP Pavilion
CPU	Inter I5@4x	Dimensity 1200@8x	Inter I5@4x
RAM	8GB	16GB	8GB
OS	Ubuntu18.04	Android 13	Ubuntu18.04
Kernel	Linux 5.4.0	Android 5.10.149	Linux 5.4.0

tasks assigned by the system to a single node. Due to geographical and efficiency requirements in large-scale tasks, nodes located in one place are unable to handle tasks originating from another location. Therefore, we build a perception environment in which a single node is assigned a small number of tasks, so ε will be closed to 1.

Table 3. One Mobile Node's Cost for Task Process.

	Unassigned task	Assigned task	Average
Computation	$2n_1 H$	$4n_1 H + 2n_2$ (PBS+M.E+NIZK)	$(2+4\varepsilon)n_1 H + 2\varepsilon n_2$ (PBS+M.E+NIZK)
Communication	$O(n_1)$	$O(n_2 N + n_1)$	$O(\varepsilon n_2 N + n_1)$
Storage	$O(n_1)$	$O(n_2 N + n_1)$	$O(\varepsilon n_2 N + n_1)$

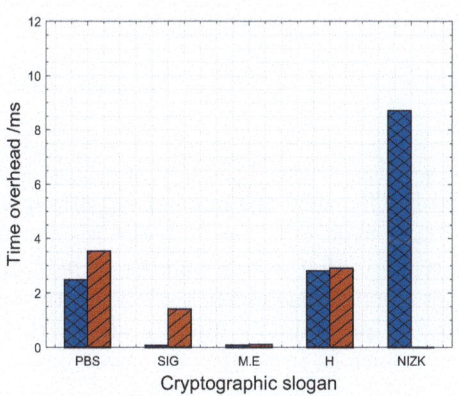

Fig. 4. Running Time of Cryptographic Primitives

We tested the running time of PBS, ELGamal signatures, modular operations, hash, and NIZK in the above model of computer, and compared them with the decentralized solution in the PPAIM [7]. To ensure that the results are reasonable, the comparison data will be obtained after simulating the scheme in the same experimental environment.

The results are presented in Fig. 4. It is worth noting that for partial blind signatures, we measure the time taken by consensus node for generating it, while the time cost of PPAIM corresponds to the aforementioned Android model. For blind signature algorithms, we utilize the ELGamal blind signature algorithm, which has a shorter running time. Since the value is too small, we are counting the time cost after the hash algorithm is expanded by 1000 times. To ensure security, we newly introduced the NIZK algorithm and separately counted its time overhead. The time overhead of NIZK refers to the time for mobile nodes to generate proofs and consensus nodes to verify proofs. As for the time overhead of transmitting proofs in the blockchain network, it is ignored. It can be inferred from Fig. 4 that the NIZK algorithm accounts for the largest proportion of running time.

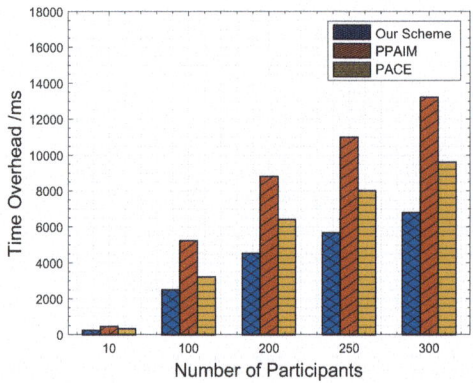

Fig. 5. Time Overhead for Different Numbers of Participants

At the same time, we also observed the time overhead of our scheme, PPAIM and [27] which named PACE when the number of participants differed and the data came from the task type of $n_1 = 256$, the results are shown in Fig. 5. Both of the overall trends is that as the number of participants increases, the overall running time of schemes also increases, but our time cost is shorter. This is because the number of participants directly affects the number of calls to cryptographic primitives such as PBS, SIG, etc. Moreover, we adopted the more lightweight ELGamal signature algorithm, and for a single task performed by a single participant, it does not need to generate a complete PBS and signature for each credit like PPAIM, but calls the $NIZK_{Pro}$ algorithm to generate a zero-knowledge proof π of the quality assessment score α, thus improving security while reducing the communication cost and time overhead. Since most of the time cost of our solution is used to generate and verify zero-knowledge proofs, if we choose a more lightweight zero-knowledge proof system, our time cost should be further reduced. But this also needs to take into account the security of the overall solution for further analysis and adjustments.

7   Conclusion

In this paper, we gave a privacy-preserving incentive mechanism in blockchain-based mobile crowdsensing, enabling users to enhance their reputation and receive rewards for contributing data without disclosing the specific data they provided, thereby safeguarding user privacy. We prioritized the preservation of user identity privacy and emphasize the equity of data quality assessment. Therefore, we designed a reputation quantification model. Simulation experiments demonstrate the security, equity, and efficiency of our scheme, without imposing additional computational burden on mobile nodes. Simultaneously, we conducted validation to confirm the reasonableness and feasibility of the proposed reputation quantification model.

References

1. An, J., Wang, Z., He, X., Gui, X., Cheng, J., Gui, R.: PPQC: a blockchain-based privacy-preserving quality control mechanism in crowdsensing applications. IEEE/ACM Trans. Netw. **30**(3), 1352–1367 (2022)
2. Capponi, A., Fiandrino, C., Kantarci, B., Foschini, L., Kliazovich, D., Bouvry, P.: A survey on mobile crowdsensing systems: challenges, solutions, and opportunities. IEEE Commun. Surv. Tutor. **21**(3), 2419–2465 (2019)
3. Chen, S., Susilo, W., Zhang, Y., Yang, B., Zhang, M.: Privacy-preserving anomaly counting for time-series data in edge-assisted crowdsensing. Comput. Stand. Interfaces **85**, 103707 (2023)
4. Huang, J., et al.: Blockchain-based mobile crowd sensing in industrial systems. IEEE Trans. Industr. Inf. **16**(10), 6553–6563 (2020)
5. Kim, J.W., Edemacu, K., Jang, B.: Privacy-preserving mechanisms for location privacy in mobile crowdsensing: a survey. J. Netw. Comput. Appl. **200**, 103315 (2022)
6. Li, B., Shi, Y., Kong, Q., Du, Q., Lu, R.: Incentive-based federated learning for digital-twin-driven industrial mobile crowdsensing. IEEE Internet Things J. **10**(20), 17851–17864 (2023). https://doi.org/10.1109/JIOT.2023.3279657
7. Li, Q., Cao, G.: Providing privacy-aware incentives in mobile sensing systems. IEEE Trans. Mob. Comput. **15**(6), 1485–1498 (2015)
8. Liu, Y., Kong, L., Chen, G.: Data-oriented mobile crowdsensing: a comprehensive survey. IEEE Commun. Surv. Tutor. **21**(3), 2849–2885 (2019)
9. Ma, Z., Wang, Y., Li, J., Liu, Y.: A blockchain based privacy-preserving incentive mechanism for internet of vehicles in satellite-terrestrial crowdsensing. In: 2021 7th International Conference on Computer and Communications (ICCC), pp. 2062–2067. IEEE (2021)
10. Mohammed, E., Emarah, A.E., El-Shennaway, K.: A blind signature scheme based on elgamal signature. In: Proceedings of the Seventeenth National Radio Science Conference. 17th NRSC'2000 (IEEE Cat. No. 00EX396), p. C25-1. IEEE (2000)

11. Papachristoudis, D., Hristu-Varsakelis, D., Baldimtsi, F., Stephanides, G.: Leakage-resilient lattice-based partially blind signatures. IET Inf. Secur. **13**(6), 670–684 (2019)
12. Peng, T., Guan, K., Liu, J.: A privacy-preserving mobile crowdsensing scheme based on blockchain and trusted execution environment. IEICE Trans. Inf. Syst. **105**(2), 215–226 (2022)
13. Shen, X., Xu, C., Zhu, L., Lu, R., Guan, Y., Zhang, X.: Blockchain-based lightweight and privacy-preserving quality assurance framework in crowdsensing systems. IEEE Internet Things J. (2023)
14. Sisi, Z., Souri, A.: Blockchain technology for energy-aware mobile crowd sensing approaches in internet of things. Trans. Emerg. Telecommun. Technol. e4217 (2021)
15. Tong, F., Zhou, Y., Wang, K., Cheng, G., Niu, J., He, S.: A privacy-preserving incentive mechanism for mobile crowdsensing based on blockchain. IEEE Trans. Depend. Secure Comput. 1–14 (2024). https://doi.org/10.1109/TDSC.2024.3368655
16. Wang, L., Zhang, D., Yang, D., Lim, B.Y., Han, X., Ma, X.: Sparse mobile crowd-sensing with differential and distortion location privacy. IEEE Trans. Inf. Forensics Secur. **15**, 2735–2749 (2020)
17. Wang, Z., Li, Y., Li, D., Li, M., Zhang, B., Huang, S., He, W.: Enabling fairness-aware and privacy-preserving for quality evaluation in vehicular crowdsensing: a decentralized approach. Secur. Commun. Netw. **2021**, 1–11 (2021)
18. Wang, Z., Hu, Q., Li, R., Xu, M., Xiong, Z.: Incentive mechanism design for joint resource allocation in blockchain-based federated learning. IEEE Trans. Parallel Distrib. Syst. **34**(5), 1536–1547 (2023). https://doi.org/10.1109/TPDS.2023.3253604
19. Wei, L., Wu, J., Long, C.: A blockchain-based hybrid incentive model for crowdsensing. Electronics **9**(2), 215 (2020)
20. Xiong, J., Chen, X., Yang, Q., Chen, L., Yao, Z.: A task-oriented user selection incentive mechanism in edge-aided mobile crowdsensing. IEEE Trans. Netw. Sci. Eng. **7**(4), 2347–2360 (2019)
21. Xiong, J., Ma, R., Chen, L., Tian, Y., Li, Q., Liu, X., Yao, Z.: A personalized privacy protection framework for mobile crowdsensing in IIoT. IEEE Trans. Industr. Inf. **16**(6), 4231–4241 (2019)
22. Yu, R., Oguti, A.M., Ochora, D.R., Li, S.: Towards a privacy-preserving smart contract-based data aggregation and quality-driven incentive mechanism for mobile crowdsensing. J. Netw. Comput. Appl. **207**, 103483 (2022)
23. Zhang, C., Zhu, L., Xu, C., Liu, X., Sharif, K.: Reliable and privacy-preserving truth discovery for mobile crowdsensing systems. IEEE Trans. Dependable Secure Comput. **18**(3), 1245–1260 (2019)
24. Zhang, M., Chen, S., Shen, J., Susilo, W.: Privacyeafl: privacy-enhanced aggregation for federated learning in mobile crowdsensing. IEEE Trans. Inf. Forensics Secur. (2023)
25. Zhang, M., Li, Z.A., Zhang, P.: A secure and privacy-preserving word vector training scheme based on functional encryption with inner-product predicates. Comput. Stand. Interfaces **86**, 103734 (2023)
26. Zhang, M., Yang, M., Shen, G., Xia, Z., Wang, Y.: A verifiable and privacy-preserving cloud mining pool selection scheme in blockchain of things. Inf. Sci. **623**, 293–310 (2023)
27. Zhao, B., Tang, S., Liu, X., Zhang, X.: Pace: privacy-preserving and quality-aware incentive mechanism for mobile crowdsensing. IEEE Trans. Mob. Comput. **20**(5), 1924–1939 (2020)

A Comparative Analysis of Phishing Tools: Features and Countermeasures

Rishikesh Sahay[1], Weizhi Meng[2,3]([✉]), and Wenjuan Li[4,5]

[1] Department of Management Information Systems, University of Illinois Springfield, Springfield, IL, USA
[2] SPTAGE Lab, Technical University of Denmark, Lyngby, Denmark
weizhi.meng@ieee.org
[3] School of Computing and Communications, Lancaster University, Lancaster, United Kingdom
[4] Department of Mathematics and Information Technology, The Education University of Hong Kong, Tai Po, Hong Kong SAR
[5] Institute of Artificial Intelligence and Blockchain, Guangzhou University, Guangzhou, China

Abstract. Phishing is a form of social engineering attack in which targets are contacted by email by someone posing as a legitimate sender to lure the target into sending them sensitive information, such as login information, credit card details, or other personal information. There are a large number of methods to perform phishing attacks, with one of the most common being website-based phishing attacks. These are attacks in which targets are lured to a website that seems to be legitimate but is a fraudulent webpage that steals all the submitted information. There are several tools that can be used for these phishing attacks, e.g., Social Engineering Toolkit (SET), Zphisher, and GoPhish. These tools set up fake websites for phishing and collect login information from the targeted users who are fooled by the legitimate website. This paper presents the method for performing a phishing attack using these three tools and compares the application of these tools to launch phishing attacks and campaigns. We specifically select these three tools because they are free and provide a good platform to create or mimic legitimate websites and use this to launch phishing campaigns to get confidential information. The comparative assessment is performed based on criteria such as GUI, integration with Windows and Linux, report generation, multiple phishing campaign, extracting victim system and browser details. The evaluation shows that GoPhish satisfies most of the features and is widely used in industry for phishing campaigns and creating cyber awareness.

Keywords: Network Security · Data Security · Phishing Tools · Social Engineering Attacks · Spear Phishing

Z. Xia and J. Chen (Eds.): ISPEC 2024, LNCS 15053, pp. 365–382, 2024.
https://doi.org/10.1007/978-981-97-9053-1_21

1   Introduction

With an increase in the number of Internet users and social media platforms, cyber attacks are increasing due to the lack of awareness of cyber security among Internet users. According to the ENISA Threat Landscape Report, cyber attacks have increased in 2023 [6]. Among the most prevalent threats organizations and end users face are social engineering attacks [8].

Social engineering attacks target end-users and organizations to disclose confidential information that can be valuable to attackers. These social engineering attacks take advantage of psychological manipulation and social interaction to trick unsuspecting users into divulging sensitive information such as usernames, passwords, and social security numbers. Attackers using these tactics pose as trustworthy organizations, service providers, and law enforcement agencies to persuade targeted users to click malicious links. Attackers bypass robust security measures such as firewalls, intrusion detection systems, and antivirus protection through social engineering attacks. This makes it difficult to defend social engineering attacks using security tools until people are aware of these attacks and the tactics used by attackers.

Attackers employ various methods, such as phishing, spear phishing, and vishing to deceive targeted users to disclose sensitive information. Spear phishing attacks refer to targeting specific individuals in the organization. A cyber attack that occurred on the Ukrainian power grid in 2015 started with a phishing attack [2]. The attackers targeted individuals in the company with phishing emails that had BlackEnergy malware as an attachment to the email. The company had a proper firewall set-up, but attackers managed to compromise an office laptop with the help of BlackEnergy malware. It is difficult to prevent this kind of phishing attacks until employees are well aware of the phishing tricks.

According to the FBI 2023 Internet Crime Report, business email compromise through social engineering attacks is on the rise, and the estimated loss was 2.9 billion dollars [7]. The FBI report also mentions phishing among the top five types of crimes. Moreover, it also highlights that phishing caused maximum loss. Some studies have reported that 84% of cyber attacks are carried out by social engineering with a very high success rate [12]. Furthermore, with several user-friendly and free tools [3,29] attackers are targeting small organizations with few defense capabilities [1]. These reports show that social engineering attacks are prevalent and that it is important to detect and mitigate them.

In this paper, we present about how social engineering attacks such as phishing can be launched using tools like the Social Engineering Toolkit (SET), Zphisher, and GoPhish. The purpose is to use these tools to create cyber awareness in organizations. The remainder of the paper is organized as follows. Related works are provided in Sect. 2. Section 3 presents about the social engineering toolkit that is installed in Kali Linux. Section 4 demonstrates the use of Zphisher, which is an open source tool for sending phishing links. Section 5 provides an overview of the GoPhish tool. The comparative analysis of SET, Zphisher and GoPhish is highlighted in Sect. 7. Section 8 presents some countermeasures to protect organizations and individual users against phishing attacks. Finally, a conclusion is given in Sect. 9.

2   Types of Phishing Attacks

Cyber criminals use different social engineering methods to trick people into divulging confidential information that compromises security. This section presents a variety of social engineering strategies used by cyber criminals to target individuals and organizations.

- **Phishing:** This is a prevalent method of social engineering employed by cyber criminals. They design a counterfeit website that mirrors a legitimate one, enticing their victims to click on a link and disclose confidential data. For a successful phishing attack, cyber criminals rely on trust and psychological manipulation of their target by creating a sense of urgency and persuasive language [18].
- **Elicitation:** It is a social engineering strategy to obtain confidential information from targeted users through friendly discussion. The main purpose of cyber criminals is to obtain sensitive and relevant information to get access to the target systems. The victim may not understand the value of the confidential information revealed and cyber criminals can use the information to compromise the system [17]. To protect themselves from elicitation, organizations should provide training and cyber awareness to employees.
- **Baiting:** In this technique, attackers provide attractive offers to their victims, such as discounted offers for the holiday season and free software in exchange for confidential information. It relies on psychological concepts such as greed and curiosity of people to trick them into performing activities such as clicking on a malicious link that will damage the security [19]. Cyber awareness and training are the best countermeasure against baiting.
- **Whaling:** It is a type of phishing attack in which cyber criminals target high-profile authorities such as the CEO, CTO, CFO, and politicians to get access to strictly confidential and valuable information. For such technique, the attacker acts as a senior executive of the organization and targets senior or other employees of the organization to obtain confidential information and steal money. In 2016, the toy manufacturer Mattel lost 3 million dollars due to the whaling attack [20]. The attackers sent an email to the top finance executive acting as a new CEO and requested a fund transfer. The fund was transferred in the account of cyber criminals but Mattel coordinated with the police and got back the money.
- **Spear Phishing:** In the spear-phishing attack, cyber criminals target a small group or specific employees in the organization to obtain confidential information such as trade secrets and log-in details. In 2016, the Ukranian power grid attack started with spear phishing attack [2].
- **Vishing:** Voice phishing also known as vishing, involves phone communication, enticing people to reveal confidential information. According to the Agari and PhishLabs threat report, there is an increase in vishing cases in 2022 [4]. In 2022, a US based telecommunication company suffered an incident due to sophisticated vishing attack [5].

– **Callback Vishing:** It is also known as "Hybrid Vishing" that is a multi-stage attack that differs from traditional vishing. The attacker first sends an email to the targeted user, alerting them about potential problems such as payment issues, malware in the system, etc. The attacker does not provide any phishing link in the email because often organizations have endpoint security that detects phishing links and malicious attachments in emails and forwards them to quarantine. Instead of phishing link, attackers provide a phone number in the email that user must call to resolve the issue. Once victim callback on the phone number attacker tricks them to reveal credentials or download a malicious attachment. Callback vishing was introduced by Ryuk ransomware group to trick users to install Bazar malware [30]. According to the Agari and PhishLabs report, there is a rise by using a hybrid vishing to target end-users and organizations [4]. An example about the vishing attack in 2022, a doctor in South Korea sent $3 million in cash, stocks, insurance and cryptocurrencies to cyber criminals [13].

3   Social Engineering Toolkit (SET)

The Social Engineering Toolkit (SET) contains a number of possible forms of social engineering attacks [29]. It is an open-source tool created by Dave Kennedy to launch social engineering attacks and create cyber awareness in the organization [14]. It provides penetration testers and ethical hackers with a collection of tools to simulate different social engineering attacks to help organizations identify and correct security vulnerabilities [9].

For example, SET enables us to clone any website that is accessible on the Internet for phishing attacks [14]. Moreover, using SET different attack vectors can be created without programming background [14]. It helps automate many complex tasks while performing a phishing campaign.

3.1   Fundamentals of SET

This section describes the method for using SET with Kali Linux [16]. SET is a menu-based tool that allows us to customize the attacks for the target. As shown in Fig. 1, once SET is launched, the menus provide different options to launch social engineering attacks. It is worth noting that our focus is to demonstrate the use of fake webpage to steal login details, i.e., credential harvesting attack.

In a credential harvesting attack, the aim of the attacker is to trick unsuspecting users into providing their credentials into the fake or cloned web page, believing it to be the genuine web page. Once the user submits their credentials on the fake web page, the attacker captures the information and then uses it for malicious purposes, such as unauthorized access to the system, identity theft, financial fraud, or further exploitation of the compromised system or network. Credential harvester attacks rely on social engineering techniques to convince users to provide their credentials, without arousing any suspicion. These attacks are conducted through various channels such as email phishing, malicious attachments, fake login webpages, or through compromised or fake mobile apps.

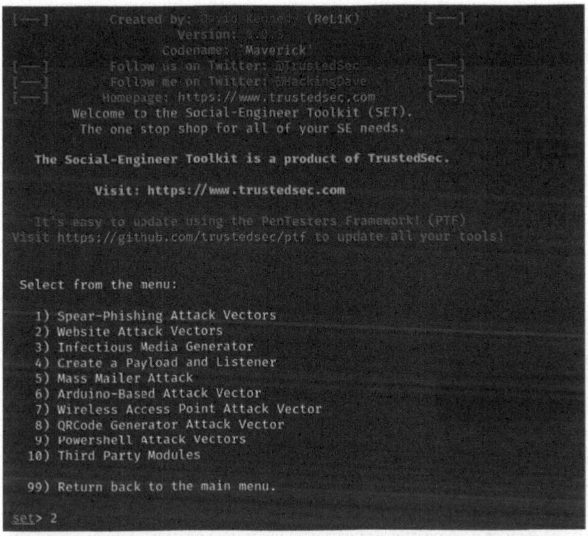

Fig. 1. Social Engineering Toolkit

3.2   Methodology of SET

As shown in Fig. 1, once SET is launched, different attack options are provided. From the list, we select option 2 which is a website attack vector that leads to a credential harvesting attack, as shown in Fig. 2. As we can see in Fig. 3, three different attack methods are provided: Web Templates, Site cloner and Custom import. We select option 2, which is the site cloner. The site cloner can clone the website for the phishing attack. Figure 4 shows that the IP address of the listener is provided along with the link to the facebook login page for the cloning. As depicted in Fig. 4, IP address of the listener is 192.168.10.6 which is the IP address of Kali Linux. As shown in Fig. 5, once the facebook login page is cloned, the listener on Kali Linux starts listening and waits for the link to be clicked and the login details to be provided.

The clone link to the Facebook login page is sent to an email address that we created for this work. As shown in Fig. 6, when the link is opened and the login details are provided, the captured details are sent to the listener on the Kali machine. Due to privacy issues, login details are hidden.

4   Zphisher-Phishing Tool

Zphisher is an open-source tool designed for phishing attacks. It offers a framework for creating and deploying phishing or fake webpages aimed at stealing confidential information such as usernames, passwords, etc. Zphisher provides various templates for popular websites such as Facebook, Gmail, Instagram, etc. It simplifies the process of setting up a fake web page for phishing attacks. The phishing website is hosted on a server managed by an attacker. The link to the phishing website is distributed through email, social networks, or other

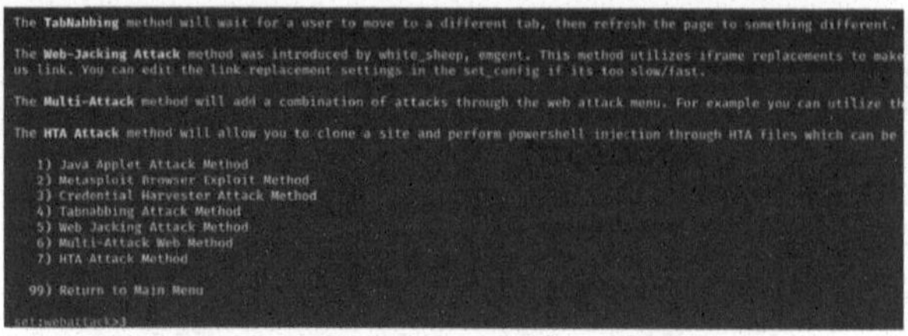

Fig. 2. Credential Harvester Attack Method

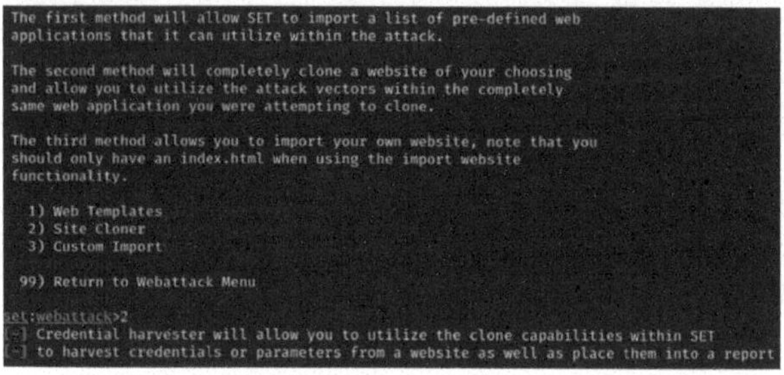

Fig. 3. Web Attack Menu

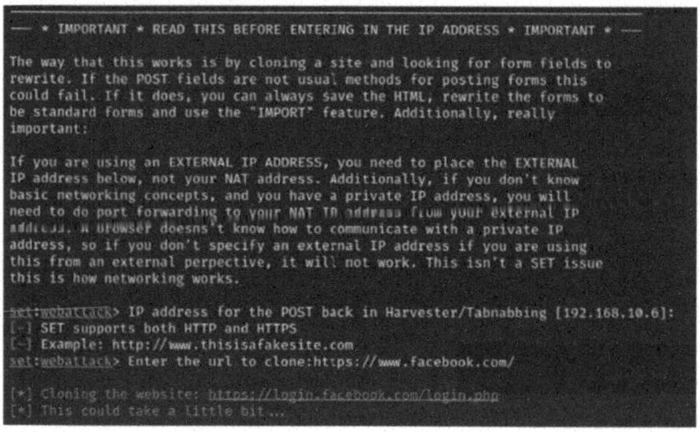

Fig. 4. Site Cloning

Fig. 5. Starting the Listener

communication channels, tricking victims into entering their credentials into a fake webpage. Once a victim enters their credentials into the phishing page, Zphisher captures all the login details. The captured information can be used by an attacker for malicious purposes such as unauthorized access to systems.

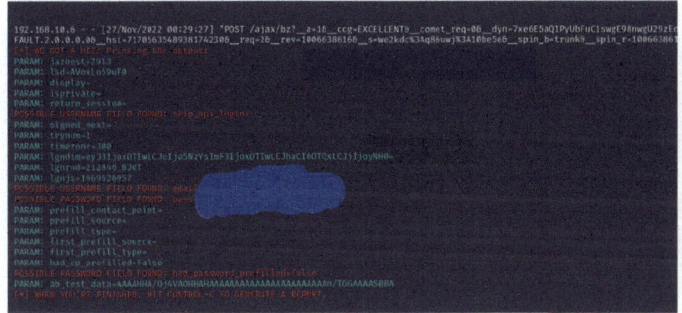

Fig. 6. Captured Credentials

The main features of Zphisher are [10]:

- It is a simple and easy-to-use tool.
- Programming experience is not required to use zphisher.
- Zphisher runs on Kali Linux.
- It provides phishing templates of 35 websites.
- It is written in Bash language.
- Zphisher is a lightweight tool.

4.1 Use of Zphisher

This part describes the method of using Zphisher. We installed Zphisher on Kali Linux. Detailed steps to install Zphisher are not described for the sake of brevity.

After installation, once in the Zphisher directory, it can be started by entering the command in the terminal, which is: "bash zphisher.sh". As shown in Fig. 7, Zphisher provides templates for many popular websites such as Facebook, Instagram, Google, etc. Phishing page can be created based on the template provided by Zphisher. In this paper, a phishing page is crafted to mimic the traditional Facebook login page. Then the phishing link to the Facebook login page is sent via emails. As depicted in Fig. 8, the login details are captured along with the IP address. IP address of the victim is also captured in the file named "IP.txt". Moreover, credentials are captured in the file named "usernames.dat", which is saved in "auth" directory of Zphisher. For privacy, the login details are not shown in Fig. 8.

5   GoPhish Background

GoPhish is an open source phishing framework that is used to Phish test the organizations. It offers a web-based interface that is very easy to use. It provides features similar to industry-grade phishing tools such as visualization and reporting of real-time results on the dashboard. GoPhish is available for all platforms such as Windows and Linux, which is also very easy to install.

Fig. 7. Zphisher

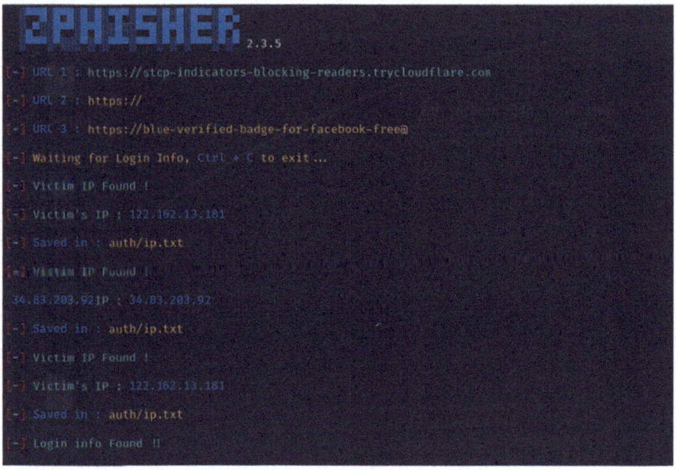

Fig. 8. Captured Details through Zphisher

To use GoPhish, a third-party SMTP server is required. For this purpose, a self-hosted SMTP server can be used or even a paid service. The selected SMTP server should be whitelisted along with the email provider to enable mail delivery.

GoPhish makes the real-world phishing simulation very simple and easy. It has been widely used in industry to create cyber awareness with a phishing campaign. GoPhish releases are compiled binaries and there are no dependencies among them because GoPhish is written in Go programming language.

6   Use of GoPhish

This section describes the process of using GoPhish for the phishing campaign. We installed GoPhish on Kali Linux, but it can also be installed on the Windows platform. GoPhish can be downloaded and installed from an official page [3]. The detailed installation process of GoPhish is not shown due to brevity.

6.1   Running GoPhish

Steps to run GoPhish on Kali Linux are described below:

– After installation, to start GoPhish, a command needs to be entered in the terminal, which is: "sudo ./gophish".
– Once GoPhish starts running, it provides "admin server" and "phishing server" IP addresses, as shown in Fig. 9. The prompt window shows that an admin server is running at IP address: "https://0.0.0.0:3333". It also shows that the phishing server is running at the IP address: "http://0.0.0.0:80". Admin credential is displayed in the command prompt window along with a message to use the credentials to log into the admin server. After the first time login, GoPhish compels to change the password.
– When the installation is complete, Fig. 10 shows the dashboard of GoPhish.

Once the initial configuration of GoPhish is complete, the sending profiles, landing page, and email templates need to be configured before launching a phishing campaign.

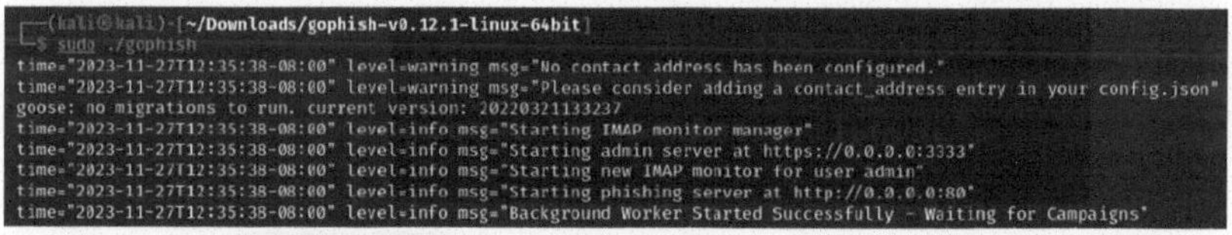

Fig. 9. GoPhish with "admin server" and "phishing server" IP addresses

6.2   Configure Sending Profiles

The sending profiles in GoPhish must be configured after the initial configuration is complete. In GoPhish, sending profiles is the configuration used to specify the way how emails will be sent out during a phishing campaign. These sending profiles comprise setting details such as the SMTP server information, the sender name, the sender email address, and any additional parameters needed to send emails effectively.

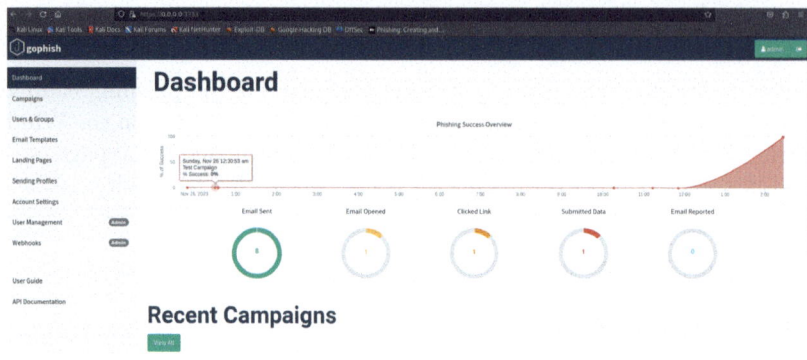

Fig. 10. GoPhish dashboard

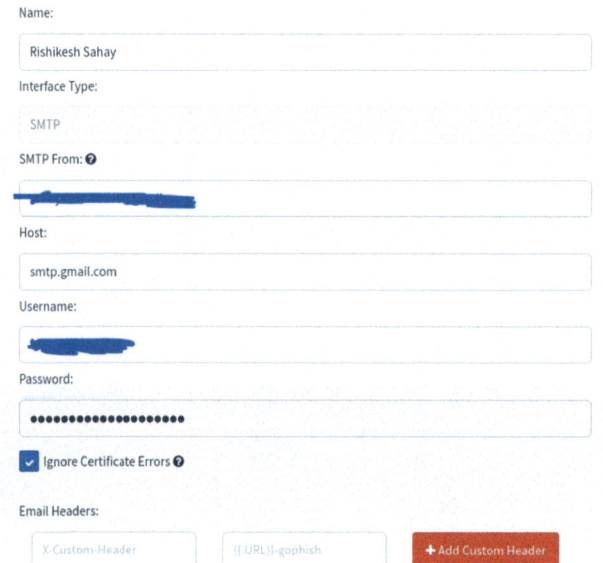

Fig. 11. Sending Profile in GoPhish

Steps to configure sending profile are described as below:

- In this work, for configuring sending profile Gmail account is used.
- Two-step verification should be enabled on the Gmail account before creating the sending profile.
- As shown in Fig. 11, password must be entered in the sending profiles setting of GoPhish. It is called the "App password" that is generated by Gmail for the GoPhish. For privacy reasons, the user name and SMTP field is not shown in Fig. 11.

6.3 Landing Page

A landing page is a web page designed to clone a legitimate website as part of a phishing campaign. It is used to trick targeted users into providing confidential information, such as usernames, passwords, or personal data (e.g., social security number), by providing them with a legitimate copy of a trusted site. GoPhish offers a variety of pre-designed templates that look like popular websites commonly used in phishing attacks, such as login pages of email providers, social media, or online banking websites. These templates can be customized to make them more authentic to targeted users and organizations. So, it is important to configure the landing page properly for the phishing campaign.

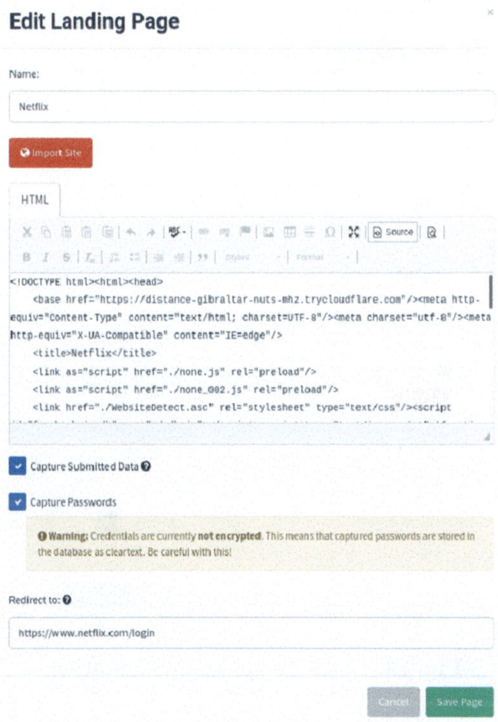

Fig. 12. Landing Page in GoPhish

Steps to configure the landing page are described as below:

- To create a landing page, we can click on the "Landing Pages" entry in the sidebar and choose the "New Page" button.
- Then, we can choose the "Import Site" button and provide the link to import the website. As shown in Fig. 12, the Netflix page is imported in this case.
- To select the "capture submitted data" and "capture passwords" checkboxes to record the credentials entered by the targeted users.

An email template is required to send the phishing link to the targeted users once the landing page is configured. The next section highlights the process of creating an email template.

6.4   Email Template

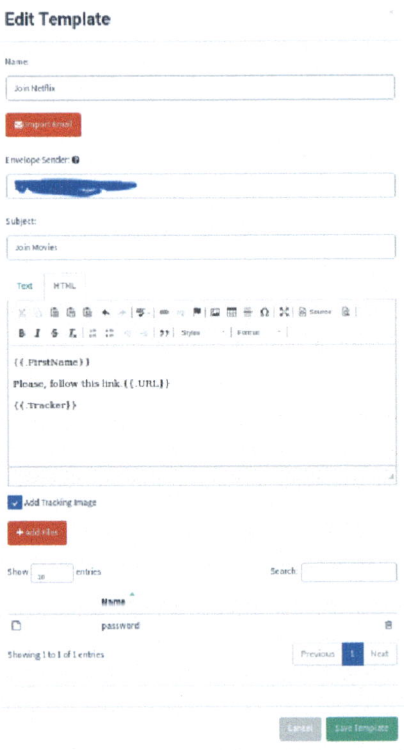

Fig. 13. Email Template Configuration

To create the Email template, we can click on the "Email Templates" button on the sidebar, as shown in Fig. 10. Then we can choose the HTML tab as depicted in Fig. 13. The phishing link is thus provided to the victim through ".URL". In this work, Email template has been kept as simple. Existing emails can also be imported into GoPhish for the phishing campaign. After saving the email templates, the receiver email is added, as shown in Fig. 14. Once the email template is configured and the recipient email is added, the phishing campaign can be launched.

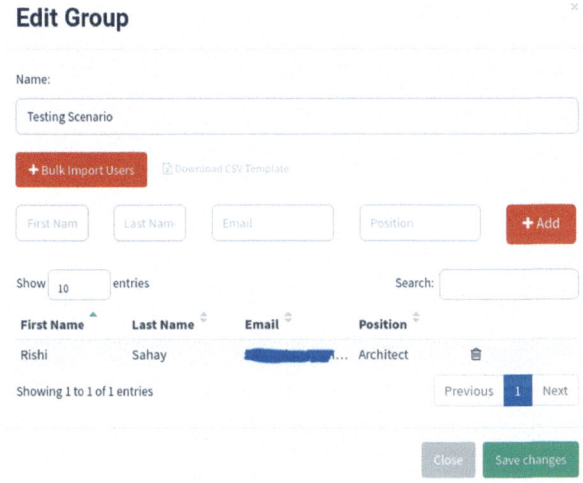

Fig. 14. Users and Groups Settings

6.5   Phishing Campaign

A phishing campaign is defined as a coordinated series of simulated phishing attacks designed to assess the security awareness of an organization's employees or stakeholders. The purpose of these phishing campaigns is to use real-world phishing tactics to trick the targeted users into disclosing confidential information, by clicking on malicious links, or performing actions that could damage the security of the organization.

As we can see in Fig. 10, "New Campaign" in the sidebar of the dashboard is used to launch a phishing campaign via GoPhish. Launching a phishing campaign requires the configured email template, landing page, sending profile, and the groups. Moreover, along with the IP address of the phishing server, we can start a phishing campaign. As shown in Fig. 15, the IP address of the phishing server in this case is: "http://0.0.0.0:80".

As shown in Fig. 16, up to 8 emails have been sent in this campaign. The results on the dashboard show that the email is opened, clicked, and some confidential information has been submitted. In this case, it is an email and a password captured as shown in Fig. 17. For privacy reasons, the captured data are not shown. Along with the captured data, GoPhish also provides information about the operating system and the browser used by the victim. Figure 17 presents that the operating system (OS) is Linux and the browser is Firefox.

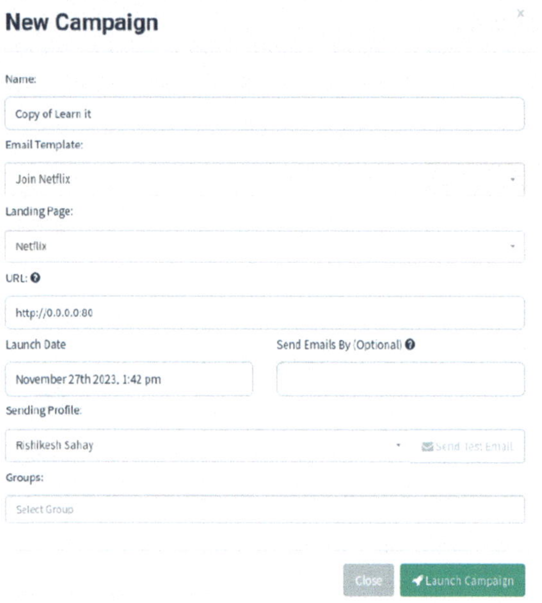

Fig. 15. Creating Phishing Campaign in GoPhish

Fig. 16. Results of the Phishing Campaign

7   Comparative Analysis of the Tools

This section provides a comparative evaluation of SET, Zphisher, and GoPhish. As shown in Table 1, all three tools are open-source and free to use. Social Engineering Toolkit (SET) is pre-installed with Kali Linux. Multiple phishing campaign refers to launching multiple simulated phishing attack simultaneously targeting different users and groups. It enables us to target multiple users and create phishing awareness in the organization. However, SET does not provide the feature of running multiple phishing campaign. The main advantage of SET is that it is integrated with metasploit framework. The metasploit framework installed in Kali is widely used for penetration testing.

Fig. 17. Captured Data

Zphisher is also an open-source and third-party tool. It is free to use but requires the installation in Kali. It is not supported on the Windows OS. The advantage of Zphisher is that it captures the system details of victims such as operating system in use and the browser that is used to open the link. However, it is not integrated with metasploit framework and does not provide a report summary of phishing campaign.

The advantage of GoPhish in comparison to Zphisher and SET is that it is very easy to install with a GUI framework. Thus, GoPhish enables us to launch multiple phishing campaigns with its GUI interface. Moreover, it can be visualized that how many Emails are opened, number of users clicked the link and submitted the data. It also provides the information about the victim system such as OS and the browser used by the victim to open the link. It is supported on Linux as well as Windows machine. However, it is not integrated with the metasploit framework.

8 Countermeasures for Phishing Attacks

Phishing attacks target human psychology (such as curiosity, panicking, etc.) to get access to victims' accounts and compromise organizations' resources. It is difficult to protect against phishing attacks because users might not be aware of the compromise. However, to protect against phishing attacks, organizations must have good security policies and procedures. Some effective strategies to prevent phishing attacks are described as follows:

– A good password policies must be defined. For example, avoid using an easy to guess password, change password frequently (e.g., every 3 months), long and complex passwords, etc.

Table 1. Comparison between SET, Zphisher and the GoPhish

Phishing tools	SET	Zphisher	GoPhsih
Open source	Yes	Yes	Yes
GUI	No	No	Yes
Linux	Yes	Yes	Yes
Windows	No	No	Yes
Report generation	No	No	Yes
Multiple phishing campaign	No	No	Yes
Victim system and browser details	No	Yes	Yes
Customizable web templates	Yes	Yes	Yes
Integration with metasploit	Yes	No	No

- Multi-factor authentication must be enforced to avoid attackers from using compromised passwords.
- Accounts must be blocked if a user exceeds the number of failed login attempts.
- Anti-phishing toolbars such as PhishTank, Netcraft should be used. These anti-phishing toolbars check whether a malicious URL is a phishing site or legitimate.
- Organizations must have cybersecurity awareness and training programs.
- To detect phishing links in email, taking the mouse over the "From" field and if the original domain name is not linked to the sender's name then it can be a phishing link.
  Organizations must perform a periodic risk analysis to identify vulnerabilities and analyze evolving attack vectors.

The above strategies are effective only if people in organizations are vigilant and alert against phishing tricks and tactics used by attackers. Thus, it is recommended for the organization to conduct a periodic phishing campaign internally and educate people about phishing tricks to prevent against these attacks. It also includes deploying proper intrusion detection systems [25,31], trust schemes [24,27] and firewall [21], which can be enhanced by software-defined networking [15,28], event filtration [26] and blockchain technology [11,22,23].

9   Conclusion

During the digital transformation period, various phishing attacks are affecting both organizations and individuals. This work presented tools that are capable of initiating phishing attacks and provided a comparative analysis of different characteristics of these phishing tools. Organizations can use these tools to create cyber awareness training for their employees. In our future work, we plan to extend this work with other phishing tools such as Hidden Eye, King

Phisher, and Shell Phish. Moreover, we plan to investigate the phishing tools such as Tycoon (2FA) that can bypass the multi-factor authentication. Techniques bypassing multi-factor authentication are on the rise, which can pose a significant threat to organizations. Furthermore, we will examine in detail the countermeasures applicable to different types of phishing tools along with concrete steps, an organization can take to protect their employees from phishing attacks.

Acknowledgement. This work was partially supported by National Natural Science Foundation of China under the No. 62102106 and U21A20463.

References

1. The year of social distancing or social engineering? Phishing goes targeted and diversifies during COVID-19 outbreak. Technical reports, Kaspersky (2020)
2. Ukrainian power grids cyberattack-A Forensic Analysis based on ISA/IEC 62443 (2020)
3. Gophish v0.12.1: (2022). https://github.com/gophish/gophish/releases/tag/v0.12.1
4. Quarterly Threat Trends and Intelligence Report: Technical reports, Agari and PhishLabs (2022)
5. Vishing Attack on the HPH Sector: Technicla report, US Department of Health and HUman Services (2022)
6. ENISA THREAT LANDSCAPE 2023: Technical report, European Union Agency for Cybersecurity (2023)
7. Federal Bureau of Investigation-Internet crime Report: Technical report, Federal Bureau of Investigation (2023)
8. Q3 2023 Threat Landscape Report Social Engineering Takes Center Stage: Technical report, Kroll (2023)
9. SEToolkit-Credential Harvester Attack: (2023). https://www.geeksforgeeks.org/setoolkit-credential-harvester-attacktutorial/
10. Zphisher-Automated Phishing Tool in Kali Linux: (2023). https://www.geeksforgeeks.org/zphisher-automated-phishing-tool-in-kali-linux/
11. Chiu, W., Meng, W., Ge, C.: Nosneaky: a blockchain-based execution integrity protection scheme in industry 4.0. IEEE Trans. Ind. Inf. **19**(7), 7957–7965 (2023)
12. Costantino, G., La Marra, A., Martinelli, F., Matteucci, I.: Candy: A social engineering attack to leak information from infotainment system. In: 2018 IEEE 87th Vehicular Technology Conference (VTC Spring), pp. 1–5 (2018). https://doi.org/10.1109/VTCSpring.2018.8417879
13. Montalbano, E.: Sophisticated Vishing Campaigns Take World by Storm. Technical report, Dark Reading (2024)
14. Engebretson, P.: Chapter 5—social engineering. In: Engebretson, P. (ed.) The Basics of Hacking and Penetration Testing, 2nd edn, pp. 127–140. Syngress, Boston (2013). https://doi.org/10.1016/B978-0-12-411644-3.00005-4, https://www.sciencedirect.com/science/article/pii/B9780124116443000054
15. Fang, L., Li, Y., Yun, X., Wen, Z., Ji, S., Meng, W., Cao, Z., Tanveer, M.: THP: a novel authentication scheme to prevent multiple attacks in sdn-based IoT network. IEEE Internet Things J. **7**(7), 5745–5759 (2020)

16. Hertzog, R., O'Gorman, J.: Kali Linux Revealed: Mastering the Penetration Testing Distribution. Offsec Press (2017)
17. Horkoff, J., Ersare, J., Kahler, J., Jörundsson, T.D., Hammouda, I.: Efficiency and effectiveness of requirements elicitation techniques for children. In: 2018 IEEE 26th International Requirements Engineering Conference (RE), pp. 194–204 (2018). https://doi.org/10.1109/RE.2018.00028
18. Ivanov, M.A., Kliuchnikova, B.V., Chugunkov, I.V., Plaksina, A.M.: Phishing attacks and protection against them. In: 2021 IEEE Conference of Russian Young Researchers in Electrical and Electronic Engineering (ElConRus), pp. 425–428 (2021). https://doi.org/10.1109/ElConRus51938.2021.9396693
19. Jain, M., Mowar, P., Goel, R., Vishwakarma, D.K.: Clickbait in social media: detection and analysis of the bait. In: 2021 55th Annual Conference on Information Sciences and Systems (CISS), pp. 1–6 (2021). https://doi.org/10.1109/CISS50987.2021.9400293
20. Yip, K.N.: Whaling Case Study: Mattel's 3 Million Phishing Adventure. Technical report, InfoSec (2016)
21. Li, D., Hu, Y., Xiao, G., Duan, M., Li, K.: An active defense model based on situational awareness and firewalls. Concurr. Comput. Pract. Exp. **35**(6), 1 (2023)
22. Li, W., Meng, W., Liu, Z., Au, M.H.: Towards blockchain-based software-defined networking: security challenges and solutions. IEICE Trans. Inf. Syst. **103-D**(2), 196–203 (2020)
23. Li, W., Tug, S., Meng, W., Wang, Y.: Designing collaborative blockchained signature-based intrusion detection in IoT environments. Future Gener. Comput. Syst. **96**, 481–489 (2019)
24. Liu, L., Ma, Z., Meng, W.: Detection of multiple-mix-attack malicious nodes using perceptron-based trust in iot networks. Future Gener. Comput. Syst. **101**, 865–879 (2019)
25. Meng, W., Li, W., Kwok, L.: Design of intelligent knn-based alarm filter using knowledge-based alert verification in intrusion detection. Secur. Commun Networks **8**(18), 3883–3895 (2015)
26. Meng, W., Li, W., Kwok, L.F.: Towards effective trust-based packet filtering in collaborative network environments. IEEE Trans. Netw. Serv. Manag. **14**(1), 233–245 (2017)
27. Meng, W., Li, W., Xiang, Y., Choo, K.R.: A bayesian inference-based detection mechanism to defend medical smartphone networks against insider attacks. J. Netw. Comput. Appl. **78**, 162–169 (2017)
28. Sahay, R., Meng, W., Jensen, C.D.: The application of software defined networking on securing computer networks: a survey. J. Netw. Comput. Appl. **131**, 89–108 (2019)
29. Thomas, V.: Chapter 11—creating simulated phishing attacks. In: Gardner, B., Thomas, V. (eds.) Building an Information Security Awareness Program, pp. 95–107. Syngress, Boston (2014). https://doi.org/10.1016/B978-0-12-419967-5.00011-9, https://www.sciencedirect.com/science/article/pii/B9780124199675000119
30. Titanadmin: What is Callback Phishing? Technical report, SpamTitan (2022)
31. Wang, Y., Meng, W., Li, W., Liu, Z., Liu, Y., Xue, H.: Adaptive machine learning-based alarm reduction via edge computing for distributed intrusion detection systems. Concurr. Comput. Pract. Exp. **31**(19) (2019)

OEIBS: A Secure Obfuscation for Encrypted Identity-Based Signatures Scheme in NB-IoT

Yudi Zhang[1,2]($\boxtimes$) (ID), Yumei Li[1] (ID), Mingwu Zhang[2] (ID), and Willy Susilo[1] (ID)

[1] School of Computing and Information Technology, University of Wollongong,
Wollongong, NSW 2522, Australia
zhangyudi007@gmail.com
[2] School of Computers, Hubei University of Technology, Wuhan 430068, China

Abstract. The Internet of Things (IoT) has become pervasive in various domains and offers unprecedented convenience to society. The Narrowband Internet of Things (NB-IoT) technology is particularly well-suited for deployment in applications such as smart manufacturing, smart homes, and smart cities. However, NB-IoT requires low power consumption and network security, which pose significant challenges. While several cryptographic schemes have been proposed for NB-IoT, most of them are infeasible due to the high computing power required by the nodes. In this paper, we propose a secure obfuscation for encrypted identity-based signatures in NB-IoT. Our approach leverages the high computational power of the IoT gateway to generate an encrypted signature, while ensuring the node's private key cannot be extracted. We prove that our scheme satisfies the virtual black box (VBB) properties and is secure against attacks by semi-honest gateways. Furthermore, we implement our scheme using the Java pairing-based cryptography library (JPBC) on a laptop and a server, and our experimental results demonstrate the practicality of our scheme in IoT applications.

Keywords: VBP Obfuscation · Identity-based Signature · Security · Privacy · NB-IoT

1 Introduction

The Internet of Things (IoT) enables the connection and communication of various devices and objects via a network. This connectivity has made it possible for users to remotely control devices, such as adjusting thermostats, even across great distances. For businesses, the IoT has created new opportunities to connect with customers and partners, while also providing an effective means of collecting, storing, and analyzing large volumes of data. According to a report by Transforma Insights [19], there were 7.6 billion active IoT devices by the end of 2019, and this number is projected to reach 24.1 billion by 2030.

© The Author(s), under exclusive license to Springer Nature Singapore Pte Ltd. 2025
Z. Xia and J. Chen (Eds.): ISPEC 2024, LNCS 15053, pp. 383–402, 2024.
https://doi.org/10.1007/978-981-97-9053-1_22

To accommodate the growing number of connected devices, the 3rd Generation Partnership Project (3GPP) developed Narrowband Internet of Things (NB-IoT) as a secure and reliable network [14,15]. NB-IoT is a cellular technology that can support a wide range of devices and services. As depicted in Fig. 1, the NB-IoT architecture typically consists of three layers: the perception layer, the network layer, and the application layer. The perception layer includes various sensors, such as temperature and humidity sensors, two-dimensional code tags, RFID tags and readers, and cameras, that can identify objects and collect data, making it the source of the IoT. The network layer is comprised of different networks, including the Internet, broadcasting and television networks, network management systems, and cloud computing platforms. It serves as the central hub of the entire IoT ecosystem and is responsible for transmitting and processing information obtained from the perception layer. The application layer connects users to the IoT and enables intelligent IoT applications that cater to industry-specific requirements.

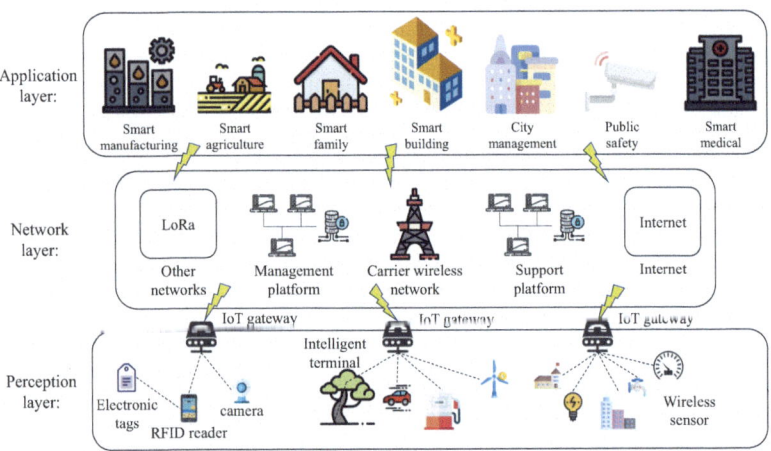

Fig. 1. A Typical Three-Layer Model NB-IoT Architecture

Narrowband Internet of Things (NB-IoT) technology has found widespread use in agriculture, industry, government, and everyday life, offering substantial convenience and business benefits to society. However, despite its advantages, NB-IoT is not immune to security threats [27]. A report by [26] indicates that attacks and threats on Operational Technology (OT) and IoT networks have increased in the first half of 2020, particularly from IoT botnets. This surge in IoT attacks may be attributed to several factors:

1. The significant increase in the number of IoT devices and connections;
2. The COVID-19 pandemic, which has forced more workers to work from home, making them more reliant on remote access and potentially exposing their devices to new security risks;

3. The proliferation of more sophisticated cyber tools, which has empowered more cybercriminals to launch successful IoT attacks.

A number of cryptographic schemes have been proposed to enhance the security of NB-IoT networks, including secure authentication schemes [6,7], encryption schemes [2,30], access control schemes [21], and more. However, as NB-IoT prioritizes cost efficiency, low device power consumption, and high connection density, most existing schemes may not be suitable for this network [10,25].

To overcome this challenge, we propose utilizing the powerful computing power of the gateway at the network layer to generate encrypted identity-based signatures for NB-IoT nodes. The encrypted signature and ciphertext can be transmitted through an open channel. While it may be intuitive to store the sensor's private key in the gateway to facilitate signature generation, in practice, the gateway is typically a semi-honest device, meaning that it is curious but can still execute the program correctly.

To solve it in NB-IoT, secure obfuscation is a ideal method for encrypted identity-based signatures (OEIBS). Program obfuscation was first proposed to protect the program's code that can change a program to a new unintelligible program. Besides, the new program still possesses the previous functionality [1,5,13,16,17,20]. From the existing notions, an obfuscator has the following properties:

1. **Preserving Functionality:** All functionalities in the original program C cannot be changed after obfuscated by the program $\mathsf{Obf}(C)$.
2. **Polynomial Slowdown:** Suppose $p(n)$ denotes a polynomial, the obfuscated program $\mathsf{Obf}(C)$ satisfies that $\mid Obf(C) \mid \leq p(\mid C \mid)$ for any $C \in C_n$.
3. **Virtual Black-Box Property (VBP):** Whatever a P.P.T algorithm can efficiently compute from the obfuscated program and can also be obtained from black-box access to the functionality.

If the encrypted identity-based signature program has been obfuscate securely, the obfuscated program satisfies **VBP**. That is to say, any information that cannot be obtained from black-box access to the original program will not be obtained from the obfuscated program either. In our scheme, the gateway can execute the obfuscated program securely without leaking any sensitive message of the NB-IoT nodes. Based on the definitions proposed by Hohenberger et al. [18] and Hada [17], we show that the identity-based signature scheme still keeps its security even if the adversary has the full access to the OEIBS program.

1.1   Application Case

NB-IoT can be applied on many service categories. Especially in some crucial applications, the data must be secure transmitted from the perception layer to the application layer, such as connected personal appliances measuring health parameters, tracking of persons, animals or objects. To protect the data, our proposed scheme can be utilized in these scenarios. As shown in Fig. 2, sensor nodes on person are responsible for collecting various data, and the data are sent to the gateway. Then the gateway can execute the obfuscated program to sign and encrypt the data, and send both the signature and the ciphertext to the application layer. Therefore, the use of the obfuscated program can ensure the security and keep the data unchanged.

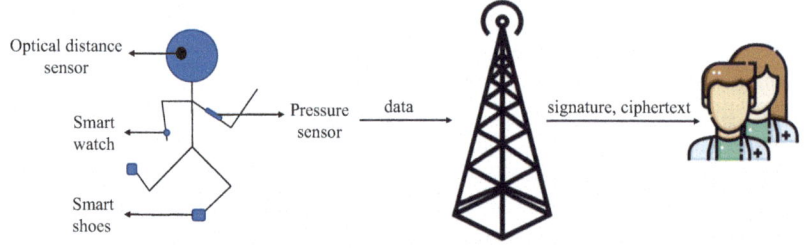

Fig. 2. Application Case

1.2   Our Contribution

We construct a special OEIBS in NB-IoT. We also implement our scheme on two different types of computers (i.e., a laptop and a server) for evaluation. The main contributions of our work are summarized as below:

1. We construct a novel obfuscation for encrypted identity-based signatures scheme in NB-IoT, which can not only protect the privacy of the NB-IoT nodes, but also guarantee the authenticity and integrity of the data. Specifically, the adversary cannot obtain the node's private key even if it possesses the white access to the obfuscated program.
2. We first propose an identity-based signature scheme and prove it is existentially unforgeable under choose message attacks (CMAs). We then construct a secure obfuscated program for the special encrypted IBS, and analyze it achieve the security requirement of the average-case virtual black-box properties (ACVBP).
3. We use the JPBC library [8] to evaluate the proposed scheme on both a laptop and a server. The evaluation results indicate that our scheme is efficient for the devices which are in the NB-IoT network layer.

1.3   Organization of This Paper

In Sect. 2, we review related literature on NB-IoT and the security of NB-IoT, then we show some related program obfuscation works. We then introduce the notations in Sect. 3, the related mathematical assumptions, the system model, and some program obfuscation properties. In Sect. 4, we introduce an efficient identity-based signature scheme and prove that the IBS scheme is secure under

CMA. We construct a special EIBS and present the obfuscation method for the EIBS, and analysis the it's security in Sect. 5. The evaluation results is showed in Sect. 6, before concluding this paper in the last section.

2 Related Work

2.1 NB-IoT

NB-IoT was launched by 3GPP, which provides low-cost devices, high coverage (20 dB higher than LTE/GPRS), longer device battery life (over 10 years) and large capacity [11]. Together with 3GPP, some telecommunication giants such as Huawei, Ericsson, Qualcomm, and Vodafone jointly put the standard.

Due to its low power consumption, NB-IoT can be more economical and can access the Internet for a longer period without maintenance. However, the focus of the market is how to ensure the security of the collected data by IoT devices. Recently, there are some schemes can be used to meet the above needs. Cao et al. [6] proposed a fast valid scheme for massive NB-IoT devices, their work supports data transmission and authentication at the same time. However, it cannot resist post-quantum attack, therefore, the authors proposed a quantum resistance access authentication and data distribution scheme which can be deployed in the large-scale NB-IoT devices [7]. Gomez et al. [23] also presented an efficient method for authentication and credential establishment, it can support 5G NB-IoT security service authentication and key establishment.

Besides, Tsaia et al. [28] introduced a secure and low-power consumption communication scheme. It reduces the terminal equipment's encryption calculation cost by reducing the AES encryption cycle. Bidgoly et al. [2] proposed a chaining encryption scheme for NB-IoT. They introduced an appropriate key finder (AKF) module, and used hash function to assign a dedicated key to each message.

However, since NB-IoT is designed for low-cost devices, many existed cryptographic schemes are not suitable for NB-IoT node. Using the gateway instead of these devices to participate in computing is a popular solution. Unfortunately, it will bring other secure problems because of implementing the node's private information by the gateway directly. Hence, how to appropriate utilize the gateway in network layer is a burning question.

2.2 Program Obfuscation

Program obfuscation technique provides a useful solution for the above problem. It was introduced to protect software intellectual property from reverse engineering attacks. In the notion of [1], an obfuscator can be viewed as a compiler, it inputs a program P and converts it into an equivalent program with *predicate black-box property*, but it cannot provide meaningful security guarantees. Wee [29] and Dodis [9] proposed some obfuscators for specific functionalities by relaxing the assumptions required for obfuscation. Despite there are some positive results, the obfuscator that has traditional cryptographic functionalities is still difficult to construct.

The first secure obfuscation for complicated cryptographic functionality was proposed by Hohenberger et al. [18] in TCC07, they securely obfuscated a proxy re-encryption scheme. Besides, they introduced the notion of average-case virtual black-box property **ACVBP**. Follow Hohenberger's idea, Hada constructed an obfuscator for encrypted signatures [17]. In recent years, Shi et al. [24] provided a special obfuscable encrypted group signature functionality. Zhang et al. [31] presented an encrypted verifiable encrypted signature (EVES) functionality, and they constructed an obfuscator for it in fair electronic transactions. Recently, Zhang et al. [32] constructed an efficient obfuscation for the IEEE P1363 signature algorithm, they utilized the high computation power of smart portable terminal to sign the data which are collected from the node.

In addition, Barak et al. [1] proposed a indistinguishability program obfuscation ($i\mathcal{O}$) which is different from before. They given the definition of an $i\mathcal{O}$ for a class of circuits $\mathcal{C}$: given two different equivalent circuits $C_1, C_2 \in \mathcal{C}$, the distribution both $i\mathcal{O}(C_1)$ and $i\mathcal{O}(C_2)$ are indistinguishable in computationally. Sahai and Waters [22] solved an open problem called deniable encryption by using indistinguishability obfuscation. Garg et al. [12] showed the constructions for indistinguishability obfuscation and functional encryption which can support all polynomial-size circuits. Bitansky and Vaikuntanathan [3] proposed a generic construction of $i\mathcal{O}$ from public-key functional encryption with succinct encryption circuits and subexponential security.

In this paper, we follow the properties of **ACVBP** program obfuscation, construct an efficient OEIBS scheme in NB-IoT.

3 Preliminaries

Let λ be the security parameter, P.P.T be a probabilistic-polynomial time algorithm. If $\mu(\lambda)$ is a negligible function, any P.P.T p satisfies $\mu(\lambda) = O(1/p(\lambda))$. Let $x \xleftarrow{r} \mathcal{R}$ be the element x is randomly chose from the set $\mathcal{R}$. $H_1 : \{0,1\}^* \to \mathbb{G}$ and $H_2 : \{0,1\}^* \to \mathbb{G}$ are two different secure hash functions.

3.1 Mathematical Assumptions

Definition 1. *[Bilinear Map] Suppose* $\mathbb{G}, \mathbb{G}_T$ *are two cyclic groups of prime order* q. *A map* $e : \mathbb{G} \times \mathbb{G} \to \mathbb{G}_T$ *is bilinear map if it satisfies the following properties:*

1. Bilinearity: for any $a, b \xleftarrow{r} \mathbb{Z}_q$ and $g \in \mathbb{G}$, the equation $e\left(g^a, g^b\right) = e(g,g)^{ab}$ holds.
2. Non-degeneracy: if g generates $\mathbb{G}$, then $e\left(g,g\right)$ generates $\mathbb{G}_T$.
3. Computability: $\forall g_1, g_2 \in \mathbb{G}$, $e\left(g_1, g_2\right)$ is efficiently computable.

Definition 2. *[DLIN (Decisional Linear) Assumption][17, 18] For each P.P.T polynomial $p(\cdot)$ and distinguisher $\mathcal{D}$, if $\lambda \in \mathbb{N}$ is a sufficiently large value and $z \in \{0,1\}^{p(\lambda)}$, DLIN assumption holds when*

$$\Pr \begin{bmatrix} params = (q, \mathbb{G}, \mathbb{G}_T, e, g); \\ a, b, r, s \xleftarrow{r} \mathbb{Z}_q; \\ \xi \leftarrow \mathcal{D}(params, (g^a, g^b), (g^{r+s}, (g^a)^r, (g^b)^s), z) : \\ \xi = 1 \end{bmatrix}$$

$$- \Pr \begin{bmatrix} params = (q, \mathbb{G}, \mathbb{G}_T, e, g); \\ a, b, r, s, t \xleftarrow{r} \mathbb{Z}_q; \\ \xi \leftarrow \mathcal{D}(params, (g^a, g^b), (g^t, (g^a)^r, (g^b)^s), z) : \\ \xi = 1 \end{bmatrix}$$

$$< \frac{1}{p(\lambda)}.$$

Definition 3. *[CDH (Computational Diffie-Hellman) Problem Assumption] For any P.P.T algorithm $\mathcal{A}$ and polynomial $p(\cdot)$, if $\lambda \in \mathbb{N}$ is a sufficiently large value, CDH problem assumption holds when*

$$\Pr \begin{bmatrix} params = (q, \mathbb{G}, \mathbb{G}_T, e, g); \\ a, b \xleftarrow{r} \mathbb{Z}_q; \\ g^{ab} \leftarrow \mathcal{A}(params, g, g^a, g^b) \end{bmatrix}$$

$$< \frac{1}{p(\lambda)}.$$

3.2   Circuit Obfuscators

We use the form $\mathcal{C} = \{\mathcal{C}_\lambda\}_{\lambda \in \mathbb{N}}$ to denote a class of polynomial size circuits, and use $l_{in}(\lambda)/l_{out}(\lambda)$ to denote the input/output length, here $l_{in}(\lambda)$ and $l_{out}(\lambda)$ are polynomials. There exists an associated P.P.T algorithm which takes as input 1^λ and outputs a random circuit $C \in \mathcal{C}_\lambda$. Similar as [32], the size of all random selection information in this algorithm depends on the security parameter 1^λ, $\mathcal{C} \leftarrow \mathcal{C}_\lambda$ denotes the generation process.

Definition 4. *Taking x as the input, for any two circuits $C_1(x)$ and $C_2(x)$, the difference in statistical between them is defined as follows: $\mathsf{StaDiff}(C_1(x), C_2(x)) = \frac{1}{2}\Sigma_{t \in \{0,1\}^{l_{out}(\lambda)}} | \Pr[s \leftarrow C_1(x) : s = t] - \Pr[s \leftarrow C_2(x) : s = t]|.$*

Definition 5. *Given a class of probabilistic circuit $C = \{\mathcal{C}_\lambda\}_{\lambda \in \mathbb{N}}$, a circuit $C' \in \mathcal{C}_\lambda$, a P.P.T circuit obfuscator Obf, $\Pr[C' \leftarrow \mathsf{Obf}(C) : \forall x, \mathsf{StaDiff}(C(x), C'(x)) = 0)] = 1$ holds.*

Definition 6. *(EU w.r.t EIBS Obfuscator) [17, 32] Given a public key encryption scheme $(\mathsf{EKG}, \mathsf{Enc}_{pk_r}, \mathsf{Dec}_{sk_r})$, and an identity-based signature scheme $(\mathsf{Extract}, \mathsf{Sign}, \mathsf{Verify})$. The obfuscator Obf takes input as C_{EIBS}. For* *every P.P.T algorithm $\mathcal{A}$ and polynomial $p(\cdot)$, all sufficiently large $\lambda \in \mathbb{N}$, and the auxiliary-input $z \in \{0,1\}^{poly(\lambda)}$, the identity-based signature scheme is existentially unforgeable w.r.t Obf if the following equation holds:*

$$\Pr \begin{bmatrix} params \leftarrow Setup(1^\lambda); \\ (pk_r, sk_r) \leftarrow EKG(1^\lambda); \\ (pk_i, sk_i) = (H_1(ID_i), H_1(ID_i)^s) \leftarrow Extract; \\ C' \leftarrow \text{Obf}(C_{params,sk_i,pk_r}); \\ (m, \sigma, M \leftarrow A^{<<S_{params,sk_i}>>}(params, pk_i, pk_r, C', z)) : \\ Verify(pk_r, m, \sigma) = 1 \text{ and } m \notin M \end{bmatrix}$$
$$< \frac{1}{p(\lambda)}.$$

3.3 Virtual Black-Box Properties

Average-case **VBP** (ACVBP) was introduced by Hohenberger et al. [18], it can provide a significant security for cryptographic schemes. We now review the definition of ACVBP briefly.

Definition 7. *(ACVBP)* *For any P.P.T algorithm $\mathcal{D}$, every polynomial $p(\cdot)$, all sufficient large $\lambda \in IN$, and every $z \in \{0,1\}^{poly(\lambda)}$, if there exists a P.P.T algorithm S satisfies the following equation, then an obfuscator Obf for circuit $\mathcal{C}$ satisfies the ACVBP.*

$$\left| \Pr \begin{bmatrix} C \leftarrow C_n; \\ C' \leftarrow \text{Obf}(C); \qquad : b = 1 \\ b \leftarrow D^{<<C>>}(C', z) \end{bmatrix} - \right.$$
$$\left. \Pr \begin{bmatrix} C \leftarrow C_n; \\ C'' \leftarrow S^{<<C>>}(1^\lambda, z); : b = 1 \\ b \leftarrow D^{<<C>>}(C'', z) \end{bmatrix} \right| < \frac{1}{p(\lambda)}.$$

However, similar with Hada's scheme [17], our proposed identity-based signature scheme does not have the *distinguishable attack property* in the context of EIBS. Therefore, we utilize the generalization of the ACVBP definition which is proposed in [17]. It is a stronger ACVBP, which allows the distinguisher to access both $<< C >>$ and a set of oracles dependent on C.

Definition 8. *ACVBP w.r.t Dependent Oracles.* *$T(C)$ denotes a set of oracles dependent on the circuit C. If the following equation holds, we say that the circuit obfuscator Obf for C satisfies the ACVBP w.r.t dependent oracle set T: There exists a P.P.T algorithm S, for every P.P.T oracle distinguisher D, every polynomial $p(\cdot)$, every $z \in \{0,1\}^{poly(\lambda)}$ where $\lambda \in IN$,*

$$\left| \Pr \begin{bmatrix} C \leftarrow C_\lambda; \\ C' \leftarrow \text{Obf}(C); \qquad : b = 1 \\ b \leftarrow D^{<<C,T(C)>>}(C', z) \end{bmatrix} - \right.$$
$$\left. \Pr \begin{bmatrix} C \leftarrow C_\lambda; \\ C' \leftarrow S^{<<C>>}(1^n, z); \quad : b = 1 \\ b \leftarrow D^{<<C,T(C)>>}(C', z) \end{bmatrix} \right| < \frac{1}{p(\lambda)}.$$

Theorem 1. *Let* $T(C_{params,sk_i,pk_r})$ *denote* $\{S_{params,sk_i}\}$. *The EU w.r.t the EIBS functionality is the EU w.r.t* Obf *if the* C_{EIBS} *obfuscator* Obf *conforms to ACVBP w.r.t dependent oracle set* T.

3.4 System Model

Figure 3 shows the detailed system model of the proposed scheme in NB-IoT. The sensors in the perception layer collect the data m in the environment, then the data are sent to the gateways in the network layer. Gateways can generate an encrypted identity-based signature by running the obfuscated program, and sends the date m and the encrypted IBS to the application layer (i.e. the smart manufacturing factory, smart family or city management). The application layer can decrypt the encrypted IBS, and checks the original identity-based signature.

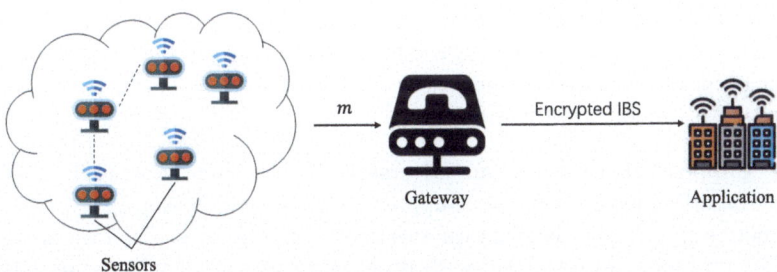

Fig. 3. System Model

4 Encrypted Identity-Based Signature Scheme

We aim to construct a special encrypted identity-based signature scheme to satisfy the above system model. Before that, we first propose an identity-based signature (IBS) scheme and prove that the proposed IBS scheme is secure in the existential unforgeability against chose-message attacks (EU-CMA) security model.

4.1 Identity-Based Signature Scheme

We propose an identity-based signature scheme, the main construction is as follows:

- Setup(λ): Input a security parameter λ, generate a group $\mathbb{G}$ of a large prime order q with generator g, a cyclic multiplicative group $\mathbb{G}_T$ with the same prime order q, and a bilinear pairing $e : \mathbb{G} \times \mathbb{G} = \mathbb{G}_T$. Choose $s \xleftarrow{r} \mathbb{Z}_q$ randomly, and set s as master secret key, then compute public value $P_{pub} = g^s$. Choose two secure hash functions $H_1 : \{0,1\}^* \to \mathbb{G}$, $H_2 : \{0,1\}^* \to \mathbb{G}$. The public parameters params $= \{g, q, \mathbb{G}, \mathbb{G}_T, e, P_{pub}, H_1, H_2\}$.

- Extract(params, ID_i): Take a user U_i's identity ID_i as input, the PKG computes U_i's public key $pk_i = H_1(ID_i)$ and its corresponding private key $sk_i = pk_i^s$.
- Sign(params, ID_i, sk_i, m): Input a message $m \in \{0,1\}^*$, the signer first selects $x \xleftarrow{r} \mathbb{Z}_q$, computes $R = g^x \in \mathbb{G}$ and $h = H_2(m, ID_i, R)$. The algorithm outputs the signature $\sigma = (\sigma_1, \sigma_2) = (sk_i \cdot h^x, R)$.
- Verify(params, ID_i, pk_i, m, σ_1, σ_2): Input the message m and its corresponding signature $\sigma = (\sigma_1, \sigma_2)$ with U_i's public key pk_i, the verifier first computes $h = H_2(m, ID_i, \sigma_2)$, then checks the equation $e(\sigma_1, g) \overset{?}{=} e(pk_i, P_{pub})e(h, \sigma_2)$. The verifier outputs 1 if the equation holds, otherwise outputs 0.

4.2   Security Proof

Theorem 2. *Suppose the hash functions H_1 and H_2 are random oracles. If the CDH problem is hard, then, our proposed identity-based scheme is provably secure in the EU-CMA security model with reduction loss $L = q_{sk} + q_s$, where q_{sk} is the number of private key extract queries to H_1 random oracle and q_s is the number of sign queries to H_2 random oracle.*

Proof. Suppose there exists an adversary $\mathcal{A}$ who has advantage ϵ against identity-based signature scheme. Suppose $\mathcal{A}$ makes at most q_{H_i} $(0 \leq i \leq 1)$ H_i hash queries, q_{sk} Private KeyExt queries and q_s sign queries. Then we prove that the CDH problem can be solved with probability at least ϵ' in polynomial-time.

Algorithm $\mathcal{B}$ is given as input the CDH parameters $\langle q, \mathbb{G} \rangle$ and a random instance $\langle g, W = g^a, U = g^b \rangle$ of the CDH problem for these parameters, i.e. g is a generator of $\mathbb{G}$ and a, b is random in $\mathbb{Z}_q$ where q is the order of $\mathbb{G}$. Let $Z - g^{ab} \in \mathbb{G}$ be the solution of CDH problem. Algorithm $\mathcal{B}$ finds Z by interacting with $\mathcal{A}$ as follows:

Initialization: $\mathcal{B}$ lets $W \in \mathbb{G}_1$ as the system public key P_{pub} and outputs the public parameters $params = \{g, q, \mathbb{G}, \mathbb{G}_T, e, P_{pub}, H_1, H_2\}$, where H_1, H_2 are the random oracles.

Query on oracles: $\mathcal{A}$ issues queries as below.

H_1 queries: $\mathcal{B}$ holds a L_1-list with three tuples $< ID_i, c_i, h_i >$. The list is initially empty. If ID_i has already appeared in the L_1-list, then $\mathcal{B}$ responds with $H_1(ID_i) = h_i$. Otherwise,

1. if $i \neq I$, $\mathcal{B}$ randomly selects $c_i \in \mathbb{Z}_q^*$, computes $h_i = g^{c_i}$, responds h_i to $\mathcal{A}$ and adds three tuples $< ID_i, c_i, h_i >$ into L_1-list.
2. If $i = I$, $\mathcal{B}$ sets $h_I = \frac{1}{U}$, responds h_I to $\mathcal{A}$ and adds three tuples $< ID_i, \perp, h_I >$ into L_1-list.

Private KeyExt queries: $\mathcal{B}$ holds a L-list with tuples $< ID_i, sk_i >$ that is empty at first. $\mathcal{A}$ issues the private key query for ID_i. If the tuple ID_i has already appeared in the L-list, then $\mathcal{B}$ responds sk_i to $\mathcal{A}$. Otherwise, $\mathcal{B}$ executes the following:

1. if $i \neq I$, If $\mathcal{A}$ has issued a H_1 query on ID_i, then $\mathcal{B}$ computes $sk_i = W^{c_i}$, returns it to $\mathcal{A}$ and adds $< ID_i, sk_i >$ into L-list.
2. If $i = I$, then $\mathcal{B}$ reports failure and terminates.

H_2 **queries:** $\mathcal{B}$ holds a L_2-list with tuples $< ID_i, m, R_i, v_i, d_i >$ that is empty at first. If the query (ID_i, m, R_i) has already appeared in the L_2-list, then $\mathcal{B}$ responds with $d_i = H_2(ID_i, m, R_i)$. Otherwise, $\mathcal{B}$ executes the following:

1. If $i \neq I$, $\mathcal{B}$ randomly selects $v_i \in \mathbb{Z}_q^*$, computes $d_i = g^{v_i}$, responds d_i to $\mathcal{A}$ and adds the tuples $< ID_i, m, R_i, v_i, d_i >$ into the L_2-list.
2. If $i = I$, $\mathcal{B}$ randomly selects $v \in \mathbb{Z}_q^*$, computes $d_I = \frac{W^{\frac{1}{v}}}{g^v}$, responds d_I to $\mathcal{A}$ and adds the tuples $< ID_i, m, R_i, v, d_I >$ into the L_2-list.

Sign queries: $\mathcal{A}$ chooses ID_i adaptively and queries the signature of ID_i on challenge message m. Two possibilities should be considered.

1. If $i \neq I$, then $\mathcal{B}$ does:
   (a) $\mathcal{B}$ takes out private key sk_i directly if $< ID_i, sk_i >$ in L-list. Otherwise, $\mathcal{B}$ executes a Private KeyExt query on ID_i.
   (b) $\mathcal{B}$ randomly selects $x_i \in \mathbb{Z}_q$, computes $R_i = g^{x_i}$. If $< ID_i, m, R_i >$ has already appeared in the L_2-list, then $\mathcal{B}$ takes out d_i. Otherwise, $\mathcal{B}$ executes a H_2 query on $< ID_i, m, R_i >$.
   (c) $\mathcal{B}$ computes $\sigma_1 = sk_i \cdot d_i^{x_i}$ as the signature of m^*. The correctness of σ_1 can be verified that $e(g, \sigma_1) = e(W, h_i) e(R_i, d_i)$
2. Otherwise, if $i = I$, then $\mathcal{B}$ does:
   (a) $\mathcal{B}$ sets $R_I = U^v = g^{bv}$, if $< ID_I, m, U >$ has already appeared in the L_2-list, then $\mathcal{B}$ takes out d_i. Otherwise, $\mathcal{B}$ executes a H_2 query on $< ID_i, m, R_i >$.
   (b) $\mathcal{B}$ generates the signature of m:

$$\sigma_1 = \left(\frac{1}{U}\right)^a \cdot \left(\frac{W^{\frac{1}{v}}}{g^v}\right)^{bv} = \frac{1}{U^{v^2}}.$$

Output: Eventually $\mathcal{A}$ outputs a tuple $(ID_I, m^*, \sigma_1^*, \sigma_2^*)$. The adversary $\mathcal{A}$ wins the game, if $\mathcal{A}$ has not issued a sign query on m^* and not issued a private keyext query on ID_I.
$\mathcal{B}$ outputs

$$g^{ab} = g^{ab} = \frac{V^{\frac{1}{v_1}}}{\sigma_1 \cdot \sigma_2^{v_1}},$$

where $V = \left(\frac{\sigma_1}{\sigma_{11}} \cdot \sigma_2^{(v_1 - v_{11})}\right)^{\frac{v_1}{v_{11}}}$.
Now using the Forking Lemma, we can obtain a result that, if there exists an adversary $\mathcal{A}$ attacks to our scheme for an adaptively chosen message m^*

and given ID_I which can produce two valid signatures $(ID_I, m^*, \sigma_1, \sigma_2)$ and $(ID_I, m^*, \sigma_{11}, \sigma_2)$. Then,

$$\frac{\sigma_1}{\sigma_{11}} = \frac{sk_I{}^* \cdot d_1^x}{sk_I{}^* \cdot d_{11}^x} = \left(\frac{W^{\frac{1}{v_1}}}{g^{v_1}}\right)^x \cdot \left(\frac{g^{v_{11}}}{W^{\frac{1}{v_{11}}}}\right)^x,$$

we have $V = W^x = \left(\frac{\sigma_1}{\sigma_{11}} \cdot \sigma_2{}^{(v_1 - v_{11})}\right)^{\frac{v_1}{v_{11}}}$, $\sigma_2 = R = g^x$.

Since

$$\sigma_1 = sk_I{}^* \cdot h_1{}^x = \frac{1}{U^a} \cdot \frac{V^{\frac{1}{v_1}}}{\sigma_2{}^{v_1}} = \frac{1}{g^{ab}} \cdot \frac{V^{\frac{1}{v_1}}}{\sigma_2{}^{v_1}},$$

Thus, we get the solution of the given CDH instance as follows.

$$Z = g^{ab} = \frac{V^{\frac{1}{v_1}}}{\sigma_1 \cdot \sigma_2{}^{v_1}},$$

as long as $\mathcal{A}$ has not issued a sign query on (m^*, ID_I) and not issued a private keyext query on ID_I. Since $\mathcal{A}$ makes at most q_{sk} private keyext queries and q_s sign queries, we have $\epsilon' \geq \epsilon - \frac{q_{sk} + q_s}{2^\lambda}$.

4.3   Linear Encryption

We use the linear encryption scheme that is proposed by Boneh et al. [4] as the base to construct our scheme. This scheme consists of the following algorithms:

– Setup:
  1. Parse params $= (q, \mathbb{G}, \mathbb{G}_T, e, g)$.
  2. Choose two distinct elements $a, h \xleftarrow{r} \mathbb{Z}_q$ at random.
  3. Set the secret key $sk_r = (a, b)$ and the public key $pk_r = (g^a, g^b)$.
– Encrypt:
  1. Input the public key $pk_r = (g^a, g^b)$ and the message $m \in \mathbb{G}$, randomly choose $s \xleftarrow{r} \mathbb{Z}_q$ and $r \xleftarrow{r} \mathbb{Z}_q$.
  2. Compute and output ciphertext $c = (c_1 = (g^a)^r, c_2 = (g^b)^s, c_3 = g^{r+s}m)$.
– Decrypt:
  1. On input $sk_r = (a, b)$ and $c = (c_1, c_2, c_3)$, compute $t = c_1^{1/a} \cdot c_2^{1/b}$
  2. Output the plaintext $m \leftarrow c_3 \cdot t^{-1}$.

In this paper, Enc_{pk_r} denotes encrypting a message with the public encryption key, and Dec_{sk_r} denotes decrypting a ciphertext with the secret decryption key. Besides, we can re-randomize the ciphertext c by randomly selecting $\Delta r, \Delta s \xleftarrow{r} \mathbb{Z}_q$ such that:

$$
\begin{aligned}
c' &= (c_1', \ c_2', \ c_3') \\
&= (c_1 \cdot (g^a)^{\Delta r}, \ c_2 \cdot (g^b)^{\Delta s}, \ c_3 \cdot g^{\Delta r + \Delta s}) \\
&= ((g^a)^{r + \Delta r}, \ (g^b)^{s + \Delta s}, \ m \cdot g^{r + s + \Delta r + \Delta s}) \\
&= ((g^a)^{r'}, \ (g^b)^{s'}, \ m \cdot g^{r' + s'})
\end{aligned}
$$

where c' is also a valid ciphertext.

Theorem 3. *If the DL assumption holds, the linear encryption scheme satisfies the indistinguishably. [4]*

4.4   Encrypted IBS

Based on the identity-based signature scheme in 4.1 and the linear encryption algorithm, we propose a special encrypted IBS (EIBS) scheme in this subsection.

The EIBS scheme include these following algorithms, EIBSSetup, EIBSExtract, EIBSSign, EIBSVerify.

- EIBSSetup(λ):
    1. The PKG randomly chooses the master secret key $s \xleftarrow{r} \mathbb{Z}_q$, and computes the public key $P_{pub} = g^s$. It outputs the system public parameter $p = (q, g, P_{pub}, \mathbb{G}, \mathbb{G}_T, e, H_1, H_2)$.
    2. The receiver sets the secret key $sk_r = (a, b)$ that $a, b \xleftarrow{r} \mathbb{Z}_q$, and computes $pk_r = (g^a, g^b)$ as the public key.
- EIBSExtract(s, ID_i): The PKG extracts uses private key by using its master secret key such that $sk_i = pk_i^s$, the corresponding public key is $pk_i = H_1(ID_i)$
- EIBSSign(sk_i, pk_r, m): The user executes the following steps:
    1. Randomly select $v \xleftarrow{r} \mathbb{Z}_q$, compute $R = g^v \in \mathbb{G}$, set $h = H_2(m, ID_i, R)$, then output

    $$(\sigma_1, \sigma_2) = (sk_i \cdot h^v, R)$$

    2. Randomly select $r, t \xleftarrow{r} \mathbb{Z}_q$, then compute

    $$c_1 = (g^a)^r, c_2 = (g^b)^t, c_3 = g^{r+t} \cdot \sigma_1$$

    3. Output $\sigma = (c_1, c_2, c_3, \sigma_2)$ as the signature in EIBS scheme.
- EIBSVerify($\sigma, P_{pub}, pk_i, sk_r$): The verifier executes as below:
    1. Decrypt the ciphertext to get the signature

    $$\sigma_1 = c_3/(c_1^{1/a} \cdot c_2^{1/b}) = sk_i \cdot h^v$$

    2. To verify the validation of the signature σ, it first computes $h^* = H_2(m, ID_i, R)$, then checks the equation

    $$e(\sigma_1, g) \overset{?}{=} e(pk_i, P_{pub})e(h, R)$$

    If the equation holds, i.e. the signature is valid, then outputs 1. Otherwise, outputs 0.

5   Secure Obfuscator for the EIBS Functionality

We construct a secure obfuscatior Obf_{EIBS} for a special EIBS Functionality in this section. Then, based on the generalized ACVBP definition, we show the security proof of our proposed scheme.

Given a circuit C_{p,sk_i,pk_r}, the obfuscator Obf_{EIBS} is defined as follows:

1. Extract (p, sk_i, pk_r) from C_{p,sk_i,pk_r}.
2. Parse $p = (q, g, P_{pub}, \mathbb{G}, \mathbb{G}_T, e, H_1, H_2)$, $sk_i = H_1(ID_i)^s$ and $pk_r = (g^a, g^b)$.
3. Using the receiver's public key to encrypt the signer's private key, $(c_1, c_2, c_3) \leftarrow \mathsf{Enc}_{pk_r}(p, pk_r, H_1(ID_i)^s)$, so we have

$$(c_1, c_2, c_3) = ((g^a)^r, (g^b)^t, g^{r+t} \cdot H_1(ID_i)^s)$$

4. Set the c_3 as the private signing key sk_i'.
5. Construct   and   output   an   obfuscated   circuit   with   values $(p, pk_r, pk_i, sk_i', c_1, c_2)$.

When the obfuscator executed on the gateway, it works as follows:

1. On input KEYS, output (p, pk_i, pk_r).
2. On given a message $m \in \{0, 1\}^*$,
   (a) Run (σ_1, σ_2) $\leftarrow$ $\mathsf{Sign}(p, sk', m)$,   then   we   get (c_1, c_2, σ_1) $=$ $((g^a)^r, (g^b)^t, g^{r+t} H_1(ID_i)^s \cdot h^v)$, and $\sigma_2 = R = g^v$ where v is selected randomly from $\mathbb{Z}_q$.
   (b) Re-randomize (c_1, c_2, σ_1) by select $r', t' \xleftarrow{r} \mathbb{Z}_q$ randomly, compute

$$(c_1', c_2', c_3') =$$
$$((g^a)^{r+r'}, (g^b)^{t+t'}, g^{r+r'+t+t'} \cdot H_1(ID_i)^s \cdot h^v)$$

   (c) Output $(c_1', c_2', c_3', \sigma_2)$.

Note that, we can simply use Enc_{pk_r} to encrypt σ_2, we can also use any other encryption algorithm to encrypt it, due to σ_2 is just a random value. Therefore, we do not encrypt σ_2 and output it directly.

5.1   Functionality Preservation (Correctness)

Now, we show that the proposed obfuscator Obf_{EIBS} preserves the original EIBS functionality.

To check the signature $(c_1', c_2', c_3', \sigma_2)$ in EIBS scheme, the receiver executes the algorithms as follows:

1. Decrypts the ciphertext to get the first part of the signature:

$$\sigma_1 = \frac{c_1'^{1/a} \cdot c_2'^{1/b}}{c_3'}.$$

2. Checks the equation

$$e(\sigma_1, g) \stackrel{?}{=} e(pk_i, P_{pub})e(h, R).$$

If the equation holds, it accepts the signature and outputs 1. Otherwise, it outputs 0.

In the above equations, the first equation is to decrypt the ciphertext to obtain the identity-based signature. Then the program on the application layer can verify the signature by using the original verification algorithm which was proposed in 4.1.

5.2 Security Analysis of ACVBP

Theorem 4. *Let $T(C)$ be S_{p,sk_i}. Obf_{EIBS} satisfies ACVBP w.r.t dependent oracle set T under DL assumption.*

Proof. Intuitively,   we   can   know   an   obfuscated EIBS circuit with $(p, pk_r, pk_i, sk_i', c_1, c_2)$ hardwired. Then we construct a simulator using the sampling access to the original circuit C_{p,sk_i,pk_r}. The public values (p, pk_r, pk_i) can be accessed from the function C_{p,sk_i,pk_r} by using KEYS. Then, we should consider how to simulate (sk', c_1, c_2), due to it is an encrypted format of $H_1(ID_i)^s$, we can construct *junk* values for them.

Suppose the simulator S possess C_{p,sk_i,pk_r}.

1. Take the security parameter 1^λ and an auxiliary-input z as input.
2. Get (p, pk_i, pk_r) from C_{p,sk_i,pk_r} by using the sampling access.
3. Parse $p = \{g, q, \mathbb{G}, \mathbb{G}_T, e, P_{pub}, H_1, H_2\}$ and $pk = H_1(ID_i)$.
4. Choose $Junk \stackrel{r}{\leftarrow} \mathbb{G}$ at random.
5. Encrypt $Junk$, such that $(c_1, c_2, c_3) = \mathsf{Enc}_{pk_r}(p, pk_r, Junk)$.
6. Set the private key as $sk' = c_3$.
7. Output $(p, pk_r, pk, sk', c_1, c_2)$.

It is sufficient for us to prove that the distribution between S's output and the real $(p, pk_r, pk, sk', c_1, c_2)$ is indistinguishable, even if the P.P.T adversary has the sampling access to $CS = \{C, S_{p,sk}\}$. Assume that there has a distinguisher $D^{<<CS>>}$ that can differentiate the two distributions with a non-negligible probability. In other words, the difference between the following two probabilities is non-negligible. That is, D outputs 1 if given the simulated and the real distributions respectively. Only the ciphertext c_3 is difference. The algorithm encrypts $H_1(ID)^s$ tn the real distribution, and the algorithm encrypts $Junk$ while in the simulated distribution.

$$\Pr \begin{bmatrix} \mathsf{params} = \{g, q, \mathbb{G}, \mathbb{G}_T, e, P_{pub}, H_1, H_2\} \leftarrow \mathsf{Setup}(1^\lambda); \\ (pk_r, sk_r) \leftarrow \mathsf{Setup}(1^\lambda); \\ (pk_i, sk_i) = (H_1(ID_i), H_1(ID_i)^s) \leftarrow \mathsf{Extract}; \\ (c_1, c_2, c_3) \leftarrow \mathbf{Enc}(p, pk_r, H_1(ID_i)^s); \\ sk' = c_3; \\ b \leftarrow D^{<<CS>>}(p, pk_i, pk_r, sk', c_1, c_2, z) : \\ b = 1 \end{bmatrix}$$

$$\text{Pr}\begin{bmatrix} \text{params} = \{g, q, \mathbb{G}, \mathbb{G}_T, e, P_{pub}, H_1, H_2\} \leftarrow \text{Setup}(1^\lambda); \\ (pk_r, sk_r) \leftarrow \text{Setup}(1^\lambda); \\ Junk \leftarrow \mathbb{G}; \\ (c_1, c_2, c_3) \leftarrow \mathbf{Enc}(p, pk_r, Junk); \\ sk' = c_3; \\ b \leftarrow D^{<<CS>>}(p, pk_i, pk_r, sk', c_1, c_2, z) : \\ b = 1 \end{bmatrix}$$

Suppose that an adversary pair $(\mathcal{A}_1, \mathcal{A}_2)$ can break the indistinguishability of the linear encryption scheme. $\mathcal{A}_1$ generates a message pair (m_1, m_2) as follows:

1. Take (params, pk_r, z as input.
2. Request the oracle, and output the user's private key $sk = H_1(ID)^s$.
3. Choose $Junk \xleftarrow{r} \mathbb{G}$ at random.
4. Set $m_1 = H_1(ID)^s$, $m_2 = Junk$, and a hint $h = pk_r$.
5. Output (m_1, m_2, h).

Upon receiving c (an encryption on m_1 or m_2), $\mathcal{A}_2$ distinguishes m_1 and m_2 by using the distinguisher D, it works as follows:

1. Take params, pk_r, (m_1, m_2, h), z, c as input.
2. Set $sk' = c_3$ as the private key.
3. Simulate $D^{<<CS>>}$(params, $pk_r, pk_i, sk', c_1, c_2, z$).
4. Output D's output.

The probability that $\mathcal{A}_2$ outputs 1 is the former probability If c is the cipher-text of m_1, otherwise, the probability is the latter. However, the DL problem is hard, it contradicts DL assumption, therefore, the probability to distinguish them is negligible.

6   Experimental Results

We run the proposed scheme by using JPBC library to evaluate it's performance. The performance of the experimental platform is given in Table 1.

Table 1. Experimental Platform's Performance.

Device	Performance	
	Laptop	Server
Processor	Intel Core i5-520M dual core	Intel Xeon E5-2678 v3
Memory	4 GB	128 GB
Operating system	Windows 10	Ubuntu 20.04

The experimental results are shown in Fig. 4. We use Setup, Extract denote the EIBSSetup algorithm and the EIBSExtract algorithm respectively. Constract_Obf denotes the time cost of constructing the obfuscator, Obf_Sign denotes the time cost of executing the obfuscated circuit to generate the signature, Obf_Verify denotes the time cost of verifying the signature that outputs from the obfuscated circuit.

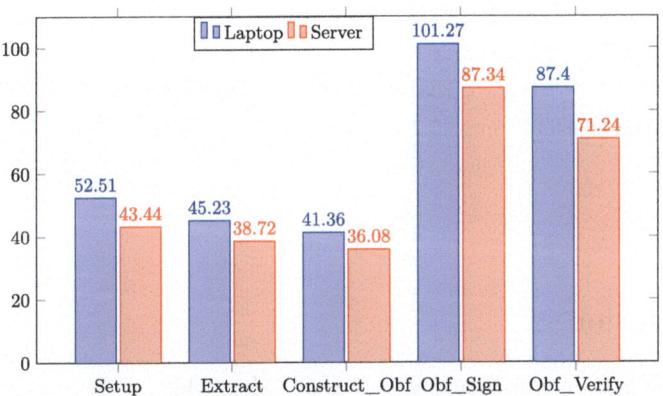

Fig. 4. Running time of each progress

We also give the time-consuming of our proposed IBS scheme proposed in Sect. 4.1 and the linear encryption scheme in Fig. 5. Note that, due to the obfuscated program are more complex than encryption and signing, therefore, the time required to generate the encrypted IBS by the obfuscated program is more than the sum of the time required for encryption and signing.

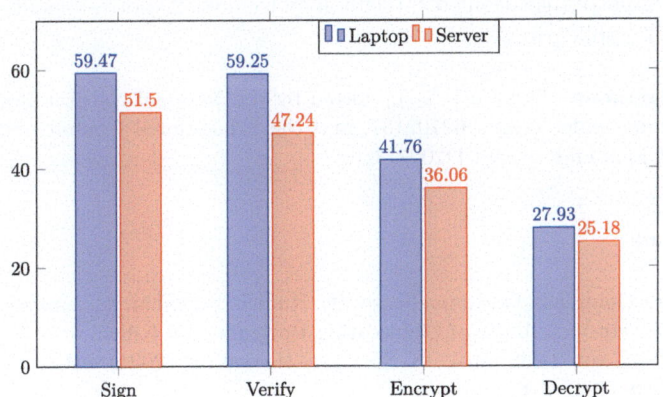

Fig. 5. Running time of The Two Original Schemes

In addition, we compared our scheme with [32] shown in Table 2, both the schemes are obfuscation for encrypted identity-based algorithms. The difference is that, our scheme uses a type-A curve (base field size is 512 bits), [32] uses a type-F curve (base field size is 160 bits). Therefore, the operations on $\mathbb{G}_1$ (type-F) is faster than $\mathbb{G}$ (type-A).

Table 2. Running Time on Laptop.

Scheme	Algorithm				
	Setup	Extract	Constract_Obf	Obf_Sign	Obf_Verify
Our scheme	52.51 ms	45.23 ms	41.36 ms	101.27 ms	87.4 ms
[32]	141.72 ms	3.75 ms	9.82 ms	39.55 ms	151.04 ms

7 Conclusion

NB-IoT technique is now being widely used. Meanwhile, it faces many security issues, which need to be solved urgently.

In this paper, we constructed a secure obfuscation for encrypted identity-based signatures scheme in NB-IoT. Specifically, we constructed a secure obfuscator for the EIBS, which contains node's sensitive information (e.g., private key), the obfuscated program can be executed on the gateways, and it is impossible to extract the node's private key. We proved that our proposed identity-based scheme is secure under random oracle model, and we also analyzed the obfuscation which can satisfy **VBP** property. The experimental results showed that the proposed scheme is suitable for NB-IoT applications in real-world.

Furthermore, we will study some different obfuscation technology, such as indistinguishable obfuscation ($i\mathcal{O}$) technology to make it more efficiently in large-scale NB-IoT applications.

Acknowledgement. This work is supported by the National Natural Science Foundation of China under grants 62102137, and the Educational Commission of Hubei Province of China under grant D20221406.

References

1. Barak, B., Goldreich, O., Impagliazzo, R., Rudich, S., Sahai, A., Vadhan, S., Yang, K.: On the (Im)possibility of Obfuscating Programs. In: Kilian, J. (ed.) CRYPTO 2001. LNCS, vol. 2139, pp. 1–18. Springer, Heidelberg (2001). https://doi.org/10. 1007/3-540-44647-8_1
2. Bidgoly, A.J., Bidgoly, H.J.: A novel chaining encryption algorithm for lpwan iot network. IEEE Sens. J. **19**(16), 7027–7034 (2019)

3. Bitansky, N., Vaikuntanathan, V.: Indistinguishability obfuscation from functional encryption. In: Guruswami, V. (ed.) 56th Annual Symposium on Foundations of Computer Science, pp. 171–190. IEEE Computer Society Press (2015)https://doi.org/10.1109/FOCS.2015.20

4. Boneh, D., Boyen, X., Shacham, H.: Short Group Signatures. In: Franklin, M. (ed.) CRYPTO 2004. LNCS, vol. 3152, pp. 41–55. Springer, Heidelberg (2004). https://doi.org/10.1007/978-3-540-28628-8_3

5. Canetti, R., Varia, M.: Non-malleable Obfuscation. In: Reingold, O. (ed.) TCC 2009. LNCS, vol. 5444, pp. 73–90. Springer, Heidelberg (2009). https://doi.org/10.1007/978-3-642-00457-5_6

6. Cao, J., Yu, P., Ma, M., Gao, W.: Fast authentication and data transfer scheme for massive nb-iot devices in 3g pp 5g network. IEEE Internet Things J. **6**(2), 1561–1575 (2018)

7. Cao, J., Yu, P., Xiang, X., Ma, M., Li, H.: Anti-quantum fast authentication and data transmission scheme for massive devices in 5g nb-iot system. IEEE Internet Things J. **6**(6), 9794–9805 (2019)

8. De Caro, A., Iovino, V.: jpbc: Java pairing based cryptography. In: Proceedings of the 16th IEEE Symposium on Computers and Communications, ISCC 2011. pp. 850–855. Kerkyra, Corfu, Greece, June 28–July 1 (2011)

9. Dodis, Y., Smith, A.: Correcting errors without leaking partial information. In: Gabow, H.N., Fagin, R. (eds.) 37th Annual ACM Symposium on Theory of Computing. pp. 654–663. ACM Press (2005).https://doi.org/10.1145/1060590.1060688

10. Feltrin, L., Tsoukaneri, G., Condoluci, M., Buratti, C., Mahmoodi, T., Dohler, M., Verdone, R.: Narrowband IoT: a survey on downlink and uplink perspectives. IEEE Wirel. Commun. **26**(1), 78–86 (2019)

11. Flore, D.: 3gpp standards for the internet-of-things. Recuperado el **25** (2016)

12. Garg, S., Gentry, C., Halevi, S., Raykova, M., Sahai, A., Waters, B.: Candidate indistinguishability obfuscation and functional encryption for all circuits. In: 54th Annual Symposium on Foundations of Computer Science, pp. 40–49. IEEE Computer Society Press (2013). https://doi.org/10.1109/FOCS.2013.13

13. Goldwasser, S., Rothblum, G.N.: On Best-Possible Obfuscation. In: Vadhan, S.P. (ed.) TCC 2007. LNCS, vol. 4392, pp. 194–213. Springer, Heidelberg (2007). https://doi.org/10.1007/978-3-540-70936-7_11

14. Grant, S.: 3gpp low power wide area technologies-gsma white paper. gsma. com, p. 1 (2016)

15. GSMA: Narrowband—internet of things (nb-iot). https://www.gsma.com/iot/narrow-band-internet-of-things-nb-iot/. Accessed 5 July 2018

16. Hada, S.: Zero-Knowledge and Code Obfuscation. In: Okamoto, T. (ed.) ASIACRYPT 2000. LNCS, vol. 1976, pp. 443–457. Springer, Heidelberg (2000). https://doi.org/10.1007/3-540-44448-3_34

17. Hada, S.: Secure Obfuscation for Encrypted Signatures. In: Gilbert, H. (ed.) EUROCRYPT 2010. LNCS, vol. 6110, pp. 92–112. Springer, Heidelberg (2010). https://doi.org/10.1007/978-3-642-13190-5_5

18. Hohenberger, S., Rothblum, G.N., Shelat, A., Vaikuntanathan, V.: Securely Obfuscating Re-encryption. In: Vadhan, S.P. (ed.) TCC 2007. LNCS, vol. 4392, pp. 233–252. Springer, Heidelberg (2007). https://doi.org/10.1007/978-3-540-70936-7_13

19. Insights, T.: Global IoT market will grow to 24.1 billion devices in 2030, generating $1.5 trillion annual revenue. https://transformainsights.com/news/iot-market-24-billion-usd15-trillion-revenue-2030. Accessed May 2020

20. Lynn, B., Prabhakaran, M., Sahai, A.: Positive Results and Techniques for Obfuscation. In: Cachin, C., Camenisch, J.L. (eds.) EUROCRYPT 2004. LNCS, vol. 3027, pp. 20–39. Springer, Heidelberg (2004). https://doi.org/10.1007/978-3-540-24676-3_2

21. Mwakwata, C.B., Malik, H., Mahtab Alam, M., Le Moullec, Y., Parand, S., Mumtaz, S.: Narrowband internet of things (nb-iot): from physical (phy) and media access control (mac) layers perspectives. Sensors 19(11), 2613 (2019)

22. Sahai, A., Waters, B.: How to use indistinguishability obfuscation: deniable encryption, and more. In: Shmoys, D.B. (ed.) 46th Annual ACM Symposium on Theory of Computing, pp. 475–484. ACM Press (2014).https://doi.org/10.1145/2591796.2591825

23. Sanchez-Gomez, J., Garcia-Carrillo, D., Marin-Perez, R., Skarmeta, A.F.: Secure authentication and credential establishment in narrowband iot and 5g. Sensors 20(3), 882 (2020)

24. Shi, Y., Zhao, Q., Fan, H., Liu, Q.: Secure obfuscation for encrypted group signatures. PLoS ONE 10(7), e0131550 (2015)

25. Sinha, R.S., Wei, Y., Hwang, S.H.: A survey on lpwa technology: Lora and nb-iot. ICT Exp. 3(1), 14–21 (2017)

26. Stahie, S.: IoT botnet attacks on the rise in 2020. https://www.bitdefender.com/box/blog/iot-news/iot-botnet-attacks-rise-2020/. Accessed July 2020

27. Tawalbeh, L., Muheidat, F., Tawalbeh, M., Quwaider, M., et al.: IoT privacy and security: challenges and solutions. Appl. Sci. 10(12), 4102 (2020)

28. Tsai, K.L., Huang, Y.L., Leu, F.Y., You, I., Huang, Y.L., Tsai, C.H.: AES-128 based secure low power communication for lorawan IoT environments. IEEE Access 6, 45325–45334 (2018)

29. Wee, H.: On obfuscating point functions. In: Gabow, H.N., Fagin, R. (eds.) 37th Annual ACM Symposium on Theory of Computing, pp. 523–532. ACM Press (2005). https://doi.org/10.1145/1060590.1060669

30. Zhang, M., Chen, Y., Huang, J.: Se-ppfm: a searchable encryption scheme supporting privacy-preserving fuzzy multikeyword in cloud systems. IEEE Syst. J. (2020)

31. Zhang, M., Zhang, Y., Jiang, Y., Shen, J.: Obfuscating eves algorithm and its application in fair electronic transactions in public clouds. IEEE Syst. J. 13(2), 1478–1486 (2019)

32. Zhang, Y., He, D., Li, Y., Zhang, M., Choo, K.K.R.: Efficient obfuscation for encrypted identity-based signatures in wireless body area networks. IEEE Syst. J. 14(4), 5320–5328 (2020). https://doi.org/10.1109/JSYST.2020.2974892

Author Index

© The Editor(s) (if applicable) and The Author(s), under exclusive license
to Springer Nature Singapore Pte Ltd. 2025
Z. Xia and J. Chen (Eds.): ISPEC 2024, LNCS 15053, pp. 403–404, 2024.
https://doi.org/10.1007/978-981-97-9053-1

GPSR Compliance

The European Union's (EU) General Product Safety Regulation (GPSR) is a set of rules that requires consumer products to be safe and our obligations to ensure this.

If you have any concerns about our products, you can contact us on ProductSafety@springernature.com

In case Publisher is established outside the EU, the EU authorized representative is:

Springer Nature Customer Service Center GmbH
Europaplatz 3
69115 Heidelberg, Germany

The manufacturer's authorised representative in the EU is Springer
Nature Customer Service Centre GmbH, Europaplatz 3, 69115 Heidelberg,
Germany. If you have any concerns regarding our products, please
contact ProductSafety@springernature.com

Printed and bound by CPI Group (UK) Ltd, Croydon, CR0 4YY

29/04/2026

02099470-0009